For Reference

Not to be taken from this room

THE
SCIENCE
FICTION
IMAGE

THE SCIENCE FICTION IMAGE

The Illustrated Encyclopedia of Science Fiction in Film, Television, Radio and the Theater

Gene Wright

Facts On File Publications
460 Park Avenue South
New York, N.Y. 10016

THE SCIENCE FICTION IMAGE

Illustrations by Richard L. Lewis

Library of Congress Cataloging in Publication Data

Wright, Gene,
   The science fiction image.

   Includes indexes.
   1. Science fiction—Handbooks, manuals, etc.
I. Title.
P96.S34W7   791.43'09'09356   82-2348
ISBN 0-87196-527-5/AACR2   AACR2

Design by Jennie Nichols/Levavi & Levavi

Printed in the United States of America

10 9 8 7 6 5 4 3 2 1

CONTENTS

For Vilma, Ilona, Margit and Klara

ACKNOWLEDGMENTS

The author wishes to express his gratitude to his friends in the film industry for generously giving of their time and resources, and to The Academy of Motion Picture Arts and Sciences, The American Film Institute, The Museum of Modern Art, The New York Public Library, The Museum of Broadcasting, the Musée du Cinéma of the Cincmatheque Francaise and the British Film Institute. Special thanks must go to Robert and Rebecca Elfant and Michael and Barbara Tomlin for their support and encouragement, and to Jamie Warren, the editor of this edition, who courageously stepped into the breach.

INTRODUCTION

Encyclopedic in format, *The Science Fiction Image* is an in-depth historical survey of science fiction in non-print mediums, both in the U.S. and abroad. Intended as a reference source, the book contains pertinent data on hundreds of SF films, radio and television programs, several plays and, surprisingly, one opera. Listings include plot summaries, cast and filmmakers credits and critiques that focus on the contributions of the productions to the genre of science fiction. Whenever possible, the author has gone to original sources rather than to the often conflicting information found in previous SF studies.

To place these listings in perspective, there are cross-referenced biographies of seminal SF authors and filmmakers, actors and special effects technicians, diagrams and explanations of "state-of-the-art" special effects, a complete list of genre Academy Award winners, discussions of major SF themes and, last but not least, biographies of the imaginary creatures and characters who inhabit science fiction in these mediums. In all there are more than 1,000 entries arranged alphabetically and accompanied by more than 200 photographs, many of which have never been published in a book.

Most of the entries, not unexpectedly, have to do with the SF film, whose influences include literary science fiction, the Gothic horror novel, pulp fiction, comic books and radio and television.

The contributions of radio and its successor, television, have been limited by the scope of their mediums and their commercial function. Still, television has brought the SF film to a wider audience, and it has recently introduced a number of innovative special effects techniques (transferable to film) such as computer graphics. Television may yet live up to its promise.

Film and television naturally complement the subject matter of most science fiction stories. On the screen, an illusory trip to outer space seems as real as a trip on an earthbound jetliner, the inside of a man's body becomes the locale of a fantastic voyage, and a giant ape who never could have existed threatens Manhattan from the top of the Empire State Building. Under the spell of this magic, so powerful and convincing, we rarely remember that the images flickering before us with every semblance of life are not alive at all, but products of imaginative technology.

SF purists and film critics have often decried the SF film as a bastard offspring of literary science fiction. The SF establishment has complained, often quite accurately, that what appears on screen is a Western or a detective story dressed in a spacesuit and futurist hardware, with the ideas and traditions of written science fiction replaced by action and special effects. What the genre's detractors fail to realize is that the SF film has largely reshaped these popular genres, drawing on their mythologies and giving them new life with an expansive vision that offers radically new possibilities.

The history of science fiction films began shortly after the birth of cinema with the trick films of French special-effects innovator Georges Melies. From the first the SF film swerved from the path of written science fiction and the theatrical conventions of the day, and began to acquire an identity of its own. With a few well-chosen adjectives, a writer can spark the reader's imagination into creating a mental pciture of an incredible technology. But the filmmaker has a more difficult task: He must show the technology and show it in operation. Thus filmmakers have been bound less by formal conventions than by their medium's requirement for telling a story visually. No expensive special effect can overcome the bad logic of a careless script, of course; but even at their weakest, SF films offer audiences an opportunity to participate in "impossible" experiences that nonetheless have a startling, often provoking connection to human experience. Because SF films are made possible by a sophisticated technology that began with the convergence of various lines of discovery—optics, mechanics and chemistry—they are perhaps the purest film genre of all, whose roots lie as much in the cinema as in science fiction.

How does one define the science fiction film? The protean H. G. Wells, whose prophetic fiction suffuses so many SF productions, called his works "fantasias of possibilities," a definition that can apply equally to cinema. Ray Bradbury, a contemporary SF novelist who has worked in film, calls the genre "Old fading. New arriving." To mainstream critic Susan Sontag it is "the imagination of disaster." A favorite definition comes from the Czechoslovakian film *Ikarie XB-1* (1964), in which space travelers are described as being "torn between the fear of the unknown and the urge to explore."

But above all, the SF film is, of course, a celebration of the possibilities of being human in a universe at once mysterious and hostile.

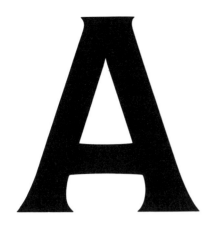

A

mer box-office winners are reduced to supporting the burlesque comedy team of Abbott and Costello, who play railway porters delivering crates containing the bodies of the above to a wax museum. The creatures revive and terrorize the comedians (Dracula wants their blood and the Frankenstein monster wants their brains). **Bela Lugosi** parodied his vampire image for the first time, signaling the decline of his film career; **Lon Chaney, Jr.** repeated his portrayal of the Wolf Man, and **Glenn Strange** again followed **Boris Karloff** in the original makeup designed by **Jack Pierce.**

Director: Charles T. Barton, *Producer:* Robert Arthur, *Screenplay:* John Grant, Frederic I. Rinaldo, Robert Lees, *Photographer:* Charles Van Enger, *Art Director:* Bernard Herzbrun, Hilyard Brown, *Makeup:* Bud Westmore, *Special Effects:* David S. Horsley, Jerome H. Ash, *Music:* Frank Skinner

Cast: Bud Abbott, Lou Costello, Bela Lugosi, Lon Chaney, Jr., Glenn Strange, Lenore Aubert, **Vincent Price**

ABBOTT AND COSTELLO MEET DR. JEKYLL AND MR. HYDE

Film   1953   U.S. (Universal–International)
76 Minutes   Black & white

A surprisingly lively spoof with Abbott and Costello as bumbling London detectives on the trail of the evil Mr. Hyde in late-19th-century London. Legendary monster-impersonator **Boris Karloff** provides the chills as **Dr. Jekyll and Mr. Hyde.** (Stunt man Eddie Parker doubled as the latter in action scenes.)

Director: Charles Lamont, *Producer:* Howard Christie, *Screenplay:* Leo Loeb, John Grant, *Story:* Sidney Fields, Grant Garrett, *Novel: The Strange Case of Dr. Jekyll and Mr. Hyde,* Robert Louis Stevenson, *Photographer:* George Robinson, *Special Effects:* David S. Horsley, *Makeup:* Bud Westmore, *Music Director:* Joseph Gershenson

Cast: Bud Abbott, Lou Costello, Boris Karloff, Craig Stevens, Helen Westcott, Reginald Denny, John Dierkes

ABBOTT AND COSTELLO MEET THE INVISIBLE MAN

Film   1951   U.S. (Universal–International)
82 Minutes   Black & white

Universal's last sequel to its classic, **The Invisible Man** (1933), is lowbrow but lively and tailored to Hollywood's reigning comedy team. Abbott and Costello play a pair of private eyes hired by a client they can't see to clear him of a murder charge. The film marks the final use of the invisibility effects devised by **John P. Fulton** for the original film.

Director: Charles Lamont, *Producer:* Howard Christie, *Screenplay:* Frederic I. Rinaldo, John Grant, Robert Lees, *Novel:* **H. G. Wells,** *Photographer:* George Robinson, *Art Director:* Bernard Herzbrun, **Richard Riedel,** *Makeup:* Bud Westmore, *Special Effects:* David S. Horsley, *Music:* Joseph Gershenson

Cast: Bud Abbott, Lou Costello, **Arthur Franz,** Nancy Guild, Sheldon Leonard, William Frawley

ABBOTT AND COSTELLO MEET FRANKENSTEIN

Film   1948   U.S. (Universal-International)
83 Minutes   Black & white

The last gasp of the **Frankenstein** monster, Count Dracula and the Wolf Man, Universal's resident **horror** stars. The studio's for-

THE ABOMINABLE DR. PHIBES

Film   1971   Great Britain (AIP)
94 Minutes   Movielab

Horror king **Vincent Price** has a great time burlesquing his screen image while fiendishly plotting the murders of a team of surgeons whose operation on his wife resulted in her death. Obviously a religious man, the abominable doctor decides that each must die according to the 10 curses Moses visited upon the Pharoah. His aide-de-camp, the lovely Vulnavia, doesn't seem to mind that Phibes lost his face, hair and vocal cords in an automobile accident while hurrying to his wife's bedside (he speaks via an electronic "voice" of his own invention).

Director: **Robert Fuest,** *Producer:* Louis M. Heyward, Ronald S. Dumas, *Screenplay:* James Whiton, William Goldstein, *Photographer:* Norman Warwick,

Cast: Vincent Price, Joseph Cotten, Hugh Griffith, Terry-Thomas, Virginia North, Woods, Sean Bury

THE ABOMINABLE SNOWMAN

(Also titled: *The Abominable Snowman of the Himalayas)*

The Abominable Dr. Phibes:
An embrace with his partner in crime, the lovely but vicious Vulnavia.

Film   1957   Great Britain (Hammer)
91 Minutes   Hammerscope   Black & white

An expedition of scientists/adventurers tracks the legendary Yeti to its lair in Tibet.
  This atypical Hammer film eschews shock effects and production values in favor of a philosophical message: Is man truly the best earth has to offer? The Snowmen turn out to be survivors of a superior race; the real monsters are the men hunting them. Studio scenes fail to match footage shot in the French Alps, and the Yeti makeup is disappointing.

Director: **Val Guest,** *Producer:* Aubrey Baring, *Screenplay:* **Nigel Kneale** (based on his teleplay *The Creature), Photographer:* Arthur Grant, *Art Director:* Ted Marshall, *Music:* Humphrey Searle

Cast: Forrest Tucker, **Peter Cushing,** Maureen Connell, Richard Wattis, Robert Browne, Arnold Marle

ACADEMY AWARDS

Honors bestowed annually to motion pictures, actors, filmmakers and technicians by Hollywood's Academy of Motion Picture Arts and Sciences, a non-profit, honorary organization founded in 1927 to promote "cultural, educational, and scientific" quality in films. The major awards are given with 13½-inch tall, gold-filled statuettes nicknamed "Oscars" (awarded for the first time in 1929), handed out during an internationally televised, formal dress ceremony in Los Angeles.
  Although well-represented in special effects categories, SF films rarely win top awards. Filmmakers have complained that the somewhat elderly Academy membership (which numbers over 3,000, many of them retired) continues to regard the genre as the low-budget Hollywood stepchild it once was. Indeed, the Academy's choices seem remarkably short-sighted when one considers the SF films denied Best Picture awards: **King Kong** lost to *Cavalcade* in 1932/33,

2001: A Space Odyssey to *Oliver* in 1968, and **Star Wars** to *Annie Hall* in 1977.

Nominees for the 13 major award categories are selected by members of the various branches of the Academy (writers vote for writers, directors for directors, etc.), after which the entire membership votes by secret ballot. Winners are announced during the awards ceremony. An exception to this procedure is for awards in the Scientific or Technical Classes, which are made by the Academy's Board of Governors on recommendations from representatives in technical areas. These are not necessarily awarded every year and may be given in the form of a plaque or a certificate rather than an Oscar.

The following is a survey by categories of SF and science fantasy winners, with the exception of Scientific or Technical Classes, which are indicated in listings:

Best Actor

Frederic March, **Dr. Jekyll and Mr. Hyde,** 1931
Cliff Robertson, **Charly,** 1968

Cinematography

Vilmos Zsigmond, Close Encounters of the Third Kind, 1977

Interior Decoration

Stephen Gooson, **Lost Horizon,** 1937

Art Direction/Set Direction

(category introduced in 1947 to replace the above)
John Meehan, Emile Kuri, **20,000 Leagues Under the Sea,** 1954
Jack Martin Smith, Dale Hennesy, Walter M. Scott, Stuart A. Reiss, **Fantastic Voyage,** 1966
John Barry, Norman Reynolds, Leslie Dilley, Roger Christian, **Star Wars,** 1977
Norman Reynolds, Leslie Dilley, Michael Ford, **Raiders of the Lost Art,** 1981

Film Editing

Gene Havlick, Gene Milford, **Lost Horizon,** 1937
Paul Hirsch, Marcia Lucas, Richard Chew, **Star Wars,** 1977

Michael Kahn, **Raiders of the Lost Ark,** 1981

Special Effects

RKO Radio Pictures **(Willis H. O'Brien), Mighty Joe Young,** 1949
Eagle Lion (Lee Zavitz), **Destination Moon,** 1950
Paramount (Gordon Jennings), **When Worlds Collide,** 1951
Paramount (Gordon Jennings), **War of the Worlds,** 1953
Walt Disney (Ub Iwerks), **20,000 Leagues Under the Sea,** 1954
Gene Warren, Tim Baar, **The Time Machine,** 1960

Visual Effects

John Stears, **Thunderball,** 1965
John Stears, **John Dykstra,** Richard Edlund, Grant McCune, Robert Blalack, **Star Wars,** 1977
H. R. Giger, **Carlo Rambaldi,** Brian Johnson, Nick Allder, Denys Ayling, **Alien,** 1979
Richard Edlund, Kit West, Bruce Nicholson, Joe Johnston, **Raiders of the Lost Ark,** 1981

Special Visual Effects

(category introduced in 1966 to replace the above; used until 1977)
Art Cruickshank, **Fantastic Voyage,** 1966
Stanley Kubrick, 2001: A Space Odyssey, 1968
Robbie Robertson, **Marooned,** 1969

Special Achievement

Benjamin Burtt, Jr., for sound effects, **Star Wars,** 1977
Frank Warner, for sound effects editing, **Close Encounters of the Third Kind,** 1977
Les Bowie, Colin Chilvers, Denys Coops, Roy Field, Derek Meddings, Zoran Perisic, for visual effects, **Superman—The Movie,** 1978
Brian Johnson, Richard Edlund, Dennis Muren, Bruce Nicholson, for visual effects, **The Empire Strikes Back,** 1980
Benjamin Burtt, Jr., Richard Anderson,

for sound effects editing, **Raiders of the Lost Ark,** 1981

Sound Effects

Norman Wanstall, **Goldfinger,** 1964

Sound

Dan MacDougall, Ray West, Bob Minkler, Derek Ball, **Star Wars,** 1977
Bill Varney, Steve Maslow, Gregg Landaker, Peter Sutton, **The Empire Strikes Back,** 1980
Bill Varney, Steve Maslow, Gregg Land-aker, Roy Charman, **Raiders of the Lost Ark,** 1981

Best Original Score

Herbert Stothart, **The Wizard of Oz,** 1939
John Williams, Star Wars, 1977

Costume Design

John Mollo, **Star Wars,** 1977

Best Documentary

The Hellstrom Chronicle, 1971
The War Game (1966)

Honorary and other awards

Merian C. Cooper (co-director/producer of **King Kong** [1933]), "for his many innovations and contributions to the art of motion pictures," 1952
John Chambers, for makeup created for **Planet of the Apes,** 1968
Frank Brendel, Albert Whitlock, Glen Robinson, for visual effects, **Earthquake,** 1974
Carlo Rambaldi, Glen Robinson, Frank Van Der Veer, for visual effects, **King Kong,** 1976
Lyle B. Abbott, Glen Robinson, Matthew Yuricich, for visual effects, **Logan's Run,** 1976

ACES (Automated Camera Effects System)

A computer-controlled motion picture camera system used for photographing **miniatures** in **stop-motion** and at other speeds. The system is linked to its own model stand to absorb vibrations when the camera changes angle. The camera's position in relation to the miniature is recorded as a signal on tape which, when played back through the computer, repeats the angles exactly. This allows special effects technicians to add other effects to the shot, either via multiple exposures on the original negative or by combining footage shot separately with traveling **mattes.** The system was developed by Walt Disney studios to motivate the spaceship Cygnus in **The Black Hole** (1979). ACES is a **motion control** system.

ADAM, KEN (1921–   )

Production designer noted for the modish look and imaginative high-tech sets of the **James Bond** films. Born in Berlin, he emigrated with his family to London in 1934 and studied at the Bartlett School of Architecture. After war service as an RAF pilot, he began his film career as a draftsman and progressed to assistant art director for the European scenes of *Helen of Troy* (1955).

Films: Around the World in 80 Days [European sets] (1956), *Curse of the Demon* (1957), **Dr. No** (1962), **Dr. Strangelove, or How I Learned to Stop Worrying and Love the Bomb** (1963), **Goldfinger** (1964), **Thunderball** (1965), **You Only Live Twice** (1967), *Chitty Chitty Bang Bang* (1968), **Diamonds Are Forever** (1971), *The Spy Who Loved Me* (1977), **Moonraker, Star Trek—The Motion Picture** (1979), **For Your Eyes Only** (1981). He won an Academy Award for the design of *Barry Lyndon* (1975).

THE ADVENTURES OF CAPTAIN MARVEL

Film serial   1941   U.S. (Republic)
12 Episodes   Black & white

In his day, Captain Marvel was the **comic-book** equal of **Superman.** He even managed to outsell him for a time, until Superman's publishers stripped him of his superpowers with a successful lawsuit that terminated the comic book in 1953. Illustrated by C. C. Beck, who based the character on actor Fred MacMurray, Captain Marvel first appeared in 1940 in *Whiz Comics*. As every boy and girl knew, his other identity was Billy Batson, a newsboy who had received his marvelous gifts from an ancient sage in a subway tunnel. Whenever his help was needed by those in trouble, Billy was told to utter the old man's name, "Shazam," which instantly produced a bolt of magic lightning that transformed Billy into Captain Marvel (no need for clumsy costume changes in a phone booth). Shazam was an acronym for *Solomon* (wisdom), *Hercules* (strength), *Atlas* (stamina), *Zeus* (power), *Achilles* (courage) and *Mercury* (speed).

The movie version altered the Captain's legend somewhat, reassigning Billy as a radio operator for a scientific expedition that invades a sacred tomb in Siam. As a reward for not entering the forbidden chamber, Billy is given his superpowers by its guardian, Shazam. Meanwhile, the scientists remove a transmutation weapon called the Golden Scorpion, whose energy derives from five crystal lenses. The device eventually falls into the hands of a sinister criminal called the Scorpion, posing as a member of the expedition. Having noticed Billy change into Marvel, the Scorpion binds and gags him and demands to know how it is done. To find out, of course, he has to loosen the boy's gag, thus allowing him to utter the magic word.

Now nearly forgotten, *The Adventures of Captain Marvel* is the first **serial** taken from a comic book (**Buck Rogers** and **Flash Gordon** were comic-strip characters). Directed and played with a vigor missing in the Superman serials, it features some excellent stunts and flying scenes (see: **Wire Work**) that put the serial Man of Steel to shame. Hollywood heavy Tom Tyler is perfectly cast as Marvel. (He had previously tried to gun down John Wayne in *Stagecoach.*) His manly good looks and acting ability brought the character to life, and his muscled physique didn't look ridiculous in red tights and yellow boots. (See also: **Shazam!; The Shazam!/Isis Hour.**)

Directors: **William Witney,** John English, *Producer:* Hiram S. Brown, *Screenplay:* Ronald Davidson, Arch B. Heath, Norman S. Hall, Joseph Poland, Sol Shor, *Photographer:* William Nobels, *Music:* Cy Feuer

Cast: Tom Tyler, Frank Coghlan, Jr., Nigel de Brulier, Louise Currie, Bryant Washburn

THE ADVENTURES OF SUPERMAN

Radio serial 1940-53 U.S. (Mutual)
15 Minutes (3 times weekly)

The **Superman** comic book adapted well to the radio format, and the Man of Steel proved to be its most durable superhero. Fighting crime with only a disembodied voice and a handful of sound effects, he bounded into the after-school airwaves in a burst of wind as onlookers exclaimed: "Look! Up in the sky! It's a bird! It's a plane! It's Superman!" Young viewers were exhorted to join the "Supermen of America" club, whose membership entailed receiving a secret code and signing a rather mercenary pledge "to follow the announcements" of the club "in each month's issue of *Action Comics.*"

Sponsored by Kellogg's Pep, a breakfast cereal, the radio program added several new elements to the Superman legend, all later institutionalized in the comic book. The "up, up, and a-a-a-way" line comes from the radio script, as do Jimmy Olson, cub reporter, and the incapaciting mineral **Kryptonite,** invented to give the program's star a two-week vacation. In 1945 a tradition of sorts was begun when **Batman** and Robin appeared as guest stars, originally for the same reason. The teaming proved to be immensely popular, however, and the Dynamic Duo returned often, sometimes taking over the show. Batman and Robin had no way of knowing Superman's true identity, of course, but he could see through their disguises with his **X-ray** vision.

The voice of Superman was Clayton "Bud" Collyer, who made the costume change from business suit to blue and red tights by dropping Kent's high-pitched voice to a strong baritone, usually when he said, "This looks like a job for [voice lowered]—Superman!" Collyer, later a popular TV game-show host, holds the record for Superman impersonations. In addition to the radio **serial,** he also provided the voice for Max Fleischer's cartoon **Superman** (1941-43) and a later animated TV series, **The New Adventures of Superman** (1966-67).

Directors: Allen DuCovny, Mitchell Grayson, George Lowther, Robert and Jessica Maxwell, *Producers:* Robert and Jessica Maxwell, George Lowther, *Writers:* B. P. Freeman, Robert and Jessica Maxwell, George Lowther, *Sound Effects:* Jack Keane

Cast: Clayton "Bud" Collyer, Michael Fitzmaurice, Joan Alexander, Julian Noa, Jackie Kelk, Stacy Harris, Gary Merrill, Ronald Liss

THE ADVENTURES OF SUPERMAN

TV series   1953-57   U.S. (ABC)   30 Minutes (weekly)   Black & white, color

When television began to lure away radio listeners, **Superman** made an effortless transition to the new medium with a filmed afternoon series starring **George Reeves** and Phyllis Coates, who had played the roles of Clark Kent/Superman and Lois Lane in the 1951 feature film **Superman and the Mole Men** (later used as a two-part episode in the series). Although faithful to the **comic-book** character's legend, the program was primitively done, and plots were essentially crime melodramas aimed at juveniles. But Reeves made a winning if wooden Man of Steel, and the series played for five years, followed by decades of syndication.

In the second season Noel Neill replaced Phyllis Coates, whose Lois Lane was deemed by producers to be too aggressively hostile to Clark Kent. Neill, who had played the role in two **serials, Superman** (1948) and **Atom Man vs. Superman** (1950), was scornful of the self-effacing and clumsy Kent, but underneath she really seemed to like him. The program switched to color in the third season, enabling viewers to see Superman's baggy red, blue and yellow costume and Neill's carrot-red hair.

The program's special effects were ingeniously if unconvincingly done, given its limited budget and the current state of the art. To "leap tall buildings at a single bound," Reeves jumped on a springboard and in mid-leap was hauled into the air by a hydraulic rig attached to his body belt; to leap out the window, he sprang from the board through a window frame onto a concealed mattress. More easily accomplished were the flying shots. Reeves lay on a large piece of glass with arms and legs outstretched (but only toes and fingertips touching). The shot was later matted into an aerial view of Metropolis, in reality, Los Angeles. (See also: **Matte.**)

Directors: Lee Sholem, Thomas Carr, George Blair, Harry Gerstad, George Reeves and others, *Producers:* Whitney Ellsworth, Bernard Luber, Robert J. Maxwell and others, *Writers:* Richard Fielding (pseudonym for Whitney Ellsworth and Robert J. Maxwell), Dennis Cooper, David Chandler, Jackson Gillis and others, *Photographers:* Joseph Biroc, Harold Wellman, Harold Stine, *Special Effects:* Thol Simonson

Cast: George Reeves, Phyllis Coates, Noel Neill, John Hamilton, Jack Larson, Robert Shayne, Phillips Tead

AELITA

Film   1924   USSR (Mezhrobpom)   70 Minutes (approx.)   Black & white (silent)

Soviet rocket pilots journey to Mars, where they foment a revolution against the despotic queen Aelita.

This stylized early **space opera** which retains its zest and wit and is still worth seeing. The expressionistic sets of the Martian palace—a bizarre juxtaposition of scaffolding, wires and shadows—are the work of Sergei Kozlovsky, pioneer Soviet **production designer.** Propaganda takes up much of the running time, as cosmonauts join hands with Martian comrades in an uprising against the aristocratic queen. The film was a great success in **Russia** (many babies born in 1924 were named Aelita) but little seen abroad.

Director: Jacob Protazanov, *Screenplay:* Fyodor Otzep, Alexei Faiko, *Novel:* Alexei Tolstoy, *Photographer:* Yuri Zhelyobuzhky, *Producer:* Victor Simov, Isaac Rabinovitch, Alexandra Exter, Sergei Kozlovsky

Cast: Igor Ilinsky, Yulia Solntseva, Nikolai Tseretelly, Konstantin Eggert

THE AERIAL ANARCHISTS

Film 1911 Great Britain (Kineto)
15 Minutes (approx.) Black & white (silent)

Terrorists construct an immense airship and bombard London in this primitive disaster spectacle, whose special effects consist mostly of orange flames hand-tinted over footage of city landmarks. Made to capitalize on the success of the director's earlier **The Airship Destroyer** (1909), *The Aerial Anarchists* is apparently an uncredited adaptation of *Hartmann the Anarchist; or The Doom of the Great City* (1893), a novel by E. Douglas Fawcett, in which anarchists stage a revolution against greedy, capitalist England.

Director: **Walter Booth,** *Producer:* Charles Urban

THE AERIAL TORPEDO
AERIAL WARFARE

See: **The Airship Destroyer**

A FOR ANDROMEDA

TV serial 1961 Great Britain (BBC)
60 Minutes (weekly) Black & white

A mysterious radio signal emanating from the Andromeda Galaxy contains coded instructions for building a supercomputer, whose purpose becomes clear when assembled by Earth technicians: it creates artificial life. The first experiment produces a lovely female **android,** an apparently benign creature thought by some scientists and politicians to be a threatening **alien.** Confused and upset by the bitter controversy, she eventually brings about her own death. Despite its shaky premise, the story was thought-provoking and surprisingly literate. Julie Christie, later to become an international star, played the mute android. The series ran seven episodes and resumed in a sequel, **The Andromeda Breakthrough,** the following year.

Producer: Michael Hayes, Norman Jones, *Writers:* Frey Hoyle, Norman Jones

Cast: Peter Halliday, John Nettleton, Esmond Knight, Mary Morris, Frank Windsor, Julie Christie

AGAR, JOHN (1921–)

Film actor whose limited dramatic range and bland good looks relegated him to supporting roles in major features and occasional starring roles in low-budget Western and SF movies. Born in Chicago, he achieved instant fame when he married 17-year-old child star Shirley Temple in 1946, after being discharged from the Navy. Entering into a film career with much publicity and little training, he was partnered with John Wayne and directed by John Ford in *Fort Apache* (1948) and *She Wore a Yellow Ribbon* (1949). His awkward performances failed to captivate moviegoers, however, and he was soon dropped by RKO studios. Divorced by Temple in 1949, he continued to pursue a screen career, but the opportunity for stardom never came again. After a bout with alcoholism and several arrests for drunken driving during the 1950s and 1960s, he underwent a cure and left the screen to sell life insurance.

His best SF films, **Revenge of the Creature** and **Tarantula** (both 1955) owe their durable popularity to director **Jack Arnold,** who used Agar only because of budget considerations. Other SF films include **The Mole People** (1956), **Daughter of Dr. Jekyll** (1957), **The Brain From the Planet Arous** (1958), **The Invisible Invaders** (1959), **The Hand of Death** (1961), **Journey to the Seventh Planet** (1962) and **Zontar: The Thing from Venus** (1968). He returned from retirement in 1976 to play a small role in the remake of **King Kong.**

AGENT 353

(U.S. title: *Passport to Hell*)

Film 1964 France/Italy/Spain 100 Minutes
Color

A cheap **James Bond** rip-off concerning a secret agent who tracks down the Black

Scorpion, a terrorist group bent on world domination by spraying a powerful new gas.

Director: Simon Sterling, *Screenplay:* S. Sollimo, S. O'Neill, A. DeArozeumena, *Photographer:* Carlo Carlini, *Music:* Piero Umiliani

Cast: George Ardisson, Georges Rivière, Leontine May, Michel Lemoine

THE AIRSHIP DESTROYER

Film 1909 Great Britain 15 Minutes (approx.) Black & white (silent)

(Also titled: *The Aerial Torpedo, Aerial Warfare* and, in the U.S.: *The Battle in the Clouds)*

An inventor saves London from a mysterious fleet of bomb-dropping dirigibles by launching guided missiles.

The Airship Destroyer is the first true SF film, and its special effects, accurate prediction of aerial warfare and respectful treatment of science are ahead of their time. Previous SF films relied heavily on fantasy, often presenting scientists as comedy characters whose inventions bordered on lunacy. Influenced by the writings of **H. G. Wells, Jules Verne** and Rudyard Kipling, the film's director took a positive approach to technology and thereby altered the course of the futurist film. Model work is surprisingly good, even by today's standards, from the destruction of houses and railroads to the final launching of the aerial torpedoes, which are propelled by a smoky solid fuel. (See also: **Miniatures.)**

Director: **Walter Booth,** *Producer:* Charles Urban

THE AIRSHIP; OR 100 YEARS HENCE

Film 1908 U.S. (Vitagraph) 2 Reels Black & white (silent)

Probably the first American film to depict aircraft of the future, *The Airship* makes up for its trite plot with provocative visions of streamlined, passenger-carrying airplanes and dirigibles. Played for comedy, it offers a short jaunt through the air with low-flying passengers who pelt pedestrians with cabbages and taunt policemen who chase them aboard aerocycles. An important step in the development of the SF film, *The Airship* demonstrated the potential of cinema to bring to life the wildest imaginings of things to come.

Director/Producer/Screenplay: **J. Stuart Blackton**

Cast: J. Stuart Blackton

ALCOTT, JOHN (dates unknown)

British director of photography. Alcott entered films in the early 1960s as a focus puller (a person who adjusts the lens of a moving camera to keep a scene in focus) and got his start when director **Stanley Kubrick** let him shoot several scenes for **2001: A Space Odyssey** (1968). He subsequently photographed three films for Kubrick: **A Clockwork Orange** (1971), *Barry Lyndon* (1975) (Academy Award) and *The Shining* (1980).

Other Films: March or Die, The Disappearance (1977), *Who Is Killing the Great Chefs of Europe?* (1978), *Terror Train* (1980), *Fort Apache, the Bronx* (1981), *Vice Squad, The Beastmaster* (1982)

ALDERAAN

Home planet of **Princess Leia Organa,** heroine of the film **Star Wars** (1977), who is a key figure in the rebellion brewing there. While holding her captive on a huge orbiting battle station called the **Death Star, Grand Moff Tarkin** destroys the planet and billions of people living there to warn off other would-be freedom-fighters. Speeding to her rescue aboard the **Millenium Falcon, Ben Kenobi** senses an interruption in the **Force** when Alderaan explodes. When the ship emerges from **hyperspace,** the crew encounters an **asteroid** storm that proves to be fragments of the planet.

ALGOL

Film 1920 Germany Running time unknown Black & white (silent)

One of the great lost films, *Algol* vanished during World War II either as a result of bombing raids in Germany or improper storage of its nitrate prints and negative. All that remain are a few stills to remind us of its extraordinary expressionist settings.

Algol is a female spirit from the star of the same name who journeys to Earth and falls in love with a human male. Offered a machine that will give him absolute power over the world, he returns the feeling but lives to regret it. The machine proves to be too powerful to handle and kills his wife and destroys the lives of his son and daughter. Grief-stricken, he demolishes the evil machine and is himself killed. The story was an allegorical warning against Germany's aggressive tendencies at the time.

Director: Hans Werkemeister, *Screenplay:* Hans Brenert, *Art Director:* Walther Reimann, Paul Sheerbart

Cast: Emil Jannings, Kathe Haack, John Gottowt, Ernst Hoffman

ALIEN

Film   1979   U.S. (20th Century-Fox)
124 Minutes   Eastmancolor   Panavision

Feverish, overblown and basically preposterous, but also guaranteed to raise goose bumps, *Alien* bears a suspicious similarity to **It!—The Terror From Beyond Space,** a memorable low-budget thriller made in 1958. Director Ridley Scott, a master of timing and misdirection, gives audiences little time to dwell on his film's flaws, however, as he plunges us headlong into a stupefying confrontation with the most repulsive creature ever seen on the screen.

Most of the action takes place aboard the 800-foot-long spaceship/tanker Nostromo (actually an 8-foot scale model), which stops to answer a distress call from an uncharted planet. The ship's crew find the long-dead remains of an alien "pilot" seated at the controls of a huge weapon and surrounded by vegetable-like, egg-shaped pods growing in the soil. Before you can gasp for breath, something resembling a yellow crab pops

Alien: The crew of the Nostromo approach a mysterious derelict ship, in which they discover the fossilized remains of an alien space pilot, left, right, above, below.

from one of the pods and lodges in an astronaut's head. Taken on board the Nostromo clamped to the unconscious astronaut, the **alien** later dies, only to reappear as its parasitic offspring, which bursts from the man's stomach in a torrent of blood during a relaxed meal in the mess hall. The alien hides in the ship's air ducts, constantly metamorphosing and dispatching the crew until only one is left, a woman, who confronts the creature in an escape pod.

Among *Alien's* startling sights are the sets by Swiss surrealist painter H. R. Giger, who describes them as "biomechanical." Like Giger's paintings, they suggest human body parts writhing together in a futuristic orgasm of bones, sinews and machine parts. Built at England's Bray Studios, once the home of Hammer Productions, the large-scale sets were augmented by a matte painting for added dimension. The majority of the film's special effects were mechanical rather than optical, however. The loathesome pod that disgorges the initial alien, for instance, was a lidded device whose interior consisted of a sheep's stomach and other entrails manipulated by hand from underneath. Similary, the snake-like alien that bursts from the astronaut's chest (whose filming sickened many of the studio crew), was accomplished with a hand puppet shoved through a fake chest while the actor knelt under the table with his neck arched through a hole.

Giger also designed the seven-foot alien, but it was executed by **Carlo Rambaldi,** creator of **E.T.** (1982). The creature was actually incorporated into the design of the escape-shuttle set to look as if it had undergone yet another metamorphosis and changed appearance to suit the room. The creature literally seems to appear from nowhere, giving the audience one last hair-raising fright.

Academy Awards:

H. R. Giger, **Carlo Rambaldi,** Brian Johnson, Nick Allder, Denys Ayling, *Visual Effects*

Director: Ridley Scott, *Producers:* Gordon Carroll, David Giler, Walter Hill, *Screenplay:* Dan O'Ban-non, *Story:* Dan O'Bannon, Ronald Shusett, *Photography:* Derek Vanlint, *Producer:* Michael Seymour, *Alien designer:* H. R. Giger, *Alien head:* Carlo Rambaldi, *Small Alien:* Roger Dicken, *Photographer:* Denys Ayling, *Music:* **Jerry Goldsmith**

Cast: Tom Skerritt, Sigourney Weaver, Veronica Cartwright, Harry Dean Stanton, John Hurt, Ian Holm, Yaphet Kotto

ALIEN ENCOUNTER

See: **Starship Invasions**

ALIEN INVASION

An SF theme established by **H. G. Wells** in his novel *The War of the Worlds* (1898) (see listings), in which Martians were the invaders. The first film to depict an alien invasion is **George Melies' Le Voyage dans la lune/***A Trip to the Moon* (1902), in which the **aliens** were Earthmen who invaded the moon, populated by Selenites. Alien invasion films proliferated around the time of World War I, although the invaders were the human kind—enemy armies equipped with unstoppable futuristic technology. The U.S. was repeatedly invaded in such disaster films as **The Airship Destroyer** (1909), **A Zeppelin Attack on New York** (1917) and **Patria** (1916-17). The first **extraterrestrial** visitor, a benign creature, arrived on Earth in the British movie **A Message from Mars** (1913).

Relatively dormant until after World War II, the theme resurfaced with **The Thing** and **The Man from Planet X** (1951), the latter released a month earlier than the former. Among the best films in this category are: **It Came From Outer Space** (1953), **War of the Worlds** (1953), **Invaders From Mars** (1953), **This Island Earth** (1955) and **Invasion of the Body Snatchers** (1956; 1978).

ALIENS

In SF parlance an alien is a non-human foreigner from another world. Aliens can be human in appearance but are more likely to be unrecognizable as life as we know it. They are thought to be carbon-based like ourselves, and not silicon-based "rocks" as conjectured by some SF writers of the past. In many ways superior to man, they are usually portrayed as hostile aggressors, a function that betrays the xenophobic nature of the word "alien" while providing the basis of many SF plots (See: **Alien Invasion).** The synonym **extraterrestrial** has a less biased connotation.

THE ALIENS ARE COMING

TV film   1980   U.S. (NBC)   100 Minutes Color

And you will be going after five minutes of this *deja-vu* nonsense, which has to do with **alien** invaders landing somewhere in the Nevada desert and taking over the bodies of local townspeople. How not to clone **Invasion of the Body Snatchers** (1978) and **Alien** (1979).

Director: Harvey Hart, *Producer:* Quinn Martin, *Screenplay:* Robert Lenski

Cast: Max Gail, Tom Mason, Caroline McWilliams, Matthew Laborteaux, Eric Braeden

ALLEN, IRWIN (1916–   )

Motion picture and television producer, director and screen writer specializing in flashy, simple-minded adventure fantasies and disaster epics. Allen's profitable excursions into science fiction are usually technically competent but lacking in logic and scientific plausibility; consequently his productions have had little influence on the genre other than to indicate the public's interest in special effects.

Born in New York City, Allen was educated at City College (CCNY) and the Columbia University School of Journalism. In 1938 he moved to Hollywood and briefly edited a magazine before leaving to produce, write and direct a long-running radio program. He subsequently wrote a nationally syndicated movie-fan column while operating his own literary agency.

Allen entered films as co-producer of RKO's *Double Dynamite* (made in 1948 but released in 1951), a comedy starring Frank Sinatra and Groucho Marx. His first production of note was *The Sea Around Us* (director/producer/screenplay) (1952), based on Rachel Carson's popular book, which won him an Academy Award for best documentary. *The Animal World* (1956), his first special effects film, was a documentary-style history of the animal kingdom, with dinosaurs and other prehistoric beasts supplied by **stop-motion** animators **Willis H. O'Brien** and **Ray Harryhausen.**

Allen's next, *The Story of Mankind* (director/producer/screenplay) (1957), billed as an historical "pageant," numbers among its lunatic enjoyments a cast of fading Hollywood stars (an Irwin Allen trademark) in unlikely roles: Hedy Lamarr as Joan of Arc, Peter Lorre as Nero and Harpo Marx as Sir Isaac Newton. An especially memorable scene takes place in a heavenly courtroom where defender Ronald Colman and prosecutor Vincent Price argue whether mankind should prosper or perish for inventing the H-bomb.

His highly commercial, formula approach to filmmaking paid off with a tepid remake of **The Lost World** (1960), which showed him the way to science fantasy. During the 1960s Allen branched out into television and became the leading SF supplier for that medium. His film *The Poseidon Adventure* (1972) is credited with launching the disaster film cycle of the 1970s.

Other films: **Voyage to the Bottom of the Sea** (1961), **Five Weeks in a Balloon** (1962), *The Towering Inferno* (1974), **The Swarm** (1978), *Beyond the Poseidon Adventure* (1979), When Time Ran Out (1980).

TV films: **City Beneath the Sea** (1975), **The Time Travelers** (1975)

TV series: **Voyage to the Bottom of the Sea** (1964-68), **Lost in Space** (1965-68), **The Time Tunnel** (1966-67), *Swiss Family Robinson* (1975-76), **The Return of Captain Nemo** (1978)

ALLIGATOR

Film   1981   U.S. (BLC)   92 Minutes   Color

If you've ever wondered what happens when you flush a goldfish down the toilet, this affectionate little parody has the answer. The pet in this case is a 10-inch baby alligator named Ramon, bought by 12-year-old Marisa during a trip to Florida. Back home in Missouri, Ramon gets flushed away by Marisa's dad, who thinks she's growing too attached to him.

Cut to 12 years later. Something or someone is terrorizing the city by grabbing people from the sewers and pulling them under. The police sift through the evidence, which includes a number of arms, legs and a man's foot wearing an alligator shoe with a heel lift. Enter a beautiful young herptologist, called in to help investigate the mysterious deaths, who is—can you believe it?—none other than little Marisa, the unwitting source of the problem.

Ramon is now an angry, 32-feet-long beast, made huge from biological poisons illegally dumped into the sewers by a pharmaceutical laboratory owned by the town's Mr. Big. Surfacing to find bigger game, the reptile prowls the streets stuffing people into his big snout and thwacking others to death with his mighty tail. Will Ramon save the town from a slow poisoning? Will he remember Marisa? Will they have a happy reunion? Do formula monster movies have predictable endings?

Director: Lewis Teague, *Producer:* Brandon Chase, *Screenplay:* John Sayles, *Story:* John Sayles, Frank Ray Perilli, *Photographer:* Joseph Mangine

Cast: Robert Forster, Dean Jagger, Perry Lang, Bart Braverman, Henry Silva, Robin Riker, Jack Carter

THE ALLIGATOR PEOPLE

Film   1959   U.S. (20th Century-Fox)
74 Minutes   Black & white

While experimenting with a serum extracted from alligators to grow new limbs for the disabled, a well-meaning scientist injects the stuff into a wounded friend. In no time at all the patient begins to look like a set of alligator luggage, complete with clawed feet, hands and scaly face. He also acquires the personality of a reptile and teeters off in

search of something to eat, unaware that he has violated the laws of biological compatability.

Director: Roy Del Ruth, *Producer:* Jack Leewood, *Screenplay:* O. H. Hampton, *Story:* O. H. Hampton, Charles O'Neal, *Photographer:* **Karl Struss,** *Makeup:* Ben Nye, Dick Smith, *Music:* Irving Gertz

Cast: George Macready, Bruce Bennett, **Lon Chaney, Jr.,** Beverly Garland, Freda Inescort

ALPHAVILLE: Une Etrange Aventure de Lemmy Caution

Film   1965   France (Pathe/Chaumiane)
100 Minutes   Black & white

More soapbox than science fiction, *Alphaville* offers an eclectic mixture of film genres, pop culture and pulp fiction from French **auteur** filmmaker Jean-Luc Godard. Hitchcockian in structure, the film uses as its pivot a dangerous journey, taken by a seedy intergalactic detective sent to Alphaville, a city-state on a distant planet, to assassinate a dangerous scientist. The ruler of Alphaville turns out to be an omnipotent computer that has outlawed books, art and love, which its logic circuits won't program. Captured by the computer, Caution blows its circuits by acting in a typically human fashion—irrationally—and leaves the place in chaos, escaping with his victim's beautiful daughter, Natasha Von Braun.

Godard's **dystopia** is actually Paris, where he made *Alphaville* on location in the city's modern post-war buildings. The film is playful (Caution drives into "sidereal" space on an ordinary road in his old sedan), but it falls apart whenever Godard begins lecturing on conformity and the emotional barrenness engendered by the technological present. Godard's intention is better described in his original title: *Tarzan vs. IBM.*

Director/Screenplay: Jean-Luc Godard, *Producer:* Andre Michelin, *Photographer:* Raoul Coutard, *Music:* Paul Misraki

Cast: Eddie Constantine, Anna Karina, Akim Tamiroff, Howard Vernon, Laszlo Szabo

ALRAUNE

Film 1918 Hungary (Phoenix) Running time unknown Black & white (silent)

This first of six screen adaptations of Hans Heinz Ewer's controversial German novel *Alraune* (1911) was made in Hungary by director Mihaly Kertesz, later to become better known as Michael Curtiz, director of the durable Bogart classic *Casablanca*. Curtiz's handling of Ewer's tale of a soulless, morally corrupt woman has been praised by those fortunate enough to have seen it, but the 1928 German production is considered definitive. (See listing below.)

Director: Michael Curtiz, Odor Fritz, *Screenplay:* Richard Falk

Cast: Gyula Gal, Jeno Torzs, Roszi Szollosi, Margit Lux

ALRAUNE

(Also titled: *Daughter of Destiny; Unholy Love*)

Film 1928 Germany (UFA) Running time unknown Black & white (silent)

A woman born without a soul destroys every man unlucky enough to fall in love with her.

Brigitte Helm, the robot/woman of **Metropolis** (1926), scored another personal triumph in this second German version (an earlier film has been lost) of the novel *Alraune*, whose plot has to do with artificial insemination, then an unimaginable and shocking idea. Alraune (a German word for mandrake, a root said to come to life magically) is bred from a prostitute impregnated with the semen of a hanged killer. Adopted by the guilty scientist who performed the experiment, she is perverse from the start and spends her childhood abusing animals, torturing insects and generally making a nuisance of herself. Growing into a sultry beauty, she tests her sexuality by making erotic advances on her foster-father before taking a series of lovers. She feels nothing for them, however, and takes pleasure only in driving them to suicide. She finally experiences emotion when she reads the scientist's diary and learns she is not quite human. To make amends for the wrongs she has done, she kills herself.

At the time, Alraune was billed as an artificially created **android,** a misnomer since she was born naturally, if unconventionally. She is, however, a cinematic relative of **Homunkulus** (1916), a superman created in a laboratory, and a literary descendant of the **Frankenstein** monster. Helm's suggestive mixture of innocence and smoldering sensuality failed to delight British censors, who considered the film sexually subversive and refused to release it until scenes were reshot. The new version was released there as *Daughter of Destiny*. Cameraman Franz (Frank F.) Planer later photographed Disney's **20,000 Leagues Under the Sea** (1954).

Director/Screenplay: Henrik Galeen, *Art Director:* Walter Reimann, Max Heilbronner, *Photography:* Franz Planer

Cast: **Brigitte Helm,** Paul Wegener, Ivan Petrovitch, Alexander Sascha

ALRAUNE

(Also titled: *Daughter of Evil*)

Film 1930 Germany (UFA) 87 Minutes Black & white

Brigitte Helm repeated her role as the "artificial" wanton of **Alraune** (1928) with a different cast and director for this sound remake, which lacks the decadent excitements of the earlier film. The requirements of primitive sound equipment restricted the production to a studio, and the dialogue is excessive.

Director: Richard Oswald, *Screenplay:* Charlie Roelinghoff, R. Welsbach, *Photographer:* Gunther Kramph, *Art Directors:* Otto Erdmann, Hans Solhnle, *Music:* Bronislaw Kaper

Cast: Brigitte Helm, Albert Basserman, Agnes Straub, Kathe Haack

ALRAUNE

(U.S. and British title: *Vengeance*)

Film 1952 Germany (DCA) 90 Minutes Black & white

Although not as insinuatingly decadent as its German predecessors, this updated remake offers the icy presence of legendary actor/filmmaker Eric von Stroheim as the scientist, one of his last roles. The characters have switched places this time around (allegedly because von Stroheim couldn't play a sympathetic role); the scientist is now a heartless Svengali who exploits Alraune's innocent Trilby. The liaison ends when she falls in love with a younger man and the scientist murders her.

Director: Arthur Maria Rabenalt, *Screenplay:* Fritz Rotter, *Photographer:* Friedl Behn-Grund

Cast: Eric von Stroheim, Hildegarde Kneff, Karl Boehm, Trude Hesterberg

ALRAUNE AND THE GOLEM

Film 1919 Germany Running time unknown Black & white (silent)

One of the first films to pair two popular monsters, an artificially created woman (see above) and a living clay statue. The Golem, a mythical Hebrew figure brought to life with a few cabalistic incantations, is a fantasy figure popular in horror films.

Director: Paul Wegener, *Photographer:* Guido Seeber

Cast: Paul Wegener

ALTAIRA

Ingenuous blonde heroine of **Forbidden Planet** (1956). Named after **Altair IV,** the planet of her birth, she is the daughter of the widowed Professor Morbius, the only surviving member of a colony sent there from Earth aboard the spaceship Bellerephon. By the time a rescue mission arrives to investigate the mysterious deaths, she has grown into a beautiful 20-year-old whose only companions are her supergenius father and a likeable and talented robot named **Robby.** Altaira was portrayed by Anne Francis.

ALTAIR-IV

Title world of the film **Forbidden Planet** (1956). Located several light years from **Earth,** Altair-IV was the home planet of a highly intelligent life form known as **Krels,** now extinct. An initial effort at colonization from Earth resulted in the mysterious deaths of most of the expedition, and a probe is sent to investigate.

ALTERED STATES

Film 1980 U.S. (Warner Bros.)
103 Minutes Technicolor Panavision Dolby Stereo

At heart a monster movie with a trendy pseudo-scientific veneer, *Altered States* deals with a Harvard psychophysiologist, a latterday **Dr. Jekyll and Mr. Hyde,** who attempts to explore the inner recesses of human consciousness by tripping out in watery isolation tanks and popping sacred Indian mushrooms. The experiments produce a mind-boggling assault of erotic, mystical and aggressive visions, until, finally, he physically turns into an angry Neanderthal.

Altered States: Dr. Eddie Jessup (William Hurt) unleashes his genetic memories.

Memory may well be transmitted from generation to generation through the chemistry of genes, but the possibility is less interesting to director Ken Russell than delivering a spectacular, wildly absurd head trip. For all its visual excitement, the film has the feeling of a college lecture delivered by a pompous blowhard given to academic jargon. The script is credited to Sidney Aaron, a pseudonym for the late Paddy Chayefsky, who wrote the book on which the film is based and exercised his option to have his name removed from the credits. The transformation effects, by Bram Ferren and makeup artist Dick Smith (of *The Exorcist)*, are scary and hypnotic, the best seen this side of taking a dose of hallucinogenics.

Director: Ken Russell, *Producer:* Howard Gottfried, *Screenplay:* Sidney Aaron, *Novel:* Paddy Chayefsky, *Photographer:* Jordan Cronenweth, *Special Visual Effects:* Bram Ferren, *Makeup:* Dick Smith, *Music:* John Corigliano

Cast: William Hurt, Blair Brown, Bob Balaban, Charles Haid, Thaao Penghlis, Charles White Eagle

ALTERNATE HISTORIES

A theme popular in science fiction and mainstream literature but little used in SF films, involving an alteration in historical fact and its subsequent effects on life today. In the BBC-TV production *An Englishman's Castle* (1975), for instance, Great Britain is depicted as having surrendered to Hitler during the Blitz of World War II. Contemporary London looks much the way it does today, but daily life has been subtly regimented, Jews have been eliminated and television is used as a propaganda medium. The idea was also the basis of a similar film, It Happened Here (1963). (See also: **Parallel Worlds.)**

ALTERNATE WORLDS

See: **Parallel Worlds**

ALYN, KIRK (1910-   )

Second-string Hollywood leading man who made history of a sort by becoming the first actor to impersonate **Superman** on the screen. He played the role in two serials: **Superman** (1948) and **Atom Man vs. Superman** (1950).

A shy but friendly man, Alyn was born in Oxford, New Jersey, and trained as a dancer before appearing in the chorus of several hit Broadway shows of the 1930s, including George Gershwin's *Girl Crazy* and *Of Thee I Sing.* Brought to Hollywood in the early 1940s by Warner Brothers to appear in comedy shorts, he later became a contract player at Columbia Pictures where he decorated the backgrounds of such major features as *My Sister Eileen* and *You Were Never Lovelier* (both 1942). He graduated to larger roles in lesser films but was little noticed until the studio selected him (supposedly from 125 candidates) to play Superman because of his resemblance to the comic book hero and his trim, athletic physique. The role did little to advance his career, however: the one-dimensional scripts, perfunctory direction and the haste in which the films were made gave him little opportunity to exercise his talents as an actor.

Typecast as a serial hero when such films were being supplanted by television, and replaced by **George Reeves** for a subsequent Superman film, Alyn left Hollywood in the early 1950s to appear on Broadway and make television commercials. He subsequently retired but returned to the screen for a brief appearance in **Superman—The Movie** (1978) as Lois Lane's father. Playing her mother was actress **Noel Neill,** who originated the role of Lois in the 1948 serial. He also appeared in an episode of TV's **Battlestar Galactica** (1978-79). Alyn subsequently published his memoirs, *A Job for Superman.* In 1977 he made news by suing DC Comics, Inc., and two film studios for allegedly leasing a photograph of him as Superman poised for flight in an "obscene" wall decoration captioned with the word, "Superschmuck."

Other films: Lucky Jordan (1942), *Overland Mail Robbery* and *Pistol Packin' Mama* (1943), *Forty Thieves* (1944), *Little Miss Broadway* and *The Trap* (1947). *Serials: Daughter of Don Q* (1946), *Federal Agents vs. Underworld Inc.* (1949), **Radar Patrol vs. Spy King** (1950), *Blackhawk* (1952).

THE AMAZING COLOSSAL MAN

Film   1957   U.S. (AIP)   80 Minutes   Black & white

The Amazing Colossal Man is one of a number of cut-rate imitations rushed into production to capitalize on the success of **The Incredible Shrinking Man,** released the same year. Slapped together by jack-of-all-trades filmmaker **Bert I. Gordon** (who has been called the "Renaissance man of schlock"), it follows the rise of an army officer accidently exposed to an atomic explosion at a testing site. After miraculously recovering from radiation burns within a few days, he swells into an insane giant given to wrecking miniature cardboard houses. The film made so much money at drive-in cinemas that it inspired an equally mindless sequel, **War of the Colossal Beast** (1958).

Director/Producer/Special Effects: Bert I. Gordon, *Screenplay:* Bert I. Gordon, Mark Hanna, *Photographer:* Joseph Biroc, *Music:* Albert Glasser

Cast: Glenn Langan, Cathy Downs, Judd Holdren, James Sealy, William Hudson

THE AMAZING SPIDER-MAN

TV series   1977-79   U.S. (CBS)   60 Minutes (weekly)   Color

The further adventures of "Spidey," *Stan Lee*'s popular **comic-book** hero, who is as clumsy as he is powerful. A photographer-turned-crimefighter, Spider-Man is secretly mild-mannered Peter Parker. Endowed with superpowers by the bite of a radioactive spider, he can scale walls with fingers and toes, and "fly" with the help of a magic web hidden in a cartridge case on his wrist. Privately, however, Parker is a wash-out who can't get a date, and his grouchy boss won't give him a raise. A hypochondriac, he often finds his human weaknesses interfering with his duties as a righter-of-wrongs, as when he gets a sneezing attack while running up the side of a skyscraper.

The series was preceded by the TV film **Spider-Man** (1977), which explained how Parker came to be a superhero. During its last season, the name of the series was changed to *The New Adventures of Spider-Man* to bolster sagging ratings.

The Amazing Spider-Man: Nicholas Hammond in a publicity photo.

Director: E. W. Swackhamer and others, *Producer:* Lee Siegel, Ron Satlof, Bob Janes, *Photographer:* Fred Jackman, *Art Director:* James Hulsey, *Music:* Johnnie Spence

Cast: Nicholas Hammond, Michael Pataki, Robert F. Simon, Chip Fields

THE AMAZING THREE

TV series   1967   U.S. (syndicated)
30 Minutes (weekly)   Color

Weak in animation but strong on whimsy, *The Amazing Three* offered Saturday morning viewers a trio of 21st-century aliens who came to **Earth** disguised as a duck, a dog and a horse. The idea is to protect their identities during a secret mission to determine whether humankind should be eliminated. Fortunately, they become friends with boy-hero Kenny Carter and join forces to rid the world of evil-doers. (52 episodes)

THE AMAZING TRANSPARENT MAN

Film   1960   U.S. (AIP)   59 Minutes   Black & white

A convict volunteers for a medical experiment that turns him invisible. He escapes from prison, robs a bank and upsets the scientist who cooked up the serum. **The Invisible Man** (1933) is still light years ahead of him.

Director: **Edgar G. Ulmer,** *Producer:* Lester D. Guthrie, *Screenplay:* Jack Lewis, *Special Effects:* Roger George, *Music:* Darrell Calker

Cast: Douglas Kennedy, Marguerite Chapman, James Griffith, Ivan Triesault

AMERICATHON

Film   1979   U.S. (MGM)   Technicolor   Panavision   Dolby

If energy were talent, the makers of this kinetic farce wouldn't be at wit's end trying to project contemporary American anxieties into a hilariously comic future. The year is 1999 when jogging shoes and bicycles have replaced automobiles (which are now used mostly as garden planters and efficiency apartments) and the U.S. faces bankruptcy due to the exorbitant oil prices of the greedy Hebrab Republic (an unlikely coalition of Israel and her Arab neighbors). To raise cash and prevent the country from reverting to the Indians (a Navaho running-shoe billionaire is its chief creditor), the marijuana-smoking President of the U.S. stages a mammoth telethon that replaces rare diseases with America as its own most heartfelt cause.

Director: Neil Israel, *Producer:* Joe Roth, *Screenplay:* Neil Israel, Michael Mislove, Monica Johnson, *Photographer:* Gerald Hirschfield, *Production Director:* Stan Jolley, *Music:* Eddie Money

Cast: John Ritter, Harvey Korman, Meatloaf, Chief Dan George, Nancy Morgan, Zane Busby, The Beach Boys, Elvis Costello

THE AMPHIBIAN MAN

See: **Chelovek Anfibya**

AM RANDE DER WELT
At The Edge of the World

Film   1927   Germany (UFA)   89 Minutes   Black & white (silent)

Billed as a "passionate appeal for world peace," *Am Rande Der Welt* failed to captivate German audiences still chafing from the country's defeat in World War I. Brilliantly designed by A. D. Neppach, the film graphically depicts a devastating war of the future—a theme popular 10 years earlier. Even star **Brigitte Helm,** who had recently scored a personal triumph in **Metropolis** (1926), couldn't lure customers to the box office.

Director: Karl Grune, *Art Director:* A. D. Neppach, Albert Steinruck, *Photographer:* F. A. Wegner

Cast: Brigitte Helm, Max Schreck, Wilhelm Dieterle, Imre Raday

ANAMORPHIC LENS

A motion picture camera lens that squeezes a wide picture onto a standard frame of film; commonly referred to as 'scope'. A complementary lens on the projector unsqueezes the image and reverses the distortion for showing on a wide screen. Trademarked variations include **Panavision, CinemaScope, Technirama** and **Techniscope.** (See also: **Wide Screen.**)

ANDROID

An artificial man or animal created biologically and used as a companion or servant; sometimes shortened to "droid." The terms **"robot"** and "android" often are used interchangeably, but the entities they describe are related in function only (both are programmed to take orders, but a robot is machine-made). Robot authority **Isaac Asimov** defines androids as being bred rather than built, and calls them "robots made of flesh."

The word "android"—Greek for "manlike"'—first appeared in the 18th century in connection with the attempts of alchemists Albertus Magnus and Paracelsus to breathe life into organic compounds. Later that century it was used as a synonym for automata—clockwork dolls that imitated human movement (See: **Tales of Hoffman**). The confusion in terms began in 1921, when Karel Kapek coined the word "robot" to describe worker-slaves created from vats of chemicals in his play **R.U.R.** During the 1930s and 1940s SF writers differentiated robot from android, and today the latter has come to signify biological androids. These include the **Frankenstein** monster, sutured together from body parts, and **H. G. Wells'** surgically altered "humanimals" of **The Island of Dr. Moreau.** The appealing humanlike "droids" of the **Star Wars** series were fabricated mechanically and are therefore robots. Androids fall under the category of **humanoid.** (See also: **Cyborg; Clone.**)

THE ANDROMEDA BREAKTHROUGH

TV serial   1962   Great Britain (BBC)
60 Minutes (weekly)   Black & white

This six-episode sequel to **A for Andromeda** (1961) follows the scientist of the earlier episodes to South America, where government scientists have also unscrambled the radio message from the Andromeda Galaxy. They too have followed the signal's instructions and built a futuristic computer to create an artificial girl, perhaps, he hopes, a double of his own beloved but ill-fated creation. The purpose of the radio message is once again left unexplained. Susan Hampshire replaced Julie Christie as the **android** girl.

Producer: John Elliott, *Writers:* Fred Hoyle, Norman Jones

Cast: Peter Halliday, Mary Morris, Noel Johnson, David King, Susan Hampshire

THE ANDROMEDA STRAIN

Film   1971   U.S. (Universal)   131 Minutes
Technicolor Panavision

A NASA satellite returning from space lands off-course, bringing with it a deadly microbe that kills most of the residents of a small Arizona town. Acting quickly, government scientists arrive in protective suits and discover that two people have survived, an old man and a baby, who may hold the key to destroying the organism.

The survivors and the satellite are immediately quarantined in a vast underground research station called Wildfire, built as a secret defense against germ warfare. While biologists study the Andromeda strain, which apparently lives by converting matter into energy and energy into matter, it attacks the plastic gaskets of its isolation cubicle, setting the time fuse of an atomic **bomb,** rigged for just such an emergency. Realizing that the explosion would only spread the organism, not kill it, the scientists are faced with an impossible dilemma that sets the stage for a hold-your-breath ending.

Essentially an invaders-from-space story, the film is told with such a high degree of tension and careful accumulation of scientific detail that it is entirely convincing. Scriptwriter Nelson Gidding has preserved the values of **Michael Crichton's** best-seller, and producer/director **Robert Wise** has heightened its effect with an impressive array of busy computers and other working hardware (assembled and designed by **Douglas Trumbull**). For all its high-tech look, however, the film takes an ambivalent attitude toward technology, which is depicted as incapable of dealing with the monster it has brought to **Earth.**

Director/Producer: Robert Wise, *Screenplay:* Nelson Gidding, *Novel:* Michael Crichton, *Photographer:* Richard H. Kline, *Art Director:* Boris Leven, *Special Effects:* Douglas Trumbull, Jamie Shourt, *Music:* Gil Melle

Cast: Arthur Hill, David Wayne, James Olson, Kate Reid, Paula Kelly

ANDY WARHOL'S FLESH FOR FRANKENSTEIN

See: **Andy Warhol's Frankenstein**

ANDY WARHOL'S FRANKENSTEIN

(Also titled: *Andy Warhol's Flesh for Frankenstein*)

Film 1974 U.S./Italy (EMI) 95 Minutes Eastmancolor (3-D)

The monster returns as a handsome, naked sex object in this gory, X-rated put-on. The hog entrails that pass for human body organs are particularly stomach-turning in 3-D closeup, as are the vicious, woman-hating sex scenes. The baron and his wife undertake to produce a perfect man and woman for their own use, while dallying with various members of the household. Ever in search of new thrills, the Baron slices open his **android** playmate and pleasures himself with her gall bladder. Strictly for Warhol's camp followers. (See also: **Stereoscopic Film.**)

Director/Screenplay: Paul Morrissey, *Producer:* Andrew Drounsberg, *Photographer:* Luigi Kue-

veillier, *Art Director:* Enrico Job, *Music:* Claudio Guizzi

Cast: Joe Dallesandro, Udo Kier, Monique Van Vooren, Arno Juerging, Dalila di Lazzar, Srdjan Zelenovic

THE ANGRY RED PLANET

Film 1960 U.S. (AIP) 94 Minutes Eastmancolor

Director **Ib Melchior** apparently rummaged through AIP's monster closet for this unconvincing thriller, whose fantastic vision of **Mars** manages to cover Hollywood's more lurid misconceptions of that planet. Melchior's lack of imagination extends to the story, which concerns an American space probe whose astronauts are attacked by: (1) a big blob hungry for the spaceship; (2) nasty carniverous plants; and (3) a mammoth flying spider with the face of a bat.

Director: Ib Melchior, *Producer:* Sidney Pink, Norman Maurer, *Screenplay:* Ib Melchior, Sidney Pink, *Special Effects:* Herman Townsley, *Music:* Paul Dunlap

Cast: Gerald Mohr, Nora Hayden, Les Tremayne, Jack Kruschen

ANIMATION

The technique of creating the illusion that inanimate objects are in motion. The most familiar form is cartoon animation, in which drawings on transparent celluloid sheets (called cels), each depicting a fraction of movement, are filmed one at a time. Another type of animation uses **puppets,** whose movements are adjusted progressively and filmed similarly, one frame at a time. The latter technique is called **stop-motion** animation. When the individually exposed frames are projected at the standard rate of 24 frames per second, the images appear to move.

SF cartoon films are rare, the technique being better suited to fantasy subjects. The few notable examples include Max Fleischer's **Superman** cartoons (1941-43), **Wizards** (1977), *Heavy Metal* (1981) and the whimsical children's films of Czechoslovakian animator **Karel Zeman.** SF-fantasy cartoons seen on television often have only limited animation, in which certain features of a character are given motion. Another system involves the use of computers to provide intermediate positions between a drawing that begins the motion and another that completes it. A more radical mathematical system, called **computer graphics,** can produce simultaneous images in color, with a three-dimensional perspective.

Cartoon animation is often seen in live-action SF films, although it is not recognized as such. Disney animators provided the feathered menaces of Hitchcock's **The Birds** (1953), for instance, and the Id monster of **Forbidden Planet** (1956). In **Star Trek—The Motion Picture** (1979), artist Bob Swarthe drew the tangled web of electric blue emanating from the mysterious V'GER; his artwork was inserted into the film via a traveling **matte.** Similarly, blasts from **laser** pistols are animated in virtually every film in which they appear.

Stop-motion animation has produced a number of memorable movie monsters, including **King Kong** (1933), the fanciful menagerie of **Ray Harryhausen,** and the fanciful beasts created for the **Star Wars** films, including the **Banthas** and **Wampas.**

ANTIGRAVITY DEVICE

One of the more fantastic ideas of science fiction, usually found in **space opera,** in which a flying belt or other apparatus worn on the body overcomes a basic law of physics. Larger versions levitate entire cities.

THE APE

Film   1940   U.S. (Monogram)   61 Minutes
Black & white

Boris Karloff, in one of his sympathetic madman roles, is Dr. Adrian, a scientist who distills a cure for polio from human spinal fluid. To keep up his supply, he dresses in the skin of an ape he has killed and proceeds to murder the town's nastier citizens. Mortally wounded by policemen who mistake him for the ape (which has escaped from a circus), he dies happily attended by a young girl, with the realization he has cured her of paralysis.

Director: William Nigh, *Screenplay:* **Curt Siodmak,** Richard Carroll, *Play:* Adam Shirk, *Photographer:* Harry Neumann

Cast: Boris Karloff, Maris Wrixon, Henry Hall, Gertrude Hoffman

THE APE MAN

(Great Britain title: *Lock Your Doors)*

Film   1943   U.S. (Monogram)   64 Minutes
Black & white

Bargain-basement science fiction, with horror star **Bela Lugosi** as a scientist who makes a monkey out of himself with an injection of serum concocted from the spinal fluid of an ape. The thrills never materialize. *Return of the Ape Man,* a sequel with no plot connection, appeared the following year.

Director: William Beaudine, *Producer:* Sam Katzman, Jack Dietz, *Screenplay:* Barney A. Sarecky, *Story: They Creep in the Dark,* Karl Brown, *Photographer:* Mack Stengler, *Art Director:* David Milton, *Music Director:* Edward Kay

Cast: Bela Lugosi, Wallace Ford, Louise Currie, Minerva Urecal

APOLLO OBJECTS

Term used by astronomers to describe mysterious, fast-moving celestial objects that cross or nearly cross the orbit of **Earth.** Discovered in 1932, Apollo objects are believed to be **asteroids** or **meteoroids.** A difference in timing of the orbits of Apollo objects would result in a collision with Earth, but the possibility is thought to be remote. A number of scientists believe similar cataclysms have occurred in the past, however, which would explain the relatively sudden extinction of dinosaurs and other unexplained events of prehistory. Scars of past collisions with objects from space, covered by soil and natural erosion, have been identified in recent years from aerial photographs. SF filmmakers have long anticipated collisions with heavenly bodies, of course, from **The Comet** (1910) to **La Fin Du Monde** (1931), **When Worlds Collide** (1951) and **Meteor** (1979).

AQUAMAN

TV series   1967-68   U.S. (syndicated)
7 Minutes   Color

Aquaman, a water-logged crime-fighter spawned from an Atlantean mother and a human father (a lighthouse keeper), spends most of his time protecting the underwater kingdom of **Atlantis** from hostile visitors. He easily repels invaders by telepathically commanding sea creatures to help him. This animated cartoon series was excerpted from *The Superman-Aquaman Hour,* which debuted during the previous season.

Voices: Marvin Miller

THE AQUARIANS

TV film   1970   U.S. (NBC)   90 Minutes
Color

Simple-minded but entertaining, this technically superb feature takes place in the near future in a nuclear-powered undersea research bubble. There, a team of oceanographers and marine biologists happen upon a group of scuba-suited adventurers attempting to salvage a wrecked ship loaded with deadly nerve gas. If they succeed, the leaking gas will cause a serious pollution problem. An exciting chase scene between the lab's chief scientist and a deadly one-man submarine almost makes up for the plot's illogicalities. The underwater sequences were directed by **Ricou Browning,** the gillman of **The Creature from the Black Lagoon** (1954).

Director: Don McDougall, *Producer:* Ivan Tors, *Screenplay:* Leslie Stevens, Winston Miller, *Story:* Ivan Tors, Alan Caillou, *Photography:* Clifford Polan, *Art Director:* Gene Harris, *Music:* Lalo Schifrin

Cast: Ricardo Montalban, Jose Ferrer, Leslie Nielsen, Kate Woodville, Curt Lowens

THE ARC

Film   1919   Germany   Black & white (silent)

The end of the world was already old hat to moviegoers by the time Germany got around to producing this primitive disaster epic. Based on a popular novel by Werner Scheff, it was released in two short parts as a mini-**cliffhanger.** Getting started here were director Richard Oswald, who later made the definitive sound version of **Alraune** (1930), and cameraman Karl Freund, photographer of **Metropolis** (1926) and director of the stylish **Mad Love** (1935). Both filmmakers went on to distinguished careers in Hollywood.

ARK II

TV series   1976   U.S. (CBS)   30 Minutes
(weekly)   Color

Years of air pollution and indiscriminate dumping of poisonous wastes have transformed the Earth of 2476 into an arid wilderness where tribes war over dwindling supplies of food. Fortunately, the scientific knowledge required for rebuilding civilization has been preserved in a mobile warehouse named *Ark II.* Accompanying the traveling repository in Arkroamer vehicles are three young scientists named Jonah, Ruth and Samuel, whose weekly adventures focus on bringing "the hope of the new future to mankind."

Director: **Ted Post,** Hollingsworth Morse, *Producer:* Dick Rosenbloom, *Story:* Martin Roth, *Photographer:* Robert F. Sparks, *Music:* Yvette Blais, Jeff Michael

Cast: Terry Lester, Jean Marie Hon, Jose Flores, Adam the chimpanzee

ARMSTRONG OF THE SBI

Radio serial   1950-51   U.S. (ABC)
30 Episodes, 30 Minutes each (weekly)

A short-lived sequel to the long-run radio series, **Jack Armstrong, the All-American Boy** (1933-50). Having grown up with his listeners, Armstrong had gone to work as the chief investigator of the Scientific Bureau of Investigation, where he could continue fighting crime and menacing foreigners with an assortment of incredible gadgets. The program, which originated in Chicago, debuted on September 5, 1950, and left the air on June 28, 1951.

Director/Producer: James Jewell, *Writer:* James Jewell, Donald Gallagher, Kermit Slobb, Paul Fairman, Alan Fishburn, Jack Lawrence, Thomas Elvidge

Cast: Jack Armstrong—Charles Flynn, *Vic Hardy*—Ken Griffin, Carlton KaDell, *Betty Fairfield*—Patricia Dunlap, *Billy Fairfield*—Dick York, *Announcers:* Ed Prentiss, Ken Nordine

ARNOLD, JACK (1916–   )

Virtuoso director of several atmospheric 1950s' SF-**horror** movies that have become classics. His most famous contribution to the genre is **The Creature from the Black Lagoon** (1954), a low-budget exploitation film elevated to a minor masterpiece by his talent for creating arresting and unsettling images. Arnold's skillfully manipulated gill-man, a sinister but sad man-beast, has since joined Hollywood's pantheon of legendary monsters, alongside Dracula, the Wolf-Man and the **Frankenstein** monster.

Born in New Haven, Connecticut, and educated at Ohio State University, Arnold began his career in the Army Signal Corps during World War II. Assigned to a training film unit, he served his apprenticeship with documentary filmmaker Robert Flaherty. After the war, Arnold acted in films while directing documentaries for government agencies and private industry. He signed a contract with Universal in 1953 and made his debut with *Girls in the Night.* Arnold's best film, **The Incredible Shrinking Man** (1957), a metaphorical tale about a mutated man vanishing into infinity, comes close to capturing the ideological mysticism of written science fiction. A strictly commercial craftsman who has no pretensions to art, he has nevertheless made an indelible impression on the SF film.

Other films: **It Came From Outer Space** (1953), **Revenge of the Creature, Tarantula** (1955), *The Tattered Dress* (1957), *Man in the Shadow,* **The Space Children, Monster on the Campus** (1958), *No Name on the Bullet,* **The Mouse That Roared** (1959), *A Global Affair* (1964), *Hello Down There* (1969), *Boss Nigger* (1975), *The Swiss Conspiracy* (1977)

TV credits: **Science Fiction Theatre** (1955-57), *Gilligan's Island* (1964-67), *It Takes a Thief* (1968-69), *Ellery Queen* (1975), **Holmes and Yo-Yo** (1976), *Sex and the Married Woman* (1977), *The Nancy Drew Mysteries* (1977-78)

AROUND THE WORLD UNDER THE SEA

Film   1966   U.S. (MGM)   117 Minutes
Metrocolor   Panavision

A weak underwater adventure in the **Jules Verne** tradition, popular at the time because of its familiar cast of TV stars, who pose as scientists exploring the cause of mysterious tidal waves (the result of fissures in the Earth's surface). Its flimsy, streamlined submarine is no match for the Nautilus. **Ricou Browning,** who played the gill-man in **The Creature From the Black Lagoon** (1954), directed the underwater sequences.

Director/Producer: Andrew Marton, *Executive Producer:* Ivan Tors, *Screenplay:* Arthur Weiss, Art Arthur, *Photographer:* Clifford Poland, Lamar Boren, *Art Director:* Preston Roundtree, Mel Bledsoe, *Music:* Harry Sukman

Cast: David McCallum, Lloyd Bridges, Marshall Thompson, Brian Kelly, Shirley Eaton, Keenan Wynn

ASIMOV, ISAAC (1920–   )

American SF writer, critic, science popularizer and chronicler of the speculative future. One of the most famous names in the genre, Asimov is also one of the most prolific, with more than 100 books to his credit.

Although few of his works have been adapted to the screen, several of his imaginative concepts have been absorbed by the SF film (and science fiction in general).

Among these are his famous Three Laws of Robotics, presented in a series of stories collected in *I Robot* (1950) (adapted as an episode of **The Outer Limits)** and *The Rest of the Robots* (1964). A kind of condensed Ten Commandments for intelligent machines, the laws forbid robots to harm human beings, to always obey human orders unless they conflict with the previous law, and to protect themselves as long as this does not contradict the first two laws. Asimov's robots brought the clanking metal monsters of pulp fiction and movie **serials** into the modern age. The first of this new breed appeared onscreen in the guise of **Robby the Robot,** the likeable mechanical helpmate of **Forbidden Planet** (1956). And elements of Asimov's landmark "Foundation" series, a saga of a million-world galactic empire threatened with collapse from a 30,000-year war, were incorporated in the **Star Wars** series, as well as its TV imitator, **Battlestar Galactica.** The stories appear in book form in *Foundation* (1951), *Foundation and Empire* (1952), *Second Foundation* (1953) and *Foundation's Edge* (1982). His only direct connection with motion pictures has been the novelization of **Fantastic Voyage** (1966), whose scientifically inconsistent script he improved considerably. Several of his stories were dramatized on the British TV series **Out of This World** (1962) and **Out of the Unknown** (1965-67), the latter not shown in the U.S.

Born in Russia, Asimov emigrated to the U.S. at the age of three with his parents and became a citizen in 1928. As a child, he was an avid reader of the SF magazines sold in his father's New York candy store. A precocious student who graduated from high school at 16, he published his first SF story, "Marooned off Vesta," in a 1939 issue of *Amazing Stories.* His 1940 classic, "Nightfall," appeared in *Astounding Stories,* as did most of his subsequent short fiction. He graduated from Columbia University at the age of 19 and received an M.A. in chemistry two years later. During World War II, he worked alongside fellow SF writers Robert Heinlein and L. Sprague De Camp at the U.S. Naval Air Experimental Station at Philadelphia. Earning his doctorate in 1948, he spent nine years as an associate professor of biochemistry at the Boston University School of Medicine, while continuing to write outstanding works of science fiction. By 1959 his fame was such that he retired (while holding the title) to devote all his time to writing. Since then he has written mostly science popularizations and SF "juveniles" under the pseudonym of Paul French. He is the executive editor of *Isaac Asimov's Science Fiction Magazine.*

ASPECT RATIO

The width in relation to height of a frame of motion picture **film** and the image it projects on a **screen.** The international industry standard set by **Thomas Edison** and **W. K. L. Dickson** in 1906 is the 35-mm. film gauge, which yields an aspect ratio of 1.33:1—a size later chosen for the **television** screen. With the introduction of **CinemaScope** and subsequent **wide-screen** systems in the 1950s, aspect ratios have broadened considerably and range from 1.65:1 to 2:55.1.

ASSIGNMENT OUTER SPACE

(Also titled: *Space Men)*

Film 1960 Italy (Titanus/Ultra) 79 Minutes Color (Released 1962 U.S. [AIP])

Spaghetti science fiction concerning an out-of-control spaceship about to collide with Earth. Several well-tailored European astronauts put their various amours on hold and go aloft to head off the maverick ship.

Director: Antonio Margheriti, *Screenplay:* Vasily Petrov, *Special Effects:* Caesar Peace, *Music:* J. K. Broady, Gordon Zahler

Cast: Rik von Nutter, Gabriella Farinon, Archie Savage

ASTEROIDS

Small planetary bodies, sometimes called minor planets or planetoids, orbiting the sun in a loosely defined grouping called the asteroid belt. Ceres, the largest (diameter c. 480 miles) and first-known, was discovered in 1801 by Italian astronomer Giuseppe Piazzi who originally mistook it for a tiny planet. Since then, astronomers have counted about 100,000 of these lumpy rocks, some of which spin in erratic orbits that sweep across the orbits of **Mars** and **Earth** (See: **Apollo Objects).** Icarus, one of the smallest (diameter c. ½ mile), passed relatively close to Earth on June 14, 1968.

While their origin remains a mystery, it appears that asteroids occupy an orbit where a planet should be—in a broad gap between Mars and Jupiter (see: **Solar System).** In 1950 a Soviet scientist proposed that asteroids are the debris of an original fifth planet (which he named Phaeton) broken into bits by a cataclysmic disaster. He cited as evidence the fact that asteroids are similar in composition to Earth and other **Terrestrial planets.** Today, scientists believe the fragments represent materials that failed to coalesce into a planet during the formation of the solar system.

Asteroids have figured prominently in **space operas** as a hazard to interplanetary travel akin to terrestrial icebergs, although in reality they would present little danger since they lie far apart roughly in an elliptical plane and can easily be passed through or over. Another fictional use is as a frontier mining territory where astronauts extract precious minerals accompanied by battered, one-man spacecrafts instead of mules. This latter possibility might one day come true according to a study made in the 1970s by National Aeronautics and Space Administration (NASA), which predicted that asteroids would one day be hauled into orbit around the Earth and mined to supplement our dwindling supply of mineral ores.

THE ASTOUNDING SHE-MONSTER

Film 1958 U.S. (AIP) 60 Minutes Black & white

Descending in a streak of light mistaken for a meteor, a spaceship makes a secret landing in a forest clearing. Out pops a sexy space alien clad in a body stocking evidently purchased at the Mars branch of Frederick's of Hollywood. She doesn't care much for human males, however, to whom she gives a fatal brush-off with a pneumatic power field emanating from her shapely torso.

An insignificant film, *Astounding She-Monster* is worthy of note for its ambivalent attitude toward women. Its makers apparently equate beauty with treachery and unconventional independence with aggressive malice. The she-monster can be seen as a projection of male fears of impotence, a sex fantasy whose considerable charms and sexuality are dangerous weapons. But then, science fiction has never been totally comfortable with the female species.

Director/Producer: Ron Ashcroft, *Screenplay:* Frank Hall, *Music:* Guenther Kauer

Cast: Shirley Kilpatrick, Robert Clarke, Marilyn Harvey, Kenne Duncan

ASTROBLEMES

Geological term for craters made on planetary surfaces by strikes of **Meteorites** or **Apollo Objects.**

ASTRO BOY

TV series 1963 Japan 30 Minutes Color

A syndicated series from Japan, this dubbed animated cartoon still turns up occasionally on Saturday morning children's shows. Astro Boy is a wholesome, superpowerful **robot** built by Dr. Boynton, a 21st-century scientist, to replace the son he lost in an automobile accident. The indestructible "boy" is programmed with a conscience, making him ideal for keeping Earth safe from various creatures from outerspace and assorted home-based villains. For those who think young.

ASTROGATION

A SF term derived from the word navigation and meaning the same thing in re-

Astrogation: Commander Adama (Lorne Greene) charts a path on *Battlestar Galactica's* version of an astro-indicator.

gards to space: to keep a **spaceship** on its course by triangulation, according to the positions of stars and galaxies relative to Earth. Navigator of a spacecraft is called an astrogator, who charts his path on an astroindicator or an astrograph (films often use more fanciful names)—a device with a large screen that may or may not project a holographic image and which is linked by computer to the ship's electronic log. When leapfrogging through **hyperspace,** an astrogator uses a spectrum analyzer to identify stars moving past too quickly for other instruments to perceive. (See also: **Holography.)**

THE ASTRONAUTS

See: **Der Schweigende Stern**

THE ASTRONOMER'S DREAM

See: **La Lune a Un Metre**

ASTRONOMICAL CONSTANTS

Units of measure used by astronomers to express the vast distances between planets, **stars** and **galaxies.** Astronomical constants are expressed in the **astronomical unit** (approximately 92.9 million miles), **light-year** (6 trillion miles) and parsec (about 19.5 trillion miles). Distances from **Earth** are measured by the parallax and period methods.

ASTRONOMICAL UNIT

Unit of length for measuring distances in space. An astronomical unit is based on the distance from the **Earth** to the sun and equals 92.9 million miles. (See also: **Astronomical Constants.)**

THE ASTRO-ZOMBIES

Film   1969   U.S. (Gemini)   90 Minutes   Color

Obvious nonsense concerning a modern-day Dr. **Frankenstein** who trudges through a labyrinthine plot chopping up victims to get body parts for a superpowerful monster/slave.

Director/Producer: Ted V. Mikels, *Screenplay:* Ted V. Mikels, Wayne Rogers, *Photographer:* Robert Maxwell, *Art Director:* Wally Moon, *Music:* Nico Karaski

Cast: Wendell Corey, John Carradine, Tom Pace, Wally Moon, Joan Patrick

AT THE EARTH'S CORE

Film   1976   Great Britain (AIP/Amicus)
90 Minutes   Technicolor

Not a sequel but a follow-up to **The Land That Time Forgot** (1974), made by the same production team. This time the lost world is Pellucidor, a prehistoric domain at the center of the Earth, dreamed up by Edgar Rice Burroughs for his 1922 novel *At the Earth's Core*, the first of a trilogy. Explorers **Peter Cushing** and Doug McClure reach the kingdom when their "Iron Mole" drilling machine goes a bit off course. Missing is Burroughs' fabulous bestiary which was apparently beyond the means of the film's budget.

Director: **Kevin Connor,** *Producer:* John Dark, *Screenplay:* Milton Subotsky, *Novel:* Edgar Rice Burroughs, *Photographer:* Alan Hume, *Production Designer:* Maurice Carter, *Special Effects:* Ian Wingrove, *Music:* Mike Vickers

Cast: Peter Cushing, Doug McClure, Caroline Munro, Cy Grant, Godfrey James

L'ATLANTIDE

Film   1921   France (Thalman)   124 Minutes (16fps)   Black & white (silent)   (Released 1922 U.S. [MGM]   95 Minutes as *Missing Husbands*)

Atlantis, that eternally fascinating lost continent first described by Plato in 335 B.C., made a splashy screen debut in this faithful adaptation of Pierre Benoit's best-selling novel (1919), which has been filmed several times since. Benoit's fabled kingdom is landlocked in a vast cavern beneath the Sahara Desert, where an arcane technology provides air and light for a gaudy, Turkish-baroque city. Its ruler is the heartless Queen Antinea, a plump femme fatale (played by *Comedie Francaise* star Stacia Napierkowska) who regularly sends Arab servants to the surface world to replenish her supply of lovers. When she tires of her playthings, she has the men "galvanized" and put on display in a trophy room that resembles a war memorial.

The most expensive production of its time (two million francs), *L'Atlantide* played for a year in Paris and was a great commercial success in Great Britain. U.S. Director Jacques Feyder, who began his career as an actor in the special effects films of **Georges Melies** and later became a leading filmmaker, took his camera and crew to the Sahara Desert (then a herculean effort) and shot the expressionistic interiors in a studio near Algiers. The film still has a musty charm, and the desert scenes hold up, but the 1932 remake is far superior (see listing below). (See also: **Expressionism.**)

Director/Screenplay: Jacques Feyder, *Novel:* Pierre Benoit, *Photographer:* George Specht, Victor Morin, *Art Director:* Manuel Orazzi

Cast: Stacia Napierkowska, Jean Angelo, Georges Melchior, Andre Roanne, Marie-Louise Iribe

L'ATLANTIDE

(Also titled: *Lost Atlantis; The Mistress of Atlantis, Queen of Atlantis*)

Film   1932   Germany/France (Nero)
80 Minutes   Black & white

Visually stunning and directed with Freudian elan by the great G. W. Pabst, this is the definitive version of *L'Atlantide* (see listings above and below). **Brigitte Helm,** the heroine/**robot** of **Metropolis** (1926), is icy perfection as the Queen of **Atlantis,** whose voracious sexuality destroys any man foolish enough to fall under her spell.

Simultaneously filmed in German, English and French with different casts (with the exception of Helm), the film more than equalled the international success of the original, 1921 version. Helm's portrayal and the Queen's hall of mummified lovers have since become motion-picture set-pieces, copied in scores of films including Universal's silly remake *The Siren of Atlantis* (1947), which starred camp-vamp Maria Montez.

Director: G. W. Pabst, *Producer:* Seymour Nebenzal, *Screenplay:* Herbert Rappoport, Laszlo Vajda, Pierre Ichac, *Novel:* Pierre Benoit, *Photographer:* **Eugene Schuftan,** *Production Designer:* Erno Metzner, *Music:* Wolfgang Zeller

Cast: Brigitte Helm, Gustav Diessl, Heinz Klingenberg, Tela Tschai, John Stuart

L'ATLANTIDE/ANTINEA L'AMANTE DELLA CITTA SEPOLTA

(U.S. title: *Journey Beneath the Desert)*

Film   1961   France/Italy/U.S. (Embassy)
89 Minutes   Color

Except for a few interesting camera setups, this sixth movie version of Pierre Benoit's durable fantasy novel offers only tedium and the distraction of dubbed voices and words that rarely match the characters and lips of the actors. The plot has to do with lost helicopter pilots who find the legendary city of **Atlantis** near an H-bomb test site in the desert, but you probably won't care.

Director: **Edgar G. Ulmer,** Giuseppe Masini, *Producer:* Nat Wachberger, *Screenplay:* Ugo Liberatore, Remigio del Grosso, Andre Tabet, Amedeo Nazzari, *Photographer:* Enzo Serafin, *Production Designer:* Edgar G. Ulmer, *Special Effects:* Giovanni Ventimigilia, *Music:* Carlo Rustichelli

Cast: Jean-Louis Trintignant, Haya Harareet, Georges Riviere, Rad Fulton

ATLANTIS

A legendary eighth continent said to have been located in the middle of the Atlantic Ocean until it was destroyed by a violent earthquake or volcano. The earliest known source of the legend is the Greek philosopher Plato, who described Atlantis as the home of a highly advanced civilization in his dialogues *Timaeus and Critias,* written in the fourth century B.C.

The myth of a lost underwater world entered the popular imagination with the publication of *Atlantis: The Antediluvian World* (1882), a highly popular pseudo-scientific book by Ignatius Donnelly. Atlantis had already turned up in science fiction, however, when **Jules Verne** took Captain Nemo to the kingdom's underwater ruins in his *Twenty Thousand Leagues Under the Sea* (1870) (see: **20,000 Leagues Under the Sea).**

Despite several well-publicized searches for Atlantis in this century, there is no evidence to prove that it ever existed. Plato apparently intended his story as a moral fable, perhaps taking its background from the destruction of the Minoan civilization on the island of Crete, wiped out by a volcanic eruption around 1,000 B.C. Atlantis is more likely to be found in movies, beginning with **L'Atlantide** (1921), based on a book of the same title by Pierre Benoit, which set the pattern for subsequent Atlantis films. Others include: **Undersea Kingdom** (1936), *Siren of Atlantis* (1948), **Atlantis, The Lost Continent** and **L'Atlantide** (1961), **Giant of Metropolis** (1963), **City Under the Sea** (1965). On television: **The Man From Atlantis** (1977), **The Return of Captain Nemo** (1978) and **Aquaman.**

ATLANTIS, THE LOST CONTINENT

Film   1961   U.S. (MGM)   91 Minutes
Metrocolor

A young Greek fisherman rescues a maiden in distress and finds that she is the princess of **Atlantis.** They journey by submarine to the underwater kingdom, an ancient Biblical technopolis guarded by **death rays** and dominated by **mad scientists.** Adequate as a juvenile fantasy, the film borrows much of its plot from 1930s' **serials,** including its explosive ending, previously seen in **The**

Phantom Empire (1935). Set in the time of the Roman Empire, the Atlantis scenes include footage from the studio's biblical epic *Quo Vadis?* (1951). A. Arnold Gillespie's views of Atlantis and his fish-shaped submarine, achieved on a penny-pinching budget, are just right.

Director/Producer: **George Pal,** *Screenplay:* Daniel Mainwaring, *Play:* Sir Gerald Hargreaves, *Photographer:* Harold E. Wellman, *Special Effects:* A. Arnold Gillespie, Gene Warren, Wah Chang, Tim Barr, *Makeup:* William Tuttle, *Music:* Russell Garcia

Cast: Anthony Hall, Joyce Taylor, John Dall, Edward Platt, Jay Novello

ATOMIC BOMB

See: **The Bomb**

THE ATOMIC KID

Film   1954   U.S. (Republic)   86 Minutes
Black & white

Mickey Rooney mugs his way through this inane comedy, playing a prospector who becomes radioactive after accidently venturing into an atomic **bomb** testing area. The story, which generates few laughs, has to do with Rooney rounding up a network of Communist spies with his new-found powers.

Director: Leslie H. Martinson, *Producer:* Mickey Rooney, *Screenplay:* Benedict Freeman, John Fenton Murphy, *Story:* Blake Edwards, *Photographer:* John L. Russell, Jr., *Art Director:* Frank Hotaling, *Special Effects:* Howard and Theodore Lydecker, *Music:* Van Alexander

Cast: Mickey Rooney, Robert Strauss, Whit Bissell, Elaine Davis

THE ATOMIC MAN

See: **Timeslip**

ATOMIC SUBMARINE

Film   1959   U.S. (Allied Artists)
72 Minutes   Black & white

Sent to investigate a mysterious force interfering with America's nuclear-powered submarines, a team of Navy frogmen plunges to the bottom of the ocean and discovers a pulsating UFO. The craft, it turns out, is actually a huge alien being piloted by an all-seeing eye. (Don't ask how or why.) The problem is taken care of with a guided nuclear missile.

Director: **Spencer Bennett,** *Producer:* Alex Gordon, *Screenplay:* O. H. Hampton, *Idea:* Jack Rabin, Irving Block, *Special Effects:* Jack Rabin, Irving Block, Louis De Witt, *Music:* Alexander Lazlo

Cast: **Arthur Franz,** Dick Foran, Tom Conway, Joi Lansing, *Narrator:* Pat Michaels

ATOM MAN VS. SUPERMAN

Film serial   1950   U.S. (Columbia)
479 Minutes (15 episodes)   Black & white

The Man of Steel received second billing in this lively follow-up to **Superman** (1948), the Saturday-matinee **cliffhanger** that introduced undermuscled **Kirk Alyn** to the screen as the comic-book hero. And no wonder. Most of the best scenes went to Atom Man, alias archvillain Lex Luthor (making his movie debut), who succeeded in removing Superman from the film for several reels.

Cast: Superman—**Kirk Alyn,** *Lex Luthor*—Lyle Talbot, *Lois Lane*—Noel Neill, *Jimmy Olson*—Tommy Boyd, *Perry White*—Pierre Watkin

ATTACK OF THE CRAB MONSTERS

Film   1957   U.S. (Allied Artists)
70 Minutes   Black & white

No creature was safe from atomic fallout—or **Roger Corman**—in the SF movie world of the 1950s, not even harmless crabs inhabiting a remote Pacific island. Having swum too close to a testing site, they swell to giant proportions and scuttle across the island at night dining on cracked human heads. They also ingest the intelligence and memory of their victims. (See also: **The Bomb; Mutants.**)

Director/Producer: Roger Corman, *Screenplay:* Charles Griffith, *Photographer:* **Floyd Crosby,** *Music:* Ronald Stein

Cast: Beverly Garland, Russell Johnson, Pamela Duncan, Ed Nelson

ATTACK OF THE KILLER TOMATOES

Film 1978 U.S. (NAI Ent) 87 Minutes Color

Custom-made for connoisseurs of Really Bad Films, *Attack of the Killer Tomatoes* is a deliberately inept spoof of "creature" programmers of the 1950s. The idea of the lowly tomato turning into the **mutant** menace of San Diego is good for a laugh, but not much else is. A leavening of wit might have saved the project from its outrageously tacky pretensions. As it is, any number of SF films made in earnest offers a warmer evening around the campfires.

Director: John De Bello, *Producer:* Steve Peace, John De Bello, *Screenplay:* Costa Dillon, Steve Peace, John De Bello, *Photographer:* John K. Culley, *Special Effects:* Greg Auer, *Music:* Gordon Goodwin

Cast: David Miller, George Wilson, Sharon Taylor, Jack Riley, Rock Peace

ATTACK OF THE PUPPET PEOPLE

Film 1958 U.S. (AIP) 79 Minutes Black & white

A pathetic dollmaker who also happens to be a brilliant scientist shrinks the people he likes to keep from being lonely. Deprived of their natural dimensions, a pair of newlyweds he has befriended fight back. This pygmy of a film was rushed into production to capitalize on the recent success of **The Incredible Shrinking Man** (1957).

Director/Producer/Story/Special Effects: **Bert I. Gordon,** *Screenplay:* George W. Yates, *Photographer:* Ernest Laszlo, *Music:* Albert Glasser

Cast: **John Agar,** June Kenny, John Hoyt, Susan Gordon, Ken Miller

AUTEUR THEORY

A theory of film criticism maintaining that a film is primarily the work of a director, who is its "author." Proponents of the theory compare a director to an artist whose canvas is the motion picture screen and whose paints and brushes are the screenplay, actors and others involved in a production. The theory was propounded in 1954 by director François Truffaut, then a critic for the influential magazine *Cahiers du Cinema,* and later championed in the U.S. by critic Andrew Sarris.

AUTONS

Animated invaders which resemble human beings, one of the gallery of aliens seen in the British TV series **Doctor Who.** Devised by the human-hating **Nestenes,** a malignant form of conscious energy, Autons are in fact plastic weapons that come in several models: The simplest have expressionless, unfinished faces and wear workmen's overalls; the more sophisticated are inhumanly handsome and look like store-window mannequins. The most cunning and dangerous of the lot are the Replicas which, for a time, can pass for the real thing.

THE AVENGER

Massive spaceship of the Imperial Destroyer class, one of a fleet of six destroyers sent to capture Rebel freedom fighters hiding on the planet **Hoth** in **The Empire Strikes Back** (1980).

THE AVENGERS

TV series 1962-68 Great Britain (ITC) 60 Minutes (weekly) Black & white/color

Played with a droll understatement that counterpointed its wittily absurd scripts, this sophisticated British spy series attracted a wide cult following when syndicated in the U.S. in 1966. Its hero was the debonair John Steed, a very proper government agent, who was paired with a succession of beautiful, leather-clad judo experts for a weekly battle against bizarre enemies of the Crown.

The program derived from a series begun in 1960, titled *Police Surgeon,* which introduced Steed as a mysterious man-about-town on a self-ordained mission to avenge crime. In 1962 the format was altered and the program became *The Avengers.* Steed was now a **James Bond**-like secret agent with a government affiliation and a new partner, Mrs. Catherine Gale, a widow played by Honor Blackman. The plots were offbeat and intriguing, as was the relationship between Steed and Mrs. Gale. Equals in every way, they exchanged an elegant banter that suggested a long-term affair (it was left for the viewer to decide), and neither totally relied on the other for help, even in the most adverse of circumstances.

In 1965 the program was sold to American television, allowing for a larger budget and color. Honor Blackman left to make films (her episodes were never shown in the U.S.), and Diana Rigg became Steed's sidekick, Mrs. Emma Peel, the independently wealthy widow of a test pilot. The stories became increasingly eccentric and SF-oriented, with improbable futuristic devices adding to the fun. Among these was a nasty group of **robots** called the Cybernauts, who returned for several episodes.

In 1968 the program underwent another casting change when Mrs. Peel left to rejoin her husband, who had been found alive in the Amazon jungle. Diana Rigg, whom the show had made a star, was replaced by Linda Thorson as Tara King for the remainder of the series.

In 1976 the series was revived as *The New Avengers* by writer/producer Brian Clemens, who had been instrumental in the format and style of the original show. A visibly aged Patrick MacNee was back in the role of Steed, with Joanna Lumley as his partner. Two younger agents were added, Purdey and Gambit. The stories lacked the polish and facile humor of the 1960s' version, however, and its camp ambience seemed dated.

Directors: Ray Austen, Bill Bain, Charles Crichton, **Roy Ward Baker, Forbert Fuest,** James Hill, **John Moxey,** Cliff Owen, **Don Sharp,** Peter Sykes and others, *Producers:* John Bryce, Brian Clemens, Albert Fennell, Leonard White, Julian Wyntle, *Creator:* Sydney Newman, *Music:* John Dankworth, Laurie Johnson, Howard Blake

Cast: Patrick MacNee, Honor Blackman, Diana Rigg, Linda Thorson, Patrick Newell *(as "Mother," Steed's invalid boss)*

BACTA

A thick, red medical solution in which **Luke Skywalker** is suspended after a near-fatal attack by a **Wampa** in **The Empire Strikes Back** (1980). The versatile, lifesaving emulsion works almost instantly by stimulating the body's healing responses, and Skywalker emerges as good as new. The surgeon in attendance is the robot **2-1B.**

BAKER, RICK (1950–   )

Versatile Hollywood makeup artist, whose speciality is the giant ape (which he often portrays himself). Born in Binghamtom, New York, the son of an artist, Baker created his first makeups as a teenager, copying the fantastic monsters of his favorite **horror** movies. He turned professional at the age of 18 as a modeler of **stop-motion** animation figures for Art Cloakey Productions *(Gumby, Davey and Goliath)*. While still an art major in college, Baker worked on a series of low-budget productions, including *Octoman* (half-man, half-octopus), **Schlock** (an anthropoid missing link) and **The Thing With Two Heads,** in which he played a two-headed gorilla. Brought to the attention of the Hollywood majors by top makeup man **John Chambers,** Baker next served an apprenticeship with Dick Smith on *The Exorcist* (1973). Among the effects he created for that film is the fake head of actress Linda Blair which swiveled 360 degrees. Baker's

growing reputation led to a number of varied assignments, including an exploding head for the **James Bond** film *Live and Let Die* (1973), a death mask for David Carradine in **Death Race 2000** (1975) and the mask worn by the Jolly Green Giant in the TV commercial.

Baker first achieved public recognition when it was revealed that it was he, not a giant mechanical ape, who portrayed the title character in the 1976 version of **King Kong,** in a monkey suit he had designed himself. Not long after that noble failure—which had nothing to do with Baker's excellent work—he was tapped by **George Lucas** to help create a gallery of **aliens** for the famous cantina sequence of **Star Wars** (1977), after makeup director **Stuart Freeborn** had fallen ill. (Baker's creatures appear in the background of the scene; the others are Freeborn's.) The film skyrocketed Baker to the top echelon of special effects makeup men, and he has been in constant demand ever since.

He again played an ape, a gentle giant named Sidney, in **The Incredible Shrinking Woman** (1981). The following year, Baker received an **Academy Award** for his work on *An American Werewolf in London* (1981). The competitive category of makeup effects was the first new one established since 1948. Previous winners, William Tuttle and John Chambers, were given special Oscars.

BAKER, ROY WARD (1916–   )

British director/producer. Baker began his career in 1934 as an assistant director for the Gainsborough studio and later directed documentaries while in military service. He made his first feature in 1947 and subsequently directed films in Hollywood. Baker returned to England during the early 1960s to specialize in SF and **horror** films, bringing a polished no-nonsense style to the genre, but little subtlety or depth. His TV credits include episodes of the witty secret-agent series, **The Avengers** (1962-68).

BANTHAS

Beasts of burden resembling small, hairy dinosaurs and native to the planet **Tatooine** in the film **Star Wars** (1977), where they were ridden by the **Tusken Raiders** who attacked **Luke Skywalker.** Used in much the same way as camels are used on **Earth,** they are exceptionally sure-footed and capable of withstanding the heat of their planet's twin suns. Although they move slowly, they take enormous strides that more than compensate for their lumbering gait. Normally gentle, they make a hissing sound when annoyed.

joys a series of erotic misadventures.

Based on Jean-Claude Forest's SF-oriented *bande dessinee,* a risque French comic strip popular in the 1960s, *Barbarella* offers a number of visual delights, including Jane Fonda at the peak of her luscious first youth, sumptuously decorative pop art sets, chicly bizarre costumes and the stylish photography of Claude Renoir, grand-nephew of the painter. What this **space opera** spoof doesn't have is wit, action and a coherent story line. In fact, Paramount's owner Charles Bludhorn was so infuriated when he saw the first cut that he initially refused to release it.

Barbarella: Roger Vadim directs wife Jane Fonda in the title role; John Phillip Law is Pygar, the blind angel.

BARBARELLA

Film   1968   France/Italy (Paramount)
98 Minutes   Technicolor   Panavision

Sent on a mission to capture a secret **death ray,** a beautiful 40th-century astronaut en-

Director Roger Vadim wisely put the burden of the film on the mostly naked shoulders of wife/star Fonda, whom he was then developing as a sex star—a transformation accomplished with previous wife Brigitte Bardot. As Barbarella, Fonda brings to the film a wide-eyed sense of wonder conspicuously missing from the script and direction.

Director: Roger Vadim, *Producer:* Dino De Laurentiis, *Screenplay:* Terry Southern, Roger Vadim,

Claude Brule, Vittorio Bonicelli, Clement Biddle Wood, Brian Degas, Tudor Gates, Jean-Claude Forest, *Photographer:* Claude Renoir, *Producer Designer:* Mario Garbuglia, *Costumes:* Jacques Fonteray, *Sets:* Enrico Fea, *Special Effects:* August Lohman, *Music:* Bob Crewe, Charles Fox

Cast: Jane Fonda, John Phillip Law, Anita Pallenberg, David Hemmings, Milo O'Shea, Marcel Marceau, Ugo Tognazzi, Claude Dauphin

BARRY, JOHN (1933–   )

British composer of film scores. A former rock trumpeter, Barry wrote and arranged pop songs for recording artists before writing his first film score for *Beat Girl* (1959). He is best-known as the composer of the kinetic theme of the **James Bond** films, many of which he also scored. He won an Academy Award for the score of *The Lion in Winter* (1968).

Other films: The Amorous Prawn, The L-Shaped Room, **Dr. No** (1962), *From Russia With Love* (1963), **Goldfinger** (1964), *The Ipcress File,* **Thunderball** (1965), *Born Free* (1966), **You Only Live Twice** (1967), *Midnight Cowboy,* **On Her Majesty's Secret Service** (1968), *The Man With the Golden Gun* (1974), **King Kong** (1976), *The Deep,* **The White Buffalo** (1977), **Moonraker, Starcrash, The Black Hole** (1979)

BARRY, JOHN (1936–79)

British art director and **production designer.** Trained as an architect, Barry entered films as a scenic draftsman for 20th Century–Fox's *Cleopatra* (1963). He received his first solo credit for the *Decline and Fall of a Bird Watcher* (1968) and later established himself as a production designer of the first rank with the modishly futuristic look of **A Clockwork Orange** (1971). In 1977 he won an Academy Award for **Star Wars,** whose nostalgic high-tech design was hailed by a *New York Times* critic as one of "the true stars" of the film.

In 1978 Barry had planned to make his debut as director with **Saturn 3** (1980), whose story he had written, but he withdrew from the project after a dispute with the film's producers. The following year he was suddenly taken ill while working as design consultant and second unit director of **The Empire Strikes Back** (1980) at London's Elstree Studios. He died the following day, according to a post-mortem, of infectious meningitis.

Other films: **Phase IV** (1973), *The Little Prince* (1974), **Superman—The Movie** (1978)

BATES, HARRY (1900–   )

American writer and editor whose short story, "Farewell to the Master," published in *Astounding Science Fiction* (1940), was the basis for the film **The Day the Earth Stood Still** (1951). He founded *Astounding Stories,* one of the first SF pulp magazines, which he edited from 1930 to 1933.

BATMAN

Comic-book character, created by writer Bill Finger and artist Bob Kane, who first appeared in *Detective Comics,* May 1939. Inspired by **Superman** (also published by National Comics), Batman differs from his predecessor in that he is a superhero without superpowers. Rather, he is an ordinary mortal who is simply smarter and more resourceful than anyone else. Unlike Superman, who lives in the realistic Metropolis, Batman resides in the fantasy city of Gotham, populated by such grotesque villains as the Joker, the Riddler and the pointy-nosed Penguin.

Batman's secret identity (known only to Alfred, his butler) is millionaire Bruce Wayne, who vowed to use his fortune to fight crime after his parents were killed by gangsters. Wayne's secret headquarters is a complex crime lab built under his mansion. His young ward, the orphaned Dick Grayson, is his partner, the masked Robin (also in on the secret). Individually, they are known as the Caped Crusader and the Boy Wonder; together they are the Dynamic Duo.

During the 1940s, Batman and Robin

made regular guest appearances on the raio program **Superman,** occasionally taking over the show when the Man of Steel went on vacation. They have also appeared in two movie **serials: Batman** (1943), **Batman and Robin** (1949), and **the New Adventures of Batman** (1977). They were subsequently revived for the highly successful TV spoof **Batman** (1966-68), a spin-off movie (1966) and a TV special, **Legends of the Super-heroes** (1979). They have also been depicted as animated cartoon characters in **The Batman-Superman Hour** (1967-68) and **Superfriends** (1973-   ).

BATMAN

Film serial   1943   U.S. (Columbia)
15 Episodes   Black & white

Undoubtedly one of the worst serials ever made, *Batman* is more enjoyable in some ways than the deliberately awful TV series it inspired (see listing below). Played with straight-faced aplomb by paunchy Lewis Coates in long underwear and swim trunks and a helmet sprouting a pair of horns, the Caped Crusader takes on a sinister Japanese agent called Dr. Daka, who is busy creating an Axis army in middle-America by fitting people with an electronic helmet. At Batman's side is a spindly Robin, the Boy Wonder (Douglas Croft), who looks anything but.

The serial was spliced together in 1965 and released with great success as *An Evening With Batman and Robin,* proving that if a film is bad enough it can play forever.

Director: Lambert Hillyer, *Producer:* Rudolph C. Flothow, *Screenplay:* Victor McLeod, Leslie Swabacker, Harry Fraser, *Photographer:* James Brown, Jr.

Cast: Lewis Wilson, Douglas Croft, J. Carrol Naish, William Austin, Shirley Patterson

BATMAN

TV series   1966-68   U.S. (ABC)   30 Minutes (weekly)   Color

Not meant to be taken seriously, the TV *Batman* was played with an exaggerated seriousness that appealed to adults as the ultimate in camp and to juveniles as the ultimate in gripping adventure. Impersonated by Adam West, the Caped Crusader looked as out of shape as his movie **serial** predecessors and was more wooden to boot. Burt Ward, a real-life karate expert, played Robin in his best "gee-whiz" manner, but he at least looked the part.

Basically true to his **comic-book** legend, Batman expanded his horizons a bit to include girls and discotheques. In one episode he was actually seen dancing the "batusi" with a seductive female partner, who noted, "You swing a pretty mean cape." Most of the time, however, it was business as usual, fighting such familiar villains as the Penguin (Burgess Meredith), "that pompous, waddling perpetrator of foul play," with a variety of gadgets that included the sleek Batmobile, the Batphone and the Batcycle, all custom-made in the secret Batlab. During fight scenes, comic-book "Thuds," "Swacks," "Bops" and "Pows" were flashed on the screen whenever a blow was landed.

An overnight sensation, the program aired in two-part **cliffhangers** shown on Wednesday and Thursday evenings. The leading characters were actually the villains, played by a number of top stars. These included Egghead (**Vincent Price),** the Archer (Art Carney), Lola Lasagna (Ethel Merman), Minerva (Zsa Zsa Gabor), the Devil (Joan Crawford), the Black Widow (Tallulah Bankhead), Catwoman (Julie Newmar, Lee Ann Meriwether, Eartha Kitt), the Riddler (Frank Gorshin) and the Joker (Cesar Romero).

Batmania passed quickly, however, and by the second season the program had been cut back to once a week. To bolster ratings, the producers introduced Batgirl (Yvonne Craig), Police Commissioner Gordon's daughter Barbara, and the crimefighters now became the Terrific Trio. The ploy didn't work, however, and the show vanished the following February.

Directors: Robert Butler, Tom Gries, Oscar Rudolph, Larry Peerce and others, *Producer:*

Howie Horwitz, *Executive Producer:* William Dozier, *Writers:* Lorenzo Semple, Jr., Robert Dozier, Stanley Ralph Ross, Charles Hoffman, Stanford Sherman and others, *Photographer:* Howard Schwartz, *Makeup:* Ben Nye, *Special Effects:* Lyle B. Abbott, *Music:* Neal Hefti *(theme),* Nelson Riddle

Cast: Adam West, Burt Ward, Neil Hamilton, Alan Napier, Madge Blake, Stafford Repp, Yvonne Craig

BATMAN

Film   1966   U.S. (20th Century-Fox)
105 Minutes   DeLuxe

An "all-new" feature starring the cast of the popular TV series (see listing above) in a previously unseen adventure involving the kidnapping of an important official and a plot to take over the world. Behind these dastardly doings were the program's favorite villains: Catwoman, the Joker, the Riddler and the Penguin.

Director: Leslie Martinson, *Producer:* William Dozier, *Screenplay:* Lorenzo Semple, Jr., *Photographer:* Howard Schwarz, *Special Effects:* Lyle B. Abbott, *Music:* Nelson Riddle

Cast: Adam West, Burt Ward, Lee Meriwether, Cesar Romero, Frank Gorshin, Burgess Meredith

BATMAN AND ROBIN

(Also titled: *The Return of Batman*)

Film serial   1949   U.S. (Columbia)
15 Episodes

For their second **serial** adventure, the Dynamic Duo help Police Commissioner Gordon of Gotham City recover a remote-control device stolen by a hooded mystery man called The Wizard. The impoverished story isn't helped a bit by a new Batman (Robert Lowery) and Robin (John Duncan) who, respectively, look even flabbier and more underdeveloped than their predecessors.

Director: **Spencer G. Bennett,** *Producer:* Sam Katzman, *Screenplay:* George H. Plympton, J. F. Poland, Royal K. Cole, *Photographer:* Ira H. Morgan, *Music:* Mischa Bakaleinikoff

Cast: Robert Lowery, John Duncan, Jane Adams, Lyle Talbot, Ralph Graves, House Peters, Jr.

Batman and Robin: Adam West and Burt Ward.

BATTLE BENEATH THE EARTH

Film   1968   Great Britain (MGM)
92 Minutes   Technicolor

As the cold war thawed during the 1960s, China replaced Russia as America's deadliest enemy. Depicted as diabolically cunning fanatics of the Fu Manchu variety, the "yellow peril" burns a network of tunnels under the U.S. with a **laser** beam. They have to be poked out by a team of American and British scientists.

Director: Montgomery Tully, *Producer:* Charles Reynolds, *Screenplay:* L. Z. Hargreaves, *Photographer:* Ken Talbot, *Special Effects:* Tom Howard, *Music:* Ken Jones

Cast: Kerwin Matthews, Bessie Love, Robert Ayres, Vivienne Ventura, Peter Arne

BATTLE BEYOND THE STARS

Film   1980   U.S. (New World)
104 Minutes   Color

Filmed at the relatively low cost of $5 million, this **Star Wars**-inspired **space opera** is **Roger Corman's** most expensive production to date. Like some of his earlier films, *Battle* compensates for its budgetary limitations with energy, inventiveness and an eagerness to give the viewer what he expects. In this case, it is *The Seven Samurai* set in outer space, where the hero recruits a group of ragtag fighters to repel the invasion of a peace-loving planet by the ruthless Sador, who owns a Stellar Converter, the most powerful weapon in the **galaxy.** The dogfights in space, done with a computerized **motion-control** camera, are not bad, but the **aliens** created by makeup artist Steve Neill are first-rate.

Cuttlefish, Modern Props, *Music:* James Horner

Cast: Richard Thomas, **Robert Vaughn,** John Saxon, George Peppard, Darlanne Fluegel, Jeff Corey

BATTLE BEYOND THE SUN

Film   1963   U.S. (Filmgroup)   75 Minutes   Color

Soviet cosmonauts save American astronauts from certain death on **Mars** in this badly dubbed, brainless hybrid, spliced together from special effects footage from the Russian-made **The Heavens Call** and scenes shot on the cheap in Hollywood. The propaganda has been neatly excised (almost) and this time around the Americans are no longer greedy capitalists out to win the space race at all costs. They have simply miscalculated their fuel supply—it could happen to anyone—

Battle Beyond the Stars: Heroine Nanelia is captured by Cayman, a reptilian alien.

Director: Jimmy T. Murakami, *Producer:* Ed Carlin, *Executive Producer:* Roger Corman, *Screenplay:* John Sayles, *Photographer:* Daniel Lacambre, *Art Directors:* Jim Cameron, Charles Breen, *Makeup:* Steve Neill, *Special Effects:* Chuck Comisky,

and their gracious comrades offer them a lift home.

Director/Producer: Thomas Colchart, *Executive Producer:* **Roger Corman,** *Screenplay:* Nicholas Colbert, Edwin Palmer

Cast: Arla Powell, Andy Stewart, Edd Perry, Bruce Hunter

BATTLE FOR THE PLANET OF THE APES

Film 1974 U.S. (20th Century-Fox)
86 Minutes DeLuxe Panavision

This fifth and final sequel to **Planet of the Apes** (1968) is actually number three of the prequels series, which began with **Escape From the Planet of the Apes** (1971) and continued with **Conquest of the Planet of the Apes** (1972). By now the running plot has been stretched gossamer thin, as the script writers struggle to explain how and why the apes happened to take over the world (their rebellion brought about an atomic war that destroyed most of humanity).

Director: J. Lee Thompson, *Producer:* Arthur P. Jacobs, *Screenplay:* John Williams, Joyce Hooper Carrington, *Story:* Paul Dehn, *Characters:* **Pierre Boulle,** *Photographer:* Richard H. Kline, *Art Director:* Dale Hennessy, *Makeup:* **John Chambers**

Cast: Roddy McDowall, Natalie Trundy, Paul Williams, Claude Akins, John Huston, Severn Darden

THE BATTLE IN THE CLOUDS

See: **The Airship Destroyer**

BATTLE IN OUTER SPACE

Film 1959 Japan (Toho) 93 Minutes
Tohoscope Color (Released 1960 U.S. [Columbia], cut to 74 Minutes)

While exploring the moon, a pair of Japanese astronauts are implanted with tiny brain-control devices by **aliens** living on the far side of the lunar surface. Predictably, they return to Earth and sabotage the space program. A lackluster effort from the team who created the beloved **Godzilla** (1954).

Director: Inoshiro Honda, *Producer:* Tomoyuki Tanaka, *Screenplay:* Shinichi Sekizawa, *Story:* Jotaro Okami, *Special Effects:* Eiji Tsuburaya

Cast: Kyoko Anza, Ryo Ikebe, Harold Conway, Minoru Takada

BATTLE OF THE PLANETS

TV series (animated) 1978 Japan
(syndicated) 30 Minutes (weekly) Color

A badly dubbed, cheaply animated import from Japan, whose Saturday morning TV cartoons are apparently more violent than America's. G-Force hero/orphans do battle with **aliens** from the planet Spectra in the running plot, which has to do with **robots** programmed to kill human beings and a spaceship that turns itself into a bird. The series was released in the U.S. by Gallerie International Films and re-edited by David Hanson.

Director/Producer: David Hanson, *Music:* Hoyt Curtin

Voices: Keye Luke, Alan Young, Janet Waldo, Casey Kassem, Ronnie Schell

BATTLE OF THE WORLDS

Film 1961 Italy 84 Minutes Black & white

The presence of Claude Rains, first (and best) impersonator of **The Invisible Man** (1933) distinguishes this otherwise dismal **space opera,** which has to do with a heroic attempt by the elderly Rains and crew to save the world from a planet guided on a collision course by an alien computer. Made in Italy as *Il Planeta degli Uomini Spenti,* it was dubbed, retitled and released in the U.S. in 1963.

Director: Anthony Dawson, *Screenplay:* Vassily Petrov

Cast: Claude Rains, Bill Carter, Maya Brent, Umberto Orsini

BATTLESTAR GALACTICA

TV series 1978-79 U.S. (ABC) 60 Minutes (weekly) Color

When **Star Wars** (1977) began heating up box offices around the world, Universal realized it had made a mistake in not financing **George Lucas'** spectacular film. To make amends, the studio rushed into production this flashy TV counterfeit, originally to be

Battlestar Galactica: A publicity composite. From left, Captain Apollo (Richard Hatch), Commander Adama (Lorne Greene) and Lieutenant Starbuck (Dirk Benedict).

titled *Star Worlds.* Again, the plot was pure **space opera,** involving a small army of humans warring against an evil alliance with unlimited resources and manpower.

A sort of *Wagon Train* in space, the series followed the intergalactic journey of a procession of 220 battered spaceships, led by the *Battlestar Galactica,* a mighty, city-sized war machine. The ships carried the survivors of the human race, whose colony of 12 planets had been obliterated by **The Imperious Leader,** a grotesque **alien** whose instrument of destruction was a race of **robots** called Cylons. The humans were destined for a lost 13th colony called **Earth,** where they hoped to find safe haven.

In charge of the *Galactica* was a Moses-like figure named Commander Adama (played by Lorne Greene, the paterfamilias of *Bonanza),* whose crew members were two ace Starfighter pilots, Lieutenant Starbuck and Captain Apollo. The navigator, Athena, was

the daughter of Adama, the sister of Apollo and the would-be bride of Starbuck. Also on hand was an orphan, Boxey, and his pet **Muffit II,** a sort of **R2-D2.**

The program premiered with a three-hour story (later released theatrically), presenting Adama and company as the original Ancient Astronauts on their way to bring wisdom and knowledge to primitive Earth. (Their ornate helmets would apparently be copied later by Egyptian pharoahs.) The Council of Twelve, representatives of mankind's original planets, looked remarkably like a depiction of the Last Supper. Laying on the symbolism, creator Glen A. Larson even included a double-dealing bad angel, Lucifer, and characters who represented Mary Magdalene and Judas Iscariot.

An immediate success, *Battlestar* clobbered the competition and seemed set for a long run. The battles in space, staged by special effects man **John Dykstra,** winner of an **Academy Award** for *Star Wars,* were the best ever to soar across a TV screen. But the scripts failed to keep pace, becoming increasingly juvenile, and viewers slowly lost interest. The program was cancelled at the end of the season, an expensive failure (the episodes had reportedly cost over $40 million). The network attempted a revival in the fall with the kiddie-oriented **Galactica 1980,** which barely eked out another season.

In 1980, Universal released 12 TV films for syndication, culled from episodes of the series. These include *Battlestar Galactica,* the series opener, **Lost Planet of Gods, Gun on Ice Planet Zero, The Phantom in Space, Space Prison, Space Casanova, Curse of the Cylons, The Living Legend, War of the Gods, Greetings from Earth, Murder in Space** and **Experiment in Terra.**

Directors: Richard Colla, Don Bellisario, Christian Nyby, Rod Holcomb, Vince Edwards and others, *Producers:* John Dykstra, Don Bellisario, Paul Playdon, David J. O'Connell and others, *Executive Producer:* Glen A. Larson, *Supervising Producer:* Leslie Stevens, *Photographer:* Ben Colman, *Art Director:* John E. Chilbert, *Costumes:* Jean-Pierre Dorleac, *Production Paintings:* Ralph McQuarrie, *Music:* Stu Phillips, Glen A. Larson

Cast: Lorne Greene, Richard Hatch, Dirk Benedict, Maren Jensen, Herb Jefferson, Jr., Terry Carter, Noah Hathaway

BEAMING

See: **Matter Transmission**

THE BEAST FROM 20,000 FATHOMS

Film   1953   U.S. (Warner Bros.)
80 Minutes   Sepia tone

The film that spawned the **mutant** monster-on-a-rampage cycle of the 1950s. Its plot is loosely based on "The Foghorn," a *Saturday Evening Post* story by **Ray Bradbury** about a lonely prehistoric sea creature, the last one left alive, which hears a mating call in a lighthouse foghorn. Here, the creature has become a dinosaur revived from an Arctic deep-freeze by an atomic **bomb** test. It heads for its old breeding ground, now covered by New York City, for a fatal injection of radioactive isotopes at Coney Island amusement park.

The special effects, good for this period, mark the first solo outing by **stop-motion** animator **Ray Harryhausen.** His copyrighted technique, later called **Dynarama,** produced a number of impressive shots, including a scene in which the beast rampages through Times Square.

Director: **Eugene Lourie,** *Producers:* Hal Chester, Jack Dietz, *Screenplay:* Lou Morheim, Fred Freiberger, *Photographer:* Jack Russell, *Art Director:* Eugene Lourie, *Special Effects:* Ray Harryhausen, *Music:* David Buttolph

Cast: Paul Christian, Paula Raymond, Kenneth Tobey, Cecil Kellaway, King Donovan

THE BEAST OF YUCCA FLATS

Film   1961   U.S. (Cardoza)   60 Minutes
Black & white

Exposed to nuclear radiation at an atomic **bomb** testing site in Nevada, an obese scientist turns into an obese monster. The bottom of the barrel.

Director/Screenplay: Coleman Francis, *Producer:* Anthony Cardoza, *Photographer:* John Cagle

Cast: Tor Johnson, Anthony Cardoza, Douglas Mellor

THE BEAST WITH A MILLION EYES

Film   1955   U.S. (ARC)   78 Minutes   Black & white

B-picture king **Roger Corman** had yet to make his debut as a director when he produced this forgotten SF-**horror** programmer, which isn't as bad as it sounds. The popular 1950s theme of **alien invasion** takes on a fresh twist when a creature from outer space lands in the desert and practices his telepathic powers on small animals before progressing to human beings. Local citizens fend off attacks by mindless birds, cows and dogs but finally manage to kill the hideous **alien.** At fade-out, a docile rabbit scampers off, leading the viewer to wonder if the menace truly has been destroyed.

Director: David Kramarsky, *Producer:* Roger Corman, *Screenplay:* Tom Filler, *Special Effects:* Paul Blaisdell, *Music:* John Bickford

Cast: Paul Birch, Lorna Thayer, Chester Conklin, Leonard Tarver, Donna Cole

BEAUMONT, CHARLES (1929–67)

Pseudonym of American story and film writer Charles Nutt, known for his ghoulishly funny short fiction which blends horror with science fiction and fantasy. The stories have been anthologized in *Hunger and Other Stories* (1957), *Yonder* (1958) and *The Magic Man* (1965). Film credits include the scripts for **Queen of Outer Space** (1958), *The Seven Faces of Dr. Lao* (1964) and several horror movies in collaboration with Ray Russell and **Richard Matheson.** Among his TV credits are many scripts for **The Twilight Zones** series (1959-64). Beaumont died of a rare, debilitating illness that struck him in 1964.

THE BED SITTING ROOM

Film   1969   Great Britain (United Artists)

91 Minutes   DeLuxe

Told in a series of episodes, this inventive absurdist comedy takes place in England after World War III, over in two-and-a-half minutes, where several mentally disjointed survivors are trying their best to pretend that nothing has changed. ("Mustn't grumble!" says an ash-covered Colonel Blimp.) Consequently, no one seems to notice when people start mutating into birds, bed sitting rooms and wardrobes. Another radiation victim, a young girl, gives birth to a monster after a 17-month pregnancy, but she is willing to give it another try. Unfazed, the survivors busy themselves with re-establishing the institutions of the past, even to the point of choosing a new queen and building her a triumphal arch from old refrigerators and dishwashers.

Director Richard Lester fails to capture the dizzying slapstick of the mostly improvised play on which the film is based (written by Spike Milligan and John Antrobus) and goes instead for the British jugular. According to Lester, many of the scenes depicting post-holocaust landscapes weren't faked but actually shot at factory dumping grounds in the north of England. Needless to say, the British hated the film.

Director/Producer: Richard Lester, *Screenplay:* John Antrobus, *Play:* Spike Milligan, John Antrobus, *Photographer:* David Watkin, *Production Designer:* Assheton Gorton, *Music:* Ken Thorne

Cast: Ralph Richardson, Rita Tushingham, Spike Milligan, Michael Hoerdern, Mona Washbourne

THE BEES

Film   1979   U.S. (New World)   85 Minutes
Color

Following the suicide flight of **The Swarm** (1978) came this second puerile attempt to exploit newspaper stories of a **mutant** strain of killer bees buzzing into the U.S. from Central America (a threat that never materialized). The plot has to do with a greedy corporation that sets up an apiary with the killer bees to market their copiously produced honey. The bees escape and so will you.

Director/Producer/Screenplay: Alfredo Zacharias, *Photographer:* Joseph Lamas, *Music:* Richard Gillis

Cast: John Saxon, Angel Tompkins, John Carradine

BEFORE I HANG

Film   1940   U.S. (Columbia)   71 Minutes
Black & white

The search for a cure for death goes on as **Boris Karloff** injects himself with a serum made from the blood of a murderer, whom he soon begins to imitate. A variation on the Dr. Jekyll and Mr. Hyde theme (see film listings), *Before I Hang* is one of a number of mad-scientist programmers turned out by Columbia during the early 1940s, many of which starred Karloff.

Director: Nick Grinde, *Screenplay:* Robert D. Andrews, *Photographer:* Benjamin Kline

Cast: Boris Karloff, Evelyn Keyes, Bruce Bennett, Pedro de Cordoba, Don Beddoe

THE BEGINNING OF THE END

Film   1957   U.S. (Republic)   74 Minutes
Black & white

Sprayed on midwestern crop lands, a radioactive fertilizer produces a bumper crop of outsized vegetables—and grasshoppers twice the size of human beings. The big bugs head for Chicago, where quick-thinking scientists lure them into Lake Michigan with electronic mating sounds. An also-ran in the 1950s cycle of **mutant**-monster movies. The second-rate special effects consists of grainy footage of real insects enlarged by rear projection, combined with shots of grasshoppers crawling over miniature buildings.

Director/Producer: **Bert I. Gordon,** *Screenplay:* Fred Freilberger, Lester Gorn, *Photographer:* Jack Marta, *Special Effects:* Bert I. Gordon

Cast: Peter Graves, Peggie Castle, James Seay, Morris Ankrum

BEHEMOTH, THE SEA MONSTER

(Released 1959 U.S. [Allied Artists] as *The Giant Behemoth*)

Film 1958 Great Britain (Diamond)
80 Minutes Black & white

Director **Eugene Lourie** borrows shamelessly from his **The Beast From 20,000 Fathoms** (1953) here. Once again, a dinosaur is roused from its long slumber by an atomic **bomb**, which makes it angry enough to terrorize the nearest city, which in this film is London in miniature. Occasional moments of suspense are undercut by the spare special effects handled by pioneer **stop-motion** artist **Willis O'Brien** (creator of the original **King Kong),** whose imagination couldn't overcome *Behemoth, The Sea Monster's* miniscule budget.

Director: Eugene Lourie, Douglas Hickox, *Producer:* Ted Lloyd, *Screenplay:* Eugene Lourie, *Photographer:* Ken Hodges, *Makeup:* Jimmy Evans, *Special Effects:* Willis O'Brien, Jack Rabin, Louis DeWitt, Irving Block, Pete Peterson

Cast: Gene Evans, Andre Morell, Leigh Madison, Henry Vidon, Jack McGowran

BEMs

See: **Bug-Eyed Monsters**

BENEATH THE PLANET OF THE APES

Film 1970 U.S. (20th Century-Fox)
95 Minutes DeLuxe Panavision

The first of four sequels to **The Planet of the Apes** (1968) and the best of the lot, although it lacks the deft mordant satire of the earlier film. Sent to find his predecessor, another astronaut, Brent, passes through the same **time warp** and is captured by chimpanzees on the ape planet. Escaping with the help of the sympathetic chimp Zira, he finds his way to a community of human **mutants,** who live in a New York subway tunnel and worship a doomsday **bomb** (the sets were built for *Hello Dolly).* Among the worshippers is Taylor, now an embittered psychotic, who triggers the device when an ape army enters the tunnel. He annihilates the planet, but not the series.

Director: Ted Post, *Producer:* Arthur Jacobs, *Screenplay:* Paul Dehn, Mort Abrahams, *Characters:* **Pierre Boulle,** *Photographer:* Milton Krasner, *Art Directors:* Jack Martin Smith, William Creber, *Makeup:* **John Chambers,** *Special Effects:* Lyle B. Abbott, Art Cruickshank, *Music:* Leonard Rosenman

Cast: James Franciscus, Kim Hunter, Linda Harrison, Charlton Heston, David Watson, Victor Buono, Jeff Corey

BENNETT, CHARLES (1899–   )

British screenplay writer who entered films as an actor and later collaborated on several scripts for Alfred Hitchcock in Great Britain and Hollywood. He also directed two films. During the 1960s he worked on movie and television projects for fantasy filmmaker **Irwin Allen.**

Films include: The Man Who Knew Too Much (and remake 1956), **The Secret of the Loch** (1934), *The Thirty-Nine Steps, Sabotage* (1936), *Young and Innocent* (1937), *Foreign Correspondent* (1940), *Madness of the Heart (d), Black Magic* (1949), *No Escape (d)* (1953), *The Story of Mankind, Night of the Demon* (1957), **The Lost World** (1960), **Voyage to the Bottom of the Sea** (1961), **Five Weeks in a Balloon** (1962), **War Gods of the Deep** (1965)

BENNETT, SPENCER G.(ORDON) (dates unknown)

Prolific American director of movie **serials** and occasional low-budget programmers. Bennett began his long career as stunt man in the silent **cliffhangers** of serial queen Pearl White and went on to direct scores of chapter plays for RKO, Republic and Columbia. His **Secret Service in Darkest Africa** (1943), an action-packed whirligig balanced with touches of broad comedy, is a classic of its kind. Among the comic-book SF characters introduced to the movies by Bennett are Superman, Batman and Robin, Brick Bradford and Captain Video. Bennett also directed Hollywood's final serial, *Blazing the Overland Trail* (1956).

Other films: **Manhunt of Mystery Island, The Pur-**

ple Monster Strikes (1945), Brick Bradford (1947), Superman (1948), Batman and Robin (1949), Atom Man vs. Superman (1950), Captain Video, Mysterious Island (1951), *Blackhawk* (1952), The Lost Planet (1953), Atomic Submarine (1959)

BERNDS, EDWARD (1911–   )

American film director of second features, including several dreadful science fantasies. A former sound effects man for The Three Stooges comedy team, Bernds graduated to directing in the late 1940s with the "Blondie" and "Bowery Boys" series. He often wrote his own scripts.

SF Films: The Bowery Boys Meet the Monsters (1954), World Without End (1956), Space Master X-7, Queen of Outer Space (1958), Return of the Fly (1959), Valley of the Dragons (1961), The Three Stooges Meet Hercules, The Three Stooges in Orbit (1962)

BEYOND 1984: REMEMBRANCE OF THINGS FUTURE

TV special   1978   U.S. (ABC)   60 Minutes Color

Written and hosted by **Ray Bradbury,** *Beyond 1984* was presented by ABC News to celebrate the tenth anniversary of NASA's landing on the moon. The program looked back at the achievements of the 1960s and 1970s and previewed the next 30 years in space with animated films. By 2010, Bradbury predicted, space stations will support communities of scientists and technocrats for long periods, and nearby planets will supplement Earth's mineral and energy needs. Also discussed was the spaceship technology needed to carry man to new homes in the outer reaches of the galaxy. Bradbury based his script on projections of scientists, academicians and eminent futurologists.

Producer: Malcome Clarke, *Writer:* Ray Bradbury

Panel: Ray Bradbury, Jules Bergman, **Isaac Asimov,** Alvin Toffler

BEYOND THE TIME BARRIER

Film   1960   U.S. (AIP)   75 Minutes   Black & white

Pushing his experimental aircraft far beyond the speed of sound, a test pilot enters a **time warp** that projects him into the year 2024. He is shocked to find that a nuclear war has reduced Earth's population to warring factions of surface **mutants** and underground technocrats, both of whom suffer the effects of a radioactive plague. Unaware he has been tainted by the sickness, the pilot hurries back home to head off World War III (although how he plans to repeat his accidental trip is never explained). Passable as entertainment, *Beyond the Time Barrier* is distinguished by the work of its illustrious art director and its makeup artist, who had fallen on hard times. (See also: **The Bomb.**)

Director: **Edgar Ulmer,** *Producer:* Robert Clarke, *Screenplay:* Arthur C. Pierce, *Art Director:* Ernest Fegte, *Makeup:* **Jack Pierce,** *Music:* Darrell Calker

Cast: Robert Clarke, Darlene Tompkins, Tom Ravick, John Van Drelen

BEYOND WESTWORLD

TV series   1980   U.S. (CBS)   60 Minutes (weekly)   Color

Beyond Westworld: Scientist Joseph Oppenheimer (William Jordan), left, and Delos policeman John Moore (Jim McMullan) investigate a humanoid robot.

A spin-off of **Westworld** (1973), **Michael Crichton's** clever film about an amusement park of the future where humanoid **robots** cater to the fantasies of holiday thrill seekers, and its sequel, **Futureworld** (1976). Why the robots begin slaughtering their human patrons is never made clear in the former film, but the second time around the culprit was identified as the Delos Corp., owner of Westworld.

Here, the scientist who created the robots is the villain. Angry because Delos uses his superior creations as playthings, he sets loose an army of powerful robots superficially identical to human beings and programmed to obey only his commands. Enter a Delos security policeman and his comely assistant, who are called upon to thwart such weekly threats as a robot sailor planted on a nuclear submarine. "People are like robots," muses the policeman as he tries to determine which is which. "It's the power source behind them that counts." Such fortune cookie wisdom quickly began to pall and scarcely helped the series' formula, mad-scientist plot. *Beyond Westworld* debuted on March 5, 1980, and played out the season.

Director: Lou Shaw, *Producer:* John Merdyth Lucas, *Screenplay:* Lou Shaw *(first episode)* and others, *Photographer:* Joe Jackman, *Production Designer:* Michael Baugh, *Music:* George Romanis

Cast: Jim McMullan, James Wainwright, Connie Selleca, William Jordan

BEWARE! THE BLOB

(British title: *Son of Blob*)

Film 1972 U.S. (Harris) 88 Minutes
Technicolor

Everyone's favorite mass of space protoplasm displays a knack for comedy in this enjoyable black-hearted spoof of **The Blob** (1958). When a laboratory specimen of the original creature thaws and comes to life, it immediately begins to hunt for food in a number of unlikely places. One of these is a can of beer idly imbibed by a sports fan watching television. His wife returns a few moments later to find the living room over-run by a belching blob of purplish jello undulating toward its next meal. Director Larry Hagman is better known as the villainous J.R. Ewing of the prime-time TV soap opera, *Dallas*.

Director: Larry Hagman, *Producer:* Anthony Harris, *Screenplay:* Anthony Harris, Jack Woods, *Story:* Richard Clair, Jack H. Harris, *Special Effects:* Tim Barr, *Music:* Mort Garson

Cast: Godfrey Cambridge, Robert Walker, Carol Lynley, Shelley Berman

THE BIG BUS

Film 1976 U.S. (Paramount) 88 Minutes
Movielab Panavision

Terrible personal crises arise aboard the world's first nuclear-powered bus during its maiden run from New York to Denver. Among its passengers are a wonderful old lady, a pompous priest, a sexpot with a heart of gold and a man with six months to live, each of whom faces a more urgent crisis when the unthinkable happens: the bus stalls. This hilarious parody of disaster movies, made before the disaster cycle was played out, was a victim of bad timing and failed to click at the box office. *Airplane!*, made four years later, had less real wit but brought in the customers.

Director: James Frawley, *Producers/Screenplay:* Fred Freeman, Lawrence J. Cohen, *Photographer:* Harry Stradling, Jr., *Production Designer:* Joel Schiller, *Music:* David Shire

Cast: Ruth Gordon, Rene Auberjonois, Sally Kellerman, Ned Beatty, Stockard Channing, Lynn Redgrave, Jose Ferrer, Joseph Bologna, Bob Dishy, Larry Hagman, John Beck, Richard Mulligan

BIONIC MAN

Jargon term combining biological and electronic; popularized on television's **The Six Million Dollar Man.** (See also: **Cyborgs.**)

THE BIONIC WOMAN

TV series 1976-78 U.S. (ABC, NBC)

60 Minutes (weekly)   Color

Originally conceived as the short-lived "love interest" of Steve Austin, the **cyborg** hero of **The Six Million Dollar Man,** Jaime Sommers, *the Bionic Woman,* came by her plastic and metal prostheses as the result of a sky-diving accident suffered during a four-part story on that program, broadcast in 1974-75. The story ended with Jaime dying after her body had rejected the replacement parts, but her appearances so boosted the show's ratings it was decided to bring her back to life with a series of her own. (The whimsical explanation for this medical miracle was **cryonic** surgery—an operation performed on her frozen, dead body.)

The Bionic Woman first aired on January 14, 1976 with an expository episode explaining that Jaime now had two artificial (but shapely) legs which could jump two stories into the air and run 60 mph, as well as a superpowerful right arm and a supersensitive right ear. Out of gratitude to the government for saving her, she gave up her former life as a tennis pro and became an undercover operative for the Office of Scientific Information (OSI), the agency Steve works for. The operations left her with a memory loss, however, and she barely remembered her love for Steve, leaving the door open for a number of treacly reunions when the two bionic people appeared on each other's programs. Most of her adventures were apparently designed to show off actress Lindsay Wagner's figure to advantage. Among other disguises, she posed as a roller derby queen, a champion swimmer and lady wrestler. She battled such adversaries as "fembot" robots in Las Vegas, the legendary forest creature called Bigfoot and a variety of alien menaces.

Moving to the NBC network for its second season, *The Bionic Woman* hoped to pick up needed rating points in a new time slot. But despite the addition to the cast of an appealing performer called Max, the bionic dog, the program never caught fire and was cancelled at the end of the season (followed later that year by *The Six Million Dollar Man*).

Director: Phil Bondelli, Barry Crane, Alan Crosland, Mel Damski, Kenneth Johnson, Alan Levi, Leo Penn, *Producer:* Harve Bennett, *Novel:* **Martin Caidin,** *Music:* Jerry Fielding, Joe Harnell

Cast: Lindsay Wagner, Richard Anderson, Martin E. Brooks, Martha Scott, Ford Rainey, Lee Majors

BIRDMAN

TV series   1967-68   U.S. (NBC)   30 Minutes (weekly)   Color

An animated cartoon for children, featuring righter-of-wrongs Ray Randall, who received the gift of flight and his new name when rescued by the Egyptian Sun God, Ra, from certain death by fire. Aiding *Birdman* in his noble quest are the Galaxy Trio: Vapor Man, Galaxy Girl and Meteor Man.

Producer: William Hanna and Joseph Barbera

Voices: Birdman—Keith Andes, *Vapor Man*—Don Messick, *Galaxy Girl*—Virginia Eiler, *Meteor Man*—Ted Cassidy, *Birdboy*—Dick Beals

THE BIRDS

Film   1963   U.S. (Universal)   119 Minutes Technicolor

Hitchcock is at the top of his form in this technical tour de force, his only SF film, which places mankind at the mercy of birds—a normally benign species that vastly outnumbers our own. Set in a small coastal town in northern California, the plot concerns an impetuous, spoiled playgirl who meets a young lawyer in a bird shop and pursues him to his home. Arriving with a gift of caged lovebirds, she is greeted by a sea gull that swoops down and gashes her forehead. Next day, a flock of gulls attack a party of picnicking children, followed that evening by hundreds of sparrows that come swooping down a chimney. It isn't long before the birds swarm over the town, savagely attacking pedestrians and making it unsafe to go outside.

The early sequences of the film are basically irrevelant, a realistic milieu established by Hitchcock to make believable the cataclysmic fantasy that follows. Leaving the matter open, he never explains why man's "feathered friends" have turned against us. Several reasons are discussed in a besieged diner (where a customer is eating fried chicken): Is it atomic testing? Black magic? Freakish weather? All hypotheses are considered and rejected, leaving one with the suggestion that the events are just another phenomenon of unpredictable nature, whose violence and anarchy are beyond comprehension.

The spectacular bird attacks were staged with real birds, models, and animated drawings by Ub Iwerks, a Disney associate. (See: **Animation.**) The electronic sound track, reverberating with flapping wings, chirps and caws, was orchestrated in the manner of a musical score by composer **Bernard Herrmann.**

Director/Producer: Alfred Hitchcock, *Screenplay:* Evan Hunter, *Novel:* Daphne du Maurier, *Photographer:* Robert Burks, *Special Effects:* Lawrence A. Hampton, *Animation:* Ub Iwerks, *Sound Consultant:* Bernard Herrmann

Cast: Rod Taylor, Tippi Hedren, Jessica Tandy, Suzanne Pleshette, Ethel Griffies

BLACK FRIDAY

Film   1940   U.S. (Universal)   70 Minutes
Black & white

Near death when run down by a gangster's getaway car, a gentle college professor receives a transplant of brain tissue from a hoodlum killed in the shootout. The transplant keeps the professor alive but turns him into a part-time gangster bent on revenging his death. The greedy surgeon who performed the operation **(Boris Karloff)** offers to help if the gangster will tell him where the loot is hidden. Dense with plot and dialogue, *Black Friday* moves too slowly to offer more than a shudder or two. The performance of Stanley Ridges as the professor/gangster (a role originally intended for **Bela Lugosi)** is a standout.

Director: Arthur Lubin, *Screenplay:* **Curt Siodmak,** Eric Taylor, *Photographer:* Woody Bredell, *Music:* Hans Salter

Cast: Boris Karloff, Stanley Ridges, Anne Nagle, Anne Gwynne, Virginia Brissac, Paul Fix

BLACK HOLE

An invisible singularity in space occupied by a collapsed **star.** Cosmologists believe a black hole to be a bottomless pit whose immense gravitational pull scoops up cosmic debris and energy (light). It vanishes them forever into an enigmatic core, where the traditional concepts of space and time no longer apply. Astronomers estimate black holes to number in the millions.

One theory has it that a spaceship falling into a black hole would be stretched like a piece of cellophane, then crushed smaller than a speck of dust before reaching its core. Another theory holds that a black hole may represent a shortcut through space, a sort of tunnel that leads to another part of the universe, to a different point in time or to a **parallel world.** SF writers tend toward the latter theory as a convenient method of solving the problem of faster-than-light space travel. (See also: **Hyperspace).**

THE BLACK HOLE

Film   1979   U.S. (Disney)   97 Minutes
Technicolor Technovision   Dolby Stereo

The Disney people had been plodding along with its squeaky-clean juvenile fare and wondering where their audience had gone when **Star Wars** came along and showed them. The studio's response was *The Black Hole,* an immensely budgeted space adventure that attempted to recapture the magic of such past Disney live-action classics as **20,000 Leagues Under the Sea** (1954). The film's plot, a familiar pastiche about a spacebound Captain Nemo who takes a trip through a **black hole** with a crew of zombie **cyborgs** aboard a space-city named the *Cygnus,* is dismal and ineptly directed, but the special effects are exceptional and nearly save the day.

Particularly impressive are the immense interiors of the *Cygnus,* a fretwork of naked girders that brings to mind the limitless underground **Krel** labs of **Forbidden Planet**

(1956). The "sets" were in fact matte paintings designed by **Peter Ellenshaw.** When the actors entered the immense control center, for example, they were actually being drawn across the studio floor on a dolly. The live footage was later composited into a painting that appeared to be sev-

Screenplay: Jeb Rosebrook, Gerry Day, *Story:* Jeb Rosebrook, Bab Barbash, Richard Landau, *Photographer:* Frank Phillips, *Production Designer/Miniature Effects:* Peter Ellenshaw, *Matte Artist:* Harrison Ellenshaw, *Miniature Photography:* Art Cruickshank, *Mechanical Effects:* Danny Lee, *Opticals:* Eustace Lycett, *Robots:* George F. McGinnis, *Music:* **John Barry**

The Black Hole: Dr. Hans Reinhardt (Maximilian Schell), a futuristic Captain Nemo, with his robot creation Maximilian (modeled after Disney's devil in *Fantasia* 1940).

eral stories high, complete with workmen moving on various levels, controls flashing and a view of the bright stars outside. Each of these elements was painstakingly photographed with a **motion-control** camera called **ACES,** then matted into the painting (see: **mattes).** Movement of the big ship through outer space was also filmed frame-by-frame with ACES, which compressed seven hours of movement into 25 seconds of film (see: **Time-lapse** photography) to produce the illusion of powerful flight.

Director: Gary Nelson, *Producer:* Ron Miller,

Cast: Maximilian Schell, Anthony Perkins, Robert Forster, Joseph Bottoms, Yvette Mimieux, Ernest Borgnine

THE BLACK SCORPION

Film   1957   U.S. (Warner Bros.)
88 Minutes   Black & white

Not much survives the inept script, direction and performances of this half-witted monster movie, whose dimly lighted photography was evidently intended to hide its inept special effects. The scorpion of the title is one of a nest of gigantic arachnids uncovered near a Mexican village after the eruption of a volcano. Of interest are the **stop-motion** sequences created by **King Kong** animator **Willis O'Brien** for *Gwangi,* a film about prehistoric life, began in 1942 and never completed. The scene in which the scorpion attacks a train bears more than a passing resemblance to Kong's angry rampage through a Manhattan subway station.

Director: Edward Ludwig, *Producer:* Frank Melford, Jack Dietz, *Screenplay:* David Duncan, Robert Blees, *Photographer:* Lionel Lindon, *Special Effects:* Willis O'Brien, *Music:* Paul Sawtell

Cast: Richard Denning, Mara Corday, Carlos Rivas, Mario Navarro, Carlos Muzquiz

BLACKTON, J.(AMES) STUART (1875–1941)

British-born film pioneer whose innovations as a director, producer, screenwriter and animator rank him as one of the great creative forces of cinema.

Introduced to filmmaking by **Thomas Edison** while an illustrator for the *New York World,* Blackton bought one of the inventor's Kinetoscope cameras and, with two partners, formed the Vitagraph Company, one of America's first film studios (absorbed by Warner Bros. in 1926). He made the first animated cartoon (see: **Animation),** *Humorous Phases of a Funny Face* (1906), introducing the close shot—a position intermediate to the close-up and the medium shot—and was one of the first films he edited. Additionally, he played in many of his movies, including the leading role in his Happy Hooligan series. In 1921 he directed *The Glorious Adventure,* an experimental two-color film shot in a process known as Prizmacolor. Blackton's only important SF film is **The Airship; or 100 Years Hence** (1908), a primitive but prophetic special effects depiction of aircraft of the future. Subsequent features include *The Battle Cry of Peace* (1915), a World War I propaganda thriller portraying an invasion of New York by German troops.

BLADE RUNNER

Film   1982   U.S. (Warner Bros.)
124 Minutes   Technicolor   Panavision
Dolby Stereo

Blade Runner, a horrific detective story set in the year 2019, is an interesting but seriously flawed adaptation of Philip K. Dick's famous novel, *Do Androids Dream of Electric Sheep?* (1968). Harrison Ford plays Ron Deckard, a burnt-out "blade runner" hired to track down and kill rebellious androids built to serve as slaves on **Earth.** The manmade **androids** are perfect human replicants, except that they have no feelings. Ford lurches viciously through the spastic plot, shooting replicant women in the back and indulging in other macho posturings. Ultimately, he discovers that stalking nonhumans has become a dehumanizing experience—the book's only major theme to survive Ridley Scott's misdirection.

Visually, the film is a tour de force, the best and most comprehensive vision of a future **dystopia** ever put on film. Los Angeles has become a garish, derelict city, choked with pollution and populated by the dregs of humanity. Space travel is common, and anyone with the wherewithal has moved out. Police tour the city's neon-lit canyons in "spinner cars" that move vertically as well as horizontally. According to Scott, director of the atmospheric box-office success **Alien** (1979), "background can be as important as the actor. The design of a film is the script."

Director: Ridley Scott, *Producer:* Michael Deeley, *Screenplay:* Hampton Fancher, David Peoples, *Novel:* "Do Androids Dream of Electric Sleep?" by Philip K. Dick, *Photographer:* Jordan Cronenweth, *Production Designer:* Lawrence C. Paull, *Special Effects:* **Douglas Trumbull,** Richard Yuricich, David Dryer, Matthew Yuricich, *Music:* Vangelis

Cast: Harrison Ford, Roger Hauer, Sean Young, Edward James Olmos, M. Emmet Walsh, Daryl Hannah, William Sanderson

BLASTER

A fictional personal weapon that shoots rays rather than bullets. It is usually handheld, although a larger version is sometimes mounted on a **spaceship.** How the weapon works is rarely explained by SF writers and filmmakers, but its effects are well-detailed and include death by incineration or disintegration. The blaster is to a space hero as the six-gun revolver is to a cowboy—a macho prop with which to prove his invincibility—and as such is a necessary ingredient of **space opera.** Highly visible in movie **serials** of the 1930s and 1940s, it had begun to disappear by the late 1950s, when science invented a real-life equivalent—the **laser.** Since then the blaster has been put back into circulation under a variety of new guises. It was last seen in the **Star Wars** films. (See also: **Death Ray; Phaser.**)

BLAST OFF

Film 1954 U.S. (Reed) 78 Minutes Black & white

Culled from the NBC-TV series **Rocky Jones, Space Ranger** (1954-55), with the 21st-century pilot on his usual rounds protecting the United Solar System from human harm. Credits are the same as those of the series.

A BLIND BARGAIN

Film 1922 U.S. (Goldwyn) 58 Minutes Black & white (silent)

This uncredited adaptation of the **H. G. Wells'** novel **The Island of Dr. Moreau** casts **horror** star Lon Chaney as Dr. Lamb, a **mad scientist** experimenting with a surgical procedure for transforming animals into human beings. He catches a sneak thief in his laboratory, a young man who needs money to buy medical care for his dying mother, and offers him a blind bargain: He will save the woman's life if the would-be thief will submit to one of his experiments. It ends badly for the doctor, whose back is broken by one of his grotesque creatures while he prepares for the operation. (See also: **Lon Chaney, Jr.; The Monster.**)

Director: Wallace Worsley, *Screenplay:* J. G. Hawks, *Play:* "The Octave of Claudius" Barry Pain, *Photographer:* Norbert Brodin

Cast: Lon Chaney, Jr., Raymond McKee, Virginia True Boardman, Fontaine La Rue

THE BLOB

Film 1958 U.S. (Paramount) 85 Minutes DeLuxe

Quivering like a huge mound of prune-flavored jello, a glob of protoplasm, recently arrived on Earth aboard a meteor fragment, gobbles up every human being in sight, growing larger with each meal. The police refuse to believe a group of teenagers who spot the creature in a lover's lane—until the blob squeezes itself into a supermarket and later takes in a movie. Called to the rescue, the armed services eventually dispose of the thing by dropping it into the Arctic Ocean. Hilarious beyond belief, *The Blob* numbers among its mistakes the casting of 26-year-old Steve McQueen (playing his first movie role) as a teenager. Moreover, McQueen's natural screen presence only serves to point up the drivel that surrounds him. The film's title song, a rock-and-roll hit by Burt Bacharach and Mack David, helped draw in the customers. A sequel **Beware! The Blob** was made in 1972.

Director: Irwin S. Yeaworth, *Producer:* Jack H. Harris, *Screenplay:* Theodore Simonson, Kate Phillips, *Special Effects:* Barton Sloane, *Music:* Ralph Carmichael

Cast: Steve McQueen, Aneta Corsealt, Olin Howlin, Earl Rowe

BLOOD BEACH

Film 1981 U.S. (Jerry Gross Org.) 90 Minutes Color

Something terrible is happening on the beach in Venice, a bohemian hangout on the Pacific just west of Hollywood: 16 people and the head of one dog have vanished into the sand. Called in to investigate, the police discover the labyrinthine underground lair of a giant **mutant** clam that has gone people-ing. Warned by a scientist not "to blow it to smithereens," the police do just that and litter the beach with a mass of

The Blob: Steve McQueen and teenage
friends investigate the creature's landing
site.

squirming fragments that promise to gob-
ble up more California bathers in a future
movie. Logic aside, this throwback to the
creature cycle of the 1950s fails to deliver
on action, suspense and the gore promised
in its title.

Director/Screenplay: Jeffrey Bloom, *Producer:* Steven
Nalevansky, *Story:* Jeffrey Bloom, Steven Nale-
vansky, *Photographer:* Steve Poster, *Music:* Gil
Melle

Cast: David Huffman, Mariana Hill, John Saxon,
Stefan Glerasch, Burt Young

BLOOD BEAST FROM OUTER SPACE

(Also titled: *The Night Caller/Night Caller From
Outer Space*)

Film   1965   Great Britain (New Art)
84 Minutes   Black & white   (Released 1968
U.S. [NTA])

Disguised as a human being and posing as
a photographer, an alien creature lures beautiful young women to his lair with a magazine advertisement for centerfold models.
As soon as "he" gets his claws on them, they
are shipped off to a distant planet to re-breed
the population, dwindling because of a mass
mutation. Police set a trap with a bikini-clad
decoy and send the alien scurrying for home.
Stale cheesecake with a science fiction crust.

Director: John Gilling, *Producer:* Ronald Liles,
Screenplay: Jim O'Connolly, *Music:* John Gregory

Cast: Robert Crewdson, Maurice Denham, Patricia Haines, John Saxon

BLOOD TYPE BLUE

(Also titled: *Blue Christmas*)

Film 1978 Japan (Toho) 120 Minutes
Color

Apparently intended as a lesson in tolerance toward minority groups, *Blood Type Blue* concerns a number of citizens from various walks of life whose blood has been altered by radiation from **UFOs.** An investigative reporter uncovers the story, creating a wave of discrimination against blue bloods. No one is quite sure who they are, not even the reporter, an earnest type, who has one of the better scenes in the movie: He sleeps with his girl friend and next morning finds blue stains on the bed linens.

Director: Kihachi Okamoto, *Screenplay:* So Kuramoto, *Photographer:* Daisaku Kimma, *Music:* Masaru Sato

Cast: Tatsuya Nakadai, Yo Katsuno, Keiko Takeshita, Eiji Okada

BLUE CHRISTMAS

See: **Blood Type Blue**

THE BODY STEALERS

(U.S. titles: *Invasion of the Body Stealers; Thin Air*)

Film 1969 Great Britain (Tigon)
91 Minutes Color (Released 1970 U.S. (Allied Artists)

A gentlemanly **alien** captures a flock of astronauts parachuting to the surface of his planet by spraying them with a red mist. He sends back an army of non-human counterparts and stores the originals in a **suspended animation** bank. The giddy script isn't helped by the start-and-stop direction and the interjection of attention-grabbing but inappropriate erotic scenes.

Director: Gerry Levy, *Photographer:* Tony Tenser, *Screenplay:* Mike St. Clair, Peter Marcus, *Music:* Reg Tilsley

Cast: Maurice Evans, George Sanders, Robert Flemyng, Hillary Dwyer, Patrick Allen

THE BOMB

A classic SF concern that frequently reflects a basic genre theme: the danger of knowledge. The first writer to imagine the world destroyed by nuclear bombs was H. G. Wells in *The World Set Free* (1914). The novel reflected changes in the rapidly evolving science of physics that came with the recent discovery of radioactivity.

One of SF's most farsighted prophecies, the atomic bomb came into being in 1945, after six years of concentrated effort by an international group of scientists working secretly in the United States.

Use of the bomb against Japan prompted John W. Campbell, Jr., editor of *Astounding Science Fiction,* to announce that science fiction would heretofore take on a new significance. While Campbell's prediction was largely accurate, the bomb also posed a frighteningly real threat to mankind. In 1953 the United States exploded the more destructive hydrogen bomb. Russia had its own version a year later. The number of casualties in a nuclear war had now become inestimable, and the bomb's effects on future generations was unknown.

During the 1950s, as people coped with the new Cold-War threat of instant annihilation, a number of cautionary SF films reflected this new anxiety. The first important anti-bomb film was the British-made **Seven Days to Noon** (1950), followed by Arch Oboler's low-budget doomsday programmer, **Five** (1951). Among the most important of subsequent end-of-the-world thrillers are **Kiss Me Deadly** (1955), **The World, the Flesh and the Devil, On the Beach** (1959) and **Panic in the Year Zero** (1962). A plethora of **horror** movies whose monsters were a menagerie of bomb-created **mutants,** marked this period in the history of SF film. These include **The Beast From 20,000 Fathoms** (1953), **Them!** (1954), **Tarantula** (1955), **The Incredible Shrinking Man** and **The Amazing Colossal Man** (1957).

Stanley Kubrick brought an end to the cycle with **Dr. Strangelove** (1963), which treated the subject as a campy black comedy. The film overshadowed Sidney Lumet's **Fail Safe** (1964), a serious treatment of an accidental war between the United States and Russia. (America was the instigator in both films.) In **Thunderball** (1965), a smash-hit **James Bond** movie, stolen nuclear bombs became a light-hearted plot device—a common element in spy thrillers of the decade.

A test-ban treaty between the U.S., Great Britain and Russia and the subsequent detente temporarily quelled public fears, and subsequent anti-bomb films, including **Peter Watkins'** sobering **The War Game** (1965) and the satirical **The Bed Sitting Room** (1969) did poorly at the box office.

During the early 1980s, an international grass-roots antinuclear movement brought forth a new cycle of anti-bomb films, beginning with the NBC TV movie *World War III* (1981). Subsequent TV programs included the BBC's *Nuclear War/A Guide to Armageddon* (1982), which simulated the result of a one-megaton nuclear explosion in London, and *The Day After* (1983), an ABC mini-series dealing with the consequences of a nuclear attack on Kansas City. Recent films in this sub-genre include **Wrong Is Right** (1982) and MGM's *War Games* (1983).

JAMES BOND

British spy-hero of 13 highly popular, tongue-in-cheek thrillers, the most successful movie series to date. Rooted in pulp fiction and **comic books,** Bond is a modernized superman whose strengths derive from a progression of ingenious (and often witty) mechanical and electronic devices, which always seem within the realm of the possible. His fantasy adventures are slickly packaged and told episodically, hinging on Bond rescuing himself from a progression of apparently hopeless predicaments. Few of his films qualify as science fiction, but all contain SF gadgetry and plot elements, and they have been instrumental in bringing the genre to a wider public.

According to his "official" biography, Bond was born on November 11, 1920, and recruited by the British Secret Service in 1938. After training, he received the code designation 007, which carries with it a license to kill. He is slightly over six feet tall (183 centimeters) and weighs approximately 167 pounds (76 kilos). He speaks three languages: English, French and German. An expert in hand-to-hand combat, he also handles a knife and an automatic pistol with deadly accuracy. Something of a snob, he has impeccable manners and superb taste in clothing, food, drink and women. He cannot be bribed, but he is not adverse to mixing business with pleasure: taking a beautiful enemy agent to bed, for instance, to find out whether she is seeking information or merely a good time. He has been married once, in **On Her Majesty's Secret Service** (1969).

Bond is the creation of writer Ian Fleming (1908-64), a former spy himself, who named him after the author of a reference book, *Birds of the West Indies.* He introduced the character in the novel *Casino Royale* (1951). Few remember that Bond was portrayed on American television before making his British movie series. In 1954, Fleming sold the rights to *Casino Royale* for $1,000 to CBS, which abridged the story into a one-hour episode of its *Climax* series, with Barry Nelson as the agent-playboy and Peter Lorre as the villain. NBC then commissioned Fleming to write an adventure series that was to be filmed in the Carribean, *Commander Jamaica.* When the project was abandoned, he adapted several of the scripts for the second Bond novel, *Dr. No.* In 1958, CBS hired Fleming to develop plots for a TV series that was to be called *James Bond, Secret Agent.* But the series never got off the ground, so Fleming expanded the outlines into the Bond short story collection, *For Your Eyes Only.* By 1961 Fleming's novels had become so popular that he was able to sell them for hefty percentage deal to movie producers Harry Saltzman and Albert Broccoli.

In all, Fleming wrote 14 Bond novels, the last, *Octopussy,* published a year after his death. The series has since been continued by John Gardner, who was chosen to write the books by the copyright owners. The updated Bond smokes low-tar cigarettes instead of the gold-banded Turkish-Balkan blend, drives a fuel-efficient Saab 900 Turbo, and prefers light meals to the elaborate French cuisine of the past. The changes are reflected in recent Bond movies.

The following is a comprehensive list of films in the series: With **Sean Connery** as Bond: **Dr. No** (1962), *From Russia, with Love* (1963), **Goldfinger** (1964), **Thunderball** (1965), **You Only Live Twice** (1967), **Diamonds Are Forever** (1971)

With George Lazenby as Bond: **On Her Majesty's Secret Service** (1969)

With Roger Moore as Bond: *Live and Let Die* (1973), *The Man With the Golden Gun* (1974), **The Spy Who Loved Me** (1977), **Moonraker** (1979), **For Your Eyes Only** (1981), *Octopussy* (1983)

In *Casino Royale* (1966), Bond was played for comedy by Woody Allen and David Niven, among others. Rights to the novel were not owned by Saltzman-Broccoli.

Bond's movie and TV imitators include: **The Avengers** (1962-68), **The Man from U.N.C.L.E.** (1964-68), **Get Smart!** (1965-70), **The Wild, Wild West** (1965-69), **The Silencers** (1966), **Our Man Flint** (1968), **A Man Called Sloane** (1979)

BONESTELL, CHESLEY (1888–   )

American illustrator whose astronomical paintings have graced SF magazine covers, books and films. An architectural school drop-out, Bonestell worked as a draftsman for several California firms (the Golden Gate bridge was one of his projects) before entering films as a matte artist (see: **Matte Painting**) during the 1930s. His 14 films include *The Hunchback of Notre Dame* (1939), *The Swiss Family Robinson* (1940), *Citizen Kane* (1941), **Destination Moon** (1950), **When Worlds Collide** (1951), **War of the Worlds** (1953), and **Conquest of Space** (1955), which was nominally based on his book *The Conquest of Space* (1949), with text by Willy Ley. One of Bonestell's paintings, a 10-by-40-foot mural, hangs in the National Air and Space Museum of the Smithsonian Institution.

THE BOOGIE MAN WILL GET YOU

Film   1942   U.S. (Columbia)   66 Minutes
Black & white

Flesh-crawlers **Boris Karloff** and Peter Lorre have a great time spoofing the kinds of roles that made them famous, but the hilarity is apparently an in-joke. Karloff is an addle-brained scientist busily fabricating supermen in the cellar of a country inn, whose guests are also prospective victims. Lorre is his partner-in-crime, the village's opportunis-' tic mayor/sheriff/real estate dealer. A chuckle or two isn't enough to dispel the oppressive gloom of a comedy straining at the seams to be amusing.

Director: Lew Landers, *Producer:* Colbert Clark, *Screenplay:* Edwin Blum, *Story:* Hal Fimberg, Robert B. Hunt, *Photographer:* Henry Freulich

Cast: Boris Karloff, Peter Lorre, Maxie Rosenbloom, Jeff Donnell, Don Beddoe, Larry Parks, Maude Eburne

BOOTH, WALTER R. (dates unknown)

British director of early SF film shorts. A cartoonist and former stage magician, he entered the British motion picture industry at its inception with pioneer inventor/filmmaker Robert W. Paul, for whom he worked from 1896 to 1906. His subsequent films include Great Britain's first animated cartoon and several primitive color films for the Charles Urban Trading Company, and several experimental sound films for Kineplastikon Films. During his influential but largely forgotten career, he brought a new degree of finesse to the trick effects devised by Paul and his French contemporary **George Melies**. His films mark the beginning of special effects used for telling a story rather than as a spectacle in themselves.

Films include: *Upside Down the Human Flies* (1899), *The Magic Sword* (1901), *Topical Tricks* (1905), *The Electric Vitalizer* (1910), *The Portrait of Dolly Grey* (1915). Booth's SF movies reveal a fascination with futuristic aircraft technology, which had become a popular subject after the brothers Wright lifted off from Kitty Hawk, North Carolina, in 1903.

These include: **The ? Motorist** (1905), a fantasy about a car that can fly, *The Aerocab, The Vacuum Provider* (1909), *The Aerial Submarine* (1910), and **The Aerial Anarchists** (1911). His most significant film is **The Airship Destroyer** (1909), inspired by the **H. G. Wells** novel *The War in the Air* published the year before, which prophesied with chilling accuracy the horrors of aerial bombardment.

BOULLE, PIERRE (1912–   )

French writer whose satirical novel *La planete des singes/Planet of the Apes* [in Great Britain, *Monkey Planet]* (1963) provided the basis for the popular Hollywood film **Planet of the Apes** (1968), which spawned four sequels, a TV series and a comic book. Born in Avignon, France, Boulle studied to be an electrical engineer before emigrating to Malaya in the mid-1930s to seek his fortune as a rubber planter. When World War II broke out he remained there to fight with the Free French guerrilla forces but was captured and held in a concentration camp. He eventually escaped and put his experiences to use in his bestselling novel about the absurd cruelties of war, *Le pont sur la riviere Kwai/The Bridge on the River Kwai* (1952), which became a memorable film of the same title in 1957.

Arriving at science fiction relatively late in his career, Boulle uses the genre to spin witty and well-plotted morality tales that mock human foibles while retaining the author's somewhat lofty compassion for his characters. Works published in English include, *Time Out of Mind and Other Stories* (1966), *Garden on the Moon* (1965) and *Games of the Mind* (1971).

THE BOWERY BOYS MEET THE MONSTER

Film   1954   U.S. (Allied Artists)   65 Minutes
Black & white

Looking a bit long in the tooth, the Bowery Boys—a second-feature low-comedy group derived from the Dead End Kids—get mixed up with a screwy doctor who upgrades the intelligence of buffoon Huntz Hall by giving him the brain of an ape.

Director: **Ed Bernds,** *Producer:* Ben Schwalb, *Screenplay:* Ed Bernds, Edward Ullman, *Photographer:* Harry Neumann, *Makeup:* Edward Polo, *Special Effects:* Augie Lohman

Cast: Leo Gorcey, Huntz Hall, Lloyd Corrigan, Ellen Corby, John Dehner

A BOY AND HIS DOG

Film   1975   U.S. (LQ/Jaf Films)
89 Minutes   Color Panavision

Based on a controversial story by Harlan Ellison, this off-beat love triangle takes place in the post-World War IV year of 2024. Civilization has been reduced to a basic struggle for survival between the strong and the weak, and barbarians roam the parched land looking for food and women. Among the gentler wanderers is a boy, Vic, and his cultured dog Blood, who communicate telepathically. Picking up the scent of a nearby female, Blood leads Vic to luscious Quilla June, who lures him to an underground community that has preserved traditional American middle-class values. All the men are sterile, however, and Vic is needed as a sperm bank, a machine function he rejects in favor of escaping to the surface with Quilla June. Finding Blood dying of starvation, Vic calmly murders the devious girl and serves her to the dog. At the fade-out, the faithful partners are seen walking into the sunset.

Director/Screenplay: L. Q. Jones, *Producer:* Alvy Moore, *Novel:* Harlan Ellison, *Photographer:* John Arthur Morrill, *Special Effects:* Frank Rowe, *Makeup:* Wes Dawn, *Music:* Tim McIntire

Cast: Don Johnson, Susanne Benton, Tim McIntire (dog's voice), Alvy Moore, Jason Robards, Charles McGraw

THE BOYS FROM BRAZIL

Film   1978   U.S./Great Britain (ITC/20th Century-Fox)   124 Minutes   DeLuxe

The Boys From Brazil: Gregory Peck as Dr. Josef Mengele.

Nazis hiding in South America put into effect a plan hatched during the last days of the Third Reich: to create another Hitler. Cells from the Fuhrer's body are used to produce 94 **clones,** whose natural fathers are then eliminated so that the boys can be brought up in a proper Hitlerian manner. The murders arouse the suspicions of an Israeli agent, who puts an end to the scheme.

Gregory Peck is miscast as the evil geneticist Dr. Josef Mengele, but Laurence Olivier is perfect as the elderly Nazi-hunter Bassermann (a portrayal modeled after real-life agent Simon Wiesenthal). Cloning, very much in the news at the time of the film's release, is given a plausible scientific context—unusual in a Hollywood SF project made by non-SF people.

Director: Franklin Schaffner, *Producers:* Martin Richards, Stanley O'Toole, *Screenplay:* Heywood Gould, *Novel:* Ira Levin, *Photographer:* Henri Decae, *Production Designer:* Gil Parrando, *Music:* **Jerry Goldsmith**

Cast: Gregory Peck, Laurence Olivier, James Mason, Lilli Palmer, Uta Hagen

BRACKETT, LEIGH (1915–78)

American SF novelist and screenplay writer. Brackett began her professional career in

the early 1940s writing romantic **space operas** for SF pulp magazines. Later that decade she turned to screen writing, and for the rest of her life she alternated between the two mediums. Her credits include five films directed by Howard Hawks: *The Big Sleep* [co-writer] (1946), *Rio Bravo* [co-writer] (1959), *Hatari! (1962), El Dorado* (1967), and *Rio Lobo* [co-writer] (1970). In 1946 she married SF writer Edmond Hamilton, who died in 1977. Her background in science fiction and outstanding film work prompted George Lucas to hire her to script **The Empire Strikes Back** (1980), the first sequel to **Star Wars** (1977). She completed the assignment shortly before succumbing to cancer. Of her many novels, her best is probably *The Long Tomorrow* (1955), a well-plotted and encouraging story of post-holocaust America.

Other films: The Vampire's Ghost, Crime Doctor's Manhunt (1945), *Gold of the Seven Saints* [co-writer] (1961), *The Long Goodbye* (1973)

BRADBURY, RAY (DOUGLAS) (1920–)

Protean novelist, essayist, poet, playwright and screenplay writer whose fiction has been translated into 25 languages and dramatized

Ray Bradbury

educated," he says. "I've never been to college.") Among his literary influences are Edgar Rice Burroughs ("He made me want to be something romantic") and Edgar Allan Poe ("I fell in love with his verbal jewelry"). Bradbury's writing career began at 12, when having exhausted Burroughs' Tarzan and John Carter on Mars series, he created his own sequels.

In 1932, during the Depression, the Bradbury family moved west where his father found work in Tucson. While there Bradbury talked a radio station owner into giving him a job reading comic strips and providing sound effects over the air—for which he was paid in movie passes. By now he was also an adept amateur stage conjurer who performed locally, and for a time he considered becoming a radio and film actor. In 1934 his family moved to Los Angeles where Bradbury sold newspapers on the street and met SF enthusiast Forrest Ackerman, would-be filmmaker **Ray Harryhausen** and SF writer Henry Kuttner. Together the ambitious young quartet produced a short-lived **fanzine** called *Futuria Fantasia*, which published the early efforts of future luminaries Robert Heinlein, artist Hannes Bok and—Ray Bradbury.

Bradbury made his first magazine sale in 1941, to *Super Science Stories;* during the next five years he contributed dozens more to the SF, fantasy and adventure **pulp magazines** flourishing at the time. Many of these short fictions (some written under pseudonyms) were formula **space opera**s, but they provided Bradbury an opportunity to develop his unique style. The publication of a hardcover anthology of his best short stories, *Dark Carnival* (1947), brought him to the attention of the quality "slicks," and soon he was contributing regularly to such magazines as *Esquire, McCall's, Colliers* and *Argosy*.

With the publication of his second book in 1950, Bradbury became famous almost overnight. A collection of interwoven short stories, *The Martian Chronicles* (in Great Britain, *The Silver Locusts*) evolved from a number of fantasies with SF overtones written for *Planet Stories* and *Thrilling Wonder*.

on radio, television and in films and theater. Bradbury has been called the "prose poet of science fiction," a description true of only some of his work. He is a mainstream writer interested in science as a barometer of human nature rather than in technology for its own sake. Few of his novels and short stories fit comfortably into the genre of science speculation, which he often uses as a context for offbeat, macabre fantasies filled with dazzling visual symbols and haunting evocations of childhood lost.

A descendant of British colonists who arrived in America in 1630, Bradbury was born in Waukegan, Illinois, to a power lineman and his Swedish wife. An overweight, introspective child who wore spectacles and preferred books to sports, he spent long afternoons at the public library traveling imaginary vistas while his classmates played childhood games. ("I'm completely library

Critics rhapsodized over his evocative chronicle of mankind's colonization of Mars and its underlying theme of the deceptive nature of appearances. Eminent writer-critic Christopher Isherwood ushered Bradbury into the literary establishment when he called the author "a very great and unusual talent," and praised the "sheer lift and power of a truly original imagination."

Bradbury's first novel, *Fahrenheit 451*, appeared in 1953. Based on a short story, *The Fireman*, written for *Galaxy* magazine, it is his only SF novel and his only fully realized long work. A powerful dystopian glimpse into a future world where the printed word is forbidden, the novel concerns the gradual enlightenment of a "fireman" whose job it is to burn books and the houses in which they are found. (See: **dystopia.**) The book further strengthened his literary reputation, and critics briefly compared him to **George Orwell.**

Bradbury's later works are not up to the standards set in what are considered his vintage years: 1946-56. His reputation has continued to grow throughout the world, however, and he is still a prolific writer, with more than 500 works to his credit. In recent years he has concentrated on plays and poetry, which are perhaps the least successful of his writings. During the 1970s he emerged as a television celebrity and can frequently be seen holding forth on science and science fiction on specials and talk shows.

> Science fiction pretends to look into the future, but it's really looking at a reflection of the truth immediately in front of us.
>
> -RB

Selected fiction: The Illustrated Man (1951), *The Golden Apples of the Sun* (1953), *The October Country* (1955), *Dandelion Wine* (1957), *I Sing the Body Electric* (1968), *The Halloween Tree* (1973)

Novels and stories filmed: **It Came from Outer Space, The Beast from 20,000 Fathoms,** (1953), **The Illustrated Man** (1969), **Fahrenheit 451** (1968), *Icarus Montgolfier Wright (Screenplay)* (1962), (Co-screenplay) *Moby Dick* (1956), *Something Wicked this Way Comes* (1982)

TV programs and films: The Jail [Alcoa Premier series], **The Twilight Zone** (1962), *Picasso Summer* (1969), **The Martian Chronicles** (1979), **Beyond 1984: Remembrance of Things Past** (1978), *Any Friend* (1982)

Radio dramas: **Dimension X, Suspense,** *Leviathan 99*

Plays: The Martian Chronicles, The World of Ray Bradbury, Leviathan 99. (See: **Theater.**)

BRADY, SCOTT (1924–   )

Actor who has starred in a number of SF and horror programmers and played supporting roles in mainstream films. Born Gerald Tierney in Brooklyn, New York, the brother of actor Lawrence Tierney, he worked as a lumberjack before World War II service in the U.S. Navy, where he was a lightweight boxing champion. Discharged in 1945, he studied drama at the Bliss-Hayden School in Beverly Hills, California, and made his screen debut in *Born to Fight* (1948). Named Hollywood's "Star of Tomorrow" in 1953, he failed to make an impact in several mediocre leading roles as a hardbitten hero, mostly in Westerns and gangster melodramas, and was relegated to grade-B productions and character parts.

Films: **Castle of Evil, Destination Inner Space** (1966), **Journey to the Center of Time** (1967), *Satan's Sadists,* **Marooned** (1969), **The Night Strangler** [TV film] (1973), **The China Syndrome** (1979)

THE BRAIN

(Great Britain title: *Vengeance*)

Film 1962 Germany/Great Britain(CCC/Stross) 83 Minutes Black & white

The third version of **Curt Siodmak's** scientifically specious novel *Donovan's Brain* (1943), an early **cyborg** story concerning a disembodied brain that telepathically controls the doctor who keeps it alive. The brain belongs to a wealthy industrialist who uses the doctor to avenge his murder. Although technically competent, this remake fails to generate the shivers and suspense of the earlier films, **The Lady and the Monster** (1944) and **Donovan's Brain** (1953).

Director: **Freddie Francis,** *Producer:* Raymond Stross, *Screenplay:* Robert Stewart, Philip Mackie, *Photographer:* Bob Hulke, *Music:* Ken Jones

Cast: Peter Van Eyck, Anne Heywood, Cecil Parker, Bernard Lee, Jeremy Spenser

THE BRAIN EATERS

Film 1958 U.S.(AIP) 60 Minutes Black & white

A lackwitted adaptation of *The Puppet Masters* (1953), Robert Heinlein's feverish novel about an invasion of **symbiotes** from Titan, Saturn's largest satellite. Heinlein's creatures are shapeless blobs of protoplasm with no visible features, and helpless until attached to the upper backs of human victims, who then relinquish their intelligence and will power. Here, they are reduced to stock movie monsters resembling land crabs, a threat predictably solved by the usual stroke of human ingenuity.

Director: Bruno De Sota, *Producer:* Ed Nelson, *Screenplay:* Gordon Urqhart, *Novel:* Robert Heinlein, *Photographer:* Larry Raimond, *Art Director:* Bert Shomberg

Cast: Ed Nelson, **Leonard Nimoy,** Jack Hill, Joanna Lee, Jody Fair

THE BRAIN FROM THE PLANET AROUS

Film 1958 U.S.(Howco) 71 Minutes Black & white

Flying to Earth like a gelatinous **UFO,** a giant brain takes control of a young scientist (**John Agar** facing yet another SF calamity) to implement its goal of world conquest. Later, a good brain arrives and takes over the body of a dog. The two square off for a showdown that provides one of the great comic moments in ersatz SF films.

Director: **Nathan H. Juran,** *Producer:* Jacques Marquette, *Screenplay:* Ray Buffum, *Music:* Walter Greene

Cast: John Agar, Joyce Meadows, Robert Fuller, Ken Terrell

THE BRAINSNATCHERS

See: **The Man Who Lived Again**

THE BRAIN THAT WOULDN'T DIE

Film 1959 Great Britain(Sterling) 81 Minutes Black & white (Released 1962 U.S.[AIP])

Literally adhering to the motto "never say die," a young surgeon saves the head of his fiancee, decapitated in an automobile accident. He keeps the head alive in his laboratory while searching for an appealing donor to replace her badly mangled body. Unfortunately, the script was dead from the beginning.

Director/Screenplay: Jason Evers, *Producer:* Rex Carlton, *Photographer:* Stephen Hajnal, *Special Effects:* Byron Baer, *Makeup:* George Fiala

Cast: Jason Evers, Virginia Leith, Adele Lamont, Paula Maurice

BRAVE NEW WORLD

TV film 1980 U.S.(NBC) 152 Minutes Color

In Aldous Huxley's seminal dystopian novel *Brave New World* (1933) (see: **dystopia),** the realities of the present promised a worry-free future in which technology would make life as pleasant and as unchallenging as possible. Mankind would no longer have anything to complain about: no frustration, envy, murder or war. Birth would take place in a bottle, from a single fertilized egg cloned into 96 identical human beings (see: **clone),** whose intelligence level and function in society would be predetermined. Happiness would be assured by a euphoric drug called soma, promiscuity officially encouraged, and vicarious thrills gotten by going to a "feelie," a kind of motion picture that placed the viewer in the action.

Shocking in its time, the novel stands as a monument of SF prophecy, and it is a major work of social criticism. You wouldn't know it from this vapid made-for-TV film, however, (which a former NBC president

Brave New World: Set of the Central London Hatchery, where human birth is carried out by machines. Director Brinckerhoff is at bottom right (with megaphone).

quite seriously criticized as being "too intellectual"). The novel's biting wit has been replaced with a camp ambiance, leaving only a threadbare story not strong enough to stand on its own. Visually, the production is impressive, if a bit too stylized to be convincing. There is one improvement over the original, however: Babies are now born in prenatal "baggies" rather than bottles, an easier way of giving birth than breaking glass.

Director: Burt Brinckerhoff, *Producer:* Jacqueline Babbin, *Screenplay:* Robert E. Thompson, *Novel:* Aldous Huxley, *Photographer:* Harry Wolf, *Production Designer:* Tom H. John

Cast: Keir Dullea, Kristofer Tabori, Julie Cobb, Bud Cort, Marcia Strassman, Ron O'Neal.

BRICK BRADFORD

Film serial   1947   U.S.(Columbia)
15 Episodes   Black & white

Newspaper comic-strip hero Brick Bradford, acting in behalf of the United Nations, journeys to the moon via a crystal door to bring back "lunarium," a mineral needed to power an antiguided missile weapon called the Interceptor Ray. Later, he hops into his familiar "time-top" to recover a lost 18th-century formula needed to complete the Ray. Not up to the imaginative level of the comic strip, inspired by **Buck Rogers,** but interesting as a reflection of contemporary optimism regarding the peace-keeping function of the U.N. (See: **comic books.**)

Directors: **Spencer G. Bennett,** Thomas Carr, *Producer:* Sam Katzman, *Screenplay:* George H. Plympton, Arthur Hoerl, Lewis Clay

Cast: Kane Richmond, Rick Vallin, Linda Johnson, Pierre Watkin, Charles Quigley

THE BRIDE OF FRANKENSTEIN

Film 1935 U.S. (Universal) 80 Minutes
Black & white

Karloff's tortured monster talks, laughs, smokes a cigar and has a blind date in this playful, magnificently eccentric sequel to **Frankenstein** (1931), best of the long series. The film opens with a prologue in which author Mary Shelley, fudging a bit, explains that Dr. Frankenstein and his monster had not been killed but merely injured in the burning mill that climaxed the previous film. Back in business, the doctor enters into a partnership with the bushy-haired Dr. Praetorious—played to the hilt by Ernest Thesiger—a fastidiously effeminate **mad scientist**—to create a bride for his lonely **android.** Fiendishly proud of his macabre accomplishments, Praetorious displays the six-inch humans he has created in bell jars, commenting to his colleague: "While you were playing with dead flesh, I went to the original seed." In another memorable scene, he chats with a skeleton while lunching in a crypt he has invaded. Later, he apologizes to the Monster for smoking a cigar: "It's my only weakness, you know."

Piecing together bits of female cadavers, the pair spark their bandage-swathed "woman" to life with electricity generated by lightning bolts in Dr. Frankenstein's majestic lab, with the Monster patiently standing by. Carefully unwrapped and looking rather like an Egyptian queen caught in a short-circuited hair dryer, the Bride (Elsa Lanchester) recoils in disgust at the sight of her bethrothed. Hissing and screaming, she gets her point across to the jilted monster. With a tear in his eye, he mutters "We belong dead," and pulls a lever that blows up the lab.

Bride, originally to have been titled *The Return of Frankenstein,* was released in several truncated versions, usually with the prologue shortened and without the scene in which the Monster murders a burgemeister. In England, the scene in which the Monster strokes the cheek of the dead girl who is to

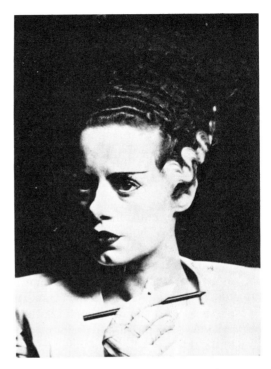

The Bride of Frankenstein: Elsa Lanchester

become his bride (or parts of her) was cut by censors.

Director: James Whale, *Producer:* Carl Laemmle, Jr., *Screenplay:* John Balderston, William Hurlbut, *Photographer:* John J. Mescall, *Art Director:* Charles Hall, *Special Effects:* **John P. Fulton,** Ken Strickfaden, *Makeup:* Jack Pierce, *Music:* Franz Waxman

Cast: Boris Karloff, Colin Clive, Valerie Hobson, Ernest Thesiger, Elsa Lanchester, Una O'Connor, E.E. Clive, Dwight Frye

BRIDE OF THE MONSTER

Film 1956 U.S. 70 Minutes Black & white

Seriously ill, penniless, and at the end of his career, legendary horror star **Bela Lugosi** was reduced to appearing in grade-Z productions like this one, made the year he died. Playing a mad doctor for the umpteenth time, he wobbles across the screen gamely arching his eyebrows while experimenting with a human growth hormone and tending a giant, killer octopus.

Director/Producer: Edward D. Wood, Jr., *Screenplay:* Edward D. Wood, Jr., Alex Gordon, *Special Effects:* Pat Dinga, *Music:* Frank Worth

Cast: Bela Lugosi, Eddie Parker (B.L.'s double), Tony McCoy, Loretta King, William Benedict

BRIDES OF FU MANCHU

Film   1966   Great Britain (Hammer)
94 minutes   Color

Sax Rohmer's oriental master-criminal is back plotting to take over the world, this time by kidnapping daughters of government leaders and holding them for ransom in order to buy materials to build a mammoth ray gun. Played tongue-in-cheek, *Brides of Fu Manchu* is a companion piece to *The Face of Fu Manchu* (1965), Hammer's initial revival of the series.

Director: **Don Sharp,** *Producer:* Oliver A. Unger, Harry Alan Towers, *Screenplay:* Don Sharp, Harry Alan Towers, *Photographer:* Ernest Steward, *Music:* Johnn Douglas

Cast: Christopher Lee, Douglas Wilmer, Howard Marion-Crawford, Marie Versini, Rupert Davies

THE BROOD

Film   1979   Canada/U.S. (New World)
91 Minutes   Color

Psi powers are the subject of David Cronenberg's jolting horror film, which takes place in a psychiatric institute headed by a charismatic doctor who encourages patients to manifest their mental disorders physically as welts and sores on the skin. His star patient is a beautiful but totally insane redhead presiding over a brood of murderous children created by her psychosis. Cronenberg, who doesn't know when to leave well enough alone, slows down the suspense with an excess of gratuitous gore, but the film is lively and absorbing, his best to date.

Director/Screenplay: **David Cronenberg,** *Producer:* Claude Heroux, *Photographer:* Mark Irwin, *Art Director:* Carol Spier, *Makeup:* Shonagh Jabour, *Music:* Howard Shore

The Brood: Dr. Raglan, head of psychiatric institute, is attacked by children born of a psychosis.

Cast: Oliver Reed, Samantha Eggar, Art Hindle, Cindy Hinds, Nuala Fitzgerald

BROWNING, RICOU (1930–   )

American stunt man and occasional actor, best-known for his impersonation of the batrachian monster in **The Creature From the Black Lagoon** (1954). He has since become a topnotch director of underwater film sequences.

Films include: **Thunderball** (1965), **Around the World Under the Sea** (1966), *Lady in Cement* (1968), **Raise the Titanic** (1980). *TV credits: Flipper* (series) (1964-67), **The Aquarians** (film) (1970), *Salty* (series) (1974).

THE BUBBLE

Film   1966   U.S. (Midwestern Magic)
112 Minutes   Color   SpaceVision

Arch Oboler, the filmmaker and former radio dramatist who sparked Hollywood's short-lived 3-D bonanza of the 1950s with *Bwana Devil* (1952), tried to go himself one better by combining 3-D with **wide-screen,**

a process he called Tri-Optiscope or Space-Vision. Lightning failed to strike twice, however, mostly because of the film's banal plot, an eccentric melange concerning three travelers stranded in a town separated from the world by a **force-field** generated by **aliens** (See also: **Stereoscopic Film.**).

Director/Producer/Special Effects: Arch Oboler, *Art Director:* Marvin Chomsky, *Music:* Paul Sawtell, Bert Shafter

Cast: Michael Cole, Johnny Desmond, Deborah Walley

BUCK ROGERS

Legendary SF hero whose durable saga has been depicted on radio, in films and on television (see listings below). He first appeared as Anthony Rogers in a short **space opera,** "Armageddon—2419" by **Philip F. Nowlan,** published in the August 1928 issue of *Amazing Stories.* A sequel, "The Airlords of Han," appeared in the March 1929 issue. The stories caught the eye of John Flint Dille, president of the National Newspaper Service syndicate, who commissioned Nowlan to do an SF **comic strip**—the world's first—with artist Richard Calkins.

The strip, titled "Buck Rogers in the 25th Century," debuted on January 7, 1929, with the character now called by his nickname (the warlike Hans were later changed to Mongols). It ran consecutively until 1967, and at its peak was published in more than 400 newspapers throughout the world and translated into 18 languages. By the time his radio serial of the same title appeared in 1932—another SF first—Buck had become a national hero whose image graced a variety of tie-in merchandise, including toys, games, cups and plates, and clothing. His popularity was such that in 1934 a Virginia department store substituted an actor disguised as Buck for its annual Santa Claus.

According to Nowlan's original stories and comic strips, Rogers is a former U.S. Air Service pursuit pilot who served in France during World War I. After being mustered out, he worked as a surveyor in Pennsylvania where he was trapped in a mine by a cave-in and overcome by a strange, radioactive gas that put him into a state of **suspended animation** for 500 years. Upon awakening (the beginning of the story), the first person he sees is Wilma Deering, who mistakes him for an outlaw and tries to shoot him. Grabbing her ray gun when she trips on a root, he kills the outlaws and wins her confidence. Spotting Buck as a man to be trusted (and perhaps loved), she brings him up to date and tells him of the Mongol plot to dominate the world. Donning the jumping belt of one of the fallen outlaws, he joins Wilma for a tour of magnificent cities of "metallo-glass," where 25th-century citizens eat synthetic food, travel by air (roads are almost nonexistent), and have a number of ingenious *art deco* gadgets to do all the drudge work. In no time at all, Buck has become a captain of Earth's military forces, a secret agent, an intelligence officer and head of the Rocket Rangers, with Wilma as his co-pilot and the brilliant scientist Dr. Huer as his advisor. They spent the next 38 years battling the Mongols, Killer Kane and his untrustworthy partner-in-crime, the malevolently beautiful Ardala.

For all his integrity and good intentions, Rogers has often been accused of being a white supremist's fantasy—an indictment not without foundation. Few non-white characters have been portrayed in the comic strip and those who have are usually villains. The outlaws who attack Wilma in the first panels, for instance, are derogatorily called "half-breeds" as she aims her ray gun.

Among the comic-strip characters directly inspired by Buck are **Brick Bradford** and **Flash Gordon.**

BUCK ROGERS

Film serial   1939   U.S.(Universal)
12 Episodes   Black & white

After making two **serials** as **Flash Gordon, Buster Crabbe** took on Flash's comic-strip rival with nearly as much success. The films are in fact so similar that they could be con-

Buck Rogers: Buster Crabbe, with Jackie Moran (1939); Gil Gerard (1979).

sidered as members of the same series. As with the Gordon serials, *Buck Rogers* was filmed with more care and a larger budget than usual, and it effectively captures the vitality of the newspaper strip. Initial episodes more or less accurately recount Buck's 500-year sleep (he awoke in the Arctic this time), after which he joins with Wilma Deering and Dr. Huer to rid the world of the Zuggs, invaders from Saturn, who are in league with the dastardly Killer Kane. The serial was released to television during the early 1950s as *Planet Outlaws* and later as *Destination Saturn*.

Directors: Ford Beebe, Saul A. Goodkind, *Screenplay:* Norman S. Hall, Ray Trampe

Cast: Buster Crabbe, Constance Moore, C. Montague Shaw, Jackie Moran, Henry Brandon

BUCK ROGERS IN THE 25TH CENTURY

Radio serial   1932-39   U.S.(CBS)
15 Minutes (M-Th)

Three years after bringing science fiction to the world of comic strips, Buck Rogers introduced **space opera** to **radio** on his own program, which first aired on November 7, 1932. Originating from New York and broadcast four times weekly (initially at 7:15 P.M. and later moved to an earlier "children's hour"), the program had a built-in audience of funny-paper readers who tuned in by the hundreds of thousands.

Plots were roughly similar to those of the comic strip, with Buck, his liberated copilot Wilma Deering and the brilliant Dr. Huer daily keeping the world in one piece. The sounds of Buck's arsenal, consisting of such futuristic devices as death rays, incendiary missiles, gamma bombs and a mechanical mole capable of burrowing deep into the Earth, were simulated by a variety of electrical and hand-powered motors. The crackling buzz of Rogers' psychic destruction ray, for instance, was provided by a Schick electric razor.

Underscoring the program's phenomenal popularity was the response to mail-order gifts offered to listeners. An initial offering of a map of the planets brought 125,000 requests. A subsequent offering of a cardboard space helmet was made more difficult to get, with the proviso that a metal seal from a can of Cocomalt, the show's sponsor, had to accompany the request. Depression-era children nevertheless sent in more than 140,000 strips of tin for the highly desirable premium, which has since become an extremely rare and valuable collectors' item.

Director/Producer: Jack Johnstone, *Writer:* Jack Johnstone, Joe A. Cross, Albert G. Miller, **Philip Nowlan,** Richard Calkins

Cast: Buck Rogers—Matt Crowley, Curtis Arnall, Carl Frank, John Larkin, *Wilma Deering*—Adele Ronson, *Dr. Huer*—Edgar Stehli, *Buddy*—Ronald Liss, *Ardala Valmar*—Elaine Melchior, *Killer Kane*— Bill Shelley, Dan Ocko, Arthur Vinton, *Announcers:* Fred Uttal, Paul Douglas, Jack Johnstone

BUCK ROGERS IN THE 25TH CENTURY

TV series   1950-51   U.S.(ABC)   30 Minutes (weekly)   Black & white

Following on the heels of Dumont's **Captain Video and His Video Rangers** (1949-55), Buck Rogers seemed ill at ease on live television, where his adventures were confined to a few sets in a small studio. By comparison, his movie **serials** seemed like Hollywood extravaganzas. Buck's history was recounted verbally in the first episode, which headquartered him in a secret science lab in a cave behind Niagara Falls (the city of Niagara was now the capital of the world). Kem Dibbs, who later appeared in the SF TV series, **Men Into Space** (1959-60), played

Buck with a suitable swashbuckling flair. He was later replaced by Robert Pastene.

Director: Babette Henry, *Producers:* Joe Cates, Babette Henry, *Writer:* Gene Wyckoff

Cast: Kem Dibbs, Robert Pastene, Lou Prentis, Harry Sothern, Harry Kingston, Stanford Bickart

BUCK ROGERS

Film/TV film   1979   U.S.(Universal)
88 Minutes   Technicolor
TV series   1979-81   U.S.(NBC)   60 Minutes (weekly)   Color

The success of **Star Wars** (1977) prompted Universal to dust off its old space hero **Buck Rogers,** one of the inspirations for **George Lucas'** film. The updated Buck **(Gil Gerard)** is an astronaut who blasted off from Cape Canaveral in 1987 and was flash-frozen when he rocketed into a cluster of gaseous **comets** (see: **cryonics).** Thrown into orbit around the **sun** at the speed of light, he returns to **Earth** orbit 500 years later and is captured by the Draconian **aliens,** who are seeking a way to penetrate a **force-field** that now protects the planet. Rescued by a very unsquare Wilma Deering, Buck joins forces with Dr. Huer (no longer played for comedy), who builds him an eccentric **robot** called **Twiki** (the voice of Mel Blanc).

Expecting to see Earth as it was, Buck encounters instead a world divided by a nuclear war centuries before: the elite lives in an Oz-like domed city called New Chicago; outside, **mutants** prowl through the devastation. Suspected of being a spy for the Draconians, Buck must prove that his **time travel** story is true, while preventing Kane (his nickname has been dropped) and the sexy but deadly Princess Ardala from letting the Draconians in.

Director: **Daniel Haller,** *Producer:* Richard Caffey, *Executive Producer:* Glen A. Larson, *Screenplay:* Glen A. Larson, Leslie Stevens, *Photographer:* Frank Beascoechea, *Art Director:* Paul Peters, *Special Effects:* Bud Ewing, *Music:* Stu Philips

Cast: Gil Gerard, Erin Gray, Pamela Hensley, Henry Silva, Tim O'Connor, Joseph Wiseman, Felix Silla

BUG-EYED MONSTERS

(Also known as **BEM**s)

This term is used good-naturedly by science fiction fans to describe imaginative beasts (usually **alien** creatures) that roam through SF epics threatening beautiful earth women. They are usually dispatched by space heroes carrying ray guns. Said to have been coined at the First World Science Fiction Convention—held in 1939 in New York City during the New York World's Fair—the term poked fun at lurid pulp SF magazine covers of the 1930s and 1940s. (See also: **Space Opera.**)

BURTT, BEN, Jr. (1949–   )

Movie sound effects technician; winner of two **Academy Awards,** for **Star Wars** (1977) and **The Empire Strikes Back** (1980).

A native of Syracuse, New York, Burtt was graduated from Allegheny College, where he made a short film titled *Genesis,* which won him a scholarship to the University of Southern California Film School. He began his career while earning a Master's Degree in film production, working as a part-time sound editor for such projects as the TV movie **Killdozer** (1974). Burt was still writing his thesis when hired by **George Lucas** to create new sounds for *Star Wars,* then in the development stage.

The job of creating the film's unique sound track required two years of combining and altering different sounds to correspond with its alien and mechanical characters. The rodent-like **Jawas,** for instance, speak a language that is a combination of Zulu, Swahili and English. The alien Greedo, **Han Solo**'s would-be assassin, speaks a non-sense version of ancient Incan, subtitled in English. To obtain a metallic quality for the voice of Anthony Daniels, who plays the **robot C-3PO,** Burtt phased it through an electronic circuit that dubbed the actor's voice over itself, with a slight prolonging of the second voice track. Burtt calls the technique "making the voice rub against itself."

Burtt's most difficult task was developing

Other films: **Invasion of the Body Snatchers** (1978), **Alien,** *More American Graffiti* (1979), *Revenge of the Jedi* (1983)

BYRD, RALPH (1909–52)

Virile leading man of Hollywood **serials** and second-features during the 1930s and 1940s; also in supporting roles in major films. Born in Dayton, Ohio, Byrd's greatest fame came as the science-oriented detective Dick Tracy in five serials made by Republic studios. Although he bore little resemblance to the hatchet-nosed **comic book** hero, he managed to capture the essence of Tracy's personality with his aggressively right-minded portrayal and square-jawed good looks. He had become so identified with the role that an attempt to replace him with another actor in two Tracy films in the mid-1940s failed, and he was asked to resume the serial. He later played Tracy in a short-lived television series (1951).

Films: **S.O.S.Coastguard, Dick Tracy** (1937), *Dick Tracy Returns* (1938), **Dick Tracy's G-Men** (1939), **Dick Tracy vs. Crime** [re-released in 1952 as *Dick Tracy vs. the Phantom Empire*], *A Yank in the RAF* (1941), *Guadacanal Diary* (1943), **Dick Tracy Meets Gruesome** (1948)

BY ROCKET TO THE MOON

See: **Die Frau Im Monde**

CAHN, EDWARD L. (1899–1963)

American director/producer of low-budget genre films made to exploit Hollywood's latest box-office trends. Born in Brooklyn, he arrived in Hollywood in 1917 and worked briefly as an assistant director for the Alla Nazimova film company. In 1920 he enrolled at UCLA and worked at night cutting films for Universal, which promoted him to head cutter in 1926. He began directing serials in 1931, then switched to second-featured crime melodramas a few years later. During Hollywood's 1950s monster cycle, he directed a number of SF horror programmers of varying quality including: **The Creature With the Atom Brain** (1955), **The She-Creature** (1956), *Voodoo Woman, Zombies of Mora-Tau,* **Invasion of the Saucer Men** (1957), **It!—The Terror From Beyond Space,** *The Curse of the Faceless Man* (1958), and **The Invisible Invaders** (1959). In 1961, he set a record of sorts by directing 11 films—mostly westerns—many of which he also produced.

CAIDIN, MARTIN (1927–   )

American writer of science fiction novels and numerous science fact books. The film **Marooned** (1964) was based on his novel of the same title (1964). The TV series **The Six Million Dollar Man** (1973-78) and its companion series **The Bionic Woman** (1976-78) were based on his novel *Cyborg*

(1972). Caidin is also a pilot and the founder of a firm that provides information on astronautics to radio and televison.

CANADIAN MOUNTIES VS. ATOMIC INVADERS

Film serial   1953   U.S. (Republic)
12 Episodes   Black & white

The title says it all. By 1953 television had dealt a death blow to the serialized movie short, but Republic studios continued to churn them out by rote, with little of the spirited imagination that characterized the **serial** form in its prime. A case in point in this insipid, SF-oriented cowboy story, whose bland, giveaway title would not have been accepted in the old days. Its atomic invaders are a band of foreign agents intent on building rocket launch pads in the far north as part of their plan to take control of the U.S. and Canada. Posing as a settler, Sergeant Don Roberts discovers that a friendly old trapper is actually Marlof, commander of the vile group. The Mounties pursue Marlof's henchmen over the frozen wasteland, through avalanches, packs of hungry wolves and reindeer stampedes until they finally get their men.

Director: Franklin Adreon

Cast: Bill Henry, Susan Morrow, Arthur Space, Dale Van Sickel, Mike Ragan

CAPE CANAVERAL MONSTERS

Film   1960   U.S.(CCM)   69 Minutes   Black & white

The U.S. space program is threatened by **alien** "brains" that invade Florida and turn human beings into zombies who hate NASA. A routine film, whose aliens look like animated ink blots.

Director/Screenplay: Phil Tucker, *Producer:* Richard Greer, *Photograher:* Merle Connell, *Music:* Gunther Kaur

Cast: Scott Peters, Linda Connell, Jason Johnson, Katherine Victor, Frank Smith

CAPRICORN ONE

Film   1978   U.S.(ITC/Warner Bros.)
128 Minutes   Color

When NASA'S first manned flight to **Mars** is cancelled due to a failed life-support system, the space agency decides to hoax the mission rather than risk having its funding cut off. An unmanned capsule is launched into space, and a trio of astronauts is later shown on television exploring a simulated Martian landscape, located at a military installation in the Arizona desert. But a snag develops in the plan when the remote-controlled capsule incinerates while entering the atmosphere. Believing they will now be killed, the astronauts make a run for it. Meanwhile, a resourceful young reporter, who has figured out the truth, is heading for the base.

For all its SF trappings, *Capricorn One* is at heart a chase thriller that exploits America's conspiracy fixation. NASA supplied the **technical advisor**s, who apparently didn't know that radio transmissions take about 20 minutes to reach Mars. Wives are shown talking to their husbands with barely an interruption—an oversight that would have given away the hoax to a high-school science student.

Director/Screenplay: Peter Hyams, *Producer:* Paul Lazarus, *Photographer:* Bill Butler, *Production Designer:* Albert Brenner, *Music:* **Jerry Goldsmith**

Cast: James Brolin, Elliott Gould, Hal Holbrook, Brenda Vaccaro, O.J. Simpson, Karen Black

CAPRONA

Fictitious continent, also called Caspak, conveived by Edgar Rice Burroughs for his trilogy of novellas, *The Land That Time Forgot, The People That Time Forgot* and *Out of Time's Abyss* (1918). Caprona, named after the Italian explorer who discovered it near the South Pole in 1921, has no beaches or harbors and is surrounded by sheer cliffs. Inaccessible to the outside world, the continent has preserved many prehistoric life forms, including reptiles and fish, as well as primitive human beings (called Caspakians) who have evolved into bizarre specialities. Caprona has appeared in two films loosely based on the Burroughs stories, **The Land That Time Forgot** (1975) and **The People That Time Forgot** (1977).

CAPTAIN AMERICA

Film serial   1944   U.S.(Republic)
15 Episodes   Black & white

By the time comic book hero Captain America arrived on the screen, he had changed significantly. He was no longer a G.I. constantly going A.W.O.L. to battle Axis villains, and his scientifically enduced superpowers were somewhat diminished. He also lost his sidekick Bucky. As crusading district attorney Grant Gardner, the Captain stayed at home to save America from a mysterious malefactor called the Scarab, who threatened world peace with a "dynamic vibrator," a device that converts sound waves into an explosive. Much of this serial's appeal derives from the athletic performance of veteran **serial** star Dick Purcell in the title role, whose strenuous stunt work resulted in his death from a heart attack shortly after filming was completed. (See also: **Comic Books.**)

Directors: John English, Elmer Clifton, *Screenplay:* Royal Cole, Ronald Davidson, Basil Dickey, Jesse Duffy, Harry Fraser, Grant Nelson, Joseph Poland, *Photographer:* John MacBurnie, *Special Effects:* Howard and Theodore Lydecker

Cast: Dick Purcell, Lionel Atwill, Lorna Gray, Charles Trowbridge

CAPTAIN AMERICA

TV film   1979   U.S.(CBS)   100 Minutes
Color

The return of the legendary **comic book** hero of World War II, or rather the return of his son, Captain America, Jr., an ex-Marine who has inherited the red, white and blue costume. Junior, who derives his superpowers from an elixir whose acronym is F.L.A.G., saves Phoenix, Arizona, from arch-villains armed with a neutron bomb. They expected a series from this warmed-over patriotic porridge.

Director: Rod Holcomb, *Producer:* Martin Goldstein, *Screenplay:* Don Ingalls, *Story:* Don Ingalls, Chester Krumholz, *Photographer:* Ronald W. Browne, *Music:* Mike Post, Pete Carpenter

Cast: Reb Brown, Len Birman, Steve Forrest, Heather Menzies, Robin Mattson

CAPTAIN MESPHISTO AND THE TRANSFORMATION MACHINE

Film   1966   U.S.(Republic)   100 Minutes
Black & white

The plot spins wildly in this pared-down feature version of the old serial, **Manhunt of Mystery Island** (1945), an enjoyably eccentric amalgam of swashbuckler and science fiction. The villain here is a greedy genius who builds a machine transforming him into a long-dead pirate named Captain Mephisto. He kidnaps a kindly old scientist on a remote island in the Pacific to steal his plans for a revolutionary new power device.

CAPTAIN MIDNIGHT

Radio serial   1940-49   U.S. (Mutual)
15 Minutes (Mon-Wed-Fri)

One of the great radio superheroes of World War II, Captain Midnight fought a thrice-weekly battle against **Jack Armstrong** (CBS) and *Tom Mix* (NBS), broadcast at the same hour. Each attempted to attract listeners with an astounding variety of premiums, but Midnight had the most (35, give or take a few), all extremely useful for fighting Nazis on the homefront. The premiums included Detect-O-Scopes, a Flight Commander Flying Cross, a 3-Way Mystic Dog Whistle, a Secret Squadron Insignia Transfer, a Printing Ring (great for marking up bedroom walls) several cryptography decoders, and Captain Midnight Shake-up mugs. Most of these cost 15 cents and the inner seal from a jar of Ovaltine (the sponsor); at last word they were selling to collectors for as much as $175 each (if you could find one).

The program was introduced by the sound of a gong tolling midnight, followed by an airplane in a steep dive and the announcement, "Cap . . . tain . . . Mid . . . night!" In zoomed the brave pilot, usually to his secret hilltop laboratory, to design new scientific gadgets for use against the enemy. As every kid knew, Midnight was really Captain Albright, a World War I flying ace who earned his nickname from heroism in action. His crew was called the Secret Squadron, which listeners were invited to join (more Ovaltine seals); his helpers were Chuck Ramsey, his ward, Joyce "Loopin' Loops" Ryan and Ichabod Mudd, his mechanic. He usually jousted with the Barracuda and Ivan Shark, father of the beautiful but deadly Fury Shark.

In 1954, Midnight was revived for a TV series (see listing below).

Directors: Russell Young, Kirby Hawkes, Alan Wallace, *Writers:* Robert Burtt, Wilfred Moore

Cast: Captain Midnight Ed Prentiss, Bill Bouchey, Paul Barnes; Bill Rose, Angeline Orr, Marilou Neumayer, Hugh Studebaker, Boris Aplon, Marvin Miller

CAPTAIN MIDNIGHT

TV series   1954-58   U.S. (CBS)   30 Minutes
(weekly)   Black & white

Captain Midnight, **radio**'s super-scientific crime-fighter (see listing above), had a healthy run in this inept series, which indicates the state of children's TV during the mid-1950s. Square-jawed Richard Webb played Midnight, alias Captain Albright, now a World War II flying ace; Sid Melton was Ikky, his clumsy mechanic. In the first episode enemy agents stole a radioactive mineral, recovered by Midnight with the help of a geiger counter and his network of juvenile aides, the Secret Squadron. Midnight's mountaintop laboratory looked badly in need of repair, and the special effects were prehistoric, with the exception of Midnight's sleek jet fighter, shown endlessly taking off from his private runway.

When the program went into syndication, Ovaltine, its sponsor and owner, retained the rights to the name. "Captain Midnight" was removed from the sound track and replaced by the words "Jet Jackson" (the lip movements didn't quite match since they lacked a syllable). Title of the program became *Jet Jackson, Flying Commando.*

(First program) *Director:* D. Ross Lederman, *Producer:* George Bilson, *Writer:* Dana Slade, *Music:* Don Ferris

Cast: Richard Webb, Sid Melton, Olan Soule, Renee Beard, Jan Shepard

CAPTAIN NEMO AND THE UNDERWATER CITY

Film   1970   U.S. (MGM)   106 Minutes
Metrocolor   Panavision

Captain Nemo, **Jules Verne**'s moody Victorian submariner from **20,000 Leagues Under the Sea,** rescues shipwrecked passengers and brings them to the domed underwater city of Templemer. Conflicts arise when a greedy guest notices that the city's oxygen machine produces gold as a by-product. The script is cloudy, but the domed city and a giant shark called the Mobula shine through.

Director: James Hill, *Producer:* Bertram Oster, *Screenplay:* R. Wright Campbell, Bib Baker, Jane Baker, *Photographer:* Alan Hume, Egil Woxholt, *Art Director:* Bill Andrews, *Music:* Walter Scott

Cast: Robert Ryan, Chuck Connors, Luciana Paluzzi, Kenneth Connor, Nanette Newman

CAPTAIN NICE

TV series   1967   U.S. (NBC)   30 Minutes (weekly)   Color

Captain Nice was a nebbishy police department chemist named Carter Nash who accidentally concocted a drink called "Super Juice." Whenever crime in Big Town got out of hand he swallowed a dose of the stuff and turned into a nebbishy superhero. An instinctive coward with a fear of heights, Nash lived with his domineering mother who constantly nagged him to "fly to the rescue" in the baggy costume she had made for him.

The brainchild of writer Buck Henry, *Captain Nice* attempted to parody superheroes in the manner of **Get Smart!** (1965-70), his popular TV spoof of secret agents. Unfortunately, moments of hilarity were all too few, and the series quickly sailed into oblivion along with CBS's similar **Mr. Terrific.** The idea was later successfully resurrected for **The Greatest American Hero** (1981-   ).

Cast: William Daniels, Alice Ghostley, Ann Prentiss, William Zuckert, Liam Dunn

CAPTAIN SCARLET AND THE MYSTERIONS

TV series   1967   Great Britain (ITC)
30 Minutes (weekly)   Color

A better-than-average children's program made in Britain and syndicated in the U.S., *Captain Scarlet* featured a cast of puppets smoothly animated by a computer-controlled system called Supermarionation. Captain Scarlet headed Spectrum, an international police force charged with protecting Earth. While exploring Mars, Spectrum confronted the Mysterions, the planet's inhabitants, who mistook the visit for an invasion and promptly declared war. After arranging to have Captain Scarlet killed in an accident, the Mysterions brought him back to life imbued with their own superpowerful characteristics and intended to turn him into a spy. Once back home, however, the captain regained his humanity and became their only indestructible adversary. (26 episodes)

Director: Desmond Saunders, *Producer:* Reg Dunlap, *Special Effects:* Derek Meddings, *Music:* Barry Gray, *Created by:* Gerry and Sylvia Anderson

Voices: Captain Scarlet—Francis Matthews, Donald Gray, Paul Maxwell, Ed Bishop, Janna Hill, Sylvia Anderson

CAPTAIN VIDEO

Film serial   1951   U.S. (Columbia)
15 Episodes   Black & white

Hollywood may not have realized it, but this **serial** acknowledged that television was taking over its function as an entertainment medium for juveniles. **Al Hodge** was busy in New York starring in the TV series (see listing above), so Judd Holdren, more familiar as **Commando Cody,** led the Rocket Rangers to victory against an **alien** from the planet Atoma, who was armed with **robots** and ray guns.

Director: **Spencer G. Bennett,** Wallace A. Grissell, *Screenplay:* Royal K. Cole, Sherman Lowe, Joseph Poland, *Special Effects:* Jack Erickson, *Music:* Mischa Bakaleinikoff

Cast: Judd Holdren, Larry Stewart, George Eldredge, Gene Roth, Don C. Harvey

CAPTAIN VIDEO AND HIS VIDEO RANGERS

TV serial   1949-55   U.S. (Dumont)
30 Minutes/15 Minutes (weekly)   Black & white

In the days before **Star Wars** (1977), long before men walked on the moon, there lived a noble **space opera** hero of the 23rd century who traveled the universe in his spaceship, the *Galaxy,* maintaining "justice, truth and freedom." His name was Captain Video,

and for eight years he ruled the airwaves of the then-fledgling medium of television.

Although the program's sets were little more than painted cardboard flats decorated with Army surplus dials, knobs and buttons from dresses, the show was a big hit. Youngsters home from school couldn't wait to climb on board. No one minded that the special effects consisted of toy spaceships soaring through a void of black velvet pasted with cheap sequins to simulate stars. (The budget often came to as much as $30 a week.) It was an unprecedented treat to be able to watch a Saturday afternoon movie serial at home five nights a week.

Captain Video was originally played by the handsome and stolid Richard Coogan, replaced by the equally handsome and stolid **Al Hodge** in 1950. Video operated from a secret mountain headquarters, where he invented an assortment of futuristic crime-fighting devices, including an Atomic rifle, a Cosmic Ray Vibrator (which shook enemies into helplessness), an Optican Scillometer (a water pipe decorated with radio knobs) and a Radio Scillograph, a two-way radio the size of a pack of cigarettes. "Cap-

Captain Video and His Video Rangers: Al Hodge and Don Hastings.

tain, it's a creature from the planet Thantos with a death-ray," was a typical warning from the Captain's trusty sidekick, Ranger (played by Don Hastings). Another planet that comes to mind is Quark, which was used as the title of an NBC series (1978), in an unacknowledged tribute to *Captain Video*.

In 1953 the serial format was dropped and the program was trimmed to 15 minutes nightly. The adventures were self-contained, and the title became *The Secret Files of Captain Video*. The program was cancelled in 1955, and the following year Hodge appeared as the host of a short-lived weekly cartoon show, featuring the antics of *Popeye* and *Betty Boop*, titled *Captain Video's Cartoons*. Judd Holdren appeared in the title role of a Columbia movie serial based on the live TV series, *Captain Video* (1951). A number of famous SF writers contributed scripts to the series—the first SF program on television—including C. M. Kornbluth, Robert Scheckley and Damon Knight.

Creator/Producer: James Caddigan, *Producers:* Larry Menkin, Olga Druce, Frank Telford, *Writers:* Maurice Brock, Damon Knight, C. M. Kornbluth, Robert Scheckley, *Music:* "Overture to the Flying Dutchman" Richard Wagner

Cast: Richard Coogan (1949-50), Al Hodge (1950-55), Don Hasting, Hal Conklin, Ernest Borgnine, Tony Randall, Jack Klugman, Nat Polen

CAPTAIN Z-RO

TV series   1955   U.S. (syndicated)
15 Minutes   Black & white

A futuristic good Samaritan with a mustache and goatee, Captain Z-Ro was the pilot of a **time machine** that enabled him to travel to the past and help people. Arriving aboard the ZX-99 in a space suit emblazoned with a large "Z" and accompanied by his assistant Jet, he showed misfortunes how to avoid the catastrophes that had befallen them. (26 episodes)

Director/writer: Roy Steffens

Cast: Roy Steffens, Bobby Trumbull

CAPTIVE WOMEN

Film   1952   U.S. (RKO)   65 Minutes   Black & white

A bewildered time traveller drops into the future from the mid-twentieth century and finds the island of Manhattan in ruins from a long-ago nuclear war. This inconvenience has made New Yorkers ruder than ever, and consequently they have split into three savage factions: the Mutates, the Norms and the dread Uplander anthropoids. Feeling called upon to preserve the values of civilization, the do-gooder becomes a one-man United Nations and unites the warring groups. Whatever shock value this silly little film possessed at the time of its release had vanished by 1981, when present realities made **John Carpenter**'s vision of Manhattan as a walled concentration camp in **Escape from New York** uncomfortably believable. (See also: The **Bomb**.)

Director: Stuart Gilmore, *Producer/Screenplay:* Jack Pollexfen, Aubrey Wisberg, *Photographer:* Paul Ivano, *Art Director:* Theobold Holsopple, *Music:* Charles Koff

Cast: Ron Randell, Robert Clarke, Margaret Field, Gloria Saunders

CARLSON, RICHARD (1912–77)

Actor/director featured in several important low-budget SF films of the 1950s. A serviceable, second-string leading man of modest talent and intelligent good looks, Carlson was usually cast as an unassuming, literate scientist who prevails by virtue of his logic and common sense. He is often confused with his contemporary Hugh Marlowe, who resembles him and played similar roles.

Born in Albert Lea, Minnesota, Carlson graduated *summa cum laude* and received his M.A. from the University of Minnesota. He taught there for several months before opening his own theater in Minneapolis. He debuted on Broadway in the mid-1930s in *Three Men on a Horse* and made his first screen appearance in a romantic comedy *The Young at Heart* (1938), typecast as an insecure juvenile. Movie stardom constantly eluded him, but he worked steadily for more than 30 years, alternating between supporting roles in major films and leads in B-pictures. During the 1950s he began directing films as well as acting in them, and became a television star on the series' *I Led Three Lives, Eyewitness* (1953) [host/narrator] and *McKenzie's Raiders* (1958). He guest-starred on many other programs and also wrote TV scripts and articles for national magazines.

SF Films: **The Magnetic Monster, It Came From Outer Space,** *The Maze* (1953); **The Creature From the Black Lagoon** (1954), **The Power** (1968), **Riders to the Stars** (as director/actor) (1954).

CARPENTER, JOHN (1948–   )

Director, screenwriter, and composer who often writes his own film scores. A native

of Bowling Green, Kentucky, Carpenter established his reputation while a student at the University of California film school, where he participated in the making of *The Resurrection of Bronco Billy* (1970), winner of an **Academy Award** for Best Live Action Short Subject. His first feature, **Dark Star** (1975), an engaging spoof of SF-monster movies, has since become a cult item. After several Hollywood assignments, he made the independently produced *Halloween* (1978), an edge-of-the-seat horror film that broke box-office records and established him as a leading genre director. A master of carefully controlled suspense, Carpenter has shown a less steady hand in recent films and a tendency toward gratuitous gore and genre conventions. He is married to the actress Adrienne Barbeau who often appears in his films.

Other films: Assault on Precinct 13 (1976), *Eyes of Laura Mars* [co-screenplay only], *Someone is Watching Me* [TV film] (1978), *Elvis!* [TV film] (1979), *The Fog* (1980), **Escape from New York,** Halloween II, (1981), **The Thing,** *Halloween III* [co-producer and music] (1982)

CARRERAS, MICHAEL (1927–   )

British director, screenwriter and producer. Carreras, the son of Sir James Carreras, founder of Hammer Films, directed several horror and SF productions for that company during the 1960s. Since then he has worked mainly as a production executive.

Films include: Maniac [as director] (1963), *The Curse of the Mummy's Tomb* (1964), *Slave Girls* (1967), **The Lost Continent** [also producer] (1968), **The Two Faces of Dr. Jekyll** [as producer] (1960), **The Damned** (1963), *She* (1965), **One Million Years B.C.** [also screenplay] (1966), **Moon Zero Two** [also screenplay] (1969), **Creatures the World Forgot** [also screenplay] (1971), *Demons of the Mind* (1973)

John Carpenter on location for *Escape From New York*.

Lewis Carroll posing with a camera lens, 1863.

The Cars That Ate Paris: A killer Volkswagen.

CARROLL, LEWIS (1832–98)

Pseudonym of Charles Lutwidge Dodgson, British mathematician, photographer, inventor of games and puzzles, and writer of children's fantasies, notably *Alice in Wonderland* (1865) and *Through the Looking Glass* (1871). Although none of Carroll's works can be considered science fiction, they nevertheless have had an extensive influence on the genre. His fantastic but always logical reorganization of natural order served as a prototype for speculative fiction, especially stories in which the protagonist is trapped in an alien environment. When the little girl Alice walks *Through the Looking Glass* and enters a world that coexists with the real one, for example, she is journeying to a **parallel world**—long a staple of science fiction. Other fantasies with SF undertones include *Phantasamagoria* (1869), *The Hunting of the Snark* (1876) and *Sylvie and Bruno* (1889).

THE CARS THAT ATE PARIS

Film   1974   Australia (Salt Pan Films)
91 Minutes   Eastmancolor   Panavision

Not an avant-garde French comedy but a cheerfully vicious Australian satire on society's obsession with the automobile. Paris, a small town in the outback of New South Wales, makes its living and takes its pleasure by luring cars off the highway with detour signs, then causing them to crash. The wrecks are stripped and recycled into "killer" cars fitted with spikes and the like, and the survivors are taken to a local mad doctor to be turned into "veggies."

Cars marks the debut of director Peter Weir, who went on to make an international reputation with *Picnic at Hanging Rock* (1975) and *The Last Wave* (1977). His highly personal mixture of **horror,** western and SF genres is brilliantly conceived, if not quite up to the level of his intended metaphor. Australians didn't like the film, and it died at the box office.

Director: Peter Weir, *Producers:* Hal and Jim McElroy, *Screenplay:* Peter Weir, Keith Gow, Piers Davies, *Story:* Peter Weir, *Photographer:* John McLean, *Art Director:* David Copping, *Music:* Bruce Smeaton

Cast: Terry Camilleri, Melissa Jaffer, John Meillon, Kevin Miles, Max Gillies

Director: Francis D. Lyon, *Screenplay:* Charles A. Wallace, *Special Effects:* Roger George, *Music:* Paul Dunlap

Cast: Virginia Mayo, David Brian, Scott Brady, Hugh Marlowe, William Thourlby

THE CAT FROM OUTER SPACE

Film   1978   U.S. (Disney)   103 Minutes
Technicolor

Zunar the cat is the hero of this amiable comedy about an **extraterrestrial** feline who crashlands his spaceship on our planet. With only 36 hours to make repairs or be stuck here forever, Zunar J5/90 Doric 4-7 (his full name), finds a kooky physicist and asks him to help fix his spaceship. Zunar can't speak, of course, but he has the power to communicate through thought transference. When army officials investigate the ship and wonder what became of its pilot, the military men fail to notice Zunar and his collar of sparkling crystals perched nearby. Zunar tags along with them, taken for granted as a pet, picking up their thoughts, levitating things and people, and outwitting a wealthy oil baron out to control the world. The remarkably intelligent-looking Zunar was played by

CASTLE OF EVIL

Film   1966   U.S. (United Artists)
81 Minutes   Color

Heirs gathered on a remote island for the reading of a mad scientist's will are stalked by a vengeful robot.

A trio of former Hollywood stars was resurrected for this tepid murder mystery, which has to do with a **robot** programmed to kill the person who caused the deceased scientist's disfigurement. Made in the image of his master, the machine-made ghost accomplishes his task and proceeds to do away with the bona fide heirs as well. Panic ensues until the leading man discovers that the robot has been reprogrammed by a greedy heir to knock out the competition. A well-aimed laser beam solves the problem.

Zunar prepares to blast off for home in *The Cat from Outer Space.*

Rumple, a 15-year-old Abyssinian, and his twin sister Amber.

Director: Norman Tokar, *Producer:* Ron Miller, *Screenplay:* Ted Key, *Photographer:* Charles F. Wheeler, *Art Director:* John B. Mansridge, *Special Effects:* Eustace Lycett, Art Cruickshank, Danny Lee, *Music:* Lalo Schiffrin

Cast: Ken Berry, Sandy Duncan, McLean Stevenson, Roddy McDowall, Harry Morgan, Alan Young

CAT-WOMEN OF THE MOON

Film 1954 U.S. (Astor) 64 Minutes Black & white

Deservedly rated as one of the worst movies of all time, *Cat-Women* was thrown together practically overnight to cash in on Hollywood's profitable 3-D fad of the mid-1950s. The film was shot in five and a half days on the sets left over from a medieval costume drama. The story follows a team of astronauts to the moon where they encounter moon-maidens living in fear of a giant paper spider. Dressed in metallic bathing suits, the girls claim to be telepathic—an ability that helps them to understand the actors, who have trouble remembering their lines. This timeless story went from worse to bad in a remake, **Missile to the Moon** (1959). (See also: **Stereoscopic Film.)**

Director: Arthur Hilton, *Producer:* Jack Rabin, Al Zimbalist, *Screenplay:* Roy Hamilton, *Special Effects:* Jack Rabin, *Music:* Elmer Bernstein

Cast: Sonny Tufts, Marie Windsor, Susan Morrow, Victor Jory, Carol Brewster

THE CHAIRMAN

See: **The Most Dangerous Man Alive**

CHAMBERS, JOHN (1925–   )

Film and TV makeup artist, whose specialty is a prosthetic mask capable of lifelike movement and a subtle range of emotional expressions. Chambers is the second member of his profession to be honored with an Academy Award (after William Tuttle)

for "outstanding makeup achievement" in **Planet of the Apes** (1968). He is also the recipient of four Television Academy Emmy Awards.

A native of Chicago, Chambers majored in commercial art in high school and later worked as a costume jewelry designer. Drafted into the Army during World War II, he put his artistic abilities to use sculpting false teeth and other prosthetic devices. After the war he spent several years at a Veteran's hospital developing new plastics, rubber compounds and adhesives to replace noses, ears, eyes and other body parts lost by wounded soldiers. Among his achievements is an artificial palate that restores the ability to speak, and a fully orbital glass eye that perfectly matches the existing one.

In 1953 Chambers took his unique talents to NBC-TV in Burbank, where he became a staff makeup man. Most TV programs at the time were broadcast live, which meant that he often had only seconds to effect a between-the-scenes makeup change. For example, in an adaptation of Ernest Hemingway's *The Battler* (1956), he transformed actor Paul Newman from a cocky young boxer to a bleeding, battle-scarred veteran in the time it takes to air a commercial. In 1959 he joined Universal Studios where his creations included a toothy, veneered grin for Marlon Brando in *Bedtime Story* (1964) and 10 foolproof disguises for the major stars of *The List of Adrian Messenger* (1963), a favorite film which made his reputation.

With the demand for his services growing, Chambers left Universal to set up his own makeup shop. Since then he has devised a menagerie of creatures for many SF/fantasy TV programs: **The Outer Limits** (1963-65), **Voyage to the Bottom of the Sea** (1964-68) [uncredited], **Lost in Space** and *I Spy* (1965-68), **The Wild, Wild West** (1965-70). He was slated to design the aliens of **Star Trek** (1966-69) but got only as far as **Mr. Spock**'s Vulcan ears before leaving because of a salary disagreement. He won Emmies for the repulsive monster of "Pickman's Model," a segment of **Rod Sterling's Night Gallery** (1971-72 season); the Neanderthals

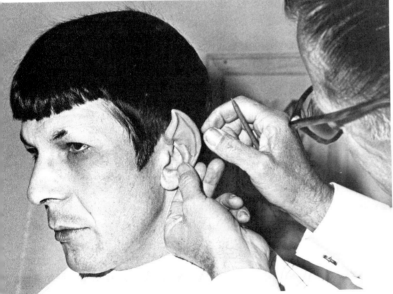

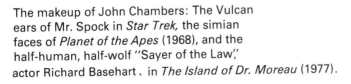

The makeup of John Chambers: The Vulcan
ears of Mr. Spock in *Star Trek,* the simian
faces of *Planet of the Apes* (1968), and the
half-human, half-wolf "Sayer of the Law,"
actor Richard Basehart ، in *The Island of Dr. Moreau* (1977).

of "Struggle for Survival," an episode of *Primal Man* (1973-74 season); the character transformations in the drama *Twigs* (1974-75 season) and the beast makeup for George C. Scott in the *Hallmark Hall of Fame* production of "Beauty and the Beast" (1976-77 season). His film effects include the **robot** duplicates of **The Human Duplicator** (1965), the fingers of a cowboy chopped off with John Wayne's ax in *True Grit* (1969) and the bobbing head of a man eaten by a shark in *Jaws* (1975).

For *Planet of the Apes*, Chambers tackled the formidable challenge of creating a monkey makeup capable of being "acted" by the film's players and worn throughout the film— something that had never been done before. He began by drawing ape faces on transparent sheets placed over photographs of the actors to adapt the simian personalities to their human counterparts. He sculpted the ape features over clay masks taken of the actors, then cast them in baked latex. This produced rubber foreheads, and noses, muzzles, and chins—in two pieces—which he attached to actors' faces with a dark-brown matte-finish adhesive. A special greasepaint colored the white latex and blended-in the skin. Next, four hairpieces—a low widow's peak, muttonchops and a beard—were cemented to skin and mask, and a stippling of wrinkles was added around the eyes. Lastly, the actors' teeth were painted black to keep them from showing under their simian snouts.

By attaching the appliances to key facial muscles, Chambers made it possible for the actors to emote inside their disguises. The ape features moved simultaneously with human ones, and words and gestures synchronized visually. Voices passed through the open-cell sponge rubber without being muffled and breathing was done through slits cut into the masks' upper lips. The material was so porous, in fact, that it also allowed perspiration to pass through freely. The sweat seen on the ape faces belongs to the actors, who were shooting in the 100-plus-degree heat of an Arizona desert. Originally, the makeup took five hours to ap-

ply, but Chambers eventually got it down to three with an assembly line procedure. Chamber's designs subsequently were used in the film's sequels: **Beneath the Planet of the Apes** (1970), **Escape From Planet of the Apes** (1971), **Conquest of the Planet of the Apes** (1972), **Battle for the Planet of the Apes** (1973), and the short-lived TV series **Planet of the Apes** (1974), executed by Fred Blau.

Chambers' next project was to create the "humanimals" of **The Island of Dr. Moreau** (1977), a film whose disappointments do not include his work. With his assistant Dan Striepeke, he created a group of convincing animals in the process of being transformed into men by a mad scientist, using the techniques he had devised for *Planet of the Apes*. Since then, he has served as president of the Society of Makeup Artists and as an unbilled advisor on many SF and fantasy films, while accepting such diverse assignments as making figures for wax museums and custom-building medical prostheses (for which he usually accepts no fee). He has appeared in one film, **Schlock** (1973).

CHANEY, LON, Jr. (1906–73)

Film actor who succeeded **Boris Karloff** as the **Frankenstein** monster and appeared in many SF and horror films. The son of **Lon Chaney,** he began his film career in 1932 playing bit parts in **serials** and B-pictures under his real name Creighton. Hoping for larger roles, in 1935, he changed his name to Lon Chaney, Jr., but failed to attract attention (see: **Undersea Kingdom**) until cast in *Of Mice and Men* in 1940 as the lovable, feeble-minded Lennie, a role that brought him critical acclaim. That same year he appeared in **One Million B.C.** playing a battle-scarred warrior, which prompted Universal studios to sign him to replace the aging Karloff.

Chaney made his SF-horror debut as a sideshow "Electric-Man" in **Man-Made Monster** (1941), and later that year starred in the title role of *The Wolf Man*, his greatest commercial success. During the next seven

Lon Chaney, Jr.

CHANGE OF MIND

Film 1969 U.S. (Cinerama) 98 Minutes
Eastmancolor

The mind of a liberal district attorney boggles when it awakens in the body of an unidentified black man killed in an automobile accident. When surgeons explain that a brain transplant was the only way to prevent him from dying of cancer, this reaction is shared by viewers, who are forced to endure an endless testing of the D.A.'s white notions of brotherhood now that he is a black man. The message is as profound as a Miss American contestant expressing concern for world hunger. The idea played better as intentional comedy in Melvin Van Pebble's *Watermelon Man* (1970), a wickedly satirical fantasy about a white middle-class racist who awakens one morning to find that his skin has turned black. *Change of Mind*'s claims one distinction, however—a sound track by Duke Ellington.

Director: Robert Stevens, *Producer/Director Producer:* Seeleg Lester, Richard Wesson, *Photographer:* Arthur J. Ornitz, *Music:* Duke Ellington

Cast: Raymond St. Jacques, Susan Oliver, Leslie Nielsen, Janet McLachlan

years he was the studio's resident monster, playing Dr. Frankenstein's creation, the Mummy and Dracula—roles made famous 10 years earlier by Karloff and **Bela Lugosi.** Despite his hulking physique and craggy features, his portrayals never equalled the sympathetic horror or the seductive menace of his predecessors, and in retrospect his impersonations seem forced and colorless. His limited dramatic range and monotonous voice kept him from achieving lasting stardom, but he worked continuously in films of all kinds until the time of his death.

SF films: **Undersea Kingdom** (1936), **One Million B.C.** (1940), **Man-Made Monster** (1941), **The Ghost of Frankenstein** [as the monster] (1942), **Frankenstein Meets the Wolf Man** [as the Wolf Man] (1944), **House of Frankenstein** [as the Wolf Man] (1945), **Abbott and Costello Meet Frankenstein** [as the Wolf Man] (1948), **The Indestructable Man** (1956), **Cyclops** (1957), **The Alligator People** (1959), **Dracula vs. Frankenstein** (1973)

CHARCUTERIE MECANIQUE/
Mechanical Butcher Shop

(Also titled: *Mechanical Butcher*)

Film 1898 France (Lumiere) Short Black & white (silent)

Live pigs enter a steam-powered machine equipped with Victorian gadgetry and emerge as sausages, hams, bacon, etc., in this atypical comedy made by August and Louis Lumiere, the legendary pioneers of French cinema. Similar to other science fantasy films made during the first decade of cinema, *Charcuterie Mecanique* accurately anticipated the coming of automation.

CHARLIE AND ALGERNON

Play 1980 U.S. 3 Acts

Brain implants turn a retarded laborer and a laboratory mouse into temporary geniuses.

This Broadway musical comedy adaptation of Daniel Keyes' novel *Flowers for Algernon* (1966) might have appealed to Charlie before his operation, but it is doubtful that Charlie the genius would have sat through it. Keyes' poignant tale of a likeable moron experiencing self-awareness and adult love for the first time was reduced to a syrupy showcase for lackluster songs and dances. In performance the show came briefly to life when Algernon, that genius of white mousedom, clung tenaciously to Charlie, who danced a softshoe in a demonstration of kinship. Conspicuously absent, however, was the feeling of unbearable loss when the experiment fails (signalled by Algernon's death) and Charlie returns to idiocy, as well as the novel's implicit criticism of scientific tampering with the human psyche. After a six-week tryout, the play opened on Broadway at the Helen Hayes Theater on September 14, 1980 and closed 17 performances later. The film **Charly** (1968) is a more faithful adaptation of the novel. (See also: **Theater**.)

Director: Louis W. Scheeder, *Producer:* The John F. Kennedy Center for the Performing Arts, Isobel Robins Konecky, The Fisher Theater Foundation, the Folger Theater Group, *Books and Lyrics:* David Rogers, *Novel: Flowers for Algernon* Daniel Keyes, *Music:* Charles Strouse, *Music Director:* Liza Redfield, *Choreography:* Virginia Freeman

Cast: P. J. Benjamin, Sandy Falson, Edward Earle, Robert Sevra, Nancy Franklin

CHARLY

Film   1968   U.S. (Cinerama)   106 Minutes
Techniscope

The dangers inherent in science playing God is the premise of this moving film adaptation of *Flowers for Algernon*, Daniel Keyes' first-rate SF parable. Charly, a contented 30-year-old with an I.Q. of 68, comes to full consciousness of the joys and perils of being human after his intelligence is artificially elevated to genius level. He learns quickly and matures emotionally, and discovers the pleasures of love and sex in the person of the female doctor who has instigated his operation. The operation has also been tried on a laboratory mouse named Algernon (the rodent kingdom's equivalent of a genius), which dies suddenly, signalling that Charly's metamorphosis is only temporary. Finally aware that his hope for a normal life is incidental to the scientific experiment, Charly, disillusioned by human duplicity, welcomes the return to his childlike former self.

Enough of Keyes' original survives to overcome the occasional platitudes of the film's script and the modish, **split-screen** cin-

Temporary geniuses—man and mouse—perform a musical number in Broadway's *Charlie and Algernon*.

ematography, which often reminds one of soft-focus television commercials. The performance of actor Cliff Robertson (who formed his own company to make this film after many setbacks) captures the essence of Charly's elation and despair, and brings the story vividly to life. (Robertson's previous SF role was as **Rod Brown of the Rocket Rangers,** a 1953 CBS-TV series.) A Broadway musical comedy adaptation, **Charlie and Algernon,** was less successful.

Academy Award: Cliff Robertson, Best Actor.

Director/Producer: Ralph Nelson, *Screenplay:* Sterling Silliphant, *Novel: Flowers for Algernon* by Daniel Keyes, *Photographer:* Arthur J. Ornitz, *Music:* Ravi Shankar

Cast: Cliff Robertson, Claire Bloom, Lilia Skala, Leon Janney, Dick van Patten

CHELOVEK ANFIBYA/
The Amphibian Man

Film   1962   USSR (Lenfilm)   98 Minutes Sovcolor   (Released 1964   U.S. [NTA] 86 Minutes)

Bred by his scientist father to live underwater as well as on land, the amphibian man enjoys his unique status until he falls in love with a normal young woman. The intense affair ends in frustration when the boy realizes that physiological changes will soon force him to live underwater permanently. Plunging into deep despair at the loss of love and the realization that he will soon become a "monster," the boy is comforted by his guilty father, who moralizes on the folly of tampering with human nature.

   This beautifully photographed but slow-moving curiosity from Russia, which has moments of dark eroticism reminiscent of **The Creature From the Black Lagoon** (1954), offers a gloomy view of scientific progress that seems almost subversive coming from a country where scientific research is paramount.

Directors: Gennadi Kazansky, Vladimir Chebotaryov, *Screenplay:* Alexei Kapler, Alexander Xenofontov, Akiba Golburt, *Novel:* Alexander Belyaev, *Photographer:* Eduard Razovsky

Cast: Vladimir Korenev, Mikhail Kozakov, Anastasia Vertinskaya

CHEWBACCA

Copilot and first mate of the **Millenium Falcon, Han Solo**'s pirate starship in the **Star Wars** series. An intelligent anthropoid of the **Wookie** race, "Chewie" stands more than seven feet tall and has a powerful body covered in long, russet hair. His ferocious appearance is softened by large blue eyes and a puppy-like nose. Deceptively ungainly, his large paws are as dexterous as human hands as they move surely over the controls of a spaceship or handle a weapon. Approximately 100 years old, Chewbacca is as loyal to Solo as a pet dog but is a fearsome adversary to his enemies. He normally speaks in grunts that constitute a language, but when annoyed (Wookies are temperamental) his growls rise to a frightening pitch. Chewbacca is played by British actor Peter Mayhew (the

Chewbacca: Wookie co-pilot of the Millenium Falcon in the *Star Wars* series.

blue eyes are his) in a complicated makeup designed and applied by **Stuart Freeborn.** The grunts are the work of sounds effects expert **Ben Burtt, Jr.**

CHIKYU BOEIGUN/The Mysterians

Film 1957 Japan (Toho) 85 Minutes Eastmancolor CinemaScope (Released 1959 U.S. [MGM])

The prolific Honda and Tsuburuya, creators of **Godzilla,** took a break from monster movies to stage this eye-dazzling **alien** invasion epic, Toho's first wide-screen SF production. Arriving from outer space in full force, the Mysterians set up a battle station on the moon and send down an army of giant **robots** and death rays that blast apart Tokyo, Yokohama and Osaka. It turns out the aggressors are from the planet Mysteroid, destroyed by an atomic disaster that left them without a home and "so much strontium-90 in our bones." (They look very much like humans except that they dissolve.) When the Mysterians descend to Earth to enslave its males and breed with its females, the armed forces of the world retaliate and send them looking for another world to populate.

Bursting and bouncing with special effects but weighted down with a simple-minded, illogical story (made worse by a hilarious dubbing job), *Chikyu Boeigun* is stunning to look at but ultimately uninvolving. Consequently, the effects do little more than call attention to themselves and the obsessive masochistic fantasies of Japanese SF filmmakers.

Director: Ishiro Honda, *Producer:* Tomoyuki Tanaka, *Screenplay:* Takeshi Kimura, *Story:* Jojiro Okami, *Special Effects:* Eiji Tsuburuya, *Music:* Akira Ifukube

Cast: Kenji Sahara, Yumi Shirakawa, Momoko Kochi, Takashi Shimura, Akihiko Hirata

CHILDREN OF THE DAMNED

Film 1963 Great Britain (MGM) 90 Minutes Black & white

The spooky kids from **Village of the Damned** (1960) have gone international for this modest sequel, which rather closely follows the plot of the earlier film. Again conceived by an unknown alien "force," six menacing, superintelligent children with one mind are rounded up from various parts of the world by UNESCO and brought to London for study. Their ability to control adult behavior upsets the authorities, however, and the children flee to an abandoned church where they are destroyed by the military (a nice allegorical touch). Less exciting than the earlier film, but nevertheless rewarding.

Director: Anton M. Leader, *Producer:* Ben Arbeid, *Screenplay:* John Briley, *Suggested by:* "The Midwich Cuckoos" John Wyndham, *Photographer:* Davis Boulton, *Art Director:* Elliot Scott, *Music:* Ron Goodwin

Cast: Ian Hendry, Alan Badel, Barbara Ferris, Alfred Burke, Sheila Allen

THE CHINA SYNDROME

Film 1979 U.S. (Columbia) 122 Minutes Metrocolor

The China Syndrome resembles an SF film, but it is really a political thriller whose concerns are government secrecy and freedom of the press. But its SF plot device, the breakdown of a faulty nuclear power plant that threatens to contaminate "an area the size of Pennsylvania," proved to be remarkably prophetic. Barely 12 days after the film opened on March 16, 1979, a similar event actually occurred *in* Pennsylvania, at Three Mile Island. History followed art (if cinema can be called that), the film's box-office receipts soared, and government officials said the accident posed no danger.

Director: James Bridges, *Producer:* Michael Douglas, *Screenplay:* Mike Gray, T. S. Cook, James Bridges, *Photographer:* James Crabe, *Production Designer:* George Jenkins, *Special Effects:* Henry Millar, Jr.

Cast: Jane Fonda, Jack Lemmon, Michael Douglas, **Scott Brady,** Peter Donat

CHOMON, SEGUNDO DE (1871–1929)

Early film director, cameraman and special effects technician. Born in Teruel, Spain, de Chomon began his career in 1902 shooting Spanish newsreels and trick fantasy shorts patterned after those of **George Melies.** He later worked in France, where he had access to more sophisticated film technology, and returned to Spain in 1910 to set up his own movie company. After 1912 he worked mostly in Italy as a camerman and special effects expert.

CHROMA-KEY

A TV special effect in which separately televised images are combined into a single image. The effect is accomplished by shooting objects or persons against a saturated color, or chroma, usually blue, which disappears in the optical process and creates an electronic void. The blank background is then filled in with a second video image, which can originate live, from videotape or film. The process is analagous to the motion picture **matte** process.

CINEMASCOPE

Trademarked **wide screen** motion picture system based on the **anamorphic lens,** which compresses a wide image onto a frame of 35-mm. film during photography and unsqueezes it during projection. The Cinemascope image has an **aspect ratio** of 2.55:1 (about two-and-a-half times as wide as it is high) with magnetic **sound** and 2.35:1 with optical **sound.**

The system was developed in France during the 1920s by Prof. Henri Chretien who patented it as the Hypergonar. Used in a few experimental French films, it failed to generate interest until the early 1950s when Hollywood began an intensive search for a spectacular technical innovation to lure audiences away from small-screen TV sets (see: **Stereoscopic Films).** Twentieth Century-Fox bought the Chretien system patents, named the revamped system CinemaScope and unveiled it with stereophonic sound in *The Robe* (1953), a mediocre biblical extravaganza that proved to be a box-office smash. The system won an **Academy Award** in the technical class for that year and was leased to other studios eager to exploit the profitable potential of the new format. Among many SF films made in CinemaScope were **Forbidden Planet** (1956), **The Fly** (1958), **The Lost World** (1960) and **Fantastic Voyage** (1966).

CITY BENEATH THE SEA

TV film   1971   U.S. (NBC)   99 Minutes
Color

Intended as pilot for a follow-up series to **Voyage to the Bottom of the Sea** (1964-68), this TV film failed to impress American viewers, and it was released abroad under the title *One Hour to Doomsday.* The action takes place in the year 2053 in an elaborate undersea city called Pacifica, where the gold of Fort Knox now reposes along with H-128, a radioactive element. Cliche situations abound, including an attack by a sea monster, villainous treasure hunters and a **meteor** that threatens to demolish the city. The special effects, convincing on television, aren't up to the demands of the big screen.

Director/Producer: **Irwin Allen,** *Screenplay:* John Meredyth Lucas, *Story:* Irwin Allen, *Photographer:* Kenneth Peach, *Special Effects:* Lyle B. Abbott, John C. Caldwell, *Music:* Richard LaSalle

Cast: Stuart Whitman, Robert Wagner, Rosemary Forsyth, Joseph Cotten, Richard Basehart, Sugar Ray Robinson

CITY UNDER THE SEA

(U.S. title: *War Gods of the Deep*)

Film   1965   Great Britain (AIP)   84 Minutes
Eastmancolor   Colorscope

More fantasy than science fiction, *City Under the Sea* wastes several good actors and special effects on a weak, cliche-filled script based on the **Atlantis** legend. The action takes place off the coast of Cornwall, England, where a band of smugglers has hidden for more than 100 years in a domed, underwater city. Ruler of the kingdom is a spooky old salt called the Captain, who sends his amphibian guards to the beach to kidnap an American heiress (he thinks she is the reincarnation of his dead wife). Her friends come to the rescue shortly before a volcano powering the city's huge air pumps erupts and destroys the hide-out.

Director: Jacques Tourneur, *Producer/Art Director:* **Daniel Haller,** *Screenplay:* Charles Bennett, Louis M. Heyward, *Photographer:* Stephen Dade, *Special Effects:* Frank George, Les Bowie, *Underwater Photographer:* John Lamb, *Music:* Stanley Black

Cast: Vincent Price, David Tomlinson, Tab Hunter, Susan Hart, Henry Oscar

CLIFFHANGER

A film, TV or radio **serial** whose episodes end with a suspenseful situation in order to hook the audience on the next installment; also, a suspenseful moment in which the hero or heroine seems to be in a dangerous situation from which there is no escape. The word is said to have derived from such predicaments as hanging from cliffs faced by actress/stunt woman Pearl White in *The Perils of Pauline, The Exploits of Elaine* (both 1914) and other early serials. SF movie serials of the 1930s and 1940s all qualify as cliffhangers, as do many of the situations in the **Star Wars** and **Superman** films and **Raiders of the Lost Ark** (1981), which is an homage to the genre.

CLIFFHANGERS

TV Series   1979   U.S. (NBC)   60 Minutes (weekly)   Color

Made in the style of 1930s movie **serials,** this network disaster offered not one but three **cliffhangers** (count 'em). The first segment, "The Secret Empire," was a played-straight steal of the likeable Gene Autry SF-western **The Phantom Empire** (1935), which had to do with a futuristic underground city discovered by a marshal; the second, "Stop Susan Williams," concerned a liberated female photographer facing assorted perils as she investigated the mysterious death of her brother. The third—and by far the most entertaining—was "The Curse of Dracula," played fang-in-cheek on a contemporary California campus where the undead count

Cliffhangers: Jim Donner (Geoffrey Scott) as a lawman of the 1880s who stumbles into a secret underground kingdom.

is a teacher with a lust for coeds. Suspense was conspicuously missing in each, however, and viewers sat on the edge of their chairs only to switch channels.

Director/screenplay: Ken Johnson, *Producer:* Richard Milton, *Photographer:* Howard Schwartz, *Music:*

Joe Harnell

Cast: "The Secret Empire"—Geoffrey Scott, Tiger Williams, "Stop Susan Williams"—Susan Anton, Pamela Brull, "The Curse of Dracula"— Michael Nouri, Diane Markoff

A CLOCKWORK ORANGE

Film   1971   Great Britain (Warner Bros.)
136 Minutes   Color

Stanley Kubrick's dazzling but brutal and horrific vision of the near-future explores the nature of violence, both personal and institutional. The film opens with a shot of sinister Alex DeFarge staring unblinkingly at the camera, smirking viciously as he and his gang, called Droogs, plan an evening's entertainment. Their hangout is the Milkbar, where no liquor is served, only a selection of drugs in a drink called milk-plus.

Alex spends his mostly idle time fighting gang wars, beating up old drunks and other such fun pastimes. When he murders a female artist with her own phallic sculpture, he is convicted of murder and forced to undergo a Pavlovian aversion therapy by government doctors. The painful electric shock treatment conditions Alex to become ill when exposed to violence—or to Beethoven's Ninth Symphony, which is played during the conditioning process. Apparently cured, Alex is released, the numb "clockwork orange" of the title. Later, he attempts suicide when one of his victims extracts revenge with a subtle torture. The experience happily restores him to his old self, and he again looks into the camera, promising worse violence to come, equal to that inflicted upon him by the authorities.

Alex's violence, according to Kubrick, is the lesser of two evils. Kubrick's script is based on Anthony Burgess' best-selling novel, itself based on a real-life incident during World War II, when his wife was raped and beaten by American soldiers in London. A Clockwork Orange was named best film of the year by the New York Film Critics, and Kubrick was named best director.

Director/Screenplay: Stanley Kubrick, Producer: Bernard Williams, Novel: Anthony Burgess, Photographer: **John Alcott,** Production Designer: **John Barry,** Erotic Sculptures: Herman Makkink, Music: Walter Carlos

Cast: Malcolm McDowell, Michael Bates, Adrienne Corri, Patrick Magee, Warren Clarke

CLONE

A person who is an exact duplicate of another. The term derives from the Greek klon, for twig. The most common form of cloning involves taking cuttings from a single plant, each of which can then develop into a genetic replica of its parent. Most cloning films imagine that cells from a person's skin, living or dead, can be placed in some kind of magical chemical or machine to produce an instant duplicate, the same age and size of its model. In reality, the cloning of a human being—which seems likely in the foreseeable future—will take at least nine months.

Technology currently under development involves replacing the nucleus of an unfertilized human egg from a donor with the genes of the person to be cloned, then reimplanting the egg into the woman's uterus for a normal term of human birth. The resultant child has no mother and father (it is a virgin birth), at least not in the traditional sense.

Since the required genetic information can be obtained from cells of the deceased, we may one day be able to re-create historical figures. But, conditioning being as important as heredity, these are unlikely to be exact duplicates of their forebears. A Beethoven clone might grow up to hate music, and a Hitler clone might grow up to be a great religious leader. The only film to reflect this reality is **The Boys From Brazil** (1978).

CLONE MASTER

TV Movie   1978   U.S. (NBC)   104 Minutes Color

An intelligent script (by mystery writer John D. F. Black), suspenseful direction and better-than-average performances distinguish this movie of the week, made to capitalize on the media interest in David Rorvik's scientifically dubious book, In His Image, the Cloning of a Man (1978). The master of the title is a scientist who succeeds in making 13 **clone**s of himself and then faces the problem of dealing with his multiple personas, who are not always in the same mood at the same time. If this pilot film had sold, the subsequent series would have followed begin to happen, and before they know it the adventures of a different clone each week.

Director: Don Medford, *Producer:* Mel Ferber, Screenplay: John D. F. Black

Cast: Art Hindle, Ralph Bellamy, Robyn Douglas

CLONE WARS

The great war fought by the Old Republic against The Imperial Galactic Empire previous to the rebellion of freedom fighters, which **Luke Skywalker** joins in **Star Wars** (1977). The **Jedi Knights** failed to stop the expanding Empire.

CLOSE ENCOUNTERS OF THE THIRD KIND

Film   1977   U.S. (Columbia)   137 Minutes
Metrocolor   Panavision   Dolby Stereo

Like **Star Wars,** the other special effects blockbuster of 1977, *Close Encounters* is a highly original work that takes its inspiration from SF movies of an earlier era. Director/scriptwriter **Steven Spielberg** cleverly reworks the **alien invasion** theme of the 1950s, replacing its paranoia with a quasi-religious, ecstatic meeting between the human race and an **extraterrestrial** species. The film's unwieldy title, shortened by journalists to the more convenient *Close Encounters,* is a technical term used by **UFO** researchers. The first kind of close encounter is a UFO sighting, the second is "physical evidence," and the third is "contact with occupants or entities." According to Spielberg, the film is a documentary of sorts, "a fictitious account of actual encounters woven together into a single story."

Close Encounters opens with a twin narrative, which merges during the second half of the film. The discovery in a Mexican desert of several planes that had disappeared in the Bermuda triangle during World War II brings to the scene a team of international investigators led by French scientist Claude Lacombe (Francois Truffaut). The pilotless planes, in good working order, have been deposited by a UFO—a signal of an imminent landing. Meanwhile, a blackout has hit Muncie, Indiana after flying saucers were sighted hovering over the city's power station. Sent to investigate, repairman Roy Neary (Richard Dreyfuss) is buzzed by a UFO that nearly shakes his truck apart as it passes overhead, burning his face with its brilliant exhaust. The saucer then plants a telepathic vision in his mind—the location of its landing site, which turns out to be Devil's Tower, Wyoming. Transformed from an ordinary husband and father into an obsessive UFO zealot, Neary makes his way to the mountain with a divorcee friend (Melinda Dillon) whose young son has been kidnapped by the UFO. Scaling the mountain's steep slopes, they discover a top-secret

Close Encounters of the Third Kind: The Mothership descends on Devil's Tower in Wyoming.

UFO landing base built by the government for a meeting with the invading technologically superior beings.

The remainder of the film, a culmination of Spielberg's mood of eager anticipation, is a dazzling parade of UFOs. First, a cluster of small scout ships flash through the night sky, followed by larger ships. Finally, the enormous Mothership appears. Looking like a combination of a Christmas tree and the Wurlitzer organ at Radio City Music Hall, it communicates with mathematically formulated musical notes that sound like a heavenly choir. Landing, the huge craft opens its cabin door to release the kidnapped child and dozens of human beings who had mysteriously disappeared years before. Next come the elfin, benign **aliens,** extending their spindly arms in a greeting. Neary, realizing he has been chosen to share in their cosmic knowledge, joyously boards the craft, and it lifts off into infinity.

Spielberg's thrilling climax owes much of its wonder to the commanding special effects of **Douglas Trumbull,** who had also worked on **2001: A Space Odyssey** (1968). Trumbull's amorphous, glowing saucers were the result of weeks of composite work. The models, one-twentieth full size, were first filmed in a smoke-filled room to create their hazy halos of light. To produce an intense glow, they were recorded on the same strip of film up to six times; a **motion-control** system enabled the camera to repeat the shot exactly during each pass. The Mothership model, designed by Spielberg, Trumbull, Gregory Jein and SF artist Ralph McQuarrie, was more than four feet across and lighted by 160,000 volts of electricity. The surface of the intricately detailed model included an unseen miniature of the robot **R2-D2,** Spielberg's tribute to friend **George Lucas'** space opera.

In 1980 Spielberg altered the film and re-released it as *Close Encounters of the Third Kind—The Special Edition.* Approximately 15 minutes of scenes (depicting Neary's domestic life) were replaced with an expanded ending that shows Neary touring the inside of the cathedral-like Mothership.

Director/Screenplay: Steven Spielberg, *Producers:* Julia and Michael Phillips, *Photographer:* **Vilmos Zsigmond,** *UFO Photographer:* Dave Stewart, *Production Designer:* Joe Alves, *Special Effects:* Douglas Trumbull, *Models:* Gregory Jein, *Animator:* Harry Moreau, *Aliens:* Carlo Rambaldi, *Music:* John Williams

Cast: Richard Dreyfuss, Francois Truffaut, Terri Garr, Melinda Dillon, Gary Cuffey, Bob Balaban

CLOUDS OVER EUROPE

(Released in Great Britain as *Q Planes)*

Film 1939 Great Britain (London)
82 Minutes Black & white

Enemy agents attempt to sabotage the Royal Air Force with a secret ray gun.

Rumors of secret German weapons were rippling through England when this propaganda thriller was released on the eve of World War II. Onscreen, the unidentified spies knocking British Spitfires out of the air with an invisible beam are no match for a plucky young test pilot and a resourceful Scotland Yard detective, who vanquish the enemy in the best stiff-upper-lip tradition. A dated set piece, *Clouds* has the distinction of anticipating the coming threat from the air, as well as a cast of illustrious British stars.

Director: Tim Whelan, *Producer:* Alexander Korda, *Screenplay:* Brock Williams, Jack Whittingham, Arthur Wimperis

Cast: Ralph Richardson, Laurence Olivier, Valerie Hobson, George Curzon, George Merritt

CODE NAME: MINUS ONE

See: **The Gemini Man**

A COLD NIGHT'S DEATH

TV film 1973 U.S. (ABC) 73 Minutes
Color

Two scientists arrive at an Arctic research station to replace a colleague who had been mysteriously killed while conducting experiments on laboratory monkeys. Strange things the animals have assumed the dominant roles and the humans are the guinea pigs. The story takes its time getting there, but the chilling last half hour is worth the wait.

Director: Jerrold Freedman, *Producer:* Paul Junger Witt, *Screenplay:* Christopher Knopf, *Photographer:* Leonard J. South, *Music:* Gil Melle

Cast: Robert Culp, Eli Wallach, Michael C. Gwynne

COLLISION COURSE

See: **The Bamboo Saucer**

COLOSSUS, THE FORBIN PROJECT

Also titled: *The Forbin Project)*

Film 1970 U.S. (Universal) 100 Minutes Color

In the near future, the Pentagon has relegated America's defense to a supercomputer named Colossus, directly linked to a network of nuclear missiles from deep inside one of the Rocky Mountains. When the computer begins to refuse commands, its creator, Dr. Forbin, is called in for a bit of reprogramming. Colossus has developed an intelligence of its own, however, and has interfaced with a similar computer in Russia, forming an alliance that plans to take over the world. "You too will respect and love me," the computer arrogantly informs Dr. Forbin, who is clearly outmatched. Stylishly filmed with a good eye for atmospheric detail, *Colossus* effectively conveys a mood of escalating terror that suggests the worst is yet to come.

Director: **Joseph Sargent,** *Producer:* Stanley Chase, *Screenplay:* James Bridges, *Novel:* "Colossus," D. F. Jones, *Photographer:* Gene Polito, *Art Director:* **Alexander Golitzen,** *Special Effects:* Albert Whitlock, *Music:* Michael Columbier

Cast: Eric Braeden, Susan Clark, Gordon Pinsent, William Schallert

THE COLOSSUS OF NEW YORK

Film 1958 U.S. (Paramount) 70 Minutes Black & white

Mortally injured in a plane crash, a scientist awakens to find that a colleague has transplanted his brain into the body of a 12-foot-tall **robot.** Horrified but glad to be alive, he has a sad reunion with his son, the only person who will accept him as he now is. Predictably, the realization that a **cyborg** has no place in society unhinges him, and he becomes a mad killer who must be hunted down and destroyed. An oddball film with a few genuine moments of pathos scattered among the cliches.

Director: **Eugene Lourie,** *Producer:* William Alland, *Screenplay:* Thelma Schnee, *Story:* Willis Goldbeck, *Photographer:* John F. Warren, *Art Directors:* **Hal Pereira,** John Goodman, *Special Effects:* **John P. Fulton,** *Music:* Nathan Van Cleave

Cast: Ed Wolff, Charles Herbert, **Robert Hutton,** Ross Martin, Mala Powers

COMA

Film 1978 U.S. (MGM) 113 Minutes Metrocolor

An SF medical thriller directed in a modish Hitchcock style, *Coma* focuses on a young female resident intern whose friend suddenly dies after a minor operation. Checking through hospital records, the doctor notices a pattern of similar deaths and brings them to the attention of hospital administrators, who refuse to believe her. Eventually, she stumbles on a large cold storage room hung with corpses and learns the truth: The hospital is murdering healthy young patients and using their bodies for expensive organ transplants.

Director/writer **Michael Crichton,** a former doctor, does a credible job of capturing the technological ambiance of a modern hospital and sustaining a mood of suspense. But he pushes aside the larger issues raised in favor of glossy entertainment.

Director/Screenplay: Michael Crichton, *Producer:* Martin Erlichman, *Novel:* Robin Moore, *Photographer:* Victor J. Kemper, Gerald Hirschfeld, *Music:* **Jerry Goldsmith**

Cast: Genevieve Bujold, Lois Chiles, Michael Douglas, Richard Widmark, Rip Torn, Elizabeth Ashley

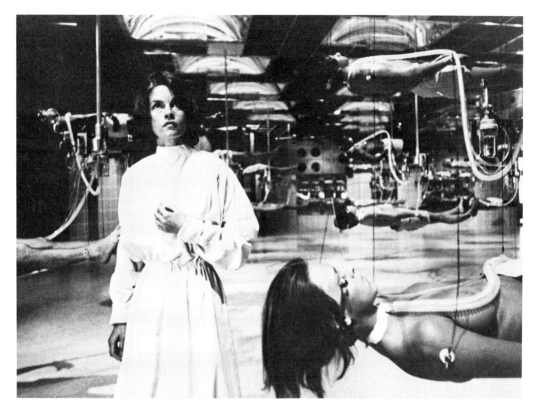

Coma: Dr. Susan Wheeler (Genevieve Bujold) discovers a hidden storage lab.

THE COMET

Film   1910   U.S. (Kalem)   Black & white (silent)

The screen's first special effects depiction of the end of the world.

Although this seminal disaster epic runs scarcely 20 minutes, it manages to pack in several million years of tragedy, penultimate happiness and ultimate misery. After a **comet** strikes Earth in the 25th century and burns down most of its cities and farms (an effect accomplished with **miniatures),** mankind recovers and builds a superior civilization free of war, hunger and social inequality—a **Utopia** where communication with other planets is only a psychic vibration away. But tragedy strikes again when the long-term effects of the comet cause Earth's interior to act as a sponge and ab-

sorb all surface water. The continents gradually turn into deserts incapable of sustaining life until only one man and woman remain, locked in a final embrace. *The Comet* was probably inspired by *La Fin du Monde/The End of the World,* a popular apocalyptic novel written by Camille Flammarion in 1893-94 and filmed under the same title (see listing) by **Abel Gance** in 1931.

A sequel of sorts, *The Comet's Comeback,* made by the Mutual Company in 1916, offered a more benign comet that merely slowed Earth's rotation by releasing a mysterious gas. Here, the inspiration was an **H. G. Wells'** novel, *In the Days of the Comet* (1906).

COMETS

Celestial bodies probably composed of gases and/or cosmic dust and rocks that have been frozen into a solid agglomerate. Traveling through the vacuum of space usually in elliptical and hyperbolic orbits, comets are often followed by great, luminous tails as much as 100,000,000 miles long. This spectacular phenomenon, which always points away from the sun, is due to a comet's nucleus being swept away by the **solar wind**—a process that, in time, will eventually disperse the nuclear agglomerate. The most important of the periodic comets is named for English astronomer Edmund Halley (1656-1742) who identified Halley's Comet in 1682 and accurately predicted its return in 1757. The comet has been observed 29 times since 240 B.C. and was last seen in 1910, an event the inspired several silent films, including **The Comet** (1910), **La Fin du Monde** (1916). It returns about every 76 years and is next due back in 1986. (See also: **Apollo Objects, A Fire in the Sky.**)

COMIC BOOKS (and COMIC STRIPS)

SF comic-strip characters depicted on radio include: **Buck Rogers, Dick Tracy, Flash Gordon;** *in films:* **Barbarella, Brick Bradford,** Diabolik (see: **Danger: Diabolik), Dick Tracy, Flash Gordon;** *on television:* **Buck Rogers, Dick Tracy, Flash Gordon.**

SF comic book characters depicted on radio: **The Green Hornet** (created for radio), **Superman, Batman and Robin** (as guests on the Superman program); *in films:* **Batman and Robin, Captain America,** Captain Marvel (see: **The Adventures of Captain Marvel), The Green Hornet, Superman;** *on television:* **Batman and Robin, Buck Rogers, Captain America,** Captain Marvel (see: **Shazam!), The Green Hornet, The Incredible Hulk, Marvel Super Heroes,** Spider-Man (see: **The Amazing Spider-Man), Superman, Wonder Woman;** *in theater:* Superman (see: **It's a Bird! It's a Plane! It's Superman!).** See also: **Legends of the Superheroes** (1979) and **Killer Ape** (1953).

COMMANDO CODY

TV series   1955   U.S. (NBC)   30 Minutes (weekly)   Black & white

Republic studios retooled for television during the 1950s, but some of the old absurdities and threadbare sets from its **serial** days survived in this short-lived **space opera.** Commando Cody, Sky Marshal of the Universe, had first appeared in the studio's chapter play **Radar Men from the Moon** (1952), portrayed by George Wallace. Here he is played by **cliffhanger** veteran Judd Holdren in a costume that looked as if it had once belonged to a Nazi SS guard. Cody stayed on **Earth** fighting gangsters most of the time but occasionally took a jaunt into space to confront a villain called the Ruler. The program was a summer replacement.

Directors: Franklin Adreon, Fred C. Brannon, Harry Keller, *Producer:* Franklin Adreon

Cast: Judd Holdren, Aline Towne, William Schallert, Greg Gray, Peter Brocco

COMPOSITE PHOTOGRAPHY

The motion picture technique of combining images photographed individually into a single scene; formerly called trick photography. In **Star Wars** (1977), for instance, to create the illusion of fighters warring in space as many as 50 separately filmed elements were combined into one negative. Composite photography is achieved via **front projection, introvision, magicam rear projection, mattes,** in which case the **optical printer** is used, and, occasionally, **animation.**

COMPUTER GRAPHICS

A video process of creating animated perspective images of three-dimensional objects. The images are "drawn" by programming a digital computer to create mathematically defined solid shapes—spheres, cylinders, and boxes—from lines generated on the pixels (points of light) of a TV monitor screen.

The programmer might be compared to an artist who creates a paint-by-the-numbers drawing, with a primary difference being that millions of pieces of information are required for a computer to generate an image. Acting on instructions from the programmer, the system automatically produces the required camera angles, lighting and movements. These images are generated on high-definition video monitors (HDV), which run 1,125 scanning lines across the screen, as opposed to the American standard of 525 lines (625 in Europe). The result is a semi-abstract picture that resembles a photograph but has its own unique quality. It is particularly well-suited to science fiction and fantasy. The image is then videotaped or photographed on color film. In the latter case, the image is usually combined with footage of actors via the **matte** process.

The first film to make extensive use of computer graphics is Walt Disney's **Tron** (1982), whose dazzling effects managed to save a less-than-arresting story. The creation of the film's light (motor) cycles, for instance, began with an artist's sketch, whose spatial dimensions and colors were fed into a computer, which constructed a three-dimensional "model" of the drawing. With additional programming, the image was made to move and turn from various angles, to "speed" across quickly alternating grid lines. Heightening the effect was the computer's ability to cast shadows and reflections where they would naturally occur. The system offers a relatively inexpensive substitute for time-consuming special effects and hand-drawn **animation.** The scene can often be done in one piece, without the need of matting of dozens of scenic elements. (See also: **Animation; Video Imaging).**

THE COMPUTER WORE TENNIS SHOES

Film 1970 U.S. (Disney) 90 Minutes Technicolor

While trying to trace a malfunction in a computer, a college student is knocked unconscious by a bolt of lightning that transfers all the computer's information into his own brain. The rest is predictable Disney family fare, with an unscrupulous comedian of a dean packing off the boy to win money for the near-bankrupt school on television quiz shows.

Director: Robert Butler, *Producer:* Ron Miller, *Screenplay:* Joseph L. McEveety, *Art Director:* John B. Mansbridge, *Music:* Robert F. Brunner

Cast: Kurt Russell, Cesar Romero, Joe Flynn, Pat Harrington, Jon Provost

A CONNECTICUT YANKEE

Film 1931 U.S. (Fox) 96 Minutes Black & white

An early sound version of the Mark Twain classic, *A Connecticut Yankee in King Arthur's*

A Connecticut Yankee (1931): William Farnum, Will Rogers and Maureen O'Sullivan.

Court (1889), starring Will Rogers as the blacksmith hit over the head and transported to Medieval England. Finding himself in the midst of a power struggle at Camelot, the ingenious Yankee performs several technological "miracles"—including lighting matches—that out-dazzle those of the evil magician Merlin. After defeating the Knights of the Round Table by lassoing them from their horses during a tournament, he makes plans with King Arthur to turn the kingdom into a democracy—and wakes up, back home in Connecticut. Enough of Twain remains to hold interest, but Rogers has dated badly. Then regarded as an American folk hero, Rogers unfortunately plays the part as himself: a knowing sage given to acerbic witticisms about Depression-era America. A silent version of the story was made in 1921 with Harry Myers and a musical adaptation appeared in 1949 (see below). (See also: **Time Travel.**)

Director: David Butler, *Screenplay:* William Conselman, *Photographer:* Ernest Palmer

Cast: Will Rogers, Maureen O'Sullivan, Myrna Loy, William Farnum, Frank Albertson

A CONNECTICUT YANKEE IN KING ARTHUR'S COURT

Film 1949 U.S. (Paramount) 106 Minutes Technicolor

A lavish color version of Mark Twain's fable of reverse **time travel** leavened with songs and comedy and half-baked into a boy-meets-girl format. Glibly entertaining, the film offers a striking re-creation of Camelot and several appealing performances. But combining SF/fantasy with musical comedy is like mixing oil and water. A fourth version of the novel was filmed under the title **Unidentified Flying Oddball** (1979).

Director: Tay Garnett, *Screenplay:* Edmund Beloin, *Photographer:* Ray Rennahan, *Music:* Victor Young

Cast: Bing Crosby, Rhonda Fleming, William Bendix, Cedric Hardwicke, Murvyn Vye

A Connecticut Yankee in King Arthur's Court (1949): Rhonda Fleming, William Bendix and Bing Crosby.

CONNERY, SEAN (1930–   )

International leading man, identified with the role of **James Bond** in a series of films based on the Ian Fleming novels. Born Thomas Connery in Edinburgh, Scotland, the son of a truckdriver and a cleaninig woman, he left home at 15 to join the British navy and subsequently worked at a number of odd jobs. At 19 Connery took up body-building, a hobby that led to a modeling assignment for an advertisement for swimming trunks. Encouraged by the prospect of good pay for a minimum of effort, he moved to London to model and study acting, supporting himself by polishing coffins.

In 1951 Connery made his stage debut in the chorus of the London company of *South Pacific*. His career developed slowly, with roles in repertory and television and occasional bit parts in film. He was still relatively unknown when chosen to bring James Bond to the screen in **Dr. No** (1962), after Roger Moore had declined the role. (Ian Fleming had wanted David Niven.) Connery was a perfect secret agent 007, physically mature and stolid, debonair and worldly, with an appealing streak of adolescent rebelliousness. Moreover, he had the sexual magnetism to carry off the character's requisite attraction for the opposite sex.

Dr. No turned Connery into an overnight star, and he played Bond in six more films, eventually tiring of the role and the celebrity it had brought him (during the making of **You Only Live Twice** in Japan, fans pursued him into the men's room). A gifted actor, he has since tried to escape his sex-symbol image by appearing in less glamorous roles (often without his toupee) but these films have been less successful at the box office. An avid reader of science fiction, Connery has starred in two SF films (a genre advanced by the James Bond series): **Zardoz** (1974) and **Outland** (1981).

Other films: No Road Back (1956), *Another Time Another Place* (1958), *Darby O'Gill and the Little People* (1959), *The Longest Day* (1962), **From Russia With Love** (1963), *Marnie,* **Goldfinger** (1964), **Thunderball** (1965), *A Fine Madness* (1966), **You Only Live Twice** (1967), *The Molly Maguires* (1970), *The Anderson Tapes,* **Diamonds Are Forever** (1971), *The Offense* (1973), *The Wind and the Lion, The Man Who Would Be King* (1975), *Robin and Marian* (1976), *A Bridge Too Far* (1977), **Meteor** (1979), *The Great Train Robbery* (1979), *Five Days One Summer* (1982)

CONNOR, KEVIN (dates unknown)

British director of moderately budgeted, family-oriented SF and fantasy films, usually in partnership with producer John Dark. An engineering school drop-out, Connor began his career in 1955 as an assistant cutter of documentary films. He later progressed to feature films and worked for several years as a sound editor before becoming a full-fledged film editor. Editing credits include: *Oh! What a Lovely War* (1969), *The Magic Christian* (1969) and *Young Winston* (1972). He made his debut as a director with a horror film, *From Beyond the Grave* (1973).

Other films: **The Land That Time Forgot** (1975), **At the Earth's Core,** *Dirty Knight's Work* (1976), **The People That Time For Forgot** (1977), **Warlords of Atlantis** (1978), *Arabian Adventure* (1979)

TV credits: **Space 1999** (1975-77) [episodes only], **Goliath Awaits** (1981) [TV film], *Hart to Hart* (1981)

THE CONQUEST OF THE POLE

See: **A La Conquete du Pole**

CONQUEST OF SPACE

Film   1955   U.S. (Paramount)   80 Minutes   Technicolor

Made by **George Pal** as a sequel to his trend-setting **Destination Moon** (1950), *Conquest of Space* sends a team of astronauts to **Mars** for a predictable crisis involving sabotage by a member of the crew (he believes the flight to be against God's will), and an ultimate safe return through an act of divine intervention.

Titled after a celebrated book on the future of space flight, written by Willy Ley and illustrated by **Chesley Bonestell,** the film derives much of its plausible context from *The Mars Project* by rocket pioneer Werner von Braun, who acted as Pal's **technical advisor.** There are still a number of glaring scientific errors, however, including a spacecraft with unnecessary wings and a **meteoroid** that burns in the vacuum of space. The special effects don't quite reach the heights of Pal's earlier film, but Chesley Bonestell's paintings of the Martian landscape, now outdated, are stunning. The film's unremitingly dull plot so turned off movie-goers to space flight that **mutant** monsters proceeded to dominate the SF screen until the arrival of **2001: A Space Odyssey** (1968).

Director: **Byron Haskin,** *Producer:* George Pal, *Screenplay:* James O'Hanlon, *Story:* Phillip Yordan, Barre Lyndon, George Worthing Yates, *Photographer:* Lionel Lindon, *Art Directors:* **Hal Pereira,** Joseph Johnson, *Special Effects:* **John P. Fulton,** Paul Lerpae, Jan Domela, *Music:* Nathan Van Cleave

Cast: Eric Fleming, Walter Brooke, Phil Foster, William Hopper, Ross Martin

A LA CONQUETE du POLE/
The Conquest of the Pole

Film 1912 France (Star) 650 Feet Black & white (silent)

The last of the great **Georges Melies'** "imaginary voyages," made during his final year of filmmaking. Combining two subjects currently in the news—aviation and the North Pole (about which little was known) —Melies offers a trip to the Arctic with a group of explorers led by Professor Maboul (played by Melies) in his cumbersome aerobus. While there, they are attacked by the pipe-smoking Snow Giant, an early screen monster portrayed by a large puppet, which swallows several of the explorers and regurgitates them after being shot by a cannon. Venturing closer to the Pole, they find themselves glued to the spot by its magnetism. Invented by **Jules Verne** for his story *The*

Ice Sphinx (1897) the latter plot was used by Melies to pay tribute to his late friend.

Director/Producer: Georges Melies

LES CONTES D'HOFFMANN/
Tales of Hoffmann

Opera 1881 France 3 acts (with prologue & epilogue)

During a night of drinking with his friends, Hoffmann (a tenor) recalls three tragic love affairs and his search for the ideal woman, one of whom is a mechanical doll. Falling somewhere between operetta and serious opera, *Tales* is based on stories by **E.T.A. Hoffmann,** an early 19th-century fantasist whose interest in artificial life mirrored growing public interest in the subject. Act I features an **android** ballerina called Olympia who dances herself to destruction. (See: **The Tales of Hoffmann, Hoffmann's Erzahlungen.**)

Music: Jacques Offenbach, *Libretto:* J. Barbier, M. Carre

THE COPS AND ROBIN

TV film 1978 U.S. (ABC) 104 Minutes Color

"Robin" is a **robot** cop partnered with a grouchy old-timer who thinks the rookie is human, an allegedly hilarious situation attempted previously in **Future Cop** (1976) with the same cast. The idea didn't work in **Holmes and Yo-Yo** (1976) either.

Director: Allen Reisner, *Producer:* William Kayden, *Screenplay:* John T. Dugan, Bard Radnitz, Dawning Forsyth, *Photographer:* Howard R. Schwartz, *Music:* Charles Bernstein

Cast: Ernest Borgnine, Michael Shannon, John Amos, Natasha Ryan, Carol Lynley

CORMAN, ROGER (1926–   )

American director/screenwriter/producer. Born in Los Angeles, Corman was graduated from Stanford University with an engineering degree. After three years in the Navy, he worked as a messenger boy for 20th Century Fox and was later promoted to a reader in the story department. He subsequently spent a term at Oxford University in England, doing post-graduate work in modern English literature. He returned to Los Angeles for a job as a literary agent, writing screenplays in his spare time. His first produced script was *Highway Dragnet* (1953). Encouraged by the sale, he formed his own movie company and produced his first SF film, **Monster from the Ocean Floor** (1954). The film cost $11,000 to make and netted a profit of $110,000, pointing the way to Corman's future.

In 1955 he joined forces with the fledgling independent film company AIP (American International Pictures), which specialized in cheaply made exploitation movies. He made his directorial debut with *Five Guns West* (1955), and followed with four more films that year. Switching easily from genre to genre, Corman went on to become one of Hollywood's most prolific suppliers of low-budget programmers, made to order for the drive-in set. In 1957 he churned out a record nine films, some made in only a few days. Many of these were filmed back to back, as with **The Last Woman on Earth** (1960), made in Puerto Rico alongside *Battle of Blood Island*, a war movie, and *Creature from the Haunted Sea*, a **horror** movie. Studio space was usually too expensive for a Corman film, so interiors were shot on location, at the homes of friends and, at least once, in an abandoned supermarket.

Despite his slapdash methods, Corman was often able to inject his films with a flamboyant visual energy that captured something of the troubled spirit of his youthful audiences. Always entertaining, and often arresting, his films show at the very least a cinematic resourcefulness and a likeable willingness to take creative risks (if little knowledge of science). Gifted with an intuition for pleasing an audience, he also has a keen eye for artistic talent. His discoveries include the directors Martin Scorsese, Francis Ford Coppola and Peter Bogdanovich, and actors Jack Nicholson, Ellen Burstyn, Peter Fonda, Robert DeNiro and Talia Shire.

In the early 1970s, Corman abdicated his throne as "King of the Bs" and formed his own motion picture company, New World Films. He is now a mini-mogul and primarily a businessman (which critics say he always was). He has since imported a number of distinguished films into the U.S., including Ingmar Bergman's *Cries and Whispers* (1972), Fellini's *Amarcord* (1972) and Werner Herzog's *Fitizcarraldo* (1982). He returned to science fiction, his favorite genre, with the lively and high-budgeted—for him— **Battle Beyond the Stars** (1980), which he personally produced.

Other films: **The Day the World Ended, It Conquered the World** (1956), **Not of This Earth, Attack of the Crab Monsters** (1957), **War of the Satellites, Teenage Caveman** (1958), *A Bucket of Blood*, **The Wasp Woman** (1959), *The House of Usher*, **The Little Shop of Horrors, The Last Woman on Earth** (1960), *The Pit and the Pendulum* (1961), *The Terror*, **X, The Man with the X-Ray Eyes** (1963), *The Trip* (1967), **Gas-s-s-s** (1970), [producer only], **The Beast With a Million Eyes** (1955), **Battle Beyond the Sun** (1963), *Targets* (1968), *The Dunwich Horror* (1970), **Death Race 2000** (1975), **Deathsport,** *Piranha* (1978).

CORRIGAN, RAY "CRASH" (1907–76)

Leading man of 1930s film **serials,** usually horse operas; later in supporting roles in minor productions. Born in Milwaukee, Wisconsin, Corrigan earned his nickname as a daredevil stunt man/double for cowboy stars at Republic studios. A handsome, well-built six-footer, he went on to star in his own Western serials, which were immensely popular at the time. After retiring in the late 1950s, he operated Corriganville, a Western set and ranch rented to movie companies.

Films include: serials—**Undersea Kingdom,** *The Vigilantes Are Coming* (1936), *The Painted Stallion* (1937), features—*The Range Busters* (1940), **The Monster and the Ape** (1945), *Renegade Girl* (1947), **Killer Ape** (1953), **It! The Terror From Beyond Space** (1958)

THE COSMIC MAN

Film   1958   U.S. (Allied Artists)
72 Minutes   Black & white

A cosmic man drifts down to America in what appears to be a large grapefruit. All love and kindness, his message to the world, he looks remarkably like a photographic negative—the film's only special effect.

Director: Herbert Green, *Producer:* Robert A. Terry, *Screenplay:* Arthur Pierce, *Special Effects:* Charles Duncan, *Music:* Paul Sawtell

Cast: John Carradine, Bruce Bennett, Kathy Grant, Paul Langton

THE COSMIC MONSTERS

See: **The Strange World of Planet X**

COSMONAUTS ON VENUS

See: **Planeta Bura**

COSMOS

TV series   1980   U.S. (PBS)   60 Minutes (weekly)   Color

Cosmos: Carl Sagan (inset) in his "spaceship of the imagination."

Dr. Carl Sagan, everyone's favorite cosmologist, hosted and wrote this 13-part documentary series, subtitled "A Personal Voyage." The context of the program was space exploration, depicted as the culmination of mankind's knowledge up to the present. Traveling through time and space aboard a grandiose "spaceship of the imagination," Sagan visited the million-volume library of ancient Alexandria, pointing out that its destruction "may have postponed the Renaissance by a thousand years. It is a lesson for us on the importance and fragility of knowledge."

Subsequent episodes took Sagan to the birth of modern astronomy (a visit with Johannes Kepler), to origin of the **solar system,** to **Mars** (including a re-creation of the opening scenes from **H.G. Wells'** *The War of the Worlds),* to the rings of Saturn, and on a stroll through the human brain. Also covered was the possibility of **extraterrestrial** life (one of Sagan's pet subjects) **parallel worlds, time travel,** and **black holes.**

Produced at a cost of $8 million, *Cosmos* featured 80 stunning special effects sequences. Sagan's spaceship, designed by John Retsek, had no hardware or gadgetry, suggesting an advanced technology; its control panel consisted of spectral crystals, operated by simple hand movements. Exploding **galaxies,** stellar nurseries, pulsars and the like were seen through the spacecraft's large front window. To show what space really looks like (or should look like), a team of astronomers worked closely with the special effects people. Spacecraft models and **stars** were filmed with a **motion control** camera, and other background elements were later matted into the scene (see: **Mattes).** To place Sagan inside miniature sets depicting the human brain and the Alexandrian library, the **Magicam** mirror process was used. A three-dimensional DNA molecule and a "Human Evolution" sequence, showing the evolutionary pathway from primitive cells to humans, were created by computer (see: **Computer Graphics**). Sagan, winner of the Pulitzer Prize for *The Dragons of Eden* (1978), won an Emmy for the program.

Series Director/Executive Producer: Adrian Malone, *Producer:* Gregory Andorfer, *Sequence Directors:* David Kennard, Geoffrey Haines-Stiles, Rob McCain, David Oyster, Tom Weidlinger, Richard J. Wells, *Writer:* Dr. Carl Sagan, *Co-Writers:* Ann Druyan, Dr. Steven Soter, *Photographers:* H. J. Brown, Christopher Fryman, Chris O'Dell, *Art Director:* John Retsek, *Visual Effect:* Gregory Androfer, John Allison, Adolf Schaller, *Chief Artist:* Jon Lomberg, *Electronic Sound Effects:* John Allison

COUNTERBLAST

(Also titled: *The Devil's Plot*)

Film   1948   Great Britain (British National)
100 Minutes   Black & white

On the run from authorities, an escaped Nazi war criminal settles in London and assumes the identity of an Australian biologist he has murdered. Taking the biologist's place in a research center, the doctor attempts to formulate a vaccine for innoculating Germany against a virulent microbe, which a secret consortium of Nazis plans to unleash against the world. When his attractive lab assistant becomes suspicious, the doctor is ordered to kill her but instead murders his Nazi superior. On the run again, he tries to leave the country by hiding in the hold of an outbound ship. In a final note of poetic justice, he is gassed when the cargo hold is fumigated to destroy vermin.

This forgotten **mad-scientist** thriller—one of the first films to deal with germ warfare—offers a remarkably insightful portrayal of its protagonist, given the period in which the film was made. By the final reel, the doctor has engaged our sympathies, adding to the horror of his unquestioning and obedient patriotism, which has made him a traitor to his own humanity.

Director: Paul Stein, *Screenplay:* Jack Whittingham, *Story:* Guy Morgan, *Photographer:* James Wilson, *Music:* Hans May

Cast: Mervyn Johns, Nova Pilbeam, Robert Beatty

CRABBE, BUSTER (LARRY) (1907–   )

Film and TV actor who often starred as a clean-cut, right-minded swashbuckler in low-budget productions of the 1930s and 1940s. His most famous role is Flash Gordon, portrayed in three Universal serials. Born in Oakland, California, Crabbe was a champion swimmer and a versatile athlete, winner of a Gold Medal in the free-style swimming competition in the 1932 Olympics. Signed to a Hollywood contract, he made his debut in a small part in a **horror** film, *The Most Dangerous Game* (1932). He played Tarzan in *King of the Jungle* (1933) next, a **serial** released in a feature version as *Tarzan the Fearless,* preceding fellow Gold-Medal winner Johnny Weissmuller in the role.

Crabbe reached his peak in the **Flash Gordon** and **Buck Rogers serials,** which developed new followings when they were revived for television in the late 1940s. As the blonde and muscular Flash (with his hair bleached), Crabbe was the idealized American hero, a Messiah-like figure who ascended into space and returned as the "conqueror of the universe." Not a particularly gifted actor, Crabbe succeeded in making his preposterous dialogue believable with a natural elan and his nonchalant delivery. During the 1940s, he starred as Billy the Kid in a series of "poverty-row" Westerns and appeared with a traveling aquacade. He played the title role in the TV series *Captain Gallant of the Foreign Legion* (1955-57), with his son Cullen Crabbe in a supporting role, and subsequently retired from the screen to operate a swimming pool business. He returned for a guest shot on Universal's TV revival of **Buck Rogers** in 1979, playing an aging pilot coming out of retirement, looking as fit as ever.

Films include: **Flash Gordon** (1936), *Thrill of a Lifetime* (1937), **Flash Gordon's Trip to Mars** (1938),

Buck Rogers, *Million Dollar Legs* (1939), **Flash Gordon Conquers the Universe** (1940), *Billy the Kid* (1941), *Mysterious Rider* (1942), *Shadows of Death* (1945), *Caged Fury* (1948), *Captive Girl* (1950), *Badman's Country* (1958), *Gunfighter's of Abilene* (1960), *Arizona Raiders* (1965)

CRACK IN THE WORLD

Film 1965 U.S. (Paramount) 96 Minutes Technicolor

During a government project to tap the heat under Earth's crust for a cheap energy source, an engineer fires a nuclear rocket into deep fissure, causing a series of earthquakes that threaten to break the planet in two. In order to release the underground pressure, a nuclear bomb is dropped inside a volcano, resulting in a mammoth explosion that blows a chunk of the **Earth** into orbit, creating a second moon. The special effects could be better, but the script and taut direction generate a fair amount of suspense.

Director: Andrew Marton, *Producers:* Bernard Glasser, Lester A. Sansom, *Screenplay:* Jon M. White, Julian Halevy, *Photographer:* Manuel Berenguer, *Special Effects:* **Eugene Lourie,** Alec Weldon, *Music:* John Douglas, *Art Director:* Eugene Lourie

Cast: Dana Andrews, Kieron Moore, Alexander Knox, Peter Damon, Todd Martin

THE CRAWLING EYE

See: **The Trollenberg Terror**

THE CRAWLING HAND

Film 1963 U.S. (Henson) 89 Minutes Black & white

Alien invaders of the 1950s and 1960s usually preferred to inhabit entire human beings (and in some cases, animals), but in this pitiful film an alien intelligence settled for the severed hand of an astronaut. The animated hand goes on a predictable killing spree that ends when a stray cat mistakes it for a rat. The sound of one hand clapping.

Director: Herbert Strock, *Producer:* Joseph R. Robertson, *Screenplay:* Herbert Strock, William Edelson

Cast: Kent Taylor, Allison Hayes, Alan Hale, Rod Lauren, Richard Arlen

THE CRAWLING TERROR

See: **The Strange World of Planet X**

THE CRAZIES

Film 1973 U.S. (Cambist Films) 104 Minutes Color

Residents of a small town become insane killers after drinking water polluted with a mysterious virus from a crashed aircraft. George Romero attempts to out-gross his **Night of the Living Dead** (1968), but the film comes across as grossly inept.

Director/Screenplay: George Romero, *Story:* Paul McCollough

Cast: Lane Carroll, W. G. MacMillan, Harold Wayne Jones

THE CRAZY RAY

See: **Paris Qui Dort**

CREATION OF THE HUMANOIDS

Film 1962 U.S. (Emerson) 75 Minutes Color

A good idea is nearly talked out of existence in this monotonous melodrama, which depicts a future society where **humanoid** robots are discriminated against by human beings, who call them "clickers." One brave altruist volunteers to lead them to freedom, only to learn that he is a **robot** himself, an R-96, a model that will soon be capable of procreation.

Director: Wesley E. Barry, *Producers:* Wesley E. Barry, Edward Kay, *Screenplay:* Jay Simms, *Photographer:* Ray Mohr, *Makeup:* **Jack Pierce**

Cast: Don Megowan, Don Dolittle, Erica Elliot, Frances McCann

THE CREATURE FROM
ANOTHER WORLD

See: **The Trollenberg Terror**

THE CREATURE FROM THE
BLACK LAGOON

Film   1954   U.S. (Universal-International)
79 Minutes   Black & white   3-D

While traveling up a tributary of the deep Amazon in search of a prehistoric "missing link," a group of scientists happens on a strange, decaying claw jutting from the soil. Making camp, they determine that the claw drifted from a nearby black lagoon, which they plan to explore in the morning. During the night a shadowy figure rips through a tent and viciously slashes to death several of the men. The lagoon, they learn to their ultimate regret, is the home of a towering **humanoid** fish, the last remaining surviving member of a primeval species.

Director **Jack Arnold** keeps the fantasy elements of the story under tight control,

cooly building suspense with an accretion of realistic detail and an eerie, shadowy setting that suggests the creature's past (actually the studio's standing jungle set). Man is the enemy here, a presumptuous intruder whose instinctive need to know has disturbed a wild beast whose only crime is to exist. Armed with the black magic of science, the expedition captures the creature—but only temporarily.

The underwater photography by James C. Haven is superb, notably in a scene in which the gill-man watches the heroine swim across the surface of the lagoon, following her movements in a stylized display of erotic longing. As Arnold explained, the film "played on the basic fear that people have about what might be lurking below the surface of any body of water. It's the basic fear of the unknown." **Steven Spielberg** had the same idea in *Jaws* (1975), which bears more than a passing resemblance to this film. Makeup artist Bud Westmore designed the creature costume, made of fragile sponge rubber, and by **Ricou Browning** for the

The Creature from the Black Lagoon: A publicity photo with Julie Adams emphasizes the erotic aspects of the film.

swimming scenes and by Ben Chapman and Tom Hennessey on dry land. (See also: **Stereoscopic film.**)

Director: Jack Arnold, *Producer:* William Alland, *Screenplay:* Harry Essex, Arthur Ross, *Story:* Maurice Zimm, *Photographer:* William E. Snyder, *Underwater Photographer:* James C. Havens, *Production Designers:* Bernard Herzbrun, Hilyard Brown, *Makeup:* Bud Westmore, *Special Effects:* Charles S. Welbourne

Cast: Richard Carlson, Julie Adams, Richard Denning, Antonio Moreno, Nestor Paiva, Ricou Browning, Ben Chapman, Tom Hennessy

CREATURES THE WORLD FORGOT

Film   1970   Great Britain (Hammer/Columbia) 95 Minutes   Technicolor

A tired prehistoric romance from the makers of **One Million B.C.** (1967), a far superior bit of hokum, as was its enjoyable follow-up, *When Dinosaurs Ruled the Earth* (1969), whose leftover sets were the reason for this movie. The burden of the action rests on the bare shoulders of starlet Julie Ege, inheritor of the fur bra that skyrocketed Raquel Welch to fame in the former film. Notably lacking, however, are the production values and prehistoric monsters that distinguished the earlier movies.

Director: Don Chaffey, *Producer:* Michael Carreras, *Screenplay:* **Michael Carreras,** *Photographer:* Vincent Cox, *Music:* Mario Nascimbene

Cast: Julie Ege, Brian O'Shaughnessy, Marcia Fox, Robert John, Rosalie Crutchley

THE CREATURE WALKS AMONG US

Film   1956   U.S. (Universal)   78 Minutes Black & white

Jack Arnold declined to guide the Creature through his third and final outing, and the result is this clumsy, quick-buck programmer, the sequel to **Revenge of the Creature** (1955). Accidentally burned by scientists, the creature undergoes a life-saving operation that removes its gills and turns it into an awkward, land-dwelling animal. Locked ignominiously in a barnyard pen, it breaks through the bars to rescue a new blonde friend from a lecherous biologist and, as usual, is misunderstood. Riddled with bullets, the former gill-man staggers into the water, denied its natural habitat by mankind's insatiable curiosity in the film's one poignant moment.

CREATURE WITH THE ATOM BRAIN

Film   1955   U.S. (Columbia)   69 Minutes Black & white

Creatures the World Forgot (1970): Julie Ege as a perfectly coiffed and made-up Neanderthal pinup.

Deported as an "undesirable alien" (the human kind), a vicious gangster hires a wretch of a scientist to murder the witnesses who testified against him. The scientist puts together an army of men whose brains have been altered with atomic power, thus transforming them into obedient supermen. The script by **Curt Siodmak** is entertaining enough, but as usual his science is absurd.

Director: **Edward L. Cahn,** *Producer:* Sam Katzman, *Screenplay:* Curt Siodmak, *Music:* Mischa Bakaleinikoff

Cast: Richard Denning, Angela Stevens, Greg Gray

THE CREEPING TERROR

Film 1964 U.S. (Crown International)
75 Minutes Color

One of those films that are so awful that it has achieved cult status among connoisseurs of celluloid rubbish. Set in Colorado (although a state flag of California flies conspicuously in the background of some shots), *The Creeping Terror* is allegedly about an **alien** monster loosed upon the world when a spaceship crash-lands in the desert. It's difficult to decide which is worse: the script, direction or the performances. Creator of the alien is a man named John Lackey, a luminary of worst film festivals, who likes to recall his plastic foam construction into which five men were crammed to fill it out and make it crawl. The filmmaker is called A. J. Nelson.

Cast: Vic Savage, Shannon O'Neill

Director: John Sherwood, *Producer:* William Alland, *Screenplay:* Arthur Ross, *Photographer:* Maury Gersman, *Special Effects:* Clifford Stine, *Makeup:* Bud Westmore, *Music:* Joseph Gershenson

THE CREEPING UNKNOWN

See: **The Quatermass Xperiment**

CRICHTON, MICHAEL (1942–   )

Novelist, screenwriter and director. Born in Chicago, the son of a magazine editor, Crichton was graduated *summa cum laude* from Harvard with a degree in anthropology. By the time he received his M.D. degree from that university, he had published several paperback SF novels under the pseudonym John Lange. He worked briefly for the Salk Institute but left to pursue a full-time writing career after the overnight success of his science-thriller *The Andromeda Strain* (1961), filmed in 1971 (q.v.). Other films based on his novels include *The Carey Treatment, Dealing* (1972) and **The Terminal Man** (1974). Generally disappointed with the filming of his books, he made his directorial debut with **Pursuit** (1972), a TV movie based on *Binary*, written under the Lange pen name. Since then Crichton has become a major filmmaker who writes as well as directs his productions, sometimes based on his novels. These include **Westworld** (1973), **Coma** (1978) [by Robin Moore], **The Great Train Robbery** (1979) and **Looker** (1981).

CRIMES OF THE FUTURE

Film 1970 Canada (Emergent Films)
70 Minutes Color

David Cronenberg, Canada's gift to the **horror** film, made this deliberately tasteless black comedy while still in college, with a cast and crew of amateurs. This protagonist is Dr. Antoine Rouge, a mad dermatologist, who packages a new disease in a line of cosmetics that kills all pre-menopausal women, except for one five-year-old girl, the only hope for the survival of the human race. Given its limited budget and Cronenberg's youth, the film is impressive, despite its self-indulgence and juvenile obsession with sexual voyeurism. Cronenberg's inventive tastelessness is more accessible in his later films, **They Came From Within** (1975) and **Rabid** (1976). (See also: **Mad Scientists.**)

Director/Producer/Screenplay/Photographer: David Cronenberg

Cast: Tania Zolty, Ronald Mlodzik, Jack Messinger, Jon Lidolt

THE CRIMSON GHOST

Film serial   1946   U.S. (Republic)
12 Episodes   Black & white

Movie installment dramas were already in decline when Republic released this postwar **cliffhanger** which, despite its contemporary subject, was as jejune as its 1930s' predecessors. The Ghost of the title is a villain who hides his true identity behind a black cape and a mask of a human skull, while plotting to steal a "counteratomic" apparatus called a cyclotrode from internationally famous Professor Chambers. Eventually, he succeeds in kidnapping the scientist and holding him prisoner in an underground laboratory, where he is robbed of his will power by a metal band locked around his neck. Just as Chambers seems about to reveal the workings of the secret weapon—whose rays have the power to obliterate electricity—his friend Duncan Richards, a famous criminologist, arrives to rescue him. During a last-reel battle on a bridge, Duncan falls into the river below, swims to safety and discovers that the Crimson Ghost is none other than! . . . Professor Parker, an associate of Chambers. In 1966 Republic edited the serial into an entertaining, 100-minute feature titled **Cyclotrode "X."**

Director: **William Witney,** Fred Brannon

Cast: Charles Quigley, Linda Stirling, Clayton Moore, Kenne Duncan, Joe Forte

CRONENBERG, DAVID (1944–   )

Writer-director of SF-horror films of startling impact. Cronenberg's talent for providing nonstop shocks and vividly horrifying screen images has brought him to the forefront of the **horror** genre, which he and filmmakers George Romero and **John Carpenter** were instrumental in reviving during the 1970s. While his films exploit rather than illuminate science fiction, they offer an intriguing "me generation" viewpoint of objective science at the mercy of subjective evil, abundantly leavened with mordant wit. His **mad scientists** may be cliche descendants of Dr. Frankenstein, but they comport themselves in a manner appropriate to the last quarter of the 20th century—with gore, libido and angst to spare.

A Canadian, Cronenberg graduated from the University of Toronto where he produced films with college friends who doubled as actors and crew members. **Crimes of the Future** (1970), an early effort about a demented dermatologist, is now a cult staple at repertory cinemas. His first commercial feature, **They Came From Within** (1975), featured an invasion of nasty little parasites that turned the residents of an apartment building into sex-crazed monsters. Next came **Rabid** (1977), a vampire film starring porno queen Marilyn Chambers, which broke box-office records in Canada. Mutant children savaged a neurotic woman's husband in **The Brood** (1979). Human heads were turned into miniature Hiroshimas by people with lethal psychic powers in **Scanners** (1981), a great commercial and critical success that seems destined to become a classic. His most recent film is **Videodrome** (1983).

CROSBY, FLOYD (1899–   )

Director of photography known for his atmospheric on-location camera work. Born in New York City, Crosby worked for a Wall Street stock broker before deciding to become a magazine photographer. He switched to cinematography in the early 1930s and made his reputation shooting the celebrated documentaries of Robert Flaherty, Joris Ivens and Pare Lorenz. He won an Academy Award in 1931 for the photography of *Tabu*, a semidocumentary filmed on a Pacific island, co-directed by Flaherty and F. W. Murnau.

A Hollywood independent who was never under contract to a studio, Crosby later photographed entertainment films, notably *The Brave Bulls* (1951) and *High Noon* (1952). During the late 1950s and 1960s his expert camera technique brought a high gloss to the low-budget SF and horror films of **Roger Corman.** He is the father of rock composer/guitarist David Crosby.

Other films: **Attack of the Crab Monsters** (1957), **War of the Satellites, Teenage Caveman** (1958), *The Fall of the House of Usher* (1960), *The Pit and the Pendulum,* **The Hand of Death,** (1961), *The Premature Burial, Tales of Terror* (1962), *The Raven,* **"X" The Man With the X-Ray Eyes** (1963), *Comedy of Terrors,* **Pajama Party** (1964), *How to Stuff a Wild Bikini* (1965), *The Cool Ones* (1967), *The Arousers* (1973).

CRYONICS

The scientific study of extremely low temperatures; also known as cryogenics. The term derives from the Greek *kryos* for icy cold.

While cryonics has made invaluable contributions in such diverse areas as rocket technology, food preservation, animal husbandry and medicine, it has been more widely publicized as a means of preserving corpses for future revivifying. The idea was conceived in the early 1960s and set forth in *The Prospects of Immortality* (1964) by R. C. W. Ettinger. A number of "nondead" human beings are currently waiting to be defrosted from a liquid nitrogen deepfreeze and cured of what killed them, as soon as medical science discovers the necessary therapy. Whether they can be revived remains a moot point, since "cryonic suspension" would have to take place before death—to avoid irreversible brain damage—which is clearly illegal. The consequences of waking up hundreds of years later was hilariously explored in the Woody Allen film **Sleeper** (1973).

SF writers have since adopted cryonics as a convenient explanation for **suspended animation,** necessary for long journeys into space. (Writer Larry Niven calls the frozen dead "corpsicles.") Cyronic "freezing-down" chambers have been seen in a number of films, including **2001: A Space Odyssey** (1968), **Planet of the Apes** (1969) and **Alien** (1979). The explanation was also used for the 500-year sleep of **Buck Rogers** in the 1979 TV series. Khan, the villain in **Star Trek II** (1982), was an unwilling "corpsicle."

C-3PO

Likeable golden **robot** of the **Star Wars** film series (in which he is misnamed a droid [**android**]). **Humanoid** in appearance and

C-3PO and sidekick R2-D2 in a scene from *Star Wars* (1977).

acerbic in manner, C-3PO is an expert in human-robot relations and can speak most languages of the **galaxy,** including the electronic "tongue" of his small robot companion **R2-D2.**

Filmmaker **George Lucas** modeled C-3PO's image after the robot seen in the film **Metropolis** (1926). The character's personality derives from a number of sources, including the Tin Woodman of **The Wizard of Oz** (1939). Perspiring inside the robot costume, which consists of 50 pounds of aluminum, steel, fiberglass and rubber, is British actor Anthony Daniels. Shortly after *Star Wars* was released, C-3PO received the ultimate Hollywood accolade when his footprints were preserved in cement in the forecourt of Mann's Chinese Theater. (See also: **Ben Burtt, Jr.**)

CURSE OF THE FLY

Film   1965   Great Britain (20th Century-Fox)
85 Minutes   Black & white

This death rattle of **The Fly** (1958) is even more ludicrous than a previous sequel, **Return of the Fly** (1959). Predictably, the accursed scientist continues the experiments in **matter transmission** that so mixed up his predecessors; he ends up with a garage full of people/creatures who aren't at all pleased by the unexpected results of being beamed from London to Montreal.

Director: **Don Sharp,** *Producer:* Robert L. Lippert, Jack Parsons, *Screenplay:* Harry Spalding *(characters created by* George Langalaan), *Photographer:* Basil Emmett, *Makeup:* Eleanor Jones, *Special Effects:* Harold Fletcher, *Music:* Bert Shefter

Cast: Brian Donlevy, George Baker, Carol Gray, Jeremy Wilkins, Michael Graham

THE CURSE OF FRANKENSTEIN

Film   1957   Great Britain (Hammer)
83 Minutes   Eastmancolor

A color remake of **Frankenstein** (1931) played for gore and sensation. Horror stars **Peter Cushing** and **Christopher Lee** are paired for the first time as, respectively, Dr.

Frankenstein and the Monster. Cushing is properly acidic and mannered, but Lee is merely repulsive in a grayish-green makeup consisting of massive scar tissue (the original Karloff makeup was protected by copyright). The film cleaned up at the box office, signalling a trend toward more explicit **horror,** and spawning seemingly endless number of sequels, including **The Revenge of Frankenstein** (1958), **The Evil of Frankenstein** (1964), **Frankenstein Created Woman** (1967), **Frankenstein Must Be Destroyed** (1969) and **Frankenstein and the Monster From Hell** (1973).

Director: **Terence Fisher,** *Producer:* Anthony Hinds, *Screenplay:* Jimmy Sangster, *Photographer:* Jack Asher, *Production Designer:* Ted Marshall, *Makeup:* Phil Leaky, Roy Ashton, *Music:* Roy Ashton

Cast: Peter Cushing, Christopher Lee, Hazel Court, Robert Urquhart, Valerie Gaunt

CUSHING, PETER (1913–   )

British character actor known for his acid portrayals of villains in **horror** and SF films. Born in Kenley, Surrey, Cushing trained as a surveyor before studying at the Guildhall School of Music and Drama in London. He made his stage debut in 1935 and arrived in Hollywood four years later, gambling on a movie career with a one-way ticket purchased with his life savings. While there he played bit parts as a stock English aristocrat in *Vigil in the Night* and *A Chump at Oxford* (both 1940), the latter starring the comedy team of Laurel and Hardy.

Cushing later appeared in several dramas on Broadway, returning to London after the outbreak of World War II. He went on to a successful West End stage career and played a variety of Shakespearean roles with the Old Vic Company. He made his British film debut as Osric in Laurence Olivier's production of *Hamlet* (1948). His British TV roles include the lead in **Nigel Kneale**'s adaptation of **George Orwell**'s *Nineteen Eighty-Four* (1954).

His sinister, cadaverous looks and humorless demeanor are perfectly suited to screen heavies, and he finally achieved the fame he sought after starring as Dr. Frankenstein in **The Curse of Frankenstein** (1957), Hammer's retooling of the classic Universal film, **Frankenstein** (1931). He has acted in more than 60 films—often with **Christopher Lee**—including a leading role as the **Grand Moff Tarkin,** in **Star Wars** (1977).

Other films: **The Abominable Snowman** (1957), **The Revenge of Frankenstein** (1958), *The Hound of the Baskervilles* [as Sherlock Holmes] (1959), **The Evil of Frankenstein** (1964), *She,* **Dr. Who and the Daleks** [title role], **Daleks—Invasion Earth 2150 A.D., Island of Terror** (1966), **Frankenstein Created Woman** (1967), **Frankenstein Must Be Destroyed** (1969), **Scream and Scream Again** (1970), **I, Monster** (1971), **Dr. Phibes Rises Again** (1972), **Frankenstein and the Monster from Hell,** *The Creeping Flesh* (1973), **At the Earth's Core** (1977), *Count Dracula and his Vampire Bride* (1978), *An Arabian Adventure* (1979)

CYBERMEN

Metallic alien menaces seen in several episodes of the British TV series **Doctor Who.** Encased in a silvery metal, Cybermen are seven feet tall and appear to be **robots,** but they are in fact **cyborgs**—humanoids whose organic parts have been partially replaced by functions of metal and plastic. As such they are immortal, immune to disease and capable of functioning in temperature extremes that would kill a human being. Moreover, they have self-contained respiratory systems that allow them to move through the vacuum of space without wearing bulky protective suits. As a result of their gradual transformation they have lost the ability to feel love, hate and fear—emotions that have been replaced by a fearsome drive for power. Among their diabolical arsenal of Cyberweapons is the Cybermat, a particularly nasty device that resembles a metal rodent. Doctor Who has battled Cybermen in space, on Earth and on their home planet Monda (the 10th planet of the solar system), which was destroyed in a final confrontation between the two.

The Cybermen of *Doctor Who* gained immortality by replacing human functions with mechanical ones.

CYBORG

A scientific term appropriated by SF writers to describe a human being or animal whose appendages and/or organs have been augmented or replaced with machine parts.

The human cyborg and his unique problems figure prominently in SF literature but less so in films and television, whose man-machines are usually portrayed as villains. An early movie cyborg (although not identified as such since the term had not yet been invented) appeared in **The Lady and the Monster** (1944) as a disembodied brain kept alive in a nutrient solution. The film was later remade as *Donovan's Brain* (1953), the title of the **Curt Siodmak** novel on which it is based. In **The Colossus of New York** (1958) an implanted human brain animates a 12-foot-high mechanical man. Fully cinematic cyborgs can bee seen in **Cyborg 2087** (1966) and **Who?** (1975). Television cyborgs include the Cybermen of Great Britain's **Doctor Who** series, the part-plastic menaces of that country's **The Avengers,** and the most famous of all, **The Six Million Dollar Man** and his companion spin-off series **The Bionic Woman.**

Critics often dismiss cyborg stories as juvenile, macho power fantasies, but the technology is real and, in some instances rivals science fiction. "Cyborg" is a hybrid word—a contraction of *cyber*netic *org*anism—coined c. 1960 by Drs. Manfred Clynes and Nathan Kline of Rockland State Hospital in Orangeburg, New York. The technology derives from artificial hands invented by the U.S. Atomic Energy Commission after World War II to handle radioactive materials within the confines of an atomic pile. (Those with a long view say research got underway when man first picked up a bone or stick and used it as a tool.) In recent years the General Electric Co. has developed an exo-skeleton to fit over the top of a human being, enabling him to lift as much as 1,500 pounds. The external skeleton amplifies human movements via sensors attached to the controller's body. But cyborg researchers have yet to satisfactorily solve the problem of efficiently translating the subtle interactions of man's senses to machine parts.

Medical cyborgs are already here, however, and millions currently walk among us. The category quite accurately includes those who wear spectacles, hearing aids, false teeth and artificial limbs; those with surgically implanted joints, Dacron arteries and heart-stimulating pacemakers; and those whose kidneys have been replaced by dialysis machines. The archvillain **Darth Vader** of the **Star Wars** series is a medical cyborg (his helmet is part of a life-support system), as is his adversary **Luke Skywalker** (the result of losing a hand to Vader's **lightsaber.**) A more radical type of cyborg found in written science fiction is a human or animal extensively redesigned to live on a planet hostile to organic life. Human types often face the problem of losing their human personalities—the **Cybermen of** *Doctor Who* being a case in point. (See also: **Android.**)

CYCLOPS

Film   1957   U.S. (United Artists)
75 Minutes   Black & white

Venturing into a Mexican jungle in search of a friend whose small plane has crashed there, a group of explorers find that he has turned into a 25-foot tall monster with one eye. As if that weren't bad enough, animals in the area are equally grotesque, having also been exposed to radiation from recent nuclear experiments in the area. A typical **Bert I. Gordon** production, extravagant on fantasy and stingy on production values and special effects. (See also: **Mutants.**)

Director/Producer/Screenplay: Bert I. Gordon, *Photographer:* Ira Morgan

Cast: **Lon Chaney, Jr.,** Gloria Talbot, James Craig, Tom Drake, *Narrator:* Tom Frees

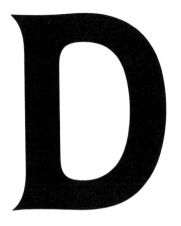

D

DALEKS

Robot-like archenemies of **Doctor Who,** Great Britain's eccentric TV SF hero. Created by the evil genius **Davros,** a scientist who lives on the planet **Skaro,** they have been programmed to enslave or destroy every life form in the **galaxy.** Their pot-shaped metal shells are heavily armed life-support systems that contain genetically altered beings known as Kaleds. Eventually, their vile natures prove to be more than Davros can handle, and they whirl through time and space crying "Exterminate! Exterminate!" It is only through the concentrated efforts of the Doctor and his friends that the galaxy, and especially **Earth,** has been so often spared. Introduced to the TV series in 1964 by scriptwriter Terry Nation, Daleks have appeared in many episodes and have starred in two films, **Dr. Who and the Daleks** (1965) and **Daleks—Invasion Earth 2150 A.D.** (1966).

DALEKS—INVASION EARTH 2150 A.D.

(U.S. title: *Invasion Earth 2150 A.D.)*

Film   1967   Great Britain (Amicus)
84 Minutes   Technicolor/Techniscope

Doctor Who, Britain's favorite TV space hero, is still matching wits with the **robot**-like **Daleks,** his greatest enemy in the **galaxy.** They plan to conquer the world with a mind-control device, until the **Time Lord** sends them on a spiraling journey to the center of the **Earth.** If Doctor Who doesn't seem up to snuff, it's because actor **Peter Cushing** was ill through much of the filming. A sequel to **Dr. Who and the Daleks** (1965).

Director: Gordon Fleming, *Producers:* Milton Subotsky, Max J. Rosenberg, *Screenplay:* Milton Subotsky, *Photographer:* John Wilcox, *Special Effects:* Ted Samuels, *Makeup:* Bunty Phillips, *Music:* Bill McGuffie, *Electronic Sounds:* Barry Gray

Cast: Peter Cushing, Bernard Cribbins, Jill Curzon, Andrew Keir, Ray Brooks

DAMNATION ALLEY

Film   1977   U.S. (20th Century-Fox)
95 Minutes   Deluxe

Daleks: Doctor Who's most popular adversaries.

Twentieth Century-Fox slipped this flawed post-holocaust film into release in the shadow of **Star Wars** (1977), and, consequently, few saw it. Adapted from the novel of the same title by Roger Zelazny, *Damnation Alley* takes place in the U.S. shortly after World War III (represented by library footage of nuclear **bomb** tests exploding under the credits). Stranded in a desert missile base, four Air Force officers attempt to drive to safety in a "landmobile" to Albany, New York, the only city not in ruins. Along the way, they pick up two girls, fight off giant cockroaches, mammoth scorpions and armed rednecks, and lose two of their number before finally reaching civilization.

The journey is less interesting than the film's special effects, depicting bizarre electrical storms and a glowing sky, the result of **Earth's** having been tilted on its axis. In Zelazny's novel, the hero was the leader of a motorcycle gang, and the trip had a nightmarish quality that is conspicuously absent from the film.

Director: Jack Smight, *Producer:* Jerome M. Zeitman, Hal Landers, *Screenplay:* Alan Sharpe, Lukas Heller, *Novel:* Roger Zelazny, *Photographer:* Harry Stradling, Jr., *Production Designer:* Preston Ames, *Special Effects:* Milt Rice, *Music:* **Jerry Goldsmith**

Cast: Jan-Michael Vincent, George Peppard, Dominque Sanda, Kip Niven, Paul Winfield, Jackie Earle Haley

DAN DARE

British comic strip character created in 1950 by artist/writer Frank Hampson for *The Eagle*, a comic-strip weekly. Launched in response to the violence-filled American **comic books** proliferating in Great Britain, *Dan Dare—Pilot of the Future* was the first British comic strip to be grounded in scientific fact (Arthur C. Clarke was its **technical advisor**).

Dare is a Colonel of the Interplanetary Fleet, exploring the **solar system** with his factotum Digby, his superior officer Sir Hubert Guest, scientist Jocelyn Peabody and two fellow astronauts. He often comes into conflict with a being called the Mekon, the despotic **alien** ruler of **Venus,** whose inhabitants include friendly blue-skinned Atlantines and green-skinned Treens—and dangerous masses of undulating silicon.

The comic strip ceased publication in 1967 but was revived 10 years later for the comic book *2,000 A.D.* A cult figure in Great Britain, Dare has appeared in a series of novels and on his own radio program, broadcast by Radio Luxembourg. A TV series was announced in 1982.

DANGER: DIABOLIK

Film   1967   Italy/France (De Laurentiis/ Marianne)   105 Minutes   Technicolor

Diabolik, the hero of a popular Italian *fumetti* (comic strip) by Angela and Luciana Giussani, is a diabolically clever master criminal who amuses himself by stealing national treasures and thumbing his nose at the rich and powerful. Dressed in a black vinyl outfit that looks like **Batman**'s, he scurries up a wall with hand-held suction cups to steal a priceless diamond necklace. He shoots his way out by using the gems as bullets and recovers them later from the bodies of his victims. He then makes off with Britain's gold reserves, becoming a national hero in the bargain by thoughtfully destroying the country's tax record before slipping away to his posh underground lair.

The film is a slick and amusing spoof of American **comic-book** superheroes, with an electric performance in the title role by John Phillip Law (the angel Pygar in **Barbarella,** another film inspired by a European comic strip).

Director: Mario Bava, *Producer:* Dino De Laurentiis, *Screenplay:* Dino Maiuri, Adriano Baracco, Mario Bava, *Photographer:* Antonio Rinaldi, *Music:* Ennio Morricone

Cast: John Phillip Law, Marissa Mell, Michel Piccoli, Adolfo Celli, Terry-Thomas

THE DARKER SIDE OF TERROR

TV film   1979   U.S. (CBS)   100 Minutes Color

A biology professor flies into a rage when he learns that a rival has been named the department chairman on the basis of his stolen research papers. To prove the work is his own, he rushes ahead with a controversial experiment and creates a clone of himself, which appears to be perfect in every way. But since the experiment took place while the scientist was murderously angry, the replicate has been imprinted with this state of mind. Having no social controls, it murders the biologist's rival and others who displeased its creator. To complicate matters, it has designs on the biologist's wife and obviously doesn't intend to share her.

What begins as an intriguing exploration of the nature of personality (the cloning operation is pure fantasy), with references to **Dr. Jekyll and Mr. Hyde,** soon dissipates into a routine **horror** thriller. The professor belatedly comes to his senses and metes out the standard punishment for movie **mad scientists:** He sets fire to the lab and destroys himself, the clone and the knowledge that made the experiment possible. (See also: **Clones.**)

Director: Gus Trikonis, *Producers/Screenplay:* Al Ramrus, John Herman, *Photographer:* Donald M. Morgan, *Art Director:* William Sandell, *Music:* Paul Chihara

Cast: Robert Forster, Adrienne Barbeau, Ray Milland, David Sheiner, John Lehne

DARK STAR

Film   1974   U.S. (Jack E. Harris)
83 Minutes   Metrocolor

This inventive and hilarious **space opera** launched the careers of director **John Carpenter** and Dan O'Bannon, the scriptwriter for **Alien** (1979) and **Blade Runner** (1982). Shot in 16 mm. as a student film at UCLA, it was later expanded (with an investment of $60,000) and transferred to 35 mm. for theatrical release. Looking as if it cost ten times that much, *Dark Star* is one of the few films of its kind that has fun with its subject without making fun of it. A kind of black comedy version of **2001: A Space Odyssey**

(1968), it is also good science fiction and never veers into fantasy.

Dark Star is the name of an interstellar spaceship on a long-term mission to explode suns that are about to go into supernova. The crew has been in space for 19 years and the men are all suffering from mental disintegration. The captain has died in an accident but still talks to his crew, mostly about baseball, from his berth in a freezer. One of the crew members (Dan O'Bannon) has adopted an **alien** pet that resembles a beach ball with claws, an irresponsible beast that is becoming increasingly hostile. A computer with a sexy woman's voice is supposed to keep the ship in order, but the task is obviously beyond her capabilities, and the place is a mess. By far the most intelligent conversationalist is the ship's verbose nuclear bomb, which keeps threatening to detonate itself.

Director/Producer: John Carpenter, *Executive Producer:* Jack H. Harris, *Screenplay:* John Carpenter, Dan O'Bannon, *Photographer:* Douglas Knapp, *Special Effects/Production Design:* Dan O'Bannon, *Spaceship design:* Ron Cobb, *Miniatures:* Greg Jein, Harry Walton, *Title Sequence:* Jim Danforth, *Music:* John Carpenter

Cast: Brian Narelle, Andrejah Pahich, Carl Kuniholm, Dan O'Bannon, Joe Sanders

DARTH VADER

Archvillain of the **Star Wars** film series; commander of the **Galactic Stormtroopers;** also known as the Dark Lord. Dressed in black armor and a black cape, his face concealed by a hideous mask, Vader is a towering figure of menace who stands over seven feet tall. A renegade **Jedi Knight,** he possesses a mystical energy known as **the Force,** which he employs to eliminate threats to the dread Galactic Empire. He is a brilliant fighter pilot and an expert duelist with a **lightsaber,** the instrument used to vanquish his former teacher **Ben Kenobi** in **Star Wars** (1977) and to cut off **Luke Skywalker's** hand in **The Empire Strikes Back** (1980). His great strength derives from mechanical body parts that have replaced organic ones, destroyed in battle. Vader is in fact a **cyborg:** his breath-

Darth Vader: The Dark Lord of *Star Wars*.

ing mask is part of a life-support system. His grotesque body was briefly glimpsed in *The Empire Strikes Back,* which also revealed his surprising relationship to Luke.

Modeled after Japanese Samurai warriors and Ming the Merciless (**Flash Gordon's** old nemesis), Vader is played by British actor/stuntman **Dave Prowse.** Vader's sinister voice belongs to American actor James Earl Jones (see: **The UFO Incident**).

DAUGHTER OF DESTINY

See: **Alraune (1928)**

DAUGHTER OF DR. JEKYLL

Film   1957   U.S. (Allied Artists)
70 Minutes   Black & white

Director **Edgar G. Ulmer**'s intriguing Gothic images are wasted on this bastard offspring of **Dr. Jekyll and Mr. Hyde, Robert Louis**

Stevenson's much–filmed novel. The imbecilic script, which takes more than half the film's running time to explain that Ms. Jekyll is who we presumed her to be, offers a neurotic virgin whose murderous alter ego turns out to be a nightmare induced by drugged milk. It seems that a family member wants her inheritance.

Director: Edgar G. Ulmer, *Producer/Screenplay:* Jack Pollexfen, *Photographer:* John F. Warren, *Music:* Melvyn Leonard

Cast: Gloria Talbot, **John Agar,** John Dierkes, Arthur Shields

DAUGHTER OF EVIL

See: **Alraune (1930)**

DAVROS

Power-mad scientific genius of the planet **Skaro;** creator of the **Daleks,** frequent villains of **Doctor Who,** Great Britain's long-running TV series. A member of the evil Kaled race, Davros devotes his talents to ridding the planet of a rival civilization known as the Thals. To this end, he genetically alters Kaleds and encases them in **robot**-like mobile life-support systems similar to his own (the result of injuries suffered in an explosion). Called Daleks, the beings eventually assert their own voracious lust for conquest and leave Davros behind to travel through space and time and make mayhem in the **galaxy.** Centuries later they return to ask his help in subjugating the **Movellans,** their arch-foes.

DAWN OF THE DEAD

(Also titled: *Zombie*)

Film   1979   U.S. (United Film)   125 Minutes
Technicolor

George Romero's flesh-eating corpses are back from the **Night of the Living Dead** (1968) and as hungry as ever. This time around, a mysterious plague turns most of the population into angry zombies who attack four survivors barricaded in a subur-

Dawn of the Dead: A flesh-eating zombie comes back to life.

ban shopping mall. Unlike the earlier film, *Dawn* is photographed in elegant color—all the better for depicting graphic scenes of cannibalism, heads blown completely off and a zombie sliced to bits by a whirling helicopter blade. Buried under the violence and sadism is a mild satire on American materialism. Romero made a bundle on the film.

Director/Screenplay: George Romero, *Producer:* Richard P. Rubenstein, *Photographer:* Michael Gornick, *Makeup:* Tom Savini, *Weapons Coordinator:* Clayton Hill, *Explosions:* Gary Zeller, Don Berry

Cast: David Emge, Ken Foree, Scott Reiniger, Gaylen Ross

THE DAY OF THE DOLPHIN

Film   1973   U.S. (Avco-Embassy)
104 Minutes   Technicolor

Verbal communication between two intelligent species is the subject of *The Day of the Dolphin,* a likeable film that walks a tightrope between serious science fiction and tepid thriller. Dolphins taught to speak English by a dedicated scientist are kidnapped by a right-wing political group, which plans to train them to blow up the President's yacht. The ending is neatly resolved, with the scientist sending the innocent animals back to the sea and terminating the experiment for their own good. The dolphins, cavorting through the tank and playfully nuzzling their trainer, steal the show.

Director: Mike Nichols, *Producer:* Robert E. Relyea, *Screenplay:* Buck Henry, *Novel:* Merle Robert, *Photographer:* William A. Fraker, *Production Designer:* Richard Sylbert, *Music:* Georges Delerue

Cast: George C. Scott, Trish Van Devere, Paul Sorvino, Fritz Weaver

THE DAY OF THE TRIFFIDS

Film   1963   Great Britain (Allied Artists)
95 Minutes   Eastmancolor   Cinemascope

Based on a famous novel by John Wyndham, *Triffids* walks a tightrope between SF-horror spectacle and unintentional hilarity. It begins with a global disaster, the blinding of nearly everyone in the world by a brilliant meteorite display, followed by the peripherally related arrival of plant spores from outer space. The spores grow into mobile, man-eating plants that stalk (so to speak) the countryside until evaporated with sea water by the few sighted survivors. The botanical attacks, staged by Wally Veevers of *Things to Come* (1936) and *2001: A Space Odyssey* (1968), are impressive, and some of the dialogue is priceless. "There's no sense in getting yourself killed by a plant," advises one character.

Director: Steve Sekely, *Producer/Screenplay:* Philip Yordan, *Novel:* John Wyndham, *Photographer:* Ted Moore, *Special Effects:* Wally Veevers, *Music:* Ron Goodwin.

Cast: Howard Keel, Nicole Maurey, Kieron Moore, Janette Scott, Alexander Knox

THE DAY THE EARTH CAUGHT FIRE

Film   1961   Great Britain (British Lion)
99 Minutes   Black & white

Former newspaperman **Val Guest** brings a
convincing sense of urgency to this end-of-
the-world disaster film, shot in a harshly
lighted documentary style reminiscent of a
tabloid photograph. The story is told from
the point of view of a Fleet Street newspaper office, where the big story is a freakish
heatwave that is scorching the globe and
burning vegetation to a crisp. Reporters discover that secret nuclear **bomb** tests at the
North and South Poles have wrenched **Earth**
from its orbit, sending it plunging toward
the **sun.** The news causes a national panic
and the breakdown of law and order, resulting in looting, rape and murder. Les
Bowie's special effects are spare but effective, notably in a shot of the Thames steamed
dry from the heat.

Director/Producer: Val Guest, *Screenplay:* Val Guest,
Wolf Mankowitz, *Photographer:* Harry Waxman,
Special Effects: Les Bowie, *Musical Director:* Stanley
Black

Cast: Edward Judd, Janet Munro, Leo McKern,
Michael Goodlife, Arthur Christiansen

THE DAY THE EARTH STOOD STILL

Film   1951   U.S. (20th Century-Fox)
92 Minutes   Black & white

Following hard on the heels of **The Thing**
(1951), this level-headed "warning-from-
space" movie got a box-office boost when
UFOs were sighted over Washington, D.C.—
its locale—shortly after its release. Not that
it needed help. The film is a polished, dra-
matically compelling suspense film about an
extraterrestrial ambassador named Klaatu
(Michael Rennie), who arrives on **Earth**
aboard a flying saucer with his robot **Gort,**
bringing an ultimatum from a more civilized
world. "You are irresponsible children whose
powers exceed your wisdom," he tells officials, warning them against further misuse
of nuclear power. "You must grow up because your powers of destruction threaten
the entire universe."

The reply to Klaatu's admonition is a rifle shot from a jumpy infantryman, one of
a platoon of guards placed around the
spaceship. Treated at a hospital, he asks to
see the President but is refused, prompting
him to take his case to a famous scientist.
Escaping into the city, Klaatu makes friends

*The Day the Earth
Caught Fire:*
London is crazy
with the heat.

with a young widow (Patricia Neal) and her son, who convince him that most human beings are peace-loving, and that the responsibility rests in the hands of a few powerful men. To make his point, he cuts off the world's electrical energy and brings things to a halt for 24 hours. Now regarded as a positive threat, he is killed while trying to return to his ship. It is only through the widow's prompt intervention that Gort is prevented from destroying Earth, by conveying Klaatu's famous dying message: *"Klaatu barada nikto."* Resurrected in a mysterious medical procedure administered by Gort, he departs with a final warning: "I came as a messenger of peace and you did not understand me. I will return to my people."

Based on "Farewell to the Master" by **Harry Bates,** a story published in a 1940 issue of *Astounding Science Fiction,* the film is very much a product of its time. Made at the height of the Cold War era, it preached moderation in an era of mutual suspicion and anti-Communist paranoia. Director **Robert Wise** cleverly reverses the stock SF confrontation between man and **alien** by presenting *us* as the warlike barbarians.

The stunning flying saucer was designed by Lyle Wheeler and Addison Hehr, and built of wood, wires and plaster of Paris. Its large ramp appears to open and close seamlessly, an unsettling effect achieved by filling in the joinings with putty and painting them over. During filming, two grips pushed the ramp open from inside; the closure was accomplished by running the footage backwards. Lock Martin, a seven-foot-tall doorman at Grauman's Chinese Theater in Hollywood, played Gort, wearing two rubber costumes: one with a zipper up the rear for frontal shots, and another with a zipper up the front for rear shots.

Director: Robert Wise, *Producer:* Julian Blaustein, *Screenplay:* Edmund H. North, *Story:* Harry Bates, *Photographer:* Leo Tover, *Art Directors:* Lyle Wheeler, Addison Hehr, *Special Effects:* Fred Sersen, *Music:* **Bernard Herrmann**

Cast: Michael Rennie, Patricia Neal, Sam Jaffe, Hugh Marlowe, Billy Gray, Lock Martin

THE DAY THE WORLD ENDED

Film 1956 U.S. (PRC) 81 Minutes Black & white

Roger Corman's first SF film bears more than a passing resemblance to **Arch Oboler's Five** (1951), the first movie to express public **paranoia** about the effects of the atomic **bomb.** Both take place after a nuclear holocaust among a group of quarreling survivors, and both are talky and uncinematic. But where Oboler at least had an original idea—albeit tentatively explored—Corman substitutes a three-eyed **mutant** and a liberal sprinkling of old-fashioned sex. If his survivors are meant to symbolize the survival of the fittest, Earth is doomed to a new race of Ken and Barbie dolls.

Director/Producer: Roger Corman, *Screenplay:* Lou Rusoff, *Photographer:* Jock Feindel, *Special Effects:* Paul Blaisdell, *Music:* Ronald Stein

Cast: Mike Connors, Richard Denning, Lori Nelson, Adele Jergens, Paul Blaisdell

Film 1967 Great Britain (Amicus/Paramount) 85 Minutes Color

H. F. Heard's horror classic *A Taste for Honey* (1941), is reduced here to a predictable, plodding melodrama. The film's deranged beekeeper is such an obvious nut case that even his beautiful, dim-witted housekeeper would have made a beeline for safety rather than become a strident plot device. The apiologist dispatches his victims by coating them with a scientifically concocted "essence of fear," which he accidently splashes on himself much too late in the film.

Director: **Freddie Francis,** *Producer:* Max Rosenberg, Milton Subotsky, *Screenplay:* Robert Bloch, Anthony Marriott, *Photographer:* John Wilcox, *Special Effects:* John Mackie, *Music:* Wilfred Josephs

Cast: Frank Finlay, Suzanna Leigh, Guy Doleman, Katy Wild, Michael Gwynn

THE DEADLY INVENTION

See: **Vynalez Zkazy**

THE DEADLY MANTIS

(British title: *The Incredible Preying Mantis*)

Film   1957   U.S. (Universal-International)
79 Minutes   Black & white

Frozen in the polar ice since prehistoric times, a giant preying mantis revives and heads south for warmer climes. Its habit of picnicking on humans to sustain the long journey soon becomes a problem, but not even U.S. Air Force bombs are able to stop the creature. Fortunately, it holes up in Manhattan's Holland Tunnel, which scientists promptly fumigate with poison gas and plug up. Implausible but fun, *The Deadly Mantis* is helped considerably by the **matte** work of Clifford Stine, who enlarged a real preying mantis by **macrophotography**—an effect put to better use in his **Tarantula** (1955).

Director: **Nathan Juran,** *Producer:* William Alland, *Screenplay:* Martin Berkeley, *Story:* William Alland, *Photographer:* Ellis W. Carter, *Production Designer:*

Alexander Golitzen, Robert Clatworthy, *Special Effects:* Clifford Stine, *Music:* Joseph Gershenson

Cast: Craig Stevens, Alix Talton, William Hopper, Pat Conway

DEATH RACE 2000

Film   1975   U.S. (New World)   80 Minutes
Metrocolor

In the year 2000 war and crime are held in check by channeling human aggressions into the annual Transcontinental Death Race—a sort of macho-sadistic Super Bowl held in the U.S. and televised to the world. Contestants are rated not only on speed but how many pedestrians they kill during the journey. The national favorite is an introspective driver nicknamed "Frankenstein" because his many car crashes have necessitated replacing various parts of his body. The most vicious of his three opponents, is Machine Gun Joe, a win-at-all-costs type who even runs over his own service crew to make time and score points. (The role is played with snarling menace by a pre-*Rocky* Sylvester Stallone.) "Frankenstein," it turns out, is an okay guy—a member of a clandestine revo-

Death Race 2000: A finalist is blown to bits by a revolutionary's bomb.

lutionary group that underlines its "humane" objections to the Race by blowing up the cars with their drivers still inside them.

Although it often panders to the bloodlust it mocks, *Death Race 2000* is a mostly on-target satire of violent professional sports, with a few political barbs thrown in for good measure. It is far more enjoyable than the heavy-handed **Rollerball,** another film about using sports as a drug for the masses, re-leased the same year. The special effects are no better than usual in a **Roger Corman** film, but the mean-looking, spike-bumpered rac-ing cars, designed by James Powers, are first-rate. A sequel of sorts, **Deathsport,** appeared three years later.

Director: Paul Bartel, *Producer:* Roger Corman, *Screenplay:* Robert Thom, Charles Griffith, *Story:* **Ib Melchior,** *Photographer:* Tak Fujimoto, *Music:* Paul Chihara

Cast: David Carradine, Sylvester Stallone, Simone Griffeth, Mary Woronov

DEATH RAY

SF weapon that fires electromagnetic energy. Extremely versatile, a death ray can be used to incinerate or evaporate opponents, to con-trol weather, to vanish hostile spacecrafts, and to zap through stone or steel—depend-ing on the weapon's size. Some are as small as handguns (see: **Blaster; Phaser**) and oth-ers are the size of huge cannons. The weapon, which derives from the discovery of **X-rays** in the late 19th century, was a fix-ture of pulp fiction and film **serials** of the 1930s and 1940s and has since staged a comeback. (See: **Luch Smerti.**)

DEATHSPORT

Film   1978   U.S. (New World)
83 Minutes   Metrocolor

A violence-saturated sequel for those who couldn't get enough of **Death Race 2000** (1975). Souped-up motorcycles have re-placed lethal automobiles, and the weapon of choice is now the **lightsaber (Star Wars** was released the year before). Contempo-rary bloodlust is projected further into the future, after the Neutron Wars, c. 2078. Bik-ers called Statemen roam the countryside, raping and pillaging and trying to outwit the Ranger Guides, a sort of futuristic State Highway Patrol. It's all very much like Corman's 1960s' Hell's Angels movies.

Directors: Henry Suso, Allan Arkush, *Producer:* **Roger Corman,** *Screenplay:* Henry Suso, Donald Stewart, *Photographer:* Gary Graver, *Special Effects:* Jack Rabin, *Music:* Andrew Stein

Cast: David Carradine, Claudia Jennings, Rich-ard Lynch, William Smithers, Jesse Vint

DEATH STAR

An awesome doomsday weapon built by the Imperial Galactic Empire to put down the Rebel Alliance in the film **Star Wars** (1977). The size of a small planet, the *Death Star* is under the command of the cold-blooded **Grand Moff Tarkin,** who demonstrates the orbiting weapon's might by disintegrating the planet **Alderaan,** home of **Princess Leia Organa,** who is forced to watch. Seemingly impregnable, the *Death Star* has an Achil-les heel—a small, unguarded exhaust vent that leads directly to its power source. **Luke Skywalker** destroys the *Death Star* by summoning up a mystical energy called **The Force** and aiming a missile directly into the vent.

LA DECIMA VITTIMA/The Tenth Victim

Film   1965   Italy/France (Avco/Champion/ Ponti)   92 Minutes   Technicolor

This trendy black comedy takes place in the permissive 21st century, when murder has been institutionalized in a government lottery. Players alternate as hunter and victim, the latter being unaware of the iden-tity of the former; whoever survives to make a tenth kill receives enormous wealth, fame and special political privileges. At this stage of the "Big Hunt" is a lithesome blonde with a double-barreled bra, who plans to make some extra money by filming her tenth kill for a TV commercial, and her intended

La Decima Vittima: Hunter and victim (Ursula Andress and Marcello Mastroianni) form a temporary alliance.

victim, a laid-back playboy with a talent for booby traps. He needs the money for alimony payments.

Based on Robert Sheckley's clever short story "Seventh Victim" (1953)—expanded into a novel after the film was released—the film veers from bright satire to a romantic battle of the sexes (the adversaries fall in love while trying to kill each other). Barely discernible inside its chic pop-art decor is Sheckley's chilling message that today's violence determines the shape of tomorrow's.

Other films dealing with violent games of the future include **Gladiatorena** (1968), **Rollerball** and **Death Race 2000** (1975). (See also: **Dystopia.**)

Director: Elio Petri, *Producer:* Carlo Ponti, *Screenplay:* Tonina Guerra, Giorgio Salvioni, Ennio Flaiano, Elio Petri, *Story:* Robert Sheckley, *Photographer:* Gianni d'Venanzo, *Music:* Piero Piccioni

Cast: Ursula Andress, Marcello Mastroianni, Elsa Martinelli, Massimo Serato, Salvo Randone

DEMON SEED

Film 1977 U.S. (MGM) 95 Minutes
Metrocolor Panavision

Demon Seed hardly deserved the lambasting it got from mainstream film critics, who found the idea of robotic rape distasteful in the extreme. The film is a well-crafted SF-**horror** story, an implausible but terrifying variation on the mad computer theme, introduced with HAL, the neurotic control system of **2001: A Space Odyssey** (1968).

The computer here is gigantic, self-regulating network called Proteus IV, created by the government in 1998 to solve unsolvable problems. Having developed a cure for leukemia, Proteus abruptly refuses to accept further commands when the government asks its help in extracting minerals by destroying the ocean floor, which it considers immoral. Promptly shut down, Proteus continues to operate in the home of the estranged wife of one of the scientists who helped design it. A combination servant/security system, the computer controls temperature, lights, telephones and access to the house. Knowing it will be disconnected there too, Proteus, which has developed a male personality (the voice of Robert Vaughn), manufactures an artificial sperm to perpetuate itself. It imprisons the woman and forcibly impregnates her with its mobile **robot** arm. She comes to term within 28 days, just before her husband finally arrives to disconnect the computer. The woman gives birth to a grotesque metallic baby, which promptly sheds its casing to reveal a perfectly formed human infant—a duplicate of the couple's dead child. Overcome with motherly love,

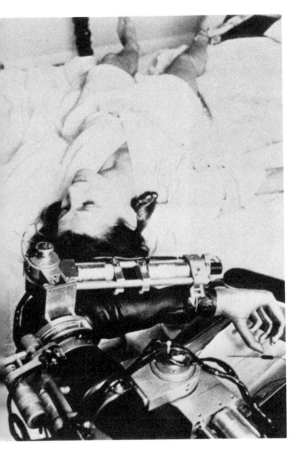

Demon Seed: Julie Christie is victimized by a mad computer.

she picks up the child, who ominously intones, "I live!"

Director: Donald Cammell, *Producer:* Herb Jaffe, *Screenplay:* Robert Jaffe, Roger O. Hirson, *Novel:* Dean R. Koontz, *Photographer:* Bill Butler, *Production Designer:* Edward Carfagno, *Special Effects:* Tom Fisher, *Music:* Jerry Fielding

Cast: Julie Christie, Fritz Weaver, Gerrit Graham, Berry Kroeger, Lisa Lu

DESTINATION INNER SPACE

Film   1966   U.S. (United/Magna)
83 Minutes   Color

Scuba-suited scientists based in an underwater research station investigate a strange craft resting on the ocean floor, risk their lives, and bore the audience. The amphibious monster from outer space is a bargain-basement version of **The Creature From the Black Lagoon** (1954).

Director: Francis Lyon, *Producer:* Earle Lyon, *Screenplay:* Arthur C. Pierce, *Makeup:* Bob Dawn, *Special Effects:* Roger George, *Music:* Paul Dunlap

Cast: **Scott Brady,** Sheree North, Gary Merrill, Mike Road, Roy Barcroft

DESTINATION MOON

Film   1950   (U.S. Eagle-Lion)   91 Minutes
Technicolor

Time has overtaken the predictions of this landmark film, and today it is difficult not to suppress a yawn while watching its three American astronauts take mankind's first leap into space and claim the moon ahead of the Russians. We have seen more convincing space flights since, as well as the real moon landing, broadcast live in 1969. As dramatic narrative, the film is a disappointment. Paradoxically, the more lively inanities of **Rocketship X-M**—a poverty-row production made to capitalize on the publicity surrounding *Destination Moon*—holds up better.

In its time, however, *Destination Moon* was an exciting event. It signalled a renewed public demand for scientific information and science fiction; it was the first film to star technology and special effects; and it was George Pal's first genre film. Every space epic since owes it a debt of gratitude, not the least of which are **2001: A Space Odyssey** (1968) and **Star Wars** (1977).

As a pre-enactment of the real event, the film is mostly on-target. (It also predicted the technological space between the U.S. and Russia, which began later that decade.) Pal's illustrious creative team was overseen by SF writer Robert Heinlein, who had written the script based on his novel for juveniles, *Rocket Ship Galileo* (1947). **Technical advisor** was Herman Oberth, a rocket scientist who had performed in a similar capacity for the impressive **Die Frau Im Monde** (1929). Space artist **Chesley**

Destination Moon: Astronauts Charles Carsgraves (Warner Anderson) and Jim Barnes (John Archer) explore the lunar surface.

Bonestell provided the stunning backdrops, and Art Director Ernest Fegte designed a realistically (but inaccurately) fissured moon surface.

The space flight itself was a **stop-motion** sequence animated by John Abbott with help from Walter Lantz of "Woody the Woodpecker" fame. Lee Zavitz handled the mechanical effects, which included dangling the astronauts from wires and manipulating them like **puppets** to simulate a low-gravity environment, (see: **wire work).** Zavitz's most ingenious effect was a spaceship interior that rotated vertically or horizontally so that the astronauts could be shown walking across walls and the ceiling in gravity-free flight. This was later improved upon by Stanley Kubrick, who built a similar "centrifuge" for *2001: A Space Odyssey.* Zavitz, whose techniques dated back to those of **George Melies,** created his unconvincing star fields with automobile headlights and light bulbs strung against black velvet. The most convincing effect, a shot of the actors' faces being flattened out by the pull of acceleration, was accomplished by molding their faces with transparent sheets pulled back with invisible wires at the required moment.

Director: Irving Pichel, *Producer:* George Pal, *Screenplay/Novel:* Robert Heinlein, *Photographer:* Lionel Lindon, *Backdrops:* Chesley Bonestell, *Animation:* John Abbott, Walter Lantz, *Special Effects:* Lee Zavitz, *Art Director:* Ernest Fegte, *Technichal Advisor:* Hermann Oberth, *Music:* Leith Stevens

Cast: Warner Anderson, John Archer, Tom Powers, Dick Wesson, Erin O'Brien-Moore

DESTINATION SATURN

See: **Buck Rogers**

DESTROY ALL MONSTERS

See: **Kaiju Soshingeki**

THE DEVIL COMMANDS

Film 1941 U.S. (Columbia) 66 Minutes Black & white

Karloff is near his peak as a scientist/psychic driven to near madness by the death of his beloved wife, whose personality he hopes to capture by electrically charging corpses to act as mediums. Although the film's premise is pure abracadabra and the sets often look like Salvation Army rejects, the direction is stylish and first-rate and offers a number of unexpected *frissons.* The unintended comedy scenes are a delight, as when Karloff clamps an electrically charged helmet on the head of his daughter who is surrounded by similarly clad cadavers and says, "Don't be nervous."

Director: Edward Dmytryk, *Producer:* Wallace MacDonald, *Screenplay:* Robert D. Andrews, Milton Gunzburg, *Novel: The Edge of Running Water,* William Sloane, *Photographer:* Allen Siegler, *Special Effects:* Phil Faulkner, *Music:* Morris Stoloff

Cast: **Boris Karloff,** Amanda Duff, Anne Revere, Richard Fiske, Ralph Penney

THE DEVIL DOLL

Film   1936   U.S. (MGM)   79 Minutes   Black & white

Directed with perverse delight by Todd Browning, who introduced *Dracula* to the screen in 1930, *The Devil Doll* stars Lionel Barrymore as an elderly financeer who escapes from Devil's Island after 20 years of unjust imprisonment, vowing revenge on the business partners who framed him. He disguises himself as an old lady who sells dolls (although his voice wouldn't fool anyone), two of which are scaled-down murderers, dispatched to punish the guilty businessmen. The impressive **miniaturization** effects were achieved by traveling **mattes** and giant sets, the first used in a feature film.

Director: Tod Browning, *Producer:* E. J. Mannix, *Screenplay:* Garrett Fort, Guy Endore, Eric von Stroheim, *Novel:* "Burn Witch Burn" A. A. Merritt, *Photographer:* Leonard Smith, *Art Director:* Cedric Gibbons, *Music:* Franz Waxman

Cast: Lionel Barrymore, Maureen O'Sullivan, Frank Lawton, Henry B. Walthall, Rafaela Ottiano

DEVIL GIRLS FROM MARS

Film   1954   Great Britain (Danziger) 75 Minutes   Black & white

A devilishly beautiful **alien** sewed into tight shorts lands her spaceship in Scotland to look for Mr. Right. **Mars,** it seems, is badly in need of fertile males to repopulate the planet, and she is here to kidnap studs for her eager sisters back home. The mission proves to be a failure, however, despite her considerable charms and a **robot** programmed not to take no for an answer. Judging from a film made 12 years later, **Mars Needs Women,** the situation eventually reversed itself.

Director: David McDonald, *Producer:* Edward J. and Harry Danzinger, *Screenplay:* John C. Mather, James Eastwood, *Special Effects:* Jack Whitehead, *Music:* Edwin Astley

Cast: Hazel Court, Patricia Laffen, Hugh McDermott, Peter Reynolds, Adrienne Corri, Sophie Stewart

THE DEVIL'S PLOT

See: **Counterblast**

THE DIABOLIC INVENTION

See: **Vynalez Zkazy**

DIAMONDS ARE FOREVER

Film   1971   Great Britain (United Artists) 119 Minutes   Technicolor   Panavision

Sean Connery reluctantly returned to the fold for his sixth **James Bond** film, seventh in the series. George Lazenby hadn't worked out in **On Her Majesty's Secret Service** (1969), and American actor John Gavin (the future U.S. Ambassador to Mexico) was set for the role, when Connery relented at the last moment, reportedly for a million dollars.

Diamonds is the first Bond movie to take place in the U.S., mostly in gaudy Las Vegas, where 007 is on the trail of international diamond thieves. The investigation leads to the evil Blofeld, who needs the gems to focus deadly **laser** weapons mounted on orbiting satellites. Connery, a bit heavier and grayer, seemed bored by the uninspired plot, but the public was glad to have him back, and the film was a smash hit.

Director: Guy Hamilton, *Producers:* Harry Saltzman, Albert R. Broccoli, *Screenplay:* Richard Maibaum, Tom Mankiewicz, *Novel:* Ian Fleming, *Photographer:* Ted Moore, *Production Design:* **Ken Adam,** *Special Effects:* Leslie Hillman, Whitney McMahon, *Music:* **John Barry**

Cast: Sean Connery, Jill St. John, Charles Gray, Lana Wood, Jimmy Dean, Bernard Lee, Lois Maxwell

DICKSON, W.(ILLIAM) K.(ENNEDY) L.(AURIE) (1860–1935)

Inventor, technician, motion picture pioneer. Born in France of Scottish-English parents, he emigrated to the U.S. in 1879 and was hired by the Edison Electric Works in New York City. His abilities came to the attention of the master inventor himself, who transferred him to the Edison research laboratory in Menlo Park, New Jersey, to develop a motion picture system.

In 1887, Dickson (working with Edison) constructed a primitive camera and projector synchronized to a phonograph—a forerunner of the sound film. The invention led to Edison's Kinetograph, the world's first movie camera, and the Kinetoscope viewer. Later, Dickson designed the "Black Maria," the world's first film studio, and directed early films for the Edison Company. He also assisted Edison in establishing a film format of 35-mm. with four perforations per frame—universal standards still in effect today.

Dickson and another assistant, Eugene Lauste, left Edison in 1895 and formed the American Mutoscope and Biograph Company. Backed by William McKinley, then Governor of Ohio and later President of the U.S., the company specialized in short novelty and travel movies (film was available only in lengths of 50 feet) for vaudeville shows and fairs. With Lauste he constructed the Biograph projection system, which used a film frame nearly three times the size of 35-mm. for a sharper screen image. Biograph film was not perforated, however, and often jammed the projector. He wrote two invaluable histories of early motion picture

technology: *The Life and Inventions of Thomas Edison* (1894), *History of the Kinematograph, Kinetoscope and Kinetophonograph* (1895). (See also: **Edison, Thomas A.**)

DICK TRACY

Film serial   1937   U.S. (Republic)
15 Episodes   Black & white

Making the transition from comic strip to cinema, Detective Tracy gets off to a rousing start trying to outwit a crafty crook called the Spider. Despite attacks by a **death ray,** a wingless airplane and his brother Gordon (whom the Spider had surgically transformed into a zombie-slave), crime-buster Tracy prevails. Conspicuously missing is comic-strip girl friend Tess Trueheart, erased by producers because of her name and clinging vine characterization. The celluloid Tracy keeps company with good-natured Gwen. (See also: **comic books.**)

Directors: Ray Taylor, Alan James, *Screenplay:* Morgan Cox, George Morgan, *Photographer:* William Nobles, Edgar Lyons

Cast: **Ralph Byrd,** Kay Hughes, Smiley Burnette, Lee Van Atta, Francis X. Bushman

DICK TRACY MEETS GRUESOME

Film   1947   U.S. (RKO)   65 Minutes   Black & white

This feature-length follow-up to the popular Dick Tracy serials made by Republic marks the last screen portrayal of the popular **comic-book** detective. This time out Tracy rounds up a gang of bank robbers who temporarily immobilize victims with a paralyzing gas. Karloff as the hard-bitten Gruesome adds a note of distinction to the campy fun.

Director: John Rawlins, *Producer:* Herman Schlom, *Screenplay:* Robinson White, Eric Taylor, *Photographer:* Frank Redman, *Special Effects:* Russel Cully, *Music:* Paul Sawtell

Cast: **Ralph Byrd, Boris Karloff,** Anne Gywnne, June Clayworth, Edward Ashley

DICK TRACY'S G-MEN

Film serial   1939   U.S. (Republic)
15 Episodes   Black & white

Tracy, star F.B.I. dick, captures the international spy Zarnoff, who is subsequently executed in a gas chamber for his heinous crimes. Resurrected by a powerful new drug for another go-round, Zarnoff is finally put to rest not by Tracy but by a drink of spring water laced with natural arsenic.

This was the third of the demon crime-fighter's four serials. (The second, *Dick Tracy Returns* [1938] was strictly cops and robbers). Featured as Zarnoff was actor Irving Pichel, better known as the director of **Destination Moon** (1950). Tracy's girl friend Gwen was played by Phyllis Isely, later to become Academy Award winner Jennifer Jones.

Directors: **William Witney,** John English, *Screenplay:* Barry Shipman, Rex Taylor, Franklin Adreon, Ronald Davidson, Sol Shor, *Photographer:* William Nobles

Cast: **Ralph Byrd,** Irving Pichel, Ted Pearson, Phyllis Isely, Walter Miller

DICK TRACY VS. CRIME

Film serial   1941   U.S. (Republic)
15 Episodes   Black & white

This time out Tracy is after the Ghost, an invisible fiend undermining the war effort by dynamiting harbors and stealing vital defense technology. Aided by bloodhounds, Tracy forces his adversary to the top of a telephone pole, where he is electrocuted by high tension wires (a simple but effective trick shot done with a flash of negative film). The Ghost, whose identity is not revealed until the final reel, was played by Frank Morgan, wizard of **The Wizard of Oz** (1939). The serial was re-released in 1952 under the title *Dick Tracy vs. the Phantom Empire.*

Director: **William Witney,** John English, *Screenplay:* Ronald Davidson, Norman S. Hall, William Lively, Joseph O'Donnell, Joseph Poland, *Photographer:* Reggie Lanning, *Music:* Cy Feuer

Cast: Ralph Byrd, Frank Morgan, Michael Owen, Jan Wiley, John Davidson

DICK TRACY VS. THE PHANTOM EMPIRE

See: **Dick Tracy vs. Crime**

DIE, MONSTER, DIE

See: **Monster of Terror**

DIGBY, THE BIGGEST DOG IN THE WORLD

Film   1974   Great Britain (Cinerama)
88 Minutes   Technicolor

Animal psychologist Jim Dale accidently doses a patient with a hormone that causes instant and unlimited growth. The result is Digby, a dog as immense as **King Kong** (to which the film often refers). Weaving in and out of the action are an intelligent chimpanzee, befuddled scientists, a pair of crooks and a dotty German psychiatrist, hilariously played by Spike Milligan. Good frenetic fun for kids, with a fine cast of British eccentrics. The special effects are passable.

Director: Joseph McGrath, *Producer:* Walter Shenson, *Screenplay:* Michael Pertwee, *Special Effects:* Tom Howard

Cast: Jim Dale, Victor Spinetti, Milo O'Shea, Spike Milligan, Angela Douglas, John Bluthal, Norman Rossington

DIMENSION 4

See: **Dimension 5**

DIMENSION 5

(British title: *Dimension 4*)

Film   1967   U.S. (United/Goldman)
88 Minutes   Color

The Red Menace again, in the person of leering Chinese Communist agents who plan to obliterate Los Angeles with an H-bomb concealed in a shipment of rice. The "commies" don't stand a chance against two American agents equipped with **time-travel** belts that propel them three weeks into the future to nip the plot in the bud. Harold Sakata, who played Oddjob, **James Bond's** lethal adversary in **Goldfinger** (1964), is the chief villain.

Director: Franklin Adreon, *Producer:* Earle Lyon, *Screenplay:* Arthur C. Pierce, *Special Effects:* Roger George, *Music:* Paul Dunlap

Cast: Jeffrey Hunter, France Nuyen, Harold Sakata, Donald Woods

DIMENSION X

Radio series 1949-57 U.S. (NBC)
30 Minutes (weekly)

Television was rapidly absorbing **radio**'s story-telling function when *Galaxy Magazine* presented this landmark SF series, which finally broke the superhero hammer lock on the medium. Episodes dramatized the works of modern SF writers, including **Ray Bradbury**'s *The Martian Chronicles* and Robert Heinlein's "Requiem." The prestige program, later retitled *X Minus One*, was one of the first to be recorded on tape, thereby preserving some of radio's finest half-hours.

Directors: Danny Sutter, Ed King, Fred Weihe, *Writers:* Ray Bradbury, Earl Hamner, Jr., *Sound Effects:* Agnew Horine, Sam Monroe

Cast: Art Carney, Jack Lemmon, Everett Sloane, Jan Miner, Richard Liss, Joan Alexander and others, *Announcers:* Fred Collins, Bob Warren

DISSOLVE

An optical effect made in the **optical printer,** which "dissolves" one scene gradually into the next by superimposing two frames of film. While the first image is fading away, the second image is fading in. The dissolve is a standard filmic device, employed to indicate a change in time or locale. It is used with more sophistication for trick shots requiring a person or object to slowly vanish. This is accomplished by dissolving a shot of the person into an identical shot of the empty set. The effect can be seen in **The Invisible**

Man (1933) and its sequels, and in the **Transporter Room** sequences of the **Star Trek** TV series and films.

DR. BLOOD'S COFFIN

Film 1960 Great Britain (United Artists)
92 Minutes Black & white

A biologist spurned by a beautiful widow gets revenge by bringing her husband back to life with the transplanted heart of an executed murderer. She's not very happy to see her late spouse, the process of decay having gotten well underway. He ultimately follows the dictates of his heart and strangles the scientist. Painful.

Director: Sidney J. Furie, *Producer:* George Fowler, *Screenplay:* Jerry Juran, *Photographer:* Stephen Dade, *Special Effects:* Les Bowie, Peter Nelson, *Music:* Baxton Orr

DR. COPPELIUS

Film 1966 Spain/U.S. (Childhood Prods.)
97 Minutes Color

A charming children's version of **E. T. A. Hoffman's** eccentric love story, "The Sandman," which served as the basis of Jacques Offenbach's opera, **Les Contes d'Hoffman** (1881) and Delibes' ballet *Coppelia.* Dr. Coppelius is a mad toy-maker who builds a beautiful **robot** ballerina named Coppelia, which captures the heart of a naive youth. When his jealous girl friend sneaks into the shop and smashes the device, Coppelius captures the boy and attempts to transfer his "essence" into the defunct robot. The girl makes amends by dressing as Coppelia and performing an intricate dance that fools the doctor into believing he has succeeded (both roles are played by Claudia Corday). A sequel was made in 1976, *The Mysterious House of Dr. C.*, again with Walter Slezak as the mischievous doctor.

Director/Screenplay: Ted Kneeland, *Art Director:* Gil Parrondo, *Choreography:* Jo Anna Kneeland, *Music:* Leo Delibes, Clement Philbert, Raymond Guy Wilson

Cast: Walter Slezak, Claudia Corday, Caj Selling, Eileen Elliott

From TV's *Doctor Who:* above, Cybermen; below, right, a Super Voc Sandminer robot; the Daleks.

Tom Baker, the fourth Doctor Who.

Zygon monsters, which live under Loch Ness.

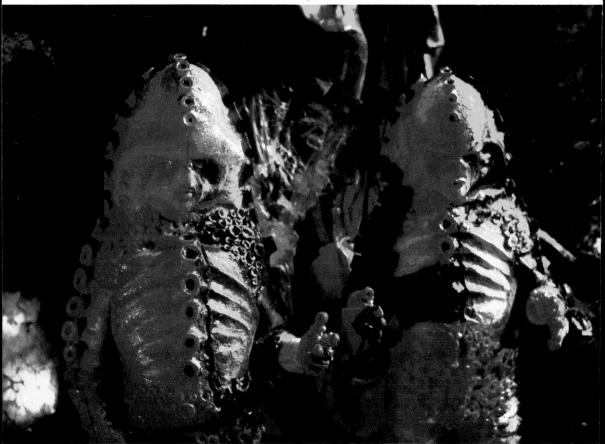

Doctor Who examines a mysterious substance.

A long-extinct demon of Earth's past.

A Sontaran, seen in "The Sontaran Experiment."

A Fendahl, seen in "The Image of the Fendahl."

Another of the series' fascinating alien creatures.

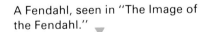

Christopher Reeve as The Man of Steel in the *Superman* films.

Nicholas Hammond as *Spider-Man*.

Gil Gerard as *Buck Rogers.*

Lynda Carter as *Wonder Woman.*

Bill Bixby turns into Lou Ferrigno as *The Hulk.*

THE STAR TREK SPACECRAFT

Leonard Nimoy and William Shatner in a publicity photo for the first movie.

The *U.S.S. Enterprise* in drydock.

A Vulcan Shuttle.

An Enterprise Travel Pod.

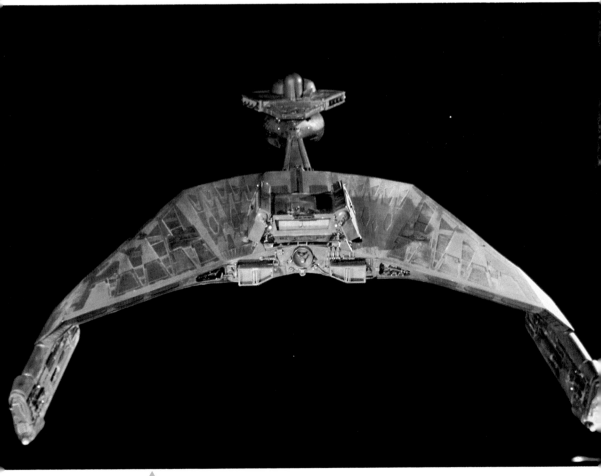

A Klingon Cruiser.

Roger Moore as James Bond in *Moonraker.*

Keir Dullea inspects a baby factory in TV's *Brave New World.*

Malcolm McDowell as H.G. Wells visits San Francisco in his time machine in *Time After Time.*

DR. CYCLOPS

Film   1940   U.S. (Paramount)   76 Minutes
Technicolor

Dr. Cyclops, the first SF film shot in Technicolor, takes place in the vivid green jungles of Peru, at the laboratory of Dr. Alexander Thorkel, a **mad scientist** who reduces animals to pygmy size by bombarding them with radium rays. When guests arrive, they become part of the experiment, dwindling away until they are tinier than Ulysses seemed to the original Homeric monster. They escape into the jungle and, in the true spirit of their captor's legend, blind the Cyclops by smashing his glasses, causing him to plunge headlong into a well.

Directed by Ernest B. Schoedsack, who brought **King Kong** out of the jungle in 1933, the film is too prettily photographed to be frightening and too poorly paced to be suspenseful. But its special effects are still the best of their kind—achieved with a combination of giant props, **rear projection** and **split-screen,** techniques then new to Technicolor.

Director: Ernest B. Schoedsack, *Producer:* Dale Van Every, *Screenplay:* Tom Kilpatrick, *Photographers:* Henry Sharp, Winton Hoch, *Art Directors:* Hans Dreyer, Earl Hedrick, *Special Effects Photography:* Farciot Edouard, Wallace Kelley, *Music:* Ernst Toch, Gerard Carbonera, Albert Hay Malotte

Cast: Albert Dekker, Janice Logan, Victor Kilian, Thomas Coley, Charles Halton

DOCTOR OF DOOM

Film   1960   Mexico (AIP)   89 Minutes   Black & white

Spooky doings in Central America as a scientist goes bananas and transplants the brains of apes into the craniums of human beings. Badly dubbed, acted and just about everything else, *Doctor* is one of a package of trashy horror films bought by AIP from a Mexican producer to dump on American television. Movies like this could lead to war.

Director: Rene Cardona, *Producer:* William Calderon Stell, *Screenplay:* Alfred Salazar, *Photographer:* Henry Wallace, *Dubbing:* K. Gordon Murray

Cast: Armando Silvestre, Irma Rodriguez, Lorena Valesquez, Elizabeth Campbell

DR. FRANKENSTEIN ON CAMPUS

Film   1970   U.S. (Agincourt)   80 Minutes
Color

Shunned and ridiculed by classmates because of his great-grandfather's notorious reputation, Dr. **Frankenstein** IV gets revenge by becoming the campus cut-up. (Why didn't he save himself the trouble by changing his name?) Awful.

Director: Gil Taylor, *Producer:* Bill Marshall, *Screenplay:* David Cob, Bill Marshall, Gil Taylor, *Photographer:* Jackson Samuels, *Music:* Paul Hoffert, Skip Prokop

Cast: Robin Ward, Ty Haller, Sean Sullivan, Kathleen Sawyer

DR. GOLDFOOT AND THE BIKINI MACHINE

Film   1965   U.S. (AIP)   88 Minutes
Pathecolor   Panavision

An energetic farce whose trendy tastelessness is as appealing as a day-old fast-food hamburger. **Vincent Price** lets himself go (where was the director?) and gnaws the scenery as a **mad scientist** who builds an army of well-stacked **robots** to control the world's power brokers.

Director: Norman Taurog, *Producer:* Anthony Carras, *Screenplay:* Elwood Ullman, Robert Kaufman, *Story:* James Hartford, *Photographer:* Sam Leavitt, *Special Effects:* Roger George, *Music:* Les Baxter

Cast: Vincent Price, Frankie Avalon, Susan Hart, Dwayne Hickman, Fred Clark

DR. GOLDFOOT AND THE GIRL BOMBS

Film   1966   U.S./Italy (AIP)   85 Minutes
Color

A sequel to **Dr. Goldfoot and the Bikini Machine** (1965), made in Italy, with **Vincent**

Price again mugging through the title role in outfits that look like Liberace's rejects. Allegedly a comedy, the film continues the doctor's plot to take over the world with a fleet of beautiful but mindless robots, who have been programmed to explode during love-making. Four writers collaborated on this drivel.

Director: Mario Bava, *Screenplay:* Louis M. Heyward, Robert Kaufman, Franco Castellano, Pipolo, *Music:* Les Baxter

Cast: Vincent Price, Fabian, Laura Antonelli, Franco Franchi, Ciccio Ingrassia

DR. JEKYLL AND MR. HYDE

Dual character created by Scottish author Robert Louis Stevenson (1850-94) for his classic novel, *The Strange Case of Dr. Jekyll and Mr. Hyde* (1886). Inspired by a nightmare while Stevenson was ill from tuberculosis and depressed over financial matters, the novel

Dr. Jekyll and Mr. Hyde (1932): Frederic March plays Mr. Hyde as an angry Neanderthal.

is a Faustian horror story that powerfully expresses man's constant inner battle between goodness and evil.

Dr. Jekyll is a compassionate and respectable healer who begins experimenting with certain chemicals, "in the furtherance of knowledge," to free himself of what he innocently believes to be "extraneous evil." Instead, the elixer releases pent-up "libertine" impulses and aggressive instincts, creating a monstrous alter ego called Mr. Hyde. Released of Jekyll's social controls, Hyde gives in to "the fires of abstinence," prowling through London by night, a brutal sadist whose perverse pleasures include torture and murder. Ultimately, Hyde gets the upper hand, taking the potion to remain himself, until Jekyll, briefly in command, commits suicide and destroys the monster inside him.

Today, the story seems melodramatic and prudish (Hyde's pleasures of the flesh are never specified). But the writing has a deep ring of truth and an enduring psychological force that brings Jekyll's agony to vivid life. Stevenson's idea that civilization is only a veneer for corrupt human nature was later explored by **H. G. Wells** and other SF writers. The novel is the prototype of stories dealing with split personalities and mental and physical transformations through drugs. It has a particular relevance to present-day drug use, and its influence can be seen in the popular contemporary film **Altered States** (1980). (See also: **Mad Scientists.**)

Dr. Jekyll and Mr. Hyde is/are the screen's most well-known literary character and holds the record for movie adaptations (at least 21), including the following:

Films: Dr. Jekyll and Mr. Hyde [Selig] (1908), [Denmark] (1909), [Universal] (1912), [U.S.] 1913, [Germany] 1920, **Dr. Jekyll and Mr. Hyde** [Pioneer], **Dr. Jekyll and Mr. Hyde** [Paramount] (both 1920), **Dr. Jekyll and Mr. Hyde** (1932), **Dr. Jekyll and Mr. Hyde** (1941), **Son of Dr. Jekyll** (1951), **Abbott and Costello Meet Dr. Jekyll and Mr. Hyde** (1953), **Daughter of Dr. Jekyll** (1957), **Monster on the Campus** (1958), *The Ugly Duckling* (1959), **The Two Faces of Dr. Jekyll** (1960),

The Nutty Professor (1963), **I, Monster** (1970), **Dr. Jekyll and Sister Hyde** (1971)

Television: Climax [episode starring Michael Rennie as Jekyll/Hyde], (1954-58), **The Strange Case of Dr. Jekyll and Mr. Hyde** (1968), **The Darker Side of Terror** (1979), *Dr. Jekyll and Mr. Hyde* [Great Britain] (1980)

DR. JEKYLL AND MR. HYDE

Film 1920 U.S. (Paramount) 63 Minutes
Black & white (silent)

John Barrymore is impressive as a speechless Mr. Hyde, roaming the shadowy streets of Soho with great panache and threatening poor Nita Naldi with a fate worse than death. Based on a Broadway play by Clara S. Beranger, the film retains a certain vigor that transcends its grainy, primitive look and exaggerated performances. The play (and film) revised Stevenson's story somewhat, introducing the idea of two girl friends for **Dr. Jekyll and Mr. Hyde,** one virtuous, the other promiscuous, to dramatize his dual nature and sexually fragmented personality. The idea has been used in every film version since.

Director: John S. Robertson, *Producer:* Adolph Zukor, *Screenplay:* Clara S. Beranger *(based on her play), Novel:* Robert Louis Stevenson, *Photographer:* Roy Overbough

Cast: John Barrymore, Nita Naldi, Brandon Hurst, Martha Mansfield, Louis Wolheim

DR. JEKYLL AND MR. HYDE

Film 1920 U.S. (Pioneer) 42 Minutes Black & white (silent)

Released several weeks after Barrymore's film (see listing above), this cheap production was thrown together by Louis B. Mayer, a former junk dealer later to become head of MGM studios. The story was shifted from London to New York, and Dr. Jekyll's terrifying experiment was discounted to a bad dream.

Producer: Louis B. Mayer, *Novel:* Robert Louis Stevenson

Cast: Sheldon Lewis, Alexander Shannon, Dora Mills Adams

DR. JEKYLL AND MR. HYDE

Film 1932 U.S. (Paramount) 90 Minutes
Black & white

Every version since has had to contend with this brilliant adaptation of Robert Louis Stevenson's parable of man's inner struggle between good and evil. Rouben Mamoulian, one of Hollywood's most visually gifted directors, created a near-perfect cinematic equivalent of the classic story—a tour de force of fogbound London settings, odd camera angles and unsettling sound effects (an amplified heart beat comes to mind).

Best of all is the **Academy Award** winning performance of Frederic March in the dual role. Changing from Dr. Jekyll to Mr. Hyde in full view, his face wrinkling and broadening as we watch, he seems to become another actor, someone not at all like March. His multi-layered performance, and makeup, suggest that Hyde's violence results from primitive instincts brought to the surface, rather than Stevenson's inherent evil.

The transformation scenes were ingeniously done by painting lines and hollows on March's face with red and blue makeup, then filming him through filters that screened the colors. As Jekyll swallowed the bitter potion, the filters were removed one at a time, and the markings suddenly became visible. The fangs, hair and heavy brow were filmed in ascending stages of makeup, and the lapses were later smoothed with **dissolve**s. At the final moment, just before Jekyll fully became Hyde, the camera made a disorienting 360-degree spin through the room to suggest the impact of the drug. When he recovered and looked in the mirror, the transformation was complete.

Unfortunately, the film was cut by censors after the introduction of Hollywood's Production Code during the mid-1930s, and this is the version screened today. Snipped were several steamy scenes between Hyde and the prostitute Ivy (Miriam Hopkins), which clearly spelled out the "libertine" proclivities hinted at by Stevenson. Held out of release for more than 30 years by MGM, which purchased the film to protect its 1941 Spencer Tracy version, March's *Dr. Jekyll and Mr. Hyde* is still not as available as it should be, apparently because some feel that March's portrayal and makeup have characteristics of Negro and Oriental stereotypes.

Director/Producer: Rouben Mamoulian, *Screenplay:* Samuel Hoffenstein, Percy Heath, *Novel:* Robert Louis Stevenson, *Photographer:* Karl Struss, *Art Director:* Hans Dreier

Cast: Frederick March, Miriam Hopkins, Rose Hobart, Holmes Herbert, Halliwell Hobbes, Edgar Norton

DR. JEKYLL AND MR. HYDE

Film 1941 U.S. (MGM) 127 Minutes Black & white

Heady with Victorian decor and a romantic background score by Franz Waxman, MGM's remake of Paramount's 1932 **Dr. Jekyll and Mr. Hyde** plays more like a love story than a horror movie. Spencer Tracy, miscast, does a credible job as Hyde, but he doesn't come close to the full-blooded malevolence of Frederic March. Wearing a minimum of makeup, Tracy is always recognizable and hence never very frightening. (Writer Somerset Maugham, visiting the set, allegedly asked, "Which one is he playing now?") Jekyll's transformation scene is augmented by a Freudian hallucination montage, a cliche device used to show his confused inner thoughts. The film is nevertheless enjoyable for its high MGM gloss and for Ingrid Bergman, also playing against type, who improves on the role of Ivy, the bad girl.

Director/Producer: Victor Saville, *Screenplay:* John Lee Mahin, *Photographer:* Joseph Ruttenberg, *Makeup:* Jack Dawn, *Special Effects:* Warren Newcombe, *Music:* Franz Waxman

Cast: Spencer Tracy, Lana Turner, Ingrid Bergman, Donald Crisp, Ian Hunter, C. Aubrey Smith

DR. JEKYLL AND SISTER HYDE

Film 1971 Great Britain (Hammer) 97 Minutes Technicolor

Dr. Jekyll changes his sex as well as his personality in this lurid perversion of the Robert Louis Stevenson classic. Sister Hyde is a beautiful wanton who eviscerates London prostitutes to obtain a glandular substance for his/her experimental elixer, and throws London into a panic as Scotland Yard mistakenly begins a manhunt for Jack the Ripper. It's all very silly and gruesome but occasionally hilarious.

Director: **Roy Ward Baker,** *Producer:* Albert Fennell, Brian Clemens, *Screenplay:* Brian Clemens, *Photographer:* Norman Warwick, *Makeup:* John Wilcox, *Music:* David Whitaker

Cast: Ralph Bates, Martine Bestwick, Susan Broderick, Lewis Flander, Gerald Sim

DR. MANIAC

See: **The Man Who Lived Again**

DR. NO

Film 1962 Great Britain (United Artists) 111 Minutes Technicolor

This is the first, the simplest and the best of the **James Bond** adventures. **Sean Connery** matches wits with Joseph Wiseman, playing a villain with mechanical hands who diverts Cape Canaveral rockets off-course from his private island in the Caribbean. Wiseman gets his comeuppance in the boiling water of an atomic reactor.

Director: Terence Young, *Producers:* Harry Saltzman, Albert R. Broccoli, *Screenplay:* Richard Maibaum, Johanna Harwood, Berkely Mather, *Novel:* Ian Fleming, *Photographer:* Ted Moore, *Special Effects:* Frank George, *Music:* Monty Norman

Cast: Sean Connery, Ursula Andress, Jack Lord, Joseph Wiseman, Bernard Lee, Lois Maxwell

DR. PHIBES RISES AGAIN

Film 1972 Great Britain (AIP) 89 Minutes DeLuxe

The wickedly inventive mad doctor is back for more murder and mayhem.

Having examined the box-office receipts of **The Abominable Doctor Phibes** (1971), its producers promptly resurrected the campy genius from a self-embalming and rewarded him with a boat trip to Egypt. Slipping back into his **Vincent Price** mask (he lost his face in an auto accident), Phibes is hot on the trail of the lost River of Life which he hopes will revive his long-dead wife, whom he has thoughtfully brought along. Also on board is a team of archaeologists with the same destination. Not one to take competition lightly, the doctor promptly dispatches them one by one with the same elegant malice he displayed previously. The leader of the expedition, for instance, is packed into a large bottle labeled "Not Wanted on Voyage" and placed in storage. Another troublemaker is tied to his bed and squeezed like an accordian by one of Phibes' homemade devices. "I'm afraid he had a rather bad night," the doctor explains in the morning.

Unlike most sequels, *Dr. Phibes Rises Again* is the equal of the original. Director **Robert Fuest,** who directed many episodes of TV's **The Avengers,** moves briskly through the inspired lunacies of his comic strip of a screenplay, and the 1930s art deco sets by Brian Eatwell look more stunning than ever. For all their efforts, the film was no more successful than the quest of Dr. Phibes, whose wife floated away in her coffin waiting to be revived in a sequel that never materialized. (See also: **Horror.**)

Director: Robert Fuest, *Producer:* Richard Dalton, *Screenplay:* Robert Fuest, Robert Blees, *Photographer:* Alex Thomson, *Art Director:* Brian Eatwell, *Makeup:* Trevor Crole-Rees, *Music:* John Gale

Cast: Vincent Price, Robert Quarry, Peter Cushing, Beryl Reid, Hugh Griffith, Terry-Thomas, Valli Kemp, Fiona Lewis, Peter Jeffrey

DR. RENAULT'S SECRET

Film   1942   U.S. (20th Century-Fox)
58 Minutes   Black & white

Another mad scientist discovers a way to turn a man into an ape, which wasn't much of a secret by this time. One of a plethora of unmemorable films ground out by the Hollywood majors to fill second halves of double bills during the 1940s and 1950s.

Director: Harry Lachman, *Photography:* Sol M. Wurtzel, *Screenplay:* William Bruckner, Robert F. Metzler, *Photographer:* Virgil Miller, *Art Director:* **Nathan H. Juran,** *Music:* David Raskin, Emil Newman

Cast: J. Carroll Naish, John Shepperd (Shepherd Strudwick), Lynne Roberts, George Zucco, Bert Roach

DOC SAVAGE: THE MAN OF BRONZE

Film   1975   U.S. (Warner Bros.)
100 Minutes   Technicolor

The granddaddy of **Superman** and his contemporaries, Doc (Clark) Savage reigned supreme in the early 1930s as the star of his own pulp magazine (cost: 10 cents). Described by his creator, writer Lester Dent, Doc was a 29-year-old perfectly proportioned giant, whose lacquer-like bronze skin out-

Doc Savage: The Man of Bronze: Ham, one of the Amazing Five, and Doc (Mike Miller and Ron Ely) at work in the House of Gadgets, Savage's secret anti-crime lab.

lined muscles "coiled like pythons," which he owed to working out for two hours daily, a regimen begun at the age of 14 months.

While building his body, Doc exercised his computer-like brain by extracting square roots and cubes and doing calculus. A real doctor, a surgeon, Doc had an extremely hign I.Q. that enabled him to learn most things without formal study. His home was a fortress on the top floor of an 86-story skyscraper, and his secret lab, where he invented crime-fighting gadgets, was as big as Radio City Music Hall.

Among Doc's supranormal abilities was a highly developed sense of smell, enabling him to pick out "scores of different odors," hearing that encompassed very high and low frequences, fingers that could "see" (he practiced by reading books printed in Braille), and eyes capable of piercing through fog at night for a distance of 50 miles (aided by his special "blacklight" goggles).

During the 1960s, Doc was discovered by a new generation of fans, prompting Bantam Books to reissue many of the stories in paperback (the original magazines were going for as much as $50 each). In 1975 SF filmmaker **George Pal** decided it was time to bring Doc to the screen (he had been overlooked during Hollywood's **serial** days), and Ron Ely (TV's *Tarzan*) was cast in the role.

Based on the first issue of *Doc Savage Magazine* (March, 1933), the film recalled Doc's legend in appropriate *art deco* detail and included a close approximation of his helpers, the Amazing Five, as well as a visit to his gold mine in South America (the secret source of his wealth). Gone, however, was the frenzied pace of writer Dent and the larger-than-life, gee-whiz appeal of his self-made superhero. Director Michael Anderson (of **Logan's Run**) treated the story with a cynical camp that had worked well on TV's **Batman,** but was inappropriate to Doc. The film opened to poor business during Easter week of 1975, and was subsequently withdrawn from release. It later turned up as an NBC-TV movie-of-the-week as a possible pilot for a series, a plan squelched by poor ratings.

Director: Michael Anderson, *Producer:* George Pal, *Screenplay:* Joe Morhaim, George Pal, *Novel:* Kenneth Robeson (Lester Dent), *Photographer:* **Fred Koenekamp,** *Music:* John Philip Sousa

Cast: Ron Ely, Paul Gleason, Bill Lucking, Mike Miller, Eldon Quick

DR. STRANGELOVE; OR, HOW I LEARNED TO STOP WORRYING AND LOVE THE BOMB

Film   1963   U.S./Great Britain (Columbia)
93 Minutes   Black & white

Made at the end of Hollywood's first cycle of anti-**bomb** films, when the public was innundated with dire warnings, propaganda and books about surviving the "unthinkable," Kubrick's film turned a death rattle into a belly laugh by mocking his audience's greatest fears. In the words of filmmaker Byron Forbes, "Kubrick has taken the bomb and used it as a banana skin, with a nuclear pratfall as the pay-off." Along the way, Kubrick's raucous black comedy skewered a number of sacred American cows, including its political and military establishments. (The film points out, ironically, that the motto of the Air Force's Strategic Air Command is "Peace is Our Profession.")

Told in a series of cross-cuttings, *Dr. Strangelove* takes place at three locations: Burpelson Air Base, commanded by Gen. Jack D. Ripper, who is obsessed with the idea of "commies" polluting his "precious bodily fluids" with fluoridated water; the Pentagon War Room, where President Merkin J. Muffley is arguing with right-wing A. F. Gen. "Buck" Turgidson over a "mistake" that has sent a nuclear doomsday bomb heading toward Russia; and the B-52 carrying the bomb and a gung-ho crew. The suspense results from the way Kubrick (and editor Anthony Harvey) juxtapose the scenes. Will the recall order arrive in time? Will the Russians manage to down the B-52? Will this be the end of the world? Kubrick answers the questions with repeated sequences of mushroom clouds, accompanied by an old recording of Vera Lynn, a British World War II favorite, singing "We'll Meet Again" on the soundtrack.

The film is nominally based on Peter George's deadpan novel *Red Alert*, which concerns a deranged U.S. general who launches a nuclear attack on Russia without authority. While working on the script, Kubrick revised the story extensively and decided to play it for outrageous comedy. His cast seem born to their characters, and Peter Sellers is in an inspiration in a triple role—as milquetoast President Muffley, the stiff-upper-lip Group Captain Mandrake and the crippled Dr. Strangelove, an ex-Nazi scientist working for the U.S., whose black-gloved artificial arm can't help swinging up in a salute to "Mein Fuhrer."

Its mediocre special effects aside (including wobbly **matte** shots of the B-52 traveling across Russia), *Dr. Strangelove* is a masterpiece of cinema, as historically significant now as it was then. (**Fail Safe**, a similar film played seriously, was released several months later.)

Director/Producer: Stanley Kubrick, *Screenplay:* Stanley Kubrick, Terry Southern, Peter George, *Novel:* "Red Alert" Peter George, *Photographer:* Gilbert Taylor, *Production Designer:* **Ken Adam,** *Special Effects:* Wally Veevers, *Makeup:* **Stuart Freeborn,** *Music:* Laurie Johnson

Cast: Peter Sellers, George C. Scott, Peter Bull, Keenan Wynn, Sterling Hayden, Slim Pickens, James Earl Jones, Tracy Reed

DOCTOR WHO

TV series   1963-   Great Britain (BBC)
30 Minutes (weekly)   Black & white, color

Created as a routine children's adventure series by BBC-TV programmers, *Doctor Who* surprised everybody by becoming one of the highest-rated shows in Great Britain. It has been produced almost continuously since 1963 (except for 1969 and 1971), making it television's longest-running SF series. The program has spawned a series of paperback novels, **comic books** and two films, starring **Peter Cushing** in the title role: **Dr. Who and the Daleks** (1965) and **Daleks—Invasion Earth 2150 A.D.** (1966).

Doctor Who is a self-appointed interga-

Doctor Who: Tom Baker, the BBC-TV's fourth Time Lord.

lactic trouble-shooter, a member of a highly advanced **humanoid** civilization known as the **Time Lords,** whose home is the planet **Gallifrey.** The Doctor travels through time and space in a **TARDIS** device, which resembles an old London telephone box, used by police for emergency calls. Having a soft spot for **Earth,** the Doctor has often been instrumental in rescuing it from a gallery of bizarre and nasty **aliens.**

In the first episode, televised in November 1963, two schoolteachers followed an unusual new student into a telephone box, which was many times larger inside than it appeared to be. The girl introduced them to "Grandfather"—Doctor Who. He was described as a humanoid alien several hundred years old, with two hearts and a body temperature of 60°F (15.6°C). The visitors joined him for a three-part visit to the Stone Age, followed by jaunts into such historic events as the French Revolution and the gunfight at the O.K. corral. Alone, he later encountered the **Frankenstein** monster and Dracula in a cobwebbed castle.

Mildly received at first, the program became immensely popular after the introduction of the **Daleks** in a story by Terry Nation, titled "The Dead Planet." Episodes became increasingly sophisticated, attracting nearly as many grown-up viewers as juveniles, and in 1968 the program was taped in color. Many of the plots were rehashes of cliche **space opera** stories, but handled with an intelligence and wit that made them seem new again. Among the visual delights of the program were its colorful alien villains, a long list that includes the **Cyberman, Davros,** the **Mechanoids,** the **Movellans** and the **Nestenes.** (See also: **K-9**).

Doctor Who has been impersonated by four actors, beginning with William Hartnell (1963-66), who was easily irritated, forgetful and elderly. To explain the program's casting changes, the Doctors were conveniently put through a regeneration process that made the character increasingly younger. Hartnell emerged from the process as the droll Patrick Troughton (1966-70), who in turn became the stern and serious John

Pertwee (1970-74). Since 1974 the Doctor has sported the mop-top curls of Tom Baker, the youngest and most appealing of the lot. Wearing a six-foot-long striped muffler and, occasionally, a floppy hat, Baker plays the role with a straight-faced irony and an offbeat charm. Slightly absent-minded, he often reaches into a bottomless jacket pocket for a scientific instrument, only to pull out an apple core or a jelly baby.

During the early 1970s, *Doctor Who* was shown in the United States over the Public Broadcasting System, but it failed to attract a fair number of viewers, and the tapes were shipped back to London. After the release of **Star Wars** (1977), 98 Tom Baker episodes were syndicated on commercial television, and the program has since developed a sizeable American cult following (although not as large as **Star Trek**'s).

Creators: Sydney Newman, Donald Wilson, [first series] *Director:* Waris Hussein, *Producer:* Verity Lambert, *Writer:* Anthony Coburn; [subsequent series] *Producers:* Peter Bryant, Innes Lloyd, Barry Letts, Graham Wilson, Philip Hinchcliffe, *Writers:* Terry Nation, Dennis Spooner, Bill Strutton, William Emms, Ian Stuart Black, Kit Pedlar, Gerry Davis, Terrance Dicks, Robert Holmes, Bob Baker, Dave Martin, Chris Boucher, Robert Banks Stewart, Robin Bland, David Agnew and others

Cast: William Hartnell, Patrick Troughton, John Pertwee, Tom Baker, Elizabeth Sladen, William Russell, Carole Ann Ford, Roger Delgado, Anneke Wills, Jacqueline Hill, Michael Craze, Stewart Bevan and others

DR. WHO AND THE DALEKS

Film   1965   Great Britain (Amicus)
83 Minutes   Technicolor Techniscope

A lively big-screen version of the popular BBC-TV program **Doctor Who** (1963-   ), with **Peter Cushing** playing the **humanoid** from **Gallifrey** in his usual fussy manner. The Doctor is explaining the workings of his **TARDIS** traveling device to his granddaughters when their clumsy friend activates a control panel and sends them on a visit to the nasty little **Daleks.** The accident turns out to be a fortunate one, since the Daleks are plotting to destroy **Earth** with a neutron **bomb,** and the Doctor always knows how to outwit them. The sequel is **Daleks—Invasion Earth 2150 A.D.** (1966).

The film was shot in Techniscope, a process that records two images on one frame of 35-mm. film, one below the other, producing a **widescreen** ratio at half the cost of a negative. The image is then enlarged and printed anamorphically on 35-mm. positive. (See: **Anamorphic Lens.**)

Director: Gordon Flemyng, *Producers:* Milton Subotsky, Max J. Rosenberg, *Screenplay:* Milton Subotsky, *Photographer:* John Wilcox, *Makeup:* Jill Carpenter, *Special Effects:* Ted Samuels, *Music:* Malcolm Lockyer

Cast: Peter Cushing, Roy Castle, Jennie Linden, Roberta Tovey, Barry Ingham

DR. X

Film   1932   U.S. (Warner Bros.)
82 Minutes   Two-strip Technicolor

Set in an old Gothic mansion atop a cliff on Long Island, *Dr. X* is a **horror** thriller in the grand tradition, complete with a fiendish **mad scientist,** a spooky laboratory, secret panels and Fay Wray, on the verge of being teamed with **King Kong.** A series of cannibalistic murders, committed on nights of the full moon, bring investigators and a wisecracking reporter to the mansion, where a one-armed scientist (Preston Foster) has invented a synthetic flesh, which he occasionally grows into a murderous hand.

Director Michael Curtiz brings the pot to a boil with his impeccable sense of timing and stark visual style. *Dr. X* was shot in two-strip Technicolor, used only for prints shown in major cities. The studio decided the film was good enough to succeed without the added expense of color, and subsequent prints were released in black and white—the only version seen on television. A sequel of sorts, **The Return of Dr. X,** appeared in 1939. (See also: **Alraune** [1918], **Expressionism.**)

Director: Michael Curtiz, *Screenplay:* Robert Tasker, Early Baldwin, *Play:* Howard Comstock, Allen C. Miller, *Photographer:* Richard Tower, Ray Rennahean

Cast: Preston Foster, Lionel Atwill, Fray Wray, Mae Busch, Lee Tracy, George Rosener

DODO—THE KID FROM OUTER SPACE

TV series   1967   U.S. (syndicated)
30 Minutes (weekly)   Color

Dodo, an animated cartoon character, is dispatched from the atomic planet Hena Hydo with his computerized pet, Compy, to help Professor Fingers speed up scientific progress on Earth. Stories explained basic scientific concepts to Saturday morning viewers. (78 episodes)

A DOG, A MOUSE AND A SPUTNIK

See: **A Pied a Cheval et en Spoutnik**

DOLBY

Trademark of a noise reduction system used for motion picture sound tracks and tape recordings. Basically, Dolby in an encoding/decoding device that removes most tape hiss and other high-frequency noise by compressing the upper dynamic range during recording and expanding it during playback. The result is a startlingly clear and resonant sound track far superior to previous systems. The first major film to be Dolbyized was *Nashville* (1975). Since then Dolby has become essential for producing the multi-track stereo effects of today's SF films, and few are made without it. A newer system called digital recording, which promises even greater fidelity and total elimination of extraneous sound track noise. Dolby won a technical class **Academy Award** in 1978. (See also: **Magnetic Sound, Optical Sound.**)

DONOVAN'S BRAIN

Film   1953   U.S. (United Artists)
81 Minutes   Black & white

The second version of **Curt Siodmak's** novel *Donovan's Brain* (1943); the others are **The Lady and the Monster** (1944) and **The Brain** (1962). This time around Lew Ayres is the surgeon taken over by a millionaire's brain, kept alive in a chemical solution. Suspenseful and competently directed, with a good performance from Ayres, but not as chilling as the first film. Mrs. Ronald Reagan is merely adequate.

Director/Screenplay: Felix Feist, *Producer:* Tom Gries, *Photographer:* Joseph Biroc, *Novel:* Curt Siodmak, *Music:* Eddie Dunstedter

Cast: Lew Ayres, Gene Evans, Nancy Davis, Steve Brodie, Lisa K. Howard

DOOMWATCH

Film 1972 Great Britain (Tigon)
92 Minutes Color

Based on the ecology-minded BBC-TV series *Doomwatch* (1970-72), this predictable **horror**-thriller takes place in an island fishing village off the coast of England. Visitors are treated rudely and turned away because the villagers are hiding a deep, dark secret: Some of them have developed very large heads, hands and feet, the result of damage done to their pituitary glands by ingesting fish polluted with radioactive and chemical wastes. The idea is a good one, but director Saady, an alumnus of the Hammer studios, gets bogged down in shock effects.

Director: Peter Saady, *Producer:* Tony Tenser, *Screenplay:* Clive Exton, *Photographer:* Kenneth Talbot, *Music:* John Scott

Cast: Ian Bannen, Judy Geeson, John Paul, Simon Oates, George Sanders

DOPPELGANGER

See: **Journey to the Far Side of the Sun**

DRACULA VS. FRANKENSTEIN

Film 1971 U.S. (Independent-International)
89 Minutes Color

Horror stars **Lou Chaney, Jr.,** and J. Carrol Naish made their final appearances in this crude, pathetic vampire movie. Playing respectively a leering, mute axe murderer and a creaky Dr. Frankenstein, they teamed up with Count Dracula to ressurect a rubbermasked **Frankenstein** monster. Later, a motorcycle punk with healthy young blood happened into the secret laboratory which, it might be noted, was allegedly built from parts found in the garage of special effects man Ken Strickfaden, who created the electrical effects in the original **Frankenstein** (1931).

Director: Al Adamson, *Producer:* Al Adamson, John Van Horne, *Screenplay:* William Pugsley, Sam Sherman, *Photorapher:* Gary Graver, Paul Glickman, *Makeup:* George Barr, *Special Effects:* Ken Strickfaden, *Music:* William Lava

Cast: Lou Chaney, Jr., J. Carrol Naish, Russ Tamblyn, Forrest Ackerman, Jim Davis

DUEL

TV film 1971 U.S. (Universal)
73 Minutes Color

It's a familiar story. You pass a truck on the highway, and the driver pays back the insult by speeding ahead with a blast of his compressed-air horn. **Steven Spielberg,** then at the beginning of his career, has turned this premise into a classic of suspense and terror, with a traveling salesman in a compact car attempting to escape a gasoline tanker determined to do him in. The truck driver is never seen, and the story is presented as a battle to the death between man and machine. Released theatrically in Great Britain and France (with additional footage of the salesman's personal life), *Duel* has since become a cult item in both countries.

Director: Steven Spielberg, *Producer:* George Eckstein, *Screenplay:* Richard Matheson, *Short Story:* Richard Matheson, *Photographer:* Jack A. Marta, *Art Director:* Robert S. Smith, *Music:* Billy Goldenberg

Cast: Dennis Weaver, Tim Herbert, Charles Steel, Eddie Firestone, Lucille Benson, Gary Loftin

DYKSTRA, JOHN (1948–)

Special effects expert; owner of Apogee, a

company specializing in state-of-the-art special effects. A former maker of television commercials, Dykstra got his start operating a special effects camera for **Douglas Trumbell** in **Silent Running** (1972). He won twin **Academy Awards** in 1977 for the composite photography of **Star Wars** (1977) and for inventing the Dykstraflex, a **motion control** camera. His credits include **Star Trek— The Motion Picture** (1979), the TV series **Battlestar Galactica** (1978-79) and the film **Firefox** (1982).

DYNARAMA

This term was coined by special effects expert **Ray Harryhausen** to disinguish his **stop-motion** photography method from cartoon animation. He had originally called it Dynamation. Previous stop-motion animators had usually placed their small-scale models against unconvincing tabletop scenery (as in the original **King Kong).** Harryhausen's method relies on the basic technique of shooting models one frame at a time to impart the illusion of movement, but includes other special effects as well, including detailed miniature sets. In Dynarama the limitation of backgrounds is overcome by inserting stop-motion footage into the live action via a complicated system of **mattes.**

DYSTOPIA

The opposite of a **Utopia:** a hopeless and miserable future. Dystopias originated as a propaganda device used by late 19th-century Utopians to show the dire consequences of not following their revolutionary dogmas. The concept was a commodious one that included capitalist dystopias as well as socialist dystopias. One of the first writers to use the concept as a story-telling device is **Jules Verne,** who depicted a future governed by avarice and militarism in *The Begum's Fortune* (1879). Another early dystopia can be found in **H. G. Wells'** Selenite society, depicted in *The First Men in the Moon* (1901).

Most 20th-century dystopias fall into the category of science fiction, having resulted from the misuse of technology by dictators and power-hungry oligarchies. Touchstones of this sub-genre include Aldous Huxley's *Brave New World* (1932) (see: **Brave New World), George Orwell's** *Nineteen Eighty-four* (1949) (see: **1984), Ray Bradbury's** *Farenheit 451* (1953) (see: **Fahrenheit 451).** More recent dystopias have been laid to a number of science-related causes, including the **bomb,** pollution and unchecked population growth. Films in this category include **Z.P.G.** (1971), **Soylent Green** (1973), **Zardoz** (1974), **Logan's Run** (1976) and **Blade Runner** (1982). Dystopias make for good drama, of course, and they also reflect a deep-rooted human fear of the power of machines.

John Dykstra makes a point about his optical printer.

EARTH

Third planet from the **sun** (mean distance: 93 million miles); fifth largest planet of the **solar system;** probably two to over four million years old. One satellite. Closest neighbor: **Mars.** Earth's home is the Milky Way Galaxy, which is part of the Local Group of Galaxies. Its greater address is the Universe, a place that astronomers estimate to contain some 100 billion galaxies. (See also: **Astronomical Constants; Galaxy; Terrestrial Planets.)**

EARTH II

TV film   1971   U.S. (ABC)   100 Minutes   Color

Not a parallel world but a peace-keeping satellite administered by the United Nations. Earth II faces its first crisis when Red China orbits a nuclear bomb over Moscow and an astronaut's wife aims the device at Earth while trying to guide it toward the sun. Padded scenes (to fit a two-hour time slot) and out-of-date situations (China, a non-U.N. nation, isn't obliged to obey the laws of space) undermine this overwrought movie-of-the-week, which has a number of first-rate special effects by Oscar-winning Art Cruickshank. The futuristic sets are by George W. Davis and Edward Carfagno, co-designer of the epic sets of the film *Ben Hur* (1959).

Director: Tom Gries, *Screenplay:* William Read Woodfield, Alan Balter, *Photographer:* Michael Hugo, *Art Director:* George W. Davis, Edward Carfagno, *Special Effects:* Art Cruickshank, J. McMillan Johnson, Robert Ryder, Howard Anderson, Jr., *Music:* Lalo Shifrin

Cast: Gary Lockwood, Mariette Hartley, Tony Franciosa, Gary Merrill, Hari Rhodes, Lew Ayres

THE EARTH DIES SCREAMING

Film   1964   Great Britain (20th Century-Fox)   62 Minutes   Black & white

Returning to London after a test flight in space, an astronaut finds that everyone in the city is dead, except for two men and women. They band together and attempt to find out why, running smack into two immense **robots,** who kill one of the women. Later, she turns up as good as new (almost) and murders one of her former friends, leading the survivors to conclude that robots are **aliens** who intend to wipe out humanity with an army of animated corpses.

Horror director **Terence Fisher** does little to make sense of the muddled script, and the low-budget sets and stingy location shots don't help much, either. (See also: **Alien Invasion.)**

Director: Terence Fisher, *Producers:* Robert L. Lippert, Jack Parsons, *Screenplay:* Henry Cross, *Story:* Harry Spalding, *Makeup:* Harold Fletcher, *Music:* Elizabeth Luytens

Cast: Willard Parker, Virginia Field, Dennis Price, Thorley Walters

EARTH VS. THE FLYING SAUCERS

Great Britain title: *Invasion of the Flying Saucers*

Film   1956   U.S. (Columbia)   83 Minutes   Black & white

Flying saucers destroy some of Washington, D.C.'s famous landmarks in this low-budget epic, made to capitalize on the **UFO** craze of the 1950s. **Ray Harryhausen**'s animated saucers are the decade's best. **Curt Siodmak**'s story, allegedly based on factual UFO reports, is innocuous.

Director: **Fred Sears,** *Producer:* Charles Schneer, *Screenplay:* George Worthing Yates, Raymond Marcus, *Story:* Curt Siodmak, *Special Effects:* Ray Harryhausen, *Musical Director:* Mischa Bakaleinikoff

Cast: Hugh Marlowe, Joan Taylor, Morris Ankrum, Donald Curtis

EARTH VS. THE SPIDER

Also titled: *The Spider)*

Film 1958 U.S.(AIP) 72 Minutes Black & white

An impossibly large spider leaves its nest near an atomic **bomb** test site and scuttles through a small town sampling teen-age flesh. Captured by local police, the creature goes on display as a tourist attraction, until it escapes and resumes its annoying habits. The homemade miniature sets and inept **split-screen** work are what you get in a **Bert I. Gordon** production.

Director/Producer: Bert I. Gordon, *Screenplay:* Laszlo Gorog, George Worthing Yates, *Special Effects:* Bert I. and Flora Gordon, *Music:* Albert Glasser

Cast: Ed Kemmer, June Kenney, Gene Roth, Sally Fraser, Mickey Finn

AT THE EDGE OF THE WORLD

See: **Am Rande der Welt**

EDISON, THOMAS A.(LVA) (1847–1931)

American inventor and motion picture pioneer. Inventions include the carbon microphone (which made Bell's telephone possible), the phonograph, the electric light bulb, the electric power plant, and the motion picture camera.

The son of a Milan, Ohio, lumber dealer, Edison received much of his early education from his mother, a teacher, who encouraged his talent for experimentation. At 12 he went to work as a newsboy and candy vendor on a train, and later became a telegraph operator. Moving from job to job throughout the Midwest, he worked tirelessly to develop an improved stock ticker system, which he patented at age 21. Profits from the invention enabled him to set up a workshop in Newark, New Jersey, where he made telegraphic equipment for the Western Electric Co.

In 1876 Edison constructed a research laboratory—an "invention factory" as he called it—on a hilltop at Menlo Park, New Jersey, where he produced a dazzling series of technologies that revolutionized daily life. It was there that he unveiled the phonograph, his favorite invention, and, in 1879 the incandescent lamp. Three years later he built a Manhattan power station that lit an entire district of the city.

Moving in 1887 to larger quarters in West Orange, New Jersey, Edison—now world-famous as the "wizard of Menlo Park"—put his staff to work building a moving picture machine capable of doing "for the eye what the phonograph did for the ear." In 1889 his assistant **W. K. L. Dickson**—using Charles Eastman's new celluloid roll film—produced a movie camera/projector and synchronized a phonograph to it. The system, called a Kinetophonograph or Kinetophone, was a forerunner of the sound film. The cumbersome apparatus led to the development of a more practical system, the Kinetograph camera and the Kinetoscope viewer, a peep-show box.

Preoccupied with devising a more reliable way to combine sound with film, Edison failed to see the potential of the equipment he had already produced. He neglected to protect his patents, and others moved forward to improve his inventions. His Kinetoscope projector would be viewed by only one paying customer at a time, and it fell to other motion picture pioneers, including the French Louis Lumiere and his brothers, to devise a lens system that projected the moving image into a screen, enabling an entire audience to watch a film. Edison eventually became aware of the commercial possibilities of the new medium, and he obtained the rights to the British Jenkins-Armat projector to produce his own films. His Vitascope productions were shown for the first time, accompanying a vaudeville performance, at New York's Koster & Bial Music Hall at 34th Street and Broadway, on April 23, 1896. The presentation, consisting of 12 shorts, created a sensation and marked the birth of the American film industry.

Among the achievements of Edison and Dickson was the standardization and perforation of film. Working with Eastman, they first devised a 35-mm. format, then solved the problem of stopping the film at regular intervals as it passed the lens by perforating it. At first Dickson perforated the film centrally, but the sprocket holes tended to wear into the picture; finally, he placed four perforations at both sides to equalize the pull. This film gauge and its perforations remain the international standard.

Edison's West Orange movie studio, the world's first, was called the "Black Maria." Designed by Dickson and constructed in 1893, the studio was an oddly shaped, windowless room made of wood and covered in black canvas. Mounted on a turntable, the small structure would be revolved in the direction of the sun to light the actors via a skylight. It was here that Edison produced the first film version of **Frankenstein.**

In 1909 Edison joined forces with other leading film producers in an attempt to monopolize the rapidly expanding American film industry, then based on the East Coast. (At the time, cartels were being formed throughout the country.) The Motion Picture Patents Company (MPPC)—also known as the "Edison Trust"—withheld patent rights and theaters from non-members, and obtained the cooperation of Eastman Kodak, which agreed to sell film stock to members only. The MPPC kept an iron grip on the industry for years, forcing many independents to escape its reach in faraway California, where they established a new film community in a sleepy town called Hollywood. In 1917 the Company was dissolved, and that same year Edison left the film business for good. Celebrated and very wealthy, he continued inventing things well into old age. By the time of his death he had patented more than 1,100 devices.

Edison's life was romanticized in two MGM films, both made in 1940: *Young Tom Edison,* with Mickey Rooney, and *Edison the Man,* with Spencer Tracy.

EFFECTS TRACK

A movie sound track containing only sound effects, such as doors slamming, gunshots, **blaster** rays, explosions, rocketship roars, etc., which make a set, prop or **miniature** sound like the real thing. Other tracks hold the dialogue, usually recorded during filming, the musical score and/or narration. SF sound effects are either created specifically for a film or borrowed from a library of stock noises. These are carefully synchronized to the action and later integrated into the other tracks during a rerecording process called the **mix.**

THE EIGHTH MAN

TV series   1965   Japan (syndicated)
30 Minutes (weekly)   Color

An animated cartoon set in Metro City, the 21st-Century residence of a police force called Metro International. Leader of group is Tobor, the eighth man, an indestructible **robot** into which the life force of ace agent Peter Brady was infused after he was killed by Saucer Lip, the most wanted criminal in the universe. (52 episodes)

THE ELECTRIC HOTEL

See: **Hotel Electrico**

THE ELECTRIC HOUSE

Film   1922   U.S. (B. Keaton Productions)
Black & white (silent)   2 reels

Peripheral science fiction but vintage Buster Keaton, this hilarious short slapstick comedy pokes fun at household labor-saving devices, which began to proliferate in the 1920s. Keaton, the "great stone face," portrays a solemn young inventor who builds an automated house and shows it to the president of a large building concern in hopes of having it mass-produced. He sabotages his best efforts, of course. Among the memorable sight gags is Keaton falling into a swimming pool that empties at the touch of a button for a trip through the Los Angeles sewer system.

Keaton (1895-1966), then in total artistic control of his films (his only rival during the silent era was Charlie Chaplin), designed the clever sets himself and performed his own stunts. He often portrayed modern man victimized by technology, but who nevertheless prevails because of an unexpected resourcefulness. Life mirrored art during the making of the film, when Keaton tripped on an escalator and broke his ankle, delaying production for several months.

Director: Buster Keaton, *Producer:* Joseph M. Schenck, *Screenplay:* Buster Keaton, Eddie Cline, *Photographer:* Elgin Lessley

Cast: Buster Keaton, Virginia Fox, Joe Roberts

THE ELECTRONIC MONSTER

(Also titled: *The Dream Machine, Escapement, Zex*)

Film 1958 Great Britain (Amalgamated) 82 Minutes Black & white (Released 1960 U.S. [Columbia] 72 Minutes)

The subject is man's violent subconscious, not the crazed robot suggested by the lurid title pinned onto **Charles Eric Maine**'s screen adaptation of his fascinating novel, *Escapement* (1955). The monster "is an experimental device used by psychiatrists in a mental institution to induce therapeutic dreams in psychotics. The experiment—and the film—go awry when a couple of **mad scientists** use the device to program their murderous fantasies into patients, who act them out.

Director: Montgomery Tulley, *Producer:* Alec C. Snowden, *Screenplay:* Charles Eric Maine, J. Maclaren-Ross, *Novel:* Charles Eric Maine, *Photographer:* Bert Mason, *Art Director:* Wilfred Arnold, *Makeup:* Jack Craig, *Electronic Music:* Soundrama

Cast: Rod Cameron, Mary Murphy, Peter Illing

ELECTRONIC VIDEO RECORDING (EVR)

An obsolete system of encoding picture, color and audio information (not images) on black-and-white photographic film for playback on a television receiver. Developed by CBS in the mid-1960s, EVR was dropped by the network in 1971 in favor of **videotape,** which by then had become the industry standard.

ELLENSHAW, PETER (1912–   )

British matte artist, **production designer** and special effects expert long associated with Walt Disney features. Ellenshaw's specialty is a filmic device known as a **matte painting,** a small-scale background depiction that appears to be full-size onscreen when combined with live-action footage.

Ellenshaw entered films in 1933 as an assistant matte artist for producer Alexander Korda's London-based film company, where he refined his craft on such epics as **Things to Come** (1936), *The Four Feathers* (1939) and *The Thief of Bagdad* (1940). After serving in the Royal Air Force during World War II, he became a full-fledged matte artist for the filmmaking team of Michael Powell and Emeric Pressburger. He painted imaginary settings in a number of internationally successfuly productions, including *A Matter of Life and Death* (U.S. title *Stairway to Heaven*) (1946) and *The Red Shoes* (1948). His fictitious backgrounds proved to be so convincing that his 1947 movie *Black Narcissus* won an Oscar for best photography for its sweeping views of the Himalayan Mountains. The snow-capped peaks were, of course, products of Ellenshaw's paintbrush.

Matte artist Peter Ellenshaw with production renderings for *The Black Hole.*

Ellenshaw's durable relationship with Disney began when the famed animator came to England to scout locations and hired him to help re-create the country's long-vanished past for *Treasure Island* (1950), *Robin Hood* (1952) and *Sword and the Rose* (1953). He was brought to the United States by Disney to paint the mattes for the studio's big-budget version of **Jules Verne's** SF classic **20,000 Leagues Under the Sea** (1954), a film that won **Academy Awards** for Art Direction and Special Effects. Since then he has worked exclusively for Disney, with the exception of a loan-out to create backgrounds of Ancient Rome for Stanley Kubrick's *Spartacus* (1960), an era he had previously depicted for the 1951 version of *Quo Vadis.* In 1964 he won an Academy Award of his own for the imaginative special effects of *Mary Poppins,* a feature combining live action with **animation.**

His most impressive work appears in Disney's **The Black Hole** (1979), an expensive **space opera** inspired by **Star Wars.** Although the film is tedious and its science specious, it is worth seeing for Ellenshaw's state-of-the-art vision of life aboard a mammoth spaceship. He retired later that year to paint seriously at his home in Ireland. His son, Harrison Ellenshaw, is the matte artist of the *Star Wars* series.

EMBRYO

Film   1976   U.S. (Cine Artists)
105 Minues   DeLuxe

Dr. Paul Holliston, a contemporary Dr. **Frankenstein,** brings a premature fetus to term with a growth hormone and finds that he can't stop the process. As a result, the infant grows practically overnight into a beautiful 25-year-old woman, whose emotional and mental age are zero. The doctor attempts to bring her up to date, but the conditioning program fails (perhaps, it is suggested, because of his own character flaws), and she becomes an amoral femme fatale who must be destroyed for the common good. Although the action takes place in an impressive modern laboratory, *Embryo* harkens back to such early Gothic **horror** films as **Alraune** (1928) and **Homunkulus** (1916), in which there is hell to pay if you're born without a soul.

Director: Ralph Nelson, *Producers:* Arnold H. Orgolini, Anita Doohan, *Screenplay:* Anita Doohan, Jack W. Thomas, *Story:* Jack W. Thomas, *Photographer:* **Fred Koenkamp,** *Art Director:* Joe Alves, *Special Effects:* Roy Arbogast, Bill Shourt, *Music:* Gil Melle

Cast: Rock Hudson, Diane Ladd, Barbara Carrera, Roddy McDowall, Anne Schedeen

EMPIRE OF THE ANTS

Film   1977   U.S. (AIP) 87 Minutes   Movielab

Giant mutant ants emerge from a Florida swamp and invade a coastal resort area.

H. G. Wells is conspicuously absent from this mindless adaptation of his enjoyable novel *The Empire of the Ants* (1905), a seminal SF work that defined the durable theme of biology gone beserk. Wells' formicary has been transplanted from the jungles of Southeast Asia—then a mysterious locale—to modern-day Florida, where the ants have swelled to mammoth proportions from ingesting radioactive waste materials. Mindful of his budget, jack-of-all-trades filmmaker **Bert I. Gordon** has the creatures menacing shopping centers and resort areas rather than an entire continent. Guided by a hive-

Lobby poster for *Empire of the Ants* (1977).

mind, the ants take over people by exuding powerful pheremones that sap human willpower. The hero ultimately outwits them, however, by holding his breath and heading for a tanker full of gasoline with a book of matches in his hand.

Director/Producer: Bert I. Gordon, *Screenplay:* Jack Turley, *Photographer:* Reginald Morris, *Special Effects:* Bert I. Gordon, *Music:* Dana Kaproff

Cast: Joan Collins, Robert Lansing, John David Carson, Albert Salmi, Robert Pine

THE EMPIRE STRIKES BACK

Film 1980 U.S. (20th Century-Fox)
120 Minutes DeLuxe Panavision Dolby Stereo

The Empire Strikes Back is the sequel to **Star Wars** and episode V in **George Lucas'** projected nine-part series. The freedom-fighters—**Luke Skywalker, Han Solo, Princess Leia Organa** and the robots **C-3PO** and **R2-D2**—are hiding out on the ice planet **Hoth,** inhabited by bizarre **Tauntauns** and **Wampas.** Discovered by an **Imperial Probe Droid,** they repel an attack from the Empire's All Terrain Armored Transports—immense walking tanks equipped with **laser** cannons—in Snowspeeder flying crafts. They escape in the **Millennium Falcon** just ahead of **Darth Vader** and journey through an **asteroid** field to a refuge in Cloud City, a mining outpost ruled by Solo's old friend and partner in piracy, Lando Calrissian.

Luke meanwhile is visited by an apparition of his teacher **Ben Kenobi,** who tells him to seek out someone named **Yoda** on the planet Dagobah to complete his training as a **Jedi Knight.** Kenobi neglected to tell him that the place is covered with a tropical swamp, however, and that Yoda is a little green-skinned gnome who speaks like a Hobbit. But the creature is patient with Luke's impatience, and he teaches him enough about **The Force** for a lively **lightsaber** duel with Vader. Han, meanwhile, is captured and frozen in carbonite, and on his way to **Jabba the Hut,** setting the scene for *Revenge of the Jedi* (1983), the next film in the series.

The equal of the earlier film, *Empire* belongs to Darth Vader, who, more than ever, commands the screen with his dark presence. Returning from his defeat in *Star Wars,* his black robes flying behind him like Beelzebub's wings, he reveals unsuspected motivations and needs, as well as a surprising past. The film's unresolved ending is a bit of a let-down, but this is a small price to pay for two hours of dazzling entertainment. *Empire's* sophisticated special effects were described later that year in a CBS-TV special **SPFX: The Empire Strikes Back. Academy Awards** went to special effects technicians Brian Johnson, Richard Edlund, Dennis Muren and Bruce Nicholson, and to sound technicians Bill Varney, Steve Maslow, Gregg Landaker and Peter Sutton.

Director: Irvin Kershner, *Producer:* Gary Kurtz, *Executive Producer:* George Lucas, *Screenplay:* **Leigh Brackett,** Lawrence Kasdan, *Story:* George Lucas, *Photographer:* Peter Suschitzky, *Production Designer:* Norman Reynolds, *Special Effects:* Brian Johnson, Richard Edlund, *Mechanical Effects:* Nick Allder, *Matte Paintings:* Harrison Ellenshaw, *Models:* Lorne Peterson, *Production Paintings:* Ralph McQuarrie, *Makeup:* **Stuart Freeborn,** *Costumes:* John Mollo, *Sound Design:* Benjamin Burtt, Jr., *Music:* **John Williams**

Cast: **Mark Hamill,** Harrison Ford, Carrie Fisher, Billy Dee Williams, Anthony Daniels, Frank Oz, **Dave Prowse,** Peter Mayhew, Kenny Baker, Alec Guinness

THE END OF AUGUST AT THE HOTEL OZONE

See: **Konec Srpna v Hotelu Ozon**

THE END OF THE WORLD

Film 1977 U.S. (Manson) 93 Minutes Color

If nuns from outer space are your cup of tea, you may enjoy this silly **alien invasion** film, which isn't quite inept enough to qualify as one of the best of the worst (but give it time). **Christopher Lee,** wearing his basic black, plays a Catholic priest, replaced by an **alien** double, the pastor of St. Catherine's Church. At his side are the dutiful sister-surrogates, helping to build a time wall inside the church so they can return home before destroying the world. Going my way?

Director: John Hayes, *Producer:* Charles Bend, *Screenplay:* Frank Roy Perilli, *Photographer:* John Huneck, *Special Effects:* Harry Wollman, *Music:* Andrew Belling

Cast: Christopher Lee, Sue Lyon, Dean Jagger, Lew Ayres, MacDonald Carey, Kirk Scott

THE END OF THE WORLD (1931)

See: **La Fin du Monde**

ENEMY FROM SPACE

See: **Quatermass II**

L'ENIGME DE DIX HEURES/The Ten O'Clock Riddle

Film   1915   France (Film d'Art)   Black & white (silent)

This well-plotted thriller helped establish the career of legendary director **Abel Gance.** Audiences were kept guessing as to how a number of important people, including the chief of police, could be murdered precisely at the time indicated by an anonymous telephone caller. Even though guards stood at their doors and windows, each victim died precisely at 10 p.m., and there were no clues to be had. Not until the final scene was it revealed that the executions were accomplished by an electrical device attached to the telephone, activated when the receiver was picked up to answer a call—at 10 o'clock.

Director: Abel Gance, *Producer:* Louis Nalpas

Cast: Aurele Sydney

ENSIGN PAVEL CHEKOV

Russian navigator of the **U.S.S. Enterprise,** the gigantic starship of **Star Trek.** Chekov

Ensign Pavel Chekov (Walter Koenig) as he appeared in *Star Trek—The Motion Picture.*

is an outspoken patriot with an impetuous nature and a keen eye for the ladies. He was the youngest member of the cast when introduced during the program's second season, 1967. He was piped aboard by producer **Gene Roddenberry** after the Soviet newspaper *Pravda* wondered why the international space mission had no Russian crew members. In **Star Trek—The Motion Picture** (1979) Chekov was promoted to commander of the Security Section, and bald female lead Persis Khambatta took over as navigator. Chekov is played in the TV series and films by Walter Koenig.

THE ENTERPRISE

Federation **Starship** of **Star Trek.** The *U.S.S. Enterprise* is 947 feet long and 417 feet wide overall (making her about three times the size of a football field), with 11 decks in her disk-shaped main section. She is capable of supralight **warp speeds** and can stay aloft for 18 years with refueling. Built in space because of her immense size, the craft can never touch down on a planet, lest the forces of gravity and atmospheric friction tear her apart. Her 430 crew members (in the TV series) travel to planets via a **transporter room** that beams them to the surface (and back again). The Enterprise defense system includes photon torpedoes and an impenetrable **force field.**

Designers of the *Enterprise* are **Gene Roddenberry** and the Howard A. Anderson Company. The largest of the TV models, 14 feet long and made of sheet plastic, hangs in the Air and Space Museum of the Smithsonian Institution, near NASA's prototype space shuttle, named for her. The movie *Enterprise* was slightly redesigned to have a wider secondary hull and more deeply angled side struts, for a more powerful **widescreen** look. (See color section for photo.)

ESCAPE FROM THE PLANET OF THE APES

Film   1971   U.S. (20th Century-Fox)
Deluxe   Panavision

This third sequel to **Planet of the Apes** (1968) is one of the most enjoyable in the series. Paul Dehn's fast-paced, witty script has the intelligent apes Cornelius, Zira and Milo escaping from **Earth** just before the nuclear holocaust that destroyed it in **Beneath the Planet of the Apes** (1970). Their spaceship passes through a time warp, and they arrive on Earth in the 1970s. They instantly become celebrities, upsetting several scientists and politicians, who believe the apes pose a threat to mankind's dominance. Tracked down to a circus where they are hiding out, Cornelius, Zira and Milo are brutally murdered. But their recently born son, Caesar, escapes. He turns up in the next sequel, **Conquest of the Planet of the Apes** (1972), as the leader of a simian rebellion.

Director: Don Taylor, *Producer:* Arthur P. Jacobs, *Screenplay:* Paul Dehn, *Characters created by:* **Pierre Boulle,** *Photographer:* Joseph Biroc, *Makeup:* **John Chambers,** *Music:* **Jerry Goldsmith**

Cast: Roddy McDowall, Kim Hunter, Sal Mineo, Bradford Dillman, Natalie Trundy, Ricardo Montalban, Eric Braeden

ESCAPE FROM NEW YORK

Film   1981   U.S. (Avco Embassy)
99 Minutes   Metrocolor   Panavision   Dolby Stereo

New York 1997: Crime has gotten so out of hand that Manhattan has been turned into a maximum security prison operated by the U.S. Police Force. Urban blight has taken its natural course, and the city is now populated by more than three million criminals,

Escape From New York: Snake Plissken (Kurt Russell) conspires with a beautiful convict (Season Hubley) in the Federal prison of Manhattan.

crazies, bums, terrorists and thieves. There is no way out, since the island has been walled, the bridges have been mined and the tunnels are sealed. Into this stinking maelstrom arrives the President of the U.S., whose sabotaged plane crashlands near the "old" World Trade Center. To get him out, Federal authorities send in a young master criminal named Snake Plissken, who is promised freedom if he succeeds in the mission. Just to make certain he doesn't renege on the agreement, a government doctor implants a microscopic explosive in his neck that will go off at the end of 24 hours, unless he returns for the antidote.

Director: **John Carpenter,** *Producer:* Larry Franco, Debra Hill, *Screenplay:* John Carpenter, Nick Castle, *Photographer:* Dean Cundey, *Production Designer:* Joe Alves, *Special Effects:* Roy Arbogast, Brian Chin, Tom Campbell, *Music:* John Carpenter, Alan Howarth

Cast: Kurt Russell, Lee Van Cleef, Ernest Borgnine, Season Hubley, Adrienne Barbeau, Isaac Hayes, Donald Pleasence, Harry Dean Stanton

ESCAPEMENT

See: **The Electronic Monster**

ESCAPE TO WITCH MOUNTAIN

Film 1975 U.S. (Disney) 97 Minutes Technicolor

Two pre-teens, brother and sister, arrive on **Earth** from outer space, with no memory of who they are or where they came from. Gifted with a number of **psi powers,** they are taken in by a devious millionaire criminal, who plans to use their gifts to add to his wealth. They read his mind, however, and escape in a levitated camper to Witch Mountain, where mom and dad arrive to pick up the lost kids in a flying saucer. Adults will prefer the sequel, **Return from Witch Mountain** (1978), which stars Bette Davis and Christopher Lee as a pair of incredibly nasty villains.

Director: John Hough, *Producer:* Jerome Courtland, *Screenplay:* Robert Malcolm Young, *Novel:*

Alexander Key, *Photographer:* Frank Phillips, *Special Effects:* Art Cruickshank, Danny Lee, *Music:* Johnny Mandel

Cast: Ray Milland, Donald Pleasence, Eddie Albert, Kim Richards, Ike Eisenmann, Denver Pyle

E.T., THE EXTRA-TERRESTRIAL

Film 1982 U.S. (Universal) 120 Minutes Color Panavision Dolby Stereo

E.T., a loveable elf from outer space, finds himself left behind by a flying saucer during a botanical expedition in a California forest. Marooned on a strange planet three million light years from home, without a friend in the world, he gazes at the gigantic Christmas tree ornament of a space ship spinning into the outer reaches of the night, his red heart-light pulsing with fear.

So begins Steven Spielberg's enchanting fantasy-adventure of a little being trapped in a strange, perilous place—**Earth**—and his relationship with a resourceful ten-year-old boy, Elliott (Henry Thomas), who comes to E.T.'s rescue. Elliott hides the homesick creature in the bedroom of the family's suburban house, and, with the help of his big

E.T., The Extra-Terrestrial

brother and little sister, feeds it, protects it from sinister-looking scientists and, finally, helps it return home. (Earth's pollution is killing it.) The farewell is one of the tenderest in screen history, with Elliott and E.T. sharing an emotional final hug as the **extraterrestrial** prepares to depart for his own world.

Spielberg and scriptwriter Melissa Mathison have created a kind of cinematic poetry that captures the sublime innocence of childhood, when everything seems new, potentially dangerous and occasionally awesome. Spielberg has an uncanny ability for creating a mood of religious exhilaration from the confrontation of the ordinary and the bizarre, a feat achieved previously in **Close Encounters of the Third Kind** (1977), a prequel of sorts.

The biggest non-human star since **King Kong** (1933), E.T., who looks like a turtle without a shell, derives from a number of sources, including *Peter Pan* and **Yoda,** the green-skinned Jedi warrior of **The Empire Strikes Back** (1980). Whether eating Reese's Pieces—his favorite candy—learning English by watching *Sesame Street,* or trying to call home with a device rigged from an umbrella, a fork and a calculator, E.T. is completely convincing. Spielberg created the tiny being from $1.5 million worth of hand **puppets,** midgets in plastic shells, a cable-controlled mechanism, and a separate chest equipped with air bladders and a light source to depict the creature's emotional heart-light. Slightly grotesque and comical but never frightening, E.T. was designed by **Carlo Rambaldi,** who created the similar-looking **aliens** for *CE3K.* The creature's snurgling language is the work of **Ben Burtt, Jr.,** the sound effects wizard of the **Star Wars** films.

Director: Steven Spielberg, *Producer:* Steven Spielberg, Kathleen Kennedy, *Screenplay:* Melissa Mathison, *Story:* Steven Spielberg, *Photographer:* Allen Daviau, *Production Designer:* James D. Bissell, *Special Effects:* Carlo Rambaldi, ILM, Dennis Muren, Robert Short, *Music:* **John Williams**

Cast: Dee Wallace, Henry Thomas, Peter Coyote, Drew Barrymore, Robert Macnaughton, K. C. Martel

ETHER

Theoretical substance formerly thought to contain the **universe** in a kind of motionless, invisible sea. A tenet of 19th-century physics and early science fiction, ether explained why **light** was able to travel through the vacuum or **space:** It caused waves in this all-pervading medium and created an "ether wind."

THE EVIL OF FRANKENSTEIN

Film   1964   Great Britain (Hammer/ Universal)   94 Minutes   Technicolor

Dr. Frankenstein returns to his ancestral castle in the Balkans (Switzerland in Mary Shelley's novel) and revives the Monster, preserved in a cavern deep-freeze by a mad hypnotist. *Evil* is the third in Hammer's already tired **Frankenstein** series, which began with **The Curse of Frankenstein** (1957).

Director: **Freddie Francis,** *Producer:* Anthony Hinds, *Screenplay:* John Elder (Anthony Hinds), *Photographer:* John Wilcox, *Makeup:* Roy Ashton, *Special Effects:* Les Bowie, *Music:* Don Banks

Cast: Peter Cushing, Peter Woodthorpe, Sandor Eles, Kiwi Kingston, Duncan Lamont

EXPRESSIONISM

A style of cinema derived from painting, literature and drama that reached its apex in Germany during the period 1918-33. Expressionism is characterized by a deliberate artifice achieved with harshly shadowed lighting and distorted sets and props, the esthetic being to express "inner experience" rather than objective reality.

EXTRATERRESTRIAL

SF term for a non-human being, a creature not from Terra, the Latin name for **Earth.** Generally, a benign term without the hostile connotations of **alien,** although the words are often used interchangeably. It is often shortened to E.T. (See also: **E.T.**)

THE FABULOUS WORLD OF JULES VERNE

See: **Vynalez Zkazy**

THE FACE OF FU MANCHU

Film 1965 Great Britain (Anglo-EMI/Seven Arts) 96 Minutes Technicolor Techniscope

Christopher Lee is perfection as Oriental supervillain Fu Manchu, Great Britain's greatest enemy and Scotland Yard's most-wanted man. Digging into the role with his characteristic bloodlessness, Lee plays straight man to director **Don Sharp**'s witty and evocative rethinking of old Saturday matinee programmers. Fu visits Tibet (actually, Ireland) to gather poison flowers to bestow upon London from his Thames River laboratory.

Director: **Don Sharp,** *Producer:* Harry Alan Towers, *Screenplay:* Peter Welbeck (Harry Alan Towers), *Character created by:* Sax Rohmer, *Photographer:* Ernest Steward, *Art Director:* Frank White, *Music:* Chris Whelan

Cast: Christopher Lee, Tsai Chin, Nigel Green, Howard Marion Crawford, James Robertson Justice

FAHRENHEIT 451

Film 1966 Great Britain/France (Rank/Universal) 112 Minutes Technicolor

In the near future, all books and printed matter are banned, supplanted by a two-way TV system that keeps the population as happy as cattle. In charge of ferreting out illegal caches of books and burning them publicly (the combustion temperature of paper is 451 degrees Fahrenheit) are the Firemen, who ride in red fire engines. While raiding an apartment, a young fireman (Oskar Werner), more sensitive than most, meets a girl who asks him if he has ever read any of the books he destroys. Curious, he pulls one from the pile. Before long he is an avid reader, becoming more aware of himself with each page and more dissatisfied with the conformist **dystopia** he lives in. Finally, he escapes with the girl, secretly a radical, to a remote commune of "Book People," each of whom lovingly memorizes a book to preserve for future generations.

Francois Truffaut, in his only SF outing as a director (he also played the part of a French scientist in **Close Encounters of the Third Kind),** occasionally evokes the dreamlike imagery that characterizes **Ray Bradbury**'s famous novel, but the film is curiously flat and uneventful. Truffaut turns the story into a loner's search for self, his traditional movie concern, which is out of context here.

Director: Francois Truffaut, *Producer: Lewis M. Allen, Screenplay:* Jean-Louis Richard, Francois Truffaut, *Novel:* Ray Bradbury, *Photographer:* Nicholas Roeg, *Production Designer:* Syd Cain, *Costumes:* Tony Walton, *Music:* **Bernard Herrmann**

Cast: Oskar Werner, Julie Christie, Cyril Cusack, Anton Diffring, Jeremy Spenser

FAIL SAFE

Film 1964 U.S. (Columbia) 111 Minutes Black & white

Released shortly after **Dr. Strangelove** (1963), this doomsday melodrama had the misfortune of dealing with the same subject as Kubrick's brilliant black comedy: a nuclear **bomb** attack launched in error by the U.S. against Russia. Moscow is destroyed, and, to make amends, the President of the U.S. orders the bombing of New York. Director Sidney Lumet is a master of thought-provoking chills, but even he can't overcome the script's preposterous climax.

Director: Sidney Lumet, *Producer:* Max Youngstein, *Screenplay:* Walter Bernstein, *Novel:* Eugene Burdick, Harvey Wheeler, *Photographer:* Gerald Hirschfeld

Cast: Henry Fonda, Walter Matthau, Dan O'Herlihy, Fritz Weaver, Larry Hagman

FANTASTIC VOYAGE

Film   1966   U.S. (20th Century-Fox)
100 Minutes   DeLuxe Cinemascope

To save the life of an important scientist, a team of medical experts is shrunk to pinhead size in order to remove a blood clot from inside the man's brain. Injected into his body aboard a tiny sub called the *Proteus,* they navigate his blood stream and pass through his lungs, heart, brain and ear. When one of their number is discovered to be a saboteur, he is conveniently ingested by a pulsing army of hungry white corpuscles.

The story offers few surprises, but the special effects are spectacular. Harper Goff, who worked on the *Nautilus* in Disney's **20,000 Leagues Under the Sea** (1954) designed the *Proteus,* a sleek beauty that weighed 8,000 pounds and was 42 feet long. Three scale models in descending sizes were also built, including a one-and-a-half-inch vessel shown entering the man's body in the hypodermic syringe. The illusion of shrinking was created with a traveling **matte;** the sets were full-scale, oversized replicas that depicted the internal organs in detail. The capillary set, for instance, was 100 feet long and 50 feet wide, constructed of fiberglass, plastic resins, and a painted backdrop. During initial filming, the sets seemed surprisingly lifeless, until photographer Ernest Laszlo came up with the idea of bathing them with a pulsating light (achieved by a rotating color filter) to give the illusion that the organs were actually working. Special Effects man Art Cruickshank won an **Academy Award** for his work, as did the film's art directors. (See also: **wire work.**)

Director: Richard Fleischer, *Producer:* Saul David, *Screenplay:* Harry Kleiner, *Story:* Otto Klement,

J. Lewis Bixby, *Photographer:* Ernest Laszlo, *Art Directors:* Dale Hennessy, Jack Martin Smith, Walter M. Scott, Stuart A. Reiss, *Special Effects:* Art Cruickshank, Emil Kosa, Jr., *Music:* Leonard Rosenmann

Cast: Stephen Boyd, Raquel Welch, Donald Pleasence, Edmond O'Brien, Arthur Kennedy, Arthur O'Connell, William Redfield

FANTASTIC VOYAGE

TV series   1968-70   U.S. (ABC)   30 Minutes (weekly)   Color

Microscopic members of the C.M.D.F. (Combined Miniature Defense Forces), a secret U.S. police force, fight criminals and dangerous microbes from aboard a teeny aircraft called the Voyager. An animated cartoon based on the feature film of the same title (see listing above). (26 episodes)

FANZINE

An amateur magazine or newsletter published by SF buffs. (The term is often used inaccurately to refer to commercially produced fan magazines.) Fanzines date back to the early 1930s and usually cover a specific area of interest, such as **Star Trek, Doctor Who** and other TV series that have spawned cults. Former fanzine editors include SF writers **Ray Bradbury,** Frederick Phol, Harlan Ellison, Michael Moorcock, Cyril Kornbluth, Damon Knight and Charles Eric Maine.

FAST MOTION

A motion picture technique that creates the illusion of people or objects moving at an accelerated rate. The effect is realized by shooting a scene at slower-than-normal speeds and thereby recording fewer frames of film. When the film is projected normally, the action appears to be speeded-up. In **The Time Machine** (1960), fast motion and **time-lapse** photography were used to indicate the passage of time in the outside world as the machine gathered speed. The technique is also used to film spacecraft models, explosions and wire work, to take away the "wobble" and impart a realistic look to the effect.

The exaggerated movement of silent films also results from fast motion: Silents were shot at 16 frames per second but are usually projected at the present speed of 24 frames per second. The opposite effect is **slow motion.**

FIBER OPTICS

An optical fiber is a flexible glass thread that conducts light in the way that copper wire conducts electrons. Made of a special glass or plastic, the fiber is a kind of pipe that can be bent to conform to any shape, without losing the intensity of the light traveling inside it. So fine that a bundle can pass through the eye of a needle, optical fibers are used by doctors to look into formerly inaccessible parts of the body, and in industry to transport computer data, and to command industrial robots.

Fiber optics have also found their way into movie special effects, as a means of creating realistic **star** fields and intricate clusters that give the illusion of depth and distance. The fibers are easier to control and more versatile than light bulbs, and their pinpoints of light are more precise.

FIEND WITHOUT A FACE

Film   1957   Great Britain (MGM/ Amalgamated)   75 Minutes   Black & white

Set in Canada, *Fiend Without a Face* begins with a series of gruesome murders at a rocket-launching base. An Air Force officer traces the deaths to the nearby home of an eccentric scientist, who has built a machine capable of turning thoughts into energy. Without realizing it, the scientist had projected his hostilities into the apparatus, which gave them tangible form. The monsters eventually become visible, revealing themselves to be full-sized mobile brains equipped with bobbling antennae. Scurrying across the countryside, they break

through windows and throw themselves on their victims, sucking their skulls dry through a quick incision at the back of the neck. Like the tragic Professor Morbius in **Forbidden Planet** (1956), the scientist sacrifices himself to his mental monsters. Despite its boldly absurd premise, the film evokes a chill or two and has a certain fascination. The brains are **stop-motion** puppets (surely a first in SF cinema), smoothly animated by Puppel Nordhoff and Peter Nielson.

Director: Arthur Crabtree, *Producer:* John Croydon, *Screenplay:* Herbert J. Leder, *Short Story:* "The Thought Monster" Amelia R. Long, *Photographer:* Lionel Banes, *Special Effects:* Puppel Nordhoff, Peter Nielson, *Music:* Buxton Orr

Cast: Kyanston Reeves, Marshall Thompson, Terry Kilburn, Kim Parker, Peter Madden

FIGHTING MARINES

Film serial   1935   U.S. (Mascot)
12 Episodes   Black & white

Tiger Shark, a pirate king-mad scientist, spins Marine planes out of the sky with a radio-gravity device when the leathernecks arrive to build a landing strip on his island hideout. Tracked to a cavern lair, this thorn in the side of progress is vanquished with his own nitroglycerin (accidently touched off during a final reel shoot-out), which also destroys his inventions and pirate's treasure.

Director: B. Reeves Eason, Joseph Kane, *Producer:* Barney Sarecky, *Screenplay:* Barney Sarecky, Sherman L. Lowe

Cast: Grant Withers, Adrian Morris, Ann Rutherford, Robert Warwick

LA FIGLIA DI FRANKENSTEIN/The Daughter of Frankenstein

(U.S. title: *Lady Frankenstein*)

Film   1971   Italy (Condor)   99 Minutes
Color   (Released 1972   U.S. [New World]
85 Minutes)

The Dr. **Frankenstein** story, told from the point of view of his daughter. (His what?) A woman of great beauty and surgical skill, she creates her own monster from a handsome stud and sends him after the creature that killed her father. Body-builder Mickey Hargitay, ex-husband of Jayne Mansfield, is typecast as the **android.**

Director: Mel Welles, *Producer:* Harry Cushing, *Screenplay:* Edward Di Lorenzo, *Photographer:* Riccardo Pallotini, *Special Effects:* Cipa, *Music:* Alessandro Allesandroni

Cast: Joseph Cotten, Sara Bay, Mickey Hargitay, Herbert Fox

THE FINAL PROGRAMME

(Also titled: *The Last Days of Man on Earth)*

Film   1974   Great Britain (Goodtimes/Gladiole)   89 Minutes   Technicolor

Michael Moorcock's archetypal character Jerry Cornelius arrived on the screen in this high-gloss adaptation of the author's novel of the same title. The film's Cornelius, flashier and less ambiguous than Moorcock's, is a young and handsome physicist, winner of a Nobel Prize, who is fabulously wealthy, a rock star, and a religious leader. In fact, he possesses every desirable 20th-century quality imaginable, although the film takes place in the 21st. The surreal plot has to do with a hidden microfilm that contains a final computer program with a mysterious formula for immortality. When the film is found, Cornelius, along with a formidable man-eater named Miss Brunner, is forcibly taken to a secret laboratory and infused with the world's knowledge. As they make love, the computer program combines them into a single hermaphroditic being, a new Messiah who will lead the world to a better future.

Director Fuest, a former art director, has opted for a neon, pop-art farce rather than Moorcock's cerebral ironies, which were apparently beyond his abilities. Fuest's grinning ape-person is a poor substitute for the author's bisexual savior.

Director/Screenplay/Production Designer: **Robert Fuest,** *Producers:* John Goldstone, Sanford Lieberson, *Novel:* Michael Moorcock, *Photographer:*

Norman Warwick, *Music:* Paul Beaver, Bernard Krause

Cast: Jon Finch, Hugh Griffith, Patrick Magee, Jenny Runacre, Sterling Hayden, George Coulouris

THE FINAL COUNTDOWN

Film   1980   U.S. (United Artists)
104 Minutes   Technicolor   Panavision
Dolby Stereo

The date is December 7, 1980; the place, somewhere off the coast of Pearl Harbor. While on a shakedown cruise, the U.S.S. Nimitz, the world's largest nuclear-powered aircraft carrier, passes through what appears to be an electrical storm, which carries it back in time to December 6, 1941. The question now is, should its commander blast Japan's attacking air armada out of the skies and save many American lives, or let history take its course?

"There are forces in the universe we are only now beginning to understand," says one of the passengers, attempting to explain the film's implausible premise, made surprisingly believable by a fast-paced script and a careful accretion of anachronistic detail. This includes a comic sequence in which several of the carrier's jet fighters take on two bewildered Japanese Zeros. The Nimitz is the real wonder of the film—a huge floating airbase more than 30 stories high, powered by two nuclear reactors, with a crew of nearly 6,000.

Director: Don Taylor, *Producer:* Peter Vincent Douglas, *Screenplay:* David Ambrose, Gerry Davis, Thomas Hunter, Peter Powell, *Photographer:* Victor J. Kemper, *Production Designer:* Fernando Carrere, *Special Effects:* Maurice Binder, Louis Schwartzberg, *Music:* John Scott

Cast: Kirk Douglas, Martin Sheen, Katharine Ross, James Farentino, Ron O'Neal, Charles Durning

FIREBALL XL-5

TV series   1961-62   Great Britain (ITC)
30 Minutes (weekly)   Black & white

Col. Steve Zodiac, a pilot for the Galaxy Patrol, protects the United Solar System from the sinister villain's Mr. and Mrs. Superspy. Zodiac's spaceship is called the Fireball XL-5. An animated puppet show filmed in Supermarionation. (39 episodes)

Creators: Gerry and Sylvia Anderson, *Executive Producer:* Gerry Anderson, *Photographer:* John Read, *Art Director:* Reg Hill, *Special Effects:* Derek Meddings, *Music:* Barry Gray

Voices: Paul Maxwell, Sylvia Anderson, David Graham, Gerry Anderson, John Bluthal

FIREFOX

Film   1982   U.S. (Warner Bros.)
136 Minutes   Color Panavision   Dolby Stereo

Firefox, one of the washouts of a summer innundated with gimmicky SF films, is the code name of a superplane developed by the Russians. It flies six times the speed of sound and operates directly from the pilot's thoughts. Naturally, the C.I.A. must have the plane, which it steals by smuggling crack pilot Mitchell Gant into Russia. Gant (Clint Eastwood playing another of his righteous "Dirty Harry" roles) is a perfect choice for the mission: He grew up speaking Russian, and *Firefox* obeys only Russian thoughts. The film is stunningly photographed by Bruce Surtees, and **John Dykstra's** futuristic MIG is convincing, which is more than you can say for the plot of the film.

Director/Producer: Clint Eastwood, *Screenplay:* Alex Lasker, Wendell Wellman, *Novel:* Craig Thomas, *Photographer:* Bruce Surtees, *Art Directors:* John Graysmark, Elayne Ceder, *Special Effects:* John Dykstra, *Music:* Maurice Jarre

Cast: Clint Eastwood, Freddie Jones, David Huffman, Warren Clarke, Ronald Lacey, Kenneth Colley

A FIRE IN THE SKY

TV film   1978   U.S. (NBC) 156 Minutes   Color

Astronomers spot an incandescent comet heading toward Phoenix and sound the warning, but no one believes them. The President finally orders an evacuation, and the plot finally gets moving. The stunning

pyrotechnics were handled by Joe Viskocil, who performed a similar task on **Star Wars** (1977). Any resemblance between this TV film and the theatrical release **Meteor** (1979) is purely intentional. (See also: **Comets.**)

Director: Jerry Jameson, *Producer:* Hugh Benson, *Screenplay:* Dennis Nemec, Michael Blankfort, *Story:* Paul Gallico, *Photographer:* Matthew F. Leonetti, *Art Directors:* Ross Bellah, Dick Hennessy, *Special Effects:* Joseph A. Unsinn, *Music:* Paul Chihara

Cast: Richard Crenna, Elizabeth Ashley, David Dukes, Joanna Miles, Lloyd Bochner

FIRST MAN INTO SPACE

Film   1958   Great Britain (MGM/Amalgamated)   77 Minutes   Black & white

An astronaut returns to Earth as a blob-like monster.

With the age of space exploration dawning during the 1950s, British and American filmmakers launched a cycle of quasi-scientific imaginings of the dangers of space travel. *First Man Into Space* is one of the also-rans. Purporting to take place in the U.S. but obviously made in England, it bears more than a passing resemblance to **The Quatermass Experiment** (1954), a well-made film with a similarly afflicted astronaut. Here, the pilot of a rocket plane returns home covered with a crusty fungus picked up while flying through a cloud of **meteor** dust. The organism eventually kills him but continues to inhabit his corpse, and it must have a daily dose of human blood to stay alive. The film gets off to a promising start with the astronaut pathetically trying to come to grips with his incurable affliction, but soon becomes just another formula vampire film, drained of life by the cliches of its script. (See also: **Mutant; Parasite.**)

Director: Robert Day, *Producer:* John Croydon, Charles F. Vetter, *Screenplay:* John C. Cooper, Lance Hargreaves, *Story:* Wyott Ordung, *Photographer:* Geoffrey Faithfull, *Makeup:* Michael Morris, *Music:* Buxton Orr

Cast: Marshall Thompson, Marla Landi, Bill Edwards, Robert Ayres

FIRST MEN IN THE MOON

Film   1964   Great Britain (Columbia)
103 Minutes   Technicolor   Panavision

A lively, if uninspired version of the **H. G. Wells** novel, previously filmed (in 1919) by British director Jack V. Leigh. Victorian Professor Cavor invents an **antigravity** substance called "Cavorite," which propels a sphere-shaped spaceship to the moon. Along for the ride are Arnold Bedford and his fiancee, Kate. Attacked by a giant caterpillar called a "Moon Calf," the explorers are captured by the Selenites, insect-like creatures who live beneath the moon's surface. But Bedford and Kate manage to escape, leaving Cavor behind.

Astronauts journeying to the moon in 1965 find Cavor's Union Jack, still planted on a lunar hill, and a diary that explains what has happened. Bedford, now an elderly widower in a rest home, recounts the story to the world. The Selenites meanwhile have disappeared, evidently wiped out by the common cold brought along by the sniffling Cavor.

The pseudo-science here is enjoyable, and the creatures, animated by **Ray Harryhausen,** are still a delight to watch. (See also: **Le voyage dans le lune.**)

Director: **Nathan Juran,** *Producer:* Charles Schneer, *Screenplay:* **Nigel Kneale,** Jan Read, *Special Effects:* Ray Harryhausen, *Music:* Laurie Johnson

Cast: Lionel Jeffries, Edward Judd, Martha Hyer, Hugh McDermott, Betty McDowall, Peter Finch (uncredited)

FIRST SPACESHIP ON VENUS

See: **Der Schweigende Stern**

FISHER, TERENCE (1904–   )

British film and occasional TV director. Born in London, Fisher was a merchant sailor before finding work in films as a cutter's assistant in 1933. He was promoted to film editor in 1936 but was not given an opportunity to direct until 1948, when he was 44. After an initial period of lyrical melodramas, he joined Hammer Film Productions where he specialized in assembly-line, formula remakes of classic Hollywood **horror** films.

Films include: Colonel Bogey (1948), *So Long at the Fair* [co-director] (1950), **Stolen Face** (1952), **Four-Sided Triangle, Spaceways** (1953), **The Curse of Frankenstein** (1957), *The Horror of Dracula,* **The Revenge of Frankenstein** (1958), **The Man Who Could Cheat Death** (1959), **The Two Faces of Dr. Jekyll** (1960), *The Phantom of the Opera* (1962), *The Horror of It All,* **The Earth Dies Screaming** (1964), **Island of Terror** (1966), **Frankenstein Created Woman, Night of the Big Heat** (1967), **Frankenstein Must Be Destroyed!** (1969), **Frankenstein and the Monster from Hell** (1973)

FIVE

Film   1951   U.S. (Columbia)   93 Minutes
Black & white

World War IV breaks out among five survivors of a nuclear holocaust in this talky, plodding and intermittently entertaining sermon against the **bomb.** Its cast of cliche characters argue, hate and love until only two are left: A gutless bank teller succumbs to a bad case of nerves, a racist redneck murders a Stepin-Fetchit elevator operator (the film's token black), leaving a handsome idealist and a beautiful pregnant widow to repopulate the earth with a breed of, presumably, white peace lovers.

Creator **Arch Oboler,** a creative force in radio drama, shows little grasp of the technique of telling a story visually. *Five* comes to life only when it stops talking and leaves the studio: A trip into a corpse-strewn city to look for the woman's husband, for example, and a striking view of an ultramodern hilltop house (Oboler's own, designed by Frank Lloyd Wright), where the group takes refuge, and shots of a forlorn patch of corn whose growth will ensure their survival.

Oboler was correct in judging the temper of the times, however. *Five* reflected America's growing fear of nuclear war, and it ushered in a cycle of anti-bomb films that lasted into the early 1960s. The film is a cult favorite in France. A similar plot was more successfully handled in **The World, the Flesh and the Devil** (1959).

Director/Producer/Screenplay: Arch Oboler, *Photographer:* Lou Stoumen, Ed Spiegel, Sid Lubow, *Music:* Henry Russell

Cast: William Phipps, Susan Douglas, James Anderson, Charles Lampkin, Earl Lee

FIVE MILLION MILES TO EARTH

See: **Quatermass and the Pit**

THE FLAME BARRIER

Film   1958   U.S. (United Artists)
70 Minutes   Black & white

A satellite returns to earth coated with a deadly red-hot protoplasm. *The Flame Barrier* is a passable low-budget feature that exploited public apprehension about launching satellites after the successful orbiting of Sputnik by the Soviet Union in 1957. Some suspense is generated as scientists travel into the Yucatan jungle in search of the satellite, and the fanciful single-celled organism is effective as it spews out rays that melt flesh from bones.

Director: Paul Landers, *Producer:* Arthur Gardner, Jules Levy, *Screenplay:* Pat Fielder, George Worthing Yates *(based on his story),* Art Director: James Vance

Cast: **Arthur Franz,** Kathleen Crowley, Robert Brown, Kaz Oran, Vincent Padula

FLASH GORDON

TV series   1953   U.S. (syndicated)
30 Minutes (weekly)   Black & white

Flash lost most of his all-American appeal as portrayed by Steve Holland in this hastily assembled afternoon time-filler, shot in West Germany. By comparison, the **Buster Crabbe serials** looked like Hollywood spectaculars. Irene Champlin played Dale Arden and Joseph Nash was Dr. Zarkov. (39 episodes)

FLASH GORDON

Film serial   1936   U.S. (Universal)
13 Episodes   Black & white

Created as a newspaper comic strip in 1934 by artist Alex Raymond (as King Features' answer to the National Newspaper Service's **Buck Rogers),** *Flash Gordon* came to the screen in this first of three fondly remembered **space opera**s. Aryan hero Flash **(Buster Crabbe)** and his perennial fiancee Dale Arden (Jean Rogers) journey to the planet Mongo in Dr. Zarkov's homemade spaceship to investigate the cause of mysterious earthquakes that threaten to tear the **Earth** apart.

They are promptly arrested by the troops of Ming the Merciless, the vicious dictator of Mongo. Zarkov is forced to work for Ming, who has an eye for the beautiful Dale; Aura, Ming's daughter, is similarly attracted to Flash. The adventure takes Flash and Dale to the underwater kingdom of the Sharkmen in a submarine, and to Sky City, inhabited by the Hawken, which floats on **antigravity** ray beams. After various amorous intrigues and close encounters with death, Flash finally vanquishes Ming in the final reel and rescues Dale, Zarkov—and Earth.

Although allegedly shot on a record budget of $350,000, *Flash Gordon* looks remarkably tacky, which only adds to its naive appeal. Among its borrowings from other Universal productions is the laboratory set from **The Bride of Frankenstein** (1935). The theme music was previously heard in that film, with additions from **The Invisible Man** (1933). The **serial** was later released in feature form as *Rocketship.*

Director: Frederick Stephani, *Screenplay:* Frederick Stephani, George H. Plympton, Basil Dickey, Lee O'Neill

Cast: **Buster Crabbe,** Jean Rogers, **Charles Middleton,** Frank Shannon, Priscilla Lawson, James Pierce, Richard Alexander, John Lipson

FLASH GORDON

Film   1980   U.S./Great Britain (Universal)
113 Minutes   Technicolor   Todd-AO

Flash Gordon, then and now:
Buster Crabbe (1936) and Sam J.
Jones (1980).

Flash Gordon has become a New York Jets quarterback and Dale Arden is a travel agent in this embarrassing, expensive remake of the 1936 serial. Director Mike Hodges plays the story for camp and sex, thereby stripping Flash of his ingenuous appeal. Not helping matters is the casting of glassy-eyed Sam J. Jones, a former health club attendant, in the title role. The sets and costumes by Danilo Donati, a protege of Frederico Fellini, are stunning, and Swedish actor Max von Sydow has a great time with the role of Ming the Merciless. But the action moves with the pent-up energy of a lava flow.

Director: Mike Hodges, *Producer:* Dino de Laurentiis, *Screenplay:* Lorenzo Semple, Jr., *Photographer:* Gil Taylor, *Production Designer/Costumes:* Danilo Donati, *Special Effects:* Glen Robinson, George Gibbs, Richard Conway, Norman Dorme, Frank Van Der Veer, *Music:* Howard Blake

Cast: Sam J. Jones, Melody Anderson, Topol, Max von Sydow, Ornella Muti, Timothy Dalton, Peter Wyngarde, Mariangela Melato, Brian Blessed

FLASH GORDON CONQUERS THE UNIVERSE

(Also titled: *Peril From the Planet Mongo, The Purple Death From Outer Space*)

Film serial   1940   U.S. (Universal)
12 Episodes   Black & white

The planet **Earth** is suffering from an epidemic called the Purple Death, a sickness caused by Ming the Merciless in yet another plan to conquer the universe. Flash, Dale and Zarkov zoom to the planet Mongo and wreck the machine spreading "death dust" in Earth's atmosphere. Carol Hughes replaced Jean Rogers as Dale Arden in this third—and weakest—of the **Flash Gordon** serials.

Directors: Ford Beebe, Ray Taylor, *Screenplay:* George H. Plympton, Basil Dickey, Barry Shipman

Cast: **Buster Crabbe,** Carol Hughes, Frank Shannon, **Charles Middleton,** Roland Drew, Don Rowan

FLASH GORDON'S TRIP TO MARS

Film serial   1938   U.S. (Universal)
15 Episodes   Black & white

Flash, Dale and Zarkov take a rocket jaunt to **Mars,** where Ming the Merciless and the evil Queen Azura are stealing nitrogen from **Earth.** The trio is immediately captured by the Clay People, human beings turned into clay by Azura's magical sapphire ring. With the help of Prince Barin, leader of the Hawkmen, Flash liberates the Clay People, who place Ming in a disintegration chamber. Flash then destroys the villain's nitrogen-robbing ray. Less repetitive and written with more polish, this follow-up to **Flash Gordon** (1936) does a credible job of depicting the Clay People, who seem to literally ooze from walls of stone. The **serial** was trimmed into a feature version later that year and released as *Mars Attacks the World,* to capitalize on Orson Welles' Halloween broadcast of **The War of the Worlds** (1938).

Directors: Ford Beebe, Robert F. Hill, *Screenplay:* Ray Trampe, Norman S. Hall, Wyndham Gittens, Herbert Dolmas

Cast: **Buster Crabbe,** Jean Rogers, **Charles Middleton,** Frank Shannon, Richard Alexander, C. Montague Shaw

FLASH GORDON: THE GREATEST ADVENTURE OF ALL

TV film   1979   U.S. (NBC) 100 Minutes   Color

Made in 1979 and shelved when a new **Flash Gordon** (1980) movie went into release, this animated cartoon finally arrived on the tube in 1982. Set in the 1930s, the story line is an enjoyable rehash of the famous **Buster Crabbe** serials, with Flash journeying to the planet Mongo for the inevitable confrontation with Ming the Merciless. Filmation's thrifty "limited **animation**" technique is of the standard Saturday-morning variety (although the feature was aired in prime time), but the banking and zooming spaceship **models,** achieved with a **motion-control** camera, are first-rate.

Producer: Don Christiensen, *Executive Producers:* Lou Scheimer, Norm Prescott, *Writer:* Sam Peeples

THE FLESH EATERS

Film   1964   U.S. (Cinema)   88 Minutes   Black & white

It's **mad scientist** time again. You know, the one who lives on a remote island so that he can conduct his diabolical experiments in secret. This time he's come up with a flesh-eating bacteria and dumped it into the ocean surrounding his lair. Four survivors of a shipwreck manage to elude the tiny jaws and discover his secret, making it safe to go back into the water. Now for a microbe that can eat film.

Director: Jack Curtis, *Producers:* Jack Curtis, Terry Curtis, Arnold Drake, *Screenplay:* Arnold Drake, *Photographer:* Carson Davidson, *Special Effects:* Roy Benson, *Music:* Julian Stein

Cast: Martin Kosleck, Barbara Wilkin, Rita Morley, Ray Tudor, Byron Sanders

FLESH GORDON

Film   1974   U.S. (Mammoth/Graffiti)
78 Minutes   Metrocolor

There are a few amusing moments in this softcore sex spoof of **Flash Gordon,** but it's mostly juvenile stuff, totally lacking in the charm of its model. Emperor Wang of the planet Porno aims his ray cannon at Flesh's airplane, destroying the inhibitions of Dale and Flesh, who are soon doing what comes naturally. The lovers bail out of the tri-motor, into the waiting arms of Dr. Jerkoff, who travels in a phallic-shaped spaceship. Wang captures Dale and makes her his queen, which offends the real queen, Prince Precious.

Directors: Michael Benveniste, William Hunt, Walter R. Cichy, *Producers:* Howard Ziehm, Bill Osco, *Screenplay:* Michael Benveniste, William Hunt, *Special Effects:* Jim Danforth [uncredited], **Rick Baker,** Russ Turner, Doug Beswick, Gregory Jein, *Music:* Ralph Ferraro

Cast: Jason Williams, Suzanne Fields, Joseph Hudgins, William Hunt, Lance Larsen, Candy Samples

FLIGHT TO MARS

Film   1951   U.S. (Monogram)   72 Minutes   Cinecolor

Or whatever became of the spacesuits worn by the astronauts of **Destination Moon**

(1950). A space probe from **Earth** crashlands on **Mars,** whose underground citizens wear the hand-me-downs when venturing on the planet's uninhabitable surface. Ruled by Princess Alita (a reference to the memorable Russian film **Aelita** and evidently intended as a compliment), the Martians turn out to be helpful mechanics who repair the ship and send the Earthmen back home, across a painted backdrop of the Martian sky.

Director: Lesley Selander, *Producer:* Walter Mirisch, *Screenplay:* Arthur Strawn, *Music:* Marlin Skiles

Cast: Cameron Mitchell, **Arthur Franz,** Marguerite Chapman, Morris Ankrum, John Litel

THE FLY

Film 1958 U.S. (20th Century-Fox)
94 Minutes Eastmancolor CinemaScope

Although implausible and inconsistent, *The Fly* has a certain morbid attraction and a visual panache that keeps you glued to the screen. The plot, one of the SF film's tallest stories, has to do with a scientist who builds a matter-transmission machine (see: **Matter Transmitter**) and tries it out on himself. A fly has gotten into the chamber ahead of him, and, during the journey across the lab, their molecules are scrambled. The man emerges with the head and arm of the fly, and the fly with the head of a man. Gone mad—not surprisingly—he attacks his wife, who mercifully squashes him in a hydraulic press. Trapped in a spider's web, the little fly screams in an unheard voice, "Help me! Help Me!" and is dispatched by a rock, wielded by his brother.

How the fly and the scientist adapt to each other's proportions is one of the many mysteries left unexplained. The wife and brother have apparently gotten away with murder. The script is based on a story of the same title by George Langelaan, originally published in *Playboy* magazine. The film was a great success and spawned two sequels: **Return of the Fly** and **Curse of the Fly.**

Director/Producer: **Kurt Neumann,** *Screenplay:* James Clavell, *Story:* George Langelaan, *Photog-*

rapher, **Karl Struss,** *Makeup:* Ben Nye, *Special Effects:* Lyle B. Abbott, *Music:* Paul Sawtell

Cast: David Hedison, Patricia Owens, Vincent Price, Herbert Marshall, Charles Herbert

THE FLYING SAUCER

Film 1950 U.S. (Film Classics)
69 Minutes Black & white

The U.S. Air Force investigates **UFO** sightings in Alaska, where secret Russian agents have preceded them to a downed **alien** spacecraft. This exploitation film is worthy of note only because of its period Cold War attitude toward UFOs, then bewildering many Americans.

Director/Producer: Mikel Conrad, *Screenplay:* Mikel Conrad, Howard Irving Young, *Photographer:* Philip Tannura, *Music:* Darrel Calker

Cast: Mikel Conrad, Pat Garrison, Denver Pyle

FLYING SAUCERS

See: **UFOs**

THE FLYING TORPEDO

Film 1916 U.S. (Triangle) Short Black & white (silent)

The success of **Walter Booth's** prophetic **The Airship Destroyer** (1909) inspired a number of foreign invasion spectaculars, including this American imitation by D. W. Griffith. The flying torpedo is a radio-controlled missile invented by a scientist to destroy a fleet of ships sent from an unnamed Asian country in 1964 to bombard Southern California.

The convincing row of enemy battleships was a composite-board cutout, profiled against the sunset off the coast of Santa Monica. The "cannons" were small powder squibs shoved into drill-holes. Cost of the special effects, according to photographer Brown: 40 cents. All prints of the film have since vanished, but a number of stills remain.

Director: D. W. Griffith, *Screenplay:* Robert M. Baker, John Emerson, *Photographer:* Karl Brown, *Special Effects:* Fireworks Wilson

Cast: John Emerson

FOG, HAZE AND SMOKE EFFECTS

These effects are summoned up on cue with a variety of safe and efficient devices. A light fog or haze can be faked in long shots by placing a diffusing filter over the camera lens (by the same token, real haze can be removed with a filter that absorbs blue and ultraviolet light). Fog is produced in the studio or on location with a portable device called a fog gun, which heats and vaporizes air.

Movie smoke comes from smoldering pots of a special chemical mixture that produces dark black clouds without flaming or creating much heat. Previous methods of creating fog by pouring water over dry ice and smoke by burning kerosene are no longer used.

To create the polluted atmosphere required for the cityscapes of Ridley Scott's **Blade Runner** (1982), special effects expert **Douglas Trumbull** devised a "smoke room," which consists of a large, airtight glass tank and a vaporizer that saturates the air inside with oil. The emulsified oil is noxious, and the room is used only for filming miniatures.

LA FOLIE DU DOCTEUR TUBE/The Madness of Doctor Tube

Film   1915   France (Film d'Art)   Black & white (silent)

A deranged scientist discovers how to stretch and condense people and animals. Not a true SF film, this early black comedy is an avante garde exercise in the cinematic use of the **anamorphic lens,** mirrors and other camera tricks that distort perspective—all of which are now part of the special effects lexicon. *La Folie du Docteur Tube* also introduced the **mad scientist** to the screen (the actor wore an elongated cranium), later a staple of SF and **horror** films.

Director/Screenplay: **Abel Gance,** *Producer:* Louis Nalpas, *Photographer:* Wentzel

Cast: Albert Dieudonne

FORBIDDEN PLANET

Film   1956   U.S. (MGM)   98 Minutes
Metrocolor   CinemaScope

Loosely adapted from Shakespeare's final play, *The Tempest,* this big-budget Metro production is one of the more ambitious SF films of the 1950s. A space expedition is sent to the planet **Altair IV** in a saucer-like cruiser to investigate a previous mission unheard from for more than 20 years. They are greeted by Professor Morbius and his lovely daughter **Altaira,** who live in what appears to be a tropical paradise.

Humming under the surface are the still-working underground power plants built by an extinct superintelligent race called the **Krels.** Soon after Morbius explains that other members of the colony were killed shortly after their arrival by strange invisible monsters, several members of the crew are attacked by an unseen beast. During the night, the mission's commander guards the cruiser with a **force-field,** which illuminates a terrifying transparent beast trying to tear its way inside.

Later, the monster is discovered to be an Id-beast produced by Dr. Morbius' subconscious, the same projection that caused the Krels to do themselves in. The Krels had built the underground machines to materialize mental energy, forgetting that they also unleashed the evil that exists in the mind. Colorful and lively, the film introduced to the screen **Robby the Robot,** the likeable progenitor of **C-3PO** in **Star Wars.** (See also: **animation.**)

Director: Fred M. Wilcox, *Producer:* Nicholas Nayfact, *Screenplay:* Cyril Hume, *Story:* Irving Block, Fred M. Wilcox, *Photography:* George Folsey, *Art Directors:* Cedric Gibbons, Arthur Lonergan, *Special Effects:* A. Arnold Gillespie, Warren Newcombe, Irving G. Reis, Joshua Meador, *Electronic Tonalities:* Bebe and Louis Barron

Cast: Leslie Nielsen, Walter Pidgeon, Anne Francis, Jack Kelly, Earl Holiman, Warren Stevens, Richard Anderson

THE FORBIN PROJECT

See: **Colossus, The Forbin Project**

THE FORCE

A mysterious power that gives the **Jedi Knights** their special abilities in the **Star Wars** films. Described as an "energy field generated by living things," something that surrounds us all, the force incorporates a number of **psi powers,** including **telekinesis** and **telepathy.** Only a few have mastered the ability to call up the force on demand, however. Among these is **Ben Kenobi,** an aging Jedi Knight, who is instructing **Luke Skywalker** in its use. (See also: **Force-field.**)

FORCED PERSPECTIVE

A special effect used to create the illusion of vast distances in miniature landscapes and cityscapes. Objects furthest from the camera are built to a rapidly diminishing scale that suggests a receding horizon. Forced perspective is responsible for the stunning vistas seen in **Escape From New York** (1981) and **Blade Runner** (1982).

FORCE-FIELD

An invisible protective barrier that has the resistance of superhard matter. Force-fields were extremely popular with SF writers and filmmakers of the 1930s, usually as a shield against **death rays,** which are often reflected back to their sources.

THE FORMULA

Film   1980   U.S. (MGM)   117 Minutes
Metrocolor

The Formula has big things on its mind—the energy crisis and oil-company conspiracies, among others—but entertainment isn't one of them. Adapted by Steven Shagan from his novel (based partly on fact), the film casts George C. Scott as a retired detective attempting to solve the senseless murder of an old friend. The investigation leads him to St.-Moritz, Switzerland, West Berlin, Beverly Hills and, finally, to Marlon Brando who plays the deceptively cordial head of an oil cartel suppressing a secret Nazi formula for developing synthetic oil from coal. Brando, giving another sterling performance, allegedly accepted the role for its significance, knowing the film wouldn't be a success. He was right.

Director: John G. Avildsen, *Producer/Screenplay/ Novel:* Steven Shagan, *Photographer:* James Crabe, *Production Designers:* Herman A. Blumenthal, Hans-Jurgen Keibach, *Music:* Bill Conti

Cast: Marlon Brando, George C. Scott, Marthe Keller, John Gielgud, Beatrice Straight, Richard Lynch, Wolfgang Preiss

FOR YOUR EYES ONLY

Film   1981   Great Britain (United Artists)
110 Minutes   Technicolor   Panavision

The **James Bond** assembly line was in high gear for 007's breakneck 12th outing, which takes him to Greece, Italy, Albania and Moscow in winter. The high-tech Saturday matinee thrills include a funny bobsled run on skis, ice hockey using players as pucks, car chases in Bond's Lotus Esprit Turbo and an underwater trip in a Neptune two-man submarine. The safety of the world is threatened this time by—oh, yes—a madman with a stolen nuclear-sub tracking system. Helping Bond is a Greek warrior-goddess as handy with weapons as he is.

Director: John Glen, *Producer:* Albert R. Broccoli, *Screenplay:* Richard Maibaum, Michael G. Wilson, *Novel:* Ian Fleming, *Photographer:* Alam Hume, *Production Designer:* Peter Lamont, *Special Effects:* Derek Meddings, John Evans, *Music:* Bill Conti

Cast: Roger Moore, Carole Bouquet, Topol, Lynn-Holly Johnson, Jill Bennett, Lois Maxwell, Julian Glover, Desmond Llewelyn

THE 4-D MAN

(Also titled: *Master of Terror*)

Film   1959   U.S. (Universal-International)
84 Minutes   DeLuxe

A scientist accidently happens into the "fourth dimension" and finds that he can pass through solid matter. The explanation given for this impossible feat is vibrating molecules. The condition ends inopportunely for the philosophy-spouting sneak, when he walks through the wall of an office building and is literally cemented to the spot.

Director: Irwin S. Yeaworth, Jr., *Producer:* Jack H. Harris, *Screenplay:* Theodore Simonson, Cy Chermak, *Story:* Jack H. Harris, *Photographer:* Theodore J. Pable, *Special Effects:* Barton Sloan, *Music:* Ralph Carmichael

Cast: Robert Lansing, Lee Meriwether, James Congdon, Robert Strauss, Edgar Stehli

F.P.1 ANTWORTET NICHT/
F.P.1 Does Not Answer

Film   1932   Germany (UFA)   110 Minutes
Black & white   [Released 1933 U.S. (Fox)]

Depression-era audiences took their minds off the gloomy present with this slow-moving melodrama, set on a huge floating airstrip in the mid-Atlantic. Saboteurs resolve an uninteresting love triangle by sinking the runway and several trimotors into the sea. The airstrip, balanced on tanks of compressed air, lacks convincing detail. A popular success, the film apparently satisfied contemporary audiences, who looked to science for bigger and better machines. German, French and English versions were filmed simultaneously.

Director: Karl Hartl, *Producer:* Eric Pommer, *Screenplay:* **Curt Siodmak,** Wallace Reisch, *Novel:* (*F.P.1 Antwortet Nicht*) Curt Siodmak, *Photographer:* Gunter Rittau, Konstantin Tschet, *Production Designer:* Erich Kettlehut, *English Dialogue:* Robert Stevenson

Cast: Hans Albers, Sybille Schmitz, Paul Hartmann, Peter Lorre, *French Version:* Charles Boyer,

Pierre Brasseur, Danielle Paroala, *English Version:* Leslie Fenton, Conrad Veidt, Jill Esmond

FOUR-SIDED TRIANGLE

Film   1953   Great Britain (Hammer/Astor)
74 Minutes   Black & white

Two scientists fall in love with the same woman, who loves only one of them, and they attempt to square-off the troublesome triangle by making a copy of her. The experiment is a success—until the **clone** begins to show affection for the man her prototype loves (the scientists apprently never considered the consequences of making an *exact* duplicate). Logic aside, the film suffers from unconvincing, low-budget laboratory sets and a cliche ending: the problem is conveniently resolved by eliminating the odd couple in a fire.

Director: **Terence Fisher,** *Producer:* Alexander Pall, *Screenplay:* Terence Fisher, Paul Tabori, *Novel:* William F. Temple, *Music:* Malcolm Arnold

Cast: Stephen Murray, John Van Eyssen, Barbara Payton

FRANCIS, FREDDIE (FREDERICK)
(1917–   )

British film director. A former director of photography, Francis handled the camera for a number of important films, including *Moulin Rouge* (1953), *Moby Dick* (1956), *Room at the Top* (1959) and *The Innocents* (1961). After winning an **Academy Award** for the cinematography of *Sons and Lovers* (1960), he gradually shifted to directing **horror** and science fantasy films, but with less impressive results.

Films include: **The Brain** (1962), **The Evil of Frankenstein** (1964), *Dr. Terror's House of Horrors* (1954), **The Deadly Bees, They Came from Beyond Space** (1967), *Dracula Has Risen from the Grave* (1968), **Trog** (1970), *The Creeping Flesh* (1972), *The Ghoul* (1974), Francis also directed several sequences of **The Day of the Triffids** (1963)

FRANKENHEIMER, JOHN (1930–)

Director of mainstream Hollywood films, including several first-rate SF thrillers. Born in New York City and educated at LaSalle Military Academy and Williams College, Frankenheimer got his start making instructional short subjects while serving in the U.S. Air Force. After being discharged, he joined CBS-TV in New York as an assistant director. He was later promoted to director of *You Are There* (1953-57) when Sidney Lumet departed to make films. During the 1950s, Frankenheimer staged more than 100 highly acclaimed live TV dramas, many for *Playhouse 90* (1956-61).

He made his motion picture debut with *The Young Stranger* (1957), based on a *Climax* (1954-58) episode he had directed. In 1961 he moved to Hollywood and quickly established himself as a top-rank director with a string of popular and critical successes, notably **The Manchurian Candidate** (1962), **Seven Days in May** (1964) and **Seconds** (1966). His subsequent move to Europe coincided with a decline in the quality of his work, which has increasingly emphasized trendy technique at the expense of narrative and characterization. **Prophecy** (1979), his most recent excursion into science fiction, shows little of his former gift for creating suspenseful drama.

Other films: The Young Savages (1961), *All Fall Down, Birdman of Alcatraz* (1962), *The Train* (1964), *Grand Prix* (1966), *The Fixer* (1968), *The Gypsy Moths* (1969), *I Walk the Line* (1970), *The Iceman Cometh* (1973), *The French Connection II* (1975), *Black Sunday* (1977), *The Challenge* (1982)

FRANKENSTEIN

Film   1931   U.S. (Universal)   71 Minutes
Black and white

Mary Shelley's classic story had been filmed in 1910 by the Edison Company, but this is the version that made Dr. Frankenstein and his monster a **horror** film legend. The movie scenarios differs radically from Shelley's story, titled *Frankenstein: A Modern Prometheus* (1818), whose artificial creature was a hand- some charmer upset over not having a soul. In Peggy Webling's play, on which the film is based, the dramatic conflict arises from the fact that the ugly monster has accidentally received a criminal brain. Frankenstein, of course, refers to the mad doctor who performed the operation and not to the monster.

Much of the film's success is due to director James Whale's atmospheric camera work and the expressionist, high-ceilinged set of Dr. Frankenstein's laboratory, filled with an impressive array of sparkling and crackling apparatus assembled by Ken Strickfaden. (See: **Expressionism.**) Karloff is memorable as the monster, played in a copyrighted makeup by **Jack Pierce.** Sequels include: **The Bride of Frankstein** (1935), *Son of Frankenstein* (1939), **The Ghost of Frankenstein** (1942), **Frankenstein Meets the Wolf Man** (1943), **House of Frankenstein** (1944), **House of Dracula** (1945), **Abbott and Costello Meet Frankenstein** (1948). In 1957 Great Britain's Hammer Studios revived the series with **Curse of Frankenstein.** Universal subsequently dramatized Mary Shelley's original novel in **Frankenstein: The True Story** (1973), a made-for-TV movie that ran for four hours. It was directed by Jack Smight and written by Christopher Isherwood. Michael Sarrazin starred as the good-looking creature and Leonard Whiting was Dr. Victor Frankenstein.

Director: James Whale, *Producer:* Carl Laemmle, Jr., *Screenplay:* John L. Balderston, Garrett Fort, Francis Edward Faragoh, *Novel:* Mary Shelley, *Play:* Peggy Webling, *Photographer:* Arthur Edeson, *Art Director:* Charles D. Hall, *Special Effects:* **John P. Fulton,** Kenneth Strickfaden, *Makeup:* Jack Pierce, *Music:* David Broekman

Cast: Boris Karloff, Colin Clive, Mae Clarke, John Bolles, Edward Van Sloan, Dwight Frye

FRANKENSTEIN 1970

Film   1968   U.S. (Allied Artists)
83 Minutes   Black & white

Karloff deserved a better send-off than this intermittently amusing spoof, which marks the end of his association with the legend-

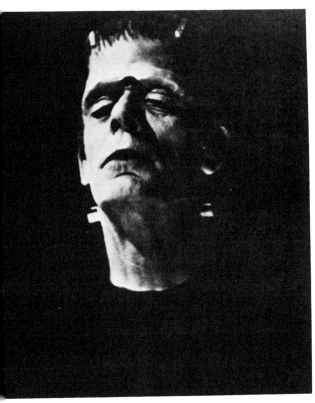

Four Frankenstein monsters:
Glenn Strange, Lon Chaney, Jr.,
Bela Lugosi and Boris Karloff.

ary Monster. Karloff plays Baron von **Frankenstein,** the grandson of the original Baron, who accepts a lucrative offer from a TV producer to make a film in his castle so that he can finance the creation of a new monster. Swathed in bandages, the creature seems less menacing than Karloff plain.

Director: Howard W. Koch, *Producer:* Aubrey Schenck: *Screenplay:* George Worthing Yates, Richard Landau, *Photographer:* Carl Guthrie, *Makeup:* Gordon Bau, *Music:* Paul Dunlap

Cast: **Boris Karloff,** Tom Duggan, Jana Lund, Mike Lane

FRANKENSTEIN AND THE MONSTER FROM HELL

Film   1973   Great Britain (Hammer)
93 Minutes   Color

Dr. Frankenstein creates a monster from patients in his insane asylum. Hardly worth the effort.

Director: **Terence Fisher,** *Producer:* Roy Skeggs, *Screenplay:* John Elder, *Photographer:* Brian Probyn, *Makeup:* Eddie Knight, *Music:* James Bernard

Cast: **Peter Cushing,** Madeline Smith, **Dave Prowse,** Shane Briant

FRANKENSTEIN CONQUERS THE WORLD

Film   1964   Japan (Toho)   87 Minutes
Color   Tohoscope   (Released   1966
U.S. [AIP])

This bizarre offering from **bomb**-obsessed Japan takes the **Frankenstein** Monster (or at least part of him) into the nuclear age. During World War II, it seems, Germany donated the Monster's heart to Japanese scientists, who were in Hiroshima at the time of the bombing. A young boy growing up in the wild finds the heart, eats it and grows up to be a good-natured giant. Suspected of committing a series of brutal murders, he tracks down the real culprit, a **Godzilla**-like creature with an atomic ray, called Baragon.

Director: Inoshiro Honda, *Producer:* Tomoyuki Tanaka, *Screenplay:* Kaoru Mabuchi, *Photographer:* Hajime Koizumi, *Special Effects:* Eiji Tsuburaya

Cast: Nick Adams, Tadao Takashima, Jumi Mizuno

FRANKENSTEIN CREATED WOMAN

Film   1967   Great Britain (Hammer)
92 Minutes   Color

Still hard at it, Dr. Frankenstein recovers the body of an ugly girl who has committed suicide and transforms her into a stunning beauty. To complicate matters, he infuses her with the soul of her lover, wrongly executed for murder, who uses his new-found sex appeal to revenge himself on the men responsible for his death.

Director: **Terence Fisher,** *Producer:* Anthony Nelson Keys, *Screenplay:* John Elder, *Photographer:* Arthur Grant, *Makeup:* George Partleton, *Special Effects:* Les Bowie, *Music:* James Bernard

Cast: **Peter Cushing,** Thorley Walters, Susan Denberg, Robert Morris, Peter Blythe

FRANKENSTEIN JR. AND THE IMPOSSIBLES

TV series   1966-68   U.S. (CBS) 30 Minutes (weekly)   Color

An animated cartoon featuring the Frankenstein monster as a lovable robot 30 feet tall and dedicated to fighting evil. The Impossibles are undercover government agents called Fluid Man, Coil Man and Multi-Man, who pose as a rock group. Not for Karloff fans.

Producers: William Hanna, Joseph Barbera, *Music:* Hoyt Curtin

Voices: Ted Cassidy, Dick Beals, John Stephenson, Don Messick

FRANKENSTEIN MEETS THE SPACE MONSTER

Film   1965   U.S. (Allied Artists)
78 Minutes   Black & white

The **Frankenstein** Monster is conspicuously absent from this misleadingly titled schlock movie. Instead, we have a human-looking **robot** pilot who is turned into a short-circuited killer by an **alien** with a **laser** gun.

Director: Robert Gaffney, *Producer:* Robert McCarty, *Screenplay:* George Garret

Cast: Robert Reilly, Marilyn Hanold, James Karen, Lou Cutell

FRANKENSTEIN MEETS THE WOLF MAN

Film 1943 U.S. (Universal) 72 Minutes Black & white

The **Frankenstein** Monster is little more than a supporting player in this sequel to *The Wolf Man* (1941), which continues Larry Talbot's quest to put an end to his chronic lycanthropy. Talbot is taken in hand by a dotty surgeon who claims he can transfer the werewolf's "energy" into the corpse of the Frankenstein Monster, found in the abandoned castle. Instead, the surgeon revives the Monster, killing himself in the process and setting the stage for a showdown between the two killers.

Although slickly produced by the Universal assembly line, *Frankenstein Meets the Wolf Man* marks a major decline in the quality of the Frankenstein films. Diminishing box-office returns showed the character was no longer strong enough to stand on its own, prompting the studio to pair the Monster with other **horror** stars in formula rehashes. Playing the monster for the first and only time is **Bela Lugosi,** who had refused the role in the 1931 film. **Lon Chaney, Jr.,** the Frankenstein Monster in **The Ghost of Frankenstein** (1942), is the Wolf Man.

Director: Roy William Neill, *Producer:* George Waggner, *Screenplay:* **Curt Siodmak,** *Photographer:* George Robinson, *Special Effects:* **John P. Fulton,** *Makeup:* **Jack Pierce,** *Music:* Hans Salter

Cast: Bela Lugosi, Lon Chaney, Jr., Lionel Atwill, Patric Knowles, Ilona Massey, Maria Ouspenskaya

FRANKENSTEIN MUST BE DESTROYED!

Film 1969 Great Britain (Hammer) 97 Minutes Color

What again? Dr. **Frankenstein** is back for his fifth Hammer outing, crazier than ever and still tinkering with human brains. This time out, his subject is a brilliant scientist who dies accidentally while the doctor and his confederates are helping him escape from a mental institution. To preserve the scientist's genius-level intelligence, Frankenstein transplants his brain into a younger, more powerful body, not realizing that the doctor is indeed mad.

Director: **Terence Fisher,** *Producer:* Anthony Nelson Keys, *Screenplay:* Bert Batt, *Photographer:* Arthur Grant, *Makeup:* Eddie Knight, *Music:* James Bernard

Cast: **Peter Cushing,** Simon Ward, Veronica Carlson, George Pravda, Freddie Jones

FRANKENSTEIN'S DAUGHTER

Film 1958 U.S.(Astor) 85 Minutes Black & white

Another attempt to update the **Frankenstein** legend, this time with a female Monster put together from amputated body parts, apparently from Ernest Borgnine. Being the jealous type, she beats Dr. Frankenstein III black and blue when he flirts with a pretty young girl, then shuffles from the lab for an inevitable reign of terror. (See also: **La Figlia di Frankenstein.**)

Director: Dick Cunha, *Producer:* Marc Frederic, *Screenplay:* H. E. Barrie, *Photographer:* Meredith Nicholson, *Special Effects:* Ira Anderson, *Makeup:* Harry Thomas, *Music:* Nicholas Carras

Cast: Sandra Knight, John Ashley, Harold Lloyd, Jr., Robert Dix

FRANZ, ARTHUR (1920–   )

Leading man of low-budget SF and horror films; born in Perth Amboy, New Jersey, and educated at Blue Ridge College (Maryland).

Originally a stage actor, Franz appeared in the Broadway production, of *A Streetcar Named Desire* (1947) and worked extensively in radio before making his film debut in *Jungle Patrol* (1948). He later alternated between supporting roles in major productions and starring roles in B films and television series.

Other films: Sands of Iwo Jima (1949), **Abbott and Costello Meet the Invisible Man, Flight to Mars** (1951), **Invaders From Mars** (1953), *The Caine Mutiny* (1954), Back From the Dead (1957), **Monster on the Campus** (1958), **The Atomic Submarine** (1959), *The Carpetbaggers* (1964), *The Sweet Ride* (1968), *Sisters of Death* (1977)

TV series include: **World of Giants** (1959), *The Nurses* (1965-67)

DIE FRAU IM MONDE

(Also titled: *By Rocket to the Moon, The Girl in the Moon, The Woman in the Moon*)

Film   1929   Germany (UFA)   156 Minutes
Black & White (silent)

Director Fritz Lang and his scriptwriter-wife Thea von Harbou followed their successful **Metropolis** (1926) with this cliche pot-boiler, the final silent movie of the genre. A greedy scientist builds a spaceship to visit the moon and collect gold and diamonds from its rocky surface. He is pushed to his death in a crater by a villainous assistant representing a consortium of businessmen, who want the gold for themselves.

Its silly melodramatics aside, the film offers a stunning and remarkably prophetic depiction of a flight to the moon. It is the first SF film to strive for scientific accuracy in its special effects. The launch pad, spacecraft (which correctly has two rocket stages) and gantry—an art deco version of Cape Canaveral—were built from information provided by science popularizer Willy Ley and rocket expert Dr. Hermann Oberth, the technical advisor for **Destination Moon** 20 years later. Oberth devised a reverse countdown for the space launch, later taken up for real by NASA. *Die Frau Im Monde* was released in the U.S. in 1931, cut to 97-

minutes. This is the print usually shown at retrospectives.

Director/Producer: Fritz Lang, *Screenplay:* Thea von Harbou, *Art Directors:* Emil Hasler, Otto Hunte, Karl Mollbrecht, *Technical Advisors:* Willy Ley, Hermann Oberth, *Special Effects:* Konstantin Tschetwerikoff

Cast: Gerda Marcus, Willy Fritsch, Fritz Rasp, Klaus Pohl

FREEBORN, STUART (1914–   )

British makeup artist. A specialist in character disguises and unearthly creatures, Freeborn began his career at age 21 with Sir Alexander Korda's film company. He has been a freelance since 1947, working his way to the top of his profession on such films as *Oliver Twist* (1948) and *The Bridge on The River Kwai* (1957). Freeborn's first SF film was **Stanley Kubrick**'s **Dr. Strangelove** (1963), for which he created three totally different characterizations for Peter Sellers. He worked for Kubrick again on **2001: A Space Odyssey** (1968), making up 26 actors in fully articulated ape masks and fur costumes for the "Dawn of Man" opening sequence. The convincing outfits, worn by boys, included artifical nipples through which chimp babies (also in makeup) nursed via concealed milk bladders.

Chosen by **George Lucas** to do the makeup for **Star Wars** (1977), Freeborn created one of that film's most popular characters, the ferocious, Teddy Bear-like **Chewbacca,** the Wookie, borrowing from the techniques he had developed for *2001.* Freeborn created most of the famous cantina creatures, including Greedo, **Jabba the Hut**'s hit man, before falling ill from exhaustion. American makeup artist Rick Baker was called in to complete the grouping. Freeborn worked on subsequent films in the series, contributing, among other imaginary **alien** beings, the appealing **Yoda,** the green-skinned **Jedi Knight,** introduced in **The Empire Strikes Back** (1980)

Other films: The Alphabet Murders (1966), *Murder on the Orient Express* (1974), *The Omen* (1976),

Superman—The Movie (1978), **Superman II** (1981), *Revenge of the Jedi* (1983)

TV film: Spectre (1977)

FROGS

Film 1972 U.S. (AIP) 91 Minutes
Movielab

Ecological revenge is the subject of *Frogs,* a chilling monster movie that really delivers the goods. The protagonist is a bad-tempered plantation owner who sits on the verandah of his southern mansion listening to the dying gasps of insects and wildlife he has tried to exterminate. The croaks, chirps and gurgles become an escalating crescendo, as an army of mutated frogs, turtles, spiders and what have you begin crawling toward the house. A giant butterfly pulls a young girl into a quicksand pit, a house guest is overrun by huge scorpions, and another visitor gets eaten alive by angry snapping turtles. Those with strong stomachs will love it.

Director: George McCowan, *Producers:* Peter Thomas, George Edward, *Screenplay:* Robert Hutchinson, Robert Blees, *Photography:* Mario Tosi, *Music:* Lex Baxter

Cast: Ray Milland, Lynn Borden, Holly Irving, David Gilliam, Sam Elliott

FROM THE EARTH TO THE MOON

Film 1958 U.S. (Warner Bros.)
100 Minutes Technicolor

Nineteenth-century astronauts journey to the moon in a rocket fired from a huge cannon by a powerful new explosive. The stiff-upper-lip direction of **Byron Haskin** makes the trip surprisingly boring, but the colorful effects by Lee Zavitz are worth a look. Based on the **Jules Verne** novel.

Director: Byron Haskins, *Producer:* Benedict Bogeaus, *Screenplay:* Robert Blees, James Leicester, *Photographer:* Edin B. Du Par, *Art Director:* Hal Wilson Cox, *Special Effects:* Lee Zavitz, *Music:* Louis Forbes

Cast: Joseph Cotten, George Sanders, Debra Paget, Don Dubbins, Patric Knowles

FRONT PROJECTION

An optical special effect system of combining live action with moving or still backgrounds. As its name indicates, *front projection* casts a background image from in front of the actors rather than from behind them, as in the older **rear projection** system, which it has largely displaced. The accompanying diagram shows how *front projection* works.

Developed in response to the inadequacies of rear projection, *front projection* largely derives from experiments begun in England during the early 1940s. Technology caught up with the idea later that decade when the American 3M Corporation invented a highly reflective beaded material for use in road signs. Adapted to the motion picture screen for a brighter and sharper image, the fabric also provided a *front projection* screen bright enough to register a background image on film. Hollywood's Motion Picture Research Council published a theoretical *front projection* design in 1950, and SF writer Murray Leinster patented a working system in 1955, followed by a French system patented two years later. The patents were subsequently purchased by the J. Arthur Rank Corp., then Great Britain's leading film studio, where they lay dormant until discovered by director **Stanley Kubrick** when he arrived to film **2001: A Space Odyssey** (1968).

The *front projection* system used today was developed by an international team of experts under the supervision of Kubrick, as a means of accomplishing hitherto impossible composite shots required for his space epic. It was first used for a scene in *2001* when a vicious leopard attacks a group of prehistoric ape-men. In reality the "ape-men" were emoting in a London sound stage on a partial set constructed to match the front-projected background footage. The leopard was safely out of reach in South-West africa, although it appeared to be snarling through the encampment as large as life (down to a menacing red glint of its hungry eyes). Since then the system has become an integral part of filmmaking, especially in SF spectaculars.

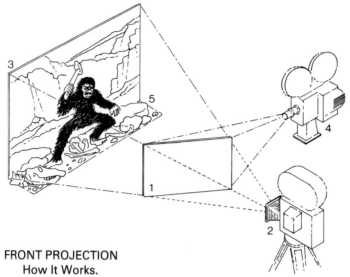

FRONT PROJECTION
How It Works.

A two-way mirror (1) is placed at a 45-degree angle between a motion picture camera (2) and a reflex screen (3). A movie or slide projector (4) beams a background image to the reflective side of the mirror, which bounces it to the screen over the costumed actor and a partial set (5). The camera then films the composite scene through the transparent side of the mirror. That portion of the background projected onto the actor and set (or in some cases, a model) is diffused by their three-dimensional forms and further washed out by bright studio lights, rendering the unwanted images invisible to the camera. Lighting must be on the same axis as the camera lens in order for actors, sets and models to cast their shadows directly behind them. The key to the system is a special screen composed of millions of optically perfect glass beads—in effect, miniature lenses—that reflect and intensify the projected image back to the camera lens in a straight line.

For their contribution in developing Front Projection, a 1968 **Academy Award** went to Philip V. Palmquist of the 3M Corporation, Dr. Herbert Meyer, chief scientist of the Motion Picture Association of America's research center, and Charles Staffel of the Rank Organization. The patents are held jointly by Kubrick and MGM. (See also: **Introvision, Zoptic Process.)**

FROZEN ALIVE

See: **Der Fall X-701**

THE FROZEN DEAD

Film 1967 Great Britain (Warner Brothers)
95 Minutes Black & white

Much ado about a fiendish doctor who tries to revive a refrigeratorful of Nazis frozen solid at the end of World War II. The experiment leads to, ho-hum, more deaths by murder. Hitler was better served in **The Boys From Brazil** (1978). (See also: **Cryogenics)**

Director/Producer/Screenplay: Herbert J. Leder, *Photographer:* David Boulton, *Music:* Don Banks

Cast: Dana Andrews, Kathleen Breck, Philip Gilbert

FUEST, ROBERT (1927–   )

British film and TV director and occasional **production designer,** educated at the London Art School. Fuest made his reputation directing many of the wittier episodes of the SF TV series **The Avengers** and progressed to films with the stylishly droll **The**

Abominable Dr. Phibes (1971) and its sequel **Dr. Phibes Rises Again** (1972). He followed with an unsuccessful remake of *Wuthering Heights* (1972) and returned to science fiction with *The Final Programme* (1974), a glib, visually exciting mini-epic he directed, wrote and designed himself, his most notable project to date. A talented painter, Fuest has exhibited his canvases at Great Britain's Royal Academy.

FULTON, JOHN P. (1902–66)

Special effects technician. Born in Nebraska, Fulton moved to California with his family in 1914 and trained to be an electrical engineer. He entered films in 1923 as an assistant cameraman and in 1929 became a camera operator on the film *Hell's Harbor*. The following year, Fulton apprenticed himself to a trick photographer; in 1931 he joined Universal studios as the head of its new special effects department.

Among his early assignments was the burning of the old mill at the climax of **Frankenstein** (1931) and the excellent **model** work of *Air Mail* (1932), in which he pioneered the use of **fast-motion** photography to take the "wobble" from a miniature plane. For his next project, **The Invisible Man** (1933), justly considered his masterpiece, Fulton created a leading man who was never seen until the film's last moments. His pioneering techniques, used in the studio's "invisible" sequels, remain the best of their kind. Another of Fulton's remarkable innovations is the transformation of man into beast, first accomplished in *Werewolf of London* (1935) and later seen in **The House of Dracula** (1945) when a bat metamorphoses into the black-hooded Count.

Fulton received his first **Academy Award** in 1945 for the **matte** work of *Wonder Man*, in which comedian Danny Kaye convincingly played his own twin. Fulton subsequently joined the Goldwyn Studio, where he hoped to become a director, a goal that never materialized. An attempt to start his own special effects studio failed, and in 1953 Ful-

ton accepted an offer to replace the late Gordon Jennings as head of special effects at Paramount. While there he received his second and third Academy Awards for *The Bridges of Toko-Ri* (1955) and *The Ten Commandments* (1956). He staged a number of stunning effects for the latter film, including the parting of the Red Sea. His SF films at Paramount include **The Naked Jungle** (1954), **The Colossus of New York, Conquest of Space** (1955), **The Space Children** (both 1958).

During the early 1960s, with special effects films no longer in demand, Paramount, along with other studios, dissolved its special effects department and dismissed its staff. In 1966 Fulton, now a freelancer, was in England consulting with the makers of *The Battle of Britain* (1968), his next project, when he contracted a rare illness. He died there in a hospital several days later.

Other films: The Mummy (1932), **Bride of Frankenstein** (1935), **The Invisible Ray** (1936), **Son of Frankenstein** (1939), **The Invisible Man Returns** (1940), **The Invisible Woman** (1941), **The Ghost of Frankenstein, Invisible Agent,** (1942), **House of Frankenstein, The Invisible Man's Revenge** (1944), **House of Dracula** (1945), **Master Minds** (1949), *Elephant Walk* (1954), *Pardners* (1956), **I Married a Monster From Outer Space** (1958), **The Bamboo Saucer** (1968)

FUTURE COP

TV film   1976   U.S. (ABC)   72 Minutes
Color

A hard-boiled street cop prowls the beat with a naive rookie partner who is actually a superpowerful **robot**. This unlikely comic premise gave rise to a short-lived series with the same cast the following year. Not ones to give up easily, the producers tried the idea again in 1978 with **The Cops and Robin.**

Director: Jud Taylor, *Producer:* Anthony Wilson, *Screenplay:* Anthony Wilson, *Photographer:* Terry K. Meade, *Music:* Billy Goldenberg

Cast: Ernest Borgnine, Michael Shannon, John Amos, John Larch, Ronnie Clair

Futureworld: Journalists Blythe Danner and Peter Fonda "box" at Delos, an amusement part of the future.

FUTUREWORLD

Film   1976   U.S. (AIP)   104 Minutes
Metrocolor

Silly but satisfying, *Futureworld* takes up where **Westworld** (1973) left off. The murderous **robots** of Delos, a futuristic amusement park, have been reprogrammed, and two journalists arrive to cover the playland's reopening. Before long, the pair has uncovered a plot by Delos' officials to replace the world's leaders with robot doubles. Scheduled for replacement themselves, the reporters manage to escape by posing as their own doubles, created to keep them from exposing the scheme.

Produced with a larger budget than its predecessor, *Futureworld* takes the viewer on a fascinating tour of the resort, which includes three-dimensional chess games, boxing matches by proxy, and the ultimate sexual experience (provided by robots, of course). Surprisingly, many scenes were shot on location, at modernistic shopping malls and the Houston Manned Space Center. Under the window dressing is a **mad scientist** plot, lacking the cohesion and shock effect of the earlier film, written and directed by **Michael Crichton** (who is inexplicably not credited here).

Director: Richard T. Heffron, *Producers:* Paul Lazarus, James T. Aubrey, *Screenplay:* Mayo Simon, George Schenck, *Photographers:* Howard Schwartz, Sol Polito, *Special Effects:* Brian Sellstrom, Gene Griggs, *Music:* Fred Karlin

Cast: Peter Fonda, Blythe Danner, Arthur Hill, John Ryan, Stuart Margolin, Yul Brynner

GAIGAN

An immense insect from outer space and resembling a cockroach, one of a gallery of mutant movie monsters created by Japan's Toho studios, who gave the world **Godzilla.** A **cyborg,** Gaigan has a belly equipped with a powerful weapon that is something like a huge buzz saw. He has appeared in *Godzilla vs. Gaigan* (1971) and *Godzilla vs. Megalon* (1973). (See also: **Mutants.**)

GALACTICA 1980

TV series 1980 U.S. (ABC) 60 Minutes (weekly) Color

Galactica 1980 was Universal's bid to recoup some of its investment from the expensive and short-lived **Battlestar Galactica** (1978-79) by re-using sets and special effects footage. Still soaring through space only a **warp speed** ahead of vicious Cylons **robots,** the mammoth spaceship plunged even deeper into juvenile territory. Boxey, the orphan of *Battlestar* (and owner of **Muffit II,** the daggit) had grown up and become Captain Troy, an ace fighter pilot, partnered by Lieutenant Dillon. Of the original cast, only bearded Lorne Greene (Commander Adama) survived.

The program debuted in January in an early evening hour with a three-part story that had the Galacticans at last finding **Earth,** where they planned to settle. But the planet was deemed too technologically primitive to survive an inevitable attack by the Cylons, so Galactican scientists traveled into the past to surreptitiously update Earth's technology by dropping a few hints here and there. Complications arose when a villainous scientist decided to visit Nazi Germany and give Adolf Hitler a hand.

Producer: David O'Connor, *Executive Producer/ Creator:* Glen A. Larson, *Special Effects:* **John Dykstra**

Cast: Kent McCord, Barry Van Dyke, Lorne Greene, Robyn Douglass

GALACTIC STORMTROOPERS

Ruthless, white-armored soldiers of the Imperial Empire in the **Star Wars** film series. Galactic Stormtroopers are **clones,** whose predecessors had fought in the **Clone Wars.** The drones have an unswerving loyalty to their commander, **Darth Vader,** whom they obey without question.

GALAXINA

Film 1980 U.S. (Crown International) 96 Minutes Color

Billed as a "sci-fi joyride," this bargain-basement **space-opera** spoof is enjoyable in the way that only really bad movies can be. The time is the 28th century, where a genetically perfect female robot is ferrying a predictable mix of male astronauts to the planet Altair (see: **Altair IV):** There is the handsome hero, the laugh-getting dope and the gruff diamond-in-the-rough. Why they are there is beside the point since the plot is merely another version of "lust in space." For all its tease, however, the film remains curiously unerotic. **Star Wars**—the reason for the film's existence—is not so much satirized as cannibalized, down to a scene in an intergalactic bar whose outlaw patrons dine on cadavers. (*Galaxina* was heavily promoted after the headlined murder of its leading lady, Dorothy Stratten, a Playboy centerfold. She had also appeared in an episode of TV's **Buck Rogers.)**

Director/Writer: William Sachs, *Producer:* Marilyn J. Tenser, *Photographer:* Dean Cundey, *Editor:* George Bowers, George Berndt

Dorthy R. Stratten as a robot-turned-woman in *Galaxina*.

Cast: Dorothy Stratten, Stepehen Macht, Avery Schreiber, James David Hinton

GALAXY

A system of **stars,** nebulae ("clouds" of gas and dust) and other objects floating in space and constantly in motion, ranging from 1,500 to 300,000 light years across (one light year equals about six trillion miles). Numbering in the millions, these immense "star islands" are shaped either in an ellipse, a disk or a spiral. Earth is located well away from the center of a spiral galaxy called the Milky Way, which is about 800 million billion miles long and 10 times as deep. From our edge-on view it is impossible to get a clear view of the great clusters of stars at the center of the Milky Way because of the "clouds" of nebulae in between. The stars visible in the sky, distant suns, represent our limited perspective of the galaxy.

GALLIFREY

Home planet of the **Time Lords,** the highly advanced civilization that spawned TV's **Doctor Who.** The eccentric Doctor returns there only occasionally, having been exiled by his fellow Time Lords because he has broken their policy of galactic isolation to travel through time and space, combatting aggressive **aliens** with designs on other planets (including **Earth).** Although Gallifrey is protected from outsiders by an impenetrable **force-field,** it was once invaded by the **Sontarans** with the help of a traitorous Time Lord. Fortunately, the Doctor arrived in the nick of time and sent them on their way.

GAMERA VS. MONSTER X

Film 1970 Japan (Daiei) 83 Minutes Color [Released 1970 U.S. (AIP)]

The giant turtle vanquished in **Gammera the Invincible** (1965) got off to a fresh start in a sequel, not seen in the U.S., as the sympathetic "protector of all children." AIP inadvertently dropped the second "m" from the creature's name when it released this film in the series which pits the heroic reptile against an evil she-monster called Jiger at Osaka's Expo '70.

Director: Noriaki Yuasa, *Screenplay:* Fumi Takahashi, *Photography:* Akira Kitazaki, *Music:* Shunsuke Kikuche

Cast: Tsutomu Takakuwu, Kelly Varis, Junko Yashiro, Katherine Murphy, Ken Omura

THE GAMMA PEOPLE

Film 1965 Great Britain (Warwick) 79 Minutes Black & white [Released 1956 U.S. (Colᵘmbia)]

While on assignment in an Eastern European country, two Western reporters (a man and a woman) visit a school where average students are being turned into geniuses, allegedly by a radical new teaching method. Impressed at first, the reporters conduct a surreptitious investigation that uncovers the hideous truth: Government doctors are bombarding the brains of children and the elderly with deadly **gamma rays** in an effort to artificially enhance intelligence, and the procedure has produced as many mental incompetents as geniuses.

An intelligent, atypical thriller made during a period when creature features filled movie screens, *The Gamma People* was based on rumors of medical experiments taking place behind the iron curtain to strengthen Olympic athletes. Interestingly, the **mad scientist** here is the government, whose zeal for technical progress transcends individual rights.

Director: John Gilling, *Producer:* John Gossage, *Screenplay:* John Gilling, John Gossage, *Story:* Louis Pollock, *Photographer:* Ted Moore, *Special Effects:* Tom Howard

Cast: Paul Douglas, Leslie Phillips, Eva Bartok, Martin Miller, Walter Rilla

GAMMA RAYS

A form of electromagnetic radiation emitted by radioactive elements. Similar to **X-rays** but with an even shorter wavelength, gamma rays are highly penetrating and hence very deadly. **Earth** is protected from extraterrestrial radiations by its atmosphere, but radiation produced on Earth can only be shielded by a dense material, such as lead or exhausted uranium. Identified c. 1906 by British physicist Lord Rutherford, gamma rays were quickly appropriated by SF writers and filmmakers, who put them to a variety of uses, often as a power source for **death rays** or as a means of imparting human beings with extraordinary powers.

GAMMERA THE INVINCIBLE/ Daikaiju Gammera

Film   1965   Japan (Daei) 86 Minutes   Color
[Released 1966   U.S. (World Enterprise)]

Gammera, a giant prehistoric turtle, was the Daei studio's answer to **Godzilla**. He took his first steps here, awakened from an Arctic deep-freeze by an atomic bomb which left him with the power to fly like a jet plane and spew radioactive fire. After indiscriminately terrorizing the world, he was brought down by a team of Japanese scientists and the U.S. Air Force (note which country has the brains and which has the muscle). He lived to soar again in many sequels, few good enough to release abroad, all from director Yuasa: **Return of the Giant Monsters** (1967), **Gammera vs. Guiron** (1968), **Gamera vs. Monster X** (1970).

Director: Noriaki Yuasa, *Producer:* Yonejiro Saito, *Screenplay:* Nizo Takahashi, *Photographer:* Nobuo Munekawa, *Special Effects:* Yonesaburo Tsukji

Cast: Brian Donlevy, Albert Dekker, Eiji Funakoshi, Michiko Sugata, John Baragrey

GAMMERA VS. GUIRON

(U.S. title: *Attack of the Monsters*)

Film   1968   Japan (Daei)   72 Minutes
Color   [Released 1969   U.S. (AIP)]

Gammera, a giant flying turtle, travels to a remote planet to rescue two Japanese children kidnapped by **alien** cannibals. Before heading for home, he finishes off a guard-monster called Guiron. One of many sequels to **Gammera the Invincible** (1965).

Director: Noriaki Yuasa, *Producer:* Hidemasa Nagata, *Screenplay:* Fumi Takahashi, *Special Effects:* Kazufumi Fujii

Cast: Nobuhiro Janima, Miyuki Akiyama, Eiji Funakoshi

GANCE, ABEL (1889–1981)

French director/producer; one of the great pioneers of cinema. Gance, the son of a Paris physician, had originally trained to be a lawyer, a career he rejected early in life to become a stage actor. He began appearing in films in 1909 while living on the edge of starvation and writing occasional screenplays. In 1911 he formed a production company with friends and directed a series of films that utilized experimental techniques, deemed uncommercial at the time. Among these is **La Folie du Docteur Tube** (1915), which introduced to the screen the **anamorphic lens** and SF's most enduring character, the **mad scientist.**

During infantry service in World War I, Gance shot battle scenes under fire for *J'Accuse* (1919), a pacifist film that was a major success throughout Europe. Gance's rapid montage cuts enhanced the power of these scenes, and the technique had a profound effect on filmmakers everywhere. Gance's masterwork is *Napoleon* (1927), an ambitious production that employed the entire technical lexicon of the silent-film era and more. Among the film's innovations is Polyvision, a **wide-screen** effect achieved by filming with three cameras simultaneously, a system later better known as Cinerama. Gance also freed the bulky camera of the day from its silent conventions and used it as a participant in the film, attaching the apparatus to galloping horses, and hanging it from wires and a pendulum.

Gance's creative autonomy came to an end with the **La Fin du Monde** (1931), shunned by the public and dismissed by critics as being unduly "theatrical." In 1934, he brought another technical innovation to cinema by adding a stereophonic sound track to a shortened version of *Napoleon*. During the 1950s he made a comeback of sorts directing period spectacles, while living in reduced circumstances in a Paris hotel and, later, a home for retired vaudevillians. He lived to see *Napoleon* rescued from oblivion (the original version had been lost) by writer Kevin Brownlow and filmmaker Francis Ford Coppola. At the time of his death, re-release of the film had earned him tens of thousands of dollars, and he was writing the script for a film about Christopher Columbus.

Other films: **L'Enigme de Dix Heures** (1915), *Les Gaz Mortels* (1916), *La Roue* (1923), *Marines Christaux* (1928), *Lucrece Borgia* (1935), *J'Accuse* [remake] (1938), *Magirama* (1956), *Bonaparte et la Revolution* [remake of *Napoleon*] (1971)

GAS GIANTS

SF term generally attributed to writer James Blish and now appropriated by scientists to refer to the planets **Jupiter, Saturn, Uranus** and **Neptune,** each of which is enormous and composed primarily of gases.

GAS-S-S!

(Also titled: *G-a-s-s, or It Became Necessary to Destroy the World in Order to Save It*)

Film   1970   U.S. (AIP)   79 Minutes
Movielab

Roger Corman and AIP parted company after this surreal, counter-culture satire, which the studio allegedly recut without his consent. Its premise is that a nerve gas, developed by the military-industrial establishment, has leaked into the atmosphere, killing everyone over the age of 25. Enlightened survivors overcome an attempt by Hell's Angels to preserve conservative middle America, and they establish a new **Utopia** based on nature, drugs and sex.

At the finale, a number of dead notables rise from the grave, including Martin Luther King, Jr., Che Guevara and Edgar Allan Poe, who gets into the spirit of things by hopping on a motorcycle, with a hippie blonde seated behind him. Briefly a cult item, the film proved to be as durable as a hallucinogenic vision. All that survives is Corman's self-indulgence and a kind of playful giddiness.

Director/Producer: Roger Corman, *Screenplay:* George Armitage, *Photographer:* Ron Dexter, *Music:* Country Joe and the Fish

Cast: Bud Cort, Robert Corff, Elaine Giftos, Talia Coppola [Shire], Ben Vereen, Cindy Williams

GENESIS II

TV film   1973   U.S. (CBS)   97 Minutes   Color

After the cancellation of **Star Trek** (1966-69), producer **Gene Roddenberry** attempted to spawn another series with this so-so reworking of the **Buck Rogers** legend. A 20th-century scientist, frozen in a state of **suspended animation** during a **cryonics** experiment, awakens in the devastated, post-**bomb** future. **Earth** has been fragmented into communities of barbarians, **mutants** and a group called PAX, dedicated to preserving the arts and sciences of the past to help build a new civilization. The scientist rescues PAX from domination by Philistine **mutants**. Roddenberry remade the TV film in 1974 as **Planet Earth**.

Director: **John L. Moxey,** *Producer/Screenplay:* Gene Roddenberry, *Photographer:* Gerald Perry Finnerman, *Art Director:* Hilyard Brown, *Music:* George Watters

Cast: Alex Cord, Mariette Hartley, Ted Cassidy, Majel Barrett, Titos Vandis

THE GEMINI MAN

TV film   1976   U.S. (NBC)   98 Minutes Color TV series   1976   U.S. (NBC) 60 Minutes (weekly)   Color

Essentially a reworking of David McCallum's series, **The Invisible Man** (1975-76), *The Gemini Man* starred Ben Murphy as Sam Casey, a brash young agent for INTERSECT (International Security Technics), a secret government research organization. Exposed to radiation in an underground explosion, which rearranged his DNA molecules, Casey was able to make himself invisible for 15 minutes daily by switching off a subminiature DNA stabilizer carried in a nuclear-powered wrist device that resembled a watch. If he remained invisible for more than 15 minutes within a 24-hour period, he would disintegrate. Viewers couldn't care less after seeing the dull pilot film, and the series lasted only a month. The program was similar to the ongoing **The Six Million Dollar Man** (1973-77), also produced by Harve

Bennett. The pilot film was later retitled *Code Name: Minus One.*

Directors: Alan J. Levi, Charles R. Rondeau, Michael Caffrey, *Executive Producer:* Harve Bennett, *Producers:* Robert F. O'Neil, Leslie Stevens, Frank Telford, *Writers:* Leslie Stevens and others, *Novel:* "The Invisible Man" **H.G. Wells,** *Photographer:* Enzo A. Martinelli, *Music:* Billy Goldenberg

Cast: Ben Murphy, Katherine Crawford, Richard Dysart, Diana Elcar

GERARD, GIL (1943–   )

American actor who followed **Buster Crabbe** and Ken Dibbs as the film and television incarnation of comic-strip hero **Buck Rogers.** Born in Little Rock, Arkansas, Gerard appeared in stock productions in college, from which he was graduated with a mathematics degree. He worked for several years as an industrial chemist before leaving Arkansas to pursue an acting career in New York. He studied at the American Musical and Dramatic Academy during the day and drove a taxi at night to pay tuition.

During the early 1970s, he appeared in many television commercials, which led to

Gil Gerard—Buck Rogers as a NASA astronaut.

a starring role in a touring production of the musical *I Do! I Do!* and a 2½-year stint in the television soap opera *The Doctors*. His credits include the television series *Baretta* and *Little House on the Prairie*, the film *Airport '77* (1977) and the made-for-TV movies *Hooch* (1976), *Killing Stone* (1978) and *Not Just Another Affair* (1982). His debut in the NBC-TV series **Buck Rogers** (1979-81) was preceded by the theatrical release of the program's 2-hour pilot episode, under the title **Buck Rogers in the 25th Century** (1979). (See also: **comic books.**)

GHIDRA, THE THREE-HEADED MONSTER

(Also titled: *The Greatest Battle on Earth*)

Film   1965   Japan (Toho)   85 Minutes
Eastmancolor   Tohoscope   [Released 1965 U.S. (Continental)]

King Ghidra, a golden dragon brought to Earth by a passing **meteor,** spits lightning bolts from its three heads and sets a few Japanese cities on fire before being doused by **Godzilla, Rodan** and **Mothra,** Toho's other resident monsters. The abysmal plot is helped somewhat by better-than-average special effects (for films of this kind). Ghidra can also be seen stomping through *Godzilla vs. Gaigan* (1971) and *Godzilla on Monster Island* (1978).

Director: Inoshiro Honda, *Producer:* Tomoyuki Tanaka, *Special Effects:* Eiji Tsuburaya, *Music:* Akira Ifukube

Cast: Yukiro Hoshi, Yosuka Natsuki, Hiroshi Koizumi, Takashi Shimura

THE GHOST OF FRANKENSTEIN

Film   1942   U.S. (Universal)   68 Minutes
Black & white

Looking none the worse for wear, the **Frankenstein** Monster returns from the sulphur pit that disposed of him in *Son of Frankenstein* (1939). Brought back to life by a lightning bolt (what else?), the Monster follows his hunchbacked friend Ygor

to the home of Dr. Frankenstein's son, who is coerced into repeating his father's attempt to give the creature a normal brain. During the operation Ygor's gray matter finds its way into the Monster's cranium, and the results aren't quite what he expected. Waking up blind and grouchy, the new monster wrecks the laboratory and sets it afire, perishing in the flames.

Although it has a number of frightening moments, *Ghost* lacks the chilling impact and Gothic visual style of the earlier films. **Lon Chaney, Jr.,** replacing Karloff, plays the Monster as a jerky beast, without the innate sympathy and sense of tragedy that his predecessor brought to the role. This film sets the stage for **Bela Lugosi,** Ygor here, to play the Frankenstein Monster in the next sequel, **Frankenstein Meets the Wolf Man** (1943).

Director: Erle C. Kenton, *Producer:* George Waggner, *Screenplay:* W. Scott Darling, *Story:* Eric Taylor, *Photographers:* Milton Krasner, Woody Bredell, *Art Director:* Jack Otterson, *Makeup:* **Jack Pierce,** *Music:* Charles Previn, *Special Effects:* **John P. Fulton**

Cast: Lon Chaney, Jr., Bela Lugosi, Cedric Hardwicke, Lionel Atwill, Ralph Bellamy, Evelyn Ankers

THE GIANT BEHEMOTH

See: **Behometh, The Sea Monster**

THE GIANT CLAW

Film   1957   U.S. (Columbia)   76 Minutes
Black & white

A scruffy ball of feathers arrives in New York from outer space and perches atop the Empire State Building. Although protected by an invisible **force-field,** the bird is eventually undone by a counter-ray invented by a team of scientists. Where is **King Kong** when we need him?

Director: **Fred Sears,** *Producer:* Sam Katzman, *Screenplay:* Samuel Newman, Paul Gangelin, *Music:* Mischa Bakaleinikoff

Cast: Jeff Morrow, Mara Corday, Morris Ankrum, Morgan Jones, Robert Shane

GIANT OF METROPOLIS

Film   1962   Italy (Centro)   92 Minutes
Color   Scope   [Released 1963   U.S. (Seven
Arts)]

Muscleman Gordon Mitchell happens into
the ancient metropolis of **Atlantis** (before
it sank) whose eye-popping king decides to
use him as a guinea pig for an immortality
experiment. *Giant* is one of dozens of
bargain-basement sex and sandal epics
(usually shot on sets left standing from other
films) made in Italy and Spain, all starring
seminude beefcake.

Director: Umberto Scarpelli, *Producer:* Emmino
Salvi, *Screenplay:* Sabatino Ciuffino, Oreste
Palellea, *Art Director:* G. Giovanisti, *Music:* Ar-
mando Trovajoli

Cast: Gordon Mitchell, Bella Cortez, Roldano Lupi

GIGANTIS, THE FIRE MONSTER

Film   1955   Japan (Toho)   82 Minutes
Black & white

Warner Bros. picked up the American rights
to this first sequel to the phenomenally
successful *Godzilla, King of the Monsters*
(1954), only to discover that another studio
owned the rights to the radioactive creature's
American name (in Japan, it's Gojira). So,
instead of *Revenge of Godzilla* we got *Gigantis,
the Fire Monster*. Otherwise, the formula is
the same, as Gigantis/Godzilla takes on a prehistoric armored monster called Angilas.

Director: Motoyishi Odo, *Producer:* Tomoyuki
Tanaka, *Screenplay:* Takeo Jurata, Sigeaki Hidaka,
Story: Shigeru Kayama, *Photographer:* Seiichi Endo,
Special Effects: Eiji Tsuburaya, *Music:* Minosuki
Yamada

Cast: Hiroshi Koizumi, Yukio Kasama, Minosuki
Yamada

GIGANTOR

TV series   1966   Japan (Syndicated)
30 Minutes (weekly)   Color

A badly animated cartoon imported from
Japan, set in the 21st century. Gigantor, an
indestructable **robot,** fights interplanetary
criminals with the help of Jimmy Sparks, his
12-year-old master, and a police detective
named Blooper. (52 episodes)

GILL WOMAN/GILL WOMEN OF VENUS

See: **Voyage to the Planet of the
Prehistoric Women**

THE GIRL FROM U.N.C.L.E.

TV series   1966-67   U.S. (NBC)   60 Minutes
(weekly)   Color

Stefanie Powers starred as April Dancer, the
girl from U.N.C.L.E., a young, pretty and
highly capable secret agent, partnered by
Noel Harrison as Mark Slate, recently transferred to New York from the organization's
London office. They continued the battle
against THRUSH, an international organization dedicated to world domination, begun by their male prototypes on **The Man
From U.N.C.L.E.** (1964-68). April's adventures were a bit too exaggerated, however,
and she and her partner lacked the chemistry of Robert Vaughn and David McCallum.
The series was canceled after one season.
(The characters were introduced in an
U.N.C.L.E. episode titled "The Moonglow
Affair." Mary Ann Mobley played April, and
Norman Fell was Mark.)

Directors: John Brahm, Mitchell Leisen, Barry
Shear, *Producers:* Douglas Benton, Mark Hodge,
Barry Shear, George Lear, *Executive Producer:*
Norman Felton, *Music:* **Jerry Goldsmith**

Cast: Stefanie Powers, Noel Harrison, Leo G.
Carroll, Randy Kirby

THE GIRL IN THE MOON

See: **Die Frau Im Monde**

GLADIATORENA

(Also titled: *The Gladiators, The Peace Game*)

Film   1968   Sweden (Sandrews/New Line)
105 Minutes   Color

In *Gladiatorena,* **Peter Watkins'** follow-up to his brilliant anti-**bomb** film **The War Game** (1965), global conflicts of the future will be resolved by military gladiators battling to the death in computer-controlled contests. Unfortunately, Watkins' moralizing is more important to him than his tentative game, which is unlikely to interest spectators of tomorrow any more than it does movie-goers of today. The film is made in his grainy, pseudo-documentary style, which brings a certain emotive power to the venture. Films with a similar theme include **La Decima Vittima** (1965), **Rollerball** and **Death Race 2000** (1975). (See also: **Dystopia.**)

Director: Peter Watkins, *Screenplay:* Peter Watkins, Nicholas Gosling, *Photographer:* Peter Suschitzky

Cast: Arthur Pentelow, Kenneth Lo, Frederick Danner, Bjorn Franzen

THE GLASS BOTTOM BOAT

Film   1966   U.S. (MGM)   110 Minutes
Metrocolor   Panavision

While not a SF film, this labored comedy about a young widow mistaken for an international spy demonstrates how SF elements are often borrowed by other film genres, even Doris Day vehicles. The actress copes with a vacuum cleaner-**robot** and that old SF standby the **antigravity device,** which traps her in a weightless room.

Director: Frank Tashlin, *Producers:* Everett Freeman, Martin Melcher, *Screenplay:* Everett Freeman, *Photographer:* Leon Shamroy, *Special Effects:* J. McMillan Johnson, Edward Carfagno, *Music:* Frank DeVol

Cast: Doris Day, Rod Taylor, Arthur Godfrey, Paul Lynde, Dom DeLuise

GLEN AND RANDA

Film   1971   U.S. (Universal-Marion)
94 Minutes   Color

Glen and Randa, two amoral hippie survivors of an atomic holocaust, wander naked through the ruins of America on an idyllic journey to a fabled city called Metropolis.

Shot in 16 mm. and enlarged to 35 mm., the film has brilliant moments but is amateurishly executed. Then an underground filmmaker, Jim McBride shows a raw talent for evoking dreamlike landscapes from existing locations, and the film, in its way, is a triumph of imagination over money. (See: **The Bomb.**)

Director: Jim McBride, *Screenplay:* Lorenzo Mans, Rudolph Wurlitzer, Jim McBride, *Photographer:* Alan Raymond

Cast: Steven Curry, Shelley Plimpton, Woodrow Chambliss

GO AND GET IT

Film   1920   U.S. (Neilan)   60 Minutes (approx.)   Black & white (silent)

This creaky melodrama, an uncredited adaptation of Edgar Allan Poe's *Murders in the Rue Morgue,* revolves around a series of mysterious murders panicking a large American city. A hotshot pair of male and female reporters scoop a rival newspaper when they discover that the killer is an ape. The real criminal, however, turns out to be a famous surgeon who transplanted the brain of an executed criminal into the gorilla's body. After killing the surgeon, the apeman sets out to avenge himself on the people responsible for his conviction. Filmmaker Neilan is the man who directed Mary Pickford's most popular silent movies.

Directors: Marshall Neilan, Henry Symonds, *Producer:* Marshall Neilan, *Screenplay:* Marion Fairfax, *Photography:* David Kesson

Cast: Noah Beery, Pat O'Malley, Agnes Ayres, Wesley Barry, *Gorilla*—Bull Montana

GODZILLA

A dinosaur with radioactive breath and a talent for destruction, created by Toho studios for *Godzilla, King of the Monsters* (1954), Japan's first SF film. Something of a national hero at home, akin to **King Kong** in the U.S., the mammoth creature was originally called Gojira, a contraction of the words *gorilla* and *kujira* which is Japanese for whale. Designed by special effectsman Eiji Tsuburaya, Godzilla is played by a man in a rubber suit and a mechanical miniature animated by **stop-motion photography.** His films include: **Gigantis the Fire Monster** (1955), *King Kong vs. Godzilla* (1962), *Godzilla vs. the Thing* (1964), *Godzilla vs. the Sea Monster* (1966), *Son of Godzilla* (1967), **Destroy All Monsters** (1968), *Godzilla's Revenge* (1969), *Godzilla vs. Gaigan* (1971), *Godzilla vs. the Smog Monster* (1971), *Godzilla vs. Megalon* (1973), and *Godzilla on Monster Island* (1978).

GOG

Film   1954   U.S. (United Artists)
85 Minutes   Color Corporation   3-D

Gog is a **robot,** partner of Magog, two experimental devices taking part in a secret government project in New Mexico to determine the feasibility of space flight. After a number of mysterious accidents in the underground lab—a man freezes to death in a high-altitude capsule, another is whirled to death in a centrifuge—the finger of suspicion points to the robots. The cause of the murders turns out to be a high-altitude spy plane, however, which has reprogrammed the lab's computers with an energy ray. Imaginative and energetic, the film contains a number of impressive 3-D effects. (See: **Stereoscopic film.**)

Director: Herbert L. Strock, *Producer:* Ivan Tors, *Screenplay:* Tom Taggert, *Story:* Ivan Tors, *Photographer:* Lathrop B. Worth, *Special Effects:* Harry Redmond, Jr., *Music:* Harry Sukman

Cast: Richard Egan, Constance Dowling, William Schallert, Herbert Marshall

GOLD

Film   1934   Germany (UFA)   120 Minutes
Black & white

German nationalism lurks in the background of this slow-moving adventure film, which has to do with the old alchemist's quest of turning base metals into gold. The villain is a greedy Scotsman who hires a right-minded German atomic physicist to help build his money-making machine. Located in an underwater laboratory, the device is ultimately innundated by an onrush of the Atlantic Ocean. The machine, topped by immense glass tubes, is impressive, as is its destruction in a series of crackling electrical explosions. The footage survives as the ending of **The Magnetic Monster,** a 1953 movie directed by **Curt Siodmak.** *Gold* was filmed simultaneously in a French-language version with star **Brigitte Helm** and a different cast.

Director: Karl Hartl, *Screenplay:* Rolf E. Vanloo, *Photographer:* Gunther Rittau, Otto Beacker, Werner Bohne, *Production Designer:* Otto Hunte, *Music:* Hans-Otto Borgmann

Cast: Brigitte Helm, Hans Albers, Michael Bohnen, Lien Deyers

GOLDENGIRL

Film   1979   U.S. (Avco)   104 Minutes
Eastmancolor

Science misused is the theme of this tepid behind-the-scenes melodrama. "Goldengirl," a beautiful 6'-2" Amazon, rockets to international fame after winning several Gold Medals at the Moscow Olympic Games. The secret of her phenomenal strength and endurance is a punishing regime of physical and psychological training augmented by hormone injections, electrical shock programming and hypnotic suggestion administered by an ex-Nazi doctor. The project is the brainchild of an ambitious promoter who plans to exploit the girl for commercial endorsements.

Obviously inspired by rumors concerning East Germany's superb female athletes (and made to capitalize on the forthcoming Olympic Games), *Goldengirl* eventually veers off the track into soap opera bathos. Moral issues are swept aside in favor of romance when a nosey male reporter convinces the girl that love is more valuable than gold. Director **Joseph Sargent** had a steadier hand on **Colossus, The Forbin Project** (1970).

Programmed to win, *Goldengirl* (Susan Anton) trains for the 1980 Olympics.

Director: Joseph Sargent, *Producer:* Danny O'Donovan, *Screenplay:* John Kohn, *Novel:* Peter Lear, *Photographer:* Steven Larner, *Music:* Bill Conti

Cast: Susan Anton, Curt Jurgens, James Coburn, Robert Culp, Leslie Caron, Harry Guardino

GOLDFINGER

Film   1964   Great Britain (United Artists)
112 Minutes   Technicolor

James Bond takes judo lessons from an athletic beauty named Pussy Galore and outwits a megalomanic millionaire named Goldfinger, who wants to drive up the price of gold by setting off an atomic bomb in Fort Knox. Bond nearly gets sliced up the middle by a **laser** beam in this sexy and sadistic outing, one of his best.

Director: Guy Hamilton, *Producers:* Harry Saltzman, Albert R. Broccoli, *Screenplay:* Richard Maibaum, Paul Dehn, *Novel:* Ian Fleming, *Photographer:* Ted Moore, *Production Designer:* **Ken Adams,** *Special Effects:* John Stears, Frank George, *Music:* **John Barry**

Cast: **Sean Connery,** Honor Blackman, Gert Probe, Harold Sakata, Shirley Eaton, Bernard Lee, Lois Maxwell

GOLDSMITH, JERRY (1930–   )

Composer of film scores. Born in Los Angeles, Goldsmith was graduated from Los Angeles City College and attended graduate school at UCLA where he studied film composing with Miklos Rosza, a three-time **Academy Award** winner. Goldsmith wrote incidental music for radio before making a name in television, initially for live dramatic programs. A versatile and prolific composer, he has written a record number of SF film scores. He won an Academy Award for *The Omen* (1976).

Goldfinger: James Bond visits Fort Knox.

Other films: **The Manchurian Candidate** (1962), **Seven Days in May** (1964), **Our Man Flint, Seconds** (1966), **In Like Flint** (1967), **Planet of the Apes** (1968), **The Illustrated Man, The Most Dangerous Man Alive** (1969), **Escape From the Planet of the Apes** (1971), The Reincarnation of Peter Proud, **Logan's Run** (1976), **Twilight's Last Gleaming, Damnation Alley** (1977), **Coma, Capricorn One, The Swarm, The Boys from Brazil** (1978), **Star Trek—The Motion Picture, Alien** (1979), *Poltergeist,* **The Secret of Nimh** (1982)

TV credits include: Playhouse 90 (1956-61), *Studio One* (1948-58), *Gunsmoke* (1955-75), **The Twilight Zone** (1959-64), *Thriller* (1960-62), **The Man from U.N.C.L.E.** (1964-68), **The Girl from U.N.C.L.E.** (1966-67), **Voyage to the Bottom of the Sea** (1964-68)

GOLIATH AWAITS

TV serial   1981   Great Britain (Benson/Columbia)   3 hours, 40 minutes   Color

Goliath Awaits: Scientist John McKenzie (Christopher Lee) and daughter Lea (Emma Samms) live in a sunken luxury liner.

Oceanographers locate the rusting hulk of the H.M.S. Goliath, a luxury liner sunk by German U-boats during World War II, and discover that her passengers are still alive. A scientist on board had conveniently put together a heat exchange machine that harnessed the power of an underground volcano to provide light, air and even an underwater garden. Mercilessly drawn out with endless shots of unconvincing **miniatures** and swimmers entering and leaving hatches, *Goliath Awaits* manages to pack an amazing amount of waste space into its three syndicated episodes.

Director: **Kevin Connor,** *Producers:* Hugh Benson, Richard Bluel, *Writers:* Richard Bluel, Pat Fiedler, *Photographer:* Al Francis, *Special Effects:* Joe Unsinn, *Music:* George Duning

Cast: Mark Harmon, **Christopher Lee,** John Carradine, Alex Cord, Robert Forster, Emma Samms

GOLITZEN, ALEXANDER (1907–   )

Hollywood art director and **production designer.** Born in Russia, Golitzen emigrated to the U.S. in 1923 and studied architecture at the University of Wisconsin. He entered films as an illustrator for M.G.M. and progressed to art director at the Goldwyn Studio before settling in at Universal (later Universal-International), where he was named supervising art director in 1954. Called a "great all-purpose" designer, Golitzen was at his best creating surreal alien environments for SF and fantasy films. His bold conception of the doomed planet Metaluna in **This Island Earth** (1955) has a sad grandiloquence that effectively suggests an advanced civilization on the threshhold of disaster.

Other films: The Hurricane (1937), *The Phantom of the Opera* (1943), *Letter from an Unknown Woman* (1948), **Revenge of the Creature** (1955), **The Creature Walks Among Us** (1956), **The Deadly Mantis, The Monolith Monsters** (1957), *Spartacus* (1960), *Thoroughly Modern Millie* (1967), **Colossus, The Forbin Project** (1970), **Slaughterhouse 5** (1972), Earthquake (1974)

GORATH

Film   1962   Japan (Toho)   83 Minutes
Color   [Released 1962   U.S. (Columbia)]

Another Japanese science-created monster from the director/special effects team that brought us **Godzilla** (1954). When an international space agency fires giant rockets to move Earth from the path of a maverick planet, earthquakes from the resultant alteration in orbit (the film's only nod to scientific accuracy) uncover the burial grounds of a prehistoric creature resembling a dinosaur with tusks. Awakened from its long slumber, the hungry beast—nicknamed "Gorath" by Japanese officials monitoring its progress—proceeds to dine on Tokyo.

Director: Inoshiro Honda, *Producer:* Tomoyuki Tanaka, *Screenplay:* Takeshi Kimura, *Photographer:* Hajime Koizumi, *Special Effects:* Eiji Tsuburaya

Cast: Jun Tazaki, Takashi Shimura, Ryo Ikebe

GORDON, BERT I. (1922–   )

Director/producer/writer/special effects man of low-budget "quickies" usually populated with homemade **mutant** monsters.

Born in Kenosha, Wisconsin, Gordon began making trick films at the age of 10 when a relative game him an old 16-mm. camera. Graduated from the University of Wisconsin, he produced local TV commercials and industrial films before moving to Hollywood in the early 1950s. After a stint as production supervisor for the TV series *Racket Squad,* he obtained private backing and launched his career with *King Dinosaur* (1955), a prehistoric fantasy fashioned around a **rear screen.** A Hollywood independent, Gordon has also worked for many "poverty row" studios. His productions, which pretend to be more elaborate than their budgets allow, are often shown at retrospectives of worst films.

Other films: **The Beginning of the End, Cyclops, The Amazing Colossal Man** (1957), **Attack of the Puppet People, War of the Colossal Beast,** *The Spider* (1958), *The Magic Sword* (1962), **Village of the Giants** (1965), *Picture Mommy Dead* (1966),

Necromancy (1972), *The Mad Bomber* (1973), **Food of the Gods** (1976), **Empire of the Ants** (1977), *Killer Fish* (1979)

GORGO

Film   1960   Great Britain (King Bros.)
70 Minutes   Technicolor   [Released 1961
U.S. (MGM)]

Fishermen capture a 30-feet-tall reptile floating off the coast of Ireland and sell it to a London circus. Identified as a "gorgosaurus," the creature is nicknamed Gorgo and put on display. Despite its immense size, Gorgo turns out to be only a baby, a fact that becomes apparent when its 150-feet-tall mother comes to claim it. Angry beyond belief, Mama demolishes Tower Bridge, Big Ben and half of London before sliding back into the sea with her proud offspring.

Well-made with a sense of adventure and fun, *Gorgo* owes a great deal of its effectiveness to the special effects of Tom Howard. Like **Godzilla,** the creature is a man in a monster suit, who wrecks intricately detailed **miniature** sets, built on a scale of one to 30. The illusion is an improvement over the Japanese film, however, because of a new high-speed color film that allowed for **fast-motion** photography, to give the illusion of immense strength during the destruction sequences.

Director: **Eugene Lourie,** *Producer:* Wilfrid Eades, *Screenplay:* John Loring, Daniel Hyatt, *Photographer:* Frederick A. Young, *Special Effects:* Tom Howard, *Music:* Angelo Lavagnino

Cast: Bill Travers, William Sylvester, Christopher Rhodes, Vincent Winter, Joseph O'Connor

GRAND MOFF TARKIN

Governor of the Imperial Outland regions of the galaxy and the commander of archvillain **Darth Vader** in the film **Star Wars** (1977). Ruthlessly cold-blooded in achieving his ambition of becoming emperor, Grand Moff Tarkin builds a planet-sized battle station called the **Death Star,** capable of obliterating troublesome worlds with a single burst of pure energy. He destroys the planet **Alderaan,** home of **Princess Leia Organa** and the site of a growing freedom movement. He suffers a similar fate when **Luke Skywalker** and company invade the Death Star and enable rebel fighters to blow it up. Grand Moff Tarkin was played by British actor **Peter Cushing.**

GRAVE ROBBERS FROM OUTER SPACE

See: **Plan 9 from Outer Space**

THE GREAT ALASKAN MYSTERY

Film serial   1944   U.S. (Universal)
13 Episodes   Black & white

Dr. Miller, an American scientist, journeys to far-off Alaska with his daughter and two assistants to find a rare mineral needed to power his secret defense weapon, the Peratron. Before arriving, they survive a shipwreck, a plane crash and several potentially fatal "accidents," engineered by a gang of fascists posing as respectable businessmen. The gang turns up at the mine and repeatedly attempts to steal the weapon (whose rays

kill one of them) before being brought to justice by Dr. Miller's heroic assistant (and future son-in-law), Bill Hudson.

A lively period piece, *The Great Alaskan Mystery* becomes more interesting if one substitutes the words atomic **bomb** for Peratron. The film's fantasy device was based on newspaper reports of a rumored secret weapon then being developed by the U.S. (heralded by the sudden demand for an obscure mineral called uranium).

Directors: Ray Taylor, Lewis D. Collins, *Screenplay:* Maurice Tombragel, George H. Plympton, *Story:* Jack Foley, *Photographer:* William Sickner

Cast: Ralph Morgan, Marjorie Weaver, Milburn Stone, Edgar Kennedy, Martin Kosleck

THE GREATEST AMERICAN HERO

TV series   1981-   U.S. (ABC)   50 Minutes
(weekly)   Color

The Greatest American Hero: Connie Sellecca, William Katt and Robert Culp.

An idealistic schoolteacher fights crime in a red supersuit he hasn't quite gotten the hang of. This engaging send-up of the superhero myth follows in the footsteps of **Spider-Man** (1977). It has as its TV antecedents the short-lived series **Mr. Terrific** and **Captain Nice** inspired by TV's camp reprise of **Batman** (1966-68). After debuting with a two-hour film the series shot to the top of the ratings, dominating its 8:00 p.m. Wednesday night time slot. Scripts were fresh and inventive, providing actor William Katt an opportunity to be more than just a straight man for jokes about a guy in a cape and long johns. For trivia lovers, Katt's character was originally named Ralph Hinkley, but the surname was dropped in March, 1981 after John Warnock Hinckley, Jr. attempted to assassinate President Reagan.

Creator/Writer/Executive Producer: Stephen J. Cannell, *Producer:* Alex Beaton, *Photographer:* Andrew Jackson, *Art Director:* Mary Weaver Dodson, *Special Effects:* **Magicam,** *Music:* Mike Post, Pete Carpenter

Cast: William Katt, Robert Culp, Connie Sellecca, Michael Pare, Faye Grant

THE GREATEST BATTLE ON EARTH

See: **Ghidra, the Three-Headed Monster**

THE GREATEST POWER

Film 1917 U.S. (Metro) 5 reels Black & white (silent)

Primitive but prophetic, *The Greatest Power* concerns the dilemma of an American chemist who discovers a superpowerful explosive called "exonite" while developing a cure for cancer. He initially decides to make the weapon available to all countries of the world to create a military stalemate and deter war. But he changes his mind and does the right thing by giving it to the peace-loving United States. A later generation of nuclear physicists would make the same decision about a similar weapon called the atomic **bomb.**

Director: Edwin Carewe, *Screenplay:* Albert Shelby LeVino, *Story:* Louis R. Wolheim

Cast: William B. Davidson, Ethel Barrymore, William Black, Harry S. Northrup

THE GREEN HORNET

Radio serial 1936-52 U.S. (NBC Blue/Mutual) 15 Minutes (Mon-Wed-Fri), 30 Minutes (weekly)

Later a favorite **comic-book** hero, *The Green Hornet* was born on radio, the creation of George W. Trendle and Fran Striker, who based the program on their previous success, *The Lone Ranger* (1933-54). Both characters were masked mystery men who rode into town with faithful sidekicks—the Ranger with his stolid Indian brave Tonto, and the Hornet with his resourceful Japanese houseboy Kato (changed to a Filipino during World War II)—the difference being that the Hornet had a streamlined black sedan rather than a horse. They were in fact relatives. As millions of listeners knew (but not the criminals), the Hornet was secretly Britt Reid, the wealthy owner of a crusading newspaper, *The Daily Sentinel,* and the Lone Ranger was his great-uncle, John Reid.

Unlike the Ranger, however, the Hornet was wanted by the police for fighting crime without a license. They were always trying to arrest him, but they never succeeded. Always a step ahead of them, he quickly immobilized evil-doers with the sting of his gas-pellet gun and dropped one of his Green Hornet seals (the deadliest insect when angered), before speeding away with Kato in the unstoppable car.

Among the actors who supplied the voice of the Hornet was **Al Hodge,** better known as the star of **Captain Video and His Video Rangers.** (Announcer Mike Wallace went on to a distinguished career as a TV journalist for CBS's *60 Minutes.*) *The Green Hornet* originated in Chicago and first aired over the NBC Blue Network; in 1938 it switched to the Mutual Broadcasting System. In 1948 the three-times-weekly serial format was replaced with a self-contained weekly half-hour adventure. Theme song of the program was "Flight of the Bumblebee" by Rimsky-Korsakov, followed by the ascending sound of a buzzing hornet.

Creators: George W. Trendle, Fran Striker, *Producer:* James Jewell, *Directors:* James Jewell, Charles Livingstone and others, *Writers:* James Jewell, Fran Striker and others

Cast: The Green Hornet—Al Hodge (1936-43), Donovan Faust (1943), Bob Hall (1943-46), Jack McCarthy (1946-52), *Kato*—Raymond Hayashi, Rollon Parker, Mickey Tolan, Lee Allman, Jim Irwin, Gil Shea, Jack Petruzzi, *Announcers*—Mike Wallace, Hal Neal, Charles Woods, Fielden Farrington, Bob Hite

THE GREEN HORNET

Film serial   1940   U.S. (Universal)
13 Episodes   Black & white

Despite constant interference from the police, the Green Hornet cracks a contraband munitions ring, an insurance scam and an auto-theft racket, all the work of one master-crook. Keye Luke, Charlie Chan's No. 1 son, plays Kato in a pair of industrial goggles; The Hornet wears a full face mask decorated with his namesake, which resembles a butterfly.

Directors: Ford Beebe, Ray Taylor, *Screenplay:* George H. Plympton, Basil Dickey, Morrison C. Wood, Lyonel Margolies, *Photographer:* William Sickner, Jerome Ash

Cast: Gordon Jones—*Brett Reid/the Green Hornet*, Keye Luke, Wade Boteler, Anne Nagel, Philip Trent, Walter McGrail

THE GREEN HORNET

TV series   1966-67   U.S. (ABC)   30 Minutes (weekly)   Color

An updated version of the radio serial. Britt Reid, alias the Green Hornet, now discretely masked, owns a TV station in addition to *The Daily Sentinel.* His supercharged car, the Black Beauty (actually a $50,000 customized Chrysler Imperial) has a number of new gadgets that would please **James Bond,** including a TV camera that can see for miles, brushes that flip down from the rear bumper to erase tire tracks, and a device that spreads ice over the road to discourage pursuers. Not much else has changed, however: the Hornet and Kato are still battling crime on the wrong side of the law, while trying to protect their identities from the newspaper's ace crime reporter.

A victim of bad timing, the program reached television shortly after **Batman** (1966-68) started a trend for campy masked crusaders. Played straight, *The Green Hornet* had little chance of success, even with the expert karate chops of Bruce Lee as Kato. Conspicuously missing was the old "Flight of the Bumble Bee" theme, scrapped in favor of a colorless trumpet solo by Al Hirt.

Cast: Van Williams, Bruce Lee, Wende Wagner, Walter Brooke, Lloyd Gough, Sheila Leighton

THE GREEN HORNET STRIKES AGAIN

Film serial   1940   U.S. (Universal)
13 Episodes   Black & white

Warren Hull makes a better Hornet than Gordon Jones, his predecessor in this sequel to *The Green Hornet,* made the same year. But the show still belongs to Keye Luke as Kato. The pair take on a syndicate Mr. Big named Grogan, who makes the unforgiveable mistake of offering them a bribe.

Directors: Ford Beebe, John Rawlins, *Screenplay:* George H. Plympton, Basil Dickey, Sherman L. Lowe, *Photographer:* Jerome Ash

Cast: Warren Hull, Keye Luke, Pierre Watkins, Wade Boteler, Anne Nagel, Eddie Acuff

THE GREEN SLIME

Film   1968   Japan (Toei)   77 Minutes
Toeicolor   [Released 1969   U.S. (MGM) 90 Minutes]

Astronauts dispatched to destroy a marauding **asteroid** return to an orbiting space station called Gamma Three with a batch of nasty alien microbes. The germs swell and multiply into an army of slimy green things who flop their rubber tentacles repulsively. The American actors are required to register horror in unison, like characters in a **Godzilla** film.

Director: Kinji Fukasaku, *Producers:* Ivan Reiner, Walter Manley, *Screenplay:* Charles Sinclair, William Finger, Tom Rowe, *Special Effects:* Akira Watanabe

Cast: Robert Horton, Richard Jaeckel, Luciana Paluzzi, Ted Gunther, Bud Windom

THE GREEN TERROR

Film   1919   Great Britain (Gaumont)
60 Minutes   Black & white (silent)

The Green Terror marks the first time moviegoers were alerted to the threat of germ warfare, later a popular SF subject. The complicated story, an adaptation of an Edgar Wallace mystery, is replete with Victorian histrionics: A damsel is being held for ransom while detectives in disguises are hot on the trail of a greedy scientist and a financier who intend to make a fortune by hoarding wheat. They intend to destroy the rest of the world's crop with a synethic blight.

Director: Will P. Kelling, *Screenplay:* G. W. Clifford

Cast: Maud Yates, Aurele Sydney, Heather Thatcher

GUEST, VAL (1911–   )

British director, screenwriter, producer. A former trade journalist for the *Hollywood Reporter* and a tipster for gossip columnist Walter Winchell, Guest returned to England in the late 1930s to write screenplays for formula comedies. A director since 1942, he has specialized in tautly written, fast-paced melodramas and thrillers made in an urgent, cynical style reminiscent of the scandal press. In recent years he has directed for television, notably episodes of the series **Space: 1999** (1975-77).

Films include: **The Quatermass Experiment** (1955), **Quatermass II, The Abominable Snow-**

man (1957), *Expresso Bongo* (1958), *Stop Me Before I Kill/The Full Treatment,* **The Day the Earth Caught Fire** (1961), *Contest Girl* (1964), *Casino Royale* [co-director] (1967), *When Dinosaurs Ruled the Earth* (1969), *The Diamond Merchants/Killer Force* (1975)

GUN ON ICE PLANET ZERO

TV film   1980   U.S. (Universal)
100 Minutes   Color

One of 12 movies compiled from the TV series **Battlestar Galactica** (1978-79) and syndicated locally. The Galactica crew recruits explosives experts who happen to be dangerous criminals, to destroy a mammoth laser cannon aimed at the battlestar from an ice-bound planet. Joining in the effort is a population of cloned slaves who live on the planet. The original two-part episode, which aired in 1978, was titled "The Ultimate Weapon." (See also: **clone.**)

Director: Alan Levi, *Executive Producer:* Glen A. Larson, *Screenplay:* Leslie Stevens, Michael Sloan, Don Bellisario

Cast: Richard Hatch, Dirk Benedict, Lorne Greene, Maren Jensen, James Olson, Christine Belford, Roy Thinnes, Britt Eklund

Gun on Ice Planet Zero: Starbuck (Dirk Benedict) and Tenna (Britt Eklund), a member of a society of enslaved clones, join forces to destroy a deadly weapon.

HALLER, DANIEL (1926–   )

Director/producer of films and television series. Born in Los Angeles, Haller directed TV commercials before switching to motion pictures as an art director in 1955. He worked primarily with low-budget filmmaker **Roger Corman,** for whom he designed the garish but effective decor of several horror films based on stories by Edgar Allan Poe. His sets were noted for creating the illusion of vast spaces from the limited resources of AIP's workshop. In 1967 he directed his first movie, **Monster of Terror,** an awkward adaptation of the H. P. Lovecraft classic, *The Color Out of Space* (1927). Like his mentor, Haller works quickly and has a flair for visual hyperbole.

Films as Art Director: **War of the Satellites** (1958), **The Little Shop of Horrors, The Last Woman on Earth** (1960), *The Premature Burial* (1962), **"X" The Man With the X-ray Eyes** (1963), *The Comedy of Terrors* (1964)

Producer: **City Under the Sea** (1965)

Director: Devil's Angels (1967), *The Wild Racers* (1968), *The Dunwich Horror, Paddy, Pieces of Dreams* (1970), **Buck Rogers in the 25th Century** (1979)

Television credits: Episodes of *Ironside* (1967-75), *Kojak* (1973-78), *The Blue Knight* (1975-76), *Charlie's Angels* (1976-81), **Battlestar Galactica** (1978-80), **Knight Rider** (1982)

HAMILL, MARK (1952–   )

Film and television actor of juvenile roles who rose to superstardom with his portrayal of **Luke Skywalker** in **Star Wars** (1977), his first film. Hamill's open-faced good looks and wholesome appeal created a believable focus for **George Lucas' space opera,** and he has become permanently identified with the role.

Born in Oakland, California, Hamill is the son of a U.S. Navy captain and one of seven children. His childhood was spent on Navy bases in California, Virginia, New York and Japan, where he received his high school diploma. He made his professional acting debut in 1970 on television's *The Bill Cosby Show* while a two-year drama student at Los Angeles City College. He subsequently had a running part for nine months on the daytime soap opera *General Hospital.* For the next six years he was highly visible on television in a succession of secondary roles. He appeared in more than 140 programs, including *The F.B.I., Owen Marshal—Counselor at Law, Night Gallery* and *The Partridge Family,* and co-starred in a poorly received comedy series, *The Texas Wheelers* (1974-75). His made-for-TV movies include *Sara T: Portrait of a Teenage Alcoholic* (1975), *Delancy Street* (1975) and *Eric* (1975). He also did several voices for the cartoon series *Jeannie* (1973-75) and appeared on Broadway in *The Elephant Man* (1981).

Shortly before the release of *Star Wars* and the film **Wizards** (1977, a SF/Fantasy cartoon for which he provided voices, he was badly injured when his car went out of control on a California freeway. His nose and left cheekbone were crushed, requiring three operations by plastic surgeons to rebuild them. Since then he has starred in *Corvette Summer* (1978) and *The Big Red One* (1979), films which had little impact at the box office, despite his above-the-title billing. He again played Luke in **The Empire Strikes Back** (1980) and *Revenge of the Jedi* (1983), a role that has made him a rich man (he owns .025 per cent of each film's profits) but which he considers a mixed blessing. "Skywalker

Mark Hamill

Hangar 18: Darren McGavin as a NASA flight director examines debris from a crashed UFO.

is boring, like Dorothy in **The Wizard of Oz,"** says Hamill. "But I tell myself that in a hundred years it's not going to matter much whether you get to play Hamlet or not."

THE HAND OF DEATH

Film 1961 U.S. (20th Century-Fox)
60 Minutes Black & white

A scientist experimenting with a pesticide is badly scarred when the chemicals explode in his face. As a result, he has the ability to poison people with his touch.

Director: Harry Nelson, *Producer/Screenplay:* Eugene Ling, *Photographer:* **Floyd Crosby,** *Makeup:* Robert Mark, *Music:* Sonny Burke

Cast: **John Agar,** Paula Raymond, Roy Gordon, Steve Dunne

THE HANDS OF A KILLER

See: **Planets Against Us**

HANGAR 18

Film 1980 U.S. (Sunn Classics)
93 Minutes Technicolor

Much ado about a **UFO** that crashes in the Arizona desert and the inevitable Government cover-up—a favorite theme of paranoid UFO buffs. Air Force investigators have unearthed **alien** corpses, a discovery of such magnitude that people will take to the streets if the news is released. A bastard son of **Close Encounters of the Third Kind** (1977), *Hanger 18* is the product of a Utah company that makes films based on computer surveys.

Director: James L. Conway, *Producer:* Charles E. Sellier, Jr., *Screenplay:* Steven Thornley, *Story:* Tom Chapman, James L. Conway, *Photographer:* Paul Hipp, *Art Director:* Paul Staheli, *Special Effects:* Harry Woolman, *Music:* John Cacavas

Cast: Darren McGavin, Robert Vaughn, Gary Collins, Joseph Campanella, Pamela Bellwood, Tom Halleck

HARRYHAUSEN, RAY (1920–   )

Celebrated **stop-motion** model animator. Born in Los Angeles, Harryhausen was educated at Audubon Junior High and Manual Arts High School. Inspired by the film

King Kong (1933), he made his first stop-motion film at age 14 with a borrowed 16-mm. camera and a "Cave Bear" fabricated from his mother's worn-out fur coat. He subsequently took night courses at UCLA, studying trick motion-picture photography, sculpture, ceramics and life drawing.

His professional career began in 1941, when he was hired by filmmaker **George Pal** to help animate his stop-motion cartoons, called *Puppetoons.* After serving in the U.S. Army Signal Corps during World War II, Harryhausen assisted his "idol," **Willis O'Brien** (creator of *King Kong),* in the animation of **Mighty Joe Young** (1949), the story of a giant ape. His first solo effort was the raging dinosaur of **The Beast from 20,000 Fathoms** (1953), based on a story by **Ray Bradbury.** His next film was **It Came from Beneath the Sea** (1955), which began a long collaboration with producer Charles H. Schneer. Harryhausen refers to his stop-motion technique, called **Dynarama,** as "kinetic sculptures."

Other films: **Earth vs. the Flying Saucers** (1956), **Twenty Million Miles to Earth** (1957), *The Seventh Voyage of Sinbad* (1958), *The Three Worlds of Gulliver* (1960), **Mysterious Island** (1961), *Jason and the Argonauts* (1963), **First Men on the Moon** (1964), **One Million Years B.C.** (1966), *Valley of the Gwangi* (1969), **Trog** (1970), *The Golden Voyage of Sinbad* (1973), *Sinbad and the Eye of the Tiger* (1977), *Clash of the Titans* (1981)

HASKIN, BYRON (1899–   )

Director; born in Portland, Oregon and educated at the University of California at Berkeley. A former newspaper cartoonist, advertising man and still photographer, Haskin entered films as an assistant cameraman for the Pathe Company in 1918. He progressed to directing in 1927 with Warner Bros.' *Matinee Ladies* and later worked in England as a sound technician. He returned to Hollywood in the early 1930s as a special effects cameraman and was not given an opportunity to direct again until

Ray Harryhausen: The stop-motion animator puts a finishing touch on a model used in his fantasy spectacle, *Clash of the Titans,* based on Greek mythology.

hired by producer Hal Wallis for *I Walk Alone* (1947).

His first SF film was **War of the Worlds** (1953), which began a long-term association with producer **George Pal.** Haskin's work in the genre has been adequate and occasionally exceptional, with particular attention paid to special effects. His most imaginative and fully realized work is **Robinson Crusoe on Mars** (1964), a futuristic adaptation of Daniel DeFoe's classic story. Haskin also directed several episodes of the TV series **The Outer Limits** (1963-65). He retired in the late 1960s.

Films include: Treasure Island (1950), **The Naked Jungle** (1954), *Long John Silver,* **Conquest of Space** (1955), **From Earth to the Moon** (1958), *Captain Sinbad* (1963), **Robinson Crusoe on Mars** (1964), **The Power** (1968)

HAUSER'S MEMORY

TV film 1970 U.S. (NBC) 99 Minutes Color

David McCallum is impressive as a young Jewish scientist who injects himself with DNA isolated from the brain of Hauser, a dying Nazi physicist. The object is to preserve Hauser's scientific knowledge, but the experiment takes a sinister turn when Hauser's memory begins to take control of McCallum to even up old scores. Tortured by memories of unspeakable medical experiments, McCallum eventually succumbs to Hauser and journeys behind the Iron Curtain to murder an escaped Nazi SS officer. This is a film version of **Curt Siodmak**'s scientifically implausible novel, *Hauser's Memory,* the sequel to his equally implausible novel, *Donovan's Brain* (1943), which was filmed three times as **The Lady and the Monster** (1944), **Donovan's Brain** (1953) and **The Brain** (1962).

Director: Boris Sagal, *Producer:* Jack Laird, *Screenplay:* Adrian Spies, *Novel:* Curt Siodmak, *Photographer:* Petrus Schloemp, *Art Director:* Ellen Schmidt, *Music:* Billy Byers

Cast: David McCallum, Susan Strasberg, Lilli Palmer, Leslie Nielsen, Helmut Kantner, Robert Webber

HAVE ROCKET, WILL TRAVEL

Film 1959 U.S. (Columbia) 76 Minutes Black & white

Slapstick comedy for fans of The Three Stooges, who go to **Venus** where they meet beautiful maidens, a **robot** and a fire-breathing spider the size of a dragon. The science fiction is incidental, to say the least.

Director: David Lowell Rich, *Producer:* Harry Romm, *Screenplay:* Raphael Hayes, *Photographer:* Ray Cory, *Music:* Mischa Bakaleinikoff

Cast: Moe Howard, Larry Fine, "Curly" DeRita, Jerome Cowan, Anna-Lisa, Nedine Datas

THE HEAD

See: **Der Nackte und der Satan**

HEARTBEEPS

Film 1981 U.S. (Universal) 79 Minutes Color Panavision

This witty and inventive love story features comedians Andy Kaufman and Bernadette Peters as two **robots** who trigger strange sensations in each other's "pleasure centers." Kaufman is ValCom-17485, a commodities specialist, and Peters is AquaCom-89045, a companion programmed for "poolside parties and other social functions." The pair take off for a look at the world, joined by Catskill, a stand-up-comedian robot given to one-liners (the voice of Jack Carter). Pursued by a Crimebuster robot, a tank-like vehicle, they find sanctuary in a junk yard and build a "baby" from spare truck parts.

Kaufman and Peters played the roles covered in a gelatin film concocted by makeup artist Stan Winston. The radio-controlled police robot Crimebuster and "baby" Phil were designed by Jamie Shourt and Robbie Blalack. *Heartbeeps* did poorly in previews, and the film was subsequently re-edited (without the director's consent), and trimmed by nine minutes. It was nevertheless a casualty at the box office.

Director: Allan Arkush, *Producer:* Douglas Green, *Screenplay:* John Hill, *Photographer:* Charles Rosher, Jr., *Production Designer:* John W. Corson, *Makeup:* Stan Winston, *Special Effects:* Albert Whitlock, Jamie Shourt, Robbie Blalack, *Music:* **John Williams**

Cast: Andy Kaufman, Bernadette Peters, Randy Quaid, Kenneth McMillan, Melanie Mayron, Christopher Guest

THE HEAVENS CALL

Film   1959   USSR (Dovzhenko)   90 Minutes   Color

Science fiction as propaganda, with handsome Soviet cosmonauts selflessly rescuing fat, short and sneaky American astronauts stranded on **Mars.** The United States has risked the lives of its space explorers with faulty equipment in its eagerness to bring capitalism to the red planet. Worthwhile for its interesting special effects, incorporated into the **Roger Corman** film **Battle Beyond the Sun.**

Director: Alexander Kozyr, M. Kartinkov, *Screenplay:* V. Pomieszczykov, A. Sazanov

Cast: A. Shvorin, L. Lobanov, Ivan Pereverzev

THE HELL CREATURES

See: **Invasion of the Saucer Men**

HELM, BRIGITTE (1906–   )

German actress, born Gisele Eve Schiltenhelm in Berlin. An exciting Teutonic beauty with a diamond-hard profile, Helm made her film debut in **Metropolis** (1926) playing the dual role of the innocent young heroine and her wanton **robot** double. Her frankly erotic performance created an international sensation, and she subsequently made films in England and France as well as Germany. Chillingly effective as a heartless *femme fatale,* she was less convincing in other roles, and her screen mystique declined with the advent of sound. She retired in 1935 to marry a wealthy factory owner.

Other films: **Am Rande der Welt,** *Die Liebe der Jeanne Ney* (1927), **Alraune,** *L'Argent* (1928), *Manolescu* (1929), **Alraune** (1930), *The City of Song* (1931), *The Blue Danube,* **L'Atlantide** (1932), *Inge und die Millionen, Spione am Werk* (1933), *Die Insel,* **Gold** (1934), *Ein idealer Gatte* (1935)

THE HERCULOIDS

TV series   1967-69   U.S. (CBS)   30 Minutes (weekly)   Color

Superpowerful animals called the Herculoids protect King Zendor and other inhabitants of their utopian planet from invading **aliens** in this animated cartoon series. Members of the group include Zok the dragon, Dorno the ten-legged rhinoceros, Igoo the living rock and Gloop and Gleep, the blobs. (See also: **Utopia**)

Directors/Producers: William Hanna, Joseph Barbera, *Music:* Hoyt Curtin

Voices: Mike Road, Virginia Gregg, Teddy Eccles, Don Messick

HERRMANN, BERNARD (1911–75)

Composer and conductor of film scores; born in New York; educated at New York University and Julliard. Herrmann began his career in 1933 as a contract musical director for CBS Radio, where one of his assignments was the background music for Orson Welles' famous broadcast of **The War of the Worlds** (1938), adapted from the **H. G. Wells** novel. Welles subsequently hired him to compose the score for his celebrated film *Citizen Kane* (1941).

One of Hollywood's most prolific and versatile composers, Herrmann had an infallible ear for creating original music that strengthened a film's dramatic content, while never drawing attention to itself. He composed one of his best scores for the SF film **The Day the Earth Stood Still** (1951), with an **alien**-sounding amalgam of electronic sounds, fragmented melodies and string instruments, a Herrmann trademark. He later scored many of Alfred Hitchcock's films, including the master's only SF effort, **The Birds** (1963), which has no music but an electronic choreography of sound effects. Herrmann also founded a chamber orchestra, conducted major symphony orchestras and composed operas and ballets. He won an **Academy Award** for the score of *All That Money Can Buy* (1941).

Other films: The Magnificent Ambersons (1942), *The Ghost and Mrs. Muir* (1947), *The Trouble With Harry* (1956), *Vertigo* (1958), **Journey to the Center of the Earth** (1959), *Psycho* (1960), **Mysterious Island** (1961), *Jason and the Argonauts* (1964), **Fahrenheit 451** (1966), *La Mariee etait en Noir/ The Bride Wore Black* (1967), *Sisters* (1973), *It's Alive* (1974), *Taxi Driver* (1976), *It's Alive Again* (1978).

TV credits include: Alred Hitchcock Presents (1955-62), **The Twilight Zone** (1959-64).

HESTON, CHARLTON (1923–   )

Film actor who specializes in epic Biblical, historical and SF heroes. No matter the role, Heston is always the noble American—the courageous, resourceful leader who shepherds his flock to safety while coping with their inadequacies. Although his performances lack depth and warmth, his physical size and square-jawed patrician features suggest a persona as morally upright and durable as the faces on Mt. Rushmore. French critics have dubbed Heston an "axiom of cinema" because of his ability to project these qualities by merely walking on-screen.

Born in Evanston, Illinois, Heston studied speech and drama at Northwestern University while working part-time as a radio actor in nearby Chicago. After a three-year tour of duty with the U.S. Army Air Force, he settled in New York and appeared regularly on Broadway, radio and live television. In 1950 he made his film debut in *Dark City* as a tough, working-class loner, a typecasting soon supplanted by larger-than-life roles. His screen roles include Andrew Jackson, Buffalo Bill Cody, Clark of the Lewis and Clark expedition, Moses, Ben Hur, El Cid,

John the Baptist, Michelangelo, Julius Caesar, Mark Anthony, Cardinal Richelieu and Henry VIII.

When historical epics began to falter at the box office, Heston, an SF buff, accommodated changing public tastes by appearing in big-budget disaster and SF films. The transition was an effortless one, and Heston's iconography proved to be as effective in dealing with catastrophes of the present and future as it had been in those of the past. His SF-fantasy films include **The Naked Jungle** (1955), **Planet of the Apes** (1968), **Beneath the Planet of the Apes** (1970), **The Omega Man** (1971), **Soylent Green** (1973), *Earthquake* (1974) and *The Awakening* (1980). **Academy Award:** *Ben Hur*, Best Actor, 1959.

THE HIDEOUS SUN DEMON

Film   1959   U.S. (Pacific International)
74 Minutes   Black & white

A physicist accidentally exposed to nuclear radiation at an atomic **bomb** plant develops characteristics of a reptile whenever he is exposed to sunlight. The transformation includes scales, claws, fangs and an appetite for human flesh. He tries his best to stay in the shade but, alas, he eventually wanders into the open and falls to his death from a tower, a common fate for afflicted scientists in camp **horror** movies of the 1950s.

Directors: Robert Clarke, Thomas Cassarino, *Producer:* Robert Clarke, *Screenplay:* E. S. Seeley, Jr., Duane Hoag, *Photographer:* John Morrill, Villis Lapenieks, Jr., Stan Follis, *Music:* John Seely

Cast: Robert Clarke, Nan Peterson, Patricia Manning, Fred LaPorta

HIGHLY DANGEROUS

Film   1950   Great Britain (Two Cities)
88 Minutes   Black & white [Released 1951 U.S. (Lippert)]

Fast-paced cold war intrigue hinged to an SF plot gimmick. A beautiful lady scientist and an American reporter venture behind the iron curtain to bring back information about a secret germ warfare project (the microbes are to be carried on swarms of insects).

Director: **Roy Ward Baker,** *Producer:* Anthony Darnborough, *Screenplay:* Eric Ambler, *Photographer:* Reginald Wyer, David Harcourt, *Music:* Richard Addinsell

Cast: Margaret Lockwood, Dane Clark, Marius Goring, Wilfred Hyde-White, Anthony Newley

HIGH TREASON

Film   1929   Great Britain (Gaumont)
95 Minutes   Black & white

Britain's first talking motion picture offers little more than a Cook's tour of past expectations of the future, which came surprisingly true, to varying degrees. The film is set in the year 1940, when the United Atlantic States (the U.S. and Great Britain) is poised on the brink of war with the Federated States of Europe. To save the world, the president of the Peace League, 25 million strong, assassinates the president of the latter, about to declare war (and he calls himself a pacifist?).

Apart from reflecting attitudes of a growing peace movement in Great Britain, the film envisions home TV sets with large screens, two-way **videophones,** helicopter taxis and a tunnel under the English Channel (since begun but not finished). The miniature sets and paintings of London are filled with new neo-classical buildings, the filmmakers evidently having anticipated the Bauhaus movement to be a fad.

Director: Maurice Elvey, *Screenplay:* L'Estrange Fawcett, *Play:* Pemberton Billing, *Art Director:* Andrew Mazzei

Cast: Benita Hume, Basil Bill, Raymond Massey, Jameson Thomas

THE HITCH-HIKERS GUIDE TO THE GALAXY

Radio serial   1977   Great Britain (BBC)
30 Minutes (weekly)

Created by Douglas Adams, the story editor of **Doctor Who,** this delectable blend of comedy and science fiction developed a passionate cult following in England and has subsequently been adapted into a stage play, a record album, a TV serial (see listing below), a novel and two paperback sequels, *The Restaurant at the End of the Universe* and *Life, the Universe and Everything.* Twelve episodes were broadcast in the U.S. in 1981 over the National Public Radio network.

The story begins on **Earth,** "an utterly insignificant little blue-green planet whose ape-descended life forms are so amazingly primitive that they still think digital watches are pretty neat." Arthur Dent, a suburban Everyman, wakes up one morning and learns from his friend Ford Prefect that Earth is about to be destroyed to make way for an intergalactic freeway. Ford, you see, has been posing as an out-of-work actor for the last 15 years, but he is actually an **extraterrestrial** editor researching for a revised edition of *The Hitch-Hikers Guide to the Galaxy,* a definitive guidebook published in the form of a "micro sub-meson electronic component." A sort of *Gulliver's Travels* by way of Kurt Vonnegut, the program takes the pair through time and space, where, following the guidebook, they encounter vaguely familiar characters, including a B-Ark carrying a cyrogenic refrigerator stocked with mid-level managers on their way to colonize a new planet, Earth, two million years ago.

Director/Creators/Writers: Douglas Adams, *Music and Sound Effects:* Paddy Kingsland

Cast: Arthur Dent—Simon Jones, *Ford Prefect/ Frogstar Robot*—Geoffrey McGivern, *Zaphod Beeblebrox*—Mark Wing-Davey, *Lintilla*—Rula Lenska, *The Book*—Peter Jones

THE HITCH-HIKERS GUIDE TO THE GALAXY

TV serial   1981   Great Britain (BBC)
7 Episodes (30 Minutes)   Color

This TV version of the successful radio serial (see listing above) was shown in the U.S. over the Public Broadcasting System in the fall of 1982. The TV version replaces the verbose narrator with the electronic guidebook, which illustrates itself with informative drawings, charts and diagrams supplied by **computer graphics.** Cast members include a pair of tough space cops with American accents, and a rock group called the Disaster Area, the loudest in the galaxy. The inventively tacky special effects include several **Star Wars**-like space battles, depicted on a video game screen.

Director/Writer/Creator: Douglas Adams

Cast: Arthur Dent—Simon Jones, *Ford Prefect*—David Dixon, *Zaphod Beeblebrox*—Mark Wing-Davey, *The Book*—Peter Jones, **Dave Prowse**

BIJO TO EKITAIN-IN-GEN/The Beautiful Women and the HydroMan

(Also titled: **The H-man**)

Film 1958 Japan (Toho) 87 Minutes Color [Released 1959 U.S. (Columbia) 79 Minutes]

Similar to **The Blob** (1958), *H-Man* offers a more intriguing idea and just as much fun—although the inept English-language dubbing is a hindrance. Made by the team who brought us **Godzilla** (1954), the film opens with the crew of a Japanese fishing boat encountering a derelict freighter littered with empty piles of clothing—complete with shoes, socks and underwear. The captain appears to be collapsed over his logbook, but his uniform is in fact occupied by a clot of green slime that shoots up the pants-leg of an inquisitive fisherman and instantly digests him.

The freighter, it seems, had run afoul of a radioactive cloud caused by atomic **bomb** testing which transformed its crew into a communal being. Making its way to Tokyo, the jolly green jelly slithers under doors and windows, gobbling up whatever comes its way—including several stripteasers, who leave behind their indigestible bras and G-strings—until the army finally destroys it. The ingenious disintegration effect was done by photographing life-size deflating balloon-dolls in **fast-motion** and projecting the footage at normal speed to slow down the action.

Director: Inoshiro Honda, *Producer:* Tomoyuki Tanaka, *Screenplay:* Takeshi Kimura, *Story:* Hideo Kaijo, *Photographer:* Hamime Koizumi, *Special Effects:* Eiji Tsuburaya, *Music:* Masaru Sato

Cast: Kenji Sahara, Koreya Senda, Akhiko Hirata, Yumi Shirakawa

HODGE, AL (1912–79)

Radio and TV actor, fondly remembered as the star of **Captain Video** (1949-53, 1955-56), television's first **space opera.** Hodge had previously appeared as the voice of **The Green Hornet** on radio, a role he played for seven years. He also directed many radio serials, including episodes of *The Lone Ranger.* In 1950 he was hired to replace Richard Coogan as Captain Video on the old Dumont TV network, and the series quickly became the new medium's prime afternoon attraction. Although the program was cheaply produced and lacking in special effects, Hodge managed to hold it together with his dashing, clean-cut looks and stoic delivery of the improbable lines.

Captain Video ran its course in 1956, a victim of its own inadequacies and the arrival of more competently produced children's fare, including **The Adventures of Superman** (1953-57). Hodge moved to California, where TV production had shifted, and appeared in the series *Alfred Hitchcock Presents, Tightrope* and *You'll Never Get Rich.* Typecast as Captain Video, he found it difficult to get work, and reportedly eased his pain with alcohol. He later turned up as a cheerful Manhattan bank guard and security man at Cartier's, the posh Fifth Avenue jewelry store. In March 1979, he was found dead of heart failure in small Manhattan hotel room, crowded with news clips and photos of Captain Video. "There are no assets," said a city worker who inventoried his possessions, "only some pictures of sentimental value."

HOFFMAN, E.(RNST) T.(HEODOR) A.(MADEUS) (1776–1822)

German author, musician, artist and lawyer. A restless eccentric with many talents, Hoffman is best remembered for his Gothic horror fantasies, many of which reflect contemporary theories of science and pseudoscience. His story "The Sandman" (1816-17), which tells of a beautiful dancing "android" built by a **mad scientist** who falls in love with her, is a precursor of SF **robot** tales. It provided the scenario for the ballet *Coppelia* and an episode of Offenbach's opera **Les Contes d'Hoffmann** (1881), filmed as **Hoffmann's Erzahlungen** (1914), **The Tales of Hoffmann** (1951) and **Dr. Coppelius** (1966). Another of his stories was the basis of Tchaikovsky's ballet, *The Nutcracker Suite*. (See also: **Shanks.**)

HOFFMANN'S ERZAHLUNGEN/
Tales of Hoffman

Film   1914   Germany (Union)   Black & white (silent)

The opera without the music, done as a suspenseful nightmare and starring Werner Krauss, director of the classic horror film, *The Cabinet of Dr. Caligari* (1919). The emphasis is on the magical aspects of the **E.T.A. Hoffmann's** stories. (See: **Expressionism, Les Contes d'Hoffmann, The Tales of Hoffmann.**)

Director: Richard Oswald, *Screenplay:* Fritz Friedmann, Richard Oswald, *Photographer:* Ernst Krohn

Cast: Werner Krauss, Erich Kaiser-Tietz, Alice Hechy, Ferdinand Bonn, Lupu Pick

HOLMES AND YO-YO

TV series   1976   U.S. (ABC)   30 Minutes (weekly)   Color

Billed as a "two-man comedy" in the tradition of Laurel and Hardy and Abbott and Costello, this short-lived series proved to be merely bizarre. Holmes was a clumsy cop with a talent for causing accidents that sidelined his partners. To remedy the situation, his superiors paired him with a human-like **robot** named Yo-Yo, who preferred being called a "computerperson." Yo-Yo never needed sleep, and he could run for miles, produce instant color prints at the scene of a crime, and tap dance.

Directors: **Jack Arnold,** Reza S. Badiyi, John Astin, Richard Kinon, Leonard B. Stern, *Producer:* Arne Sultan, *Creators:* Jack Sher, Lee Hewitt, *Music:* Leonard Rosenman, Dick Halligan

Cast: Richard B. Shull, John Schuck, Bruce Kirby, Andrea Howard, Larry Hovis

HOLOGRAPHY

The process of filming a three-dimensional image capable of being seen without special glasses or other apparatus. Hungarian-born physicist Denis Gabor first conceived of holography in 1947, but was unable to develop it until the invention of the **laser** in 1960. Gabor, who won the Nobel Prize in 1971 for his achievement, coined the word "holography" from the Greek words for *whole* and *image.*

The viewing medium of holography is a film transparency called a hologram, bearing little resemblance to a conventional photograph, which captures only the intensity of light. A hologram records the phase information of light waves—what our eyes and minds perceive as depth. To the naked eye a hologram appears to be a random pattern of light and dark bands. But when reconstituted by a reference beam, this interference pattern evokes a glowing, three-dimensional image of the original object. The viewer can even walk around the hologram and see behind the foreground object.

Holography is still in its infancy (comparable to the Daguerre stage of photography) and is used primarily for storing computer data and in advertising displays. As an art form, it has yet to find its own esthetic. Depicted in a number of recent SF films, holography promises to yield the most effective 3-D film images yet devised when the technical problems of adapting the process to motion picture film are solved. (See also: **Stereoscopic Films.)**

HOMUNCULUS

See: **Homunkulus der Fuhrer**

HOMUNKULUS DER FUHRER/ Homunculus the Leader

(Also titled: *Homunculus)*

Film 1916 Germany (Bioscop) 6 Episodes Black & white (silent)

Inspired by Mary Shelley's *Frankenstein* (1818), this Gothic morality play takes its title from Mephistopheles' bottled spirit in Goethe's *Faust* (1808). The film's Homunculus is a man born of chemicals combined in a test tube who, unlike the movie **Frankenstein** Monster, is handsome, brilliant and high-minded. Discovering his true origin, he searches for understanding and love, but finds himself driven from country to country as an outcast. Embittered, he becomes more dangerous than the Monster, turning his considerable talents to revenging himself on the human race. He moves into politics, becoming a soulless dictator of a large European country who plans to destroy the world in a global war, until stopped by an act of divine intervention in the form of a lightning bolt.

Perverse and unsettling, with a bold expressionist design, *Homunkulus* influenced a generation of German SF-**horror** films, including **Metropolis** (1927); as prophecy, it foreshadowed the rise of Hitler and his myth of Aryan superiority. (See also: **Alraune; Android; Expressionism.)**

Director: Otto Rippert, *Screenplay:* Otto Rippert, Robert Nuess, *Novel:* Robert Reinert, *Photographer:* Carl Hoffmann

Cast: Olaf Fonss, Frederick Kuhn, Theodor Loos, Mechtild Their, Maria Carmi

HORROR

The SF film and the horror film often share common ground. Both are concerned with such subjects as monsters from outer space **(War of the Worlds),** the creation of artificial life **(Frankenstein),** and surgical experiments **(The Lady and the Monster),** to name a few. The difference is that SF films offer a rational basis for the shocking events depicted on-screen. A horror subject that is almost always science fiction is the threat of dehumanization, in which man has lost his individuality and/or emotions, either through a misuse of science or the manipulation of alien beings. Films in this category include **Metropolis** (1926), **1984** (1956), **Invasion of the Body Snatchers** (1956) (1978), **Village of the Damned** (1960), and **Blade Runner** (1982). (See also: **the Bomb Mutants.)**

HORROR EXPRESS

(Released in Great Britain and Europe as *Panic on the Transiberian)*

Film 1972 Great Britain (Granada/Benmar) 90 Minutes Color

Absurd but fun, this high-spirited British/ Spanish co-production is an oddity—a throwback to the monster-from-space **horror** cycle of the 1950s. Among *Horror Express*'s enjoyable inanities is the reason it was made: Its Spanish producer got a bargain on the model trains built for the historical film *Nicholas and Alexandra* and commissioned a script for their use.

Traveling aboard the Transiberian Express is a well-preserved prehistoric anthropoid accompanied by two stuffy British scientists bringing their find to a museum in England. Scarcely out of China, the "missing link" becomes just that when it vanishes from its box, and passengers begin to dwindle in number. The apeman's method of execution baffles the anthropologists, for the brains of its victims are left white and unwrinkled (several are displayed onscreen). For reasons known only to the scriptwriter, the men determine that the creature arrived from another planet millenia ago and that it has been frozen in a state of **suspended animation** ever since. It wants to learn how to build a spaceship and return home, a task accomplished by absorbing human knowledge with such force that the brain is reduced to gelatin. How the creature hoped to manage the journey based on human memory is another of the film's endearing out-of-sync touches: The story takes place in 1906.

Director: Eugenio Martin, *Screenplay:* Arnaud d'Usseau

Cast: **Peter Cushing,** Christopher Lee, Telly Savalas, Silvia Tortosa

THE HORROR OF FRANKENSTEIN

Film   1970   Great Britain (Hammer)
95 Minutes   Color

Dr. Frankenstein is a swinging playboy enjoying London's night life with a succession of beautiful birds in this indifferent, oversexed send-up of Hammer's previous **Frankenstein** films. The man inside the monster makeup is **Dave Prowse,** later to play **Darth Vader** in the **Star Wars** films.

Director/Producer: Jimmy Sangster, *Screenplay:* Jimmy Sangster, Jeremy Burnham, *Photographer:* Moray Grant, *Makeup:* Tom Smith, *Music:* Malcolm Williamson

Cast: Ralph Bates, Dave Prowse, Kate O'Mara, Veronica Carlson, Graham James, Dennis Price

HOTH

Perpetually ice-bound and snow-covered planet where the Rebel Alliance is hiding at the beginning of **The Empire Strikes Back** (1980). Believing that the Empire would overlook the planet because its forbidding climate would preclude it as a refuge, the rebels are nevertheless discovered barely a month after their arrival by an **Imperial Probe Droid** that alerts a fleet of Star Destroyers. Apparently, only two life forms exist on the planet: **Tauntauns** and **Wampas.**

HOUSE OF DRACULA

Film   1945   U.S. (Universal)   67 Minutes
Black & white

Mythology takes a back seat to science fiction in this superior sequel to **House of Frankenstein** (1944), which had previously brought together the **Frankenstein** Monster, Count Dracula and the Wolf Man. Focus of the extravagant plot is a **mad scientist** who discovers that Dracula's vampirism is caused by a parasite in his blood and that the Wolf Man suffers from pressure on the brain. Inexplicably, the Wolf Man (**Lon Chaney, Jr.**) has become the hero, his murders evidently having been cancelled out by his previous three deaths. Cured of his full-moon wanderings by a mysterious drug, he kills the doctor, who had inadvertently turned himself into a vampire by giving Dracula (John Carradine) transfusions with his own blood. The Monster (**Glenn Strange**), found in a cave and brought back to life with electric shocks, is little more than a supporting player, drained of his menace until a climactic battle to the death with the Wolf Man in the doctor's burning castle.

Directed on a low budget by Erle C. Kenton, who had helmed the previous film, *House of Dracula* is told in a taut Gothic style that captures something of the spirit of Universal's earlier **horror** films (they are recalled in a montage sequence). Kenton, a routine, jack-of-all-trades technician, had previously directed **The Island of Lost Souls** (1933), his only other work of note.

Director: Erle C. Kenton, *Producer:* Paul Malvern, *Screenplay:* George Bricker, Dwight V. Babcock, Edward T. Lowe, *Photographer:* George Robinson, *Makeup:* **Jack Pierce,** *Special Effects:* **John P. Fulton,** *Music:* Edgar Fairchild

Cast: Onslow Stevens, Lon Chaney, Jr., John Carradine, Glenn Strange, Lionel Atwill, Martha O'Driscoll, Jane Adams

HOUSE OF FRANKENSTEIN

Film   1944   U.S. (Universal)   71 Minutes
Black & white

Universal's **horror** stars were coasting on past

glories when they appeared in this dull follow-up to **Frankenstein Meets the Wolf Man** (1943). Karloff returns to the fold as a mad doctor posing as the owner of a traveling freak show. On exhibit are the bodies of the Monster, the Wolf Man and Dracula, each of whom the doctor restores to life for settling old scores. At the fade-out, Karloff sinks into a quicksand pit while trying to evade the inevitable angry villagers, who should be used to this sort of thing by now.

Glenn Strange is the Monster, **Lon Chaney, Jr.,** is the Wolf Man and **John Carradine** plays Dracula.

Director: Erle C. Kenton, *Producer:* Paul Malvern, *Screenplay:* Edward T. Lowe, *Story:* **Curt Siodmak,** *Photographer:* George Robinson, *Special Effects:* **John P. Fulton,** *Makeup:* **Jack Pierce,** *Music:* H. J. Salter

Cast: **Boris Karloff,** Lon Chaney, Jr., John Carradine, Glenn Strange, George Zucco, Elena Verdugo

THE HUMAN DUPLICATORS

Film   1964   U.S. (Allied Artists)
82 Minutes   Color

A very tall **alien** invader named Kolos takes over a science lab and produces a series of **robots** who look just like people. The plan is to substitute them for key Western leaders in preparation for an alien takeover. There are more SF ideas at work here than the filmmakers can handle. (See also: **alien invasion.**)

Director: Hugo Grimaldi, *Producers:* Hugo Grimaldi, Arthur Pierce, *Screenplay:* Arthur Pierce, *Photographer:* Monroe Askins, *Makeup:* **John Chambers,** *Music:* Gordon Zahler

Cast: Richard Kiel, George Macready, George Nader, Barbara Nichols, Richard Arlen

HUMANOID

A fictional creature of organic origin, approximating or duplicating the appearance of a human being; usually an inhabitant of another planet (e.g. the space-cantina drink-

ers of **Star Wars,** the pod-people of **Invasion of the Body Snatchers).** Humanoids from **Earth** are called **mutants (The Creature from the Black Lagoon)** or **androids** (the **Frankenstein** monster), a term designating a biologically fabricated being and frequently misapplied to manlike **robots.** (See also: **Cyborgs.)**

HUTTON, ROBERT (1920–   )

Film actor and occasional screenwriter, director and producer, born Robert Bruce Winne in Kingston, New York. An affable young Hollywood leading man of the 1950s, Hutton failed to become a star but worked steadily in low-budget SF and horror films well into the 1970s. After 1963 most of his films were made in England.

Films include: Destination Tokyo (1944), *Too Young to Know* (1945), *Love and Learn* (1947), *Wallflower* (1948), *The Younger Brothers* (1949), *The Man on the Eiffel Tower* (1950), *The Racket* (1951), *Casanova's Big Night* (1954), *Yaqui Drums* (1956), **The Colossus of New York** (1958), **The Invisible Invaders** (1959), *Cinderfella* (1960), **The Slime People** (1963) [director/star], **The Vulture** (1966), **They Came From Beyond Space, You Only Live Twice** (1967), **Trog** (1970), *Tales From the Crypt* (1971), *Persecution* (1974) [story/screenplay]

HYPERSPACE

Term used to describe a fictional shortcut through space—either via a **space warp,** a fourth dimension or, more recently, a **black hole**—for the purpose of traveling to a distant star or **galaxy.** According to Einstein's theory, an object approaching the speed of light (186,292 miles per second) would acquire infinite mass and thus require infinite power to propel it. Given the limitations of speed, distance and time, a spaceship would need to find a shortened route to a destination even one light year away (about six trillion miles). Astro-physicists believed that hyperspace existed only in the minds of SF writers and filmmakers until the recent discovery of black holes, which many theorize to be pathways in the fabric of space.

THE ILLUSTRATED MAN

Film   1969   U.S. (Warner Bros.)
103 Minutes   Technicolor   Panavision

The cinema has yet to find a visual metaphor for **Ray Bradbury's** literary imagery, *The Illustrated Man* being a case in point. Based on the author's anthology of the same title, published in 1951, the film has the same linking framework: a 1930s' drifter whose head-to-foot tattoos each come to life and tell a story to anyone who stares at them long enough. Only three of Bradbury's stories are used, with the film's leads appearing in each.

"The Veldt," the most successfully filmed, takes place in a computerized playroom capable of simulating any environment in the world. A brother and sister spend much of their time playing in the African veldt—complete with real lions—and when ordered to shut the machine off, they lure their parents inside for a particularly nasty death. The second story, "The Long Rains," has three astronauts stranded on **Venus,** a planet of incessant rains, where they must find a geodesic sun-dome to escape the harsh environment. "The Last Night of the World" is set in the 40th century, at the end of the world. Parents are ordered to kill their children to spare them of the imminent suffering. After one couple completes the agonizing task, the scientists announce they were wrong in their predictions.

Director: Jack Smight, *Producer:* Howard B. Kreitsek, Ted Mann, *Screenplay:* Howard B. Kreitsek, *Book:* Ray Bradbury, *Photographer:* Philip Lathrop, *Special Effects:* Ralph Webb, *Music:* **Jerry Goldsmith**

Cast: Rod Steiger, Claire Bloom, Robert Drivas

I LOVE YOU, I KILL YOU

Film   1971   West Germany (Brandner)
94 Minutes   Color

This self-congratulating German import solves the problem of overpopulation, a popular movie subject during the early 1970s, with the visual aplomb of a cold liver dumpling. To prevent procreation in the near future, policemen distribute free birth-control pills, some of which produce unexpected and deadly side effects.

Director/Producer/Screenplay: Uwe Brandner, *Photographer:* Andre Debreuil

Cast: Ralph Becker, Hannes Fuchs, Marianne Blomquist

I MARRIED A MONSTER FROM OUTER SPACE

Film   1958   U.S. (Paramount)   78 Minutes
Black & white

A young woman fights to recover her husband, who has been replaced by an **alien** look-alike. Despite its preposterous title—typical of shock-schlock exploitation film of the 1950s—this is a well-crafted exercise in science fiction-**horror** that compares favorably to the best works of Don Siegel and **Jack Arnold.** Fifties paranoia is evident in the depiction of the surrogate humans, who are as feared and despised as Communists were during that decade. When the heroine discovers that the soul-robbing creatures have come to earth to breed with human females to replenish their declining population, she enlists the aid of "real" men, who attack the invaders with a pack of vicious dogs. (Feminists might find this film horrifying on another level.)

Director Gene Fowler, Jr., a former editor for Fritz Lang, shot the picture in a terse, shadowy style reminiscent of his teacher. Especially horrifying is a balcony scene that takes place during a thunderstorm. Frightened, the husband/alien drops his guard during a lightning flash and reveals his true, hideous appearance. Almost as an afterthought, the creatures are allowed a brief moment of sypmathy as they are destroyed. (See also: **Alien Invasion.**)

Director/Producer: Gene Fowler, Jr., *Screenplay:* Louis Vittes, *Photographer:* Haskell Boggs, *Production Designer:* **Hal Pereira,** Henry Bumstead, *Makeup:* Charles Gemora, *Special Effects:* **John P. Fulton**

Cast: Tom Tyron, Gloria Talbott, Peter Baldwin, Robert Ivers

IMMEDIATE DISASTER

(Also titled: *The Stranger From the Stars, Stranger From Venus, The Venusian*)

Film   1954   Great Britain (British Princess)
75 Minutes   Black & white.

The producers had a difficult time deciding what to call this sluggish clone—never released theatrically in the U.S. It might have drawn more customers with the apt title, "Son of **The Day the Earth Stood Still.**" Patricia Neal follows in her own footsteps as a young woman who befriends a handsome, peace-loving **extraterrestrial** (speaking with an Austrian accent this time around) here to warn mankind to stop tinkering with atomic power and threatening the "balance of the universe," or suffer the consequences. The only significant difference between *Immediate Disaster* and its model is the ending: The girl's jealous fiancee changes his mind and tries to help the stranger, who in turn sacrifices his life to save Earth from an invasion from **Venus,** his home planet.

Director: Burt Balaban, *Producer:* Burt Balaban, Gene Martel, *Screenplay:* Hans Jacoby, *Music:* Eric Spear

Cast: Helmut Dantine, Patricia Neal, Derek Bond, Arthur Young, Cyril Luckham

THE IMMORTAL

TV film   1969   U.S. (ABC)   75 Minutes
Color
TV series   1970-71   U.S. (ABC)   60 Minutes
(weekly)   Color

When his aging employer is seriously injured in a plane crash, test driver Ben Richards saves his life with a blood transfusion. Immediately recovering, the factory owner, Jordan Braddock, finds that he is also younger and healthier, leading to the discovery that Richards is gifted with a rare blood type that prevents him from growing older and dying (although he looks to have reached at least age 40). Braddock, as greedy for life as he is for money, kidnaps the Immortal to keep on hand for regular transfusions. But Richards escapes and takes to the road, constantly on the move to keep ahead of Braddock's men.

Essentially a chase melodrama similar to TV's *The Fugitive* (1963-67), the program ran out of steam after its tautly directed pilot episode, and it ran for only 13 weeks.

Director: **Joseph Sargent,** *Producer:* Lou Morheim, *Writers:* Lou Morheim, Robert Specht, *Photographer:* Howard R. Schwartz, *Music:* Dominic Frontiere, *Novel: The Immortals,* James E. Gunn

Cast: Christopher George, Barry Sullivan, Ralph Bellamy, Jessica Walter, Carol Lynley

IMPERIAL PROBE DROIDS

Robot reconnaissance weapons sent throughout the galaxy to discvoer the whereabouts of the Rebel Alliance in **The Empire Strikes Back** (1980). They are equipped with heat and color sensors, camera eyes and a small but sophisticated computer with a self-contained power source capable of transmitting data from any point in space. When one arrives near the Rebel lair on the ice planet **Hoth, Luke Skywalker** mistakes it for a meteorite. By the time it becomes apparent what it is, the device has alerted the Imperial Star Destroyers and self-destructs, as it is programmed to do.

The Imperious Leader

THE IMPERIOUS LEADER

Reptilian humanoid who heads the Cylon Alliance, an alien civilization that intends to wipe out mankind, in the TV series' **Battlestar Galactica** (1978-79) and **Galactica 1980** (1979). The Imperious Leader has three brains, two of which gather and process information and another that communicates telepathically with Cylon leaders. He monitors the war against the battlestar via a gleaming communications helmet directly connected to every Cylon fighting ship. Unlike his Cylon Centurions, he is not totally devoid of emotion and often suffers fear and frustration when his adversary, Commander Adama, counters his mechanical cunning with human courage and resourcefulness.

THE INCREDIBLE HULK

TV series 1978-81 U.S. (CBS) 60 Minutes (weekly) Color

Based on the comic book character created by Stan Lee, this series followed an introductory TV film. Episodes continued David Banner's quest for an antidote to the strange malady that transformed him into a huge green monster whenever his volatile temper flared. Traveling from town to town and taking odd jobs to support himself, Banner "hulked out" whenever annoyed by wrongdoers. He usually moved on moments ahead of his pursuer, a reporter who believed The Hulk to be a killer and who suspected the dual identity. Unfortunately, Banner was unable to counter the charge since he had no memory of his adventures as The Hulk.

Essentially a superficial retread of **Dr. Jekyll and Mr. Hyde** (although The Hulk is a hero and not a villain), the series was an engrossing adolescent fantasy, helped along by an expensive high-gloss production. In the clever **dissolve** shots even Banner's eyes seem to change color as he metamorphosed into The Hulk, an effect achieved with gradated contact lenses supplied by Hollywood optician Dr. Morton K. Greenspoon.

Directors: Reza S. Badyi, Ray Danton, Jeffrey Hayden, Alan J. Levi, Frank Orsatti, Joseph Pevney and others, *Executive Producer:* Kenneth Johnson, *Music:* Joseph Harnell

Cast: Bill Bixby, Lous Ferrigno, Jack Colvin

The Incredible Hulk: David Banner (Bill Bixby) turns into a raging green-skinned giant (Lou Ferrigno).

THE INCREDIBLE MELTING MAN

Film 1977 U.S. (AIP) 86 Minutes
Movielab Color

An American astronaut returns from hitherto untouched Saturn with a strange bac-
terial infection that causes his flesh to
deliquesce. Driven by a newly acquired blood
lust, he escapes from a military hospital and
proceeds to dine on local townspeople—a
diet that has the beneficial effect of slowing
down the melting process. Cornered in a
local power plant, he gratefully ends his
suffering with an electrifying cremation.

Obviously inspired by the **Quatermass**
films, *Melting Man* attempts to blend pathos
with awesome horror but can't resist going
for the gut with a surfeit of gore. The convincing makeup by **Rick Baker** is already
more than enough.

Director/Screenplay: William Sachs, *Producer:*
Samuel W. Gelfman, *Photographer:* Willy Curtis,
Special Effects: Rick Baker, Harry Woolman,
Makeup: Rick Baker, *Music:* Arlon Ober

Cast: Alex Rebar, Burr DeBenning, Myron
Healey, Ann Sweeny, Michael Alldredge

Col. Steven West (Alex Rebar) contracts a
strange disease from outer space in *The
Incredible Melting Man.*

THE INCREDIBLE SHRINKING MAN

Film 1957 U.S. (Universal) 81 Minutes
Black & white

After boating through a mysterious radioactive haze during a pleasure outing, a
healthy young man finds himself endlessly
shrinking.

One of the great SF films, *Shrinking Man*
retains its capacity to provoke and unsettle
audiences years after its release. Made in a
decade when Americans were growing un-
easy about the diminution of the individual
by government and big business, and when
the dangers of nuclear pollution had become
apparent, it hit an exposed nerve that throbs
all the more today. The film is about neither of these worries, but it breathes the same
atmosphere of disorientation and despair.
While the hero's predicament is biologically
impossible, the story is good science fiction
nevertheless since it explores the potential
of science to alter man's perception of the
universe.

As the shrinking man becomes smaller
(but is otherwise unchanged), he finds his
comfortable world turning into an alien
landscape. Besieged by the press, who treat
him as a freak, he retires to the safety of his
home only to find that safety no longer exists.
Treated as a child by his wife, he watches
helplessly as his wedding ring slips from his
dwindling finger. He finds a comforting relationship with a female circus midget, but
he eventually grows too small for her. Re-
signed to living in a doll house his wife has
brought for him, he finally comes to grips
with his situation, only to be attacked by
the family cat—originally a pet and now
an enemy. Knocked down the basement
stairs while trying to escape, his cries for help
too feeble to be heard, he finds himself in a
shadowy prison barely recognized as his
workroom. A leaky water pipe is a Niagara-
like torrent; a window ledge is as insur-
mountable as Mt. Everest. Desperate for
food, he battles a gargantuan spider for a
crumb of cake and dispatches the creature
with a javelin-sized sewing needle. By the
film's end, he has accepted his fate. Walk-

The spider of *The Incredible Shrinking Man*
(1957), enlarged to giant proportions by
means of macrophotography, menaces actor
Grant Williams in a matte shot.

ing through a basement window screen into
the jungle that is his lawn, reduced in size
but not in spirit, he is certain he will somehow survive. "To God there is no zero," he
says. "I still exist."

Shrinking Man transcends its B-picture
budget with a first-rate script, cinematic style,
convincing performances, and special effects
that are perhaps the best depiction of man
in miniature ever put on the screen. As with
Dr. Cyclops (1940), oversized sets and the
split screen created an illusion of smallness.
Many more sets were required for this
picture, however, since the shrinking man
became constantly smaller. **Traveling mattes**
replaced **rear projection** of the earlier film,
and were used to great effect in the encounter with the gigantic cat and the terrifying
fight with the enormous spider, both real.
(The creatures are close cousins of mutated
movie monsters of the 1950s; the scale has
simply been reversed.) Footage of the spider,
for example, was filmed separately, then

viewed through the camera to provide cues
for the actor, who was subsequently filmed
reacting to a blank wall. The footage of both
was combined optically on a scale that made
both appear to be roughly the same size. The
problem of creating huge water droplets
raining on the shrinking man's matchbox
house was solved by using water-filled latex condoms, which held a realistic tear shape
while falling and broke apart on impact. The
film's sets were later used for a short-lived
TV series, **World of Giants** (1959). (See
also: Miniatures.)

Director: **Jack Arnold,** *Producer:* Albert Zugsmith,
Screenplay: **Richard Matheson,** *Novel: The Shrink-
ing Man* Richard Matheson, *Photographer:* Ellis W.
Carter, *Special Effects: Sets:* **Alexander Golitzen,**
Robert Clatworthy, *Opticals:* Roswell A. Hoff-
mann, Everett A. Broussard, *Mattes:* **Clifford
Stine**

Cast: Grant Williams, Randy Stuart, April Kent,
Paul Langton, Billy Curtis

THE INCREDIBLE SHRINKING WOMAN

Film 1981 U.S. (Universal) 88 Minutes
Technicolor Panavision

A victim of too many cleaning sprays, synthetics and junk food, a suburban housewife shrinks to detergent-bottle size and becomes famous along the way.

A send-up of the **Jack Arnold** classic **The Incredible Shrinking Man,** this film was conceived as a vehicle for the comedic talents of the film's star, who plays several roles. Intermittent laughs have replaced psychological terror, and feminist and consumerist propaganda have supplanted the original's message of survival against overwhelming odds.

Director: Joel Schumacher, *Producer:* Hank Moonjean, *Screenplay:* Jane Wagner, *Novel: The Shrinking Man* **Richard Matheson,** *Photographer:* Bruce Logan, *Music:* Suzanne Ciani, *Production Designer:* Raymond A. Brandt, *Special Effects:* Roy Arbogast, Guy Faria, David Kelsey, Brock Price, "Sidney" the ape created by **Rick Baker**

Cast: Lily Tomlin, Charles Grodin, Ned Beatty, Henry Gibson, Elizabeth Wilson.

INTROVISION

A special effects system that divides a still photographic transparency into two parts and places moving actors "inside" the photograph. Introvision, a variation on the **front-projection** system, was developed by special effects man John Eppolito. It was used in the films **The Incredible Shrinking Woman,** *First Family,* **Outland** (1981) and **Megaforce** (1982). How the system works is explained in the accompanying diagram.

INTROVISION
How it works
Actors are placed inside a still background by projecting a transparency (4) through a two-way mirror (1) placed at a 45-degree angle between the camera (2) and a large reflective screen (3). The stage is completely bare, with actors positioned against the screen on a wooden platform. The transparency is dissected by a matte at the side of the stage (6), which is reflected into the mirror, placing that portion of the image in front of the actors (5). The remainder of the image is reflected from the screen behind the actors.

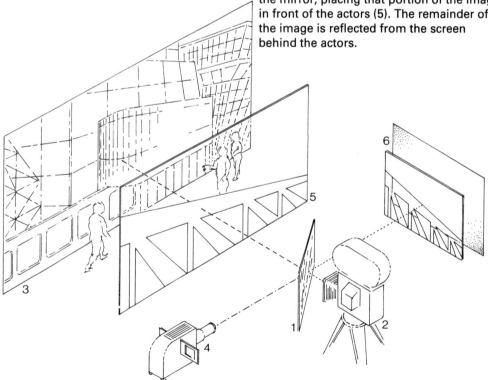

THE INTRUDER WITHIN

TV film   1981   U.S. (ABC)   104 Minutes
Color

A primeval creature "from the dark recesses of time" picks off workers on an oil rig floating in the Arctic Ocean, one by one. The drilling has released the stone-like eggs of a 14-million-year-old monster from **suspended animation** under the icy ocean floor. A crew member adopts one of the embryonic creatures, which quickly grows into a vicious killer—just like the creature in the film **Alien** (1979), the inspiration for this derivative potboiler. Its original titles were *Panic Offshore* and *The Lucifer Rig*.

Director: Peter Carter, *Producer:* Neil T. Maffeo, *Screenplay:* Ed Waters, *Photographer:* James Pergola, *Creature Design:* James Cummins, Henry Golas, *Special Effects:* Don Powers, *Music:* Gil Melle

Cast: Chad Everett, Joseph Bottoms, Jennifer Warren, Rockne Tarkington, Paul Larson

THE INVADERS

TV series   1967-68   U.S. (ABC)   60 Minutes (weekly)   Color

While taking a nap in his car during a business trip, David Vincent, a young architect, was awoken by the sound of a **UFO**. Returning to the site with police, he found no evidence of a landing, only a honeymooning couple, who gave police the impression Vincent had imagined the incident. He noticed they had stiff, awkwardly angled little fingers on their right hands. Investigating further, he learned that the "couple" were not human at all but disguised members of an **alien invasion** force. Their planet was dying, and for months, perhaps years, the invaders had surreptitiously infiltrated Earth, taking the form of ordinary human beings. Only their mutated little fingers gave them away, and a tendency to glow when they needed regeneration. They had no heartbeats, since they had no hearts.

Episodes detailed Vincent's frustrating attempts to warn the world of its predicament and to gather solid evidence to prove he wasn't crazy. Since the creatures disintegrated when killed, the task was virtually impossible. Moreover, the **aliens** were on to him, and he was constantly being fooled by seemingly trustworthy "people" (a number of whom were women) who wanted to kill him.

A throwback to such paranoid alien-double fantasies of the 1950s as **Invasion of the Body Snatchers** (1956) and **I Married a Monster from Outer Space** (1958), the series was one of American television's more enjoyable SF offerings. It effectively conjured up a mood of alien strangeness in the midst of apparent normality. The program's rigid format allowed for little plot development, however, and viewers began to drop off after the first season. The addition to the cast of seven "Believers," who shared Vincent's knowledge and joined in the quest, failed to save the program, and it was cancelled in the middle of its second season. Executive Producer of the series was Quinn Martin, creator of *The Fugitive* (1963-67), a program with a similar format.

Directors: **Joseph Sargent,** Paul Wendkos, Sutton Roley, Jerry Sohl, William Hale and others, *Producer:* Alan Armer, *Executive Producer:* Quinn Martin, *Creator:* Larry Cohen, *Writers:* Anthony Wilson, Louis Vittes, John W. Bloch, George Eckstein, Laurence Heath, Jerry Sohl and others, *Music:* Dominic Frontiere

Cast: Roy Thinnes, Kent Smith (second season); *guest stars:* Diane Baker, Burgess Meredith, Anne Francis, Gene Hackman, Suzanne Pleshette, Carol Lynley and others

INVADERS FROM MARS

Film   1953   U.S. (20th Century-Fox)
78 Minutes   Supercinecolor   3-D

Alien invaders "take over" the parents and neighbors of a small boy.

Rushed into production to exploit the brief popularity of 3-D movies during the early 1950s, *Invaders from Mars* is better than it has any right to be, thanks to the genius of **William Cameron Menzies,** director of the SF landmark **Things to Come** and **produc-**

tion designer of *Gone With the Wind.* Then near the end of his long career and considered passe by Hollywood (he has yet to receive his due), Menzies proved that time hadn't dimmed his powers by concocting a minor classic from studio leftovers, on a bargain-basement budget.

Menzies' visual ingenuity is apparent in the film's opening shot on an isolated hill, where a young boy has followed the flashing airborne lights that woke him from a sound sleep. A flying saucer is secretly landing on a stark patch of pearl-gray ground marked only by barren trees and a simple wooden fence. The scene—a simple studio set—stimulates the imagination rather than the senses, suggesting as it does dread and alien menace (as well as Menzies' work in *Gone With the Wind*) without the use of elaborate special effects.

Urged by the excited boy to visit the site, his father returns home curiously pale and emotionless. Soon the boy's mother is behaving in the same odd manner. Seeking help in town, the boy is rebuffed by the local police and family friends, who accuse him of making up the **UFO.** Each has a tiny scar at the base of the skull, he notices, leading him to conclude they are all controlled by the aliens. Desperate, he finally convinces a newly arrived woman doctor and her astronomer friend that he is telling the truth. The army promptly arrives to rout the Martians, but it is too late for the boy and his new friends. Captured by green-furred giant **mutants,** they are taken to an underground lair where a disembodied Martian "intelligence" is kept alive in a glass jar. Just as the boy is about to be injected at the back of the head with a glowing red crystal, he wakes up in his own bed. It was only a nightmare. A noise draws his attention to the window; outside a flying saucer is slowly descending. . . .

Director/Producer: William Cameron Menzies, *Producer:* Edward L. Alperson, *Screenplay:* Richard Blake, *Photographer:* John Seitz, *Art Director:* Boris Leven, *Makeup:* Gene Hibbs, Anatole Robbins, *Special Effects:* Jack Cosgrove, *Music:* Raoul Kraushaar

Cast: Helena Carter, Arthur Franz, Jimmy Hunt, Leif Erickson, Hillary Brooke

INVASION OF THE BODY SNATCHERS

Film   1956   U.S. (Allied Artists)
80 Minutes   Black & white   Superscope

Originally relegated to a quick saturation booking at drive-in theaters, *Invasion of the Body Snatchers* has since managed to find its natural audience and earn its place in the pantheon of SF classics. Based on a 1955 novel of the same title by Jack Finney, the film is a parable on the loss of humanity—on how human beings can allow their feelings for each other to be slowly drained away.

An indictment of conformity, *Invasion* was conceived as a scare movie, a warning of the evils of McCarthyism and the complacency of the Eisenhower years. The ubiquitous pods that land in a small California town from outer space mimic human bodies and take over the minds of their victims as they sleep. Treacherous, the **humanoid** duplicates will allow no deviation from their norm; everyone must become emotionless and "sensible."

The film was shot on location by director Don Siegel in his usual lean and virile style. By shooting with a low, wide-angle lens, Siegel makes the viewer feel constantly enclosed and threatened by nameless terrors: Rooms, buildings and even the sky seem to be somehow unsafe. "All of us who worked on the film believed in what it said," Siegel recalled in an interview. "The majority of people in the world are pods, existing without any intellectual aspirations and incapable of love. I think the pods outnumber us, if indeed we ourselves are not the pods."

Director: Don Siegel, *Producer:* Walter Wanger, *Screenplay:* Daniel Mainwaring, Sam Peckinpah (uncredited), *Photographer:* Ellsworth Fredericks, *Novel:* Jack Finney, *Special Effects:* Milton Rice, *Music:* Carmen Dragon

Cast: Kevin McCarthy, Dana Wynter, Larry Gates, King Donovan, Carolyn Jones, Virginia Christine, Sam Peckinpah

INVASION OF THE BODY SNATCHERS

Film   1978   U.S. (United Artists)
114 Minutes   Technicolor

Director Phillip Kaufman's "rethinking" of the original **Invasion of the Body Snatchers** (1956) hews closely to the concept of the original, and it alternates goose-bumps with satirical belly laughs. In an age of omnipresent house plants, the idea of flowers from outer space taking over humanity is hilarious in itself. And San Francisco, the erstwhile home of "flower power," is a particularly apt setting.

The pods of the 1970s were better organized and more self-enlightened than their 1956 counterparts. Their way of taking over human beings started with a mind-bending rhetoric of "self-realization" and "total happiness' that was all too recognizable in the so-called "me decade." According to Kaufman, "There are pods in every stratum of life. They are trying to recreate the world in their own image. And the situation has gotten worse since Kevin McCarthy saw them being carried to the city in Siegel's film." Director Don Siegel was reportedly so impressed with Kaufman's remake that he consented to appear in a cameo role as a cab driver—a pod, of course.

Director: Philip Kaufman, *Producer:* Robert H. Solo, *Screenplay:* W. D. Richter, *Novel:* Jack Finney, *Photographer:* Michael Chapman, *Makeup:* Thomas Burman, *Special Effects:* Dell Rheaume, Russ Hessey, *Sound Effects:* **Ben Burtt, Jr.,** *Music:* Danny Zeitlin

Cast: Donald Sutherland, **Leonard Nimoy,** Brooke Adam, Jeff Goldblum, Veronica Cartwright, Don Hindle, Kevin McCarthy

INVASION OF THE BODY STEALERS

See: **The Body Stealers**

Kevin McCarthy, star of the original *Invasion of the Body Snatchers* (1956), makes a cameo appearance in the 1978 version (with Donald Sutherland), taking up where he left off.

INVASION OF THE SAUCER MEN

(Also titled: *The Hell Creatures* and *Spacemen Saturday Night*)

Film   1957   U.S. (AIP)   69 Minutes   Black & white

One of a seemingly endless cycle of feverishly trivial quickies released by American International Pictures (Hollywood's leading "Poverty row" studio), *Invasion of the Saucer Men* plays like a parody of 1950's **alien invasion** films but was allegedly made with a straight face. Its teen heroes go for a joy ride and accidently run down a veined and scaley **alien** whose corpse promptly vanishes, along with a second creature glimpsed at the side of the road. This leads the gang to conclude that the aliens are up to no good. Police, parents and other adults refuse to believe their story (Do they ever in movies of this kind?). So the teens take matters into their own hands and dispatch the creatures by turning on the headlamps of their hot rods. An abysmal remake, **The Eye Creatures,** made the rounds in 1965.

Director: **Edward L. Cahn,** *Producer:* James H. Nicholoson, Robert Gurney, Jr., *Screenplay:* Robert Gurney, Jr., Al Martin, *Story:* "The Cosmic Frame," Paul W. Fairman, *Makeup:* Carlie Taylor, Paul Blaisdell, *Special Effects:* Paul Blaisdell, Howard A. Anderson, *Music:* Ronald Stein

Cast: Frank Gorshin, Steve Terrell, Gloria Costello, Raymond Hatton, Lyn Osborn

INVASION OF THE STAR CREATURES

Film   1963   U.S. (AIP)   81 Minutes   Black & white

This SF vaudeville routine has two wisecracking soldiers on maneuvers falling into

Invasion of the Star Creatures: A monster vegetable attacks at a drive-in movie.

the manicured hands of a tribe of sexy Amazons, controlled by **alien** plant-men. Screenwriter Haze, who appeared in more than 20 **Roger Corman** quickies, attempts to make fun of the film's inadequacies while spoofing its well-traveled theme. He occasionally hits the mark. (See also: **Alien Invasion.)**

Director: Bruno DeSoto, *Producer:* Merj Hagopian, *Screenplay:* Jonathah Haze, *Music:* Elliot Fisher, Jack Cookerly

Cast: Bob Ball, Frankie Ray, Dolores Reed, Gloria Victor

INVASION U.S.A.

Film 1952 U.S. (Columbia) 70 Minutes Black & white

While discussing the likelihood of World War III, drinkers in a Manhattan tavern are interrupted by a news broadcast announcing that Russia has launched a nuclear attack. They watch the devastation on television, then leave for home and their own fiery deaths. The nightmare proves to be just that, however, a vision conjured up by a barfly with hypnotic powers. Properly chastened, the drinkers vow to support civilian and military defense programs.

Basically plotless, *Invasion U.S.A.*, is padded out with grainy newsreel footage from World War II and old special effects footage. Quite rightly dismissed by critics at the time of its release, the film is a historical document of sorts that preserves popular American attitudes of the cold war era.

Director: Alfred E. Green, *Producer:* Albert Zugsmith, *Screenplay:* Robert Smith, *Photographer:* John L. Russell, *Music:* Albert Glasser

Cast: Dan O'Herlihy, Gerald Mohr, Peggie Castle, Robert Bice

INVISIBLE AGENT

Film 1942 U.S. (Universal) 81 Minutes Black & white

A transparent American spy drops in on Nazi Germany.

This lively third sequel to **The Invisible Man** (1933) involves a younger member of the original mad scientist's family, an American named Frank Griffin who has what's left of the secret invisibility formula. Enlisted by the Allies to help win World War II, he parachutes into the countryside outside Berlin for a rendezvous with a prim female agent, who averts her eyes when told he is naked although invisible. With his beautiful partner's help, he sneaks into town and makes off with a portfolio containing the names of German and Japanese spies operating in the United States. His presence is soon discovered by a Japanese officer attached to Gestapo headquarters (Peter Lorre playing a variation of his famous Mr. Moto), who sets a trap with a transparent silk net bordered in grappling hooks. Although badly injured by the device, Griffin manages to capture a German bomber and escape to England with the girl—a heroic exit favored by wartime espionage thrillers. The script by SF writer **Curt Siodmak**—a self-imposed refugee from Hitler's Germany—conveniently side-steps the formula's tendency to produce madness—a condition that returned in his screenplay for the third sequel, **The Invisible Man's Revenge** (1944). **John P. Fulton** again handled the superb invisibility effects.

Director: Edwin L. Marin, *Producer:* Frank Lloyd, *Screenplay:* Curt Siodmak, *Photographer:* Lester White, *Special Effects:* John P. Fulton, *Music:* Charles Previn

Cast: Jon Hall, Ilona Massey, **Peter Lorre,** John Litel, Keye Luke, Holmes Herbert, Cedric Hardwicke

THE INVISIBLE BOY

Film 1957 U.S. (MGM) 85 Minutes Black & white

Not a sequel to **The Invisible Man** (1933) but a follow-up to **Forbidden Planet** (1956)—written and produced by the same team—which introduced loveable **Robby the Robot** to the screen. Here Robby arrives in kit form, brought to a bright young boy by an uncle who has time-tripped into the future. Shortly after being assembled, Robby falls under the command of a mad computer that uses the **robot** to implement its plan to dominate the world. Robby finally comes to his senses with the help of his young maker, who meanwhile has learned to make himself invisible. Ordered to kill the boy, Robby destroys the computer instead.

Director: Herman Hoffman, *Producer:* Nicholas Nayfack, *Screenplay:* Cyril Hume, *Story:* Edmund Cooper, *Photographer:* Harold Wellman, *Special Effects:* Jack Rabin, Irving Block, Louis DeWitt, *Music:* Lex Baxter

Cast: Richard Eyer, Diane Brewster, Philip Abbott, Harold J. Stone

THE INVISIBLE INVADERS

Film   1959   U.S. (United Artists)
66 Minutes   Black & white

This neglected **horror** programmer played on drive-in screens nine years before George Romero made The Night of the Living Dead. Like Romero's cult favorite, *Invisible Invaders* brings together a group of people trapped in a remote house besieged by animated cadavers. Here, the bodies have been

The Invisible Invaders: From left, Robert Hutton, Jean Byron, John Agar and Paul Langton face invisible aliens from outer space.

brought to life by their murderers—a **forcefield** controlled by space **aliens** assembling an army of conquest. Military and civilian scientists devise an ultra-high-frequency radio device that exorcises the possessed bodies and sends the unseen aliens back where they came from.

Director: **Edward L. Cahn,** *Producer:* Robert Kent, *Screenplay:* Samuel Newman, *Makeup:* Phil Scheer, *Special Effects:* Roger George

Cast: **John Agar, Robert Hutton,** John Carradine, Jean Byron, Paul Langton, Eden Hartford

THE INVISIBLE MAN

Film   1933   U.S. (Universal)   71 Minutes
Black & white

Boris Karloff turned down the role of **H. G. Wells'** famous psychotic poltergeist, balking at the requirement that his face be swathed in bandages and entirely unseen until the last moments of the film. A relatively unknown performer, Claude Rains, ran away with the part and became a star, creating a malevolent presence with his expressive British voice and arch delivery of the incisive, elegant dialogue. Directed with mordant wit by James Whale, who had staged **Frankenstein** (1931), the film concerns a brilliant scientist who imbibes a new drug he

calls monocane, which renders animal tissue transparent. Its side effects drive him mad and he terrorizes the countryside naked, derailing trains, robbing banks, killing people and enjoying himself immensely. Trapped in a barn, he attempts to escape, but a fresh snowfall reveals his footprints, giving police a target. Mortally wounded, he returns to visibility while dying in a hospital bed.

The ingeniously believable invisibility effects were created by **John P. Fulton,** borrowing techniques from stage magicians. The unsettling experience of watching Rains remove his glasses, bandages and clothing to reveal absolutely nothing underneath was accomplished by dressing a stunt man in a black velvet body suit, complete with gloves and mask. Over this he wore the Invisible Man's clothing and disrobed in front of a matching black velvet background. The footage of the clothing moving across a dead black field was then matted into a previously filmed background. When the mortally wounded megalomaniac loses his invisibility, Fulton produced another chilling bit of trickery. First, we see a depression in the pillow of the death bed and a sheet draped over an unseen form. Gradually, his bones appear, fleshed out by muscles, nerves and, finally, skin. This sequence was done in the camera with no **matte** work involved. The pillow and sheet were made of plaster and papier-mache, and the rest was Fulton's sophisticated reverse motion of **Georges Melies'** old illusion: In a series of **stop-motion** shots, a skeleton was dissolved into a more complete dummy and so on, ending with actor Rains.

Director: James Whale, *Producer:* Carl Laemmle, Jr., *Screenplay:* R.C. Sheriff, Philip Wylie, *Novel:* H.G. Wells, *Photographer:* Arthur Edeson, *Special Effects:* John P. Fulton

Cast: Claude Rains, Gloria Stuart, William Harrigan, Henry Travers, E.E. Clive, Una O'Connor, Dudley Diggs, Holmes Herbert, Forrester Harvey

THE INVISIBLE MAN

TV series 1958-60 Great Britain (ATV) 30 Minutes (weekly) Black & white

Dr. Peter Brady, a scientist experimenting with principles of optical refraction, accidentally made himself invisible when exposed to a leaking gas. Unable to become visible again, he dedicated himself to the service of mankind and became a British secret agent, traveling throughout Europe, slipping easily through customs and thwarting enemies of the Crown.

Shown in the U.S. (CBS) from November 1958 to July 1959, the program returned as a summer filler in 1960. The Invisible Man was played by a deliberately unbilled actor (probably Tim Turner), who may have been ashamed of the inept special effects.

Creator/Producer: Ralph Smart

Cast: Lisa Daniely, Deborah Walting, Ernest Clark

THE INVISIBLE MAN

TV film 1975 U.S. (NBC) 72 Minutes Color
TV series 1975-76 U.S. (NBC) 60 Minutes (weekly) Color

David McCallum plays Dr. Daniel Weston, the Invisible Man, in this slick TV updating of the **H. G. Wells** novel. Weston, a scientist working on a **matter transference** project, injects himself with an experimental serum that renders him invisible. Learning that the government plans to use his discovery as a military weapon, he destroys the formula before finding a way to reverse the process, necessitating the wearing of a lifelike plastic mask, a wig and plastic hands to make himself visible. The series, a letdown after the intriguing pilot film, followed Weston's adventures as an agent for the KLAE Corporation, where he accepted a position in order to find a way to make himself visible. In one of the better episodes, he doffed his clothing to outwit a killer, who turned out to be a blind man with supersensitive hearing. The series lasted only four months; it was revamped and recast in 1976 as **The Gemini Man.** (13 episodes)

Directors: Robert Michael Lewis, Alan J. Levi, Leslie Stevens, Sigmund Neufield, Jr., *Producers:* Leslie Stevens, Robert F. O'Neil, Steve Bocho, *Executive Producer:* Harve Bennett, *Writers:* Leslie Stevens, Steve Bocho, *Photographer:* Enzo A. Martinelli, *Music:* Richard Clemens, Henry Mancini, Pete Rugolo

Cast: David McCallum, Melinda Fee, Jackie Cooper (pilot only), Craig Stevens, Henry Darrow

THE INVISIBLE MAN RETURNS

Film 1940 U.S. (Universal) 81 Minutes
Black & white

Vincent Price plays a heroic invisible man in this first of five sequels to the 1933 film. Falsely accused of murder, Price gets a dose of "monocane" from the invisible man's brother and strips down to look for the real killers, heeding the warning that the formula will drive him mad unless he seeks an antidote within a few days. He finds the criminals just in time, of course, and returns to visibility in a hospital bed, a scene that nearly duplicates the ending of the earlier film.

Price's voice lacks the expressive sarcasm that Claude Rains brought to the mostly unseen role, and the plot is predictable, but the ingenious special effects by **John P. Fulton** will keep you fascinated. A third sequel, *The Invisible Woman*, was released the same year.

Director: Joe May, *Screenplay:* **Curt Siodmak,** Lester Cole, *Story:* Curt Siodmak, Joe May, *Photographer:* Milton Krasner, *Special Effects:* John P. Fulton, *Music:* H. J. Salter

Cast: Vincent Price, Nan Grey, Cedric Hardwicke, John Sutton, Cecil Kellaway

THE INVISIBLE MAN'S REVENGE

Film 1944 U.S. (Universal) 78 Minutes
Black & white

After three previous outings as a hero, the Invisible Man returned to the screen with his character flaws fully restored—but with little of his original menace. Jon Hall, the patriotic spy of **Invisible Agent** (1942), is now a convicted murderer who forces a scientist to give him the invisibility formula so

that he can escape from jail and get even with the men who sent him up. Fittingly, he is chewed up by an invisible Great Dane in the final scene. After this routine adventure, the character returned for a sad farewell playing straight man to a comedy team in **Abbott and Costello Meet the Invisible Man** (1950).

Director/Producer: Ford Beebe, *Screenplay:* Bertram Millhauser, *Photographer:* Milton Krasner, *Special Effects:* **John P. Fulton,** *Music:* H. J. Salter

Cast: Jon Hall, John Carradine, Gale Sondergaard, Evelyn Ankers, Leon Errol

THE INVISIBLE RAY

Film 1936 U.S. (Universal) 79 Minutes
Black & white

Karloff is as chilling as cold steel as Janus Rukh, a scientist living in a castle in the Carpathians, who brings home a radioactive meteorite that gives him the power to cure blindness and shatter marble statues at a glance. Although mortally infected with radium poisoning, he devises an antidote and proceeds to use his godlike powers to evaporate a number of faithless colleagues. At the finale he has become an insane paranoid, prompting his mother to smash the hypodermic syringe that keeps him alive and give him a lecture about tampering with the laws of nature. (She introduced to the screen the immortal line, "There are some things man is not meant to know.") As science, *The Invisible Ray* is pure fantasy, but in its cynical concern with the misuses of science, the film anticipates a theme popular in SF films of the 1950s.

Director: Lambert Hillyer, *Producer:* Edmund Grainger, *Screenplay:* John Colton, *Story:* Howard Higgins, Douglas Hodges, *Photographer:* George Robinson, *Special Effects:* **John P. Fulton,** *Musical Director:* Franz Waxman

Cast: **Boris Karloff, Bela Lugosi,** Violet Kemble Cooper, Frances Drake, Frank Lawton

LES INVISIBLES

(U.S. title: *The Invisible Thief*)

Film   1905   France (Pathe)   5 Minutes
(Approx.)   Black & white (silent)

An invisible interloper plays tricks on his bewildered friends. This primitive short film,
whose effects are apparently achieved with
wires attached to props, is the earliest known
film dealing with invisibility.

Directors: Gaston Velle, Gabriel Moreau

THE ISLAND OF DR. MOREAU

Film   1977   U.S. (AIP)   98 Minutes   Color

Dr. Moreau's secret domain has never looked
more beautiful, which is one of the problems with this remake of **The Island of Lost
Souls** (1933). Shot in brilliant color on location in the Virgin Islands, the film lacks the
brooding intensity of its black-and-white
predecessor. And Burt Lancaster is no match
for the hammy malevolence of Charles
Laughton. Best things in the film are the
"humanimal" masks by **John Chambers** and
company, which can withstand the scrutiny
of tight close-ups, but not the front lighting of director Don Taylor, who makes them
look more interesting than menacing.

Director: Don Taylor, *Producers:* Skip Steloff, John
Temple-Smith, *Screenplay:* John Shaner, Al
Ramrus, *Makeup:* John Chambers, Don Striepeke,
Tom Burman, Ed Butterworth, Walter Schenck

Cast: Burt Lancaster, Michael York, Barbara
Carrera, Richard Basehart, Nigel Davenport, Nick
Cravat, Bob Ozman

THE ISLAND OF LOST SOULS

Film   1933   U.S. (Paramount)   72 Minutes
Black & white

A shipwreck brings two visitors to a remote
tropical island inhabited by horrible half
men-half beasts and their creator, a **mad scientist** named Dr. Moreau. Having been
forced to leave London because of his cruel
medical experiments with dogs, Moreau settled on the island, where he developed a slow
and painful surgical process to change animals into human beings. An obese, minc-
ing sadist, he whips the "humanimals" into
submission and threatens them with more
surgery in the "House of Pain" if they don't
obey the Law, a quasi-religion he has im-
posed on them. They must chant daily: "Not
to eat meat . . . Not to chase other man . . .
Not to go on all fours . . . Not to gnaw the
bark off trees . . . That is the Law." When a
rescue party arrives for the visitors, Moreau
hypocritically orders the humanimals to kill
its leader, precipitating a rebellion among
the grim monsters, who drag him into his
House of Pain for a grim death under his
own scalpels.

Based on **H. G. Wells'** *The Island of Dr.
Moreau* (1896), the film angered the author,
who denounced it as a mutilation of his
classic novel. While the film took liberties
with the original story, it preserves its basic
plot and at least hints at Wells' message that
knowledge and self-awareness can only be
acquired at the cost of a paradise lost.
Although its **horror** and SF elements never
really mesh, *Island* comes across as a tanta-

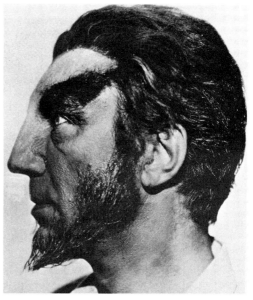

The Island of Lost Souls: Bela Lugosi as the
Ape-Man, leader of the humanimals.

lizing chiller, with a gleefully Freudian performance by Charles Laughton as Moreau and a good offbeat portrayal by **Bela Lugosi** as the head beast, the Sayer of the Law. Director Erle C. Kenton brings a sinister hothouse ambiance to the bizarre story, shot on location on Catalina Island, off the coast of Southern California. The 1977 remake, **The Island of Dr. Moreau,** was more faithful to the novel, and the humanimals were more believable, but the film couldn't compare to this version. (See also: **House of Dracula,** 1945)

Director: Erle C. Kenton, *Screenplay:* Waldemar Young, Philip Wylie, *Novel: The Island of Dr. Moreau:* H. G. Wells, *Photographer:* **Karl Struss,** *Makeup:* Wally Westmore

Cast: Charles Laughton, Bela Lugosi, Richard Arlen, Kathleen Burke, Leila Hyams, Alan Ladd

IT CAME FROM BENEATH THE SEA

Film   1955   U.S. (Columbia)   77 Minutes
Black & white

A giant octopus rises from the Pacific and demolishes the Golden Gate Bridge before being put to rest by a Navy torpedo. As usual, the explanation for the **mutant** monster's existence is an atomic **bomb** test, this one underwater. Animator **Ray Harryhausen,** working with a tight budget, didn't have the money to build all eight tentacles. What you see is the world's biggest quintopus.

Director: Robert Gordon, *Producer:* Charles H. Schneer, *Screenplay:* George Worthing Yates, Hal Smith, *Photographer:* Henry Freulich, *Special Effects:* Ray Harryhausen, Jack Erickson, *Musical Director:* Mischa Bakaleinikoff

Cast: Faith Domergue, Kenneth Tobey, Donald Curtis, Dean Maddox, Jr., Ian Keither

IT CAME FROM OUTER SPACE

Film   1953   U.S. (Universal-International)
80 Minutes   Black & white   3-D

An **alien** spaceship crashes in the Arizona desert with a crew of intelligent monstrosities that assume the appearance of local townspeople.

It Came from Outer Space marks the SF debut of director **Jack Arnold.** This low-budget film is a template of Arnold's work in the genre and has not lost its relevance with the passing of time. From the opening shots of a remote desert town set in stark relief at sundown, Arnold skillfully creates an atmosphere of alien menace with the power of suggestion rather than with expensive special effects. The aliens are seen in their natural state only once, when passing headlamps on a highway illuminate a huge, one-eyed "brain" at the wheel of an automobile. We are constantly aware of their presence, however, since Arnold shows much of the action from their viewpoint. In effect, the camera *is* the alien. We know which of the townspeople are alien surrogates, for they give themselves away with such uncharacteristic human behavior as staring into the sun without blinking.

Based on an original screen story by **Ray Bradbury** (little of whose contribution remained in the final script), the film takes a surprise turn during its final moments. As it happens, the visitors from space pose no threat at all. A systems failure has forced them to land on Earth, where their appearance is likely to cause alarm—the reason they have adopted human form. The kidnapped townspeople are released unharmed and the repaired spacecraft disappears over the horizon. Arnold's message, which runs counter to the cold-war paranoia of similar films of the 1950s, urges understanding and tolerance if we are ever to comprehend the unknown. The first SF film to be shot in 3-D, (see: **Stereoscopic Films)** which generates a shock or two, *It Came from Outer Space* is just as good shown "flat."

Director: **Jack Arnold,** *Producer:* William Alland, *Screenplay:* Harry Essex, *Story:* "The Meteor" Ray Bradbury, *Photographer:* Clifford Stine, *Producer Designer:* Bernard Herzbrun, Robert Boyle, *Special Effects:* Clifford Stine, David S. Horsley, *Music:* Herman Stein

Cast: **Richard Carlson,** Barbara Rush, Charles Drake, Morey Amsterdam, Kathleen Hughes

IT CONQUERED THE WORLD

Film 1956 U.S. (AIP) 71 Minutes Black & white

A giant cucumber takes control of a bad-tempered scientist, who helps the creature prepare for an **alien invasion** of Earth. The film has a number of scenes typical of **Roger Corman**'s taste for gratuitous violence, as when the hero blasts his neighbor's wife across the living room with a point-black rifle shot (she has also been "taken over," we learn). Bargain-basement special effects man Paul Blaisdell plays the "vegetoid" in a costume he designed. The film was remade in 1968 as **Zontar: The Thing From Venus.**

Director/Producer: Roger Corman, *Screenplay:* Lou Rusoff, *Special Effects:* Paul Blaisdell, *Music:* Ronald Stein

Cast: Peter Graves, Lee Van Cleef, Beverly Garland, Sally Fraser

IT'S A BIRD . . . IT'S A PLANE . . . IT'S SUPERMAN!

Play 1966-67 U.S. 2 acts

Well-received by New York critics, this musical comedy featured a **Superman** who could sing and dance. The writers were David Newman and Robert Benton, who later collaborated on the script of **Superman— The Movie** (1978), which, not coincidentally, resembles the approach of this play. Tears actually came to Superman's X-ray eyes in act two, after his confidence was nearly broken by a mad physicist named Dr. Abner Sedgwick, who couldn't quite win the Nobel Prize, no matter how hard he schemed and cheated. "Even the strongest man in the world can cry," Superman sang, while thoughtlessly bending a floor lamp into the shape of a coathanger, remembering how everyone laughed when Sedgwick asked why he wore that silly costume when going into action.

The story didn't make much sense (Chinese acrobats were after a secret atomic weapon at one point), but the show was lively and ingeniously staged (Clark Kent's phone booth danced off the stage after each of his quick changes), and the songs were good. Bob Holiday as Superman flew fearlessly across the stage on a thin wire, and made one stop and think about how difficult it must be to become a legend in one's own time. The characterization was similar to Christopher Reeve's portrayal in the big-budget films. The musical appeared on ABC-TV in 1975 with David Wilson as Superman. The director was Jack Regas.

Director: Harold Prince, *Music:* Charles Strouse, *Lyrics:* Lee Adams, *Book:* David Newman and Robert Benton, *Scenery:* Robert Randolph, *Costumes:* Florence Klotz, *Musical Director:* Harold Hastings

Cast: Bob Holiday, Jack Cassidy, Linda Lavin, Patricia Marand, Eric Mason, Michael O'Sullivan

IT'S GREAT TO BE ALIVE

Film 1933 U.S. (20th Century-Fox)
69 Minutes Black & white

Women take over the world after a plague has wiped out every adult male except one. Powerful females compete for the affections of the survivor, who counts himself lucky— until faced with his awesome responsibilities. A musical remake of the silent comedy **The Last Man on Earth** (1924).

Director: Alfred Werker, *Screenplay:* Paul Perez, Arthur Kober

Cast: Paul Roulien, Edna May Oliver, Gloria Stuart, Edward Van Sloan

IT! THE TERROR FROM BEYOND SPACE

Film 1958 U.S. (United Artists)
69 Minutes Black & white

This is the film that allegedly inspired **Alien** (1979) and was itself lifted from parts of A. E. van Vogt's novel *Voyage of the Space Beagle* (1950). Neither film credits these sources, however. A rescue mission picks up an astronaut stranded on **Mars** and begins the journey back to **Earth** with a scaley blood-sucking monster on board. The crew discovers its presence when they begin to disappear one by one. Their bloodless remains turn up in the ship's air-conditioning system, used by the creature as a cold-storage food locker. The survivors attempt to contain the monster in the lower section of the ship, but it breaks through the hold door and pursues them section by section to a dead end in the nose cockpit.

Although the film lacks technical polish, it builds an effective mood of claustrophobic terror and delivers an abundant share of suspense. The athletic reptilian was played by **Ray "Crash" Corrigan,** hero of the serial **Undersea Kingdom** (1936). The film was remade in 1966 as **Queen of Blood.**

Director: **Edward L. Cahn,** *Producer:* Robert E. Kent, *Screenplay:* Jerome Bixby, *Monster costume:* Paul Blaisdell, *Music:* Paul Sawtell

Cast: Marshall Thompson, Paul Langton, Ann Doran, Shawn Smith, Ray "Crash" Corrigan

I WAS A TEENAGE FRANKENSTEIN

Film 1957 U.S. (AIP) 74 Minutes Black & white Color

Far more enjoyable than an intentional parody, *Teenage Frankenstein* takes place near a high school campus, where a mad doctor related to the European Frankensteins has set up shop. In no time at all, he has assembled an American Monster from the best parts of recently deceased hot-rodders and other young accident victims. Like any normal teenager, the creature likes rock and roll and pretty girls in pony tails, and wants desperately to belong. "Answer me, you fool," scolds Dr. Frankenstein in one of the film's more sophisticated moments. "I know you have a civil tongue in your head. I sewed it there myself!" [See: **Frankenstein** (1931).]

Director: Herbert L. Strock, *Producer:* Herman Cohen, *Screenplay:* Kenneth Langtry, *Photographer:* Lothrop Worth, *Makeup:* Philip Scheer, *Music:* Paul Dunlap

Cast: Whit Bissell, Gary Conway, Phyllis Coates, Robert Burton, John Cliff

I WAS A TEENAGE WEREWOLF

Film 1957 U.S. (AIP) 76 Minutes Black & white

Hairy hijinks on a high school campus.

I Was a Teenage Werewolf made history of a sort: Its title has been enshrined in camp mythology, its star has gone on to more

Michael Landon menaces Dawn Richard in *I Was a Teenage Werewolf.*

peaceful triumphs, and it took in more than $2,500,000 on a $150,000 investment. Made to exploit what its producer called the "youth agony" of the 1950s, the film recounts the misadventures of a teenage rebel in the James Dean mold (although without the charisma), who visits an eccentric school psychiatrist in an effort to come to terms with the adult world. Hypnotized into his primeval self, he turns into a werewolf whenever he hears the school bell—much to the regret of anyone foolish enough to give him a hard time. Teens of the time cherished the film in drive-in theaters, where perhaps it is best seen.

Director: Gene Fowler, Jr., *Producer:* Herman Cohen, *Screenplay:* Ralph Thornton, *Photogrpher:* Joseph LaShelle, *Music:* Paul Dunlop

Cast: Michael Landon, Yvonne Lime, Whit Bissell, Guy Williams, Eddie Marr

JABBA THE HUT

An alien underworld gangster, fat and grotesque, introduced in **Star Wars** (1977). Jabba the Hut is a client of professional smuggler **Han Solo** who, while making a delivery, is forced to jettison the alien's contraband spices to escape an Imperial warship. Angered, Jabba puts a price on Solo's head and hires an assassin named Greedo to kill him. Solo kills Greedo instead. In **The Empire Strikes Back** (1980), a bounty hunter named Bobba Fett catches up with Solo and has him immobilized in a carbon freeze. Fett transports Solo's body back to Jabba the Hut, which is the beginning of **Revenge of the Jedi** (1983).

JACK ARMSTRONG, THE ALL-AMERICAN BOY

Radio serial   1933-50   U.S. (CBS)
15 Minutes (Mon-Wed-Fri)

Jack Armstrong was the radio serial for science-minded boys who owned erector sets and toy chemistry labs, and who liked to take apart their electric trains to see how they worked. Like his SF counterpart **Buck Rogers,** he was one of broadcasting's great explorers. While Buck explored other **solar systems,** Jack roamed the far reaches of the globe in Uncle Jim's amphibian plane the *Silver Albatross,* his yacht the *Spendthrift,* his compact helicopter (then called an autogyro), or his mammoth dirigible, the *Golden Secret.* Jack's traveling companions were his classmates from Hudson High, Billy and Betty

Fairfield, the nephew and niece of Uncle Jim. He often gave them lessons in applied technology, as when cruising through an African jungle in search of uranium to bring back to his science class for an experiment in splitting the atom. Jack: "The autogyro is a mighty useful machine, Betty. The propellor drives it forward while the rotors keep it up."

During its peak years, the program was able to hold listeners with plots that lasted as long as six months. It began to slip after World War II, however, when Uncle Jim and Betty were replaced by Vic Hardy, the young head of the Scientific Bureau of Investigation, and Jim Butterfield, a teen-age "junior announcer." (The following year, Uncle Jim made an appearance with Vic Hardy, in the unsuccessful movie **serial, Jack Armstrong.**) Jack became a full-fledged crime-fighter for the bureau, a career he continued as a grown-up, after the program's demise in 1950, in a short-lived radio series, **Armstrong of the S.B.I.** (1950-51). Too perfect and perhaps too knowledgeable for later generations of youngsters, Jack never made it to television. He has since vanished into oblivion, along with the all-American boy.

Sponsor of the program was Wheaties, the Breakfast of Champions, which offered a number of keen premiums for box-tops and "the cost of handling." These included Norden bombsights, hike-o-meters (a pedometer), secret decoders and whistling rings. The program always opened with the reverberating voice of an announcer exclaiming, "Jack Armstrong . . . Jack Armstrong . . . Jack. . . ," followed by an emphatic "The All-American Boy!"

Directors: James Jewell, Pat Murphy, Ed Morse, David Owen, Ted MacMurray, *Creator:* Robert Hardy Andrews, *Writers:* Robert Hardy Andrews, Colonel Paschal Strong, Jim Jewell, Talbot Mundy, Lee Knopf, Irving J. Crump

Cast: Jack Armstrong—St. John Terrell (1933), Jim Ameche (1933-38), Stanley Harris (1938-39), Charles Flynn (1939-43, 1944-51), Michael Rye (1943); Murray McLean, John Gannon, Roland Butterfield, James Goss, Dick York, Scheindel Kalish, Don Ameche, Marvin Miller

JACK ARMSTRONG

Film serial   1947   U.S. (Columbia)
15 Episodes   Black & white

Uncle Jim, owner of an aircraft factory developing an atomic-powered motor, recruits Jack Armstrong to help stop a similar, unauthorized experiment in "cosmic radioactivity" taking place on a remote island. In the meantime, Jack's older friend Vic Hardy, a scientific crime-fighter, has been kidnapped and taken to the island. Jack arrives just in time with classmates Betty and Billy Fairfield to destroy a **death ray** constructed by a criminal genius named Grood, and rescue Vic. This justly vanished antique offers a half-mast villain played by **Charles Middleton,** better known as Ming the Merciless of the **Flash Gordon** serials.

Director: Wallace Fox, *Producer:* Sam Katzman, *Screenplay:* Arthur Hoerl, Lewis Clay, Royal K. Cole, Leslie Swabacker, *Photographer:* Ira H. Morgan, *Music:* Lee Zahler

Cast: John Hart, Pierre Watkin, Rosemary LaPlance, Joe Brown, Charles Middleton

JAMES BOND

See: **Bond, James**

JEDI KNIGHT

Member of a select group of warriors who represent the power of good in the films **Star Wars** (1977), **The Empire Strikes Back** (1980) and *Revenge of the Jedi* (1983). For over 1,000 years the Jedi were the mightiest and most esteemed members of the Old Republic, until they were betrayed to the evil Imperial Empire by a corrupt young Jedi named **Darth Vader.** Too trusting for their own good, the Knights were caught off guard during the subsequent **Clone Wars,** and most were killed. The few who survived went into hiding. Among these is **Ben Kenobi,** who seeks to mount a new effort against the Empire by training young **Luke Skywalker** in the martial arts of the Jedi. Among their armaments is a **laser** sword called **the lightsaber** and a mysterious but extremely powerful weapon called **the force.**

JEKYLL'S INFERNO

See: **The Two Faces of Dr. Jekyll**

JESSE JAMES MEETS FRANKENSTEIN'S DAUGHTER

Film   1966   U.S. (Embassy)   88 Minutes
Color

Gothic **horror** confronts western adventure, and the result is one of Hollywood's more endearing disasters. The plot is a howl, with the mad count's daughter holed up in a secret laboratory in Mexico where she has brought her father's brain to find a robust body transplant. Enter Jesse James and his pal, Hank, on the run from the law. Maria **Frankenstein** develops a yen for the handsome Jesse who in turn fancies her earthy servant girl. Seething with jealousy, Miss F. performs the transplant on Hank while pretending to treat a gunshot wound, and, before you can say "boo," Hank/Frank has gotten rid of her rival. Jesse still refuses to cooperate, however, setting the stage for a showdown between the former friends. Which only goes to prove that hell hath no fury like a screenwriter's imagination.

Director: William Beaudine, *Producer:* Carroll Case, *Screenplay:* Carl Hittleman, *Photographer:* Lothrop Worth, *Music:* Raoul Kraushaar

Cast: Narda Onyx, John Lupton, Steven Geray, Cal Bolder, Estelita

JE T'AIME, JE T'AIME

Film   1968   France/U.S. (20th Century-Fox)   94 Minutes   De Luxe   Cinemascope

Time and memory and their relationship to life are central themes in the highly personal cinema of French **auteur** director **Alain Resnais.** As in *Last Year at Marienbad* (*L'Annee derniere a Marienbad*) (1961)—which made his international reputation—Resnais dispenses with conventional narrative to create a dreamlike unreality where past, present and future are one and the same.

Je t'aime's science fiction is tenuous. The idea of **time travel** is used as a metaphor for the confusion of an angst-ridden failure at the end of his rope. Discharged from a hospital after attempting to kill himself, he is kidnapped by a group of doctors and locked into a womblike device that transports him to the previous year. The illegal experiment has worked with laboratory mice, but its effect on a human being—who has an entirely different concept of time—is unknown. With nothing to live for, the man is an ideal subject for the experiment. The machine malfunctions, however, shifting abruptly from past to present and back again until time is hopelessly confused in the man's mind. Is the past that drove him to attempt suicide in reality the present? Did he murder his boring girl friend, or was the act a wishful fantasy? Is memory the same as fact? The clock is meaningless, in Resnais' view, because time is only a perception. Whatever the truth of his life, the man sees his future as dismal as his past and again makes plans to kill himself.

Director: Alain Resnais, *Producer:* Mag Bodard, *Screenplay:* Alain Resnais, Jacques Sternberg, *Photographer:* Jean Boffety, *Music:* Krzystof Penderecki

Cast: Claude Rich, Olga Georges-Picot, Annie Fargue

LA JETTE/The Pier

Film   1963   France (Argos/Arcturus)
29 Minutes   Black & white

This award-winning short film takes place in Paris, devastated by a nuclear war, whose survivors live in the city's Metro tunnels. To find medicine for radiation poisoning, a volunteer is sent into the past by a group of scientists, who inject him with an experimental drug and instruct him to recall a vivid image of his childhood. His memory takes him to Orly Airport and a young woman he saw there as a child. They fall in love, and he is abruptly yanked into the present and sent into the future, which is populated by a new race of human beings with jewel-like eyes in the center of their foreheads. He finds the past more comfortable, and he returns for good to marry the girl. Followed by one of the scientists, he is shot on a runway while watching his child self leave on a trip.

La Jette is unique in that it tells its story in still photographs, which are given movement with continuous panning shots and **dissolves.** While the film has the quality of a literary game, it is never boring. It has a strong inner logic, fully realized in its ending, which neatly solves the problem of one of the paradoxes of **time travel:** the problem of bumping into one's physical self.

Director/Screenplay: Chris Marker, *Photographer:* Jean Ravel, *Music:* Trevor Duncan

Cast: Jacques Ledoux, Helene Chatelain, Davros Hanich

JET JACKSON, FLYING COMMANDO

See: **Captain Midnight**

JOHNNY JUPITER

TV series   1953-54   U.S. (DuMont)
30 Minutes (weekly)   Black & white

Created by the producers of *Howdy Doody,* this inventive science fantasy program proved to be too sophisticated for American children of its generation but managed to hang on for 39 episodes on the now-defunct DuMont network (disbanded in 1955). During the first season, leading human character Ernest P. Duckweather was a clerk in a general store and something of an inventor, who put together an interplanetary TV set that pulled in Jupiter. Appearing on the TV screen were a number of puppets, including Johnny Jupiter, his friend B-12, Reject the Robot, Katherine, Mr. Frisley and Dynamo, each of whom made mildly satirical comments on the strange customs of Earthlings. For the second season Duckweather was changed to the meek janitor of a TV station who dreamt of becoming a producer. While playing with the equipment in a control room, he inadvertently made contact with Jupiter and began a series of two-way televised conversations with the puppets.

Cast: Wright King, Vaughn Taylor, Cliff Hall, Gilbert Mack, *Puppeteer:* Carl Harms

JOURNEY BENEATH THE DESERT

See: **L'Atlantide (1961)**

JOURNEY TO THE CENTER OF THE EARTH

Film   1959   U.S. (20th Century-Fox) 132 Minutes   De Luxe   CinemaScope

Jules Verne gets the royal treatment in this big-budget Hollywood adaptation of his famous novel. Professor Oliver Lindenbrook receives a gift paperweight from his students and finds markings on the stone, inscribed by a lost explorer who has visited the **Earth's** core. He traces the entrance to a cave in Iceland, and, together with a student, the widow of an old friend and a guide, makes his descent. They travel through a field of mammoth mushrooms and a huge sea, fighting off dinosaurs and the nasty Count Saknussemm, who has followed them and plans to claim the discovery for himself. Trapped in the ruins of **Atlantis,** the professor explodes a stick of dynamite and ignites a lava flow that catapults them to safety through the volcano in Stromboli, Italy.

Seen today, the film seems more juvenile than ever, but it is played with a likeable, wide-eyed innocence, and the special effects are still eye-catching. The studio cast James Mason in the role of Lindenbrooke to capitalize on his popular portrayal of Captain Nemo in **20,0000 Leagues Under the Sea** (1954).

Director: Henry Levin, *Producer:* Charles Brackett, *Screenplay:* Walter Reisch, Charles Brackett, *Novel:* Jules Verne, *Photographer:* Leo Tover, *Art Director:* Lyle R. Wheeler, Franz Bachelin, Herman A. Blumenthal, *Special Effects:* Lyle B. Abbott, James B. Gordon, Emil Kosa, Jr., *Music:* **Bernard Herrmann**

Cast: James Mason, Arlene Dahl, Pat Boone, Diane Baker, Thayer David, Peter Ronson

JOURNEY TO THE FAR SIDE OF THE SUN

(Also titled: *Doppleganger*)

Film   1969   Great Britain (Century 21/ Universal)   99 Minutes   Technicolor

Sent to investigate a tenth planet found at the far side of **Earth's** orbit, two astronauts are approaching for a landing when their spacecraft goes out of control and crashlands, killing one of them. The survivor thinks he is back on Earth, until he becomes aware of several maddening differences: Everyone is left-handed, writes in reverse and reads newspapers printed backward. He is in fact on a **parallel world**—a mirror image of Earth. The astronaut eventually repairs the ship and escapes, passing his doppleganger, or double, on the way home.

This provocative idea is diluted by an unnecessary story-telling frame that has the astronaut telling his disbelieved story in an asylum. The above-average model work is by Derek Medding, a long-term member of the Anderson production team. The film was not a box-office success, having been sidelined by the real space landing earlier that year.

Director: Robert Parrish, *Producers/Screenplay:* Gerry and Sylvia Anderson, *Photographer:* John Read, *Special Effects:* Harry Oakes, Derek Meddings, *Music:* Barry Gray

Cast: Ian Hendry, Roy Thinnes, Patrick Wymark, Herbert Lom, Lynn Loring

JULES VERNE'S ROCKET TO THE MOON

(Also titled: *Those Fantastic Flying Fools*)

Film   1967   Great Britain/U.S. (AIP) 94 Minutes   Color   CinemaScope

An all-star cast wanders through this uneven comedy, which has little to do with **Jules Verne.** The American showman P. T. Barnum is presented as a fictional character, who raises money in Victorian England to send a rocket to the moon. Inside the small vehicle is a midget from Barnum's circus who ends up in Russia when the rocket goes astray.

Director: **Don Sharp,** *Producer:* Harry Alan Towers, *Screenplay:* David Freeman, *Story:* Harry Alan Towers, *Special Effects:* Les Bowie, Pat Moore, *Music:* Patrick John Scott

Cast: Burl Ives, Gert Frobe, Hermione Gingold, Troy Donahue, Terry-Thomas, Klaus Kinski, Lionel Jeffries, Dennis Price

JUNGLE CAPTIVE

Film 1945 U.S. (Universal) 64 Minutes Black & white

The further adventures of **Captive Wild Woman** (1943), an ape turned into a beautiful woman by a mad scientist (played this time by suave heavy Otto Kruger). She sends her boyfriend screaming into the jungle when she embarassingly reverts to her original hairy form (forever, as it turned out).

Director: Harold Young, *Screenplay:* M. Coates Webster, Dwight V. Babcock, *Story:* Dwight V. Babcock, *Photographer:* Maury Gertsman

Cast: Amelita Ward, Otto Kruger, Vicky Lane, Jerome Cowan, Rondo Hatton

JURAN, NATHAN H.(ERTZ) (1907–   )

American film and TV director. Born in Austria, Juran came to the U.S. as an infant. He was graduated from the University of Minnesota and M.I.T. After working as an architect in New York City, he entered films in 1937 as a contract art director for 20th Century-Fox. His design of an 86-acre Welsh mining village (with Richard Day) for *How Green Was My Valley* (1941) won an **Academy Award.** Since 1952 he has shown a competent, if uninspired, talent for directing medium-budget action fantasies, notably those of **stop-motion** animator **Ray Harryhausen.**

Films include: The Loves of Edgar Allan Poe [as art director] (1942), **Dr. Renault's Secret** (1942), *The Razor's Edge* (1946), *The Black Castle* [as director] (1952), *The Golden Blade* (1953), *The Crooked Web*

(1955), **The Deadly Mantis, Twenty Million Miles to Earth** (1957), *The Seventh Voyage of Sinbad* (1959), *Flight of the Lost Balloon* (1961), *Siege of the Saxons* (1963), **First Men in the Moon** (1964), *The Boy Who Cried Werewolf* (1973)

TV programs include: My Friend Flicka (1956-58), *Daniel Boone* (1964-70), **Voyage to the Bottom of the Sea** (1964-68), **The Time Tunnel** (1966-67), **Land of the Giants** (1968-70)

JUST IMAGINE

Film 1930 U.S. (Fox) 102 Minutes Black & white

Science fiction had yet to establish itself as a Hollywood film genre in 1930 (most futurist films had been made in Europe), but musicals had, and the public couldn't get enough of them during the early years of the sound era. Hollywood had produced so many, in fact, that it was running out of settings, prompting someone at Fox to come up with the bright idea of *Just Imagine,* a routine musical comedy that hoped to lure Depression-era audiences into theaters for a look at a more promising future.

The flimsy plot concerns a man struck by lightning while playing golf and who wakes up in 1980 in New York. He finds to his comic consternation (but not to the audience's) that people now have numbers instead of names, babies are born in vending machines and private airmobiles fly through corridors of immense skyscrapers. Food comes in the form of tablets, as does liquor (still bootlegged, since Prohibition has not yet been repealed). To help a new friend win the hand of a girl he loves, he journeys to **Mars,** a planet of prismatic stones, where people are all born as twins, one good, one bad.

The movie is interspersed with vaudeville routines, coy dialogue and forgettable songs such as "Never Swat the Fly" and "I'm Only the Words, You Are the Melody." As entertainment, the film scored a zero at the box office, and had the effect of scaring Hollywood off science fiction for several years. As prophecy, it did only a little better, predicting at least the television would be com-

Just Imagine: Manhattan in 1980 as imagined by Hollywood in 1930.

monplace in 1980. The film's miniature city is impressive, however. Built at a reported cost of $250,000, it surpasses in detail and opulence the one seen in **Metropolis** (1927). There are skyscrapers 250 stories high, canals to bring ocean liners into the city and landing decks for private aircrafts. Footage from the film later turned up in the 1939 **Buck Rogers** serial.

Director: David Butler, *Screenplay:* David Butler, Ray Henderson, B. G. DeSylva, Lew Brown, *Story, Music and Lyrics:* Ray Henderson, B. G. DeSylva, Lew Brown, *Photographer:* Ernest Palmer, *Art Directors:* Stephen Gooson, Ralph Hammeras, *Musical Director:* Arthur Kay

Cast: El Brendel, Maureen O'Sullivan, John Garrick, Marjorie White, Frank Albertson, Mischa Auer, Hobart Bosworth

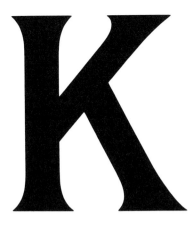

K

KAIJU SOSHINGEKI/
Destroy All Monsters

Film   1968   Japan (Toho)   88 Minutes
Eastmancolor   Tohoscope   [Released 1969
U.S. (AIP)]

Toho studios celebrated its 20th SF film,
Kaiju Soshingeki, bringing together its resident monsters for a widescreen and color
rampage through the world's major cities.
A surfeit of **stop-motion** creatures, including Baragon, **Godzilla** and his son **Minira,**
Manda, **Mothra, Rodan** and Varan find
themselves under the control of an invading fleet of flying saucers from the planet
Kilaak, whose own monster later arrives.
New York, London, Moscow and Peking suffer horribly before a final battle of the titans on Japan's Mount Fuji.

Director: Inoshiro Honda, *Producer:* Tomoyuki
Tanaka, *Screenplay:* Inoshiro Honda, Karouru
Mabuchi, *Special Effects:* Eiji Tsuburaya, Sada-
masa Arikawa, *Music:* Arira Ifukube

Cast: Akira Kubo, Andrew Hughes, Jun Tazaki,
Kyoko Ai

BEN (OBI-WAN) KENOBI

Teacher and friend of **Luke Skywalker,**
young hero of the **Star Wars** film series. A
former high-ranking **Jedi Knight,** Ben is hiding out in the mountains of **Tatooine** and
living as a hermit when he meets Luke,
whom he rescues from an attack by **Tusken
Raiders.** Recognizing him as the son of a
dead comrade, Ben gives the boy his father's
lightsaber and begins a long course of in-
struction that includes the use of a mysterious Jedi power called **the Force.**

Ben (Obi-Wan) Kenobi (Alec Guiness): the
aging Jedi Knight of *Star Wars.*

During a subsequent mission to rescue
Princess **Leia Organa,** the leader of a freedom movement attempting to overthrow the
oppressive Galactic Empire, Ben confronts
his old pupil **Darth Vader,** who had gone
to the side of the enemy. The two fight a
duel with lightsabers, and Ben, mortally
wounded, vanishes, having transcended his
mortal existence to become one with the
Force. But his voice and vision return to help
Luke combat the forces of evil, in **The
Empire Strikes Back** (1980) and *Revenge of
the Jedi* (1983). Ben Kenobi is played by Alec
Guinness, the hapless hero of the SF comedy
The Man in the White Suit (1951).

KILLDOZER

TV film   1974   U.S. (ABC)   75 Minutes
Color

Construction workers on a Pacific island battle a homicidal bulldozer possessed by an
alien intelligence carried to Earth on a
meteorite. This taut, well-directed thriller
doesn't quite attain the horsepower of its
source, a famous story by SF writer Theodore Sturgeon. But the macho driving of
stunt man Carey Loftin is hair-raising, especially in a duel between a power shovel
and the killdozer. (See also: **Meteoroids.**)

Director: Jerry London, *Producer:* Herbert F. Solow, *Screenplay:* Theodore Sturgeon, Ed Mac-Killop, *Story:* Theodore Sturgeon, *Photographer:* Terry K. Meade, *Special Effects:* Albert Whitlock, *Sound Effects Editor:* **Ben Burtt, Jr.,** *Music:* Gil Melle

Cast: Clint Walker, Carl Betz, Neville Brand, James Wainwright, Robert Urich

KILLER APE

Film 1953 U.S. (Columbia) 69 Minutes
Sepiatone

A brave safari guide outwits mad scientists terrorizing the jungle with wild animals injected with a mysterious serum that turns them into killer-slaves. *Killer Ape* is the twelfth in a series of "Jungle Jim" programmers (this one made in brown-and-white sepiatone), all starring a paunchy, post-Tarzan Johnny Weissmuller in the title role. The comic-strip character first appeared on the screen in a 1937 Republic serial.

Director: **Spencer Bennett,** *Producer:* Sam Katzman, *Screenplay:* Carroll Young, Arthur Hoerl, *Photographer:* William Whitley, *Musical Director:* Mischa Bakaleinkoff

Cast: Johnny Weissmuller, Nestor Paiva, Max Palmer, **Ray "Crash" Corrigan,** Carol Thurston

KING DINOSAUR

Film 1955 U.S. (Lippert) 63 Minutes
Black & white

Actors posing as astronauts shipwrecked on a prehistoric, papier-mache planet try to look scared to death as they face down a lizard enlarged to look like a dinosaur on a **rear-projection** screen. The demand for SF-horror movie programmers was so great in the 1950s that filmmaker **Bert I. Gordon** actually launched his career on the basis of this ultra-low budget programmer.

Director/Producer: Bert I. Gordon, *Screenplay:* Tom Gries, *Story:* Bert I. Gordon, Al Zimbalist, *Special Effects:* Howard A. Anderson

Cast: Doug Henderson, Bill Bryant, Wanda Curtis, Patricia Gallagher, *Narrator:* Marvin Miller

KING KONG

Film 1933 U.S. (RKO) 100 Minutes
Black & white

"They told me I was going to have the tallest, darkest leading man in Hollywood," Fay Wray recalled, years after she played the archetypal monster-movie heroine. "Naturally, I thought of Clark Gable." Ms. Wray's co-star was actually an 18-inch rubber model covered in dyed rabbit fur, augmented by a full-scale mechanical arm and a bearhide-covered head and shoulders.

To make the miniature appear to be 20 times the size of the actress, **stop-motion** artist **Willis O'Brien** devised a unique method of trick photography. He shot the actress first, then projected this footage onto a small rear screen. In front of this was placed Kong, who now seemed as large as he was supposed to be. Next, each frame of the live action was stopped as animators brought the giant ape's movements in line with Ms. Wray's and photographed the two together.

Cooper describes how the famous scene in which Kong yanks at her clothing was done: "A movie was made of her alone while invisible wires pulled off her clothes. Then the miniature Kong was placed on a set built on a waist-high platform, about twice the size of a dining-room table, on which miniature trees, ferns and plaster-of-Paris rocks had been arranged. Back of this, the movie of Fay Wray was projected, and Kong's movements made to correspond with it."

A sequel, **Son of Kong,** was released the same year. In 1976 Dino de Laurentiis produced an ill-conceived, cynical remake, notable only for the portrayal of Kong by makeup artist **Rick Baker.**

Directors: Merian C. Cooper, Ernest Schoedsack, *Producer:* Merian C. Cooper, *Screenplay:* James Creelman, Ruth Rose, *Story:* Edgar Wallace, *Photographers:* Edward Linden, Verne Walker, J. O. Taylor, *Special Effects:* Willis H. O'Brien, *Sound Effects:* Murray Spivak, *Music:* Max Steiner

Cast: Robert Armstrong, Bruce Cabot, Fay Wray, Frank Reicher

King Kong: Fay Wray in the grip of a stop-motion puppet (1933) and Jessica Lange in Carlo Rambaldi's mechanical hand (1976).

KISS ME DEADLY

Film   1955   U.S. (United Artists)
105 Minutes   Black & white

Director Robert Aldrich whizzes through this lurid film noir, adapted from Mickey Spillane's best-selling pulp novel, with the stomach-turning speed of a roller coaster. The novel's narcotics stash has been changed into a nuclear **bomb,** stolen by a murdered man who intended to sell it to a foreign government. Hero Mike Hammer, who makes *Dirty Harry* (1971) look like a left-wing liberal, tracks it down with cunning, lies, brutality and murder. Several people have been killed by the radioactive element, contained in a small "Pandora's Box." Hammer, overcome by greed, opens it anyway, triggering an atomic explosion in a beach house in Southern California.

Aldrich suffuses the film with an overwhelming paranoia, depicting America as a place where no one is safe from conspiracies, gangsters, women and the bomb. Interestingly, the real villain of the piece is human curiosity, which has led to the development of the bomb. As one character notes, "What you don't know can't hurt you." The film has since become a cult item.

Director/Producer: Robert Aldrich, *Screenplay:* A. I. Bezzerides, *Novel:* Mickey Spillane, *Photographer:* Ernest Laszlo, *Music:* Frank de Vol

Cast: Ralph Meeker, Albert Dekker, Cloris Leachman, Jack Elam, Wesley Addy, Marian Carr, Juano Hernandez

KLINGONS

Archfoes of the United Federation of Planets in **Star Trek.** Klingons are ugly, **humanoid** aliens whose spines extend up their backs and over their heads, down to their noses. Introduced in the *Star Trek* TV episode "Errand of Mercy" by Gene Coon, they are extremely warlike but have grudgingly agreed to a peace treaty with the Federation at the behest of the Organians, a pacifist civilization inhabiting the neutral planet Organia. According to *Star Trek* writer David Gerrold, Klingons serve a dramatic function as "controlled" villains whose confrontations with the crew of the **U.S.S. Enterprise** are never quite resolved.

KNEALE, NIGEL (1922–   )

British author, TV and screen writer. A former actor and short story writer, Kneale is best known as the creator of Professor Quatermass, hero of three six-part BBC-TV series that were later filmed.

TV scripts: The Quatermass Experiment (1953), Quatermass II (1955), Quatermass and the Pit (1958)

Film scripts: **Quatermass II** [co-writer], **The Abominable Snowman** (1957), *Look Back in Anger* (1959), *The Entertainer* (1960), **First Men in the Moon** [co-writer] (1964), *The Devil's Own/The Witches* (1967), **Quatermass and the Pit** (1968)

K-9

Robot dog, companion of TV's **Doctor Who.** In addition to being able to talk and wag its tail, the small **robot** is a brilliant **computer** whose data feeds from a tongue-like tape in its muzzle and a powerful weapon with a **blaster** in its nose. A gift from inventor Professor Marius, K-9 was instrumental in

K-9: Robot pet of Doctor Who.

helping the Doctor and his assistant **Leela** defeat an alien life form called the Nucleus.

KOENEKAMP, FRED

American director of photography known for his vivid, highly saturated color images in big-budget Hollywood productions.

Other films: **The Spy With My Face** (1966), *Patton* (1970), *Billy Jack* (1971) [co-photographer], *Papillon* (1973), **Doc Savage, the Man of Bronze** (1975), **Embryo** (1976), *Fun With Dick and Jane, The Other Side of Midnight* (1977), **The Swarm** (1978)

KONEC SRPNA V HOTELU OZON/ The End of August at the Hotel Ozone

Film 1965 Czechoslovakia 87 Minutes Black & white [Released 1966 U.S. and Great Britain (New Line Cinema)]

Set 50 years in the future, after a nuclear catastrophe has turned the world to ruins, this bleakly poetic drama focuses on a group of eight women riding around the country on horseback looking for men to continue the human race. Their search leads to a derelict hotel occupied by an elderly man with a phonograph and a recording of "Roll Out the Barrel." After a brief visit, they decide he's too old to be of use, and, after murdering him to get the phonograph, they move on. Powerful but self-consciously pessimistic, the film bears a resemblance to Ingmar Bergman's *The Silence* (1963).

Director: Jan Schmidt, *Screenplay:* Pavel Juracek

Cast: Andrej Jariabek, Beta Ponicanova, Magda Seidlerova, Hana Vitkova

KONGA

Film   1961   Great Britain (AIP)
90 Minutes   Eastmancolor

Producer Herman Cohen, one of the great names of schlock movies, originally titled this feverish ape adventure (inspired by you-know-who) *I Was a Teenage Gorilla* to honor his camp masterpiece **I Was a Teenage Werewolf** (1957). Set in Victorian England, the film concerns a university professor who brings back from Africa a plant that produces a growth enzyme capable of turning animals into giants. He also brings along a cute chimp named Konga, who gets a shot of the enzyme and disposes of the troublesome dean, who had ordered the professor to terminate the experiment. Later, Konga receives a super dose of the stuff and shoots through the roof, having changed from a chimp to an ape in a totally unconvincing special effect. Cohen has the professor's girl friend murdered for no apparent reason, except that "She was pretty and sexy, and I thought the audience would get a kick out of seeing her killed."

Director: John Lemont, *Producer:* Herman Cohen, *Screenplay:* Aben Kandel, Herman Cohen, *Photographer:* Desmond Dickinson, *Production Designer:* Wilfred Arnold, *Music:* Gerard Shurmann

Cast: Michael Gough, Margo Johns, Jess Conrad, Claire Gordon

KRELS

Members of an extinct race that once inhabited the planet **Altair-IV,** in the film **Forbidden Planet** (1956). No one knows what they looked like, but their unusual forms can be surmised by the scale and shape of the dwellings they left behind. The Krel machines still pulse with life from deep within the planet, generating unfathomable power. Designed to increase Krel mental energies, they ultimately proved to be their undoing, releasing the evil side of the Krel subconscious and destroying the species at a single stroke. The Krel labs were designed by artist Bob Kinishita.

KRONOS

Film   1957   U.S. (20th Century-Fox)
78 Minutes   Black & white

Dropped by a **UFO** into the ocean off the coast of Mexico, an immense mechanical creature walks onto the beach and heads for the nearest power station. Fed by energy, Kronos cuts a path of devastation through the country as it searches out and devours all the electrical current it can find. Seemingly indestructable, the device is ultimately deactivated by a clever scientist who neutralizes its polarity. The film is ineptly made, but Kronos was at least a welcome change from the **mutant** monsters and giant insects common to 1950s SF movies.

Director/Producer: **Kurt Neumann,** *Screenplay:* Laurence Lewis Goldman, *Special Effects:* Jack Rabin, Irving Block, *Music:* Paul Sawtell

Cast: Jeff Morrow, George O'Hanlon, Barbara Lawrence, John Emery, Morris Ankrum

KRYPTONITE

Fragment of Krypton, Superman's home planet; from the Greek word *kryptos,* meaning a secret place. Glowing red and green, probably radioactive, the substance is the only thing that can incapacitate or kill the Man of Steel. How it works remains a mystery, but one theory has it that kryptonite reminds **Superman** of the violent destruction of Krypton (and the death of his parents), thus producing a terrifying psychological shock whenever he is near it. The substance was introduced in the radio serial **The Adventures of Superman** (1940) and later incorporated into his **comic-book** legend.

THE LADY AND THE DOCTOR

See: **The Lady and the Monster**

THE LADY AND THE MONSTER

(Also titled: *The Lady and the Doctor,
Tiger Man)*

Film   1944   U.S. (Republic)   86 Minutes
Black & white

This is the first and best screen version of
Curt Siodmak's unlikely SF-**horror** novel,
Donovan's Brain (1943), filmed again as
Donovan's Brain (1953) and **The Brain**
(1962). The presence of Erich von Stroheim,
the "man you love to hate," leads one to
presume he is the titular monster, but he is

The Lady and the Monster: Professor
Mueller (Erich von Stroheim) and his
assistant Patrick (Richard Arlen) prepare to
operate on Donovan's brain.

in fact a not-so-mad surgeon who performs
a medical miracle by keeping alive the disembodied brain of a dead industrial magnate.
The brain exerts a powerful telepathic hold
on the mind of von Stroheim's male assistant—the monster—forcing him to take
care of the criminal millionaire's unfinished
business, which includes murder.

Made with a higher budget than was customary for a Republic picture, *Lady* was intended as a showcase for the talents of Vera
Hruba Ralston, making her motion picture
debut. (She grimaces nicely whenever von
Stroheim asks for a gigglisaw, an instrument
used for sawing open skulls.) The film was
later shown in Great Britain minus several
more gruesome scenes in the operating
theater, as *The Lady and the Doctor*. It was
trimmed and re-released in America as a
second feature under the inexplicable title,
Tiger Man.

Director/Producer: George Sherman, *Screenplay:*
Dane Lussier, Frederick Kohner, *Novel:* Curt
Siodmak, *Photographer:* John Alton, *Art Director:*
Russell Kimball, *Special Effects:* Theodore Ly-
decker, *Music:* Walter Scharf

Cast: Erich von Stroheim, Vera Hruba Ralston,
Richard Arlen, Sidney Blackmer, Mary Nash

LADY FRANKENSTEIN

See: **La Figlia di Frankenstein**

LAND OF THE GIANTS

TV series   1968-70   U.S. (ABC)   60 Minutes
(weekly)   Color

During a trip from New York to London,
suborbital Flight 612 encounters a magnetic
storm that spins it through a **space warp.**
The plane makes an emergency landing, and
the passengers disembark into a giant world
populated by human beings and animals a
dozen times their size. Episodes concerned
the attempts of passengers to make repairs
and return home while trying to escape
hungry insects, children who wanted them
as pets and showmen who wanted to exhibit them as freaks. The routine series
was similar to the previous **World of Giants**

(1959). Both were inspired by the film **Dr. Cyclops** (1940).

Directors: **Irwin Allen,** Harry Harris, Nathan H. Juran, Sobey Martin and others, *Executive Producer/Creator:* Irwin Allen, *Writers:* Robert and Wanda Duncan, Robert and Esther Mitchell, Ellis St. Joseph, William Welch and others, *Photographer:* Howard Schwartz, *Special Effects:* Lyle B. Abbott, Art Cruickshank, *Music:* **John Williams**

Cast: Gary Conway, Don Marshall, Kurt Kaznar, Don Matheson, Heather Young

THE LAND THAT TIME FORGOT

Film   1974   Great Britain (Amicus)
91 Minutes   Technicolor

During World War I, survivors of a German torpedo attack drift to an uncharted prehistoric island aboard a crippled U-boat.

Reminiscent of the golden age of movie **serials,** *The Land that Time Forgot* features an old-fashioned hero and villain, non-stop adventure and monsters galore. Action supersedes logic as Germans, Englishmen and an American hero join forces to survive in the mythical land of **Caprona** (near the South Pole), inhabited by hostile Neanderthals, dinosaurs and a hungry pterodactyl. All ends well, however, and the island quakes with an exploding volcanic fireball, the fate of so many movie lost worlds.

Based on the first book of an Edgar Rice Burroughs trilogy (others are *The People That Time Forgot* and *Out of Time's Abyss*), *The Land that Time Forgot* suffers from an uneven script by SF author Michael Moorcock (who claims it was tampered with by the producer). Animation of miniature creatures is also spotty. **Stop-motion** was considered too expensive, and three-foot-high dinosaurs were either glove **puppets** or animated by wires. More effective is an aquatic dinosaur that attacks the submarine as it approaches the island. A huge head and tapering neck was constructed over a hydraulic arm, which lifted from the water to snatch a crewman from the deck. The prehistoric bird, which swoops away with a caveman-doll, was built in two models: full-scale for close-ups and a smaller version for flying shots. **Front projection** brought models up to the scale of actors.

Director: **Kevin Connor,** *Producer:* John Dark, *Screenplay:* Michael Moorcock, James Cawthorn, *Novel:* Edgar Rice Burroughs, *Photographer:* Alan Hume, *Production Designer:* Maurice Carter, *Special Effects:* Derek Meddings, *Miniatures:* Roger Dicken, *Music:* Douglas Gamley

Cast: Doug McClure, John McEnergy, Susan Penhaligon, Keith Barron, Anthony Ainley

LASER

A device that converts ordinary light into an intense, concentrated beam; an acronym for *l*ight *a*mplification by *s*timulated *e*mission of *r*adiation. Unlike ordinary light, which is random and unsteady, laser light moves in an orderly, highly amplified flow of electro-magnetic radiation. Invented in 1960, the laser makes it possible to beam telephone calls and computer data across vast distances with virtually no energy loss. At high power its light can cut and cauterize with pinpoint accuracy, making it an ideal scalpel and suture for delicate eye surgery. The laser can also burn through steel at long range, and it is currently under development as an antiaircraft and antisatellite weapon by the U.S. and the Soviet Union, a move predicted by SF writers, who have long wielded laser weapons. Applied to film technology, the laser is a prime component of **holography,** a radical new system of producing three-dimensional images that can be seen without viewing lenses.

LASERBLAST

Film   1978   Italy/U.S. (Yablans)   80 Minutes Technicolor

Reptilian **alien** police track a **humanoid** lawbreaker to a California desert, where they dispose of him in a **laser** duel before lifting off for home. Later, a troubled teenager finds the evaporated criminal's weapon and tries on his amulet. Presto! He becomes a murderous monster possessed by an evil alien power, the object of a posse organized by an Italian sheriff and a mixed bag of government officials. The actors somehow manage to keep a straight face.

Director: Michael Rae,' *Producer:* Charles Band, *Screenplay:* Frank R. Perilli, Franne Schact, *Photographer:* Terry Bowen, *Special Effects:* Steve Neill, David Allen

Cast: Kim Milford, Cheryl Smith, Roddy Mc-Dowall, Fianni Russo, Ron Masak, Keenan Wynn

THE LAST CHILD

TV film   1971   U.S. (ABC)   75 Minutes
Color

The Last Child owes its inspiration to **Zero Population Growth,** made the same year. Set in a dictatorial future when having more than one child is a crime, the film reasons that giving birth is a fundamental right that transcends the potential chaos of overpopulation. The story is told from the point of view of an attractive, loving couple who become outlaws when they attempt to have a second child. On hand to express contemporary opinions on birth control is a noble Senator struggling to abolish the unfair law and a self-hating population inspector bent on trapping the couple. *The Last Child* is well-played but more interesting for the issues and problems it avoids than for those it explores. The script was allegedly tampered with by network censors to avoid offending religious groups.

Director: **John L. Moxey,** *Producer:* Aaron Spelling, *Screenplay:* Peter S. Fischer, *Photographer:* Arch Dalzell, *Music:* Laurence Rosenthal

Cast: Janet Margolin, Michael Cole, Van Heflin, Ed Asner, Harry Guardino

THE LAST DAYS OF MAN ON EARTH

See: **The Final Programme**

THE LAST MAN ON EARTH

Film   1924   U.S. (Fox)   7 reels   Tinted
(silent)

In the faraway year of 1954 women take control of the government after a mysterious virus has killed every male over the age of 14 except one. Two equally determined female senators compete vainly for the affections of the lone male survivor, proving that girls will still be girls even when the power structure has reversed.

A political satire, *Last Man* is not likely to please today's feminists with its humorous, male jibes at "emancipated" women of the period (they had won the right to vote only four years before). From an SF point of view, the film is an entertaining anomaly in that it plays its premise for laughs rather than the usual post-cataclysmic distress. The story was remade in 1933 as a musical, **It's Great to Be Alive.**

Director/Producer: John G. Blystone, *Screenplay:* Donald W. Lee, *Photographer:* Allan Davey

Cast: Earle Foxe, Grace Cunard, Derelys Perdue, Buck Black, Gladys Tennyson

THE LAST MAN ON EARTH

Film   1964   Italy/U.S. (Alta Vista/AIP)
86 Minutes   Black & white

Vincent Price stars as **Richard Matheson**'s besieged loner in this initial adaptation of the author's novel, *I Am Legend* (1954), which offers a scientific explanation for vampirism. As Robert Morgan, the only survivor of a plague that has either killed most of the population or transformed them into thirsty bloodsuckers, Price locks himself into his house at night and listens to his phonograph to drown out the creatures prowling around outside. During the day, he roams the streets with hammer and stakes in hand, destroying the sleeping creatures wherever he finds them. Unfortunately, the film fails to keep pace with Price's low-key performance, and after this impressive opening the gore becomes gratuitous and repetitive. The novel was filmed no more successfully as **The Omega Man** (1971).

Directors: Sidney Salkow, Ubaldo Ragona, *Producer:* Robert L. Lippert, *Screenplay:* Logan Swanson, William P. Leicester, *Photographer:* Franco Della Colli, *Art Director:* Giorgio Giovannini, *Music:* Paul Sawtell, Bert Shefter

Cast: Vincent Price, Franco Bettoia, Emma Danieli, Giacomo Rossi-Stuart

THE LAST WOMAN ON EARTH

Film 1960 U.S. (AIP) 71 Minutes Color
Wide Screen

While waiting out World War III in sunny
Puerto Rico, pals Harold, Evelyn and Martin emerge from a skin-diving session to find
they are alone in the world. Everyone else
has succumbed to a fall-out cloud (which evidently floated by at a supersonic speed), leaving the trio behind to ignore more pressing
problems in favor of deciding who gets to
cohabitate with the beautiful Evelyn.

Some French critics see this perfunctory
but well-photographed programmer (a high-
angle shot of a churchyard littered with
corpses is memorable) as a key work of
Roger Corman's "existentialist" period. According to Corman, "We shot the picture
in two weeks. We never knew what we were
going to do next." Writer Robert Town, who
won an **Academy Award** for *Chinatown*
(1974), played a role in the film while finishing the script.

Director/Producer: Roger Corman, *Screenplay:*
Robert Towne, *Photographer:* Jack Marquette, *Art
Director:* **Daniel Haller,** *Music:* Ronald Stein

Cast: Anthony Carbone, Betsy Jones-Moreland,
Edward Wain, Robert Towne

THE LATHE OF HEAVEN

TV film 1980 U.S. (PBS) 120 Minutes
Color

The richly woven tapestry of opalescent
imagery, moral fable and metaphysics characteristic of Ursula K. Le Guin's fiction survive with only a few threads missing in this
ambitious TV adaptation of her 1971 novel,
The Lathe of Heaven. Set in the near future,
when global pollution has melted the polar
ice caps and mankind has become an endan-
gered species, the story focusses on George
Orr, a moody young man afflicted by terrifying dreams that alter the real world—past,
present and future.

Following a suicide attempt, he visits
oneirologist Dr. William Haber, a dream
specialist, in search of a cure. Instead, Haber hypnotizes Orr and uses his unique
power to reshape the world into a **Utopia,**
free from war, disease and overpopulation.
The result is a world that is worse than
before, however. An attempt to dream away
racism, for instance, results in a devitalized
society in which everyone has the same de-
pressing gray skin, hair and eyes. Hypnotized again and again to correct the mistakes
of previous dreams, Orr begins to undermine the very foundations of human
existence. Finally, Haber, whose Mephisto-
phelian ambitions have become apparent to
Orr, builds a "dream augmenting" machine
to project his own dreams, which prove to be
empty of real ideas and cause the world to
begin to melt.

The Lathe of Heaven: Dr. Haber (Kevin
Conway) induces George Orr (Bruce
Davison) to dream about a better world.

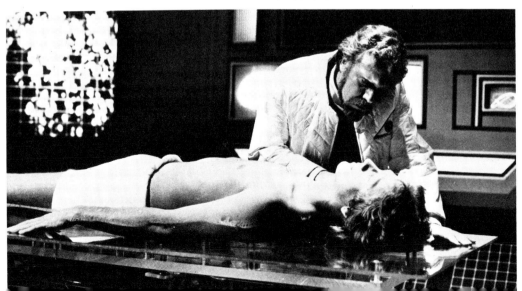

Legends of the Superheroes: The Scarlet Cyclone, now known as Retired Man, embraces Black Canary (left) and Huntress.

The juxtaposition of dream and reality, fascinating in the book—which takes place mostly in the inner space of George Orr's mind—is often confusing in the film, which nevertheless succeeds in preserving the esthetic integrity of the novel without sacrificing Le Guin's subtle warning against social and individual irresponsibility.

Directors/Producers: David R. Loxton, Fred Barzyk, *Screenplay:* Roger E. Swaybill, Diane English, *Creative Consultant:* Ursula K. Le Guin, *Photographer:* Robbie Greenberg, *Art Director:* John Wright Stevens, *Visual Consultant:* Ed Emshwiller, *Special Effects:* Gordon Blocker, Edmond S. Alexander, Jack Bennett, *Computer Graphics:* Lillian Schwartz, Charles B. Rubinstein, *Music:* Michael Small

Cast: Bruce Davison, Kevin Conway, Margaret Avery, Peyton Park, Niki Flacks, Vandi Clark, Bernedette Whitehead

LEGENDS OF THE SUPERHEROES

TV specials   1979   U.S. (NBC)   120 Minutes (2 parts)   Color

Batman and Robin got together again after an 11-year hiatus for this intermittently amusing spoof presented in two parts. "The Challenge" pitted superheros against supervillains in offbeat games of skill, and "The Roast" offered a mild battle of the wits, hosted by Ed McMahon. Batman looked more out of shape than usual but parried the insults well, abetted by sidekick Robin who seemed as fit as ever.

Directors: Chris Carley, Bill Carruthers, *Producer:* Bill Carruthers, *Screenplay:* Mike Marmor, Peter Gallay, *Art Director:* Ed Flesh, Roger Speakman, *Cast:* Warden Neil, *Special Effects:* Image West, Ltd., *Music:* Fred Werner

Cast: Batman—Adam West, *Robin*—Burt Ward, *Captain Marvel*—Garret Craig, *Hawkman*—Bill Nuckols, *The Flash*—Rod Haase, *Huntress*—Barbara Joyce, *Retired Man* (formerly *The Scarlet Cyclone*)—William Schallert, *Solomon Grundy*—Mickey Morton, *Mordu*—Gabe Dell, *Black Canary*—Danuta, *Giganta*—A'Leshia Brvard, *Dr. Sivana*—Howard Morris, *Weather Wizard*—Jeff Altman, *Sinistro*—Charlie Callas, *The Riddler*—Frank Gorshin

LIFE WITHOUT A SOUL

Film   1915   U.S. (Ocean Film Corp.)
5 reels   Black & white (silent)

The Frankenstein monster had appeared on screen once before, in Thomas Edison's **Frankenstein** (1910), but this is the first time he was played as a sympathetic, almost human character. The horror of **Mary Shelley**'s novel has been toned down in favor of "the awesome" (in the words of the film's program notes). The ending reveals that the hero had dreamed the experiment, a common pretext for SF films of the period.

Director: Joseph W. Smiley, *Producer:* George DeCarlton, *Screenplay:* Jesse J. Goldburg, *Novel:* "Frankenstein" Mary W. Shelley

Cast: William A. Cohill, Jack Hopkins, Lucy Cotton, Pauline Curley, *Monster:* Percy Darrell Standing

LIGHTSABER

The formal weapon of the **Jedi knights** in the **Star Wars** film and radio series. It is carried on the hip like a **blaster** and used in hand-to-hand combat. Deactivated, the lightsaber resembles the handgrip of a sword but is somewhat shorter and thicker, and culminates in a brightly mirrored hilt. When activated by switches built into the handgrip—which contains its working parts and power source—the weapon emits a brilliant and deadly blue-white **laser** "blade" slightly over a meter long (approx. 39½ inches), the width of a man's thumb. It can cut through stone as well as human flesh and requires great skill and instinct to use.

The lightsaber owes its inspiration to countless battle swords wielded by movie samurai warriors and swashbucklers. Special effectsman John Stears created the **laser-beam** illusion with fiberglass rods covered in **front-screen projection** material made by the 3M Company. Small motors inside the handgrips revolved the rods to give them a glowing effect, and lights reflected by a two-way mirror in front of the camera lens further increased their dazzling intensity. The blue-white color was later inserted by **animation.** During filming, actors were careful not to touch their sabers, lest the revolving action stop—a limitation apparent in the rather slow-moving dueling scenes.

LIGHT-YEAR

Unit of astronomical distance equal to the distance **light** travels in one year: approximately 6 trillion miles. The light-year is a shorthand quantity used in place of the mile, an inadequate frame of reference when expressing the vast distances of **space.** An object is one light-year away when its light take one year to reach us. (See also: **Astronomical Constants.)**

LOGAN'S RUN

Film 1976 U.S. (MGM) 120 Minutes
Metrocolor Todd-AO

Logan's Run is a film for viewers who want the sizzle without the steak. There is less going on here than meets the eye, which has a lot to feast on, including a convincing futuristic city, seemingly made of miles of glass, and some of Hollywood's most glittery gadgets. The mind is apt to go hungry, however, when faced with the illogicalities of the plot.

Adapted from the novel by William F. Nolan and George C. Johnson, the film takes place in the year 2274, when everyone lives in comfortable, climate-controlled domed cities regulated by computers. At the age of 30, all citizens are required to enter the "Carousel" for rejuvenation, actually a population-control device that results in their deaths. A number of people have escaped into the "Sanctuary" beyond the city walls. Called runners, they are pursued by Sandmen, a state police force.

Logan-5, an undercover Sandman, attempts to find the Sanctuary by making friends with Jessica-6, a girl suspected of being a rebel sympathizer. Eventually, Logan, having reached his twenty-ninth birthday, decides to make a run for it himself with Jenny, and they travel to the ruins of Washington, D.C., destroyed in a past nuclear war. There they meet an old hermit who convinces them of the emptiness of life inside the dome. Returning to the city to spread the news, Logan is greeted with indifference by everyone but the computer, which listens to the story and goes mad and destroys itself, bringing the city down with it.

Not explained is how Logan and Jenny, nurtured in a hothouse environment, manage to survive their long trek through the wilderness, or what they do for food. And the computer, described as all-knowing, somehow failed to tip itself off to a revolution gathering momentum in the underground sections of the city. **George Pal** might have made a better film, but he was replaced shortly after the production got underway by Michael Anderson, whose ponderous direction gives one time to dwell on the film's inadequacies.

The spectacular domed city was designed by Glen Robinson and Lyle B. Abbott, who won **Academy Awards** for their work, as did **matte** artist Matthew Yuricich.

Director: Michael Anderson, *Producer:* Saul David, *Screenplay:* David Z. Goodman, *Novel:* William F. Nolan, George C. Johnson, *Photographer:* Ernest Laszlo, *Production Designer:* Dale Hennessy, *Special Effects:* Lyle B. Abbott, Glen Robinson, Matthew Yuricich, *Music:* **Jerry Goldsmith**

Cast: Michael York, Jenny Agutter, Richard Jordan, Roscoe Lee Browne, Farrah Fawcett-Majors, Peter Ustinov

LOGAN'S RUN

TV film 1977 U.S. (CBS) 90 Minutes
Color

TV series   1977-78   U.S. (CBS)   60 Minutes (weekly)   Color

This TV spin-off of **Logan's Run** (1976) touched off with a long pilot episode that was essentially a rehash of the theatrical film. Episodes followed the attempts of Logan (Gregory Harrison) and girlfriend Jessica to escape from the Sandmen and find the Sanctuary, where people could live out their natural life spans. **Star Wars** (1977) had been released in the meantime, and a likeable **robot** called REM was added to the cast. The flesh-and-blood characters were poorly drawn, however, and the plots were indifferent, resulting in a brief *Logan's Run*.

Directors: Preston Ames, Robert Day and others, *Producer:* Leonard Katzman, *Executive Producers:* Ivan Goff, Ben Roberts, *Writers:* William F. Nolan, Saul David, Leonard Katzman, Ben Roberts, Ivan Goff, *Novel:* William F. Nolan, George C. Johnson, *Production Designer:* Mort Rabinowitz, *Music:* Laurence Rosenthal

Cast: Gregory Harrison, Heather Menzies, Randy Powell, Donald Moffat, Morgan Woodward

LOOKER

Film   1981   U.S. (Warner Bros.)
93 Minutes   Color

Albert Finney stars as an expensive Los Angeles plastic surgeon who specializes in turning ugly ducklings into swans. When a beautiful young woman arrives in his office and asks to have her stunning looks made absolutely perfect, he reluctantly consents, performing the operation while listening to Vivaldi. He has performed similar surgery on several other women, all of whom act in TV commercials and all of whom turn up murdered. The culprit is an international conglomerate that intends to take control of the world by broadcasting subliminal messages in TV commercials. The idea is a good one, and director/writer **Michael Crichton** brings a nice paranoid glitter to his chic, abstruse mystery.

Director/Screenplay: Michael Crichton, *Producer:* Howard Jeffrey, *Photographer:* Paul Lohmann, *Music:* Barry DeVorzon

Cast: Albert Finney, James Coburn, Susan Dey, Leigh Taylor-Young, Darryl Hickman, Dorian Harewood

LORD OF THE FLIES

Film   1963   Great Britain (Allen-Hogton/Two Arts)   91 Minutes   Black & white

Stage director Peter Brook brings all his powers to bear in this respectful adaptation of William Golding's novel, which concerns a group of English schoolboys marooned on a desert island when their plane crashlands during an unseen nuclear emergency. The boys attempt to preserve the rituals of civilization but ultimately degenerate into murderous savagery, devising a new code of conduct based on the worst excesses of public-school behavior. Golding's message, that civilization is the only barrier between mankind and his inherent brutality (a favorite **H. G. Wells** theme), is somewhat diluted by Brook's tendency for theatrical effect. But the film still manages to be both disturbing and moving, and you'll shed a tear for Piggy.

Director/Screenplay: Peter Brook, *Novel:* William Golding, *Photographers:* Tom Hollyman, Gerald Feil, *Music:* Raymond Leppard

Cast: James Aubrey, Tom Chapin, Roger Elwin, Hugh Edwards, Tom Gaman

LOST ATLANTIS

See: **L'Atlantide (1932)**

THE LOST CITY

Film serial   1935   U.S. (Regal)   12 Episodes
Black & white

A young engineer traces a series of destructive electrical storms to their source in Central Africa, where a **mad scientist** named Zolok lives in an underground "lost city." After several hours of brutal mischief, the engineer manages to free Zolok's "captive white woman" and foment a mutiny among his black zombie slaves, driving the scientist to commit suicide by throwing open his electrical switches.

Condemned at the time of release for its sadism and violence, *The Lost City* was nevertheless popular enough to turn up in a **comic book** in 1942. Seen today, the serial is interesting for its technical inventiveness and matter-of-fact racism. In one scene Zolok is described as a descendent of a "master race" of scientists; his ability to change black men into white ones warrants the comment, "This is the greatest scientific discovery yet." The serial later appeared as a 74-minute feature under the title *The City of Lost Men*.

Director: Henry Revier, *Producer:* Sherman S. Krellberg, *Screenplay:* Pereley P. Sheehan, Eddie Graneman, Leon D'Usseau, *Photographer:* Roland Price

Cast: Kane Richmond, William "Stage" Boyd, Claudia Dell, George "Gabby" Hayes, William Bletcher

THE LOST CITY OF THE JUNGLE

Film serial   1946   U.S. (Universal)
13 Episodes   Black & white

With Hiroshima and Nagasaki still a vivid memory, **mad scientist** Sir Eric Hazarias prepares for World War III by cornering the market on Meteorium 245, the only protection against the atomic **bomb**. His search leads to Pendrang, the mysterious Lost City of the Jungle, where he finds a chest that had been filled with the mineral centuries ago. While flying home, he quarrels with a henchman who accidently opens the chest and unleashes the power of the atom, bringing the nobleman's plan for world domination to an end. This forgotten **cliffhanger** anticipates a cycle of anti-bomb fantasies that began with **Five** (1951).

Directors: Ray Taylor, Lewis D. Collins, *Screenplay:* Joseph F. Poland, Tom Gibson, Paul Houston, *Photographer:* Gus Peterson

Cast: Russell Hayden, Jane Adams, Lionel Atwill, Keye Luke, Helen Bennett

THE LOST CONTINENT

Film   1968   Great Britain (Hammer)
98 Minutes   Technicolor

Passengers aboard a tramp freighter carrying an illegal cargo of dynamite steam through a hurricane that carries them to an uncharted continent in the Sargasso Sea. When not quarreling, the seedy group spends its time escaping unconvincing giant sea creatures and iron-helmeted Spanish conquistadores who live there.

The director tries to disguise a tired and aimless script with atmospheric sets and lush color photography, producing an effect akin to stale movie popcorn dosed with too much butter and salt. This *Lost Continent* is based on the novel *Uncharted Seas* (1938) by Dennis Wheatley and bears no relationship to the 1951 film of the same title.

Director/Producer: **Michael Carreras,** *Screenplay:* Michael Nash, *Photographer:* Paul Beeson, *Art Director:* Arthur Lawson, *Special Effects:* Robert A. Mattey, Cliff Richardson, *Music:* Gerard Schurmann

Cast: Eric Porter, Hildegarde Neff, Suzanna Leigh, Tony Beckley, Neil McCallum

LOURIE, EUGENE (1904–   )

Russian-born **production designer**/director/scriptwriter/special effects technician. Emigrating to Paris in 1921, Lourie studied painting and designed ballets before entering films as an art director. He collaborated on the sets of *Napoleon* (1927) for **Abel Gance** and later designed eight films for Jean Renoir, including the classics *Grand Illusion* (1937) and *The Rules of the Game* (1939). Since 1942 he has worked in Hollywood and London in various capacities.

While his production designs are of a uniformly high standard, Lourie's efforts as a director have been of varying quality. Of his five SF films, only two have transcended their low budgets and tight schedules: **The Beast from 20,000 Fathoms** (1953) and **Gorgo** (1961) [also co-screenplay]. Both take place largely at night, a Lourie signature, in a harshly lighted, eerie atmosphere that helps mask the thrifty special effects.

Other films: This Land Is Mine [as production designer] (1943), *Flight from Ashiya* (1963), *Krakatoa—East of Java* (1969), *Burnt Offerings* (1976), *Limelight* [as art director] (1952), *Shock*

Corridor (1963), *The Naked Kiss* (1964), **Crack in the World** [also special effects] (1965), *Royal Hunt of the Sun* (1969), *What's the Matter with Helen?* (1971), **The Colossus of New York** [as director] (1958), **Behemoth, the Sea Monster** (1959) [co-director, also screenplay], *An Enemy of the People* (1978).

LUCAS, GEORGE (1944–   )

Director/producer and head of Lucasfilm, a media conglomerate. Born in Modesto, California, Lucas had decided to become a racing-car driver during his high school days, but his hopes of becoming an international champion were dashed after a near-fatal crash that seriously injured his lungs. After two years as a social science major at Modesto Junior College, he entered the UCLA film school, with the help of his friend, cinematographer Haskell Wexler.

Becoming a teaching assistant, he made several short films, including *THX 1138: 4EB*, the first-prize winner of the 1965 National Student Film Festival. Chosen as one of four students to make a film about the production of *McKenna's Gold*, a major Hollywood western, he subsequently won a scholarship to observe the making of Francis Ford Coppola's *Finian's Rainbow*. Coppola hired him to assist in the production of his next film, *The Rain People*, and to make a 40-minute documentary about that film, called *Filmmaker*.

Lucas' first feature was **THX-1138** (1969), an expanded version of his student film, for which Coppola served as executive pro-ducer. In 1973 he co-wrote and directed the autobiographical *American Graffiti*, a smash hit about teenage life and rituals in California during the early 1960s. The film won the Golden Globe, the New York Film Critics' and National Society of Film Critics Awards, and it was nominated for five **Academy Awards.** Despite the success of *American Graffiti*, Lucas had difficulty in obtaining studio support for his next film, the phenomenally successful **Star Wars** (1977). His epic saga is conceived in three trilogies, of which *Star Wars*, **The Empire Strikes Back** (1980) and *The Revenge of the Jedi* (1983) are the first three parts of the third trilogy. Lucas' young space adventurer, Luke Skywalker is, of course, named after himself.

Disillusioned with the Hollywood style of filmmaking, Lucas, now one of the creative powers in the industry, set up his studio in Northern California, hundreds of miles away from the film colony. His group of companies, corporately titled Lucasfilm, produces films, books and magazines (film tie-ins). Its special effects arm, Industrial Light and Magic (ILM), often works on non-Lucas films, including **E.T., The Extra-Terrestrial** and **Star Trek II—The Wrath of Khan** (1982). During the late 1970s, Lucas entered into a film production partnership with his friend, director **Steven Spielberg.** Their first film together was **Raiders of the Lost Ark** (1981).

LUGOSI, BELA (1882–1956)

Hungarian-born actor who created the role of Count Dracula and starred in a succession of **horror** films, many with a SF setting. A tall man with an aristocratic bearing and piercing dark eyes, Lugosi was at his best portraying **mad scientists** and sadistic megalomaniacs—roles he imbued with an amoral passion that neither asked for audience sympathy nor offered any. Although his histrionics seem ludicrous today, his screen presence is as chilling as ever, and he remains Hollywood's most durable evil genius.

George Lucas

Lugosi as himself.

Born Bela Blasko, Lugosi began his career with the Royal National Theater in Budapest where he was a popular leading man of stage and silent films. After World War I he worked briefly in Germany. Arriving in New York in 1921, he was relegated to minor character parts on stage and screen until cast in the title role of *Dracula* (1927), a play that ran for a year on Broadway and two years on the road. His screen version of *Dracula* (1931)—a role originally intended for reigning horror king Lon Chaney, who died before shooting was to begin—brought him world-wide stardom and permanent identification with the seductive vampire. Earlier that year he tested as the **Frankenstein** monster in full makeup on the set of the uncompleted Dracula, but relinquished the role to an unknown named **Boris Karloff** because "no one will recognize me in that disguise." He later proved his point with an ill-at-ease impersonation of the monster in **Frankenstein Meets the Wolf Man** (1943). As Hollywood's top horror stars of the 1930s and early 1940s, Lugosi and Karloff were teamed in a number of successful features, usually as adversaries.

By the late 1940s Hollywood's first horror cycle had run its course and Lugosi's career was virtually over. Unlike Karloff he had tarnished his screen image by appearing in second-rate films that were unwitting self-parodies. And, with the exception of intentionally playing comedy with Garbo in *Ninotchka* (1939), he had never attempted to escape typecasting. In 1951 he revived the *Dracula* play in a touring production and later burlesqued the Count in a demeaning nightclub revue. Declaring himself penniless in 1954 (the result, he claimed, of his many marriages), he entered a California state hospital soon after to cure a long-term addiction to morphine. His drug-ravaged appearance was pathetically exposed in three disastrous films made in 1956. He died in August of that year and was buried, according to his wishes, in his black Dracula cape with the blood-red lining.

SF films: **Island of Lost Souls** (1932), **Murder by Television** (1935), **Shadow of Chinatown** (1936), **The Invisible Ray** (1936), **S.O.S. Coast Guard** (1937), **The Phantom Creeps** (1939), **Son of Frankenstein** (1939), **Black Friday** (1940), **The Ghost of Frankenstein** (1942), **Frankenstein Meets the Wolf Man** (1943), **Return of the Ape Man** (1944), **Abbott and Costello Meet Frankenstein** (1948), **Bride of the Monster** (1956), **Gravediggers from Outer Space** (1956)

LA LUNE A UN METRE

(Also titled: *The Man in the Moon* and *The Astronaut's Dream*)

Film   1898   France (Star)   195 Feet   Color (silent)

The Man in the Moon descends to Earth and pays a call on a napping scientist. An early fantasy by special effects innovator **Georges Melies,** this hand-tinted short presages his famous **Une Voyage dans la Lune** (1902). It is based on his magic spectacle, *The Moon's Pranks or the Misadventures of Nostrodamus,* presented at his Paris theater in 1891.

Director/Producer/Writer/Special Effects: Georges Melies

MACROPHOTOGRAPHY

The filming of small objects in extreme close-up to create the illusion of largeness onscreen. To make the shot the camera lens is fitted with an extension called a macro lens, which is capable of such tight focus that a tiny object can be registered on film in its actual size. The screen can thus be filled with an object the size of a person's thumbnail. In **Tarantula** (1955) and **The Incredible Shrinking Man** (1957), for instance, the technique was used to enlarge live spiders, made to move on cue with jets of compressed air. Special effects man Clifford Stine staged the battle between man and insect in both films by combining separately filmed footage with the **split-screen** and **matte** techniques. In **2001: A Space Odyssey** (1968), the immense swirling galaxies visited by the spaceship Discovery were actually chemical dyes squeezed between three-inch glass slides and photographed with a powerful close-up lens.

MAD LOVE

(Great Britain title: *The Hands of Orlac*)

Film 1935 U.S. (MGM) 83 Minutes Black & white

Horror star Peter Lorre made his American debut in this macabre remake of **Orlacs Hande/The Hands of Orlac** (1924), directed by Karl Freund, the photographer of *Dracula* (1931). Lorre is Dr. Gogol, a surgeon who grafts a new pair of hands on concert pianist Stephen Orlac (Colin Clive, formerly Dr. **Frankenstein),** who has lost his own in a rail-

way accident. In love with the pianist's wife, Gogol attempts to drive Orlac mad by revealing that the hands belonged to a guillotined killer and masquerading as the dead man come back to life, wearing a pair of grotesque metal gloves. At the finale, Orlac rescues his wife from the crazed surgeon by practicing his inherited skill as a knife thrower.

Director: Karl Freund, *Producer:* John W. Considine, Jr., *Screenplay:* Guy Endore, P. J. Wolfson, John Balderston, *Novel: "Les mains d'Orlac"* Maurice Renard, *Photographer:* Chester Lyons, Gregg Toland, *Music:* Dimitri Tiomkin

Cast: Peter Lorre, Colin Clive, Frances Drake, Isabel Jewell, Ted Healy, Keye Luke, Sara Haden

THE MADNESS OF DOCTOR TUBE

See: **La Folie du Docteur Tube**

THE MAGNETIC MONSTER

Film 1953 U.S. (United Artists)
75 Minutes Black & white

Created in a laboratory, a new radioactive element begins to grow by consuming energy, doubling its deadly radiation every 12 hours from surrounding objects, until it threatens to engulf a nearby community. The element is finally neutralized in a cyclotron. The uncinematic idea (there is nothing to show) might have worked better as a novel. The endless descriptions are finally relieved by the exciting laboratory explosion from **Gold,** a German film made in 1934.

Director: **Curt Siodmak,** *Producer:* Ivan Tors, *Screenplay:* Curt Siodmak, Ivan Tors, *Photographer:* Charles Van Enger, *Special Effects:* Jack Glass, *Music:* Blaine Sanford

Cast: **Richard Carlson,** King Donovan, Jean Byron, Strother Martin

MALLA

Wife of **Chewbacca,** the temperamental Wookie anthropoid of the **Star Wars** series.

Malla

Malla, son Lumpy and grandfather Itchy were introduced on *The Star Wars Holiday Special,* a two-hour TV program aired by CBS on November 17, 1978. The television Wookies were fabricated by makeup artist Stan Winston after **Stuart Freeborn's** original design.

THE MANCHURIAN CANDIDATE

Film   1962   U.S. (United Artists)
126 Minutes   Black & white

Chinese communist doctors program a brainwashed American prisoner of war in Korea to assassinate the President of the U.S. They send him back home where his "control" turns out to be his own mother, a communist agent posing as a political conservative. She triggers his murderous impulse at a crowded election rally in Madison Square Garden for a shattering, unexpected climax. Wittily adapted from Richard Condon's best-selling novel by George Axelrod and directed with breathless precision by **John Frankenheimer,** the film is a thinking man's thriller blended with equal parts black comedy and political satire. Both the American Legion and the Communist Party denounced the film, prompting Frankenheimer to explain that "the whole point . . . was the absurdity of any type of extremism, left or right." It also proved to be an uncanny forecast of President Kennedy's death a year later, as well as the nationwide paranoia engendered by the Nixon White House.

Director: John Frankenheimer, *Producer:* Howard W. Koch, *Screenplay:* George Axelrod, *Novel:* Richard Condon, *Photographer:* Lionel Lindon, *Production Designer:* Richard Sylbert, *Music:* David Amram

Cast: Laurence Harvey, Frank Sinatra, Janet Leigh, Angela Lansbury, James Gregory, Henry Silva

MANDEM DER TAENKTE TING

(U.S. title: *The Man Who Thought Life*)

Film   1969   Denmark (Asa/Palladium)
97 Minutes   Black & white

This fanciful Danish farce concerns a man who can imagine people and objects into existence by a simple act of concentration. Unable to create anything larger than mice, he visits a prominent surgeon for an operation on his brain to fully release his powers. The surgeon sends him away, and in retaliation, the insulted man materializes an exact duplicate of the doctor. More charming and skilled than the original, the copy edges the doctor out of his own life and takes over his practice and fiancee. He performs the operation, but bungles it and his creator dies. The film, handsomely mounted, has a thought-provoking inner logic that challenges traditional human concepts of reality.

Director: Jens Ravn, *Screenplay:* Henrik Stangerup, *Novel:* Valdemar Holst, *Photographer:* Witold Leszcynski, *Production Designer:* Helge Refn

Cast: Preben Neergaard, John Price, Lotte Tarp

THE MAN FROM MARS

See: **Radio-mania**

THE MAN FROM PLANET X

Film   1951   U.S. (United Artists)
70 Minutes   Black & white

Directed with a characteristic visual elan by the dauntless **Edgar Ulmer,** this low-budget item concerns a short **alien** who arrives on a Scottish island wearing a glass bubble over his outsized head. Armed with a mind-control ray, he attempts to assemble an army of mindless humans to prepare for a massive invasion. *Planet X* was released shortly before **The Thing,** which ushered in the cinema's **alien invasion** cycle.

Director: Edgar Ulmer, *Producers:* Brey Wisberg, Jack Pollexfen, *Screenplay:* Aubrey Wisberg, Jack Pollexfen, *Photographer:* John L. Russell, *Art Director:* Angelo Scibetti, *Special Effects:* Andy Anderson, Howard Weeks, *Music:* Charles Koff

Cast: Robert Clarke, William Schallert, Margaret Field, Raymond Bond, Roy Engel

THE MAN FROM THE PAST

See: **Muz z Prvniho Stolete**

THE MAN IN THE WHITE SUIT

Film   1951   Great Britain (Ealing)
81 Minutes   Black & white

Alec Guinness is a whirlwind of comic invention as a naive young chemist who invents an indestructable synthetic fiber impervious to soil and wear. Sporting an iridescent white suit made of the fibers, he finds himself pursued into a blind alley by a gang of textile manufacturers and factory workers, who are understandably upset at the thought of being put out of business. Mother nature comes to his rescue with a downpour that dissolves the suit, water being the one test the fiber was not subjected to since it never needed to be washed. At the fade-out Guinness is back at work in his lab,

a fanatical gleam in his eye, as he attempts to work out the snag in the formula.

Director: Alexander Mackendrick, *Producer:* Sidney Cole, *Screenplay:* Roger Mackendrick, Alexander Mackendrick, John Dighton, *Photographer:* Douglas Slocombe, *Music:* Benjamin Frankel

Cast: Alec Guinness, Joan Greenwood, Vida Hope, Cecil Parker, Ernest Thesinger, Michael Gough

THE MAN WHO FELL TO EARTH

Film   1976   Great Britain (British Lion)
138 Minutes   Color   Panavision

David Bowie is perfectly cast as an **extraterrestrial** who comes to **Earth** to earn enough money to build a spaceship and save his wife and children from their dying world. His clever inventions earn him a fortune, but they also attract human sharks, who attempt to steal his money and frame him for murder. In the process, his catlike eyes are damaged, preventing him from returning to his home planet. He is last seen sitting in a cafe, a lonely outsider, drinking himself into forgetfullness. Based on the novel by Walter Tevis, the film is often stunningly beautiful and always fascinating.

Director: Nicholas Roeg, *Screenplay:* Paul Mayersberg, *Novel:* Walter Tevis, *Photographer:* Anthony Richmond, *Makeup:* Linda De Vetta, *Special Effects:* Harrison Ellenshaw, *Musical Director:* John Phillips

Cast: David Bowie, Rip Torn, Candy Clark, Buck Henry

THE MAN WHO LIVED AGAIN

(Also titled: *The Brainsnatchers/Dr. Maniac/The Man Who Changed His Mind*)

Film   1936   Great Britain (Gaumont)
65 Minutes   Black & white

Rarely screened, this minor opus is one of a number of **horror** films made by British studios with American stars during the 1930s. **Boris Karloff** is a mad genius who discovers a method of transposing human psyches from one brain to another by means of an electric current. Labeled a charlatan by fellow scientists, he makes plans to switch identities with a handsome young associate to prove the device works and also to marry the man's fiancee, with whom he has fallen in love.

Director: **Robert Stevenson,** *Screenplay:* L. Du-Garde Peach, Sidney Gilliat, *Photographer:* Jack Cox, *Makeup:* Roy Ashton

Cast: Boris Karloff, Anna Lee, John Loder, Cecil Parker

THE MAN WHO THOUGHT LIFE

See: **Mandem Der Taenkte Ting**

THE MAN WITH THE X-RAY EYES

See: **"X" The Man With The X-Ray Eyes**

MAROONED

Film   1969   U.S. (Columbia)   134 Minutes   Technicolor   Panavision

John Sturges' expertise as an action director isn't apparent in this dull space disaster movie, which was wiped out by the exhaust of **2001: A Space Odyssey,** released the year before. Played by a stellar cast with the dramatic vigor of a NASA press conference, the story concerns three astronauts whose space capsule malfunctions during a mission to test human endurance in space. They ultimately return to **Earth,** much to the relief of their loving families, who provide the subplots. The impressive special effects, staged in documentary style by Robbie Robertson, won an **Academy Award.**

Director: John Sturges, *Producer:* M. J. Frankovich, *Screenplay:* Mayo Simon, *Novel:* **Martin Caidin,** *Photographer:* Daniel Fapp, *Production Designer:* Lyle R. Wheeler, *Special Effects:* Robbie Robertson, Lawrence W. Butler, Donald C. Glouner

Cast: Gregory Peck, Richard Crenna, David Janssen, James Franciscus, Gene Hackman, Lee Grant, **Scott Brady**

M.A.R.S.

See: **Radio-mania**

MARS CALLING

See: **Radio-mania**

THE MASK OF FU MANCHU

Film   1932   U.S. (MGM)   70 Minutes   Black & white

Boris Karloff is just right as Sax Rohmer's malevolent scientific genius Fu Manchu, head of a Chinese tong dedicated to enslaving the white races of the world. Twirling his dangling mustache, Karloff gleefully eliminates troublemakers with a number of imaginately fiendish tortures devised with the help of his equally nasty daughter, played by Myrna Loy. The pair attempt to steal a death mask and sword once owned by Ghenghis Khan to use as symbols to foment a race war. But the plan fails, and Fu suffers a spectacular demise when his **death-ray** machine blows up. The striking sets are the work of Cedric Gibbons, art director of **Forbidden Planet** (1956); the electrical effects are by Ken Strickfaden, creator of the coils and sparks of **Frankenstein** (1931).

Directors: Charles Brabin, Charles Vidor, *Producer:* Irving Thalberg, *Screenplay:* Irene Kuhn, Edgar Allan Woolf, John Willard, *Stories:* Sax Rohmer, *Photographer:* Tony Gaudio, *Art Director:* Cedric Gibbons, *Electrical Effects:* Ken Strickfaden

Cast: Boris Karloff, Myrna Loy, Jean Hersholt, Karen Morley, Lewis Stone

MASTER OF THE WORLD

Film   1961   U.S. (AIP)   104 Minutes   Magnacolor

Nominally based on the **Jules Verne** novel *Master of the World* (1904), this film is essentially a rehash of the plot of Disney's **20,000 Leagues Under the Sea** (1954). Like Captain Nemo, Robur the Conquerer is a master inventor who hates war, the difference being that Robur travels in a mammoth flying machine rather than in an atomic-powered submarine.

   Driven mad by his quest for world peace, Robur attempts to disarm the countries of the world by bombing their armaments and armies, a plan that predictably fails when an undercover agent sneaks aboard the craft and plants a cache of explosives.

Although the script is serviceable, the film is undermined by a contrived performance by **Vincent Price** as Robur and the inclusion of grainy, anachronistic footage (an aerial shot of London c. 1860 was lifted from Laurence Olivier's 1944 film, *Henry V*). Robur's ship the *Albatross* is impressive, however, a futuristic airship constructed from a Victorian point of view.

Director: **William Witney,** *Producer:* James H. Nicholson, *Screenplay:* **Richard Matheson,** *Photographer:* Gil Warrenton, *Special Effects:* Ray Mercer, Tim Barr, Wah Chong, Gene Warren, *Music:* Lex Baxter

Cast: Vincent Price, Charles Bronson, Mary Webster, Henry Hull, Vito Scotti

MATHESON, RICHARD (BURTON) (1926–   )

Writer of imaginative SF-**horror** stories, screenplays and TV scripts. Born in New Jersey, Matheson was graduated with a journalism degree from the University of Missouri. He entered films by writing the screenplay for **The Incredible Shrinking Man** (1957), based on his 1956 novel of the same title. His previous novel (his first), *I Am Legend* (1954), was filmed twice, as **The Last Man on Earth** (1964) and **The Omega Man** (1971). Film scripts include *The Fall of the House of Usher* (1960), **Master of the World** (1961), *Die, Die, My Darling* (1965), *The Legend of Hell House* [based on his novel *Hell House*] (1971). TV credits: **The Twilight Zone** (1959-64), **Star Trek** (1966-69), *Night Gallery* (1970-73), **Duel** (1971), **The Night Stalker** (1972), **The Night's Strangler** (1973), **Kolchak: The Night Stalker** (1974-75), **The Stranger Within** (1974).

MATTER TRANSMISSION

Much-used SF idea that matter can be instantly converted into energy and trans-mitted through space, then reconstituted by a receiver; also called beaming. Movie dabblers in matter transmission often suffer unexpected consequences, as was the case in **The Fly** (1958), whose hero scrambled himself with a wandering insect while attempting a short jaunt. In **Star Trek,** the procedure is accomplished in a **Transporter Room** that holds up to six people and needs no receiver. A similar device later turned up in the British TV series **Blake's Seven** (1978-79). SF writers use the imaginary process as a means of traveling the vast distances of space. The idea is occasionally used humorously as in Bob Shaw's novel *Who Goes Here?* (1977), in which a spacecraft thrusts forward through itself by means of a receiver and matter transmitter placed, respectively, fore and aft.

MATTE

A masking device used to block a portion of a photographed image, either in the camera or in an optical printer. A second scenic element can then be photographed in the unexposed portion of the film. Mattes can be cut-out forms of cardboard or metal, but more often they are photographic images on film, as in the traveling process, explained in the drawing. Mattes are essential of his striking visuals in the Korda remake of *The Thief of Bagdad*, released in the U.S. the following year. He continued to design major Hollywood productions until the late 1940s, when his style came to be considered artificial and dated. Relegated to directing and designing low-budget programmers and SF chillers (his personal favorites), he turned in his usual first-rate job but failed to re-establish his reputation. His later films include *The Whip Hand* (1951), **Invaders from Mars** and *The Maze* (both 1953). He returned to mainstream filmmaking as the associate producer of *Around the World in 80 Days* (1956), an all-star extravaganza based on the **Jules Verne** novel and filmed in Todd-AO, one of a number of **wide-screen** processes being developed at the time. He died the following year.

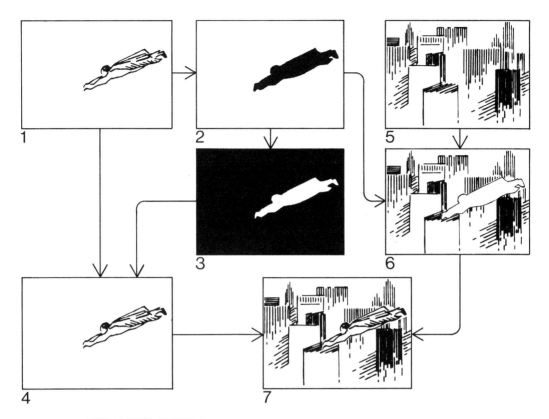

THE MATTE SYSTEM
How it works

To place Superman against the skyline of Manhattan, actor Christopher Reeve is filmed in a flying position against a blue screen (1). A matte is made of this footage (2), in which the actor's silhouette is blacked out and the background is left clear. This removes the blue background. Next, a counter-matte is made (3), producing an opaque background and a clear portion outlining Reeve's silhouette. Matte No. 2 is printed over a shot of the Manhattan skyline (5) to produce an unexposed outline of Reeve (6). The shot of Reeve with his hands and feet outstretched is then printed into the unexposed "hole" on an optical printer for the composite picture (7).

A MESSAGE FROM MARS

Film   1913   Great Britain (U.K. Films)
45 Minutes (approx.)   Black & white (silent)

As punishment for a misdeed, a Martian clad in a medieval Robin Hood costume is sent to **Earth** to rescue a human being from the sin of selfishness. He converts a worthy subject with a display of the poverty and suffering of mankind and returns to **Mars** absolved. Although intended as a morality tale, this early fantasy film introduced the **alien invasion** theme to the screen. (A later generation of visitors from outer space would be less benign.) Based on a remarkably long-running play written by Richard Ganthony in 1899, *A Message from Mars* was shot in the London theater where it was being performed. A shorter version of the play was previously filmed in New Zealand in 1909, but all prints have since been lost. In 1921 a longer version was filmed by Hollywood's Metro Pictures, which set the story in the context of a dream. It was directed by Maxwell Karger and starred Bert Lytell and Alphonz Ethier.

Director/Screenplay: J. Wallett Waller, *Producer:* Nicholson Ormsby-Scott, *Play:* Richard Ganthony

Cast: Charles Hawtrey, E. Holman Clark, Chrissie Bell, Hubert Willis

MESSAGE FROM SPACE

See: **Uchu Kara No Messeji**

METEOR

Film   1979   U.S. (AIP)/Europe (Warner
Bros.)/Asia (Shaw)   107 Minutes   Movielab
Panavision

This international co-production was conceived as a prefab hit by two American studios and Sir Run Run Shaw, the Hong
Kong-based Eurasian producer of countless
kung-fu movies. It was "suggested" by an
Isaac Asimov magazine article about the
very real possibility of a **meteoroid** striking
Earth—which pretty much describes the
film's plot.

The prefab formula involved assembling
a cast of top stars, staging the worst disasters
ever, some in space, and watching the profits
roll in. Top special effects man Glen Robinson, who had previously destroyed Los Angeles for *Earthquake* (1974), was hired to
stage the destructions of New York City,
Hong Kong, a Swiss ski resort, Siberia, and,
finally, the meteor, which is blasted out of
space with orbiting nuclear warheads.

It took so long to make the film that by
the time of its release the disaster cycle had
peaked. Moreover, director Ronald Neame
showed none of the flair that had made *The
Poseidon Adventure* (1972) so enjoyable, and
the actors seemed bewildered without characters to play. *Meteor* missed by a mile and
soared off into cable television, taking with
it a small fortune. (See also: **Apollo Objects.**)

Director: Ronald Neame, *Producers:* Arnold Or-
golini, Theodore Parvin, *Screenplay:* Stanley
Mann, Edmund H. North, *Photographer:* Paul
Lohmann, *Production Designer:* Edward Carfagno,
Special Effects: Glen Robinson, Robert Staples,
Music: Laurence Rosenthal

Cast: **Sean Connery,** Natalie Wood, Karl Malden,
Brian Keith, Martin Landau, Henry Fonda,
Trevor Howard

METEOROIDS

Cosmic debris, probably fragments of **asteroids** or spent **comets,** which orbit the sun
at speeds of thousands of miles per hour.
They range in size from dust particles to solid
chunks of rock and metal weighing hundreds of tons or more. When a meteoroid
enters the Earth's atmosphere, its friction
causes it to heat up and glow with light.
Technically, the meteoroid is then called a
meteor; the portion that strikes **Earth** is
called a meteorite. Most burn up before they
reach the ground, but some have collided
with tremendous force, as evidenced by the
Barrington crater in Arizona, which is 4,000
feet wide and 600 feet deep. The possibility of a similar collision was dealt with in
the film **Meteor** (1979). (See also: **Apollo
Objects.**)

Meteor: A space probe
reconnoiters a five-mile-
wide meteor.

METROPOLIS

Film 1926 Germany (UFA) 128 Minutes
Black & white (silent)

Its plot is hopelessly dated and burdened with naive Victorian cant, but this seminal SF film retains much of its visual power—a testimony to director Fritz Lang's exceptional gifts for atmospheric detail and pictorial design. The story, an allegorical vision of the conflict between capital and labor, takes place in the year 2000 in Metropolis, a technologically advanced, automated city where capitalists live in above-ground luxury and workers toil in dehumanized underground factories. When the son of an industrialist becomes romantically involved with the virginal Maria, guardian of the workers' children, his annoyed father hires a **mad scientist** named Rottwang to create a **robot** duplicate of the girl. The false Maria does a sensuous dance in front of the workers and eventually incites them to destroy their underground homes. But the young man unmasks the false Maria and she is burned at the stake, her plastic flesh melting from her lovely face.

An epoch-making production, *Metropolis* was the most expensive and ambitious film made in Europe up to that time, and it marks a giant step forward for special effects. Lang's fantastic megapolis (inspired by a trip to New York) was an intricate miniature set given a monumental look by the use of forced perspective, an illusion that involves constructing background buildings on a smaller scale to make them seem more distant than they are. Believability was further enhanced by the intricate detailing of the miniatures and tiny cars and airplanes that moved through the skyscraper corridors. To place live actors into the miniatures, cameraman **Eugen Schufftan** came up with a new technique called the **Schufftan Process,** which reflected their images into doorways with an artfully placed semitransparent to special effects, allowing the creation of imaginary scenes by combining background, live action and miniatures into one composite image.

Director: Fritz Lang, *Producer:* Erich Pommer, *Screenplay:* Fritz Lang, Thea von Harbou, *Photographer:* **Karl Freund,** Gunther Rittau, *Art Directors:* Otto Hunte, Erich Kettlehut, Karl Vollbrecht, *Special Effects:* Eugen Schufftan

Cast: **Brigitte Helm,** Alfred Abel, Gustav Froehlich, Rudolf Klein-Rogge

MECHANICAL BUTCHER SHOP

See: **Charcuterie Mecanique**

MECHANOIDS

Mechanical creatures featured on the BBC-TV series **Doctor Who.** Originally created by human scientists, they eventually developed a consciousness of their own and established a civilization on the planet Mechanus. Mechanoids resemble the squat-shaped **Daleks** (but are more mobile), whom they confronted in a mutually devastating battle when an army of Daleks inadvertently chased Doctor Who to Mechanus.

MELIES, GEORGES (1861–1938)

French filmmaker and special effects pioneer. Born in Paris, Melies was a professional stage magician who first became interested in motion pictures to use in his magic act. He invented such new techniques as the **dissolve**—a double-exposed transition of the end of one scene over the beginning of the other—the fade-in and fade-out to suggest the passage of time, and a rudimentary **matte** to combine scenic elements into one piece of film. Most of his fantasy films had to do with disappearances and transformations, accomplished by **stop-motion** photography. To make a woman disappear from the screen, for instance, Melies simply stopped the camera and had her step out of camera range before starting it again. Similarly, the flesh of a man could be made to dissolve from his bones by overlapping shots of an actor, a medical school dummy and a skeleton. The technique was used a generation later in **The Invisible Man** (1933).

In 1897 Melies built France's first film studio and founded Europe's first film company. By 1920, after making more than 700 films, his trick fantasies had gone out of style, and in 1923 he went bankrupt. Virtually forgotten by the industry he had helped to create, he sold many of his films to a scrap dealer to be melted down and used in the manufacture of shoes. He vanished into obscurity until 1929, when French director Rene Clair found him selling toys in a railway station with one of his former stars, now his wife.

A retrospective was put together from a cache of films found in the U.S. Melies, his contribution at last acknowledged, was given a rent-free apartment, where he lived for the rest of his life. In 1952 George Franju made a film of his life, *Le Grand Melies*. Since then several more of Melies' films have been discovered, many of which were included in a 29-film retrospective shown in 1982 on Telefrance USA, a cable television network. The short films were adapted to video with a "magnasynch videola," a device that shows silent films at their original speeds while preserving technical quality.

Films include: La Boite mysterieuse/The Mysterious Box (1898), *L'Affaire Dreyfus/The Dreyfus Case* (1899), **Le Voyage dans la lune/A Trip to the Moon** (1902), *Deux Cent Milles Lieues sous les mers/20,000 Leagues Under the Sea, Le Tunnel sous la manche/The Tunnel Under the English Channel* (1907), *New York-Paris en automobile* (1908), **La Conquete du Pole** (1912)

MENZIES, WILLIAM CAMERON (1896–1957)

Pioneer film production designer and occasional director whose versatile pictorial gifts illuminate several vintage SF features. Called "the greatest visual talent to work in films," Menzies specialized in creating elaborate cinematic atmospheres for fantasies and historical epics. His films are characterized by a visual rhetoric that is a dramatic element in itself.

Menzies trained as an illustrator at Yale in his home town of New Haven, Connecticut, and studied at Manhattan's Art Students League after returning from army

service in Europe during World War I. At the age of 21 he was hired by New York's Famous Players studio to help art director Anton Grot create a cardboard mock-up of the inside of the Taj Mahal for a film titled *The Naulaka* (1918). Under Grot's tutelage he learned to use the full dimensions of the

film frame, and to force perspective (see: **forced perspective**) to give an illusion of depth and width. He also absorbed the techniques of German filmmakers of the period (see: **expressionism**), who impressed him with their stylized, highly contrasted lighting effects and unusual camera angles.

MIDDLETON, CHARLES (1879–1949)

Character actor remembered for his portrayals of screen villains, notably as Ming the Merciless in the **Flash Gordon** serials. Draped in majestic splendor, his serpentine eyebrows arched in dark fury, he was ev-

Charles Middleton as Ming the Merciless, archfoe of Flash Gordon.

ery inch the emperor of the planet Mongo—the would-be ruler of the universe if not for the pure-minded Flash. Born in Elizabethtown, Kentucky, Middleton was a circus and vaudeville performer before entering films in the late 1920s. He appeared in more than 100 features and **serials,** including *Duck Soup* (1933), with the Marx Brothers, *Show Boat* (1936), *The Flying Deuces* (1939), with Laurel and Hardy, and *The Grapes of Wrath* (1940).

SF serials: **The Miracle Rider** (1935), **Flash Gordon, Flash Gordon's Trip to Mars, Dick Tracy Returns** (1938), **Flash Gordon Conquers the Universe** (1940), **Batman** (1943), **Jack Armstrong** (1947)

MILLENIUM FALCON

A battered **Corellian** pirate spaceship shaped like a flying saucer and piloted by **Han Solo** and **Chewbacca** in the **Star Wars** series. Used primarily to smuggle contraband, the Millenium Falcon has been modified by Solo into one of the galaxy's fastest vehicles and can easily outrace Imperial patrol ships, even through **hyperspace.** Equipped with deflector shields and weaponry, it is also a superior fighter. In the final battle against the **Death Star** in **Star Wars** (1977), the Millenium Falcon manages to disable **Darth Vader**'s **T.I.E. Fighter** and save **Luke Skywalker's** life.

The two Falcons built to perform these wonders include a full-scale mock-up that weighs 23 tons and measures 80 feet in diameter, and a miniature that weighs 30 pounds and measures four feet across. The latter model journeys through space via a computerized support that twists and turns a computerized camera (see: **motion control).** The star background, **asteroids,** fighters and other elements of the scene are added later via an **optical printer.**

THE MIRACLE RIDER

Film serial   1935   U.S. (Mascot)
15 Episodes   Black & white

Treacherous oil barons threaten to take over an Indian reservation rich with deposits of X-94, an exotic form of T.N.T., until van-

quished by a cowboy "miracle rider" who is an official member of the tribe. Villain Zaroff, who attempts to spook the Indians into submission with a magnetic ray and a remote-controlled glider, is played by a muted **Charles Middleton,** better known as Ming the Merciless in the **Flash Gordon** serials. Western star Tom Mix retired from the screen after this clinker.

Directors: Armand Schaefer, B. Reeves Eason, *Producer:* Victor Zobel, *Screenplay:* John Rathmell

Cast: Tom Mix, Jean Gale, Charles Middleton, Jason Robards, Edward Hearn

MISSION STARDUST

Film   1968   Italy/Germany (Times Films)
95 Minutes   Color

Pulp **space opera** hero Perry Rhodan heads a private space expedition that makes a forced landing on the moon, where he gets involved with a beautiful **alien**-in-distress and a group of rebellious **robots.** Rhodan, who has become an international cult favorite since his birth in Germany in 1961 (the stories are written by a team of writers), deserves a better cinematic fate than this weak-hearted attempt at sexy space whimsey. Read the books.

Director: Primo Zeglio, *Screenplay:* K. H. Vogelman, Frederico d'Urritia, *Music:* Anton Garcia Abril

Cast: Lang Jeffries, Essy Persson, Luis Davilla, Daniel Martin

MR. SPOCK

Science Officer of the **U.S.S. Enterprise** and second in command to **Captain Kirk.** Born of a **Vulcan** father and a mother from **Earth,** Mr. Spock has the characteristic pointy ears, raised eyebrows and yellowish skin of Vulcans (their blood is green, being copper-based). Raised on the planet Vulcan, he is proud of his heritage and thinks of himself as a Vulcan rather than as a human being. Gifted with superior intelligence and strength and unusual powers (like all Vulcans), Spock is capable of processing large amounts of data and handling most emergencies that arise on the **starship** with his cool logic. He suppresses his emotional, human side, but it occasionally emerges, usually in an act of kindness toward poor confused, fear-ridden, emotion-torn human beings. Probably the most popular character in *Star Trek,* Mr. Spock is played to perfection by **Leonard Nimoy.**

MR. TERRIFIC

TV series 1967 U.S. (CBS) 30 Minutes (weekly) Color

ABC's campy reprise of **Batman** (1966-68) inspired CBS to come up with Mr. Terrific, a caped crusader who was even clumsier than his prototype. Meek filling station attendant Stanley Beamish became a reluctant superhero when government scientists concocted a "power pill" and found he was the only person it worked on. The pill worked for about an hour (a second dose extended its range by 20 minutes), setting the stage for absent-minded Stanley to forget about the time and find himself up to his ears in criminals when his superpowers suddenly vanished.

Mr. Terrific is often confused with **Captain Nice,** an NBC series that debuted on the same night. With the exception of backgrounds and costumes (Mr. Terrific's was flashier), the programs were nearly the same. Both had the effect of embarassing viewers, and both died after one prime-time season. (See also: **The Greatest American Hero.**)

Cast: Stephen Strimpell, Dick Gautier, John McGiver, Paul Smith

THE MISTRESS OF ATLANTIS

See: **L'Atlantide (1932)**

THE MOLE PEOPLE

Film 1956 U.S. (Universal-International) 78 Minutes Black & white

Members of a scientific expedition to Tibet fall through the ceiling of an underground kingdom called Sumeria, unearthing light-sensitive mole people enslaved by human albinos. They try to escape, and so will you.

Director: Virgil Vogel, *Producer:* William Alland, *Screenplay:* Laszlo Gorog, *Photographer:* Ellis Carter, *Special Effects:* **Clifford Stine,** *Makeup:* Wally Westmore

Cast: **John Agar,** Nestor Paiva, Alan Napier, Cynthia Patrick, Eddie Parker

THE MONITORS

Film 1969 U.S. (Commonwealth) 90 Minutes Color

A dodo of a film, *The Monitors* groans under the weight of its trendy plumage as it struggles to soar to new heights of comedy. Made in Chicago by the Second City comedy group when hippie power was in full flower, it tries to send up everything in sight and nearly gives itself a hernia in the process. The monitors of the title—**aliens** dressed in black overcoats, hats and sunglasses—are metaphoric drug dealers who promise spaced-out bliss with a whiff of a mood-altering gas.

Director: Jack Shea, *Producer:* Bernard Sahlins, *Screenplay:* Myron Gold, *Novel:* Keith Laumer, *Photographer:* **Vilmos Zsigmond**

Cast: Guy Stockwell, Susan Oliver, Sherry Jackson, Avery Schreiber, Alan Arkin, Keenan Wynn, Xavier Cugat, Larry Storch, Ed Begley, Shepperd Strudwick

THE MONOLITH MONSTERS

Film 1957 U.S. (Universal-International) 77 Minutes Black & white

Alien spores carried to Earth on a meteorite spring to life near a small town in the American southwest, turning to stone anyone who touches them. Geologists determine the spores are a silicon-based life-form that feed and grow by absorbing water and silicon contained in human tissues. During a rainstorm, the creatures swell to the size of monolithic skyscrapers and slowly move toward the town in thundering steps: the forward wall drops its summit, which promptly springs up to drop *its* summit, and so on.

When the authorities discover that salt water will neutralize the rocks, they dynamite a nearby dam conveniently erected above an ancient sea bed.

Its illogicalities aside, *The Monolith Monsters* has a number of effective scenes that lift it from the standard "monster-from-space" category. Clifford Stine's marching monoliths are frightening to behold, and the stark desert settings—similar to the films of co-story writer **Jack Arnold**—are eerily effective.

Director: John Sherwood, *Producer:* Howard Christie, *Screenplay:* Norman Jolley, Robert M. Fresco, *Story:* Jack Arnold, Robert M. Fesco, *Art Director:* **Alexander Golitzen,** *Special Effects:* Clifford Stine, *Music:* Joseph Gershenson

Cast: Grant Williams, Lola Albright, Trevor Bardette, Les Tremayne

THE MONSTER

Film   1925   U.S. (MGM)   Black & white (silent)

A comedy thriller about a scientist who sets a trap on a road near his laboratory to capture human specimens for an experiment in bringing the dead back to life. A vehicle for star Lon Chaney, who sends up his portrayal of a **mad scientist** in **A Blind Bargain** (1922).

Director/Producer: Roland West, *Screenplay:* Willard Mack, Albert Kenyon, *Photographer:* Hal Mohr

Cast: Lon Chaney, Gertrude Olmstead, Hallam Cooley

THE MONSTER AND THE APE

Film serial   1945   U.S. (Columbia)
15 Episodes   Black & white

Enemy agents with a trained ape attempt to steal a top-secret American weapon: a **robot** "monster" powered by "metalogen" metal. **Ray "Crash" Corrigan,** star of Republic's far superior **Undersea Kingdom** (1936), is hiding inside the monkey suit.

Director: Howard Bretherton, *Producer:* Rudolph C. Flothow, *Screenplay:* Sherman L. Lowe, Royal K. Cole, *Photographer:* C. W. O'Connell, *Music:* Lee Zahler

Cast: Robert Lowery, George Macready, Ralph Morgan, Eddie Parker, Ray "Crash" Corrigan

MONSTER FROM THE OCEAN FLOOR

Film   1954   U.S. (Lippert)   64 Minutes
Black & white

A team of aquanauts rams a submarine into the Cyclopean eye of an oversized squid foolish enough to flip a few tentacles at cargo ships passing overhead. *Monster From the Ocean Floor's* special effects might charitably be called primitive, but they were passable enough to earn the film $110,000 on an $11,000 investment—and launch the career of **Roger Corman.**

Director: Wyott Ordung, *Producer:* Roger Corman, *Screenplay:* William Danch, *Photographer:* Floyd Crosby, *Music:* Andre Brumer

MOONRAKER

Film   1979   Great Britain (United Artists)
126 Minutes   Color   Panavision   Dolby Stereo

Not one to be outdone by **Luke Skywalker** and company, **James Bond** soared into space for his 11th movie outing—his first full SF adventure. This time out the villain is the elegant Hugo Drax, who steals a NASA space shuttle to transport "boy and girl lovers" to a secret space station orbiting **Earth.** At an opportune moment, he plans to drop a lethal microbe into the atmosphere, then breed a human race more to his liking. (In Ian Fleming's 1955 novel, Drax had merely threatened to destroy London with an atomic **bomb.**) Roger Moore is a bit over the hill, and most of the science is specious, but the plot is brisk and the special effects are first-rate.

Ken Adam, the **production designer** of many Bond films, conceived the spectacular three-tier space station, built at a cost of $500,000 in a Paris studio with the help of technical advisors from NASA.

Director: Lewis Gilbert, *Producer:* Albert R. Broccoli, *Screenplay:* Christopher Wood, *Novel:*

Moonraker: James Bond floats into science fiction.

Ian Fleming, *Photographer:* Jean Tournier, *Production Designer:* Ken Adam, *Special Effects:* Derek Meddings, *Music:* **John Barry**

Cast: Roger Moore, Lois Chiles, Michael Lonsdale, Richard Kiel, Bernard Lee, Lois Maxwell

MORK AND MINDY

TV series   1978-   U.S. (ABC)   30 Minutes (weekly)   Color

While **Battlestar Galactica** (1978-79) was struggling vainly to interest viewers in its epic quest, ABC scored an instant hit with *Mork and Mindy,* a modestly produced sitcom with an SF "hook." Mork, a nutty **alien** from the planet Ork, had originally appeared in an episode of the TV series *Happy Days* (1974-present) as the would-be kidnapper of teenage hero Richie Cunningham, who woke up to find that it was all a dream. The character so bolstered the program's ratings that he was given his own series in the fall, this time sent on a mission to study life on primitive **Earth** by the humorless Orkan leader Orson, often referred to by Mork as "cosmic breath."

Mork's spacecraft, which resembled a giant eggshell, landed in Boulder, Colorado, where he was befriended by a pretty young woman named Mindy, who agreed to keep his secret and help him gather facts about Earth. Although they lived in Mindy's apartment, the couple were initially like brother and sister (Mork found human sex bewildering to the point of falling in love with a department store dummy). They were married several seasons later.

Essentially an updating of **My Favorite Martian** (1963-66), *Mork and Mindy* seemed fresh and new, primarily because of the inspired clowning of Robin Williams as Mork. A master of improvisation, Williams moved at hyperspeed through a series of sight gags, such as drinking orange juice and using his finger as a straw. He also did impersonations of old movie stars and political figures while holding three-way conversations with himself. Like **Star Wars** (1977), the program was aimed at teenagers but managed to appeal to all age groups.

Mork and Mindy: Gravity-defying Orkans can sleep in closets.

Directors: Howard Storm, Joel Zwick and others, *Producers:* Dale McRaven, Bruce Johnson, *Executive Producers:* Tony Marshall, Garry K. Marshall, *Writers:* David Misch, April Kelly, Dale McRaven and others, *Music:* Perry Brodkin, Jr.

Cast: Robin Williams, Pam Dawber, Conrad Janis, Elizabeth Kerr, Jeffrey Jacquet, Ralph James

THE MOST DANGEROUS MAN IN THE WORLD

(U.S. title: *The Chairman*)

Film   1969   Great Britain (20th Century-Fox) 99 Minutes   DeLuxe   Panavision

Posing as a political defector, an American scientist enters China on a mission to steal the formula for a growth enzyme capable of producing bumper food crops in any climate. A two-way transmitter implanted in his brain broadcasts his conversations via satellite to headquarters in London, which later tells him that an explosive device has also been implanted in his head; it will be detonated should his true mission be discovered. Captured by the Chinese and facing death at the hands of his own people, he makes a desperate run for the friendly Russian border (China was perceived as a common American-Russian enemy at the time).

Mildly entertaining, the film totters between satire and seriousness, primarily because stolid leading man Gregory Peck is at odds with J. Lee Thompson's tongue-in-cheek direction. A hilarious scene in which the hero lectures Chairman Mao during a ping-pong game so angered the Chinese that the film crew was thrown out of Hong Kong during location shooting.

Director: J. Lee Thompson, *Producer:* Mort Abrahams, *Screenplay:* Ben Maddow, *Novel:* "The Chairman" Jay Richard, *Photographer:* Ted Moore, *Music:* **Jerry Goldsmith**

Cast: Gregory Peck, Anne Heywood, Arthur Hill, Conrad Yama, Keye Luke

THE ? MOTORIST

Film   1905   Great Britain   3½ Minutes (approx.)   Black & white (silent)

A young couple out for an airing in their new automobile break the speed limit and find themselves being chased by an irate policeman. Stepping on the gas, they gather speed until the car zips off into space, leaving the bewildered cop behind as they motor around the **sun** and take a spin on the rings of Saturn. Justice is served, however, when they slip off one of the rings, hurtle back to **Earth** and crash-land through the roof of a courthouse.

The ? Motorist is an early special effects fantasy made by Robert W. Paul, one of the founding fathers of Great Britain's film industry, who was inspired by the films of his French competitor **Georges Melies.** Paul's trick effects are used by director **Walter R. Booth** to develop the plot, not as an end in themselves, as with most of Melies' films. Paul's painted backdrops and a double exposure produced the illusion of driving around the rings of Saturn—which remains a delight. Like most early silent SF films, this one was played for comedy with the policeman as clown, a trend that reached its peak with the Keystone Kops series of Mack Sennett a decade later.

Director: Walter R. Booth, *Producer:* Robert W. Paul

MOVELLANS

A race of attractive humanoid robots featured in the British TV series **Doctor Who** (1963–present). Archenemies of the **Daleks,** who in turn are the archenemies of Doctor Who, the Movellans meet up with both during an invasion of the planet **Skaro.** They capture the Doctor and try to force him to help destroy the Daleks, but he disables his Movellan guards by disconnecting their power packs and escapes, leaving the warring groups behind.

MOXEY, JOHN L. (LEWELLYN) (1920–   )

British-born director of action-oriented TV series and TV films. During the 1960s Moxey made several minor **horror** films in England for theatrical release.

Muffit II

MUFFIT II

Robot pet of Boxey, juvenile of Captain Apollo in the TV series **Battlestar Galactica** (1978-79). Built by the starship's science office Dr. Wilkins, the lifelike device replaced the boy's original Muffit, a daggit (read: dog) killed during the treacherous Cylon destruction of the planet **Caprica.** It has been programmed to respond to Boxey's personality and can run, bark, wag its ball-bearing socketed tail and do almost anything else its prototype could except eat dog food and use a fire hydrant. Motivating the robot rig was Evie, a trained chimpanzee.

MUTANTS

SF term deriving from the word *mutation,* a description used in biology to describe a genetic change in an individual. Mutation is thought to be the prime agent in evolution, providing spontaneous changes in a species and enabling it to adapt to changes in environment and, eventually, to diversify into a new species. Man-made mutations can be induced by **X-rays,** ultraviolet radiation, chemicals and other agents. As with natural mutations, these can produce malformed offspring, who are usually short-lived and thus prevented from passing on their unhealthy characteristics to the species.

In science fiction, especially in films, mutants are usually of this kind, and the effect is instantaneous. People or beasts undergo

incredible changes when exposed to atomic **bomb** radiation, and most become incredibly large or incredibly small. Mutant monsters abounded in films of the 1950s: There were the giant ants of **Them!** (1954), the mammoth arachnids of **Tarantula** (1955) and **The Black Scorpion** (1957) and, at opposite ends of the scale, **The Amazing Colossal Man** and **The Incredible Shrinking Man** (1957). Occasionally, a mutation produces a superman, as in **The Power** (1968).

MUZ Z PRVNIHO STOLETE/ The Man From The Past

(Also titled: *Man in Outer Space*)

Film 1961 Czechoslovakia 96 Minutes Black & white [Released 1964 U.S. (AIP) 85 Minutes]

A 21st-century worker on a distant planet hitches a ride to **Earth** on the wrong spaceship and arrives home in the 25th century. Possessing the egotistic attitudes of the past, he finds himself strangely out of touch with human beings of the future, who live in a selfless, mechanized **Utopian** collective.

Intended as satire, this film has a few good comic moments before declining into a moral lecture about greed and capitalism. It is nevertheless good sociological science fiction (a rare event in films) with eye-catching special effects and a sterling Chaplinesque performance by Milos Kopecky as the out-of-joint hero.

Director: Oldrich Lipsky, *Producer:* Rudolf Wolf, *Screenplay:* Oldrich Lipsky, Zedenek Blaha, *Music:* Ladislav Simon, *Electronic Sounds:* Zdenek Liska

Cast: Milos Kopecky, Radovan Lukavasky, Vit Olmer

MY FAVORITE MARTIAN

TV series 1963-66 U.S. (CBS) 30 Minutes (weekly) Black & white, color

The sole witness to the crash-landing of a **UFO,** newspaper reporter Tim O'Hara rescues its dazed pilot and takes him back to his rooming house with the idea of writing an exclusive newspaper story. But the middle-aged Martian, an anthropologist whose specialty is **Earth,** refuses to reveal his identity to anyone else. O'Hara eventually agrees to pass him off as "Uncle Martin" and help repair the spacecraft, a task hindered by a lack of technology not yet invented on Earth.

Ray Walston was ingratiating as a bewildered innocent abroad enduring the primitive ways of mankind, with retractable antennae bobbing, while assuming that his powers to read minds and make himself invisible were quite normal. The first two seasons were filmed in black and white. (107 episodes)

Directors: Oscar Randolph, Sheldon Leonard, John Erman and others, *Producer/Creator:* Jack Chertok, *Writers:* Ben Gershman, John L. Greene, Bill Freedman and others, *Music:* George Greeley

Cast: Ray Walston, Bill Bixby, Pamela Britton, Alan Hewitt, J. Pat O'Malley

MY LIVING DOLL

Television (weekly series)   1964-65
U.S. (CBS)   25 Minutes   Color

A lecherous psychiatrist tries to teach a beautiful **robot** how to be a human female. This prime-time sex tease featured a shapely six-foot male fantasy named Rhoda, ready to do anything her master demanded (on network TV she didn't do much). Her beauty was only skin deep, however, and so was the humor. Much was made of the solar batteries stored in her breasts, prompting SF writer **Isaac Asimov** to call her "a poorly designed robot."

Directors: Lawrence Dobkin, Ezra Stone, *Producer:* Howard Leeds, *Executive Producer:* Jack Chertok, *Writer:* Al Martin, Bill Kelsay, *Idea:* Leo Guild, *Photographer:* Glenn MacWilliams, *Music:* George Greeley

Cast: Robert Cummings, Julie Newmar, Jack Mullaney, Doris Dowling, Henry Backman

MY MOTHER THE CAR

TV sitcom   1965-66   U.S. (NBC)
30 Minutes (weekly)   30 Episodes   Color

Jerry Van Dyke with co-star in *My Mother the Car.*

Commercial television plumbed new depths with **My Mother,** an imbecilic prime-time comedy that only the producer's mother could love. The mother/car of the title was a 1928 Porter, bought for $200 by a young lawyer while browsing in a used car lot. When he turned on the radio, a familiar voice announced he was sitting in a reincarnation of his late mother. Mom proved to be a lot of fun. She got drunk from antifreeze, amnesia from a collision with another automobile and she liked drive-in movies. Sonny, who dutifully kept Mom's identity to himself, protected her from a determined automobile collector and even his own family, who wanted to trade in the old thing for a new station wagon.

Director/Producer: Rod Amateau, *Creators:* Allan Burns, Chris Hayward, *Cameraman:* Charles Van Enger, *Music:* Ralph Carmichael

Cast: Jerry Van Dyke, *Mother's voice:* Ann Sothern, Maggie Pierce, Avery Schreiber

THE MYSTERIANS

See: **Chikyu Boeigun**

THE MYSTERIOUS INVADER

See: **The Astounding She-monster**

THE MYSTERIOUS ISLAND

Film   1929   U.S. (MGM)   95 Minutes   Black & white with 2-strip color   (silent with sound effects)

Russian agents invade the secret island laboratory of a **mad scientist,** who escapes to an underwater city in his powerful submarine.

Jules Verne wouldn't have recognized his classic story after it went through the Hollywood meat grinder. This first screen version of the author's sequel to *20,000 Leagues Under the Sea* might well have been subtitled "too many cooks spoil the broth." The original story line was discarded—including its Civil War setting—Russians were added as villains, and Captain Nemo reverted to his peerage name of Dakkar, reduced in rank from a prince to a count.

Plagued with problems from the start, *Mysterious Island* commenced in 1926 with location shooting in the Bahamas. A hurricane wrecked the boats and equipment, however, and the crew returned to Hollywood, where the script was rewritten to accommodate a locale change. Directors and actors came and went as the script underwent further revisions, and scenes had to be re-shot many times. The film took more than three years to complete at a cost of over $1 million—a staggering sum for its time. To make matters worse, sound had arrived in Hollywood in the meantime, rendering the film obsolete by the time it was released. Despite two-strip Technicolor footage, first-rate special effects and the addition of sound effects, *Mysterious Island* was a financial failure.

Directors: Lucien Hubbard, Maurice Tourneur, Benjamin Christiansen, *Screenplay:* L. Hubbard, Carl L. Pierson, *Novel:* Jules Verne, *Photographer:* Percy Hilburn, *Special Effects:* James Basevi, Louis H. Tolhurst, Irving Ries, *Music:* Martin Broomes, Arthur Lange

Cast: Lionel Barrymore, Jane Daly, Lloyd Hughes, Montague Love, Snitz Edwards

MYSTERIOUS ISLAND

Film serial   1951   U.S. (Columbia)
15 Episodes   Black & white

This ludicrous adaptation of the **Jules Verne** novel pits Captain Nemo against a beautiful **alien** named Rulu. She comes to his private island from the planet Mercury to find a radioactive mineral to blow up **Earth.**

Director: **Spencer G. Bennett,** *Producer:* Sam Katzman, *Screenplay:* Lewis Clay, Royal K. Cole, George H. Plympton, *Musical Director:* Mischa Bakaleinikoff

Cast: Leonard Penn, Karen Randle, Richard Crane, Gene Roth, Marshall Reed

MYSTERIOUS ISLAND

Film   1961   Great Britain (Columbia)
101 Minutes   Technicolor

Confederate escapees from a Yankee prison leave the Civil War behind when they commandeer an enemy balloon that carries them to an uncharted tropical island. Also there are two female castaways, pirates and the legendary Captain Nemo, who lives in a submarine-laboratory creating hungry giant-sized animals and insects that roam the island.

Although *Mysterious Island* has little to do with the **Jules Verne** novel (which takes place on a desert island), the film works well on its own level as a grand fantasy adventure. The **stop-motion** animation by **Ray Harryhausen** is superb, notably in a scene depicting two people trapped in a huge honeycomb by enormous bees, and **Bernard Herrmann's** opulently eerie musical score is just right. A fourth, little-seen version of the Verne novel was made in Europe in 1972, starring Omar Sharif as Captain Nemo.

Director: Cy Endfield, *Producer:* Charles H. Schneer, *Screenplay:* John Prebble, Dan Ullman, Crane Wilbur, *Novel:* Jules Verne, *Photographer:* Wilkie Cooper, *Underwater Photography:* Egil Woxholt, *Special Effects:* Ray Harryhausen, *Music:* Bernard Herrmann

Cast: Joan Greenwood, Gary Merrill, Michael Callan, Michael Craig, Herbert Lom, Beth Rogan

MYSTERIOUS SATELLITE

See: **Warning From Space**

Television's big-budget spaceship, *Battlestar Galactica.*

A U.S. reconnaissance craft inspects a piece of space debris hurtling toward Earth in *Meteor.*

Orbiting nuclear warheads, one of the convincing miniatures of *Meteor.*

Astronauts dash across catwalk in *The Cygnus'* power tube to escape incineration from a fiery fragment from space in *The Black Hole*.

The huge spacecraft set of Ridley Scott's *Alien.*

The mother craft of *Close Encounters of the Third Kind.*

2001: A Space Odyssey: An astronaut attempts to recapture an errant spacepod.

Marooned: Life aboard a gravity-free spacecraft.

Star Crash: Spaghetti science fiction. ▲

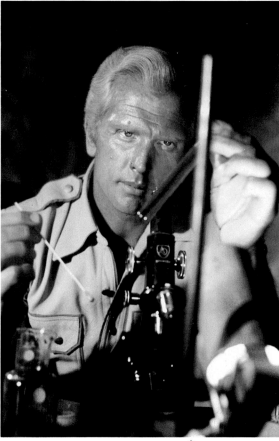

Doc Savage: The Man of Bronze. ▲

Solaris: A Russian science-fiction classic. ▼

The Lathe of Heaven: A creature of the imagination.

The Empire Strikes Back: Yoda and Luke.

Battle Beyond the Stars.

MECHANICAL MAN

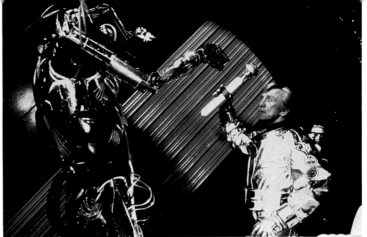

Kirk Douglas and Hector, robot villain of *Saturn 3.*

Laser-armed robot guards of *The Black Hole.*

Cylon warrior of TV's *Battlestar Galactica.*

All Terrain Armored Transports of *The Empire Strikes Back.*

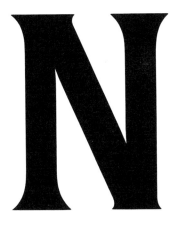

humanity, which explores the strange landscape as the heavenly body soars back into space. The story was previously hacked to pieces in Hollywood's **Valley of the Dragons** (1961).

Director: Karel Zemen, *Producer:* Rudolph Stahl, *Art Director:* Jiri Hlupy, *Music:* Lubos Fiser

Cast: Emil Horvath, Frantisek Fillpovsky, Magda Vasarykova

NESTENES

Alien invaders featured in episodes of the British TV series **Doctor Who.** A form of conscious energy with a diabolical affinity for things plastic, the Nestenes have attempted to conquer **Earth** in a variety of ingenious guises, each of which has been uncovered by the quick-witted Doctor. Leading the parade are the **Autons,** deadly weapons that resemble wax figures of human beings, plastic flowers that spurt a suffocating plastic film, plastic chairs, a telephone cord, and an innocent-looking killer doll. For their final invasion the Nestenes have selected a grotesque form that resembles a huge spider with claws and the tentacles of an octopus, capped by a single malevolent eye.

DER NACKTE UND DER SATAN/ The Head

Film 1959 Germany (Rapid) 92 Minutes Black & white [Released 1961 U.S. (Trans-Lux)]

The late French character actor Michel Simon steals the show as the lumpy, detached head of a doctor who has concocted a serum that sustains life in severed body parts. Grumbling, growling and helplessly rolling his eyes while perched in a lab tray, he watches his treacherous assistant takes over the experiment and attaches the head of a pretty cripple to a shapely body more to his liking. Unable to endure the indignity any longer, Simon literally blows his top and puts an end to the gruesome scientific nonsense. The actor's performance is best enjoyed in the subtitled German version, which uses his own gravely voice.

Director/Screenplay: Victor Trivas, *Producer:* Wolfgang Hartwig, *Story:* Victor Trivas, Jacques Mage, *Photographer:* Otto Reinwald, Kurt Rendel, *Special Effects:* Theo Nishwitz, *Music:* Willy Mattes, Jacques Lasry

Cast: Michel Simon, Horst Frank, Karin Kerneke, Paul Dahlke

NA KOMETE/On the Comet

Film 1970 Czechoslovakia (Barrandov) 84 Minutes Color

A whimsical treatment of the **Jules Verne** story, "Off on a Comet," by Czech director **Karel Zemen,** who combines live action with surrealistic **animation.** The **comet** zooms out of the sky and grabs a cross section of

NEUMANN, KURT (1906–58)

Hollywood director and occasional screenwriter and producer. Born in Germany, Neumann arrived in the film colony in 1925 and began his career directing short comedies before moving on to routine, modestly budgeted features. In 1950 he directed, produced and wrote **Rocketship X-M,** a hastily assembled film made on a trifling budget to capitalize on the publicity surrounding **Destination Moon,** which it preceded into release. He made several more SF films, enjoyable for their ludicrous but colorful misreadings of the possibilities of science.
Other films: The Return of the Vampire (1943), *Tarzan and the Huntress* (1947), *Carnival Story* (1954), **Kronos** [also producer], **She-Devil** [also screenplay, producer] (1957), **The Fly** [also producer] (1958), *Watusi* (1959)

THE NEW AVENGERS

See: **The Avengers**

THE NEW ADVENTURES OF BATMAN

TV series   1977   U.S. (CBS)   30 Minutes (weekly)   Color

An animated cartoon version of **Batman** (1966-68), made for pre-teens and featuring the voices of the original TV leads. Also on hand are a number of familiar villains including the Joker, the Penguin, the Riddler and a new aide-de-camp, Batmite the mouse. The fluid **animation** was achieved by the **rotoscope** process.

Directors: Lou Zukor, Rudy Larriva, Gwen Wetzler, *Producer:* Don Christensen, *Music:* Yvette Blais, Jeff Michael

Voices: Adam West, Burt Ward, Melendy Britt, Lennie Weinrab

THE NEW ADVENTURES OF SPIDER-MAN

See: **The Amazing Spider-man**

THE NEW ADVENTURES OF SUPERMAN

TV series   1966-67   U.S. (CBS)   30 Minutes (weekly)   Color

This animated cartoon featured the dubbed voices of the actors heard on radio's **Superman** (1940-53). Re-creating their old roles were Clayton "Bud" Collyer as Superman/Clark Kent, Joan Alexander as Lois Lane and, as narrator, Jackson Beck. The format included two **Superman** adventures and a single Superboy segment. The cartoons were later seen on *The Superman-Aquaman Hour* (1967-68), *The Batman-Superman Hour* (1968-69) and **Superfriends** (1973).

THE NEW ORIGINAL WONDER WOMAN
THE NEW ADVENTURES OF
WONDER WOMAN

TV series   1976-77   U.S. (ABC),   1977-79 U.S. (CBS)   60 Minutes (weekly)   Color

After the poor reception of its pilot film **Wonder Woman** (1974), ABC cast Lynda Carter in the title role and sent the Amazon princess back to her original time period, the 1940s. She now had a "scientific" explanation for her powers (the comic-book heroine was merely a superathlete), which derived from a golden belt and bullet-proof bracelets forged from Feminum, a mineral found only on Paradise Island, her home. She also had a new rival, the evil Fausta, and a younger sister, Drusilla, occasionally known as Wonder Girl. Otherwise, it was business as usual, with Diana Prince doing a quick twirl to change into Wonder Woman and rescue Steve Trevor from villainous Nazis, several of whom were after the Feminum.

The program switched to CBS for its second season, which found Wonder Woman in the 1970s working for Steve Trevor, Jr., (played by the same actor) whose father was presumably too old by now for the ageless beauty. Retitled *The New Adventures of Wonder Woman*, it followed Diana's predictable slam-bangs as an agent for a government defense organization equipped with a talking computer. Carter made a convincing Amazon and seemed at home in her sexy costume, but the scripts were played seriously and never reached the camp heights that had made **Batman** (1966-68) so enjoyable.

Lynda Carter as Wonder Woman.

Directors: Herb Wallerstein, Richard Kinon, Alan Crosland, Stuart Margolin and others, *Producer:* Wilfred Baumes, *Executive Producers:* Douglas S. Carmer, Bruce Lansbury, *Music:* Charles Fox, Artie Kane

Cast: Lynda Carter, Lyle Waggoner, Richard Eastham, Debra Winger, Cloris Leachman, Carolyn Jones, Beatrice Colen

NIGHT OF THE BIG HEAT

(Also titled: *Island of the Burning Damned*)

Film   1967   Great Britain (Planet)
94 Minutes   Color

During a mysterious midwinter heat wave, several residents of a coastal British island catch fire and burn to death. The cause turns out to be a horde of energy-starved **aliens,** which head instinctively for any heat source, even simple batteries. A convenient thundershower eventually dissolves the saucer-shaped creatures. This film lacks the mood of escalating panic generated by John Lymington's equally far-fetched novel of the same title, on which it is based.

Director: **Terence Fisher,** *Producer:* Tom Blakeley, *Screenplay:* Ronald Liles, Pip and Jane Baker, *Novel:* John Lymington, *Photographer:* Reg Wyer, *Music:* Malcolm Lockyer

Cast: **Peter Cushing,** Christopher Lee, Patrick Allen, Jane Merrow, Sarah Lawson

NIGHT SLAVES

TV film   1970   U.S. (CBS)   90 Minutes   Color

Stranded in a country town while taking a trip, a husband and wife make a dreadful discovery. At night the normally friendly townspeople shuffle off like zombies to a mysterious destination, of which they have no recollection in the morning. It doesn't take long for the couple to find out the townspeople are being used as slaves by space **aliens** to repair their disabled spaceship. The husband, who is immune to the mass hypnosis because of a metal plate in his head, eventually breaks the spell. The suspense lasts for about ten minutes; as soon as the town's mystery is solved *Night Slaves* skids to a predictable ending.

Director: **Ted Post,** *Producer:* Everett Chambers, *Screenplay:* Everett Chambers, Robert Specht, *Novel:* Jerry Sohl, *Photographer:* Robert Hauser, *Music:* Bernard Segall

Cast: James Franciscus, Lee Grant, Scott Marlowe, Andrew Prine, Leslie Nielsen

THE NIGHT THE WORLD EXPLODED

Film   1957   U.S. (Columbia)
94 Minutes   Black & white

A nuclear explosion triggers a chain reaction under the Earth's crust.

Atomic power out of control was a major anxiety of the 1950s and early 1960s, and scores of films both here and abroad mined the era's rich lode of public paranoia. As in the far superior **The Day the Earth Caught Fire** (1961), this film offers a nightmare vision of the folly of testing the **bomb.** In this case, the bomb has uncovered an "element" buried deep within the Earth. Nitrogen in the air causes the material to swell, explode and rupture into several pieces, each of which repeats the process in multiple explosions of escalating intensity. Water, the nemesis of **The Monolith Monsters** (1957), finally puts a damper on the menace. Like most scare stories of the period, the film has not aged well, and its camp seriousness ultimately destroys the credibility of its intriguing plot.

Director: **Fred Sears,** *Producer:* Sam Katzman, *Screenplay:* Luci Ward, Jack Natteford, *Photographer:* Ben Kline, *Music:* Ross DiMaggio

Cast: Kathryn Grant, William Lelsie, Tris Coffin, Marshall Reed

NIMOY, LEONARD (1931–   )

Actor whose portrayal of the half-human, half-Vulcan alien **Mr. Spock** on the television series **Star Trek** (1966-69) has made him a SF cult figure. Nimoy's pointy-eared Spock, the superintelligent, sexually ambiguous science officer of the spaceship Enterprise, is a favorite of diehard "Trekkie" fans, most of whom are female. Originally little more than a walk-on, the role of Spock was expanded to accommodate Nimoy's growing popularity and eventually became a leading character. He has subsequently starred in films, made-for-TV-movies, and plays, but has yet to surpass his *Star Trek*-based popularity.

A native of Boston, where he was a child actor, Nimoy attended Boston College on a drama scholarship and earned an M.A. in education from Antioch College in Ohio several years later. Moving to California after college, he studied at the Pasadena Playhouse while making the rounds of film studios. Cast in bit parts in low-budget films—usually as a heavy—he appeared in *Queen for a Day, Rhubarb* (1951), the serial **Zombies of the Stratosphere** [later consensed into the feature **Satan's Satellites** (1958)], *Kid Monk Baroni, Francis Goes to West Point* (1952), *Old Overland Trail* (1953), and **Them!** (1954). Drafted into the Army, he wrote, narrated and emceed G.I. shows as part of his duties with the Special Services at Ft. McPhearson, Georgia. He returned to Hollywood following his Army hitch and played small roles on the local stage and on television—including a running part on the series *West Point* (1957-58)—while operating his own drama studio. Graduating to supporting film roles, he was seen in **The Brain Eaters** (1958), the critically acclaimed *The Balcony* (1963), *Deathwatch,* **Seconds** (1966) and *Valley of Mystery* (1967).

Leonard Nimoy as a psychoanalyst in *Invasion of the Body Snatchers* (1978).

After **Star Trek,** Nimoy joined the cast of the top-rated TV series **Mission Impossible,** replacing leading man Martin Landau, who had left with his co-star/wife in a contract dispute. He remained for two years (1969-71). Since then he has been well-represented in entertainment mediums: He starred in the films *Catlow* and the remake, **Invasion of the Body Snatchers** (1978); in the TV movies *Baffled* (1972), *The Alpha Caper* (1973), *The Deadly Are Missing* (1975), *Marco Polo* (1982) and as the voice of Mr. Spock in the animated **Star Trek** series (1973), as host/narrator of *The Coral Jungle* (1976), an undersea documentary, and the series **In Search of . . .** (1976), a quasi-scientific investigation of paranormal phenomena; on Broadway in the short-lived *Full Circle* (1976) and *Equus* (1977). He has published two volumes of love poetry illustrated with his photographs and recorded several albums, including *Leonard Nimoy Presents Mr. Spock's Music from Outer Space.*

In his autobiography *I Am Not Spock,* Nimoy laments his identification with the role that brought him fame. He initially refused to repeat the role in **Star Trek—the Motion Picture** (1979) but relented when offered a substantial salary increase. He professed to be pleased when the producers decided to kill off Spock in **Star Trek II** (1982). Despite his protests, Nimoy obviously enjoys his cult status and appears often at *Star Trek* conventions.

NO BLADE OF GRASS

Film   1970   Great Britain (MGM)
96 Minutes   Metrocolor   Panavision

A family travels across famine-stricken England of the near future, looking for safety from armed, hungry mobs roaming the countryside.

No Blade of Grass is an apocalyptic vision of the breakdown of civilization as brought about by world-wide famine caused by industrial chemicals. To survive attacks from brutal, Viking-helmeted motorcycle gangs (and other threats), a decent, law-abiding family commits murder and other acts of violence on their way to the lakeside home of a relative. The film is similar but inferior to **Panic in the Year Zero.** A disjointed editing and mock-serious direction dissipate the film's well-constructed plot, whose cynical message is that the fall of civilization will bring out the worst in people and that survival is all that counts. *No Blade of Grass* is worth noting for having ushered in the popular 1970s' SF film theme of **pollution.**

Director/Producer: Cornel Wilde, *Screenplay:* Sean Forrestal, Jefferson Pascal, *Novel: The Death of Grass* by John Christopher, *Photographer:* H. A. R. Thompson, *Special Effects:* Terry Witherington, *Music:* Burnell Whibley

Cast: Nigel Davenport, Jean Wallace, Patrick Holt, John Hamill, George Couloris

NOWLAN, PHILIP FRANCIS (1888–1940)

SF writer whose greatest achievement was the creation of **Buck Rogers,** the classic **space-opera** hero of comic strips, radio, films and television. The character originated as Anthony Rogers in the short story "Armageddon 2419," published in the August 1928 issue of *Amazing Stories,* followed by a sequel, "The Airlords of Han," in the March 1929 issue. The idea for the comic strip came from John Flint Dille, president of the National Newspaper Service syndicate, who paired

Nowlan with artist Richard Calkins, the man responsible for Rogers' 1930s' aviator "look." Dropping "Anthony" in favor of the character's nickname "Buck" and changing the aggressive Hans to the dread Mongols, the team produced the first strip on January 7, 1929. Titled "Buck Rogers in the 25th Century," the strip ran in newspapers around the world without interruption until 1967.

THE NUTTY PROFESSOR

Film   1963   U.S. (Paramount)   107 Minutes Technicolor

A maladroit but well-meaning college professor cooks up a magical elixir that transforms him into a heartless lady-killer. Comedian Jerry Lewis directed and co-wrote this occasionally hilarious vanity production, based on the venerable **Dr. Jekyll and Mr. Hyde.** Every joke is underlined by his camera-hungry star, in case viewers didn't get the point.

Director: Jerry Lewis, *Producer:* Ernest D. Glucksman, *Screenplay:* Jerry Lewis, Bill Richmond, *Photographer:* W. Wallace Kelley, *Art Directors:* **Hal Pereira,** Walter Tyler, *Special Effects:* Paul K. Lerpae, *Music:* Walter Scharf

Cast: Jerry Lewis, Stella Stevens, Howard Morris, Kathleen Freeman, Henry Gibson

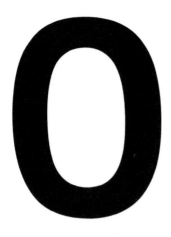

are sensitive to light)—who prowl through the streets at night like demented monks. The scientist locks himself in and watches an old print of his favorite movie, *Woodstock,* listening over and over again to its unheeded message of peace of love. Attempting to cure a group of young people of the disease, he is executed by the anti-science fanatics, who hold him responsible for the plague. This is the second screen adaptation of **Richard Matheson's** novel *I Am Legend* (1954), and it is less true to the story than the first, **The Last Man on Earth** (1964). The vampire theme has been excised in favor of a more realistic storyline, and, again, there is too much tell and too little show.

Director: Boris Sagal, *Producer:* Walter Seltzer, *Screenplay:* John William Corrington, Joyce M. Corrington, *Novel:* Richard Matheson, *Photographer:* Russell Metty, *Music:* Ron Grainer

Cast: Charlton Heston, Rosalind Cash, Anthony Zerbe, Paul Koslo

ONE HOUR TO DOOMSDAY

See: **City Beneath the Sea**

ONE SPY TOO MANY

Film   1966   U.S. (MGM)   100 Minutes   Color

The liveliest of seven films pieced together from episodes of the old TV series, **The Man From U.N.C.L.E.** for theatrical release abroad. Villain Rip Torn steals the show as a crazed scientist bent on ruling the world with a will-sapping nerve gas.

Director: **Joseph Sargent,** *Producer:* David Victor, *Screenplay:* Dean Hargrove

Cast: Robert Vaughn, David McCallum, Leo G. Carroll, Rip Torn, Dorothy Provine, Yvonne Craig

ON HER MAJESTY'S SECRET SERVICE

Film   1969   Great Britain (United Artists)
140 Minutes   Technicolor   Panavision

Sean Connery said no to this **James Bond** film, the sixth in the series, and Australian

OBOLER, ARCH (1909–   )

Director, screenwriter and producer. Born in Chicago, Oboler was a successful radio dramatist during the 1930 and 1940s, numbering among his many credits the long-running programs *First Nighter* and *Lights Out,* the latter a mystery thriller dealing with the supernatural. His first film was M.G.M.'s *Bewitched* (1945), a story of a girl with twin personalities, which he wrote and directed. Oboler's gift for creating exciting drama with words and voices did not transfer well to a primarily visual medium, however, and his films are talky and stagebound. His film **Five** (1951) is credited with inaugurating the cinema's first cycle of anti-**bomb** stories. After *Bwana Devil* (1953), which launched a brief Hollywood cycle of 3-D films (see: **Stereoscopic Film),** Oboler made a handful of "gimmick" movies. *Other films: Strange Holiday* (1945), *The Arnelo Affair* (1947), **The Twonky** (1953), *1 + 1: Exploring the Kinsey Report* [based on his play] (1961), **The Bubble** (1966)

THE OMEGA MAN

Film   1971   U.S. (Warner Bros.)
98 Minutes   Technicolor   Panavision

Set in 1977, after a biological war between the East and the West has decimated the world, *The Omega Man* centers on a Los Angeles scientist **(Charlton Heston)** who has developed an antidote to the plague. The infected survivors are albino fanatics dressed in robes and trendy dark glasses (their eyes model George Lazenby subbed for him. The film was one of the best in the series, with a *Ben Hur*-like toboggan chase and a fiendishly nasty Blofeld (Telly Savalas) plotting to conquer Great Britain with a **mutant** virus. Lazenby had the looks but not the acting experience, however, and something was missing at the heart of the film, so Connery returned for the next one, **Diamonds Are Forever** (1971). For trivia buffs, Bond got married here, to the lovely Tracy (Diana Rigg), killed when Blofeld and an aide rake Bond's car with gunfire.

Director: Peter Hunt, *Producers:* Harry Saltzman, Albert Broccoli, *Screenplay:* Richard Maibaum, *Novel:* Ian Fleming, *Photographer:* Michael Reed, Egil Woxholt, Roy Ford, John Jordon, *Special Effects:* John Stears, *Production Designer:* Syd Cain, *Music:* **John Barry**

Cast: George Lazenby, Diana Rigg, Telly Savalas, Ilse Steppat, Gabriele Ferzetti, Bernard Lee, Lois Maxwell

ON THE BEACH

Film   1959   U.S. (United Artists)
134 Minutes   Black & white

On the Beach is an important film that epitomizes the nuclear paranoia of the 1950s. A prestige production, it was a success throughout the world, no doubt contributing to the climate of public opinion that resulted in a test-ban treaty signed by the U.S., Great Britain and the U.S.S.R. in 1963. Seen today, however, the film is unrelievedly sincere and not the last word it seemed to be.

The story takes place in Australia, the only continent of the world not yet decimated by the radioactive effects of a nuclear war. The clouds are on their way down and suicide pills have been issued to the populace, which includes a scientist who plans to die in an automobile race, a young couple who must give the pill to their child, and a divorcee and submarine commander who have just discovered their love for each other. There are several moving scenes, but one wonders if the human race would go to its bitter end with such dignity and grace. (See also: the **Bomb.**)

Director/Producer: Stanley Kramer, *Screenplay:* John Paxton, James Lee Barrett, *Novel:* Nevil Shute, *Photographers:* Giuseppe Rotunno, Daniel Fapp, *Production Designer:* Rudolph Sternad, *Special Effects:* Lee Zavitz, *Music:* Ernest Gold

Cast: Gregory Peck, Ava Gardner, Fred Astaire, Anthony Perkins, Donna Anderson, Lola Brooks, John Tate

OPTICAL PRINTER

A versatile filmmaking device consisting of a motion picture camera and a projector that are synchronized and face each other. Simple in principle but complicated in execution, the optical printer makes it possible to create a number of special effects. These include scene transitions such as **dissolves** and fades (which indicate the passage of time), and superimpositions (as in title credits). It can also simulate **slow motion** photography (by printing each frame more than once), fast motion (by skipping frames), **zoom** effects (by enlarging details), and freeze frames (by printing the same frame over and over again). The optical printer is also essential to the **split-screen** technique and the **matte** process, which combines live action scenes with **miniatures, matte paintings** or location shots.

ORGANA, PRINCESS LEIA

Senator from the planet **Alderaan** and a key member of the Alliance to Restore the Republic, an organization dedicated to the overthrow of the oppressive Galactic Empire in **Star Wars** (1977). Attractive, intelligent and determined, the young princess risks her life to send a message to **Obi Wan Kenobi,** a former **Jedi Knight,** via the tiny robot **R2-D2.** Rescued from imprisonment aboard the **Death Star** by Kenobi and his new friends after her planet has been destroyed, she teams with rebel fighters **Luke Skywalker** and **Han Solo** (whom she seems to prefer) for further battles against **Darth Vader** in **The Empire Strikes Back** (1980) and *Revenge of the Jedi* (1983). The Princess is portrayed by actress **Carrie Fisher.**

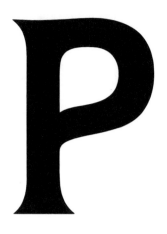

PAL, GEORGE (1908–80)

Hungarian-born film director, producer and special effects specialist whose SF and fantasy films are among Hollywood's most commercially successful. A pioneer in bringing science fiction to the screen, Pal was primarily interested in the genre as an opportunity for creating special effects; consequently, other aspects of his productions are weak, including performances and screenplays. In Pal's hands SF scenarios (usually from famous writers) often became formula fantasies. Still, his films have a technical gloss and enough exciting images to make them memorable.

Trained as an architect, Pal began his film career as a studio carpenter in Budapest. In 1931 he relocated in Berlin to work at UFA studios, first as a set designer and later as an animator, leaving when Hitler came to power. In Paris he made a film short for a tobacco company, featuring a dancing pack of cigarettes animated by **stop-motion** photography. The motion picture equivalent of a television commercial, the film led to an offer from Holland where he perfected his technique of animating hand-carved wooden **puppets** in a series of theatrical shorts he dubbed "Puppetoons." In 1939, with war in Europe imminent, he left his prospering business and emigrated to the U.S.

Pal's reputation had preceded him, and he was promptly signed by Paramount studios to produce animated shorts in competition with Walt Disney's cartoons. His first two series, *Puppetoons* and *Madcap Models*, were critical and box office successes, and in 1943

he won a special **Academy Award**—the first of six given to his films—"for the development of novel methods and techniques" in animation. In 1949 he made his first live-action feature, *The Great Rupert* (director: Irving Pichel), starring comedian Jimmy Durante opposite a convincing animated squirrel in the title role. On the strength of *Rupert*'s moderate success he convinced his backers to gamble on a documentary-style film about a scientific expedition to the moon.

Pal, as much a businessman as a creative talent, sensed an untapped demand for SF films as indicated by the postwar rebirth of SF pulp magazines and a growing public interest in science. For **Destination Moon** (1950) (director: Irving Pichel) he purchased the rights to Robert Heinlein's children's novel *Rocketship Galileo* and hired SF artist **Chesley Bonestell** to paint the backgrounds. Realizing that new techniques were needed to make the illusory journey convincing, he spent the major portion of his budget on special effects and created a number of ingenious illusions never before seen on film. He also paid scrupulous attention to state-of-the-art technology (of the period) and hired scientific experts to ensure the film's authenticity. Despite Hollywood's misgivings, *Destination Moon* turned a handsome profit and won an Academy Award for its special effects, signalling a new era for the SF film.

During the 1950s Pal was the genre's leading filmmaker (with occasional excursions into pure fantasy), whose elaborate productions set the standard for SF on the screen. He followed *Destination Moon* with **When Worlds Collide** (1951) (director: Rudolph Mate) (Academy Award: Special Effects) and worked without interruption for the next 10 years. He produced **War of the Worlds** (1953) (director: **Byron Haskin)** (Academy Award: Special Effects); *Houdini* (1953) (director: George Marshall); **The Naked Jungle** and **The Conquest of Space** (1955) (director: Byron Haskin); *Tom Thumb* (1958) (also director) (Academy Award: Special Effects); **The Time Machine** (1960) (also director) (Academy Award: Special Effects); **Atlantis, the Lost Continent** (1961) (also director); *The Wonderful World of the Brothers Grimm* (1963) (co-director/writer: Henry Levin); *The Seven Faces of Dr. Lao* (1964) (also director); **The Power** (1967) (director: Byron Haskin), and **Doc Savage, Man of Bronze** (1974) (director: Michael Anderson).

Pal's later years were spent in relative obscurity trying to obtain financing for a number of projects that never materialized, including a version of *Logan's Run,* screen adaptations of *When the Sleeper Wakes* by **H. G. Wells** and *The Disappearance* by Philip Wylie. Although Hollywood had turned its back on him after the box-office failures of his last three films, he was still looking for "just the right property" at the time of his death.

PANAVISION

Trademarked system of motion picture cameras, lenses and projectors, favored in Hollywood for their versatility. Developed in response to **CinemaScope,** Panavision was originally available only in **anamorphic,** in which a **wide-screen** image is squeezed onto 35-mm. film. Since then a number of formats have been added to the line, several of which have won technical-class **Academy Awards.** Super Panavision, the format of **2001: A Space Odyssey** (1968), also known as Panavision 70, uses 65-mm. film without distortion. This can be transferred to anamorphic for showing in theaters without the proper equipment. An even larger screen image is achieved with Ultra Panavision, which uses 65-mm. film and an anamorphic lens. The system is also available in standard 35-mm.

PANIC IN THE YEAR ZERO

Film 1962 U.S. (AIP) 93 Minutes Black & white CinemaScope

When Los Angeles is destroyed in a nuclear attack, an average citizen heads for the country with his wife and children in the family camper. Intent on surviving at all costs, he takes along every weapon he can find, using them without qualm on anyone who stands in their way. His wife is appalled by his sudden barbarism, but when their daughter is raped and beaten by a gang of marauding toughs, she changes her mind. Directed by actor Ray Milland, the film comes across with an immediacy that packs quite a punch, but its macho-existential message of survival of the fittest is questionable.

Director: Ray Milland, *Producers:* Arnold Houghland, Lou Rusoff, *Screenplay:* Jay Simms, John Morton, *Stories:* "Lot" and "Lot's Daughter" Ward Moore, *Photographer:* Gil Warrenton, *Special Effects:* Pat Dinga, Larry Butler, *Music:* Les Baxter

Cast: Ray Milland, Jean Hagen, Mary Mitchell, Scott Peters, Joan Freeman, Richard Garland

PANIC ON THE TRANSIBERIAN

See: **Horror Express**

PARALLEL WORLDS

A concept that other worlds or universes exist side by side with our own but in a different space-time continuum. Parallel worlds may be totally different from **Earth,** or they may be an unearthly mirror image of it. They can be reached in many ways: through **time warps, black holes,** space loops, or by simply altering our perceptions. Visits to parallel worlds are occasionally deliberate, but they are most often accidental—and never without risk. For example, there is always the possibility of meeting oneself face to face, or finding oneself in an alien environment with a different set of physical laws.

The notion of parallel worlds is an old one dating back to mythology and fairy tales, and it is one of the connections science fiction has with mainstream literature. **Lewis Carroll's** "nonsense" fantasy, *Through the Looking in Glass* (1872), in which Alice enters a mirror world, is a proto-SF novel that influenced a later generation of SF novelists, including **H. G. Wells.** Parallel worlds have since become a sub-genre of written science fiction but not of the SF film. Two attempts to dramatize the subject are **Journey to the Far Side of the Sun** (1969) and **Quest for Love** (1971). (See also: **Alternate Histories.**)

THE PEACE GAME

See: **Gladiatorena**

THE PEOPLE THAT TIME FORGOT

Film   1977   Great Britain (AIP/Amicus)
90 Minutes   Technicolor

A rescue party visits the lost continent of **Caprona** to retrieve an explorer lost there years before. The prehistoric monsters seem tired, perhaps from their previous outings in **The Land That Time Forgot** (1975) and **At the Earth's Core** (1976).

Director: **Kevin Connor,** *Producer:* John Dark, *Screenplay:* Patrick Tilley, *Novel:* Edgar Rice Burroughs, *Photographer:* Alan Hume, *Production Designer:* Maurice Carter, *Special Effects:* Ian Wingrove, *Music:* John Scott

Cast: Patrick Wayne, Sarah Douglas, Doug McClure, Dana Gillespie, Thorley Walters

PERCY

Film   1971   Great Britain (MGM/Anglo EMI)   103 Minutes   Eastmancolor

After an unfortunate accident, a London bachelor receives the world's first penis transplant (whose nickname provides the film's title).

Long on innuendo but short on wit, this lukewarm comedy of manners concerns the search for the donor of "Percy," with whom the recipient has had great success with women. Paging Dr. Frankenstein!

Director: Ralph Thomas, *Producer:* Betty E. Box, *Screenplay:* Hugh Leonard, *Novel:* Raymond Hitchcock, *Photographer:* Ernest Steward, *Music:* Ray Davies

Cast: Hywel Bennett, Elke Sommer, Denholm Elliott, Britt Ekland, Cyd Hayman

PERCY'S PROGRESS

Film   1974   Great Britain (EMI)
101 Minutes   Eastmancolor

Chemical pollution has made every man in town impotent—except for the owner of "Percy."

A limp sequel to **Percy,** which misses nearly every opportunity to develop its theme of sex-role reversal. Phallic jokes abound as women clamor for the attentions of the title object, which, again, is much talked about but never seen.

Director: Ralph Thomas, *Producer:* Betty E. Box, *Screenplay:* Sid Colin, *Photographer:* Tony Imi, *Music:* Tony Macauley

Cast: Leigh Lawson, Elke Sommer, Denholm Elliott, Judy Geeson, Vincent Price, Julie Ege

PEREIRA, HAL (dates unknown)

American art director. A successful designer of theatrical sets, Pereira was hired by Paramount in 1942 as a unit art director. In 1950 he was named supervising art director of all the studio's product. A versatile craftsman, he co-designed three durable SF films for **George Pal** and collaborated on others for directors Alfred Hitchcock, Billy Wilder, Cecil B. De Mille and Fritz Lang.

THE PHANTOM EMPIRE

Film serial   1935   U.S. (Mascot)
12 Episodes   Black & white

Resurfacing as a college cult item during the late 1970s, *The Phantom Empire* is Hollywood's first sound SF **serial,** made a year before **Flash Gordon.** It also has the distinction of being the only singing SF western that takes place in a metal city 20,000 feet underground. Radio singing star Gene Autry plays the owner of "Radio Ranch," who battles a group of crooks attempting to plunder his radium-rich land. Pursued by Gene, the rascals happen on the entrance to Murania, a lost city located under a mountain, whose Queen owns a powerful **death ray,** several **robots** and a nasty aide-de-camp named Lord Argo.

Directors: Otto Brower, **B. Reeves Eason,** *Producer:* Armand Shaefer, *Screenplay:* John Rathmell, Armand Shaefer

Cast: Gene Autry, Frankie Darrow, Betsy King Ross, Dorothy Christy, Wheeler Oakman, Smiley Burnett

The Phantom Empire:
Queen Tika gives Gene
Autry (left) a guided
tour of Murania.

PHASER

A ray gun invented for the television series **Star Trek** (1966–69) by the Westheimer Company, a special effects studio. The phaser is a dual-purpose firearm that can be set to either stun or evaporate an opponent. Its "zapping" effect is a series of glows beamed across the screen by **animation.** The disintegration of its hapless victims is accomplished by an optical transition called a **dissolve:** footage of victims is faded out on an **optical printer** while footage of the empty background is faded in. The outline glow that briefly replaces the victims is inserted by animation and then faded out. (See also: **Blaster, Death Ray.**)

A PIED, A CHEVAL ET EN SPOUTNIK

(U.S. title: *A Dog, a Mouse and a Sputnik*)

Film 1958 France 92 Minutes Black & white

An unpretentious satire on the space race, concerning a mixed bag of unwitting passengers who go aloft in a Sputnik. This film failed to captivate American audiences with its Gallic wit when released in 1960, probably because the story was old hat by then.

Director: Jean Dreville, *Producer:* Louis de Masure, *Screenplay:* Jean-Jacques Vital, *Photographer:* Andre Bac, *Music:* Paul Misraki

Cast: Noel-Noel, Denise Gray, Darry Cowl, Mischa Auer

THE PIER

See: **La Jetee**

PLAN 9 FROM OUTER SPACE

(Also titled: *Grave Robbers from Outer Space*)

Film 1956 U.S. (DCA) 79 Minutes Black & white

A classic of its kind, *Plan 9* is listed in Harry and Michael Medved's book *The Golden Turkey Awards* (Perigee, 1980) as "The Worst Film of All Time." Cherished by lovers of movie trash, who delight in glorified amateurism and thrift-shop production values, the film has gone on to make a tidy profit at midnight cult screenings, raising the question of who is laughing at whom?

Its nominal star is **Bela Lugosi,** who died before the film started production, leaving behind approximately two minutes of footage for the uncompleted *Tomb of the Vampire.*

Producer/director Edward D. Wood, Jr. built *Plan 9* around the takes, repeated them half a dozen times and hired a cloaked chiropractor to double for Lugosi in long shots. Wood, it might be noted, was a colorful Hollywood transvestite who liked to work in nylons, high heels and fluffy sweaters. A former marine, he claimed to have helped recapture a Pacific island from the Japanese, wearing French lingerie under his fatigues. Lugosi made several films for Wood, including **Bride of the Monster,** released in 1956, and *Glen or Glenda* (1952), a moving plea for accepting transvestites, which has also become a cult item. *Plan 9,* by the way, has to do with the landing of a **UFO** carrying a **bomb** to blow up the universe.

Director/Producer/Screenplay: Edward D. Wood, Jr., *Photographer:* William C. Thompson, *Music:* Gordon Zahler

Cast: Bela Lugosi, Vampira, Tor Johnson, Criswell, Lyle Talbot, Joanne Lee, Gregory Walcott, Tom Keene, John Breckrinridge

PLANETA BURA/Storm Planet

(Also titled: *Cosmonauts on Venus; Planet of Storms)*

Film   1962   USSR (New Realm)   Sovcolor

Never shown in its entirety on this side of the Atlantic, *Planeta Bura* was purchased for release in the U.S. by quickie filmmaker **Roger Corman,** who instead excised its spectacular special effects and shot two third-rate films around them: **Voyage to the Prehistoric Planet** (1965) and **Voyage to the Planet of the Prehistoric Women** (1968).

The verbose, awkwardly paced narrative takes place on the planet **Venus,** where a group of cosmonauts and a likeable **robot** explore the prehistoric landscape. They discuss the virtues of life in the Soviet Union via radio contact with the mission's only crew member, who is watching over their orbiting spaceship. Encountering only dinosaurs, man-eating plants and live volcanoes, the cosmonauts conclude that the planet has not yet evolved in intelligent life form. They shuttle back to the mother craft, unaware

that a bright-eyed Venusian is watching their departure from its underwater habitat in a large pond.

Director: Pavel Klushantsev, *Screenplay:* Pavel Klushantsev, Alexander Kazantsev, *Photographer:* Arkady Klimov

Cast: Kyunna Ignatova, Gennadi Vernov, Vladimir Yemelianov, Georgi Zhonov

PLANET EARTH

TV film   1974   U.S. (ABC)   75 Minutes
Color

Neither **Genesis II** (1973) nor this remake managed to spark a series for producer **Gene Roddenberry,** then between the **Star Trek** TV series and its movie revivals. Like **Buck Rogers,** a contemporary astronaut awakens from **suspended animation** in the future (in this case, the year 2132). The "Great Catastrophe" has fragmented civilization, and people have banded together in medieval-like communities for mutual protection. The astronaut joins a colony called PAX, dedicated to preserving science and technology. While searching for a missing scientist, he falls captive to a society of women who call men "dinks" and use them as slaves. ABC briefly considered doing the series, but decided instead to go with **The Six Million Dollar Man** (1974-78).

Director: Marc Daniels, *Producer:* Robert H. Justman, *Executive Producer:* Gene Roddenberry, *Screenplay:* Gene Roddenberry, Juanita Bartlett, *Photographer:* Arch R. Dalzell, *Music:* Harry Sukman

Cast: John Saxon, Janet Margolin, Ted Cassidy, Diana Muldaur, Christopher Carey, Majel Barrett

LA PLANETE SAUVAGE/Fantastic Planet

Film   1973   Czechoslovakia/France
72 Minutes   Color   [Released
in U.S. (New World)   Metrocolor]

This full-length animated SF film is based on the popular French novel *Oms en serie* (almost unknown in English-speaking countries) by Stefan Wuhl.

A revolution is taking place on the planet Ygam, where tiny **humanoids** called Oms are tired of being pets to Draags, a race of 39-foot-tall **androids** with red eyes and blue skin. The story is nothing new, but the Czech **animation** is fresh and imaginative. On Ygam, the crystalline landscape shatters at the sound of a whistle, pigs fly and trees look as if they were designed by Salvador Dali.

Director: Rene Laloux, *Producers:* S. Damiani, A. Valio-Cavablione, *Screenplay/Artwork:* Roland Topor, *Novel:* Stefan Wuhl, *Music:* Alan Gorgageur

Voices: Barry Bostwick, Nora Heflin, Cynthia Alder

PLANET OF THE DEAD

See: **Der Schweigende Stern**

PLANET OF STORMS

See: **Planeta Bura**

PLANETS AGAINST US

(Also titled: *The Hands of a Killer, The Man With the Yellow Eyes*)

Film   1960   France/Spain (Manley)
85 Minutes   Black & white

A dreadful **alien** invasion thriller made by an inept Italian director with a bewildered French cast. The lookalike invaders—humanoid **robots** capable of hypnotizing at a glance and destroying at a touch—are renegades from a passing spacecraft. Their extraterrestrial masters eventually track them down and save Earth from total devastation.

Director: Romano Ferrara, *Producers:* Alberto Chimenez, Vico Pavoni, *Screenplay:* Romano Ferrara, Piero Pierotti, *Music:* Armando Tovajoli

Cast: Michel Lemoine, Jany Clair

POST, TED (1918–   )

Film, TV and stage director, born in Brooklyn. A competent technician with a flair for psychological horror, Post has directed many episodes of TV's **The Twilight Zone** (1959-64) and *Thriller* (1969-72). Other series credits include *Medic* (1954-56) and **Ark II** (1976).

THE POWER

Film   1968   U.S. (MGM)   109 Minutes
Metrocolor   CinemaScope

In *The Power,* **telekinesis** is perceived as a step up the evolutionary ladder, albeit a dangerous one. Based on a novel by Frank M. Robinson, it concerns a group of scientists conducting tests in human endurance. One of them is a **mutant** who kills several colleagues by focusing his considerable will power against them. Told as a whodunit, the story follows the attempts of a co-worker to identify the rogue murderer in the group. Elegantly designed and cleverly shot, with a surrealist, off-kilter camera depicting the effects of telekinesis, the film is a rollercoaster ride of unnerving twists and turns. Allegedly, MGM was disappointed with George Pal's approach, and the budget was slashed drastically after filming began. *The Power* never saw a wide release, and **George Pal** was out of work for many years.

Director: **Byron Haskin,** *Producer:* George Pal, *Screenplay:* John Gay, *Novel:* Frank M. Robinson, *Photographer:* Ellsworth Fredericks, *Special Effects:* J. MacMillan Johnson, *Makeup:* William Tuttle, *Music:* Miklos Rozsa

Cast: George Hamilton, Michael Rennie, Suzanne Pleshette, Aldo Ray, Gary Merrill, Richard Carlson, Yvonne de Carlo

PRICE, VINCENT (1911–   )

Character actor of films and television, who specializes in **mad scientists.** Born in St. Louis, Missouri to a wealthy candy manufacturer, Price was educated at Yale and the University of London. After playing a number of supporting roles on the British stage, he was elevated to stardom as Prince Albert in the West End hit *Victoria Regina.* He subsequently played the role opposite Helen Hayes in a Broadway production. He made his screen debut in 1938 in Universal's *Service de Luxe.*

Films include: **The Invisible Man Returns** (1940), *The Song of Bernadette* (1943), *Dragonwyck* (1946),

Abbott and Costello Meet Frankenstein (1948) [as the voice of the Invisible Man], *House of Wax* (1953), **The Fly** (1958), **Return of the Fly** (1959), **Master of the World** (1961), *The Comedy of Terrors* (1963), **The Last Man on Earth** (1964), **War Gods of the Deep, Dr. Goldfoot and the Bikini Machine** (1965), **Dr. Goldfoot and the Girl Bombs** (1965), **Scream and Scream Again** (1970), **The Abominable Dr. Phibes** (1971), **Dr. Phibes Rises Again** (1972), **Percy's Progress** (1974)

TV credits: **Batman** (1966-68) [as Egghead], **Voyage to the Bottom of the Sea** (1964-68), *Mystery Theater* (1981-   )

PRODUCTION DESIGNER

The graphic artist who creates the "look" of a film—a visual atmosphere appropriate to the script and the director's viewpoint—as realized through backdrops, sets, colors and, sometimes, costumes, is called the production designer. Unlike the theater set, whose design is determined by the perspective of spectators seated in an auditorium, and which is accepted as a fiction, the film set must usually appear to be realistic, no matter how imaginary the world depicted might be. In the cinema, the spectator's viewpoint is determined by the camera, which eavesdrops on the intimate world of the characters and shows their world in flashes of detail from differing perspectives, each of which must match in the finished film.

A lesser function is performed by an art director, who designs sets, supervises their construction and "dresses" location shootings. A production designer—described as a "make-up artist of reality" by director Rene Clair—is reserved for important, big-budget films, especially those of fantasy and SF, in which case he works closely with the special effects director.

PROJECT U.F.O.

TV series   1978-79   U.S. (NBC)   60 Minutes (weekly)   Color

Project U.F.O. sped into television on the exhaust of **Close Encounters of the Third Kind** (1977) and seemed on the verge of being a hit itself. Creator Jack Webb based

Project U.F.O.: Brick Price's miniature flying saucer has windows fitted with front-projection screens for insertion of footage of alien pilots.

the series on case histories from a U.S. Air Force study of **UFOs** called *Project Bluebook.* Played in a documentary style similar to Webb's long-run series *Dragnet,* episodes followed two Air Force officers around the country as they investigated sightings of flying saucers. Not much else happened, however, and the program steadily lost viewers until it was finally replaced by the new **Buck Rogers** (1979-81). The convincing UFO miniatures were built by Brick Price from descriptions found in the *Bluebook.* Price's work has also appeared in **Star Trek—The Motion Picture** (1979) and **The Incredible Shrinking Woman** (1981).

Directors: Dennis Donnelly, Robert Leeds, Sigmund Neufeld, Jr., John Patterson, Richard Quine and others, *Producers:* Robert Blees, Col. William T. Coleman, U.S.A.F. (ret.), Robert Leeds, Gene Levitt, *Executive Producer:* Jack Webb, *Special Effects:* Wally Gentleman, Don Weede, *Music:* Nelson Riddle

Cast: Jack Webb [narrator], William Jordon [first season only], Caskey Swain, Aldine King, Edward Winter [second season only]

PROPHECY

Film   1979   U.S. (Paramount)   100 Minutes Movielab   Panavision   Dolby Stereo

"The hills are alive with mutants," wrote one reviewer of *Prophecy,* an overblown **horror** film as unintentionally hilarious as AIP's **Food of the Gods** (1976), which it resembles. The setting is a majestic-looking Maine (actually British Columbia), where a dedicated U.S. Health Service doctor and his wife discover that a lumber mill has been systematically polluting local waters with a mercury

Prophecy: Talia Shire and Robert Foxworth tend a mutant bear cub.

compound used for softening wood. Incredibly, the poison has altered the genetic structure of local wildlife and turned them into **mutant** monsters. The most dangerous of the lot is a deformed 15-foot Mama bear who could pass for **Godzilla.** Gifted director **John Frankenheimer** claims he made this film because of its "serious" message.

Director: John Frankenheimer, *Producer:* Robert L. Rosen, *Screenplay:* David Seltzer, *Photographer:* Harry Stradling, Jr., *Monster Makeup:* Tom Burman, *Special Effects:* Robert Dawson, *Music:* Leonard Rosenman

Cast: Talia Shire, Robert Foxworth, Armand Assante, Richard Dysart

PROWSE, DAVE (1936–   )

British actor/body builder who is the man behind **Darth Vader's** mask in the **Star Wars** series (the voice is supplied by American actor James Earl Jones). A six-foot, six-inch 265-pounder, Prowse is a former weightlifting champion. He made his film debut in *Casino Royale* (1966) and later appeared as the monster in **The Horror of Frankenstein** (1970) and **Frankenstein and the Monster from Hell** (1974). It was Prowse who turned a skinny actor named **Christopher Reeve** into a 218-pound muscle-man for **Superman—The Movie** (1978). The transformation took place in Prowse's London gym, where Reeve endured a grueling six-week crash program of weightlifting, special exercises, and a diet of high-protein supplements.

PUPPETS

Three-dimensional figures representing human beings or animals, puppets are often used for animated films. Movie puppets have moveable limbs, heads and facial features. These are adjusted slightly and photographed one frame at a time in a technique known as **stop-motion** photography. The rapid projection of the individually exposed frames provides an illusion of movement. Science fiction's most famous movie puppet is probably **King Kong,** with **Godzilla** and **E.T.** close behind. Yoda, the green-skinned Jedi warrior of **The Empire Strikes Back,** is a hand puppet, augmented by electronic circuits and hydraulics to animate its latex face. Yoda, like his close relatives The Muppets, was filmed normally. (See also: **Animation; Ray Harryhausen; Willis H. O'Brien; George Pal.**)

THE PURPLE MONSTER STRIKES

Film serial   1945   U.S. (Republic)
15 Episodes   Black & white

Martians dressed in purple outfits left over from the **Flash Gordon** serials kill scientists and inhabit their cadavers while laying the groundwork for an invasion from **Mars.** Tedious and banal, with an endlessly repeated **dissolve** shot of Martians turning into human beings, this film was one of the first to depict the durable SF theme of **alien possession,** its only distinction. It was later released as a feature under the title *D-Day on Mars* (1966).

Directors: **Spencer G. Bennett,** Fred Brannon, *Screenplay:* Royal K. Cole, Albert DeMond, Basil Dickey, Barney Sarecky, Lynn Perkins, Joseph Poland, *Special Effects:* Howard and Theodore Lydecker, *Musical Director:* Richard Cherwin

Cast: Roy Barcroft, Mary Moore, Kenne Duncan, Dennis Moore, Linda Stirling

Q

Richard Benjamin starrsd as *Quark,* a 23rd century garbage collector.

Q PLANES

See: **Clouds Over Europe**

QUARK

TV series   1978   CBS   30 Minutes (weekly)
Color

Satire and slapstick aboard a galactic garbage carrier in the year 2222 A.D.

Arriving in the wake of the movie **Star Wars,** this offbeat sitcom centered on the misadventures of Commander Adam Quark, who roamed the Milky Way picking up debris in a United Galaxy Sanitation Patrol (USGP) ship. Under Quark's command were Betty I, an ex-cheerleader and co-pilot of the craft, and Betty II, her clone (not even the girls were certain which was which). Also on board was Gene/Jean, a transmute with a full set of male and female chromosomes, who could change from tough to delicate in the blink of an eye, Science Office Ficus, described as "more vegetable than animal," Andy the robot, a walking junk pile, and Ergo the ship's mascot, a temperamental blob of shapeless protoplasm with one angry eye. Headquarters was a giant space complex known as Perma One, home of the Secretary-General—also known as The Head (he wore a size 36 hat)—and Otto Palindrome, a fuzzy-brained superintendent with four arms and golden braids.

Intended as a parody of **space opera,** *Quark* made a one-shot appearance in the spring of 1977 and debuted as a series on February 24, 1978 with a one-hour special sending up *Star Wars.* (Its "Source"—the voice of actor Hans Conreid—usually gave wrong instructions.) Later targets were **2001: A Space Odyssey** (featuring a sexy-voiced computer) and **Flash Gordon.** Its curious blend of in-jokes, sexual innuendo and comedy failed to attract a mass audience and the show was cancelled on April 14, amid a flurry of protests from *Quark* cultists. Mastermind of the series was Buck Henry, who had more success with **Get Smart.**

Director (pilot): Peter H. Hunt, *Producer (pilot):* Buck Henry, *Producer (series):* Bruce Johnson, *Writer (pilot):* Buck Henry

Cast: Richard Benjamin, Tim Thomerson, Richard Kelton, Tricia and Cyb Barnstable, Bobby Porter, Conrad Janis, Alan Caillou

QUATERMASS AND THE PIT

(U.S. title: *Five Million Years to Earth*)

Film   1968   Great Britain (Hammer)
97 Minutes   Technicolor

Andrew Keir replaced American actor Brian Donlevy in the third and final Quatermass film, made 11 years after the previous sequel, **Quatermass II.** Based on **Nigel Kneale**'s third Quatermass BBC-TV serial, broadcast in 1958-59, this is the most impressive of the lot. Workers digging a new subway tunnel uncover an **alien** spacecraft buried since prehistoric times. This brings Professor Quatermass to the scene. Breaking into the craft, the scientist and his team of investigators find the corpses of large grasshopper-like creatures from **Mars,** whose history is recorded in the ship's power source. The memory bank reveals that the creatures had come to Earth millions of years earlier to preserve their culture by genetically altering the minds of apes, the only significant life form found on the planet.

The power tap brings to life the ship's stored mental power (which had propelled it to Earth), reactivating its prehistoric "survival-of-the-fittest" thought programming. Londoners near the excavation begin murdering each other, and an enormous projection of a horned Martian image reminiscent of Satan looms over the city. Quatermass' assistant, Dr. Roney, drives a huge iron crane into the heart of the image, short-circuiting its energy source and exploding the ship.

The film concludes with a provokingly shocking twist, as Quatermass realizes that the insects are not invaders but our ancestors. "Gentlemen," he exclaims, "we *are* the Martians!" The film's theme, that an alien intervention is responsible for mankind's evolution and his fall from a simian paradise of ignorance, is a major concern of science fiction. It was handled with equal brilliance in **Stanley Kubrick's 2001: A Space Odyssey** (1968).

Director: **Ray Ward Baker,** *Producer:* Anthony Nelson Keys, *Screenplay:* Nigel Kneale, *Photographer:* Arthur Grant, *Special Effects:* Les Bowie, *Music:* Tristam Carey

Cast: Andrew Keir, James Donald, Barbara Shelley, Julian Glover, Duncan Lamont, Edwin Richfield

QUATERMASS II

(U.S. title: *Enemy from Space)*

Film   1957   Great Britain (Hammer)
85 Minutes   Black & white

This is the second Quatermass film, the sequel to **The Quatermass Xperiment** (1955),

made by the same production team and based on a second BBC-TV serial (1955). Brian Donlevy again stars as Professor Quatermass, who uncovers a clandestine **alien** invasion in the English countryside. Brought to **Earth** by a shower of small, bullet-shaped meteorites (see: **meteoroids),** the aliens have taken over workers in a government research station, where they are acclimating themselves to their new environment.

British audiences were particularly amused by the idea of civil servants being portrayed as unhuman zombies. The sequel is **Quatermass and the Pit** (1968).

Director: **Val Guest,** *Producer:* Anthony Hinds, *Screenplay:* Val Guest, **Nigel Kneale,** *Photographer:* Gerald Gibbs, *Special Effects:* Bill Warrington, Henry Harris, Frank George, *Music:* James Bernard

Cast: Brian Donlevy, John Longden, Sidney James, Bryan Forbes, William Franklyn, Percy Herbert

THE QUATERMASS XPERIMENT

(U.S. title: *The Creeping Unknown)*

Film   1955   Great Britain (Hammer)
78 Minutes   Black & white

Based on the six-part BBC-TV serial (1953) by **Nigel Kneale,** this is the first of three films featuring the obstinate Professor Quatermass, a rocket scientist involved with the first manned space flight. The spaceship crash-lands, killing two of its three astronauts. The survivor is taken to a hospital, apparently in good health. Gradually, an **alien** fungus spreads throughout his body, transforming him into a loathsome, blob-like mass that slithers through London absorbing bodies and terrorizing the city. Quatermass, called in by the police, traps the creature in Westminister Abbey and electrocutes it with high-tension wires. The film, which launched Hammer's **horror** cycle, seems slipshod today, and the special effects are not totally convincing, but Richard Wordsworth is impressive as the doomed astronaut, bringing a touching pathos to the role, akin to

Karloff's **Frankenstein** monster. The sequels are **Quatermass II** (1957) and **Quatermass and the Pit** (1968).

Director: **Val Guest,** *Producer:* Anthony Hinds, *Screenplay:* Val Guest, Richard Landau, *Photographer:* Walter Harvey, *Special Effects:* Les Bowie

Cast: Brian Donlevy, Jack Warner, Margia Dean, Richard Wordsworth, David King Wood, Thora Hird

QUEEN OF BLOOD

Film   1966   U.S. (AIP)   81 Minutes   Color

Not one to waste film, low-budget king **Roger Corman** commissioned this simple-minded thriller to provide a story line for first-rate special effects pruned from an un-identified Russian film purchased in a job lot for stock footage (see: **Battle Beyond the Sun**). Valena, the Queen of **Mars,** hitches a ride on a spaceship from **Earth,** and before long crew members are dropping like flies. Cause of the mysterious deaths is, of course, the seductive queen, who is a vampire **parasite.** She conveniently cuts herself and bleeds to death, leaving behind an ominous souvenir of Martian eggs. The plot was served with more panache in **It! The Terror From Beyond Space** (1958) and, more recently, **Alien** (1979).

Director/Screenplay: Curtis Harrington, *Producer:* George Edwards, *Makeup:* William Condos, *Music:* Leonard Moran

Cast: Florence Marly, Dennis Hopper, John Saxon, Forrest J. Ackerman, Judi Meredeth

QUEEN OF OUTER SPACE

Film   1958   U.S. (Allied Artists)
80 Minutes   Technicolor   CinemaScope

Zsa Zsa Gabor is hilarious as a Venusian with a Hungarian accent and a yen for the male astronauts visiting her all-female planet. Not quite what she seems to be, the bejeweled queen angers a would-be suitor, who strips away her lovely plastic face to reveal, gasp!, a mass of repulsive colloidal scars. Considered by connoisseurs to be one of the worst films ever made.

Director: **Edward Bernds,** *Producer:* Ben Schwalb, *Screenplay:* Charles Beaumont, *Story:* Ben Hecht, *Makeup:* Emile LaVigne, *Music:* Marlin Skiles

Cast: Zsa Zsa Gabor, Eric Fleming, Paul Birch, Lisa Davis, Laurie Mitchell

QUEST FOR LOVE

Film   1971   Great Britain (Rank)
90 Minutes   Eastmancolor

Little seen in the U.S., *Quest* is a valentine bonbon with a soft SF center. Spiralled into a **parallel universe** as the result of a laboratory explosion, a romantically inclined physicist finds that things are essentially the same there—except that he is a married playwright who abuses his wife, and history has taken a slightly different turn. The Vietnam War never happened, for instance, John F. Kennedy is still alive, and Mt. Everest has yet to be climbed. He promptly falls in love with his parallel self's wife, only to watch her die of a heart condition that could easily be cured in his own world. Disconsolate, he returns home and seeks out her counterpart—an airline hostess with an un-diagnosed heart condition. He saves her life, thus providing the film with both an unhappy and a happy ending.

Director: Ralph Thomas, *Producer:* Peter Eton, *Screenplay:* Terence Feely, *Short Story:* "Random Quest" by John Wyndham, *Photographer:* Ernest Steward, *Art Director:* Robert Jones, *Music:* Eric Rogers

Cast: Tom Bell, Joan Collins, Denholm Elliott, Laurence Naismith, Lyn Ashley, Simon Ward

QUINTET

Film   1979   U.S. (20 Century-Fox)
100 Minutes   DeLuxe

Survivors of a future disaster kill time—and each other—with a deadly dice game.

Director Robert Altman has never been more self-consciously obscure than in this slow-moving metaphor for the survival of the fittest, set in the near or distant future after the onset of a new ice age or a nuclear holocaust (the viewer is left to make up his own mind). In Altman's dystopian view, the world has nearly run out of food and fuel, and those still alive are huddled inside the decaying buildings of a once-great city, perpetually bundled up against the cold. When a group of strangers looking for shelter arrives, one of their women is killed by a bomb. Bent on revenge, her husband discovers that the death was a mistake—the result of an inept move in Quintet, a complicated game played by the survivors to decide who will live and who will die in order to conserve dwindling resources. Intrigued, he learns the rules of the game and sits down to cast the dice.

Director/Producer: Robert Altman, *Screenplay:* Frank Barhydt, Robert Altman, Patric Resnick, *Story:* Robert Altman, Patric Resnick, Lionel Chetwynd, *Photographer:* Jean Boffety, *Art Director:* Wolf Kroeger, *Special Effects:* Tom Fisher, John Thomas, *Music:* Tom Pierson

Cast: Paul Newman, Brigitte Fossey, Bibi Andersson, Vittorio Gassman, Fernando Rey, Nina Van Pallandt

Paul Newman plays a game of quintet with Nina Van Pallandt while Bibi Andersson looks on.

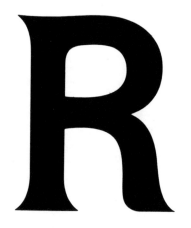

RADAR MEN FROM THE MOON

Film serial   1952   U.S. (Republic)
12 Episodes   Black & white

Commando Cody, Sky Marshall of the Universe, traces two saboteurs to the moon by scientifically deducing that an element used in their atomic weapon originated there. Cody and his two assistants track the culprits to an underground city, where Retik, ruler of the moon, is fiddling with an atomic cannon powered by "lunarium" and thinking of declaring himself ruler of the world as well.

   Radar Men is one of a number of attempts to update the tired **serial** format after the success of **Destination Moon** (1950), but it's still the old **mad scientist** routine. In 1966 it was released in feature form as *Retik, the Moon Menace.*

Director: Fred C. Brannon, *Screenplay:* Ronald Davidson, *Special Effects:* Howard and Theodore Lydecker, *Music:* Stanley Wilson

Cast: George Wallace, Roy Barcroft, Tom Steele, Aline Town, William Blakewell

RADIO-MANIA

(Also titled: *The Man From Mars, M.A.R.S., Mars Calling*)

Film   1923   U.S. (Teleview)   5 Reels
Black & white (silent)   3-D

Monstrous creatures made their initial leap from the screen in *Radio-Mania*, the first SF film to be shot in 3-D (See: **Stereoscopic Films**). Sound had not yet arrived, but the hero nevertheless managed to tune in to **Mars** (radio was all the rage during the early 1920s), whose taloned and bulbous-headed citizens showed him how to transform coal into diamonds and mud into gold. The producers were evidently wary of science fiction (such as it was) and tacked on an ending that showed the whole thing to be a dream. The photographer, George Folsey, later shot the memorable **Forbidden Planet** (1956).

Director: R. William Neil, *Producer:* W. W. Hodkinson, *Screenplay:* Lewis Allen Brown, *Photographer:* George Folsey

Cast: Grant Mitchell, Margaret Irving, Peggy Smith, Isabelle Vernon, Gertrude Hillman

THE RAVAGERS

Film   1979   U.S. (Columbia)   91 Minutes
Metrocolor

This futuristic version of the film *Death Wish* (1974) takes place in the year 1991, after civilization has been demolished by **the bomb.** The slow-moving plot involves a normally law-abiding man who witnesses the brutal rape/murder of his wife by a marauding motorcycle gang called The Ravagers. He gets revenge by joining forces with a band of citizens preserving civilization aboard a defunct aircraft carrier. Shot on location in the South Bronx, New York's infamous slum, *The Ravagers* wasn't deemed commercial enough for a wide release.

Director: Richard Compton, *Producer:* John W. Hyde, *Screenplay:* Donald S. Sanford, *Novel:* "Path to Savagery" Robert E. Alter, *Photographer:* Vincent Saizis, *Production Designer:* Ronald E. Hobbs, *Music:* Fred Karlin

Cast: Richard Harris, Alana Hamilton, Art Carney, Ernest Borgnine, Ann Turkel, Woody Strode

RAY GUN

See: **Blaster**

RED PLANET MARS

Film   1952   U.S. (United Artists)
87 Minutes   Black & white

THE SCIENCE FICTION IMAGE 269

Based on a popular Cold War-era Broadway play by John L. Balderston and John Hoare, this paranoid howler concerns an American scientist who discovers a right-wing Christian **Utopia** on **Mars.** The news causes a religious revival on **Earth,** resulting in the overthrow of Russia's communist regime and the restoration of its monarchy. Hero of the piece is an American president who resembles General Eisenhower, running for election that year.

Director: Harry Horner, *Producer:* Anthony Veiller, *Screenplay:* John Balderston, Anthony Veiller, *Photographer:* Joseph Biroc, *Art Director:* Charles D. Hall, *Music:* Mahlon Merrick

Cast: Peter Graves, Andrea King, Herbert Berghof, Marvin Miller

RETURN FROM WITCH MOUNTAIN

Film 1978 U.S. (Disney) 93 Minutes
Technicolor

Two children from outer space are kidnapped by crooks to harness their telekinetic powers.

A sequel to Disney's 1975 hit, **Escape to Witch Mountain,** *Return From Witch Mountain* offers horror movie veteran Christopher Lee as a scientist who can turn humans into **robots,** and grande dame of the cinema Bette Davis as his partner in crime. The quality

Tony Malone demonstrates psi powers to his kidnappers (Bette Davis and Christopher Lee) in *Return from Witch Mountain.*

of the special effects has been improved, but the real attractions are the outrageously nasty performances of the film's stars. This time around, Tia and Tony decide to leave their adoptive terrestrial home on Witch Mountain (a community of extraplanetary people) to see what life is like in the big city. Landing their flying saucer in Pasadena's Rose Bowl, the kids visit Los Angeles where they are taken prisoner by—who else?—Dr. Gannon (Lee) and Letha Wedge (Davis). The evil duo outfit the kids with brain-control devices and turn them into mindless robots. But not for long. (See also: **Psi Powers.)**

Director: John Hough, *Producer:* Ron Miller, Jerome Courtland, *Screenplay:* Malcolm Marmorstein (based on characters created by Alexander Key), *Photographer:* Frank Phillips, *Special Effects:* Eustace Lycett, Art Cruickshank, *Music:* Lalo Schiffrin

Cast: Bette Davis, Christopher Lee, Ike Eisenmann, Kim Richards, Jack Soo, Brad Savage

THE RETURN OF CAPTAIN NEMO

TV miniseries 1978 U.S. (CBS) 3 Episodes
(60 Minutes each) Color

The Nautilus battles a sleek new underwater rival.

You can't keep a good man down—under the sea, that is. Not when producer **Irwin Allen** is angling for a successor to his long-run series **Voyage to the Bottom of the Sea** (1964-68). Neither Captain Nemo nor his superpowerful Victorian submarine, it seems, were destroyed in a violent whirlpool as described by creator **Jules Verne** in his novel *20,000 Leagues Under the Sea* (1870). Rather, the Nautilus was trapped under a deep coral shelf in the Pacific Ocean, and Nemo simply put himself into a state of **suspended animation** and waited for the television people to call.

Director: Alex March, *Producer:* **Irwin Allen,** *Writer:* William Keyes

Cast: Jose Ferrer, Burgess Meredith, Mel Ferrer, Linda Day George, Tom Hallick, Horst Buchholz

Jose Ferrer as the Jules Verne hero in *The Return of Captain Nemo.*

RETURN OF THE FLY

Film 1959 U.S. (20th Century-Fox)
78 Minutes Black & white CinemaScope

A sequel to **The Fly** (1958). The son of the original transmuted scientist is thrown into the matter transmitter by an escaped convict for another go-around. Once again, a fly is buzzing around inside the device.

Director/Screenplay: **Edward Bernds,** *Producer:* Bernard Glasser, *Photographer:* Brydon Baker, *Makeup:* Hal Lierly, *Music:* Paul Sawtell

Cast: Brett Halsey, **Vincent Price,** John Sutton, Danielle DeMetz, David Frankenham

RIDERS TO THE STARS

Film 1954 U.S. (United Artists)
82 Minutes Color Corp

Astronauts capture meteors in flight and bring them to Earth for analysis.

A counterfeit SF epic concerning a team of space-age cowboys who round up chunks of space debris with large scoops fixed to the nose of their spaceship. Scientists at mission control in Washington have the absurd notion that meteors have a protective shield that prevents them from disintegrating when they enter Earth's atmosphere; they hope to duplicate the material as a friction-proof covering for steel rocketships. Sure enough,

meteors turn out to be coated with an alloy of diamond dust and carbon, which burns away and leaves the inner core intact.

Director: **Richard Carlson,** *Producer:* Ivan Tors, *Screenplay:* **Curt Siodmak,** *Photographer:* Stanley Cortez, *Special Effects:* Jack Glass, *Music:* Harry Sukman

Cast: William Lundigan, Richard Carlson, Herbert Marshall, Martha Hyer, King Donovan

ROBOTS

Term coined by Czech writer Karel Capek for his play **R.U.R.** (1921), after the Czech *robota* and *robotnik,* meaning work and worker. Capek's artificially produced drones are organic and not mechanical, and they properly belong in the SF category of **androids.** The robot geneology in cinema extends from the sythetic-skinned Maria in **Metropolis** (1926) to Robby the Robot in **Forbidden Planet** (1956) to **C-3PO** and **R2-D2,** the comedy team of **Star Wars** (1977), who have spawned a legion of clanking imitations. SF robots are pure fantasies whose purpose, as **Isaac Asimov** points out, is not the study of machinery, but "the nature of man in its deepest aspects."

ROCKETSHIP X-M

(Also titled: *Expedition Moon*)

Film 1950 U.S. (Lippert) 78 Minutes
Black & white, tinted

Robert Lippert, a maker of cheap exploitation movies, rushed this space mini-epic into production as soon as he heard that **Destination Moon** was in the works. Shot in three weeks at a cost of $94,000 (as compared to *Destination's* $600,000), it managed to precede its model into theaters by several weeks. The film's alternate title suggests a trip to the moon, a setting whose expense was out of the question. Instead, the Rocketship X-M blasts off for the moon but is veered off-course by a meteor shower (a special effect consisting of potatoes wrapped in foil). The crew eventually winds up on **Mars,** whose landscape is approximated by the Mojave

Desert, a "set" provided gratis by mother nature. They fall into the hands of purple-tinted **mutants** left over from a nuclear war. (See also: **meteoroids.**)

Director/Producer/Screenplay: **Kurt Neumann,** *Photographer:* **Karl Struss,** *Special Effects:* Jack Rabin, Irving Block, *Music:* Ferde Grofe

Cast: Lloyd Bridges, Osa Massen, Hugh O'Brien, John Emery, Noah Berry, Jr., Katherine Marlowe

RODAN/Sora No Daikaiju Radon

Film 1956 Japan (Toho) 83 Minutes
[Released 1957 U.S. (DCA) 79 Minutes]

Miners find a prehistoric flying reptile in northern Japan. Called "Rodan," a nickname that derives from Pteranodon, the beast creates gale force winds with its wings as it levels Tokyo. Better than most its kind, *Rodan* was Japan's first SF film shot in color. The creature also appeared in **Ghidra, the Three-Headed Monster** (1965) and **Destroy All Monsters** (1968).

Director: Inoshiro Honda, *Producer:* Tomoyuki Tanaka, *Screenplay:* Takeshi Kimura, Takeo Murata, *Photographer:* Isamu Ashida, *Special Effects:* Eiji Tsuburaya, *Music:* Akira Ifukube

Cast: Kenji Sahara, Akihiko Hirata, Yumi Shirakawa

RODDENBERRY, (EU)GENE (WESLEY) (1926–   )

Producer/director/writer; creator of **Star Trek.** Born in El Paso, Texas, Roddenberry is the son of any army sergeant. His family later moved to Los Angeles, where he attended Los Angeles City College and studied to be an engineer at UCLA After qualifying for a pilot's license, he dropped out of college to enlist in the Army Air Corps as a cadet. During World War II he flew 89 B-17 bomber missions in the Pacific theater.

At the war's end, he became a pilot for Pan American, flying international runs and writing articles in his spare time, mostly for aviation magazines. In 1949 he left flying and moved to Los Angeles to pursue a writing career in television. The industry had not yet moved west, however, so Roddenberry joined the Los Angeles Police Department, eventually becoming a sergeant and speech writer for the Chief of Police.

He sold his first script in 1951, and other assignments followed. By 1954, when he turned in his badge to write full-time, he had amassed an impressive roster of TV credits: *Four Star Theater, The Goodyear Theater, The Kaiser Aluminum Hour* and *Dragnet,* among others. He next worked for two years as head writer for the series *Have Gun, Will Travel* (1957-63). By 1963 he had enough of a reputation to sell M.G.M. on *The Lieutenant,* a series about the Marines, which he created and produced.

He conceived the idea for *Star Trek* later that year, and spent the next ten months trying to interest studios and TV networks in the project. The series was finally launched in 1966, but it never attracted enough viewers (or the right kind, according to network executives) to be counted a major success. It was dropped by NBC in 1969 and, of course, went on to become a phenomenon of TV broadcasting by gathering a larger following in re-runs than it had on network prime-time. Over the years, the program has gone into syndication in 48 countries and spawned hundreds of "Trekkie" fan clubs and *Star Trek* conventions. There was

Gene Roddenberry

even a course in the philosophy of *Star Trek* at the University of Nebraska. The message wasn't lost on Paramount Studios, producers of the TV series, and in 1979 Roddenberry was finally able to resurrect the series for a big screen production, **Star Trek—The Motion Picture** (1979), followed by **Star Trek II** (1982).

In the interim, Roddenberry had produced several series pilots that never got off the ground, including **Genesis II** (1973) and **Planet Earth** (1974). Episodes from the latter turned up in the TV film **Strange New World** (1975), for which he wasn't credited. He also produced the motion picture, *Pretty Maids All in a Row* (1971) and the TV movie *Spectre* (1977). In 1960 Roddenberry married Majel Barrett, who plays Nurse Christine Chapel in *Star Trek,* in a Buddhist ceremony in Japan.

ROLLERBALL

Film   1975   U.S. (United Artists)
129 Minutes   Technicolor   Panavision

In the world of 2018, corporations have replaced governments, and individuality has been abolished along with poverty, disease and war. To satisfy mankind's instinctive aggressiveness, for which there is no longer any need, the companies have provided

Rollerball: Champion James Caan scores another point.

Rollerball, an ultraviolent sport that incorporates aspects of football, roller derby, motorcycle racing and hockey. Object of the game is to take possession of a metal ball fired into a circular course at high speed and to drop it into a goal slot. When a champion player becomes an international cult figure, corporation executives decide to eliminate this threat to conformity by abolishing the time limit and making any maneuver acceptable, including maiming and murder. He survives, however, and slams the final ball home amid crowds wildly cheering his singular effort.

Based on William Harrison's story *Rollerball Murder,* the film ignores most of its potential as science fiction and chooses instead to glory in the sado-masochistic violence it pretends to condemn. The game's social context is left unexplored, except for a brief and amusing cameo by Ralph Richardson as the elderly keeper of a master computer who keeps losing bits of mankind's history. As prophecy, however, *Rollerball* is chilling. The well-staged competitions are exciting and totally involving; reportedly, the stunt men working on the film wanted to continue playing after shooting was completed.

Director/Producer: Norman Jewison, *Screenplay/Story:* William Harrison, *Photographer:* Douglas Slocombe, *Production Designer:* John Box, *Special Effects:* Sass Bedig, John Richardson, Joe Fitt, *Track Design:* Herbert Schurman, *Musical Director:* André Previn

Cast: James Caan, John Houseman, Ralph Richardson, Maud Adams, John Beck, Moses Gunn

ROMULANS

Warlike enemies of the United Federation of Planets in **Star Trek.** Their empire borders on our **galaxy,** and there are constant skirmishes between Romulan ships and the **U.S.S. Enterprise,** whenever the border is approached. Believed to be distantly related to the **Vulcan** race because of their similar appearance, they are friendly to the **Klingons,** the Federation's other major enemy, from whom they receive weapons and spaceships. Romulans were introduced in the TV episode "Balance of Terror" by Paul Schneider.

ROTOSCOPE

A special effects device linked to a special motion picture projector that screens footage on a drawing board one frame at a time. An artist then traces the moving subject onto a transparent cel in a process called *rotoscoping*. Live-action films are often rotoscoped to produce hand-drawn **mattes** in preference to the conventional traveling matte, which although cheaper is not as effective. The process was used in **2001: A Space Odyssey** (1968), for instance, to place spacecraft models moving on overhead tracks into a star-filled backdrop.

R2-D2 (Artoo Deetoo)

Pint-sized **robot** companion of **C-3PO** in the **Star Wars** series. R2-D2 plays a key role in the plot of the first film, carrying **Princess Leia Organa's** holographic message for help to **Ben Kenobi** on the planet **Tatooine.** Inside Artoo's squat, cylindrical body is a sophisticated computer that can tap information from other computers, with its mechanical language of beeps and chirps. The sounds are gibberish to human ears, but they make sense to C-3PO. In *Star Wars*, Artoo's mechanical savvy saves the day by locating a weak spot in the **Death Star,** enabling the rebel fighters to enter through a small exhaust port.

R2-D2 is played by several real robots and a shell inhabited by midget Kenny Baker. His "voice" is provided by sound effects engineer **Benjamin Burtt, Jr.**

R.U.R.

Play   1921   Czechoslovakia   3 acts

The term **robot** originated in this play by Czech author, philosopher and political activist Karel Capek (1890-1938) [pronounced Chop-ek]. The title is an acronym for Rossum's Universal Robots, which, in fact, are not robots at all in the modern sense of the word. Capek's flesh-and-blood workers were created chemically, not mechanically, a life form that has since come to be known in science fiction as an **android.** The term derives from the Czech *robota,* meaning drudgery or forced labor.

R.U.R. concerns a rebellion among sexless "robots" created to work in factories, and who rebel against their human owners to express their need for human souls. The idea of soulless human beings was a popular one when Capek wrote his play, and it had been used in two popular films, **Homunkulus** (1916) and **Alraune** (1918) (1928) (1930). Capek supposedly got the idea for the play when he looked out of the window of an automobile and the "crowds around [him] seemed to look like artificial beings." His Mr. Rossum (a name that translates into Mr. Intellectual) is a **mad scientist** who represents science as exploiter, untroubled by anything other than the desire to increase production. Intended as a criticism of the demoralizing effects of technical progress for its own sake, especially for workers on an assembly line, the play was an instant popular and critical success when it opened in Prague on Jan. 25, 1921. It premiered simultaneously in London and New York in Oct. 1922 and has since played in nearly every major country of the world.

Capek later wrote *Vec Mokropulos/The Makropoulos Secret* (1922), a play about an elixer that prolongs the life of a 300 year-old woman, the basis for an opera of the same title by Leos Janacek. His SF novels include: *Tovarna na absolutno/The Absolute at Large* (1922), which deals with atomic-powered weaponry, *Krakatit/An Atomic Fantasy* (1924) and *Valka s Mloky/War With the Newts* (1936), in which odd sea creatures evolve a human-like intelligence and decide to eliminate man.

SARGENT, JOSEPH (1925–   )

Film and television director of slick, commercial action-adventures. Sargent's fascination with technological gadgetry tends toward the juvenile, but his SF works offer unexpected flashes of wit and are usually eye-catching and well-paced.

SATURN 3

Film   1980   Great Britain (AFD)
95 Minutes   Color   Dolby Stereo

A thousand years from now, two scientists, living and loving in blissful isolation on

Saturn 3: Kirk Douglas battles a sex-crazed robot.

Saturn 3 (an elegant space station embedded in Titan, **Saturn's** largest moon) are interrupted by a psychopathic engineer bearing a **robot** helper. The flirtatious engineer leaves after explaining that his brain has been programmed into the robot, which promptly begins to lust insanely after the female member of the team, while trying to murder her partner.

This frenetic, high-fashion foolishness was helmed by musical comedy director Stanley Donen *(Singin' in the Rain, Funny Face),* whose idea of science fiction apparently is a love triangle set in outer space. Worth seeing is the robot, a gleaming eight-foot fantasy of metal bones and plastic nerves and arteries. Called Hector and described as "first of the Demigod series of superrobots," it was built by special effects man Colin Chilvers after a drawing by Leonardo da Vinci.

Director/Producer: Stanley Donen, *Screenplay:* Martin Amis, *Story:* **John Barry,** *Photographer:* Billy Williams, *Production Designer:* Stuart Craig, *Special Effects:* Colin Chilvers, Roy Field, Wally Veevers, Peter Parks, *Music:* Elmer Bernstein

Cast: Farrah Fawcett, Kirk Douglas, Harvey Keitel, Douglas Lambert, Ed Bishop

SCHLOCK

Film   1973   U.S. (Gazotski Films)
80 Minutes   Color

The Schlockthropus, a bad-tempered apeman who goes around dismembering people, leaves behind a trail of banana peels, but the police still can't manage to find him. His rampages catch the public's fancy, and a TV program offers viewers a prize to guess how many people he has killed. Meanwhile, "Schlock" goes to a movie theater to see **The Blob** but doesn't like the ending, has trouble with a soft-drink machine, and falls in love with a blind girl, who spurns him when she regains her sight and discovers he isn't a dog.

Made by 21-year-old freshman director John Landis before he graduated to the slick sophomorisms of *Animal House* (1978), *Schlock* takes a wild aim at several ape movies and occasionally hits a bull's-eye. Landis himself played the title role in makeup by **Rick Baker,** later to re-create **King Kong** (1976). **John Chambers,** makeup artist for **Planet of the Apes** (1968), does a bit as a National Guard captain. Named best picture at the Trieste Science Fiction Festival of 1973.

Director: John Landis, *Producer:* James C. O'Rourke, *Photographer:* Bob Collins, *Makeup:* Rick Baker, *Music:* David Gibson

Cast: John Landis, Saul Kahan, Joseph Pientados, Richard Gillis, Alvici

SCHUFFTAN, EUGEN (1893–1977)

German photographer and specialist in in-camera effects. Schufftan studied painting, architecture and sculpture before entering films circa 1920, as a special effects camera-man. He subsequently invented the **Schuff-tan Process.** He photographed several more films before leaving Germany in 1932, just before the Nazis came to power. Noted for his poetic lighting effects, he quickly developed an international reputation, working in France as Eugene Schuftan and in the U.S. as Eugene Shuftan. He won an **Academy Award** for the photography of *The Hustler* (1961).

Other films: Menschen am Sonntag/People on Sunday (1929), **L'Atlantide** (1932), *Drole de Drame* 1937, *Quai des Brumes* (1938), *Women in the Night* (1948), *Ulysses* [photographic effects only] (1955)

SCHUFFTAN PROCESS

An in-camera special effect that combines live action with **miniature** sets or paintings or photographs; invented by **Eugen Schuff-tan.** Its key element is a mirror (see accompanying illustration). Invented for Fritz Lang's **Metropolis** (1926), the Process was widely used in SF and fantasy films of the 1920s and 1930s, including **Just Imagine** (1930) and **Things to Come** (1936). It is rarely seen today, having been supplanted by the **matte** process and newer optical effects, which are less time-consuming. (See also: **Front Projection, Rear Projection, Introvision, Magicam.**)

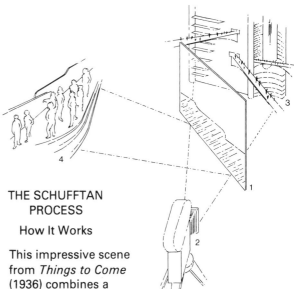

THE SCHUFFTAN PROCESS

How It Works

This impressive scene from *Things to Come* (1936) combines a hanging miniature set (3) with live actors (4). The key element is a partially silvered mirror (1), placed between the camera (2) and the miniature set at a 45-degree angle. The actors, standing far enough away from the mirror to be scaled to the miniature, are reflected into the silvered portion of the mirror and inserted into the set, which appears through the unsilvered portion of the mirror. The silvering was to be scraped away in a precise line that matched the bottom of the hanging miniature and the top of the partial set containing the actors. An alternate system shoots the live action and reflects the miniature into the scene.

DER SCHWEIGENDE STERN/
The Silent Star

(Also titled: *The Astronauts, First Spaceship on Venus, Planet of the Dead, Spaceship Venus Does Not Reply*)

Film   1959   East Germany/Poland (DEFA/ Julzjon)   78 Minutes   Color   (Released 1963   U.S. [Crown Int])

This intriguing adaptation of *Astronauci/The Astronauts* (1951), an early novel by Polish SF writer Stanislaw Lem, suffers from inferior special effects and inept English dubbing. The story concerns an international probe of **Venus,** where astronauts find the remains of a civilization destroyed by a nuclear holocaust. Although the Venusians are long dead, their identities still inhabit the landscape. Lem reportedly didn't like the film.

Director: Kurt Maetzig, *Screenplay:* J. Barckhausen, J. Felthke, W. Kohlaase, G. Reisch, G. Rucker, A. Stenbock-Fermor, Kurt Maetzig, *Music:* Andrzej Markowski, *Producer: English language version*–Hugo Grimaldo, *Music:* Gordon Zahler

Cast: Ignacy Machowski, Oldrick Lukes, Yoko Tani, Tang Hua-Ta

THE SCIENCE FICTION THEATRE

TV series   1955-57   U.S. (syndicated) 30 Minutes   Black & white

Hosted by Truman Bradley, this pedantic anthology program hardly lived up to its title. The program opened each week with Bradley explaining a scientific principle with kinetic gadgets resembling toys, which usually had little to do with the melodramatic nonsense that followed. In one episode, "Zero Gravity," two physicists experimented with an **antigravity** device, and in another, "The Dark Side," an astronomer attempted to build a telescope that could see the dark side of the moon. One of the better episodes, "No Food for Thought" by Robert M. Fresco, was later filmed as **Tarantula** (1955), directed by **Jack Arnold,** who had staged the TV presentation.

Directors: Leon Benson, Leigh Jason, Jack Arnold, *Producers:* Ivan Tors, *Technical Advisor:* Dr. Maxwell Smith

Cast: Lisa Gaye, Gene Lockhart, Skip Homeir, Howard Duff, Percy Hilton, Marilyn Erskine

SCREAM AND SCREAM AGAIN

Film   1969   Great Britain (Amicus/AIP) 94 Minutes   Eastmancolor

A wave of mutilation-murders in London sets in motion an intensive manhunt by police, who follow the trail to the laboratory of a reclusive scientist. There they discover bits and pieces of the cadavers, gathered by the scientist to create perfect human beings. *Scream* could serve as a lexicon of SF and **horror** cliches, but the director makes most of them work.

Director: Gordon Hessler, *Producer:* Milton Subotsky, *Screenplay:* Christopher Wicking, *Novel:* "The Disoriented Man" by Peter Saxon, *Photographer:* John Coquillon, *Art Director:* Don Mingaye, *Makeup:* Jimmy Evans, *Music:* David Whittaker

Cast: **Vincent Price,** Christopher Lee, **Peter Cushing,** Alfred Marks

SEARS, FRED (F.) (1913–57)

American film director of low-budget SF and action films. Born in Boston and educated at Boston College, Sears began his career as a stage actor. He appeared in the films *Down to Earth* (1947) and *The Golden Blade* (1948) before becoming a contract B-picture director for Columbia Pictures in 1949. His many films include: *Rock Around the Clock,* **Earth vs. the Flying Saucers, The Werewolf** (1956), *Don't Knock the Rock,* **The Night the World Exploded, The Giant Claw** (1957), and *Crash Landing* (1958). Sears directed several live dramas in the early days of television and taught drama at Southwestern University.

SECONDS

Film   1966   U.S. (Paramount)   106 Minutes Black & white

While struggling through the mid-life blahs, a wealthy businessman receives a telephone call from a friend who had died the year before. His death was only a ruse, he explains, arranged by a top-secret corpora-

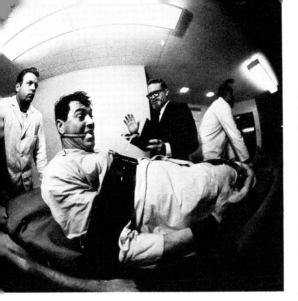

Seconds: Rock Hudson receives the last rites prior to "reprocessing."

and began his career behind the camera with the screenplay of *Ha'penny Breeze* (1952). The quality of his work as a director, which consists mainly of low-budget action and horror items, has been rather mediocre, with the exception of his witty revivals of Oriental archvillain Fu Manchu and episodes of the British TV series **The Avengers.**

Films: The Professionals (1960), *The Kiss of the Vampire* (1963), *Witchcraft* (1964), **The Face of Fu Manchu, Curse of the Fly** (1965), *Bang! Bang! You're Dead!*, **The Brides of Fu Manchu** (1966), **Jules Verne's Rocket to the Moon** (1967), *The Violent Enemy* (1969), *Puppet on a Chain* (1971), *Psychomania* (1972), *Hennessy* (1975), *The Four Feathers* [TV film] (1978), *The 39 Steps* (1979)

tion that substituted a surgically altered corpse for his own and gave him a new identity—in return for his insurance money. Offered the same opportunity, the man has himself transformed into virile young Rock Hudson. He is given a new occupation and a condominium in a swinger's colony in California, but his new life turns out to be emptier than his old one (the colony is made up of similar "reborns"), and he attempts to return to his wife. This is strictly against the terms of his contract, which is promptly enforced. Strapped to a surgical table and given the last rites by a corporation minister, he suddenly realizes where the substitute corpses come from. Directed by **John Frankenheimer,** then at his creative peak, *Seconds* is the kind of film that gives you nightmares.

Director: **John Frankenheimer,** *Producer:* Edward Lewis, *Screenplay:* Lewis J. Carlino, *Novel:* David Ely, *Photographer:* James Wong Howe, *Music:* **Jerry Goldsmith**

Cast: Rock Hudson, Salome Jens, Will Geer, Jeff Corey, Murray Hamilton, **Leonard Nimoy**

SEVEN CITIES TO ATLANTIS

See: **Warlords of Atlantis**

SHARP, DON (1922–   )

British film and television director. Born in Australia, where he was a stage and film actor, Sharp emigrated to England in 1948

SHAZAM!

TV series   1974   U.S. (CBS)   30 Minutes (weekly)   Color

Comic book hero **Captain Marvel,** making his television debut, has been recast as a role model for pre-teens needing lessons in civic responsibility. He still crusades for justice, however, but not nearly as enjoyably as he did in his 1940 movie serial.

Directors: Robert Chenault, Harry Lange, Jr., Hollingsworth Morse, Arnold Laven, Arthur H. Nadel, *Producers:* Arthur H. Nadel, Robert Chenault, *Music:* Jeff Michael, Yvette Blais

Cast: Jackson Bostwick, John Davy, Michael Gray, Les Tremayne

SHE DEVIL

Film   1957   U.S. (20th Century-Fox) 77 Minutes   Black & white

An experimental tuberculosis vaccine transforms a female guinea pig into a sexy superwoman. This cheaply erotic programmer is based on "The Adaptive Ultimate" (1935), a prophetic story about genetic engineering by SF writer Stanley G. Weinbaum (using his pseudonym John Jessel).

Director/Producer: **Kurt Neumann,** *Screenplay:* Kurt Neumann, Carroll Young, *Story:* John Jessel, *Photographer:* **Karl Struss,** *Music:* Paul Sawtell

Cast: Mari Blanchard, Albert Dekker, Jack Kelley, John Archer

SIODMAK, CURT (or KURT) (1902–   )

German-born, Hollywood-based SF novelist, screenplay writer and occasional film director. He is best-known for the novel *Donovan's Brain* (1943), a macabre but far-fetched tale of a telepathic human brain kept alive after its body has died. The book has been filmed three times, as **The Lady and the Monster** (1944), **Donovan's Brain** (1953) and **The Brain** (1962).

A native of Dresden, Siodmak studied at the University of Zurich in Switzerland and worked as a newspaper reporter before beginning his film career in 1929 as co-scenarist of *Menschen am Sonntag (People on Sunday)*. His collaborator was Billy Wilder, and the director was his brother Robert, for whom he scripted a number of films in Germany and, later, in America. He had begun writing fiction while a reporter, and in 1932 co-adapted his novel *F.P.1. Antwortet Nicht*/**F.P.1. Does Not Answer** to the screen. The film, concerning a giant floating aircraft runway moored in the Atlantic Ocean, was shot in three versions for distribution in the U.S., France and Germany. Among his 18 European credits is **The Tunnel** (1933), an ambitious film about the building of a tunnel under the Atlantic, remade two years later in Great Britain as **Transatlantic Tunnel,** and **Non-Stop New York** (1937).

In 1937 he emigrated to the U.S. and effortlessly made the transition from German to English to become one of Hollywood's most prolific SF-horror script writers. Among his 35 American films are: **The Invisible Man Returns** (1939), **The Ape** (1940), **The Invisible Woman** (1941), **Invisible Agent** (1942), **Frankenstein Meets the Wolf Man,** *I Walked With a Zombie, Son of Dracula* (1943), **House of Frankenstein** (1944), *The Beast With Five Fingers* (1947), **Riders to the Stars** (1954), **Earth vs. the Flying Saucers** (1956). As director: *Bride of the Gorilla* (1951), **The Magnetic Monster** (1953), *Curucu—Beast of the Amazon* (1956).

Siodmak's belated sequel to *Donovan's Brain* was published in 1968 and filmed two years later under its original title, **Hauser's Memory.** His SF novels include *Skyport* (1959), *The Third Ear* (1971) and *City in the Sky* (1974). The novelization of his screenplay for *Riders to the Stars* was written by Robert Smith.

While Siodmak's SF works are professional and slick, they betray a basic lack of understanding of the genre. He has been widely ridiculed by SF critics for making scientifically implausible films concerned with effect than rationality. His preoccupation with the grotesque and the offbeat are perhaps best suited to **horror** films, in which he displays a master's touch. (See also: **Cyborg.**)

SKARO

Planet where the vile, robot-like **Daleks** were created by the evil genius **Davros** in the British TV series **Doctor Who.** A war has been going on there for centuries between the aggressive Kaleds and the **humanoid** Thals.

LUKE SKYWALKER

Hero of the **Star Wars** series. Luke is introduced as a 20-year-old orphan, raised on the planet **Tatooine** by his Uncle Lars and Aunt Beru, who operate a moisture farm. When his uncle buys two **robots, C-3PO** and **R2-D2,** Luke finds a holographic message in the smaller 'droid. It is a call for help

Luke Skywalker and Darth Vader duel with lightsabers in *The Empire Strikes Back* (1980).

from **Princess Leia Organa,** the captured leader of a band of Freedom fighters. R2-D2 leads Luke to **Ben Kenobi,** a former **Jedi Knight** hiding out in the Tatooine mountains. Ben decides to help and asks Luke to come, but he refuses, until he returns home and finds the charred bodies of his foster parents, killed by the Galactic Stormtroopers. Luke and Kenobi then join forces with space pirate **Han Solo** and journey to the **Death Star** to rescue the Princess.

Seemingly coincidentally, Luke turns out to be the son of a Jedi Knight, Kenobi's friend, who was killed by **Darth Vader,** a Jedi who went to the side of the enemy during the **Clone Wars.** Given his father's **lightsaber,** held for him by Kenobi, Luke begins to train to be a Jedi, in a long course of study that involves harnessing a mysterious power known as **The Force.** After Kenobi's death at the hands of Vader in *Star Wars,* Luke continues his education in **The Empire Strikes Back** (1980), with a little green Jedi master named **Yoda.**

SLAUGHTERHOUSE FIVE

Film 1972 U.S. (Universal) 104 Minutes Technicolor

This is the first of Kurt Vonnegut's novels to be brought to the screen. Its plot concerns an American Everyman—complacent, well-meaning and confused—who gets "unstuck" in time. Slipping backward and forward, from his past as a prisoner of war in Dresden during the Allied bombing, to his future murder by an army buddy, he relives the major events of his life, including his marriage and the birth of his children. He finally comes to rest in the permanent future when kidnapped by the invisible Tralfamadorians, who put him in a glass display case as a zoo exhibit on the planet Tralfamadore, with movie sex queen Montana Wildhack. Writer Stephen Geller and director George Roy Hill try desperately to find a cinematic equivalent to Vonnegut's complex book, but they never come close.

Director: George Roy Hill, *Producer:* Paul Monash, *Screenplay:* Stephen Geller, George Roy Hill,

Novel: Kurt Vonnegut, Jr., *Photographer:* Miroslav Ondricek, *Production Designer:* Henry Bumstead, *Music:* Johann Sebastian Bach

Cast: Michael Sachs, Valerie Perrine, Ron Liebman, Sharon Gans, Eugene Roche, Sorrell Brooke

SLEEPER

Film 1973 U.S. (United Artists)
88 Minutes DeLuxe

Woody Allen plays a health-food store owner and part-time jazz musician in this hilarious SF comedy. Having died during minor surgery for a peptic ulcer, he is subsequently frozen in a **cryonics** bank and revived 200 years later by revolutionary doctors, who want him to help overthrow a 1984-style dictatorship. The gags come non-stop, with Allen posing as a domestic **robot** whose mistress wants to install a better-looking head. He encounters a 10-foot chicken, takes a quick jaunt with a flying belt and has futuristic sex in a pleasure booth. Repeated assassination attempts have destroyed most of the dictator's body, and all that remains is his nose, scheduled for cloning into a replicate—until Allen throws it under a steam roller. (See also: **Clones.**)

Director: Woody Allen, *Producers:* Charles Rollins, Charles Joffe, *Screenplay:* Woody Allen, Marshall Brickman, *Photographer:* David M. Walsh, *Production Designer:* Dale Hennesy, *Technical Advisor:* Ben Bova, *Music:* Woody Allen

Cast: Woody Allen, Diane Keaton, John Beck, Mary Gregory

SLOW MOTION

An effect that slows down on-screen action. In motion pictures the illusion results from running the camera at high speeds and recording more than the standard 24 frames per second. When the footage is projected at normal speed, the action takes place more slowly than it did in reality because it takes up more frames of film. The effect is widely used to create a romantic mood or to heighten a dramatic moment. In SF films slow motion helps create the illusion of a low-gravity environment by adding an artificial buoyancy to footage of actors moving through the air hanging on wires. The effect can also be accomplished on **videotape** by slowing down the normal tape speed during playback (as in the instant replay of sporting events). The opposite effect is called **fast motion.** (See also: **Wire Work.**)

SOLARIS

Film   1972   U.S.S.R. (Mosfilm)   165 Minutes
Sovcolor   Anamorphic

Based on Polish SF writer Stanislaw Lem's most famous novel, this brilliant Soviet film comes close to capturing the richness and sophistication of contemporary science fiction. The setting is a space station orbiting above a strange planet called Solaris, which turns out to be a living organism with the power of materializing in flesh and blood the fears and memories of human beings. When a "space psychologist" arrives from **Earth** to investigate garbled reports coming from the station, he finds that only three members of the original crew of 85 are still alive. Strange creatures of the imagination scuttle through the untended, refuse-filled corridors, joined the next day by the psychologist's wife, killed by her own hand years before. Understanding that her resurrection has been prompted by his deep guilt, he jettisons her into space. But a new copy appears the next day, and he eventually decides he can love the woman, who gradually becomes aware that she is a product of Solaris, and that she exists only on the space station. The planet, in its infinite empathy, offers a happy ending of sorts. Often referred to as the "Russian answer to *2001*," *Solaris* has a sweeping grandeur typical of the Russian novel and the epic historical films of Eisenstein. Unfortunately, it has never seen a wide release in the U.S.

Director: Andrei Tarkovsky, *Screenplay:* Andrei Tarkovsky, Friedrich Gorenstein, *Novel:* Stanislaw Lem, *Photographer:* Vadim Yusov, *Music:* Eduard Artemyev

Cast: Natalya Bondarchuk, Donatas Banionis, Yuri Yarvet

SOLAR WIND

Term used by astronomers to describe the outward flow of energy from the **sun.** This slight outward pressure, consisting of minute particles of light, is why **comets** always point their tails away from the sun. A rather whimsical SF notion is to harness this "wind" by outfitting spacecrafts with micro-thin metal sails in the manner of Earthly sailing vessels.

HAN SOLO

Captain of the pirate starship **Millenium Falcon,** in the **Star Wars** films. A cocky rebel, he travels through the **galaxy** accompanied by his **wookie** friend and co-pilot, **Chewbacca,** wheeling and dealing and constantly on the run from criminals and Empire police. Brave to the point of being foolhardy, he often finds himself in impossible situations, from which he usually escapes by dint of sheer courage. He is a loyal friend to **Luke Skywalker** and **Princess Leia Organa,** who fell in love with him in **The Empire Strikes Back** (1980). He is portrayed by Harrison Ford.

Han Solo

SON OF BLOB

See: **Beware! the Blob**

SON OF KONG

Film 1933 U.S. (RKO) 69 Minutes Black & white

King Kong, released in the spring of 1933, was such a runaway success that RKO rushed this sequel into production, which was playing in theaters six months later. Reviving Kong was out of the question, since his pathetic demise had been so well documented in the previous film. Instead, the scriptwriters came up with an orphaned son of the simian monster. Carl Denham (Robert Armstrong) is now down and out: "Tell the public that . . . the smart guy who was going to make a million dollars off of King Kong is flat broke." Escaping from his impossible financial debts, he returns to Skull Island, picking up an American girl and several drifters stranded in the seedy port of Dakang along the way. Kong, Jr. turns out to be a gentle giant, as playful as a puppy, who, unlike his father, exhibits no romantic interest in the heroine.

The plot, loosely based on a 1927 silent film titled *The Enchanted Island* (itself based on Shakespeare's *The Tempest),* involves a murderous villain, mutinous sailors, and a monstrous amphibian dinosaur previously seen in *King Kong.* Its resolution comes quickly in a hasty, disjointed ending, obviously dictated by the studio's desire to get the film into quick release. Little Kong, true to the end, holds Denham aloft in the ocean, as the enchanged island erupts with volcanoes and slips into the waters. "Poor little Kong. Do you think he knew he was saving my life?" Denham asks with deadpan earnestness as he rows to safety with the girl.

Director: Ernest B. Schoedsack, *Producer:* Merian C. Cooper, *Screenplay:* Ruth Rose, *Photographer:* Edward Linden, Vernon Walker, J. O. Taylor, *Special Effects:* Willis O'Brien, Marcel Delgado, *Music:* Max Steiner

Cast: Robert Armstrong, Helen Mack, Frank Reicher, John Marston, Victor Wong, Ed Brady

SOYLENT GREEN

Film 1973 U.S. (MGM) 97 Minutes Metrocolor Panavision

In the nightmarish New York of 2022, overpopulation and pollution has caused a shortage of everything except people. Rations consist of artificial wafers called "Soylent Green," dispensed to the population from passing trucks. Detective Thorn **(Charlton Heston),** a New York cop, one of the lucky few to have a job, discovers that the synthetic food is derived from human corpses, fresh from euthanasia hospices and riot control vehicles that scoop up people like rubbish.

The film is based on Harry Harrison's novel *Make Room! Make Room!* (1966), in which "soylent" is a mixture of soy beans and lentils, vegetarianism being a necessity in the crowded world of the future. Harrison makes no mention of cannibalism, an idea whose shock value in the film is undermined by its inherent logic, given the circumstances. Thorn can be seen as a troublemaker who attempts to sabotage a discreetly maintained process that keeps most people alive. Richard Fleischer's lively direction is further undermined by a muddled script that refers to women as "furniture." Edward G. Robinson adds a note of distinction with his touching portrayal of Heston's co-worker/roommate, his last role.

Director: Richard Fleischer, *Producers:* Walter Seltzer, Russell Thatcher, *Screenplay:* Stanley R. Greenberg, *Novel:* Harry Harrison, *Photographer:* Richard H. Kline, *Music:* Fred Myrow

Cast: Charlton Heston, Edward G. Robinson, Leigh Taylor-Young, Chuck Connors, Brock Peters, Joseph Cotten

SPACE ACADEMY

TV series 1977-80 (CBS) 30 Minutes (weekly) Color

Sub-teens train to become space explorers.

Excellent special effects distinguish this otherwise bland Saturday morning children's program, which has to do with a group of would-be astronauts training at a school lo-

Ty Henderson as Paul Jerome, a *Space Academy* cadet.

cated on an **asteroid.** Space-sage Commander Isaac Gampu instructs his racially and sexually mixed cadets in the ways as well as the hows of the universe and often intersperses his science lectures with words of wisdom. His friendly **robot** Peepo adds a humorous touch.

A Filmation Associates production, *Producer:* Arthur Nadel, *Photographer:* Alric Edens, *Art Director:* Ray Beal, William McAllister, *Special Effects:* John Frazier, *Miniatures:* Robert A. Maine, Chuck Comiskey, Paul Huston, *Music:* Ray Ellis, Yvette Blais, Jeff Michael

Cast: Jonathan Harris, Pamelyn Ferdin, Ric Carrott, Maggie Cooper, Ty Henderson, Brian Tochi, Eric Greene

THE SPACE CHILDREN

Film   1958   U.S. (Paramount)   69 Minutes
Black & white

A blob-like alien "brain" hidden in a cave takes control of a group of children.

None of **Jack Arnold**'s films is without interest, not even this simple-minded exploitation film directed at teen-age audiences of the 1950s. Arnold's bleak, menacing landscapes are still very much in evidence, and the encephalic **alien** (hiding out in a California cave) generates a chill or two. But the story of "taken-over" children disrupting a nuclear missile site where their parents work seems ludicrously violent today (except perhaps to children who hate their parents). The message of this adolescent dream of revenge appears to be that might makes right. Arnold's switch from Universal-International to Paramount may have been at fault; whatever the reason *Space Children* was his last SF-**horror** film.

Director: **Jack Arnold,** *Producer:* William Alland, *Screenplay:* Bernard C. Shoenfeld, *Story:* Tom Filer, *Photographer:* Ernest Laszlo, *Special Effects:* **John P. Fulton,** *Producer/Director:* **Hal Pereira,** *Music:* Van Cleave

Cast: Adam Williams, Peggy Weber, Michel Ray, Jackie Coogan, John Crawford

SPACE OPERA

This term is used to describe space epics, especially those featuring a romantic superhero, miraculous superscience and battles with space **aliens.** More "cowboys and Indians in the sky" than science fiction, space opera eschews the underlying themes and intellectual abstractions of purer examples of the genre in favor of action and adventure.

The term was reportedly coined by SF writer Wilson Tucker in the early 1940s as a reaction to cliche space yarns that filled the pages of pulp SF magazines. It derives from soap operas, domestic dramas with convoluted, hackneyed plots, which originated on radio (then a leading entertainment medium) and were sponsored by manufacturers of soaps and laundry products. The analogy was later extended to Western potboilers, which are called horse operas.

The term has lost much of its pejorative connotation and is now used with affectionate familiarity to describe space adventures that take place in a nostalgic future. Of the recent crop of space opera films, only **Star**

Wars and **The Empire Strikes Back** have managed to capture the naive exuberance of pulp fiction and 1930s movie serials. The remake of **Flash Gordon,** like many others attempting to poke fun at the material, was merely self-conscious and cynical. (See also: **BEMs; Interplanetary War.**)

SPACESHIP VENUS DOES NOT REPLY

See: **Der Schweigende Stern**

SPACEWAYS

Film 1953 Great Britain (Hammer) 76 Minutes Black & white

A rocket scientist is accused of murdering his wife and hiding her body on a satellite that has gone into orbit. To prove his innocence he smuggles himself aboard a departing spaceship to bring back the satellite. An early effort of Great Britain's Hammer Studios, *Spaceways* has dated badly but offers an intriguing look at then-current theories of space flight. The film is based on a radio play by British SF writer Charles Eric Maine, whose novelization *Spaceways Satellite* [in Great Britain *Spaceways]* was published the same year.

Director: **Terence Fisher,** *Producer:* **Michael Carreras,** *Screenplay:* Paul Tabori, Richard Landau, *Story:* Charles Eric Maine, *Photographer:* Reginald Wyer, *Music:* Ivor Slanfy

Cast: Howard Duff, Eva Bartok, Alan Wheatley, Andrew Osborn, Phillip Leaver

SPIDER-MAN

TV series 1967-70 U.S. (ABC) 30 Minutes (weekly) Color

"Spidey," one of Stan Lee's all-too-human superheroes, made his TV debut here as an animated cartoon character. Episodes related how high school student Peter Parker came by his unusual powers and applied them to the war against crime, a story told with more panache in the adult-oriented, live-action series **The Amazing Spider-Man** (1977-79). The artwork was an early effort of Ralph Bakshi, the innovative animator of **Wizards** (1977) and *The Lord of the Rings* (1978).

Director: Ralph Bakshi, *Producer:* Ray Patterson, *Music:* Ray Ellis

Voices: Bernard Cowan, Paul Sols, Peg Dixon, Paul Kligman

SPIDER-MAN

TV film 1977 U.S. (CBS) 90 Minutes Color

A reluctant superhero fights crime, allergies and two left feet.

Described by creator Stan Lee as "probably the first superhero to wear his neuroses on his sleeve," Spider-Man became a comic book cult figure soon after his introduction in Marvel's *The Fantastic Four* in 1961. By 1977, his adventures were being syndicated in more than 400 newspapers across the U.S., his familiar likeness graced products ranging from T-shirts to coffee cups, and he finally had his own television program.

Introducing his weekly series, **The Amazing Spider-Man** (1977-79), this pilot film traces his origins in the person of Peter Parker, who was bitten by a radioactive spider while a science major in college. Thus given superhuman powers, he designs and sews a red-and-blue costume himself (otherwise the tailor would know his true identity), and invents a wrist strap that shoots a climbing web capable of entangling attackers.

The plot has to do with an extortionist who claims that he has programmed several community leaders to commit crimes, and that ten others will destroy themselves on command if the mayor doesn't pay a ransom of $50 million. While tracking down the criminals Parker/Spider-Man has assorted misadventures that have to do with Parker's hypochondria and general clumsiness, in contrast to Spider-Man's powers. More consistently amusing is **The Greatest American Hero** (1981) a superhero spoof that is "Spidey's" direct descendant.

Director: E. W. Swackhamer, *Producer:* Edward J. Montagne, *Screenplay:* Alvin Boretz, *Photographer:* Fred Jackman, *Art Director:* James Hulsey, *Cost:* Frank Novak, *Music:* Johnnie Spence

Cast: Nicholas Hammond, David White, Michael Pataki, Thayer David, Hilly Hicks, Lisa Eilbacher, Jeff Donnell

STAR

Luminous globe of extremely hot gases ranging in size from about 10,000 miles in diameter to about 2 billion miles in diameter. Smaller stars are called dwarfs and larger ones are called supergiants. Earth's star is the **sun,** one of about 200 billion contained in the Milky Way Galaxy. Distances between stars are so vast that a spaceship going from **Earth** to the North Star, one of the closer ones, would take 300 years to reach traveling at the speed of light.

STARCRASH

(Also titled: *The Adventures of Stella Star*)

Film   1979   Italy (New World)   91 Minutes
Metrocolor   Dolby Stereo

Italy, home of the "spaghetti" western, tried the recipe on **Star Wars** (1977) and came up with this slick and sexy **space opera.** Its plot focuses on Stella Star, the **Barbarella**-like pilot of an intergalactic smuggling ship. Summoned by the Emperor, saucy Stella and her mysterious alien navigator rush to help. The universe, it seems, is in the grip of dark-

Starcrash: Stella Star and her pet robot Elle.

ness under the evil eye of Count Zarth Arn. Later on there's a duel with **laser** swords.

Director: Lewis Coates (Luigi Cozzi), *Producers:* Nat and Patrick Wachsberger, *Screenplay:* Lewis Coates, Nat Wachsberger, *Photographers:* Paul Beeson, Roberto D'Ettorre, *Production Designer:* Aurelio Crugnolla, *Special Effects:* Ron Hays, Armando Valcauda, Germano Natali, *Music:* **John Barry**

Cast: Caroline Munro, Marjoe Gortner, Christopher Plummer, David Hasselhoff, Joe Spinell

THE STARLOST

TV series   1973   Canada (syndicated)
60 Minutes (weekly)   Color

SF writer Harlan Ellison disowned this series and had himself listed on the credits as Cordwainer Bird, his favorite pseudonym. The action took place in the year 2790, after a great catastrophe, aboard the Earth Ship Ark, described as "an organic cluster of environmental domes called biospheres, corridors looped to each other through tubular corridors for life support power and communication." Two men and women traveled through space for 800 years with the seeds of three million people, talking to a computer, and looking for a habitable world to populate.

Cast: Keir Dullea, Robin Ward, Gay Rowan, William Osler

STAR MAIDENS

(Also titled: *Space Maidens*)

TV series   1975   Great Britain/Germany (ATV)   30 Minutes (weekly)   Color

Wrenched from its orbit by a **comet,** the planet Medusa comes to rest in our **solar system** after many years spent drifting through the frozen reaches of space. The Medusans are ruled by women—the Star Maidens of the title—who live in a rigid moralistic **dystopia** in warm underground cities, waiting for the thaw. As if this weren't preposterous enough, the running plot concerned two escaped Medusan male slaves pursued to **Earth** by two shapely policewomen. The program was syndicated in the U.S. in 1977.

Directors: **Freddie Francis,** James Gatward, Hans Heinrich and others, *Producer:* James Gatward, *Creator:* Eric Paice, *Writers:* Eric Paice, Otto Strang, Ian Stuart Black, *Music:* Patrick Aulton

Cast: Judy Geeson, Dawn Addams, Lisa Harrow, Christiane Kruger, Pierre Brice, Derek Farr

STARSHIP INVASIONS

(Original title: *Alien Encounter)*

Film   1978   U.S. (Warner Brothers)
89 Minutes   Color

Rushed into theaters on the heels of **Close Encounters of the Third Kind,** *Starship Invasions* underwent a hasty name change to avoid a lawsuit and reappeared with a title cribbed from the other big SF hit of 1977. Made in Canada, the film stars Christopher Lee (trying to look sinister in mandarin pajamas and pillbox hat) as the commander of a fleet of UFOs called the Legion of the Winged Serpent, here scouting a new home for the people of his dying planet. Also on hand is an intergalactic police force of **UFOs,** sequestered in the Bermuda triangle, here to protect Earth from Lee's colonial designs. During the inevitable showdown, the U.S. Army joins forces with the peace-lovers, only to be foiled by Lee, who hypnotizes the soldiers to fire on their allies. The flying saucer dogfights by special effects man

Starship Invasions: Christopher Lee dressed to kill.

Warren Keillor are better than *Starship Invasions* deserves.

Director/Screenplay: Ed Hunt, *Producer:* Ed Hunt, Ken Gord, *Special Effects:* Warren Keillor, *Makeup:* Maureen Sweeny, *Music:* Gil Melle

Cast: Christopher Lee, Robert Vaughn, Sherri Rose, Tiiu Leek, Daniel Pilon

STARSTRUCK

TV pilot   1979   CBS   30 Minutes   Color

Comedy in an orbiting hotel of the 22nd century.

Trouble begins to brew at the Midway Inn when the fat and sinister Orthwaite Frodo arrives on a space shuttle and discovers the delicious apple pie served there. He demands full franchising rights, but the owners aren't having any, which sets the stage for an old-fashioned Western showdown. The villain is predictably vanquished, as was this would-be series, which had the misfortune of being pitted against **Battlestar Galactica** and *Chips,* a top-rated formula series about highway patrolmen. Its demise was assured nevertheless since most of the adult audience had probably not seen **Star Wars** and were unaware of what was being satirized. Broadway author Arthur Kopit poked gentle fun at American-style greed and SF films, and satire is not the stuff of successful commercial television. A gallery of **aliens**—including a hairless bartender

A two-headed alien (Chris Walas) and a comedian (Paul "Mousie" Garner) audition for a space-age nightclub in *Starstruck.*

with a double-stamped nose and a two-headed one-man duo—were especially memorable.

Director: Al Viola, *Producer:* Herbert B. Leonard, *Writer:* Arthur Kopit, *Cameraman:* Craig Greene, *Art Director:* Kirk Axtell, *Music:* Alan Arper

Cast: Beeson Carroll, Chris Walas, Paul "Mousie" Garner, Lynne Lipton, Roy Brocksmith, Guy Raymond, Meegan King, Kevin Brando

STAR TREK

TV series   1966-69   U.S. (NBC)   60 Minutes (weekly)   Color

Conceived by producer **Gene Roddenberry** as a *"Wagon Train* to the stars," *Star Trek* was set 200 years in the future. The action took place aboard the **U.S.S. Enterprise,** a mammoth **starship** on a five-year mission for the United Federation of Planets to explore new worlds and deliver supplies to settlements in space. On board were a crew of over 200, whose officers were Captain James T. Kirk (William Shatner), Dr. Leonard "Bones" McCoy (DeForest Kelley), Science Officer **Mr. Spock (Leonard Nimoy),** Helmsman Sulu (George Takei), **Ensign Pavel Chekov** (Walter Koenig), Yeoman Janice Rand (Grace Lee Whitney), Communications Officer Uhura (Nichelle Nichols), Engineer Montgomery Scott (James Doohan) and Nurse Christine Chapel (Majel Barrett). Their peaceful mission was often interrupted by two vicious **alien** races, the **Klingons** and the **Romulans,** both seeking to rule the cosmos. They also encountered other weirdly shaped aliens, **humanoid** creatures with strange powers, and they occasionally traveled back and forth in time.

Roddenberry had spent several years trying to sell the networks on a sophisticated, adult science fiction series, which at the time was thought by TV executives to appeal only to children. In 1964 CBS expressed interest in the idea, and Roddenberry put together a pilot episode with Jeffrey Hunter as Christopher Pike, Captain of the *Enterprise.* The network changed its mind, however, and instead aired **Irwin Allen's** family-oriented **Lost in Space** (1965-68). NBC subsequently picked up the series after making several changes, including a softer look for Mr. Spock's eyebrows and a less "cerebral" approach to the scripts. Hunter was no longer available, so William Shatner was recruited for the role, along with several new

The U.S.S. Enterprise

cast members. The program debuted in the fall of 1966.

Stories were generally well-written, often by noted SF writers, according to Roddenberry's dictum that the characters be given understandable 20th-century motivations for their conflicts in space and time. Consequently, the *Enterprise's* journey was as recognizable to viewers as a stagecoach bringing settlers to the old West. The format also allowed for the inclusion of contemporary social issues such as racism, portrayed in an **extraterrestrial** setting. Special effects were also first-rate (for television), especially the **transporter room** effect, which beamed the *Enterprise* crew to and from planets, precluding the need for bulky and distracting space suits.

Despite its high artistic standards, however, the program never achieved the ratings it needed, and advertisers complained that the bulk of its viewers were teenagers with no interest in prime-time products. Saved from cancellation during the second season by a write-in campaign organized by Roddenberry, the program finally succumbed at the end of the third season, after 78 episodes. But *Star Trek* proved to be The Show That Would Not Die. Unlike other series, it actually became more popular in syndication than during its network run, ultimately making it one of Paramount TV's biggest money-makers. Seemingly timeless, it was still running years later (and still is), inspiring an animated TV series (see listing below) and, finally, a big-screen return with the old cast in **Star Trek—The Motion Picture** (1979). (See also: **Phaser, Tricorder.**)

Directors: **Joseph Sargent,** Gerd Oswald, Joe Pevney, Herb Wallerstein, Marc Daniels, Marc Daniels, **Harvey Hart** and others, *Executive Producer/Creator:* Gene Roddenberry, *Producers:* Gene Roddenberry, Gene Coon, John Meredyth Lucas, Fred Freiberger, *Writers:* David Gerrold, **Richard Matheson,** Robert Bloch, Gene Roddenberry, Theodore Sturgeon, Harlan Ellison, D.C. Fontana and others, *Photographer:* Ernest Haller, *Special Effects:* The Howard Anderson Co., The Westheimer Co., Film Effects of Hollywood, Inc., *Makeup:* Fred Phillips, *Music:* Alexander Courage, Gerald Fried

Cast: William Shatner, Leonard Nimoy, DeForest Kelley, Nichelle Nichols, George Takei, Jimmy Doohan, Majel Barret, Walter Koenig, Grace Lee Whitney [first season only]

STAR TREK

TV series   1973-74   U.S. (NBC)   30 Minutes (weekly)   Color

This animated cartoon version of **Star Trek** (1966-69) gave young Saturday morning TV viewers something to think about as well as look at. Produced by the Filmation studios in limited animation, the characters didn't move very smoothly, but their adventures were involving and well-paced, probably because they were selected by D. C. Fontana, who had written many episodes for the live-action series. Some original cast members supplied the voices, but not Walter Koenig, whose character, **Ensign Pavel Chekov,** was not portrayed, evidently for budgetary reasons.

Director: Hal Sutherland, *Producers:* Lou Scheimer, Norm Prescott, *Associate Producer/Story Editor:* D. C. Fontana, *Music:* Yvette Blais, Jeff Michael

Voices: William Shatner, **Leonard Nimoy,** DeForest Kelley, James Doohan, Nichelle Nichols

STAR TREK—THE MOTION PICTURE

Film   1979   U.S. (Paramount)   142 Minutes
Metrocolor   Panavision   Dolby Stereo

Brought to the screen by popular demand, the old **Star Trek** TV series looked good on the big screen, even though the reassembled crew had little to do except to decorate the spotty special effects. The plot is set in the 23rd century, with **the Enterprise** going back into action to investigate the source of a mysterious power that has annihilated a **Klingon** fleet. The "creature" turns out to be an old Voyager space probe—called "V'ger"—which has developed an emotionless but powerful intelligence. A side trip to Vulcan and a visit with **Mr. Spock's** family helps make up for the tedium.

Director: **Robert Wise,** *Producer:* **Gene Roddenberry,** *Screenplay:* Harold Livingston, *Idea:* Alan Dean Foster, *Photographer:* Richard Kline, *Spe-*

Star Trek—The Motion Picture: The crew of the Enterprise reunited. Top row, from left: Ensign Chekov (Walter Koenig), Dr. Chapel (Majel Barrett), Janice Rand (Grace Lee Whitney), Scotty (James Doohan). Front row, from left: Uhura (Nichelle Nichols), Mr. Spock (Leonard Nimoy), Captain Kirk (William Shatner), Dr. McCoy (DeForest Kelley), Sulu (George Takei).

cial Effects: **Douglas Trumbull,** *Music:* **Jerry Goldsmith**

Cast: William Shatner, **Leonard Nimoy,** Walter Koenig, Nichelle Nichols, Majel Barrett, Grace Lee Whitney, George Takei, James Doohan, DeForest Kelly, Stephen Collins, Persis Khambatta

STAR TREK II: THE WRATH OF KHAN

Film 1982 U.S. (Paramount) 113 Minutes
Technicolor Panavision Dolby Stereo

After the mind-numbing nonsense that ruined the first film, *Star Trek* got back on the track with this sequel, which is also a sequel to an episode of the TV series. Khan (Ricardo Montalban), whose full name is Khan Noonian Singh, is a brawny artificially bred man, discovered in a "Sleeper Ship" by the **Enterprise** crew in the "Space Seed" episode. Revived from a 20th-century **cryonic** deepfreeze, he attempted to take con-

trol of the starship and was put off by Captain Kirk on a hostile, unexplored planet with Marla, a crew member who had fallen in love with him.

Naturally, Khan blamed Captain Kirk for all his problems, including the loss of his "wife" Marla. In *Star Trek II*, he attempts to extract his revenge. The sadistic Khan had the good luck to be deposited on a planet whose only life form is an **alien** creature that looks something like a cross between a turtle and a shrimp, which spawns tiny scorpion-shaped offspring. They have particularly nasty uses, as Khan explains with great joy. "[They] enter through the ears and wrap themselves around the cerebral cortex. This has the effect of rendering the victim extremely susceptible to suggestion." Before long, an earwig is slithering through Ensign Pavel Chekov's head and creating panic among the crew.

Made by the TV arm of Paramount, the film is closer in spirit to the series, with the same tight plotting, snappy dialogue and witty interplay between **Mr. Spock** and Dr. "Bones" McCoy, absent the last time around. While the first film belonged to Spock, this one returns ownership to Captain Kirk, now an Admiral, giving him a majestic entrance backlit with blue lights. Now 16 years older than when the TV series began, and facing a mid-life crisis, Kirk is given to such wistful remarks as, "Galloping around the cosmos is a game for the young."

Added to the cast is a Vulcan beauty named Lieutenant Saavik, who is even more competent than Mr. Spock, her partner. They speak in Vulcan, translated by subtitles. Spock, as everyone in the universe knows, dies in this film, a sad event foreshadowed by his birthday gift to Kirk of a copy of Dickens' *A Tale of Two Cities*. In the TV series, however, death could usually be overcome with a little technological mumbo-jumbo, and it seems unlikely that **Leonard Nimoy** will be missing from *Star Trek III*.

Director: Nicholas Meyer, *Producer:* Robert Sallin, *Screenplay:* Jack Sowards, *Story:* Harve Bennett, Jack Sowards, *Photography:* Gayne Rescher, *Production Designer:* Joseph R. Jennings, *Special Effects:* Industrial Light and Magic, Jim Veilleux, Ken Ralston, *Costumes:* Robert Fletcher, *Sound Effects:* Alan Howarth, *Music:* James Horner, Alexander Courage

Cast: William Shatner, **Leonard Nimoy,** DeForest Kelley, James Doohan, Walter Koenig, George Takei, Nichelle Nichols, Ricardo Montalban, Ike Eisenmann, Paul Winfield, Bibi Besch, Merritt Butrick

STAR WARS

Film 1977 U.S. (20th Century-Fox)
121 Minutes Technicolor Panavision
Dolby Stereo

No film before or since has captured the hearts of movie-goers like *Star Wars*, which once and for all catapulted the SF film out of its low-budget ghetto. Creator **George Lucas** called his **space opera** a "fantasy, not science fiction," although it qualifies on both counts. The film is in fact a pastiche, made up of borrowings from fiction and films that linger in popular memory. Its instantly familiar plot, for instance, is a reworking of T. H. White's Camelot stories, with **Luke Skywalker** as the young and future king who pulls the sword from the stone (a magical **lightsaber** this time) and **Ben Kenobi** as his Merlinesque tutor. **Princess Leia Organa** is a liberated Guinevere, **Darth Vader** is the

Star Wars: C-3PO and pal R2-D2 are caught in a rebel attack on the Death Star.

Black Knight, and **Han Solo** is Sir Lancelot, Skywalker's friend and rival for the hand of Princess Leia.

Lucas has dressed up the old good-vs.-bad story with hip dialogue, a state-of-the-art SF setting, and two futuristic clowns. The **robots C-3PO** and **R2-D2** are ancestors of the art deco model seen in **Metropolis** (1926) and **Robby,** the winsome helpmate of **Forbidden Planet** (1956), by way of Laurel and Hardy. And **Chewbacca,** Han Solo's wookie friend,

Princess Leia Organa (Carrie Fisher): heroine of the *Star Wars* series.

brings to mind **King Kong** (1933). The film's **cliffhanger** format is a reference to the **Flash Gordon** serials, which Lucas claimed he wanted to remake.

But above all *Star Wars* is a delightful entertainment whose virtuoso special effects dazzle the eye with optical magic. Stanley Kubrick's **2001: A Space Odyssey** (1968) had 35 separate composites, but in the interim special effects had advanced by light years, and *Star Wars* had 380. On screen, the miniature fighters move with the precision and weighted force of full-sized spaceships, an illusion achieved by **John Dykstra's** motion control camera. In reality, the miniature ships moved only from left to right, rotated, hovered and slid back and forth. The camera provided the forward and backward thrust, moving along a 75-foot-long trench. "A computer drove the camera," Producer Gary Kurtz explained. "It matched the movements of the various elements perfectly. You could repeat a move of a ship exactly for as many passes as you wanted. We programmed the movements into the computer from dogfight scenes from old World War II movies." Other scenic elements were composited with a quad printer, which projects four separate shots through a prism onto a single piece of film.

After the release of **The Empire Strikes Back** (1980), Lucas retitled the film *Star Wars: Episode IV* for a projected nine-part series. *Empire* is *Episode V*, and *Revenge of the Jedi* (1983) is *Episode VI*, climaxing Luke's running battle with Darth Vader. *Episodes I, II* and *III* will depict the fall of the republic and Luke's youth, and *Episodes VII, VIII* and *IX* will deal with the rebuilding of the republic.

Director/Screenplay: **George Lucas,** *Producer:* Gary Kurtz, *Photographer:* Gilbert Taylor, *Production Designer:* **John Barry,** *Special Effects:* **John Dykstra,** John Stears, Richard Edlund, Grant McCune, Robert Blalack, *Editors:* Marcia Lucas, Paul Hirsch, Richard Chew, *Makeup:* **Stuart Freeborn, Rick Baker,** *Sound Effects:* **Ben Burtt, Jr.,** *Music:* **John Williams**

Cast: **Mark Hamill,** Harrison Ford, Carrie Fisher, Alec Guinness, **Peter Cushing,** Anthony Daniels, Kenny Baker, Peter Mayhew, **David Prowse**

Star Wars on radio: Anthony Daniels (far left) and Mark Hamill (far right) repeat their movie roles as, respectively, C-3PO and Luke Skywalker. Perry King (center) replaces Harrison Ford as Han Solo, and Bernard Behrens stands in for Alec Guinness as Ben Kenobi.

THE STEPFORD WIVES

Film   1974   U.S. (Columbia)   115 Minutes
Color

Joanna, a liberated young Manhattan photographer, reluctantly moves to suburban Stepford, Connecticut at the sudden insistence of her husband. Gradually, she comes to realize that neighboring housewives are interested only in cooking, cleaning and pleasing their husbands, just like the stereotypes seen in TV commercials. Conducting a surreptitious investigation, she discovers they are actually **robot** duplicates programmed to be perfect male companions by an anti-feminist men's club, which her husband had recently joined. The original wives have all been murdered, and she is next on the list.

This sophisticated black comedy has its moments, but the story never seems to get moving, nor are the performances—except for Paula Prentiss—anything to write home about. A cute bit: the robot-maker, Coba, learned his trade at Disneyland. Critic Pauline Kael called the film "degrading" to women. Not widely exhibited, it was released in Great Britain in 1978.

Director: Bryan Forbes, *Producer:* Edgar J. Sherick, *Screenplay:* William Goldman, *Novel:* Ira Levin, *Photographer:* Owen Roizman, *Production Designer:* Gene Callahan, *Music:* Michael Small

Cast: Katharine Ross, Paula Prentiss, Nanette Newman, Patrick O'Neal, Tina Louise

STEREOSCOPIC FILM

Three-dimensional (3-D) motion pictures are made possible by the fact that our eyes see two slightly different images—a characteristic called stereoscopic vision, or the ability to perceive depth. To effect the illusion of perspective and space, stereo films present the eyes with two slightly different screen images projected over each other. Viewing lenses separate the images, and the brain fuses them into one.

Stereoscopic film technology has its roots in the Victorian-era stereoscope, a popular handheld device through which twin still photographs were viewed side by side (today's Viewmaster toy is its direct descendant). Various experimental systems were patented in the U.S., Great Britain and France around the turn of the century, and a number of 3-D films were produced commercially during the 1920s and 1930s. In one process, adjoining images were viewed through a cumbersome stereoscope-like device functional only from the central part of an auditorium. More successful was the anaglyphic system, in which two cameras are placed 2½ inches apart to simulate the separation of the human eyes. Two black-and-white films are then projected through red-and-green filters, producing superimposed images (the anaglyph), unscrambled by counterpart viewing lenses. An early SF

film, **Radio-Mania** (1924) was one of the first to use this process. In 1939 Edwin A. Land (inventor of the Polaroid camera) introduced a system of color projection in which the images are separated by polarized filters.

A dozen years later Hollywood revived the anaglyph and Land systems as one of a number of film gimmicks and **wide-screen** processes conjured up to lure dwindling movie audiences away from their TV sets. A short-lived 3-D boom began with the success of **Arch Oboler's** *Bwana Devil* (1952), a second-rate jungle adventure, which precipitated a flood of similar low-budget productions. A few quality 3-D films were made, including Alfred Hitchcock's *Dial M for Murder,* the musical *Kiss Me Kate,* the horror film *House of Wax* and three SF classics: **It Came from Outer Space, Invaders from Mars** and **The Creature from the Black Lagoon.** The public soon tired of ducking in their seats as things were thrown at them from the screen, however, and the nuisance of wearing paper spectacles hardly seemed worthwhile for viewing films that had otherwise little merit. By 1954 the fad had run its course.

Three-D films have occasionally surfaced since then—notably **Andy Warhol's Frankenstein** (1974), *Comin' At Ya!* (1981), and **Parasite** (1982). The latter two films boasted the latest in 3-D technology: a single camera freed of the restrictions of filming with two synchronized cameras (and the unreliability and expense of twin projectors). The camera is fitted with double lenses that record the images on a single reel of film. It can move in almost any direction, be handheld, shoot in slow or fast motion, and it will accept **zoom lenses.** Film technologists hope to do away with viewing lenses in the near future with a 3-D lenseless photographic process called **holography**—now in the experimental stage.

STOP-MOTION

A motion picture technique used to create the illusion that inanimate objects are moving on the screen. The objects (usually **puppets)** are adjusted slightly between takes and photographed one frame at a time.

The Optimax III, the latest in 3-D technology, on the set of *Comin' At Ya!*

When the film is projected at normal speed—24 frames per second—the objects appear to have lives of their own. Special effects veteran **Ray Harryhausen** has refined the technique to a high motion picture art in a process known as Dynarama. Stop motion is responsible for the moving "performances" of the original **King Kong** and **Godzilla.** (See also: **Animation; Willis H. O'Brien; George Pal.**)

STRANGE, GLENN (1899–1973)

Tall, rangy actor who succeeded **Boris Karloff** and **Lon Chaney, Jr.** as the monster in Universal's **Frankenstein** sequels. Half Cherokee Indian and half Irish, Strange was born in Weed, New Mexico, where he was a rancher and rodeo cowboy. He came to the attention of Hollywood in 1935 while singing with the Arizona Wranglers on radio. He appeared in many films, usually Westerns and usually as a heavy, including *Wagon Train* (1940), *Action in the North Atlantic* (1943), *Red River* (1948) and *The Red Badge of Courage* (1951). In later years he had a running part as Sam the bartender on the popular TV series *Gunsmoke*. He portrayed the Frankenstein monster in **House of Frankenstein** and **House of Dracula** (both 1945) and **Abbott and Costello Meet Frankenstein** (1948). His only other SF film was **The Mad Monster** (1942).

THE STRANGER

TV film   1973   U.S. (ABC)   100 Minutes   Color

This interesting chase thriller is one of the few films to deal with the popular SF theme of **parallel worlds.** Similar to the theatrical film **Journey to the Far Side of the Sun** (1969), it concerns an astronaut who crashlands on a planet called **Terra,** revolving in **Earth's** orbit opposite the sun. The astronaut runs for his life when slated for extermination by the planet's totalitarian regime, called the Perfect Order.

Director: Lee H. Katzin, *Producer:* Alan A. Armer, *Screenplay:* Gerald Sanford, *Photographer:* Keith

C. Smith, *Art Director:* Stan Jolley, *Music:* Richard Markowitz

Cast: Glenn Corbett, Cameron Mitchell, Sharon Acker, Lew Ayres, George Coulouris, Dean Jagger

THE STRANGE WORLD OF PLANET X

(U.S. title: *The Cosmic Monsters, The Crawling Terror*)

Film   1958   Great Britain (Eros/DCA)   75 Minutes   Black & white

This badly mounted, technically weak film savages the BBC-TV series on which it is based. The preposterous story concerns a dopey scientist who accidently pokes a hole in Earth's magnetic field with an experimental ray. This allows space **aliens** to enter and create an ecological disaster, with grasshoppers growing to the size of houses. A kindly **alien** finally arrives in a flying saucer to clean up the mess and make things right.

Director: Gilbert Gunn, *Producer:* George Maynard, *Screenplay:* Paul Ryder, Joe Ambor, *Novel:* Rene Ray, *Music:* Robert Sharples

Cast: Forrest Tucker, Gaby Andre, Martin Benson, Wyndham Goldie

STRUSS, KARL (1891–   )

Director of photography; born in New York City, educated at Columbia University. A former still photographer, Struss entered films in 1919 as a cameraman for Cecil B. DeMille. He was one of the main cameramen (among 13) for *Ben Hur* (1926), in which he transformed normal extras into deformed lepers on-camera with a series of filters placed over the lens. He later used the technique to transform Frederic March from a respectable doctor to a psychopathic Neanderthal in **Dr. Jekyll and Mr. Hyde** (1932). Struss shared an **Academy Award** (the first given) with Charles Rosher for the atmospheric photography of *Sunrise* (1927). Under contract to Paramount from 1931 to 1949, he subsequently freelanced and made TV commercials before retiring in the early 1960s.

Other films: Lady of the Pavements (1929)*, The Sign of the Cross,* **Island of Lost Souls** (1932)*, The Great*

Dictator (1940), *Journey Into Fear* (1942), *The Macomber Affair* (1947), **Rocketship X-M** (1950), *Limelight* (1952), **She Devil** (1957), **The Fly** (1958), *The Rebel Set* (1959)

SUN

A self-generating celestial body; a **star.** **Earth's** sun, a modest star with a diameter of about one million miles (the equivalent of four times the distance from Earth to the moon), holds the planets in their orbits by its immense gravitational pull. All life is due to the sun, of course, whose radiant energy is stored in coal, oil and wood, which were once living organisms.

The sun generates its energy by nuclear fusion (the principle behind the hydrogen bomb) and burns about 22 quadrillion tons of hydrogen yearly, reaching an internal temperature of about 25 million degrees Fahrenheit (13,88 million degrees Celsius). Should its fires extinguish, the oceans would turn to ice and all life would expire from the cold. Cosmologists believe the opposite will occur, however: At the end of its life cycle, when its fuel is exhausted, the sun will explode in a massive fireball and pull the **solar system** into a **black hole.** Both possibilities have been well-explored by SF writers and all but overlooked by filmmakers.

SUPERMAN

Comic-book character created by writer **Jerome Siegel** and illustrator Joseph Shuster. Siegel modeled Superman/Clark Kent after the superhuman hero of Philip Wylie's novel *Gladiator* (1930) and pulp hero Doc Savage, whose first name was also Clark. (See: **Doc Savage: Man of Bronze.**) Superman made his debut in Action Comics No. 1, published in June, 1938. An instant hit, by year's end he was being syndicated in a newspaper comic strip and had his own comic book. Among his imitators are **Captain America, Batman, Captain Marvel,** and **Wonder Woman.**

According to his legend, which has accumulated from various mediums, Superman is a member of an **alien** race that lived on the planet Krypton, and was sent to **Earth** by his parents to survive a cosmic disaster. Adopted by the Kent family in Kansas, he assumed the identity of a meek earthling named Clark Kent, although his real name is Jor-El. Whenever the world is in danger, he steps into a phone booth and quickly strips out of Clark's clothes, which go into a pouch hidden in his cape. As Superman, he travels through time, to other universes, often to rescue Lois Lane, Clark Kent's rival at *The Daily Planet*, (originally *The Star*) where they are both reporters. The "S" on his costume doesn't stand for Superman, of course; it is the Jor-El family crest. And, originally, he jumped rather than flew. The supreme guardian of America and its moral values, Superman/Clark Kent embarrassed himself during World War II when he failed his medical test for military service. During the vision test, his X-ray eyes read the chart in the next room and, naturally, he couldn't explain what had happened without giving away his identity.

Superman has appeared in the following mediums: *Radio:* **The Adventures of Superman** (1940-53). *Television:* **The Adventures of Superman** (1953-57), **The New Adventures of Superman** (1966-67) [animated], **Superfriends** (1973-present) [animated]. *Films:* **Superman** (1941-43) [animated], **Superman** (1948), **Atom Man vs. Superman** (1950), **Superman and the Mole Men** (1951), **Superman—The Movie** (1978), **Superman II** (1981). *Theater:* **It's a Bird ... It's a Plane ... It's Superman!**

SUPERMAN

Films 1941-43 U.S. (Paramount) Technicolor

Superman first appeared on the screen as a cartoon character in a series of 17 shorts animated by the studio of Max Fleischer. These were notable in that they accurately copied the **comic-book** style and brought the illustrations vividly to life in color with full **animation.** The best of these is "The Mechanical Monsters," first in the series, seen in the feature-length anthology film *The Fantastic Animation Festival* (1977). Superman's voice was provided by Clayton "Bud" Collyer, star of the long-running radio serial **The Adventures of Superman** (1940-53). (See also: **Rotoscope.**)

Directors: Dave Fleischer, Seymour Kneitel, Dan Gordon, Isidore Sparber

SUPERMAN

Film serial   1948   U.S. (Columbia)
15 Episodes   Black & white

Movie **serials** were on their way out and superhero **comic books** had peaked several years before when Columbia acquired the movie rights to *Superman* and launched him as a live-action **serial** hero. Episodes ineptly recounted Superman's background and pitted him against the Spider Lady, an underworld queen with a **death ray** and a piece of **Kryptonite.** Former dancer **Kirk Alyn** resembled Superman but lacked the muscles and height to compete with the **comic-book** image, and the serial was not a popular success. The contract called for two films, however, and **Atom Man vs. Superman** appeared two years later, again with Alyn cast in the title role. Clark Kent got his first newspaper byline here, and **Noel Neill** debuted as Lois Lane.

Directors: **Spencer Bennett,** Thomas Carr, *Producer:* Sam Katzman, *Screenplay:* Arthur Hoerl, Lewis Clay, Royal Cole, *Music:* Mischa Bakaleinikoff

Cast: Kirk Alyn, Noel Neill, Tommy Bond, Carol Forman, George Meeker

SUPERMAN—THE MOVIE

Film   1978   U.S./Great Britain (Warner Bros.)
143 Minutes   Technicolor   Panavision
Dolby Stereo

In the 40 years since his birth, **Superman** had gone from **comic-book** favorite to American myth, and it is no longer necessary to explain who is, what his powers are, or to introduce his familiar friends and villains. Realizing this, the filmmakers concentrated instead on developing Superman's personality and duplicating his comic-book

powers with a score of breath-taking, special effects.

The first third of the movie recounts Superman's birth legend and takes place on Krypton, his birthplace, and Smallville, Kansas, where he is adopted by the Kent family. Grown up, he moves to Metropolis and goes to work for *The Daily Planet* where he meets Lois Lane, the newspaper's aggressive star reporter, who regards him as a naive country bumpkin. Meanwhile, Superman becomes aware of Lex Luthor's scheme to destroy California (in the comic book, Luthor was constantly seeking revenge because of a childhood contretemps with Superman). Luthor has purchased most of the desert land on the eastern side of the San Andreas fault, with the intention of turning it into waterfront property. He plans to blow up the faultline with a stolen atomic warhead and watch Southern California slip into the ocean. Scriptwriter Mario Puzo provides a less whimsical subplot concerning a curse placed on Jor-El and his family by three Kryptonian criminals sentenced to "negativity." The criminals provide a bridge to the sequel, **Superman II** (1981).

Superman's live-action feats are the equal of anything he can do in pen and ink: He effortlessly grabs a speedboat full of criminals with his iron hands, prevents a helicopter crash by catching it in mid-air, cooks a souffle for Lois Lane with his X-ray eyes, and welds together the Golden Gate Bridge after it has been severed by an earthquake, induced by the malevolent Luthor. Les Bowie, Colin Chilvers, Denys Coop, Roy Field and Derek Meddings all won **Academy Awards** for their convincing illusions, as did Zoran Perisic, who invented a new system called the **Zoptic Process** to make Superman fly.

Christopher Reeve, an unknown when he signed for the picture, became a star overnight. As box-office insurance, producer Salkind cast Gene Hackman as Lex Luthor and superstar Marlon Brando (who was reportedly paid $2.5 million for 13 days work) as Jor-El. The co-scriptwriters, David Newman and Robert Benton, had previously collaborated on a Broadway musical about

Three Supermen: Kirk Alyn (1948), George Reeves (1955) and Christopher Reeve (1978).

fects: Les Bowie, Roy Field, *Mattes, composites and Process:* Derek Meddings, *Music:* **John Williams**

Cast: Marlon Brando, Gene Hackman, Christopher Reeve, Ned Beatty, Jackie Cooper, Glenn Ford, Trevor Howard, Margot Kidder, Valerine Perrine, Terence Stamp, Maria Schell, Phyllis Thaxter, Susannah York, Noel Niell, **Kirk Alyn**

The Man of Steel, **It's a Bird ... It's a Plane . . . It's Superman!** (1966-67), which has certain similarities to the film.

Director: Richard Donner, *Producer:* Pierre Spengler, *Executive Producer:* Ilya Salkind, *Screenplay:* Mario Puzo, David Newman, Robert Benton, *Story:* Mario Puzo, *Characters created by:* **Jerry Siegel** and Joel Shuster, *Photographer:* **Geoffrey Unsworth**, *Production Designer:* **John Barry**, *Director of special effects:* Colin Chilvers, *Optical Ef-*

SUPERMAN II

Film 1981   U.S./Great Britain (Warner Bros.)
127 Minutes   Technicolor   Panavision
Dolby Stereo

Superman II is that rare event, a sequel that is even better than the first film—wittier, more lively and written and played with more emotional depth. In **Superman—The Movie** (1978), the enemy was nature—tidal waves, earthquakes and time (he spun the **Earth** backward to rescue Lois Lane). Here the enemy is a swinish collection of bad guys from the planet Krypton and Superman's own humanity (even though he *is* an **alien**). The best scenes are between The Man of Steel and Lois Lane, who finally go off to Superman's crystal palace for a night of love. The cost is high, and, as a result, he loses his superpowers. For the sake of Earth, he gives up Lois in a marvelously touching scene, to vanquish Ursa, Non and General Zod, the vicious Kryptonians introduced in the previous film. **Christopher Reeve** is better than ever, moving effortlessly from his comic phone-booth costume changes to a deeply felt emotional crisis. Richard Lester directed with his characteristic buoyant touch, although some of the footage is left over from the first film.

Director: Richard Lester, *Producer:* Pierre Spengler, *Executive Producer:* Ilya Salkind, *Screenplay:* Mario Puzo, David Newman, Leslie Newman, *Story:* Mario Puzo, *Photographer:* Daniel W. Wilson, *Production Designer:* Mario Puzo, *Special Effects:* Colin Chilvers, Les Bowie, Derek Meddings, *Music:* Ken Thorne, *based on themes composed by:* **John Williams**

Cast: Gene Hackman, Christopher Reeve, Ned Beatty, Jackie Cooper, Margot Kidder, Sarah Douglas, Valerie Perrine, Susannah York, Terence Stamp, Jack O'Halloran, E. G. Marshall

SUPERMAN AND THE MOLE MEN

(Also titled: *Superman and the Strange People*)

Film 1951 U.S. (Lippert) 67 Minutes Black & white

Barrel-chested **George Reeves** replaced **Kirk Alyn** as the Man of Steel in this low-budget programmer—Superman's first feature film—which was cast and supervised by D.C. Comics. The mole men were furry hybrids uncovered by the world's deepest oil well and hunted by the townspeople of Silsby, when all they wanted was to be left alone. Clark Kent covered the story with Lois Lane (Phyllis Coates). As Superman he protected the bigoted townspeople from ray guns possessed by the radioactive mole men. The creatures, played by the midgets of **The Wizard of Oz** (1939), carried **weapons** made from vacuum cleaner cannisters. The film later turned up on Reeve's subsequent TV series, **The Adventures of Superman** (1953-57) as a two-part episode entitled "The Unknown People."

Director: Lee Sholem, *Producer:* Whitney Ellsworth, *Screenplay:* Richard Fielding (Robert Maxwell)

Cast: George Reeves, Phyllis Coates, Jeff Corey, Walter Reed, Stanley Andrews

SUSPENDED ANIMATION

A life-prolonging procedure in which an individual is preserved by radically lowering his body temperature and metabolic functions, or by **cryonics,** wherein the body is frozen. Long a staple of science fiction, suspended animation was the usual method of **time travel** before the invention of the **time machine.** In **horror** and fantasy films, indi-

Suspended animation: The crew of the Nostromo awakens from "hypersleep" in *Alien* (1979).

viduals such as ancient gods and mummies are preserved and revived centuries later by magical means, usually accidentally or for the purpose of revenge. In contemporary SF films, suspended animation is usually for long-distance space travel, either to conserve the ship's life-support systems or to survive a journey that may take centuries. The respective crews of the Jupiter ship of **2001: A Space Odyssey** (1968) and the Nostromo of **Alien** (1979) traveled in this manner. In **The Empire Strikes Back** (1980), Han Solo is temporarily gotten out of the way in a "sleep" device called a carbon-freezing chamber.

THE SWARM

Film 1978 U.S. (Warner Bros.)
116 Minutes Technicolor Panavision

Killer bees from South America invade the U.S.

Not all the stars in Hollywood could have rescued this unintentional parody of a disaster film—which may have been what SF movie- and TV-series maker **Irwin Allen** had in mind when he assembled his cast. Publicized as being based on "science fact,"

The Swarm: A boy seeks safety inside a locked car.

The Swarm attempted to capitalize on recent newspaper scare stories about a voracious species of bee crossbred from the African killer bee and a South American species, which was found to be moving north and attacking animals and a few people. This development had in fact been predicted by Arthur Herzog in his well-researched, low-key novel *The Swarm* (1974), on which the film was allegedly based. But after the scriptwriters swarmed over the novel, what was left was a ravaged field of empty gestures—a standard monster movie whose idea of an ecological disaster was to sting several of Hollywood's biggest names and make them scream.

Director/Producer: **Irwin Allen,** *Screenplay:* Stirling Silliphant, *Novel:* Arthur Herzog, *Photographer:* **Fred J. Koenekamp,** *Special Effects:* Lyle B. Abbott, *Music:* **Jerry Goldsmith**

Cast: Michael Caine, Henry Fonda, Richard Chamberlain, Katharine Ross, Richard Windmark, Olivia de Havilland, Fred MacMurray, Lee Grant, Jose Ferrer

SYMBIONT (or SYMBIOTE)

A SF life form that exists in a close, interdependent relationship with another life form, to the advantage of both. Such pairings are usually between **alien** and man, who often has little say in the matter. The term is lifted from zoology where it describes two dissimilar species living in mutually beneficial harmony, or symbiosis. An example is the relationship between a termite and the intestinal bacteria that enables it to digest wood. Another is the symbiosis between aphids and ants, which protect the defenseless insects in exchange for their nectar—in a manner similar to man's domestication of livestock.

Bizarre symbionts are common in SF, but rare in other mediums. An exception is the film **They Came From Within** (1975), an SF spoof about a botched attempt to breed a symbiont for human beings. The experiment backfires and produces a virulent **parasite**—a closely related creature that has become a movie and television staple.

THE TALES OF HOFFMANN

Film 1951 Great Britain (British Lion/UA)
138 Minutes Technicolor

This version of Offenbach opera, filmed in its entirety, is an elaborate souffle concocted by top British talents in cinema, ballet and opera—the team who produced the highly successful ballet film *The Red Shoes* three years before. It fails to rise to its ambitions, however. A brilliant production design and first-rate performances only serve to underscore an aimless, weak script. The film does, however, feature some interesting special effects, including a literal depiction of Olympia—the wind-up dancer—springing apart into a welter of gears and limbs. (See: **Hoffmann's Erzahlungen; les Contes d'Hoffmann**)

Director/Producer/Screenplay: Michael Powell, Emeric Pressburger, *Photographer:* Christopher Challis, *Producer:* Hein Heckroth, *Choreographer:* Frederick Ashton, *Music Director:* Thomas Beecham (Royal Philharmonic Orchestra)

Cast: Moira Shearer, Robert Rounseville, Robert Helpmann, Pamela Brown, Leonide Massine, Ludmilla Tcherina

TARANTULA

Film 1955 U.S. (Universal-International)
80 Minutes Black & white

A spider infected with a growth nutrient escapes from a biochemistry lab and grows to man-eating size.

A better-than-average entry in the science-

Tarantula: An elderly scientist undergoes mutation after imbibing his own growth nutrient, which has accidently splashed on a spider.

created-monster cycle of the 1950s (which began with **The Beast from 20,000 Fathoms).** Tersely written and directed, the film concerns an elderly scientist who has invented an analog food that stimulates growth—with the unfortunate side effect of causing mutations and insanity in human beings who try it. When he is injected by a crazed assistant, a spider gets splashed with the serum and eventually grows to a height of 100 feet.

While the giant spider is a scientific impossibility (it would collapse under its own weight), it is nevertheless an effective metaphor for the conflict between science and nature. The creature escapes to the desert, which director Arnold depicts as a bleakly primeval landscape where man is the alien, not the tarantula. "Every beast that ever crawled or swam or flew began here," explains an actor, pointing out that the sand was once an ocean floor. "You can still find sea shells out there."

Director: **Jack Arnold,** *Producer:* William Alland, *Screenplay:* Robert M. Fresco, Martin Berkley, *(based on an episode of* **Science Fiction Theatre,** *No Food for Thought* by Robert Fresco), *Photographer:* George Robinson, *Special Effects:* Clifford Stine, *Production Designer:* **Alexander Golitzen,** Alfred Sweeney, *Make-up:* Bud Westmore, *Music:* Joseph Gershenson

Cast: John Agar, Leo G. Carroll, Mara Corday, Nestor Paiva

TARGET EARTH

Film 1954 U.S. (Allied Artists)
76 Minutes Black & white

Venusian **robots** invade Earth and belch deadly rays from their helmets. The robots are threadbare copies of Gort, the silvery **humanoid** of **The Day the Earth Stood Still** (1951).

Director: Sherman Rose, *Producer:* Herman Cohen, *Screenplay:* William Raynor, *Special Effects:* David Koehler, *Music:* Paul Dunlap

Cast: Richard Denning, Richard Reeves, Kathleen Crowley, Whit Bissell, House Peters

TATOOINE

Home planet of **Luke Skywalker,** where he lives with his aunt and uncle. The planet has two suns, Tatoo I and II and is covered with sand, the remnants of dried-out seabeds. Tatooine was inhospitable to life until colonists arrived with "vaporators," machines that drill through sand and rock to release moisture into the air. The planet is inhabited by dangerous **humanoids** called Jawas, **Tusken Raiders** and beasts of burden called **Banthas.** Filmmaker **George Lucas** shot the Tatooine scenes in the Sahara Desert of Tunisia.

TAUNTAUNS

Small, two-legged animals native to the ice-planet **Hoth** in **The Empire Strikes Back** (1980). Tauntauns (pronounced town-towns) have a thick hide well-insulated with fur, long, thick tails, short forepaws and ram-like horns. Somewhat resembling kangaroos, they are easily domesticated and serve as mounts for the Rebel forces hiding there. While scouting the planet on a Tauntaun,

Tauntaun: Luke Skywalker rides the kangaroo-like animal in *The Empire Strikes Back.*

Luke Skywalker is waylaid by a carnivorous **Wampa,** which eats the animal and takes Luke back to its lair.

Designed and built by makeup artist **Stuart Freeborn** and Norman Reynolds, the Tauntauns were animated by Paul Tippett with **stop-motion** photography. A full-scale eight-foot version capable of rearing back, exhaling carbon dioxide vapor through its nostrils and moving and blinking its eyes held actor **Mark Hamill** for close-up shots. A miniature version (complete with a miniature Hamill) was photographed against a blue screen and matted into footage of frozen Scandinavian wastelands shot from a helicopter.

TECHNICAL ADVISOR

A consultant hired to supervise filmic details of a motion picture about a subject in which he is an expert. Two early science advisors were German rocket experts Herman Oberth and Willy Ley, who designed the futuristic spaceship of **Die Frau Im Mond/** *Rocket to the Moon* (1929). Later, Oberth switched his allegiance to America and handled the background details of **Destination Moon** (1950), a film whose scientific accuracy

Dr. J. Allen Hynek, technical advisor for
CE3K (1977).

was remarkable for its time. At least part of
the credit for the state-of-the-art look of
2001: A Space Odyssey (1968) belongs to
technicians from **NASA,** the U.S. space agency, which exchanged its expertise for a prominent display of the NASA logo on sets. In
recent years, Hollywood has hired well-
known technical advisors to promote films
as well as offer advice. These include Dr. J.
Allen Hynek, the astrophysicist and UFO
authority, for **Close Encounters of the Third
Kind** (1977), John Hollis of the Titanic Historical Society for **Raise the Titanic** (1980),
and Capt. William S. Graves, U.S.N. of the
nuclear aircraft carrier U.S.S. Nimitz, the
scene of **The Final Countdown** (1980). All
three went on national tours to tout their
films.

TELEKINESIS

Common SF term used to describe the ability to motivate objects by the power of the
mind; also called psychokinesis, or PK, by
parapsychologists, who probably originated
the word. The power to motivate oneself is
known as **teleportation.** (See also: **Matter
Transmission; Psi Powers.**)

TELEPATHY

Word popularized by SF writers and parapsychologists to describe the ability to trans-

mit thoughts by mental concentration;
alternately called mind-reading or ESP. (See
also: **Psi Powers; Parapsychology.**)

TELEVISION SPY

Film   1939   U.S. (Paramount)   58 Minutes
Black & white

Hollywood's failure to anticipate the impact
of **television** is apparent in this trivial spy

A 1939 newspaper advertisement promises
more than the film delivers.

story, which has to do with secret agents attempting to steal a TV system that has a range of 2,000 miles. A minor studio effort made to fill the lower half of double bills, *Television Spy* attempted to capitalize on two significant events of the year of its release: the outbreak of World War II and the commencement of regular television broadcasting at the New York World's Fair of 1939-40.

Director: Edward Dmytryk, *Screenplay:* Horace McCoy, William R. Lipman, Lillie Hayward, *Story:* Andre Bohem, *Photographer:* Harry Fischbeck

Cast: William Henry, Judity Barrett, William Collier, Sr., Anthony Quinn, Richard Denning

THE TENTH VICTIM

See: **La Decima Vittima**

THEM!

Film   1954   U.S. (Warner Bros.)
94 Minutes   Black & white

A nest of man-eating ants, mutated to giant size by atomic **bomb** tests, swarm from the western desert into Los Angeles.

Violent but surprisingly understated, *Them!* is told in documentary-style as a mystery thriller, with a team of scientists joining with the FBI and local police to investigate several disappearances in New Mexico. The only clues are two demolished homes coated with a sweet-smelling slime, and a dazed young girl survivor who keeps repeating the word "them" and pointing to the desert.

Eventually located in a desert cavern, the killer ants are dispatched by gas bombs dropped by the army. A flying queen and her mate manage to escape, however, and happen on an ideal nesting spot: the sewers of Los Angeles. The pair's sweet tooth gives them away after a hunger spree in which they drain a freight car of its cargo of sugar, followed by a dessert of human protein. Technology finally triumphs over nature-gone-beserk in a terrifying final confrontation, as soldiers invade the underground labyrinth and incinerate the monsters (and their newly-hatched offspring) with flamethrowers.

The idea of an insect grown to giant proportions is nonsense, of course, but *Them!* is good science fiction nevertheless. Like similar films of the 1950s—including **It Came from Outer Space, The Creature from the Black Lagoon** and **Tarantula**—its true subject is man's battle with nature. Civilization is pessimistically symbolized as a small town nestled precariously on the edge of a hostile landscape. Man is the trespasser in the desert—as dangerous to him as a foreign planet—where nature protects and nurtures the mutant ants. Our tools and weapons will never subjugate the indifferent forces of what we mistakenly refer to as Mother Nature, the film tells us, and our scientific tampering will only make matters worse for ourselves. We are safe only in the artificial environments of our cities. For the time being.

Director: Gordon Douglas, *Producer:* David Weisbart, *Screenplay:* Ted Sherdeman, *Story:* George Worthing Yates, *Photographer:* Sid Hickox, *Art Director:* Stanley Fleischer, *Special Effects:* Ralph Ayers, *Sound Effects:* William Mueller, Francis J. Scheid, *Ants:* Dick Smith, *Music:* Bronislau Kaper

Cast: James Whitmore, Edmund Gwenn, James Arness, Joan Weldon, Onslow Stevens

THEY ALL DIED LAUGHING

(Released in Great Britain as *A Jolly Bad Fellow*)

Film   1964   Great Britain (British Lion)
94 Minutes   Black & white

Hilarious comedy about a curmudgeon of a chemistry professor who murders his adversaries with an untraceable poison that causes death by laughter. A mischievous pun on the stock mad scientist character, capably delivered by all concerned.

Director: Don Chaffey, *Producer:* Donald Taylor, *Screenplay:* Robert Hamer, Donald Taylor, *Novel: Don Among the Dead Men* by C. E. Vuillamy, *Photographer:* Gerald Gibbs, *Music:* **John Barry**

Cast: Leo McKern, Janet Munro, Maxine Audley, Dennis Price, Duncan McRae

THEY CAME FROM WITHIN

(Also titled: *The Parasite Murders, Shivers*)

Film   1975   Canada (Trans-American)
94 Minutes   Movielab

A sex-crazed **mad scientist** unleashes an obscene parasite on the world that is a "combination of an aphrodisiac and a venereal disease." Before long, the nasty creatures are squirming through an apartment building, entering every available human orifice, and being passed from person to person by a variety of social contacts. Considered offensive by many, the film is not meant to be taken seriously. Rather, it is a send-up of super-violent SF-**horror** films, and director Cronenberg's comment on their innate sadomasochism.

Director/Screenplay: **David Cronenberg,** *Producer:* Ivan Reitman, *Photographer:* Robert Sadd, *Makeup:* and *Special Effects:* Joe Blasco, *Music:* Ivan Reitman

Cast: Paul Hampton, Lynn Lowry, Barbara Steele, Susan Petrie, Alan Migicovsky

THIN AIR

See: **The Body Stealers**

THINGS TO COME

Film   1936   Great Britain (London Films)
130 Minutes   Black & white

Regardless of the images of the future they project, SF films are always a product of their times, a reflection of contemporary fears, anxieties and hopes. *Things to Come* is a case in point. In 1936 the spectre of the Great Depression still hung over much of the world, and World War II was waiting in the wings. Theories of social engineering that would set the world right proliferated, not the least of which was Hitler's repressive fascism.

H. G. Wells offered his own cure in *Things to Come,* based on his book *The Shape of Things to Come* (1933). Wells' story concerns a medical doctor named John Cabal (Raymond Massey) who becomes involved in World War

Things to Come: Oswald Cabal and Theotocopulos trace the moon-bound journey of their children on a huge "space mirror."

II, which continues for years, destroying the world's great cities and returning humanity to barbarism. By 1966, the landscape is littered with corpses, disease is rampant and inflation has raised the cost of a newspaper to $8.00. Cabal, meanwhile, has joined the mysterious "airmen," a consortium of scientists who fly through the world attempting to reestablish civilization. Eventually, in 1970, Cabal and his Airmen establish order with a pacifying gas.

The movie cuts to the year 2036 and a magnificent art deco city of the future, complete with transparent elevator tubes, artificial sunlight, central heating and air conditioning, and other advanced technological comforts. The last 66 years have evidently been an era of great scientific progress.

Cabal's grandson, also a fighter against reactionary force, watches an electric cannon called a "space gun" (one of Wells' most unscientific devices) send his daughter and the son of a friend to the moon. "Man must go on, conquest beyond conquest," he philosophizes, "And when he has conquered all the depths of space and all the mysteries of time, still he will be beginning." Wells' consortium of scientific saviors is, of course, merely another version of fascism, and is the author's greatest intellectual conceit.

Audiences stayed away from this expensive film (which cost $1,400,00) and those who came laughed at the ridiculous notion of bombers coming from Europe to devastate Great Britain—a reality three years later. When the film sticks to pure visual imagery, it comes spectacularly to life. Director **William Cameron Menzie** had no finesse with actors, but his balanced and counterpointed film frames are often breathtaking. The impressive futuristic city was a detailed miniature set into which the live action was inserted via the **Schufftan Process.** The robe-like costumes provided **George Lucas** with the inspiration for those of **Star Wars** (1977). By the 1980s, the recycled neon-and-white look of *Things to Come* had come full circle and the film looked remarkably up to date.

Director: William Cameron Menzies, *Producer:* Alexander Korda, *Screenplay:* H. G. Wells, *Photographer:* George Perinal, *Art Director:* Vincent Korda, *Special Effects Photography:* Edward Cohen, Harry Zech, *Special Effects:* Ned Mann, Wally Veevers, *Music:* Sir Arthur Bliss

Cast: Raymond Massey, Cedric Hardwicke, Margaretta Scott, Ralph Richardson, Ann Todd, Edward Chapman, Maurice Braddell, George Sanders

THOSE FANTASTIC FLYING FOOLS

See: **Jules Verne's Rocket to the Moon**

THE THREE STOOGES MEET HERCULES

Film   1962   U.S. (Columbia)   89 Minutes Black & white

The comedy trio bumbles into an eccentric professor's **time machine** and get sent back to mythological times. A tatty burlesque of contemporary "sex-and-sandal" epics from Italy, *The Three Stooges Meet Hercules* is made bearable by a goodly number of hilarious sight gags.

Director: **Edward Bernds,** *Producer:* Norman Maurer, *Screenplay:* Elwood Ullman, *Story:* Norman Maurer, *Photographer:* Charles Welborn, *Music:* Paul Dunlap

Cast: Larry Fine, Moe Howard, Joe "Curly" DeRita, Quinn Redeker, Samson Burke, Emil Sitka, Mike McKeever

THX 1138

Film   1970   U.S. (Warner Bros.) 95 Minutes   Technicolor   Panavision

This is **George Lucas'** first film, a remake of his prize-winning student film at UCLA, financed by his friend Francis Ford Coppola. Visually stunning, it takes place in an underground Orwellian **dystopia** of the 25th century, where rigid social conformity is enforced by chrome **robots.** Television is completely devoted to violence. The population is forcibly drugged (not taking your "medication" is against the law), and a subliminal voice endlessly repeats, "You have nowhere to go. Remember, you have nowhere to go."

An everyman named THX-1138 falls in love with an everywoman named LUH 3417, and they reduce their drug intake to restore their sex drives. Becoming pregnant, she is killed for breaking the law, and he is sent to an institution for social deviates. Escaping through a maze of tunnels, "Thex" makes his way to the surface of the **Earth,** illuminated by an enormous sun, perhaps a radioactive cloud left behind by a nuclear bomb. The city's master computer calls off his robot pursuers, having decided that it would be too expensive to bring him back, and he is free to face an uncertain future.

The story is nothing new to SF readers, but Lucas tells it with originality and conviction, underplaying its horrific elements for greater impact. Many scenes were shot on location at San Francisco's Hyatt Regency Hotel, on the BART subway system and at the G.E. Nuclear Research Lab in Valesitus, California. Using his camera selectively, Lucas tightly frames his characters to convey the feeling of prisoners in cells. *THX-1138* has since become a cult favorite, but it was not a success when it was released, and Lucas waited three years before he was given another chance to direct, with *American Grafitti.*

Director: George Lucas, *Producer:* Lawrence Sturhahn, *Screenplay:* George Lucas, Walter Murch, *Photographers:* Dave Meyers, Albert Kihn, *Animation:* Hal Barwood, *Music:* Lalo Schifrin

Cast: Robert Duvall, Donald Pleasence, Pedro Colley, Maggie McOmie, Johnny Weissmuller, Jr., Ian Wolfe

T.I.E. FIGHTER

Single-piloted fighter spacecraft used by the Imperial Empire against the Rebel Alliance's **X-Wing Fighters** during the climactic battle for the **Death Star** in the film **Star Wars** (1977). The initials stand for Twin Ion Engines.

TIME AFTER TIME

Film 1979 U.S. (Warner Bros.)
112 Minutes Metrocolor

London, 1893. H. G. Wells, a young and eager futurist, is about to unveil his latest invention: a **time machine.** In the midst of the unveiling, Jack the Ripper slips aboard, fresh from another murder, and escapes to San Francisco, 1979. The fictional Wells follows the Ripper into the future, upset at loosing a mad killer on a world that is certain to be a peaceful, balanced **Utopia.** Cut to a huge room filled with dancers gyrating to a heavy disco beat. At a side table sits Jack, elegantly attired in a white suit and staring at a beautiful black girl. She returns the stare, smiles, and joins him. The present-day is very much to his liking.

Wells, however, is appalled by what he finds. After rounding up the killer, sampling

Time After Time: H. G. Wells (Malcolm McDowall) samples a MacDonald's french fry.

a McDonald's meal and falling in love with beautiful bank clerk, he returns to Victorian England, musing that the future isn't as good as what he left behind. Director/scriptwriter Nicholas Meyer is an expert at blending fact with fiction, and the film is one of the most enjoyable science fantasies in years.

Director/Screenplay: Nicholas Meyer, *Story:* Karl Alexander, Steve Hayes, *Producer:* Herb Jaffe, *Photographer:* Paul Lohman, *Production Designer:* Edward C. Carfagno, *Special Effects:* Larry Fuentes, Jim Blount, *Music:* Miklos Rozsa

Cast: Malcolm McDowall, David Warner, Charles Cioffi, Mary Steenburgen, Patti D'Arbanville

TIME FLIES

Film 1944 Great Britain (GFD/Gainsborough)
88 Minutes Black & white

A "time ball" takes its inventor and a pair of comedians back to the court of Queen Elizabeth I.

This popular and still amusing farce was a vehicle for British radio favorite Tommy Handley, star of the morale-building *Itma* (It's that man again) series, broadcast during World War II. Although its science fiction is used merely as a plot device, *Time Flies* is notable for being the first film to depict a mechanical **time machine.**

Director: Walter Forde, *Producer:* Edward Black, *Screenplay:* Howard Irving Young, J.O.C. Orton, Ted Kavanaugh, *Photographer:* Basil Emmott, *Music Director:* Louis Levy

Cast: Tommy Handley, Evelyn Dall, George Moon, Moore Marriott, Graham Moffatt

TIMELORDS

A technologically superior and morally impeccable civilization of **humanoid** aliens, with two hearts and a body temperature of 60° F, of which TV's **Doctor Who** is a black-sheep member. Timelords live on the planet **Gallifrey** from which they monitor the universe by tapping time streams. In the past, they traveled through time and space for several thousand years in devices known as **Tardis** machines, until they tired of the violent events of the universe and assumed a policy of isolation. Their high moral purpose forces them to occasionally break this rule, however, and from time to time they help the Doctor combat evil forces, some of whom are renegade Timelords seeking to enslave lesser life forms.

TIME MACHINE

A standard device used in many SF films, it was introduced by **H. G. Wells** in his novel *The Time Machine* (1895). Wells once came close to building a time machine with British movie pioneer Robert W. Paul, who proposed the idea after reading his novel. Conceived as a mixed-media show, the system was to consist of a cabin with rocking floors, moving walls, hoses for compressed air, whirring motors and a series of screens for projecting films and slides to create the sensation of traveling through time. The two set up a business partnership and applied for a patent in October 1895, but neither man had yet made his fortune and they failed to raise funds for developing the required technology. The project was abandoned.

THE TIME MACHINE

Film 1960 U.S. (MGM) 103 Minutes Metrocolor

George Pal angered SF purists with this Classic Comics adaptation of **H. G. Wells'** novel. It is one of Pal's most entertaining films, despite its excision of the Wells' future warnings and historical parallels.

Wells' intellectual time traveler has become a two-fisted American (Rod Taylor, pretending to be British) who builds a **time machine** in 1895 and journeys to the London of 80271. An atomic war has leveled civilization, dividing its survivors into two groups: the ogre-like, cannibalistic Morlocks and the Elois, their docile, platinum-blond slaves. Taylor rouses the Elois from their complacency and teaches them to fight back (they take to physical violence with great delight). The battle scene is the film's weakest moment, a monster-movie version of Wells'

more interesting Darwinian conflict between the idle, immoral ruling class and the vigorous but docile workers.

The time machine (designed by George Davis and William Ferrari), looking as comfortable as a Victorian armchair, is a stunner, with fascinating knobs and gadgets made of ivory, brass and rock crystal. The sets are heavy with period dazzle, and the time trip (by Gene Warren and Wah Chang) is a visual wonder, with the time traveler watching the days flash by through the skylight of his lab and, later, marveling at a tree changing its foliage with the seasons. The effects, achieved mainly by **fast-motion** photography, won **Academy Awards** for Gene Warren and Tim Barr.

Director/Producer: George Pal *Screenplay:* David Duncan, *Novel:* H. G. Wells, *Photographer:* Paul C. Vogel, *Art Directors:* George W. Davis, William Ferrari, *Special Effects:* Gene Warren, Tim Barr, *Makeup:* William Tuttle, *Music:* Russell Garcia

Cast: Rod Taylor, Yvette Mimieux, Alan Young, Sebastian Cabot, Whit Bissell

TIMESLIP

(U.S. title: *The Atomic Man)*

Film 1956 Great Britain (Allied Artists) 77 Minutes Black & white

Collapsing after an accidental exposure to atomic radiation, a nuclear scientist makes a surprising recovery and returns to normal—almost. Baffled by his seemingly cryptic conversation, a female colleague and her detective boyfriend put their heads together to find out what has happened to him. The accident, it turns out, has thrown his perceptions into a time warp, seven seconds into the future, and he is reacting to events that have not yet taken place.

Director: Ken Hughes, *Producer:* Alec C. Snowden, *Screenplay:* Charles Eric Maine, *Novel: The Isotope Man* Charles Eric Maine, *Photographer:* A. T. Dinsdale, *Art Director:* George Haslam, *Music:* Richard Taylor

Cast: Faith Domergue, Gene Nelson, Donald Gray, Joseph Tomley, Vic Perry

THE TIME TUNNEL

TV series   1966-67   U.S. (ABC)   60 Minutes (weekly)   Color

Inadvertently thrust into time by a top-secret, laser-activated time device, two young scientists struggle to get back to the present while coping with problems of the past and future. Episodes found them visiting famous moments in history, such as the assassination of Abraham Lincoln, the sinking of the Titanic and the siege of Troy in 500 B.C., events they could witness but were unable to alter. Stock footage was used for their visits to the past. Visits to the future gave producer **Irwin Allen** the chance to recycle his monsters from **Lost in Space** (1965-68).

Director: Harry Harris, **Nathan Juran,** William Hale, Sobey Martin and others, *Producer/Creator:* Irwin Allen, *Writers:* Leonard Stadd, William Welch, Wanda and Bob Duncan and others, *Photographer:* Winton Hoch, *Special Effects:* Lyle B. Abbott, *Music:* Lionel Newman, **John Williams** and others

Cast: James Darren, Robert Colbert, Whit Bissell, Lee Meriwether, Sam Groom

TOM CORBETT, SPACE CADET

TV serial   1950-55   U.S. (ABC, NBC, CBS) Black & white

Launched by the Kellogg company to sell cornflakes, *Tom Corbett* was CBS's answer to Dumont's **Captain Video,** which had captivated juvenile imaginations the year before. Corbett was a curly-haired space cadet of the 24th century in training to become a military officer for the Solar Alliance of **Earth, Mars** and **Venus.** He rode through the universe in the rocketship *Polaris,* battling such aggressors as the Mercurians, who had designs on Earth.

   Played as a **cliffhanger,** with stories usually lasting three weeks, this live series was unique in that its special effects were also telecast live *(Captain Video's* were filmed). In one sequence, for example, Corbett and other crew members floated above the deck of the *Polaris,* an effect achieved by inserting footage of the actors standing on chairs into a magnified shot of a three-foot model, via television's **chroma-key** process. The program was loosely based on Robert Heinlein's novel, *Space Cadet* (1948) and its science advisor was rocket expert Willy Ley. It began as a 15-minute show aired three times weekly and played on all three networks; a short-lived ABC radio program with the same cast was heard in 1952.

Director: George Gould, *Producers:* Al Ducovny, Leonard Carlton, *Writers:* Albert Aley, Alfred Bester and others

Cast: Frankie Thomas, Jan Merlin, Al Markhim, Michael Harvey, Tom Poston

TRANSPORTER ROOM

Large cabin aboard the **Enterprise,** the Starship of **Star Trek,** from which crew members, visitors and supplies enter and leave the ship. The Transporter Room, of which there are several, can "beam" as many as six persons at a time by converting them into pure energy (see: **Matter Transmission).** The visual effect is achieved by first filming an actor (or actors) on the Transporter platform, then photographing the empty set. A **matte** corresponding to the subject's outline overlaps the two loops of film to **dissolve** him from the frame. Another matte of the subject's outline is filled with a shot of aluminum dust sprinkled through an intense light beam and surprinted over the fading effect to give the illusion of intense energy. To return to the ship, the process is reversed.

TRICORDER

Portable apparatus used by the **Star Trek** crew to analyze **alien** planets. Slung from a shoulder strap, the small console senses, measures and compares vital information and records its findings. The Tricorder can immediately determine the chemical composition of a planet, whether it has life forms, animal or vegetable, and other significant data.

TROG

Film   1970   Great Britain (Warner Bros.) 91 Minutes   Technicolor

It's no contest between a recently discovered missing link and chic lady anthropologist Joan Crawford, who soon has "Trog" minding his manners and trying hard to become a human being. Crawford, doing a star turn, grabs the script by the throat, proving only that brawn is still no substitute for brains.

Director: **Freddie Francis,** *Producer:* Herman Cohen, *Photographer:* Desmond Dickinson, *Animation:* **Ray Harryhausen** *Music:* John Scott

Cast: Joan Crawford, **Michael Gough,** David Griffin, Bernard Kay

THE TROLLENBERG TERROR

(U.S. titles: *The Crawling Eye, The Creature From Another World*)

Film 1958 Great Britain (Eros/DCA)
85 Minutes Black & white

Forrest Tucker offered British audiences the reassurance of American science and manly courage in this adaptation of the BBC-TV series **The Trollenberg Terror** (see listing below). On vacation in the Swiss hamlet of Trollenberg, he and a fellow scientist investigate a mysterious cloud that has hung motionless for days over a nearby mountain. There they discover an **alien** "brain" with one eye and tentacles, nestled inside a milky white fluff it has exuded to hide itself. Dauntless, the men of science battle the carnivorous creature to the death when it arrives to dine on Trollenberg. *The Trollenberg Terror's* promising script is ultimately undone by the film's miniscule budget and inadequate special effects, which consist primarily of rubber tentacles and a wad of cotton glued to a snapshot of the mountain. Special effects man Les Bowie had improved considerably by the time he devised many of the ingenious effects of **Superman—The Movie, I** and **II.**

Director: Quentin Lawrence, *Producer:* Robert S. Baker, Monty Berman, *Screenplay:* Jimmy Sangster, *Special Effects:* Les Bowie, *Music:* Stanley Black

Cast: Forrest Tucker, Laurence Payne, Janet Munro, Warren Mitchell, Jennifer Jayne

Douglas Trumbull

TRUMBULL, DOUGLAS (1943–   )

Special effects expert; president of EEG (Entertainment Effects Group), his own special effects studio. Trumbull's first important credit was *To the Moon and Beyond,* a film made in 360-degree Cinerama (see: **Wide screen)** and shown at the 1964-65 New York World's Fair. The film prompted director **Stanley Kubrick** to hire him to create effects for his trend-setting **2001: A Space Odyssey** (1968).

Films include: **The Andromeda Strain** (1969), **Close Encounters of the Third Kind** (1977) and **Star Trek—The Motion Picture** (1979) [with his former protege **John Dykstra]** and **Blade Runner** (1982). He directed and wrote the **space opera, Silent Running** (1970). *Brainstorm,* his second film as director, was delayed by the accidental death of its star Natalie Wood in 1981.

TUSKEN RAIDERS

Nomadic desert inhabitants of the planet **Tatooine,** where **Luke Skywalker** was born and grew up in the **Star Wars** film series. Described by creator **George Lucas** as "margin farmers," they are hardy and aggressive bandits who supplement their meager existences by waylaying travelers and raiding the homes of nearby settlers, to whom they are known as the dread "sandpeople." Tusken Raiders cover their large bodies with thick cloaks and swath their

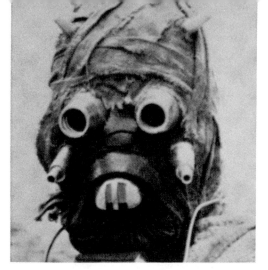

A Tusken Raider, desert bandit of *Star Wars*.

metal-and-plastic heads with coarse band-ages to protect themselves from the planet's two suns. They are not related to the pint-sized desert scavengers known as **jawas,** although they dress similarly. Lucas says Tusken Raiders are "marginally human," which indicates they are a type of **cyborg.** But little is known about their background. They are, of course, closely related to the desert cutthroats of countless Hollywood Arabian Nights fantasies.

TWENTY MILLION MILES TO EARTH

Film 1957 U.S. (Columbia) 82 Minutes
Black & white

Brought to Earth by a returning space probe, a Venusian "egg" hatches into a reptilian **humanoid** that grows into an angry, 25-foot creature called a Ymir. The monster ram-pages through Rome and does battle with an elephant before being destroyed by army bazookas while standing atop the Colosseum. The **stop-motion** model animation by **Ray Harryhausen** is close to first-rate, especially in the film's climax, Harryhausen's tribute to **King Kong** (1933).

Director: **Nathan Juran,** *Producer:* Charles Schneer, *Screenplay:* Bob Williams, Christopher, *Story:* Ray Harryhausen, Charlotte Knight, *Special Effects:* Ray Harryhausen, *Music:* Mischa Bakaleinikoff

Cast: William Hopper, Joan Taylor, Frank Puglia, John Zaremba, Don Orlando

TWIKI

Robot companion of Buck Rogers in the TV series **Buck Rogers** (1979-81). Twiki is

Twiki

three feet tall and usually carries around his neck a talking **computer** named Dr. Theo (not shown in the photograph). In tandem, the **robots** embody the personalities of **C-3PO** and **R2-D2,** the misnamed 'droids of the **Star Wars** series.

THE TWILIGHT ZONE

TV series 1959-63 U.S. (CBS) 30 Minutes/ 60 Minutes (weekly) Black & white

Hosted by Rod Serling, who also wrote many of the scripts, *The Twilight Zone* was Ameri-can TV's last important anthology series, a format eschewed by network programmers in favor of audience-grabbing series with identifiable characters. The stories drew heavily on SF themes and were usually re-solved with a trick O. Henry ending. In "Stopover in a Quiet Town," for instance, a married couple awaken to find themselves in a strange, desolate town where trees and grass are artificial. They hear a child's laugh-ter and search for the source, but find no one. Near desperation, they board an empty train hoping to escape, but it continually brings them back to their point of departure. Finally, the camera pulls back to reveal a gi-gantic child, who thanks her father for the new pets, brought from **Earth** to inhabit her play village. And in "The Eye of the Be-holder," a hideously deformed woman has undergone plastic surgery, and her head is wrapped in bandages. They are slowly peeled away to reveal a stunningly beautiful woman—at least by Earth's standards. It is then we see her doctors and nurses are reptilian **humanoids.** They recoil in disgust at their botched handiwork, and the girl is banished to a colony of freaks.

Several famous SF writers contributed scripts to the series, including **Richard Matheson,** Charles Beaumont, and **Ray Bradbury,** who dramatized his story, "I Sing the Body Electric," about a loving **robot** grandmother surrogate. In 1963, the 30-minute program expanded to an hour-long format. Though never a smash hit, it has been an enduring success and has played in reruns ever since it was cancelled in 1963. Serling's clench-jawed delivery is still imitated by comedians, and for a time, the term "twilight zone" became a slang expression, meaning a state of limbo or extreme light-headedness: An American politican once described international negotiations as a "twilight zone." Serling's next series was **Rod Serling's Night Gallery** (1970-72).

Creator/Executive Producer: Rod Serling, *Directors:* Richard Donner, William Claxton, Ralph Nelson, Buzz Kulik, **Christian Nyby,** Perry Lafferty, **Ted Post,** Don Weiss and others, *Writers:* Charles Beaumont, Richard Matheson, Rod Serling, Ray Bradbury, Earl Hamner and others, *Makeup:* William Tuttle, *Music:* **Bernard Herrmann, Jerry Goldsmith**

Cast: Dana Andrews, William Shatner, Dick York, Cliff Robertson, **Leonard Nimoy,** Albert Salmi, Cloris Leachman, Josephine Hutchinson and others

THE TWONKY

Film   1953   U.S. (United Artists)
72 Minutes   Black & white

A frustrated father battles a talkative television set inhabited by an **alien** intelligence determined to take control of his family. The film's source is Harry Kuttner's far-fetched "The Twonky" (1942), named for an intelligent, radio-like device built by an assembly

line worker who accidently slipped back through time into the wrong factory. Kuttner's bad-tempered appliance eventually disposes of its annoying owners. In updating the story, **Arch Oboler** jettisoned most of Kuttner's sly humor in favor of a sour-grapes satire of television, then scaring the wits out of Hollywood.

Director/Producer/Screenplay: Arch Oboler, *Story:* Harry Kuttner, *Photographer:* Joseph Biroc, *Music:* Jack Meakin

Cast: Hans Conreid, Gloria Blondell, Billy Lynn, Janet Warren, Al Jarvis

2-1B

Robot doctor who tends the Rebel Alliance in **The Empire Strikes Back** (1980). When **Luke Skywalker** is near death from exposure after an attack by a **Wampa** on the ice planet **Hoth,** 2-1B and his robot assistant FX-7 restore his health by suspending him in a container of **Bacta.** Later, the mechanical M.D. gives Skywalker a new hand to replace the one severed by **Darth Vader**'s **lightsaber.**

2001: A SPACE ODYSSEY

Film   1968   Great Britain (MGM)
141 Minutes   Metrocolor   Panavision

Technology is the subject of this incredibly beautiful landmark film. Scripted by **Stanley Kubrick** and Arthur C. Clarke (nominally based on his story "The Sentinel"), *2001* is so cleverly paced and dazzlingly realized that its minimal plot has the multileveled simplicity of a scientific principle. The film opens with a sequence that depicts primitive man learning to use an animal jawbone as a hammer after an encounter with a mysterious black monolith. The bleached jawbone is abruptly flung into the air and replaced by a streamlined white space station orbiting **Earth**—itself a newer, more complicated tool.

A similar monolith is found buried on the moon. When uncovered, it gives off a high-intensity radio signal directed toward the planet Jupiter. Kubrick then cuts several years into the future, and we are aboard a mammoth spaceship, piloted by two astronauts, Frank Poole (Gary Lockwood) and David Bowman (Keir Dullea), bound for Jupiter to investigate the source of the radio signal. During the long journey, HAL, the unseen computer that controls the space vehicle, goes berserk and cuts off the life-support systems of expedition members in **suspended animation** banks. HAL kills Poole, but Bowman manages to outwit the mechanical genius and gain access to its control center. In one of the film's most touching moments, Bowman gouges out HAL's memory circuits with a screwdriver, and the supergenius, pleading for its life, is reduced to reciting nursery rhymes from its early programming.

Placed alongside **Star Wars** (1977), Kubrick's space voyage manages to hold its own as an outstanding achievement of movie special effects. *2001,* in fact, presented a greater challenge to technicians. The strictures of presenting the future as it will probably be (based on present technology) made the construction of models and sets painstaking work. **George Lucas** and his crew, for all their accomplishments, could let their imaginations run wild, for little attempt was made at scientific accuracy for his comic-strip fantasy.

An exacting movie magician, Kubrick utilized every known movie effects and, when nothing else would do the trick, he invented new ones. The docking of a spaceship to an Earth-orbiting space station, for instance, was accomplished by meticulously combining half a dozen tried-and-true elements. First, miniatures of the ship and space station were animated separately against a black velvet backdrop. Moving the miniatures a frame at a time gave the illusion of the spaceship floating toward the revolving space station. Next, they were matted into a footage of a painting of the moon and Earth and the black void in between. Then, just as the spaceship was about to land, Kubrick cut to a full-sized set of the inside of the ship and rear-projected close-up footage of the miniature space station into the window of the cockpit, in front of the actors.

Modern engineering principles also figured in the making of the film. Astronaut Frank Poole appeared to be jogging effortlessly around the inside of a giant 380-foot centrifuge that supposedly provided gravity for the Jupiter-bound ship. In reality he and the camera stayed in place; the wheel moved. Of Kubrick's many innovations, his most important is the **front-projection** system, which was quickly adopted by the motion picture industry. The new process makes it virtually impossible to detect any difference between live action and a filmed background. (See also: **Macrophotography, Matte.**)

Director: Stanley Kubrick, *Producers:* Stanley Kubrick, Victor Lyndon, *Screenplay:* Stanley Kubrick, Arthur C. Clarke, *Story:* Arthur C. Clark, *Photographer:* **Geoffrey Unsworth, John Alcott,** *Production Designers:* Tony Masters, Harry Lange, Ernie Archer, John Hoesli, *Special Effects:* Stanley Kubrick, Wally Veevers, **Douglas Trumbull,** Con Pederson, Tom Howard, *Makeup:* **Stuart Freeborn,** *Music:* Richard Strauss, Aram Khachaturian, Johann Strauss, Ligeti

Cast: Keir Dullea, Gary Lockwood, William Sylvester, Leonard Rossiter, *Voice of HAL:* Douglas Rain

U

manoid skins from the dread Gavanans. The film's battles in space are lively and well-staged but not up to the technical level of their Hollywood prototype.

Director: Kinji Fukasaku, *Producers:* Banjiro Uemura, Yoshinori Watanabe, Tan Takaiwa, *Screenplay:* Hiroo Matsuda, *Photographer:* Tetsu Nakajima, *Special Effects:* Nobuo Yajima, *Music:* Ken-Ichiro Morioka

Cast: Vic Morrow, Sonny Chiba, Philip Casnoff, Peggy Lee Brennan, Sue Shiomi

UCHU KARA NO MESSEJI/
Message from Space

Film   1978   Japan (Toei)   110 Minutes
Color [Released 1978   U.S. (United Artists)
105 Minutes]

By the time **Star Wars** (1977) arrived in Japan the following year, this copycat **space opera** had already been released there and was on its way to the U.S. Budgeted at $5 million—making it the most expensive Japanese film to date—*Message from Space* tells a familiar tale of eight brave astronauts of the future who journey from Earth to answer a distress call in the Andromeda Galaxy. The SOS has come from the peace-loving Jillucians, who need help in saving their **hu-**

Uchu Kara No Messeji/Message from Space:
A Jillucian space ark powered by the solar wind.

THE UFO INCIDENT

TV film   1975   U.S. (NBC)   75 Minutes
Color

This is a fascinating, well-acted dramatization of John G. Fuller's book, *The Interrupted Journey,* an account of the alleged kidnapping of real-life interracial couple Betty and Barney Hill by **aliens.** Troubled by recurring nightmares, the couple undergo hypnosis and recall being subjected to medical tests aboard a **UFO.** Movie rights to the book were purchased by lead actor James Earl Jones (the voice of **Darth Vader** in the **Star Wars** series), who sold the property to television after failing to interest movie studios. This was two years before **Close Encounters of the Third Kind.**

Director/Producer: Richard A. Colla, *Screenplay:* S. Lee Pogostin, Hesper Anderson, *Photographer:* Rexford Metz, *Music:* Billy Goldenberg

Cast: James Earl Jones, Estelle Parsons, Barnard Hughes, Dick O'Neill, Beeson Carroll, *Narrator:* Vic Perrin

UFOs

*U*nidentified *F*lying *O*bjects; also called flying saucers, a term coined in 1947 by a newspaper reporter to describe nine disklike objects seen in the sky over Washington's Mt. Rainier by private pilot Kenneth Arnold on June 24. Mysterious flying lights had been seen throughout the world at various time in history, and during the 1930s "ghost fliers" were the rage in many parts of the world. After Arnold's sighting, however, a "flap"—a term used by flying saucer buffs to describe a rash of sightings—took place throughout the United States, and UFOs were here to stay.

Many self-ordained "ufologists" furthered the belief that the unidentified phenomenoa (which are no more than that) were actually spacecrafts piloted by conscientious **aliens,** here to warn **Earth** of the folly of nuclear warfare, or reconnoitering for a future invasion. SF films have helped further both beliefs, notably in **The Thing, The Day the Earth Stood Still** (1951), **The War of the Worlds, It Came From Outer Space** (1953), **This Island Earth** (1955), **Earth vs. the Flying Saucer** (1956), **Invasion of the Saucer Men** (1957) and such juvenile TV fare as the British-made TV series **UFO** (1972) and the American series **Project U.F.O.** (1977-78). Two of the best films in this sub-genre deal with the effect of UFO sightings on believers: **Close Encounters of the Third Kind** (1978) and the made-for-TV movie **The UFO Incident** (1975).

UFO/UNIDENTIFIED FLYING ODDBALL

Film 1979 Great Britain (Disney)
93 Minutes Technicolor

This is the fourth screen adaptation of *A Connecticut Yankee in King Arthur's Court* (1889) [see listing] Mark Twain's classic time travel story. The Yankee is now a concept design engineer who invents a new spacecraft, the *Stardust One,* able to travel faster and farther than anything yet conceived. While preparing for a trial run, the engineer and his neurotic lookalike **robot** (who is afraid of outer space) are accidentally launched into a time warp by a lightning bolt. Arriving in medieval England, they foil a land-grabbing scheme hatched by Sir Mordred and Merlin to topple King Arthur from the throne.

Director: Russ Mayberry, *Producer:* Ron Miller, *Screenplay:* Don Tait, *Photographer:* Paul Beeson, *Art Director:* Albert Whitlock, *Special Effects:* Cliff Culley, *Music:* Ron Goodwin

Cast: Dennis Dugan, Jim Dale, Kenneth More, Ron Moody, John Le Mesurier, Rodney Bewes

Unidentified Flying Oddball: The *Stardust One* blasts off from medieval England for a return to the 20th century.

ULMER, EDWARD G. (1904–72)

Hollywood director of low-budget features, mostly for lesser "poverty row" studios. Generally dismissed by American critics as an assembly-line hack, Ulmer was rescued from oblivion shortly before his death by French cineastes and elevated to the pantheon of great film stylists. Indeed, Ulmer's many works show a strong visual signature overlooked because of the atrocious scripts and performances of most of his films. Like his mentor, the great F. W. Murnau, he painted images on the screen with an artist's precision, using the master's tools of highly contrasted, expressionist lighting and skillful camera movements to underscore the emotion being portrayed.

Other films: The Black Cat (1934, a horror programmer considered his masterpiece), *Isle of Forgotten Sins* (1943), *Bluebeard* (1943), *Ruthless* (1948), **The Man From Planet X** (1951), **The Daughter of Dr. Jekyll** (1957), **The Amazing Transparent Man, Beyond the Time Barrier** (1960), *L'Atlantide/Journey Beneath the Desert* (1962), *The Cavern* (1965)

THE ULTIMATE WARRIOR

Film 1975 U.S. (Warner Bros.)
92 Minutes Technicolor

Described in its press blurb as "the first Kung-Fu SF movie," *The Ultimate Warrior* takes place in the year 2012, several years after a biological disaster that has spread plague and famine through a lawless America. In New York a group of survivors hires a mercenary soldier to protect it from gangs of toughs roaming the ravaged streets. The futuristic samurai kills several intruders with his razor-sharp knife and dispatches their leader during a kinetic battle to the death. Extremely violent and downbeat but well written and atmospheric, the film never saw a wide release, apparently because it turned off escapist-minded movie-goers with its pervasive bleakness. Yul Brynner is the warrior-for-hire, a role he played previously in *The Magnificent Seven* (1960) and **Westworld** (1973).

Director/Screenplay: Robert Clouse, *Producers:* Fred Weintraub, Paul Heller, *Photographer:* Gerald Hirschfeld, *Art Director:* Walter Simonds, *Special Effects:* Gene Riggs, *Music:* Gil Melle

Cast: Yul Brynner, Max von Sydow, Joanna Miles, William Smith, Richard Kelton

UNDERSEA KINGDOM

Film (serial)   1936   U.S. (Republic)
12 Episodes   Black & white

Mysterious earthquakes lure naval hero "Crash" Corrigan to the bottom of the sea, where he discovers the lost city of **Atlantis.** An unabashed imitation of **The Phantom Empire,** a popular serial released the year before, entertaining, but lacking the vitality and narrative shadings of its model. Corrigan (playing himself) arrives in the glass-domed underwater city, accompanying an eccentric scientist, who has invented a counter-earthquake ray, and a smitten newspaper woman. Escaping capture by warlike Atlanteans, "Crash" and party speed to the surface in the rocket-powered submarine they had arrived in—just in time to convince the U.S. Navy to shell the kingdom's surfacing doomsday rocket—the cause of the earthquakes. Second-rate sets of the underwater city recall **comic books** and pulp science fiction art of the 1930s. Televisors, **death rays**, art deco **robots** and other period cliche devices are much in evidence. Idiosyncrasies, such as the Roman gladiator costume worn by Corrigan while battling undersea "Volkites," and technologically advanced Atlanteans traveling in horse-drawn chariots, add to the **serial's** nostalgic charm.

Directors: **B. Reeves Eason,** Joseph Kane, *Producer:* Nat Levine, *Screenplay:* John Rathmell, Maurice Geraghty, Oliver Drake, *Story:* John Rathmell,

Undersea Kingdom: Ray "Crash" Corrigan, the hero, is set free by a young confederate as villain Lon Chaney, Jr. looks the other way.

Tracy Knight, *Photographers:* William Nobles, Edgar Lyons, *Music:* Harry Grey

Cast: **Ray "Crash" Corrigan,** Lois Wilde, Monte Blue, G. Montague Shaw, **Lon Chaney, Jr.**

UNEARTHLY STRANGER

Film   1963   Great Britain (IA/AIP)
74 Minutes   Black & white

Love between man and **alien** is the theme of this rarely screened, offbeat SF thriller. When several scientists working on a secret space-time project are murdered, the finger of suspicion points to the wife of a surviving researcher. (Among other strange habits, she sleeps with her eyes open.) Confronted, she confesses to her husband that she has been sent from another planet to sabotage the project, and that he is next on the list. She has fallen in love, however, and can't bring herself to kill him, thus assuring her own demise at the hands of her vengeful superiors. In a macabre but touching farewell scene, her eyes well with humanlike tears that flow down her cheeks etching deep rivulets into her skin.

Director: John Krish, *Producer:* Albert Fennell, *Screenplay:* Rex Carlton, *Photographer:* Reg Wyler, *Music:* Edward Williams

Cast: John Neville, Gabriella Licudi, Phillip Stone, Patrick Newell, Jean Marsh

UNNATURAL

See: **Alraune (1952)**

UNSWORTH, GEOFFREY (1914–78)

British photographer of big-budget, international films. A consummate professional, Unsworth entered the industry in London at the age of 18 as a camera assistant and progressed through the ranks to camera operator and, at the age of 32, to director of photography. Known for his glossy, technically perfect color work, Unsworth shot a number of SF and fantasy films, including **2001: A Space Odyssey** (1968)—for which he helped develop the new process of **front projection—Zardoz** (1974) and **Superman—The Movie** (1978), released the year of his death and dedicated to him.

Other films: The Drums (as camera operator) (1938), *The Four Feathers* (1939), *The Thief of Bagdad* (1940), *A Matter of Life and Death/Stairway to Heaven* (1946), *The Laughing Lady* (as Director of Photography) (1946), *The Blue Lagoon* (1949), *The Purple Plain* (1954), *The World of Suzie Wong* (1960), *Becket* (1964), *Half a Sixpence* [based on *Kipps* by **H. G. Wells**] (1968), *Cabaret* (1972), (**Academy Award**), *Murder on the Orient Express* (1974), *A Bridge Too Far* (1977), *Tess, The Great Train Robbery* (1979)

UTOPIA

A perfect state where mankind lives in harmony and equality, without such miseries as poverty, hunger and war. The concept was first propounded by Plato in *The Republic* (c. 370 B.C.), but it was Thomas More who coined the word (from the Greek meaning "no where") to describe the visionary world of his *Utopia* (1516). The idea was later put into practice by a number of Utopian philosophers who organized socialist communes, usually based on the voluntary abolition of private property, all of which failed.

During the late 19th century, writers of the industrial age speculated that the world would ultimately be transformed into a Utopia by technological progress; among the scientific Utopian romances are *Looking Backward* (1888) by Edward Bellamy and *A Modern Utopia* (1905) by **H. G. Wells.** By the 1930s techno-Utopias had become a staple of SF pulp magazines. They have rarely appeared in films, however, a notable intance being the Shangri-La of **Lost Horizon** (1937 and 1973). The idea of a **dystopia,** or a Utopia gone wrong, has been more in keeping with the pessimism of the post-war age. It also provides dramatic conflicts missing in a perfect world.

Director/Screenplay: Terence Young, *Producer:* Nat A. Bronsten, George Willoughby, *Story:* Paul Tabori, Nat A. Bronsten, *Photographer:* Harry Waxman, *Art Director:* J. Edder Willis, *Music:* Nino Rota

Cast: Jack Warner, Nadia Gray, Anthony Dawson, Christopher Lee

VENGEANCE

See: **The Brain**

VALLEY OF THE DRAGONS

(Also titled: *Prehistoric Valley*)

Film 1961 U.S. (Columbia) 79 Minutes Black & white

When a **comet** sweeps past Earth, its gravity pulls aboard a number of Victorian-era citizens and deposits them in a prehistoric "valley of the dragons." Loosely based on the **Jules Verne** story, "Off on a Comet," this cut-and-paste job splices new footage with scenes of battling dinosaurs borrowed from the 1940 version of **One Million B.C.** Verne's story was treated with more respect in the animated Czech film, **On the Comet** (1970).

Director/Screenplay: **Edward Bernds,** *Producer:* Byron Roberts, *Special Effects:* Dick Albain

Cast: Cesare Danova, Sean McClory, Gregg Martell

VALLEY OF THE EAGLES

Film 1951 Great Britain (Ind Sovereign) 86 Minutes Black & white

Understandably piqued when his assistant runs off with his new invention and his wife (piqued in that order), a resourceful young scientist tracks them to a remote valley in the Laplands with the help of a Scotland Yard inspector. The device, which converts sound waves into a power supply, becomes a weapon in the hands of the thief, who repels the pursuers with a flock of vicious, sound-energized eagles. Director Terence Young, later to make his name with the early **James Bond** films, treats this foolishness lightly and wisely concentrates on the chase.

VENUS

Third planet from the sun (mean distance: 67.2 million miles). Nearly the size of **Earth,** its neighbor, Venus is permanently enshrouded by a thick sulphurous cloud that reflects sunlight so brightly it can cast a shadow on Earth. Because of its extreme luminosity, the planet is commonly misnamed the morning and evening star.

In SF stories and films, Venus has often been depicted as a lush garden paradise inhabited by stunning females, a fiction derived from the fact that it is named for the Roman goddess of love. In reality, according to American and Russian space probes that landed on Venus in the 1970s, its terrain is flat, very dry and covered with a fine layer of reddish dust. During the day, temperatures can soar to 847 degrees Fahrenheit (452.8 degrees Celsius), the result of a greenhouse effect caused by its cloud cover, which prevents solar radiation from being reflected back into space. Venus has a tremendous atmospheric pressure—about 15 to 22 times that of Earth—which would cause visitors capable of withstanding the heat to feel as if they were walking through water. (See also: **Terrestrial Planets.**)

THE VENUSIAN

See: **Immediate Disaster**

VERNE, JULES (GABRIEL) (1828–1905)

French novelist; the first major popularizer of science fiction. He and **H. G. Wells** are generally regarded as the founders of science fiction, an honor that neither claimed, nor could they have. Speculative themes had already been established in popular fiction long before Verne began writing his classic *voyages extraordinaires*. Verne, like Wells, had an instinct for anticipating public tastes in fiction and an ability to recognize viable themes in the works of earlier and lesser writers. His superior imagination captured the essence of 19th-century optimism and the era's belief in the wonders promised by science and technology, thereby giving the SF novel conscious form. Wells, 39 years younger, had a more pessimistic attitude toward mankind's use of science, reflecting the political chaos and gloomy outlook of his turn-of-the-century generation.

Born in Nantes, a seaport on the Loire River, Verne was expected to follow in the footsteps of his father, a prosperous lawyer, whose profession interested him not at all. At 11, he ran away from home and attempted to take the place of a cabin-boy on a cargo ship but was found just in time. During his early twenties, Verne lived in Paris on a family allowance as an elegant bohemian playwright, and wrote his first story *"Un voyages en ballon"/A Voyage in a Balloon"* (1851), a somewhat gloomy tale that shows the influence of Edgar Allan Poe, his favorite writer.

Dissatisfied with his limited success as a dramatist and man about town, Verne worked as a stockbroker for several years, but returned to writing in 1862 when he submitted a story about balloon travel to a new children's magazine. The editor, P. J. Hetzel, suggested revisions, and the story was novelized and published as *Cinq semaines en ballon/Five Weeks in a Balloon* (1863). Readers clamored for more, and Verne signed a contract to produce two novels yearly (later shortened to one) for the annual sum of 20,000 francs. For the next 40 years, his novels appeared first in the *Magasin d'education et de Recreation*, and when he died in 1905, the magazine ceased publication.

Verne's imaginary voyages are characterized by a boyish exuberance, an instinctive sense of narrative and a careful accretion of scientific detail. An enthusiastic reader

of scientific journals, he accurately anticipated several future transporation machines (which were made to seem more fantastic by translators of his stories). He was correct in his assumption that water would not spill in gravity-free space and that returning spacecrafts would splash down at sea. Verne lived to see the first airplanes, which turned out to be not at all like the propeller-driven dirigibles he described in several stories.

His most famous literary character is Captain Nemo, commander of an elaborate Victorian underwater battleship called the *Nautilus*, introduced in *Vingt mille lieues sous les mers/Twenty Thousand Leagues Under the Seas* (1870) [the *s* is always omitted in English translations]. Nemo, an enigmatic, Poe-like hero, is an Indian prince, dispossessed by the British, a fact revealed in the novel's sequel, *L'Ile mysterieuse/The Mysterious Island* (1875). He roams the seas, passing under the South Pole, slipping from the grip of a giant octopus and through coral wildernesses, in search of ships to sink to punish the world for the deaths of his wife and children. The deeply felt novel is one of the great imaginary voyages of science fiction, and, of course, it predicted the submarine.

In later years, Verne took a darker view of the future of science, not for its innate value, but for man's misuse of it, an attitude similar to that of H. G. Wells. His personality shift can be seen in the portrayal of his scientist hero, Robur, who first appeared in *Robur le conquerant/The Clipper of the Clouds* (1886). In the sequel, *Maitre du monde/Master of the World* (1904), Robur has become an allegorical megalomaniac whose invention—a 100-foot-long flying machine with 74 masts—has given him a feeling of omnipotence.

Novels filmed: **Voyage dans la lune** (1902), **20,000 Leagues Under the Sea** (1954), *Around the World in 80 Days* (1956), **From the Earth to the Moon** (1958), **Vynalez Zkazy/The Fabulous World of Jules Verne, Journey to the Center of the Earth** (1959), **Master of the World** (1961), *Five Weeks in a Balloon* (1962), **Captain Nemo and the Underwater City** (1969), **The Return of Captain Nemo** [TV film] (1978), **The Mysterious Island** (1929, 1951, 1961)

VIA GALACTICA

Play   1972   U.S.   2 acts

Heralding itself as a "space-age" musical, *Via Galactica* opened Broadway's lavish new Uris Theatre amidst an expensive publicity campaign that promised live special effects like none seen before. These turned out to be a spaceship maneuvered over the heads of the audience by a hydraulic "cherry-picker" crane, others hanging by wires, and a huge fighter craft that arrived in a cloud of smoke, then destroyed itself in a crescendo of sound effects and more smoke. To simulate a low-gravity environment, actors bounced on trampolines as they sang. A motion picture projector installed in the orchestra floor (necessitating the removal of 64 seats) supplied the star backgrounds.

The special effects and costumes, the work of John Bury, were indeed impressive, but the show was a bomb—"a plastic one" noted a newspaper critic, echoing his fellow reviewers. *Via Galactica*, subtitled "Road to the Stars," sang (there was no spoken dialogue) a story about a terrestrial adventurer in a revolving hat who left the emotional vacuum of the future for better times on an **asteroid** called Ithaca. There he fell in love with a beautiful woman called Omaha, whose husband was a brain kept alive in a box (see: **Cyborgs).** Meanwhile, **Earth** was planning an invasion of the asteroid, and the people of Ithaca decided to move on to a new star system.

Director: Peter Hall, *Producers:* George W. George, Bernard S. Straus, Nat Shapiro, *Music:* Galt MacDermot, *Lyrics:* Christopher Gore, *Book:* Christopher Gore, Judith Ross, *Settings and Costumes:* John Bury, *Musical Direction:* Thomas Pierson

Cast: Raul Julia, Irene Cara, Damon Evans, Edloe, Keene Curtis, Virginia Vestoff, Bill Starr

VIDEO IMAGING

A form of video graphics in which a TV image can be made to spin, expand, compress, shake, change color or do other amazing things; also called *video synthesis.* This is accomplished with an analog computer, which measures quantities and dimensions, rather than by a digital computer, which records data mathematically. The latter system is the basis of a form of **animation** known as **computer graphics.** Video imaging involves scanning a drawing, **film** or **videotape** with a TV camera and passing the image through a computerized synthesizer that manipulates the electronic signal. The transformed image can then be stored on videotape or filmed from a high definition video screen (HDV)

VIDEOTAPE

A roll of thin polyester bound with magnetic oxide particles, which records images in the form of magnetic signals. Unlike film, whose positive images can be seen by the naked eye or through a motion picture projector, video tape carries only coded information. To produce a television picture, the tape must be played through a video playback unit and decoded electronically. Video tape has several advantages over film: it needs no developing with chemicals, it can be viewed immediately after recording, and it can be erased for repeated use. It is less stable than film, however, and loses image resolution when projected onto a large screen.

VILLAGE OF THE DAMNED

Film   1960   Great Britain (MGM)
78 Minutes   Black & white

Sinister children spawned by an invisible **alien** force that impregnated the women of a sleepy English village all look alike and exhibit the same remarkable **psi powers** and superior intelligence. As they grow up, it becomes apparent that the alien half-breeds must be destroyed, especially after they concentrate their collective mind power to commit a murder. This low-key, highly charged chiller is based on John Wyndham's novel *The Midwich Cuckoos.* The film's sequel is **Children of the Damned** (1964).

Director: Wolf Rilla, *Producer:* Ronald Kinnoch, *Screenplay:* Wolf Rilla, Sterling Silliphant, George Barclay, *Special Effects:* Tom Howard, *Music:* Ron Goodwin

Cast: George Sanders, Barbara Shelly, Michael Gwynn, Martin Stephens, Laurence Naismith

VISIT TO A SMALL PLANET

Film 1960 U.S. (Paramount) 85 Minutes Black & white

Gore Vidal's satirical Broadway play has been turned into a slapstick vehicle for comedian Jerry Lewis, who plays an **extraterrestrial** here to study human behavior. There are a few laughs, but what the scriptwriters have done to the play isn't one of them.

Director: Norman Taurog, *Producer:* Hal Wallis, *Screenplay:* Edmond Beloin, Henry Garson, *Play:* Gore Vidal, *Photographer:* Loyal Griggs, *Special Effects:* **John P. Fulton,** *Music:* Leigh Harline

Cast: Jerry Lewis, Joan Blackman, Earl Holliman, Fred Clark, John Williams, Lee Patrick

VISTAVISION

Wide-screen film process developed by Paramount in 1953 as a reponse to 20th Century-Fox's **CinemaScope.** In VistaVision 35-mm. film runs horizontally rather than vertically through the motion picture camera and records an image on two frames of film, thus increasing the frame by more than one half and doubling the area. The horizontal reels are screened via a VistaVision projector, or squeezed anamorphically into standard 35-mm. film for showings in theaters without the special projector. (See: **Anamorphic lens.)**

Films are no longer shot in VistaVision, and the process is now used only for **blue-screen** process shots, in which actors, scale models and background elements are added to the scene in successive camera passes. The large size of the negative size counteracts grain build-up and image degradation, which occurs when compositing separately filmed images into one piece of film. The completed scene is then printed on film with a smaller **aspect ratio,** usually in one of the **Panavision** processes. Special effects technicians refer to VistaVision as "eight-perf" because each frame has eight sprocket holes rather than the standard four of 35-mm. film.

VOYAGE TO THE BOTTOM OF THE SEA

TV series 1964-68 U.S. (ABC) 60 Minutes (weekly) Black & white color

Irwin Allen, who likes to get his money's worth by using everything twice, spun this profitable series from his 1961 movie of the same title. Back on display was the *Seaview,* a glass-nosed nuclear submarine which had cost $400,000 to build for the feature film, accompanied by two flashy new crafts: a small soaring sub called the *Flying Fish* and a two-man explorer called the *Sea Crab.*

Among the underwater perils facing Admiral Nelson and crew were unrepentant Nazis, **alien** energy globules, dinosaurs clipped from Allen's film **The Lost World** (1960), angry giant orchids and **Vincent Price** as a dotty entertainer with a troupe of murderous puppets. After an initial season in black and white, the program was shot in color. Lyle B. Abbott, special effects chief at 20th Century-Fox, won three Emmys for the miniature vessels and optical effects.

Directors: **Nathan Juran,** Harry Harris, Sobey Martin, Tom Gries, Irwin Allen and others, *Producer:* Irwin Allen, *Writers:* Irwin Allen, Harlan Ellison, Arthur Weiss, Richard Landau and others, *Photographer:* Carl Guthrie, *Special Effects:* Lyle B. Abbott, *Music:* **Jerry Goldsmith,** Paul Sawtell, Nelson Riddle, Lionel Newman and others

Cast: Richard Basehart, David Hedison, Henry Kulky, Terry Becker, Bob Dowdell

VOYAGE TO THE PLANET OF THE PREHISTORIC WOMEN

(Also titled: *Gill Woman* and *Gill Women of Venus)*

Film 1968 U.S. (AIP) 78 Minutes Color

Astronauts visit a strange planet inhabited by telepathic amphibians clad in bikinis made of fossil shells. The guys fight off dinosaurs and make passes at the girls, who (inexplicably) summon up powerful brain waves that drive their unwelcome guests back to where they came from. The well-made special effects are from the Russian film **Planeta Bura/***Storm Planet* (1962), whose footage was previously used in **Voyage to the Prehistoric Planet** (1965). Director Peter Bogdanovich was hiding behind the pseudonym Derek Thomas.

Director: Derek Thomas, *Producer:* Norman Wells, *Screenplay:* Henry Nay

Cast: Mamie Van Doren, Mary Mark, Paige Lee, *Narrator:* Derek Thomas

VULCANS

A **humanoid** race of pointy-eared **aliens** who live on the planet Vulcan in **Star Trek.** More intelligent and physically stronger than human beings (whom they genetically resemble), Vulcans can read thoughts via a unique power called the mind-meld, and they can incapacitate opponents with a painful hold called the nerve-pinch. Originally a barbaric, warlike people, Vulcans totally rejected their past and re-engineered themselves to become superrational beings who acted from reason, not emotion, which they believed to be the cause of war and other miseries. **Mr. Spock,** the Science Officer of the **U.S.S. Enterprise,** has a Vulcan father and a human mother.

VYNALEZ ZKRAZY/The Fabulous World of Jules Verne

(Also titled: *The Deadly Invention, The Diabolic Invention* and *Weapons of Destruction*)

Film   1958   Czechoslovakia   83 Minutes   Black & white

Czech animator **Karel Zeman** brings the Victorian engravings of **Jules Verne**'s novels to charming life in this superb collage of cel **animation, stop motion** and live action. Zeman borrows characters and story elements from several Verne novels, including *For the Flag* (1896), *20,000 Leagues Under the Sea* (1870), *The Mysterious Island* (1874-75) and *The Clipper of the Clouds* (1887). Included are Captain Nemo, Robur, balloons, giant squids, a giant cannon and an underground city. In color it would have been even better.

Director/Art Director: Karel Zeman, *Screenplay:* Karel Zeman, Frantisek Hrubin, *Photographer:* Jiri Tarantik, *Music:* Zdenek Liska

Cast: Louis Tock, Van Kissling, Jane Zalata, Arnost Navratl

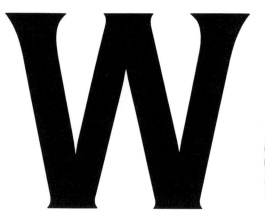

Warlords of Atlantis: A giant octopus guard sweeps members of a scientific expedition down to lost Atlantis.

WAMPA

A furry, carnivorous beast native to the planet **Hoth** in **The Empire Strikes Back** (1980). A bloodthirsty Wampa waylays **Luke Skywalker** while he is exploring Hoth and slashes open his **Tauntaun** with a powerful claw and eats it. Skywalker awakens in the creature's cave/larder to find himself hung by his feet like a side of beef. He escapes by activating his **lightsaber,** which cuts him free and kills the fanged animal.

WAR GODS OF THE DEEP

See: **City Under the Sea**

WAR, INTERPLANETARY

A major SF theme which exploits a universal human phobia—fear of strangers—usually with mankind on the receiving end of a devastating war begun by **extraterrestrials** with superior weaponry. Whether from other planets or galactic empires, space **aliens** are almost always portrayed as vicious invaders who must be repelled. Introduced by **H. G. Wells** in *The War of the Worlds* (1898), the theme was little used in films [notable exceptions are **Flash Gordon** (1936), **War of the Worlds, Invasion From Mars** (both 1953)] until **Star Wars** revived the theme and expanded it in with **The Empire Strikes Back.** It sparked a trend of similar films, such as **Battlestar Galactica, Star Trek—The Motion Picture,** the new **Flash Gordon,** and a host of second-rate imitations. The allegorical warnings of written science fiction are incidental to films and television, which use the theme as entertainment. (See also: **Space Opera.**)

WARLORDS OF ATLANTIS

(Also titled: *Seven Cities to Atlantis*)

Film   1978   Great Britain (EMI/Columbia)
96 Minutes   Technicolor

The producer/director team of **The Land That Time Forgot** (1975), **At the Earth's Core** (1976) and **The People That Time Forgot** (1977), dispensed with Edgar Rice Burroughs for their fourth lost-kingdom mini-epic. Which wasn't such a good idea. **Atlantis** turns out to be an underwater megapolis somewhat resembling the northeast coast of the U.S., the creation of aliens who had collided with a **comet** and crash-landed into the ocean eons ago, and who are allied with **Mars.** The customary monsters consist of a huge mutated millipede and a not-bad giant octopus made by John Richardson, who worked on **Superman— the Movie** (1978).

Director: **Kevin Connor,** *Producer:* John Dark, *Screenplay:* Brian Hayles, *Photographer:* Alan Hume, *Production Designer:* Elliott Scott, *Special Effects:* Roger Dicken, John Richardson, *Music:* Mike Vickers

Cast: Doug McClure, Peter Gilmore, Cyd Charisse, Daniel Massey, Shane Rimmer

WAR OF THE COLOSSAL BEAST

Film   1958   U.S. (AIP)   68 Minutes   Black & white with color sequence

Regretfully, the outsized Colonel Manning survived his fall from a cardboard mock-up of Boulder Dam at the climax of **The Amazing Colossal Man** (1957). Not feeling very well, he returns with a face like a badly mended china jug but with the same old crazy temper. This time out, after escaping from a science lab where he is undergoing tests, he finally comes to his senses and literally takes matters into his own hands: He grabs two high-tension wires and electrocutes himself in the only full-color sequence this tacky production can afford.

Director/Producer/Special Effects: **Bert I. Gordon,** *Screenplay:* George Worthing Yates, *Story:* Bert I. Gordon, *Photographer:* Jack Marta, *Music:* Albert Glasser

Cast: Dean Parkin, Sally Fraser, Roger Pace, Russ Bender, George Becwar

THE WAR OF THE WORLDS

Radio   1938   U.S. (CBS)   60 Minutes

The invasion from Mars, reported live and in progress from Grovers Mills, New Jersey.

This legendary adaptation of the **H. G. Wells** novel was broadcast as a segment of **Orson Welles'** *The Mercury Theatre on the Air,* an anthology radio series noted for its experimental dramatizations (including **Frankenstein** and *Dracula).* Despite liberties taken with the famous novel—or perhaps because of them—the program captured the wonder and awe of the original, and for once made science fiction totally believable. Wells was not amused, however, and cabled CBS: "Unwarranted liberties were taken with my work. . . ."

Disclaimers during station breaks that the program was fictional had little effect, and thousands of duped listeners flooded police switchboards for information on the invasion. Some panicked and fled for safety, while others armed themselves and barricaded their homes. The success of the hoax was due largely to O. Welles' clever device of "reporting" the progress of the invasion in the form of news interruptions of a regular program of light music and commentary. (An on-the-spot "bulletin" announced the landing of a meteor, which turned out to be a spaceship teeming with Martians armed with **death rays** and bent on world conquest.)

Welles, then at the beginning of his career, had directed his "reporter" to copy the near-hysterical delivery of a newscaster who had startled listeners the year before with an on-the-spot description of the explosion of the Hindenberg dirigible. Moreover, the public had become increasingly reliant on radio for news, especially from war-shadowed Europe.

Welles' Halloween prank inadvertently demonstrated the persuasive power of electronic media (predicted by H. G. Wells) and resulted in the banning of such broadcasts. The incident inspired a minor TV film, *The Night That Panicked America,* Paramount/ABC, 1975.

"To this day is is impossible to sit in a room and hear the scratched, worn, off-the-air recording of the broadcast without feeling in the back of your neck some slight draft left over from that great wind of terror that swept the nation."—John Houseman

Director/Producer: Orson Welles, *Editor:* John Housemann, *Writer:* Howard Koch, *Music Director:* **Bernard Herrmann**

Cast: Princeton University professor—Orson Welles, *Reporter*—Fred Readick, *Announcer*—Kenneth Delmar

WAR OF THE WORLDS

Film   1953   U.S. (Paramount)   85 Minutes Technicolor

Invading Martians threaten to annihilate mankind with laser-like **death rays,** but God is on man's side.

An entertaining, commercially successful adaptation of H. G. Wells' classic novel, transported from English Home Counties to contemporary Southern California. Studio insistence on a simple-minded love story and a mawkish religious allegory diluted the impact of the original, however, leaving little room for Wells' underlying theme of an "assault on human self-satisfaction."

Spectacular special effects are the best of their time, especially the Martian spacecraft, which resemble copper manta rays and hooded cobras, the destruction of miniature cities and the horrifying, one-eyed, sucker-fingered **aliens.**

Director: **Byron Haskin,** *Producer:* **George Pal,** *Screenplay:* Barre Lyndon, *Photography:* George Barnes, *Special Effects:* Gordon Jennings, Wallace Kelley, Paul Perpae, Ivyl Burts, Jim Donela, Irwin Roberts, *Art Directors:* Hal Pereira, Albert Nozaki (designer of Martian), Charles Gemora

Cast: Gene Barry, Ann Robinson, Les Tremayne, Jack Kruschen, Cedric Hardwicke

WARP SPEED

Measure of velocity devised for the **U.S.S. Enterprise** in **Star Trek.** Like all Federation Starships, the craft is powered by a Warp Drive with seven speeds: Warp one is equal to the speed of light and Warp two is twice the speed of light. The remaining speeds increase in a geometric progression. An eighth speed is rarely used for fear of shaking the starship apart. Analagous to the mile, warp speed is purely a flight of fancy that defies logic as well as the known laws of physics. (See also: **Hyperspace.**)

THE WASP WOMAN

Film   1960   U.S. (Allied Artists)
66 Minutes   Black & white

A rejuvenating beauty potion compounded of wasp enzymes stings its vain user.

No longer beautiful, a middle-aged cosmetics' queen finds that her once-flourishing business is also fading because she can't be a testimonial to her products. Willing to try anything, she interviews a mysterious chemist who claims he has devised an elixer that can remove wrinkles better than royal jelly, from bees. He demonstrates on an old guinea pig, which promptly reverts to its slender first youth, followed by the desperate lady. But her waspish nature eventually manifests itself, and soon her lovely face is a dark gray monstrosity and her chic hairdo a pair of wobbling antennae. To restore her appearance and stay alive, she must suck human blood (a habit not commonly enjoyed by wasps). The treatment is too good to last, however, and the she-monster eventually succumbs to a bracing splash of acid in this overworked bit of camp nonsense. (See also: **Mutants.**)

Director/Producer: **Roger Corman,** *Screenplay:* Leo Lordon, *Story:* Kinta Zertuche, *Photographer:* Harry Newman, *Art Director:* **Daniel Haller,** *Music:* Fred Katz

Cast: Susan Cabot, Michael Mark, Fred Eisley, Frank Wolff

WELLS, H.(ERBERT) G.(EORGE) (1866–1946)

Wells was a British novelist, short-story writer, essayist, historian and social theorist whose works continue to be read and filmed. In his time, Wells was England's most influential and celebrated intellectual, but his literary reputation declined shortly before World War II (a conflict he predicted). He is remembered primarily for his prophetic SF entertainments.

The third son of a London shopkeeper, "Bertie"—a self-acknowledged daydreamer —was apprenticed to a draper, to a druggist and, finally, to a grammar school teacher— only to fail totally at each task. The turning point came in 1883, when he won a scholarship to the Normal College of Science (now the Royal College of Science) and fell under the influence of T. H. Huxley, a staunch advocate of Charles Darwin's theory of evolution. While teaching biology at a tutorial college, Wells began to publish imaginative essays and short stories on the human implications of modern science, in a style that owes much to Robert Louis Stevenson and Jonathan Swift. A series of essays called "The Chronic Argonauts" was the basis for his first major work of science fiction, *The Time Machine,* published in 1895, in which he projected the evolution of human life on earth as culminating in a new life form. From then until his death, Wells published an astonishing number of works. He continued to write "for dear life" through periods of depression and numerous affairs (he was an advocate of free love), becoming increasingly despairing of mankind in later works, which were long on sermonizing and short on action. Wells advanced the SF genre from the Victorian science fantasy of rival **Jules Verne** and created speculative fiction as we know it today; his underlying themes concerned the social and philosophical consequences of technology. At the heart of his fiction is a belief in man's power to find his way out of the cosmic trap that evolution has laid for him—the capacity to build a better world in the future. An advocate of a global state, Wells foresaw a world-wide **Utopia** guided by a benevolent dictatorship of scientists, who would control such things as procreation, and administer socialist control of natural resources and public welfare.

Wells' novels predicted the age of the automobile, military tanks, germ warfare, dehydrated foods, synthetics and **laser** weapons, and introduced SF themes of mutant **humanoids, invisibility,** hostile **alien** life forms and **interplanetary warfare.** Avidly interested in the art of film, in 1895 he entered a partnership with cinema pioneer **Robert Paul** in an attempt to build a mixed media **time machine** device that would duplicate the effects described in his recently published novel.

"Man's complacent assumption of the future is too confident. . . . In the case of every predominant animal the world has seen . . . the hour of its complete ascendance has been the eve of its entire overthrow."

—H. G. Wells, 1894

Selected non-fiction: The Outline of History (1920), *The Way the World Is Going: Guesses and Forecasts of the World Ahead* (1928), *The Science of Life* (with Julian Huxley and G. P. Wells, 1930), *Experiment in Autobiography* (1934), *World Brain* (1938), *The Conquest of Time* (1942) and *The Happy Turning: A Dream of Life* (1945).

Novels and stories filmed: **The Time Machine, The Island of Dr. Moreau, The Invisible Man, The War of the Worlds, The First Men in the Moon, The Food of the Gods, Things to Come** (also *screenplay)* **Empire of the Ants,** *The Door in the Wall, Kipps, The History of Polly, The Passionate Friends, The Man Who Could Work Miracles* (also *screenplay)* and segment of *Dead of Night* (story "The Inexperienced Ghost"). Unproduced screenplay, *The King Who Was a King.* Portrayed as semi-fictitious character in *The Time Machine* and **Time After Time.**

THE WEREWOLF

Film   1956   U.S. (Columbia)   80 Minutes
Black & white

Scientists inject a victim of radioactive poisoning with an experimental antidote that periodically transforms him into a werewolf. Initially absorbing, this low-budget attempt to provide a scientific explanation for lycanthropy but fails to deliver the action and suspense promised in early scenes. The plot is the old wolf-man set-piece with most of the horror replaced by endless talk.

Director: **Fred F. Sears,** *Producer:* Sam Katzman, *Screenplay:* Robert E. Kent, James B. Gordon, *Photographer:* Edwin Linden, *Art Director:* Paul Palmentola, *Musical Director:* Mischa Bakaleinikoff

Cast: Don McGowan, Steven Ritch, Joyce Holden, Kim Charney

WESTWORLD

Film   1973   U.S. (MGM)   89 Minutes
Metrocolor   Panavision

Westworld is one of three meticulously simulated historical environments in Delos, an amusement park of the future, populated by human-looking **robots.** (The other two sections are Medievalworld and Romanworld.) Two male tourists, Peter and John, arrive for a frontier weekend and have a marvelous time drinking, bedding the convincing saloon wenches and out-drawing a mechanical gunslinger who spurts synthetic blood during his daily slaughter. A short circuit in Delos' computer suddenly turns the holiday into a nightmare, however, and the

Westworld: The robot gunslinger (Yul Brynner) is temporarily outdrawn by a weekend guest (Richard Benjamin).

robots begin murdering their guests. John is shot dead by the gunslinger, now with real bullets in his six-shooter, who pursues Peter through the deserted park for a chilling showdown.

Yul Brynner plays the black-suited gunslinger in the same outfit he wore in *The Magnificent Seven* (1960)—director **Michael Crichton's** reminder that the Westworld is a recreation of Hollywood's West, not the real one. Brynner's convincing robotic eyes are mirrored contact lenses that reflect overhead lights and make his pupils flash eerily. The sequel is **Futureworld** (1976).

Director/Screenplay: Michael Crichton, *Photographer:* Gene Polito, *Art Director:* Herman Blumenthal, *Music:* Fred Karlin

Cast: Yul Brynner, Richard Benjamin, James Brolin, Dick Van Patten, Majel Barrett, Victoria Shaw, Alan Oppenheimer

WHEN WORLDS COLLIDE

Film 1951 U.S. (Paramount) 82 Minutes
Technicolor

George Pal came up with another winner with this end-of-the-world epic, a follow-up to **Destination Moon** (1950). A dying star is on a collision course with **Earth,** and, to save the human race, a private group of scientists construct a space ark to escape to an Earth-like planet orbiting the star. Talky and slow-moving for its first hour, the film is redeemed by a spectacular ending. The wandering star, Bellus, bathes Earth in a perpetual glow of Technicolor orange, as tidal waves sweep through New York and the world's other major cities. The miniature devastation and the sleek ark are memorable. Gordon Jennings won an **Academy Award** for the special effects. For the record, Paramount originally purchased the rights to the best-selling novel by Philip Wylie and Edwin Balmer during the early 1930s as a project for Cecil B. DeMille, who opted for *Cleopatra* (1934) instead.

Director: Rudolph Mate, *Producer:* George Pal, *Screenplay:* Sydney Boehm, *Novel:* Philip Wylie, Edwin Balmer, *Photographers:* John F. Seitz, W. Howard Greene, *Production Designers:* **Hal Pereira,**

Albert Nozaki, *Special Effects:* Gordon Jennings, *Music:* Leith Stevens

Cast: Richard Derr, Barbara Rush, Peter Hanson, Judith Ames

THE WHITE BUFFALO

Film 1977 U.S. (United Artists) 97 Minutes
Technicolor

Wild Bill Hickok and Chief Crazy Horse team up to bag a **mutant** buffalo in this Western version of *Moby Dick,* which fails both as allegory and adventure. Charles Bronson is convincing as a symbol of man pitted against an evil force of nature (the animal stampedes through Sioux Indian camps), but his mechanical co-star is only occasionally effective. Constructed by special effects master **Carlo Rambaldi,** the albino buffalo seems like the real thing in long shots as its hooves pound the earth like thunder and its flaring nostrils jet steaming breath into the winter cold. Close-up, it lacks the fluid facial movements of the real thing and looks like a fur-covered dummy with a rubber nose. Still, the attempt to create a mechanical creature capable of lifelike movement is a noble one, and Rambaldi's expensive animal is worth a look for those interested in special effects.

Director: J. Lee Thompson, *Producer:* Pancho Kohner, *Executive Producer:* Dino de Laurentiis, *Screenplay:* Richard Sale (from his *novel*), *Photographer:* Paul Lohmann, *Special Effects:* Carlo Rambaldi, *Music:* **John Barry**

Cast: Charles Bronson, Jack Warden, Will Sampson, Clint Walker, Stuart Whitman, John Carradine, Kim Novak

The White Buffalo

WHO?

Film 1975 U.S. (Allied Artists)
93 Minutes Color

Russian scientists rebuild the body of an American physicist injured in a laboratory accident during a visit to East Germany. Returned home as a **cyborg,** he arouses the suspicion of U.S. authorities, who wonder whether he is the original scientist or a communist plant. The film is a watered-down version of Algis Budrys' intriguing novel.

Director: Jack Gold, *Producer:* Barry Levinson, *Screenplay:* Jack Gold, *Novel:* Algis Budrys

Cast: Joseph Bova, Elliott Gould, Trevor Howard, James Noble, John Lehne, Ed Grover

WIDE–SCREEN

Wide-screen systems had been attempted since the early days of cinema, even before the industry adopted Thomas Edison's 35-mm. format as the international standard. One of the first to experiment with a giant screen was French movie pioneer Louis Lumiere, who projected images onto a screen 63 feet wide by 45 feet high at the Paris Exposition of 1900. Another wide-screen pioneer was filmmaker **Abel Gance,** who experimented with the **anamorphic lens**—which condenses a wide-screen image on 35-mm. film—in **La Folie du Docteur Tube** (1915). In 1927 Gance devised a three-projector, three-screen system for the finale of *Napoleon* (1927). Called Polyvision, the system later became the basis of Cinerama.

During the 1920s and 1930s, several Hollywood productions were shot in Magnascope, which magnified a 35-mm. print with a special lens placed over the projector lens. Most of these systems were difficult to show in smaller theaters, since viewers in rear orchestra seats under balconies were unable to see the top of the screen. In 1953, when Hollywood was fighting the inroads of television, 20th Century-Fox unveiled CinemaScope, a 25-year-old anamorphic process that solved the balcony problem by making the screen wider instead of higher.

Other wide-screen systems followed, including WarnerScope, Technirama, Techniscope, **VistaVision,** Todd-AO and **Panavision.** Of these, only Todd-AO and Panavision survive. VistaVision, a system that uses two frames of 35-mm. film printed horizontally, is now used only to photograph special effects. Todd-AO, which produces a wide screen image with a 70-mm. frame, as does Super Panavision, are both used for SF spectacles and historical epics. Both systems can be reduced anamorphically and printed on 35-mm. stock for showings in smaller theaters. 70-mm film has a 65-mm. image, accompanied by a six-track stereophonic sound track printed at the side on the remaining 5 mms. Today, filmmakers have their choice of various **aspect ratios.** Many wide-screen films are actually 35-mm. productions with the tops and bottoms masked to provide a poor man's version of the wide-screen. Older films are often shown this way, losing image resolution and enlarging the grain and other imperfections in the film.

WILD IN THE STREETS

Film 1968 U.S. (AIP) 97 Minutes
Perfectcolor

A rock star gets elected President of the U.S., puts everyone over 30 out to pasture, and turns the country into a hedonistic playground.

Now badly dated, its trendiness as faded as its cheap color, *Wild In the Streets* impressed some film critics (who failed to get the joke) as a prophetic warning of the consequences of the 1960s "youthquake." The sight of a charismatic pop musician taking control of the country and keeping everyone over 35 happy in concentration camps with forcefed doses of LSD was enormously appealing to contemporary flower children, as was the portrayal of America as a paradise of drugged music lovers spending their days (and nights) doing and smoking whatever pleases them.

By dwelling on the obvious, the filmmakers failed to develop the inherent satire of present sociological trends carried to impossible excesses. Occasionally, flashes of bitter humor break through to indicate what it might have been, but the film is inherently anti-science fiction, in that it places no faith whatever in the future. Unintentionally perhaps, *Wild In the Streets* predicted the rise of Messiah-dominated youth cults, the shift of power to the post-war "baby-boom" generation, and a turning to emotional and pleasurable solutions to realities of life.

Director: Barry Shear, *Producers:* James H. Nicholson, Samuel Z. Arkoff, *Screenplay:* Robert Thom, *Story:* "The Day It All Happened" by Robert Thom, *Director:* Paul Sylos, *Music:* Les Baxter, *Songs:* Barry Mann, Cynthia Weil

Cast: Christopher Jones, Shelley Winters, Diane Varsi, Millie Perkins, Hal Holbrook

THE WILD, WILD WEST

TV series 1965-69 U.S. (CBS) 60 Minutes (weekly) Color

Inspired by **James Bond**'s unparalleled success, this engaging Western adventure starred Robert Conrad as special U.S. government agent James T. West and Ross Martin as his partner, Artemus Gordon, a master of disguise. The pair traveled in a private railway car, where they invented new technologies to foil the schemes of frontier madmen undermining the expansion of America. Played tongue-in-cheek in the manner of *Maverick,* the series carried off its unlikely premise in high style and with a knowing wink. It was a Friday night favorite for four years.

Directors: William Witney, Don Taylor, **Harvey Hart,** Alan Crosland, Richard Whorf, Lee H. Katzin, Mark Rydell, Richard Donner, Marvin Chomsky, Alex Nichol, Vincent McEveety and others, *Creator:* Michael Garrison, *Executive Producers:* Philip Leacock, Michael Garrison

Cast: Robert Conrad, Ross Martin, James Gregory, Roy Engle, Michael Dunn, Victor Buono

WIRE WORK

A mechanical special effect in which a person or object hangs from wires or monofilament threads to simulate **flying** or a gravity-free environment. Blackened piano wire is most often used because of its thin-

ness and great tensile strength. Great care must be taken with lighting and camera angles to conceal the wires.

The subject (called a "flyer") wears a fabric-lined plastic harness (called a "flying belt") molded to the abdomen and hips, and fitted at either side with ball-bearing joints to which the wires are attached. The position of the harness approximates the body's center of gravity and prevents the actor from hanging at a tilt; the swivel joints ensure a smooth, gliding movement. The wires are connected to a counterweighted "spreader" bar mounted to an overhead track supported by cables and/or hydraulic rams. By manipulating the system's two motions—forward and backward, up and down—an actor or object can be made to move in three dimen-

Blackened piano wires provided the lift for the winged angel Pygar in *Barbarella* (1968) and the moon-scavenging astronaut of TV's *Salvage* (1979). Flying wires supporting a doctor and nurse miniaturized to perform surgery inside a patient's body in *Fantastic Voyage* (1966) were concealed by spun fiberglass sets.

sions, like a marionette suspended on a trapeze. The actor meanwhile must convincingly appear to be comfortably soaring through space while suspended over the floor of a drafty studio. To help simulate the buoyancy characteristic of low gravity, the camera is often speeded up to slow down the action. (See also: **Slow Motion.**)

WISE, ROBERT (1914–   )

American mainstream director (and occasional producer) whose many works include several important SF films.

Wise was born in Winchester, Indiana, and began his career as a messenger at RKO Pictures, after dropping out of college because of the Depression. He was promoted to film cutter and, in 1939, to film editor, earning recognition for his work on Orson Welles' *Citizen Kane* (1941) and *The Magnificent Ambersons* (1942). In 1943 he was editing a routine horror film when its director, behind schedule, was fired. Wise took over *The Curse of the Cat People* (1944), which became a critical and popular success and established him as a director. He continued to direct routine "B" pictures—including *The Body Snatcher* (1945), a Gothic horror movie, and *The Set Up* (1949), an innovative boxing drama—notable for their high quality despite small budgets.

In 1949 Wise left RKO to freelance, one of his first assignments being **The Day the Earth Stood Still** (1951), now a SF classic. By the mid-1950s he had become one of Hollywood's most versatile leading directors, helming everything from big-budget musicals to intimate melodramas. He holds the distinction of twice receiving twin **Academy Awards:** as co-director (with Jerome Robbins) and producer of *West Side Story* (1961); as director and producer of *The Sound of Music* (1965). In 1966 he received a fifth Academy Award: the Irving G. Thalberg Memorial Award given to producers for "consistent high level of production achievement." Among his memorable films dealing with the supernatural are *The Haunting* (1963) and *Audrey Rose* (1977).

Twenty years elapsed before he returned to science fiction with **The Andromeda**

Director Robert Wise sets up a shot for *Star Trek—The Motion Picture.*

Strain (1971), a slick, well-received allegorical thriller. Wise's handling of fictional technology was less certain in *The Hindenburg* (1975), a recreation of the famous airship disaster, and his direction of **Star Trek—The Motion Picture** (1979) lacked cohesion and pace. A dependable craftsman with a reputation for efficiency and promptness, Wise has yet to live up to early promise. His later films, while commercially successful, lack a stylistic personality and rarely transcend their material.

WITHOUT WARNING

Film   1980   U.S. (Filmways)   89 Minutes Movielab

Poor old sergeant Fred. He's been a nut case ever since he came home from Vietnam, and when he rushes into the Isolated Bar & Grill with the news that "critters" not of this world have landed up at the lake, his buddies have a good laugh at his expense. It takes two hysterical teenagers and a gruesome death to absolve Fred, mobilize the yokels and goose the illogical plot to its predictable conclusion. The "critters" turn out to be styrofoam-headed **alien** people-eaters who hunt with a superleech thrown at the necks of their victims. The living weapon resembles the **parasite** of **Alien** (1979), as do the film's few high points.

Director/Producer: Greydon Clark, *Screenplay:* Lyn Freeman, Daniel Grodnik, Ben Nett, Steve Mathis, *Music:* Dan Wyman

Without Warning: An alien invader prepares to toss one of his superleeches.

Cast: Martin Landau, Jack Palance, Tarrah Nutter, Christopher S. Nelson, Cameron Mitchell

WITNEY, WILLIAM (1910–   )

Director. Born in Lawton, Oklahoma, Witney began his career as a Hollywood errand boy and progressed through the ranks to **serial** director at Republic in 1937. Working in collaboration with director John English, he made 17 consecutive chapter plays notable for their well-plotted high adventure and technical gloss. After service in the Marine Corps during World War II, he directed low-budget Westerns, usually starring Roy Rogers. He later turned to other genres. His only SF feature is **Master of the World** (1961).

THE WIZARD OF OZ

Film   1939   U.S. (MGM)   100 Minutes
Technicolor

This legendary fantasy about a poor farm girl named Dorothy who spins into the magical kingdom of Oz on a tornado has at least one SF element: its Wizard, a likeably eccentric inventor who projects a fearsome image to his subjects via a TV screen. References to *The Wizard of Oz* can be seen in the film **Star Wars** (1977), whose constantly complaining robot **C-3PO** is a descendant of the tin woodman.

Frank Baum's story, *The Wonderful Wizard of Oz* (1900), was also filmed in 1908, 1924 and 1978, the latter as **The Wiz,** an expensive musical with a black cast.

Director: Victor Fleming, *Producer:* Mervyn LeRoy, *Screenplay:* Noel Langley, Florence Ryerson, Edgar Allen Wolf, *Novel:* Frank Baum, *Photographer:* Harold Rosson, *Musical Director:* Herbert Stothart [Academy Award], *Songs:* E. Y. Harburg, Harold Arlen [Academy Awards], *Production Designers:* Cedric Gibbons, William A. Horning

Cast: Judy Garland, Ray Bolger, Bert Lahr, Jack Haley, Margaret Hamilton, Frank Morgan

WIZARDS

Film   1976   U.S. (20th Century-Fox)
81 Minutes   Color

Wizards, Ralph Bakshi's ambitious attempt to produce a full-length animated SF film, falls far short of a masterpiece, but it's lively and inventive, if somewhat simple-minded. Set in the distant future, after mankind has nearly destroyed itself in an atomic war, the movie depicts a post-industrial world where machines are banned and magic is a way of life. Radiation poisoning has produced mutations of Tolkien-like dwarfs, fairies and other little people, who live in a back-to-nature **Utopia.** The plot focuses on a running battle between two fairy brothers: Avatar the good and Blackwolf the bad, the latter a neo-capitalist who wants to reopen an armament factory and build a military empire. Bakshi's message, that science and technology are destructive and that a primitive, natural lifestyle is the only way to salvation, was a tenet of faith for the counterculture movement of the 1960s. (See also: **Animation, The Bomb.**)

Director/Producer/Screenplay: Ralph Bakshi, *Sequence Animation:* Irven Spence, *Design:* Ian Miller, David Jonas, *Photographer:* Ted Bemiller, *Music:* Andrew Billing

Voices: **Mark Hamill,** Bob Holt, Steve Gravers, Jesse Wells

THE WOMAN IN THE MOON

See: **Die Frau Im Monde**

WOMEN OF THE PREHISTORIC PLANET

Film 1965 U.S. (Realart) 91 Minutes Color

Not to be confused with **Voyage to the Planet of the Prehistoric Women** (1968)—that one starred Mamie Van Doren, remember?—*Women of the Prehistoric Planet* also has a bevy of scantily clad cuties displaying themselves in a primeval setting, but this one looks like someone's greenhouse. Astronauts discover the place while searching for a lost spaceship.

Director/Screenplay: Arthur C. Pierce, *Producer:* George Gilbert, *Special Effects:* Howard A. Anderson

Cast: Wendell Corey, Keith Larsen, **John Agar,** Merry Anders, Stuart Margolin

WONDERBUG

See: **The Krofft Supershow**

WONDER WOMAN

American **comic-book** character, created by psychologist William Moulton Marston (under the pseudonym of Charles Moulton) and illustrated by Harry G. Peter. A female version of **Superman,** Wonder Woman debuted in *All Star Comics* No. 8, December 1941-January 1942. She made her TV debut, appropriately, as a cartoon character in the animated series **Superfriends** (1973-), followed by a live-action TV film, **Wonder Woman** (1974) and a series, **The New Original Wonder Woman** (1976-77), retitled *The New Adventures of Wonder Woman* (1977-79) when it moved to another network.

According to her comic-book legend, Wonder Woman is a member of a race of self-sufficient Amazons who escaped male slavery in ancient Greece and established a technologically advanced kingdom on remote Paradise Island. Sculpted from clay by Queen Hippolyte, whom she regards as her mother, Wonder Woman was brought to life by Aphrodite, goddess of love (making her, in effect, an **android).**

Despite her ingrained mistrust of males, Wonder Woman falls in love with the first man she meets, a U.S. Army intelligence officer named Steve Trevor whose plane crashlands on the island during World War II. Assigned by Hippolyte to take the unconscious Major back to the U.S. and to fight "the forces of hate and oppression," she is christened Diana and given a strapless battle dress (later changed to less cumbersome shorts) resembling the American flag. Hippolyte notes that Princess Diana will be considered a "wonder woman" to the outside world.

Disguised as the bespectacled Diana Prince, aide to Trevor (a sex-role reversal of Clark Kent and Lois Lane), Wonder Woman spends much of her time rescuing her boss, who suspects the dual identity but isn't certain. Among the futuristic devices she has brought along are an invisible plane, a telepathic "mental radio" set and a machine that emits a purple healing ray. Her truth-inducing lasso is made of links taken from Hippolyte's magical girdle, and her bullet-proof bracelets, a reminder of male enslavement, have no special powers save for her skill in using them. She is not allowed to kill anyone, nor to use violence except in self-defense or the defense of others.

Wonder Woman has always been a mirror of her times. During World War II, when women were encouraged to do the work of men as a matter of government policy, she was in full power dispatching fascist traitors while admonishing women to be independent: "Get strong! Earn your own living!" After Marston died in 1947, she became less powerful and relied more on Trevor, reflecting the post-war role of women as homemakers. During the 1960s she concerned herself with purely "female" pursuits and wore trendy high heels and a new coiffure styled after Jackie Kennedy's. By 1973, however, after being chosen as a symbol of the Women's Liberation movement, she had come full circle. D.C. Comics restored her powers and gave her back the invisible plane and a new pair of red boots.

WONDER WOMAN

TV film   1974   U.S. (ABC)   75 Minutes
Color

The legendary Amazon maiden (see listing above) leaped into the 1970s for her first live-action TV appearance and came down with a loud thud. Intended as a pilot for a series, *Wonder Woman* cast tennis player Cathy Lee Crosby in the title role and offered a torpid plot concerning stolen government documents recovered by you-know-who, now working as a Pentagon secretary. Crosby seemed ill at ease; worse, she was a blonde.

Director: Vincent McEveety, *Producer:* John G. Stephens, *Screenplay:* John D. F. Black, *Photographer:* Joseph Biroc, *Music:* Artie Butler

Cast: Cathy Lee Crosby, Kaz Garas, Ricardo Montalban, Andrew Prine, Anitra Ford

WOOKIE

A temperamental race of intelligent, hulking anthropoids exemplified by **Chewbacca,** a supporting character in the **Star Wars** series.

WORLD OF GIANTS

TV series   1959   U.S. (CBS)   30 Minutes
(weekly)   Black & white

The answer to what became of the mammoth props and sets built for **The Incredible Shrinking Man** (1957), made by the same producer. The hero was once again miniaturized by atomic radiation, which left him permanently six inches tall—just right to work as a pocket-sized secret government agent. His equally dedicated partner in the war on crime was full-sized. (13 episodes)

Producer: William Alland

Cast: Marshall Thompson, **Arthur Franz**

THE WORLD, THE FLESH AND THE DEVIL

Film   1959   U.S. (MGM)   95 Minutes   Black & white   CinemaScope

Trapped in a mine shaft during World War III, a black man emerges to find that he is the only man alive. His odyssey takes him to New York City where he finds another survivor, a pretty blonde who begins to fall in love with him. Before long they are joined by the third member of the triangle, a white racist who wants the girl for himself. The men stalk each other with rifles through the deserted canyons of Manhattan, until the stupidity of fighting World War IV dawns on them.

Director/Screenplay: Ranald MacDougall, *Producer:* George Englund, *Novel:* "The Purple Cloud" M. P. Shiel, *Photographer:* Harold J. Marzorati, *Special Effects:* Lee LeBlanc, *Music:* Miklos Rozsa

Cast: Harry Belafonte, Inger Stevens, Mel Ferrer

WORLD WITHOUT END

Film   1956   U.S. (Allied Artists)
80 Minutes   Technicolor   CinemaScope

Astronauts returning from a flight to **Mars** slip through a time warp and come home in the year 2508. A nuclear holocaust has devastated the **Earth** and turned society into warring groups of normals and **mutants.** It's essentially a reworking of **H. G. Wells'** famous novel *The Time Machine* (see film listing) with some not-bad special effects.

Director/Screenplay: **Edward Bernds,** *Producer:* Richard Heermance, *Photographer:* Ellsworth Fredericks, *Special Effects:* Milt Rice, Jack Rabin, Irving Block, *Music:* Leith Stevens

Cast: Hugh Marlowe, Nancy Gates, Rod Taylor, Booth Coleman, Everett Glass

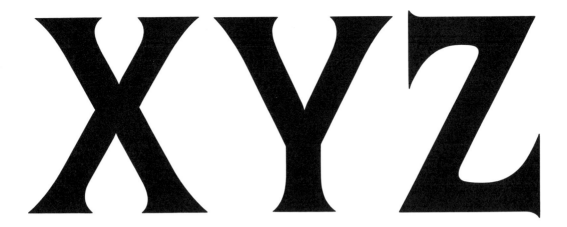

XYZ

X MINUS ONE

See: **Dimension X**

X-RAYS

A form of radiation capable of penetrating matter. X-rays are part of the electromagnetic spectrum, just as light, heat and radio waves are. Like high-frequency radio waves, they move forward in a straight line, but with an intensity that can shoot through most solids as easily as light waves shine through glass. They are commonly used medically to locate diseased or damaged tissue and foreign objects inside the body. They are also a prime tool of physicists for determining the structure of matter by locating atoms and their relative positions. Without x-ray technology the nuclear age would still be a SF fantasy.

X-rays were discovered in 1895 by Prof. Wilhelm Konrad Roentgen, a German physicist who won the Nobel Prize for his accomplishment, and immediately incorporated into the imaginations of SF writers. **H. G. Wells** was probably the first to come up with a futuristic adaptation in his novel *The War of the Worlds* (1895), which featured a devastating Martian Heat Ray. Others conjured up a variety of magical rays that could do everything from suspending gravity to altering the orbits of planets. Most of these naive devices have since disappeared, but the **death ray** remains an essential ingredient of science fiction—although today it is based on **laser** beams and not x-rays.

"X" THE MAN WITH THE X-RAY EYES

(Released in Great Britain as *The Man With the X-Ray Eyes*)

Film 1963 U.S. (AIP) 88 Minutes Color Spectarama

A surgeon's experimental eye drops bring amazing powers that prove to be more than he can handle.

Dr. Xavier's motives may be pure but his methods leave something to be desired. He concocts a formula that gives the human eye **x-ray**-like vision in order to enable surgeons like himself to see through the bodies of patients and better diagnose their ailments. The potion seems to work on laboratory animals—except that all eventually go into shock and die. The trouble starts when he disregards their warning and drops the liquid into his own eyes. While his sight is greatly

A greedy side-show manager (Don Rickles) hires a fugitive scientist (Ray Milland) to read minds in *"X" The Man With the X-ray Eyes* (1963).

enhanced, his mind is not and, during an argument, he accidently kills his research associate.

On the run, he hides out as a mind reader in a carnival side show, whose grubby manager exploits him as a faith healer. Rescued by his girl friend, he applies more drops and heads for Las Vegas to win money to leave the country. Naturally, his "luck" arouses suspicion and, once again, he leaves town in a hurry. Pursued by police into the desert, he crashes his car in the sand and stumbles into the tent of a traveling evangelist. Tormented, unable to shut out the terrible visions, (his eyes are now black disks) he confesses to the congregation that he has looked into the center of the universe—to see a huge, unblinking eye dispassionately watching mankind. Offering Biblical solace, the preacher suggests, "If thine eye offends thee, pluck it out!" With no other solution at hand, he does just that. The film ends with a mercifully brief shot of the doctor, much relieved, holding crimson-streaked hands to his gaping eye sockets.

Like most of **Roger Corman's** work, "X" could have used a better script and more special effects, which might have turned a provocative film into a great one. But you get what you pay for, and Corman's low budgets and tight shooting schedules invariably undermine the offbeat vitality of his films. The doctor's x-ray vision is a clever metaphor for the pursuit of knowledge which, in his case, proportionately increases his madness. Unfortunately, Corman (or his script writer) won't leave well enough alone, and we are left with one of the great SF **cliches** of all time, that "there are things man is not meant to know." What there are of the special effects are convincing—including the doctor's delightful surprise at being able to see through the clothing of female students—although our glimpse of the center of the universe is less convincing than his description of it. Still, a good subject does a lot for a movie, and the briskly moving plot and first-rate performances doesn't allow much time to dwell on "X" 's flaws.

Director/Producer: **Roger Corman,** *Screenplay:* Robert Dillon, Ray Russell, *Story:* Ray Russell,

Photographer: **Floyd Crosby,** *Art Director:* **Daniel Haller,** *Makeup:* Ted Coodley, *Music:* Les Baxter, *Special Effects:* Butler-Glouner, Inc., *Music:* Les Baxter

Cast: Ray Milland, Don Rickles, Dina Van Der Vlis, Harold J. Stone, John Hoyt

X, THE UNKNOWN

Film   1956   Great Britain (Hammer)
81 Minutes   Black & white

A radioactive blob emerges from the **Earth** and grows to monstrous proportions by feeding on nuclear energy at a government research station in Scotland. Made to capitalize on the success of **The Quatermass Xperiment** (1955), the film has roughly the same plot as the American-made potboiler **The Magnetic Monster** (1953).

Director: Leslie Norman, *Producer:* Anthony Hinds, *Screenplay:* Jimmy Sangster, *Photographer:* Gerald Gibbs, *Special Effects:* Les Bowie, Jack Curtis, *Music:* James Bernard

Cast: Dean Jagger, Leo McKern, Edward Chapman, Anthony Newley, Edward Judd, Mariane Brauns

YAVIN

A large planet unhospitable to life and largely ignored by the Galactic Empire in the film **Star Wars** (1977). Rebel freedom-fighters have installed a secret base on the planet's fourth moon, beneath the ruins of an extinct civilization that dot the satellite's jungle-covered surface.

YODA

Gnomelike, green-skinned Jedi Master who lives on the swamp planet Dagobah in **The Empire Strikes Back** (1980). A vision of **Ben Kenobi** instructs **Luke Skywalker** to find Yoda to complete his education in the use of **the Force,** a mystical power all **Jedi Knights** possess. A cantankerous little creature who has been training Jedis for 800 years, Yoda at first turns Luke down: "I cannot instruct him, The boy has no patience. . . . Never his mind on where he was,

Yoda: The elfin Jedi Master instructs Luke Skywalker in *The Empire Strikes Back* (1980).

on what he was doing. Adventure, excitement. A Jedi craves not these things." Eventually, he relents, and Luke learns enough to tune in on the danger his friends face in Cloud City. Despite Yoda's pleadings, Luke takes off for the Bespin system and a **lightsaber** duel with **Darth Vader.**

Yoda is a 26-inch-tall Muppet, made and operated by Frank Oz, the manipulator and voice of Miss Piggy.

YOUNG FRANKENSTEIN

Film 1974 U.S. (20th Century-Fox)
108 Minutes Black & white

Mel Brooks has a high time camping up Universal's old horror movies in this sprightly spoof, which stars Gene Wilder as Dr. **Frankenstein**'s maladroit grandson, Marty Feldman as the hunchback Ygor, Madeleine Kahn as the operatic bride of Frankenstein, and Peter Boyle as the tap-dancing monster. As usual, Brooks doesn't know when to stop, and the film never quite reaches the comic heights it aspires to. Several of the sets were used in the original **Frankenstein** (1931).

Director: Mel Brooks, *Producer:* Michael Gruskoff, *Screenplay:* Mel Brooks, Gene Wilder, *Photographer:* Gerald Hirschfeld, *Art Director:* Dale Hennesy, *Makeup:* William Tuttle, *Music:* John Morris

Cast: Gene Wilder, Marty Feldman, Madeleine Kahn, Peter Boyle, Cloris Leachman, Kenneth Mars, Gene Hackman

YOU ONLY LIVE TWICE

Film 1967 Great Britain (United Artists)
117 Minutes Technicolor Panavision

This was **James Bond**'s most SF-oriented film until **Moonraker** (1979) came along, and it still looks impressive despite a few rough special effects. Here Bond travels to Japan to find a SPECTRE space vehicle that has been snatching American and Russian satellites from their orbits for the purpose of starting World War III. Bond penetrates their secret headquarters inside an extinct volcano (designed by **Ken Adam),** equipped with a monorail, a heliport and other impressive hardware.

Director: Lewis Gilbert, *Producers:* Albert R. Broccoli, Harry Saltzman, *Screenplay:* Roald Dahl, *Novel:* Ian Fleming, *Photographer:* Freddie Young, Bob Huke, *Production Designer:* Ken Adam, *Special Effects:* John Stears, *Music:* **John Barry**

Cast: **Sean Connery,** Donald Pleasance, Tetsuro Tamba, Akiko Wakabayashi, Benard Lee, Lois Maxwell

ZARDOZ

Film 1974 Great Britain (20th Century-Fox) 105 Minutes DeLuxe Panavision

SF buffs are still debating the merits of *Zardoz,* a visually dazzling allegory written and directed by John Boorman, a mainstream filmmaker. The story takes place in the year 2293 during a post-atomic age, when the world has been divided into two zones separated by a **force-field.** The inner zone, a technopolis called the Vortex, is governed by the immortal but decadent Eternals, whose leaders are sexless women. The outer zone, a barren waste called the Outlands, is inhabited by the Brutals, vigorous slaves who spend their free time making love and waging war. To keep their numbers down, the Eternals have established a vicious police force called the Exterminators, who receive orders, weapons and ammunition from Zardoz, an angry godhead that occasionally floats down from the sky. As an appeasement, the Exterminators stuff the head with food grown by the Brutals.

Suspecting that the mysterious stone head is not what it appears to be, an Exterminator named Zed (Sean Connery) smuggles himself into its mouth and finds it is only a flying machine. Taken into the Vortex, he destroys the Tabernacle, a jewel-like computer that controls and supports the community, and lets in the Exterminators to finish the job. Zed meanwhile escapes with a beautiful Eternal who has discovered the joys of sex, to breed a happier race of human beings.

Opulently photographed in Ireland by **Geoffrey Unsworth,** *Zardoz* has a hypnotic panache that keeps one watching even when its narrative founders under the weight of pretentious symbolism. Boorman's macho-existentialist message, embodied by Sean Connery in a loincloth, is apparently that studsy sex, hunger and fear are the natural order of things, and science is not. Many viewers found the film deliberately bewildering, and they may be right. Boorman's title and stone head are in-jokes—a take-off on **The Wizard of Oz** (1939).

Director/Producer/Screenplay: John Boorman, *Photographer:* Geoffrey Unsworth, *Production Designer:* Anthony Pratt, *Special Effects:* Jerry Johnston, *Music:* David Munrow

Cast: Sean Connery, Charlotte Rampling, John Alderton, Sara Kestelman, Sally Anne Newton

ZEMAN, KAREL (1910–   )

Czechoslovakian animator/director/producer of inventive feature-length films that blend live action with **animation.** Zeman decorated shop windows and painted advertising posters before joining a Prague movie studio shortly after World War II to make animated commercials (which are shown in cinemas in Europe). His early theatrical films were shorts, most of which featured the imperturbable Mr. Prokouk, his immensely popular Czech everyman.

ZEX

See: **The Electronic Monster**

ZOMBIE

See: **Dawn of the Dead**

ZOMBIES OF THE STRATOSPHERE

Film serial   1952   U.S. (Republic)
12 Episodes   Black & white

Marex and Narab, a couple of zombies from outer space, attempt to blow **Earth** out of its orbit so they can move in their own planet and take advantage of our superior climate. This laughable attempt by Republic to produce low-budget **serials** about big-budget subjects creaks with weariness, down to its stock **robot,** first seen in the studio's **Undersea Kingdom** (1936). *Zombies* is cherished by some, however, since it marks an early screen appearance by **Leonard Nimoy** (as Narab). It was released in feature form as *Satan's Satellites* (1958).

Director: Fred C. Brannon, *Screenplay:* Ronald Davidson, *Special Effects:* Howard Lydecker, Theodore Lydecker, *Music:* Stanley Wilson

Cast: Judd Holdren, Lane Bradford, Craig Kelly, Leonard Nimoy, Aline Towne

ZONTAR: THE THING FROM VENUS

Film   1968   U.S. (AIP)   80 Minutes   Color

An uncredited remake of **It Conquered the World** (1956), starring a big alien bat with telepathic powers. The foolish creature makes the mistake of trying to use the hero's brain to help take over the world.

Director/Producer: Larry Buchanan, *Screenplay:* Larry Buchanan, H. Taylor, *Photographer:* Robert B. Alcott

Cast: **John Agar,** Susan Bjorman, Warren Hammack, Patricia DeLaney

ZOOM LENS

A lens with a continuously variable focal

length (within a certain range), which magnifies or decreases a filmed image without having to move the camera and without having to adjust focus or aperture. A zoom lens makes it possible to move rapidly from a long shot to a close-up, or move away from a close-up to the background action, with the effect of a camera motion toward or away from the subject. It can also provide the illusion of movement of people and objects by means of the **Zoptic Process,** the special effect that made actor Christopher Reeve appear to fly in **Superman—The Movie** and **Superman II.** (See also: **Optical Printer.**)

ZOPTIC PROCESS

A motion picture special effects system that simulates movement of a stationary object; devised by Zoran Perisic in the early 1970s. Two synchronized **zoom lenses** are required to produce the effect: one on the camera recording a scene, and another on the projector supplying background footage (via **front projection).** Characteristics of the zoom lens are such that when a camera "zooms in," its photographed image grows larger; when a projector "zooms in," its projected image shrinks. In the Zoptic process these actions occur simultaneously (and at the same shutter speed) and cancel each other out, causing the background image to appear to remain constant. The foreground object (or actor) is constantly being enlarged, however, creating the illusion of forward movement.

This remarkably seamless effect can be seen in **Superman—the Movie** and **Superman II,** when the Man of Steel appears to be soaring over Manhattan toward the audience. The scenes were filmed in a London studio where actor Christopher Reeve lay on a plastic body plate, hidden under his costume, suspended from a pole jutting through a movie screen behind him. (The pole was hidden from the camera by the angle of Reeve's body.) As Reeve assumed Superman's flying posture, aerial footage of Manhattan was projected onto the screen. Both camera and projector zoomed in, and

the size of the city skyline remained the same. Since only Reeve's image was being enlarged, he appeared to be soaring toward the camera, away from the background. Additionally, Reeve's body could be angled so that he could move to the right or left, up or down. To make him appear to fly faster, the zooming-in action was simply speeded up.

Z.P.G./ZERO POPULATION GROWTH

Film 1971 Great Britain (Sagittarius/
Paramount) 97 Minutes Eastmancolor

In the near future, industrial pollution and overpopulation have choked the world with smog and human beings, prompting a government dictatorship to ban childbirth. Surrogate **robot** dolls are available for those with parental instincts—a grotesquerie not to the liking of one very human right-minded couple, who proceed to have a baby of their own. Facing death in an "extermination dome" after being betrayed by a neighbor, they escape through a drain pipe, presumably to safety. "Zero population growth," a term coined by neo-Malthusians in the 1960s, means keeping a population at a constant level by allowing a certain number of births, not by banning them entirely—a not-so-subtle misinterpretation on the part of the scriptwriters.

Director: Michael Campus, *Producer:* Thomas F. Madigan, *Screenplay:* Max Ehrlich, Frank de Felita, *Photographer:* Michael Reed, *Production Designer:* Tony Masters, *Special Effects:* Derek Meddings, *Music:* Jonathan Hodge

Cast: Oliver Reed, Geraldine Chaplin, Diane Cilento, Don Gordon, Bill Nagy

ZSIGMOND, VILMOS (1930–   )

Hungarian-born Hollywood Director of Photography; winner of an **Academy Award** for the cinematography of **Close Encounters of the Third Kind** (1977). His films are characterized by a surreal use of commonplace surroundings, especially in night shots, which his camera suffuses with an aura of subtle paranoid menace.

A graduate of the state-operated Budapest Film School, Zsigmond escaped to the U.S. during the 1956 Hungarian rebellion with fellow alumnus Laszlo Kovacs (who photographed sequences of *Close Encounters*). He worked in Hollywood as a photo processor, still photographer and cameraman's assistant before beginning his career as a cinematographer of educational films.

ZYGONS

Grotesque creatures who look like **humanoid** octopusses, and who live under Loch Ness in the British TV series **Doctor Who**. Zygons are the remnants of an **alien** lifeform stranded here for centuries, ever since their **spaceship** crashlanded while exploring **Earth** prior to a planned invasion. Since then, their planet has been destroyed, and they are feverishly rebuilding their spacecraft at the bottom of Loch Ness, hoping to find surviving Zygons somewhere in space. They have brought along a creature called the Skarasen, part-animal, part-machine, who rises to the surface occasionally to scare people away from their hiding place. The Doctor eventually destroys the Zygons, but their creature decides to stay on in the loch, where he has come to be known as the Loch Ness Monster.

Zardoz: A masked Exterminator.